The Art of Medieval French Romance

The Art of Medieval French Romance

Douglas Kelly

The University of Wisconsin Press

Publication of this book has been supported by a grant from the National Endowment for the Humanities, an independent federal agency.

The University of Wisconsin Press
114 North Murray Street
Madison, Wisconsin 53715

3 Henrietta Street
London WC2E 8LU, England

for Sandra

Memories of memories are not necessarily distorting or pale reflections of the original; they may be re-collections of re-collections, deepenings through meditation of the primary experiences. We shall therefore take the latest and uppermost layer as seriously as the earlier ones.

—Leo Strauss

Contents

Preface

Jeder Archetypus ist unendlicher Entwicklung und Differenzierung fähig.
[Every archetype is susceptible of endless development and differentiation.]
— C.G. Jung

How would or could medieval authors have addressed the problems we perceive in their works? Problems like those of source and intertextuality, of structure in its manifold modern meanings, of character psychology and individuality? Did those problems exist for them? The answers to these questions may not be essential to modern readings of medieval works, but they are essential to historically valid readings. They may also offer a useful corrective or complement to those which are not.

Romance is usually defined by reference to Chrétien de Troyes and Marie de France. Although these authors are central to the art of romance, that art is comprehensible only if one draws on the other available sources, including prose romance, non-Arthurian romance, thirteenth-century verse romance, and variant versions, especially from the later Middle Ages. Deepening the context of romance as this study seeks to do, it functions not as an introduction but as a disquisition on the historically obvious and critically identifiable art of romance as it was presented to French-speaking audiences in the medieval period.

To describe the art of romance as French romancers and their contemporaries do, one must rely on so-called authorial interventions. Taken together, these interventions reveal a paradigm for invention adopted and adapted principally from medieval Latin traditions. The romancers fitted the paradigm to narrative material derived from heterogeneous sources. This is especially obvious in the earlier romances. The seminal achievements of the great twelfth-century writers established romance as a recognizable genre. In the thirteenth century and after, romancers consolidated, built on, and adapted the achievements of their predecessors. I shall concentrate here on French romances of the twelfth and thirteenth centuries.

Those who have studied romances written after 1300 may sense how in-complete my survey has been. This is to some extent unavoidable. We still lack good editions, so that serious study of these works is only now begin-ning.[1] Variant versions and adaptations of twelfth- and thirteenth-century romances that include authorial or scribal interventions lie still buried in any number of unpublished manuscripts. Still, there is enough for the twelfth and thirteenth centuries to justify my study, and from the fourteenth and fifteenth centuries to permit discrete use of illustrations from later romances and compilations. Occasional references to romances in other languages, es-pecially in German, suggest the critical usefulness—but not the certain validity—of the French art for the study of its counterparts in other languages.

The more cogent or suggestive illustrations from French romances prior to 1300 are quoted as samples representative of all varieties of romance. I have tried to provide enough primary references in the notes to support my analyses and interpretations. An exhaustive index of all references would have been of great use to the scholar. But that would have made an already lengthy book longer still. The interested reader is referred to the appropriate documen-tary volumes in the *Grundriß der romanischen Literaturen des Mittelalters (GRLMA)*, especially vols. IV/2, VI/2, and the forthcoming vol. VIII/2. The mass of primary material to be surveyed, sifted, and integrated into this lengthy study precludes critical discussion or debate except on the most im-portant current issues. I have discussed controversial readings or interpreta-tions only when absolutely necessary; some issues will no doubt surface in reviews and future work. My goal here has been to set forth what medieval romances say about how they were written and to integrate these statements into a coherent conception of the art of romance invention which those state-ments suggest. I have therefore also noted illustrations of the application of the art of romance as well as studies and interpretations by other scholars when these help clarify authorial interventions or when they corroborate them by practice.

Terms in foreign languages appear frequently in the following pages. Al-though this "scholasticism" is irritating to some, it is also unavoidable. It is useful to remember that medieval words had medieval meanings which, by and large, do not fit modern usage, even if the words have not changed. For example, although *roman* can be rendered by "romance," the English word is not synonymous with Old French *roman;* the same is true of *mer-veille* and marvel. It may also be that a given word such as *conjointure* has no precise English equivalent. Many terms, especially technical ones in Latin, no longer convey the specific meaning or meanings they once had. I have fol-lowed the example of Latin and Greek scholarship, using the original terms simply to guarantee good sense and precision, and hoping they may appear useful enough to become current once again. I have in all cases endeavored to use that term or word which is both accurate and least cumbersome. That modern critical vocabulary lacks equivalents to that of medieval languages is a defect of modern critical thought. It is therefore essential for the medievalist to identify that defect rather than try to twist medieval language into the straitjackets of modern theories.

All quotations in foreign languages except modern French have been translated, except in the notes. *Matiere* (without an accent) refers to the Old French word, *matière* to the modern French word.

D. W. Robertson, Jr., has suggested that medieval literature "may have 'languages' made up of conventions of expression which we should learn to 'read' just as we learn to read an earlier language or a foreign language."[2] I have tried to foster just this kind of "learning" here: to discover and to delineate the art of medieval romance as its authors themselves do. The result is, therefore, a work of scholarship, not of literary criticism. I cannot guarantee that the art was practiced as authorial interventions describe it. But evidence is available that it was, and I have identified it in notes and elsewhere. It would indeed be a curious case of secular schizophrenia if it were not. In the last analysis, this study is meant to return the reader to medieval romance, so that he or she can appreciate its art and its practitioners' accomplishments, their originality, profundity, ability to entertain; or, conversely, so that he or she can recognize failures—superficiality, stupidity, and narrow-mindedness. I also hope that it will assist and confirm others in their critical study of discrete romances or groups of romances, and, perhaps, will serve to caution or chasten those overly prone to reading without a historical sense. Historical criticism and modern methodologies are compatible, provided those who practice them are.

I am very beholden to friends and colleagues who, *nolens volens,* have given me ideas, perceptions, and criticism in conversations, lectures, publications, and reviews. My indebtedness is obvious in the notes. Institutional support has been very generous. The University of Wisconsin has provided grants, leaves of absence, and a tenure at the Institute for Research in the Humanities without which I should not have been able to complete this work even by this late date. The American Council of Learned Societies also assisted with a research fellowship. I owe special thanks to Professor SunHee Gertz, who had the knowledge, patience, and kindness to read and critique the penultimate version of the manuscript, thus making it intelligible. For their perceptive and intelligent criticism I am equally indebted to Professor Norris J. Lacy and Professor Daniel Poirion, who read the final manuscript for the University of Wisconsin Press.

The Art of Medieval French Romance

Introduction

Some years ago William A. Nitze wrote that "we lack a discriminating book on Old French literary technique, centering upon that original and observant writer, Chrétien de Troyes."[1] To correct the lack today would be difficult, given the expansion of knowledge and critical studies since 1950 on *chansons de geste,* the *grand chant courtois,* fabliaux, *Dits,* and other kinds of writing in medieval French. Romance itself, the kind Chrétien contributed most to,[2] is by no means an easily manageable subject. Although there are numerous studies of Old French literary technique, none delineates thoroughly and to everyone's satisfaction the art of medieval romance as medieval romancers understood and practiced it. Yet an art of romance did emerge; it evolved and was adapted during the twelfth and thirteenth centuries and beyond.[3] That art, however, was not set forth systematically or theoretically in those times. How may we approach the art of medieval romance in a manner useful for critical interpretation?

Recorded Statements

To begin with, Wesley Trimpi has provided some helpful suggestions as to the study of the theoretical presuppositions of premodern writers.

> The proper subject of the history of literary theory is not literature itself but the recorded statements about literature. The historian is not primarily concerned with why literature emerged in the ways that it did but with why people began to discuss it in the terms that they did. The nature and sources of their initial terminology indicate the premises upon which an "art" of literature was conceived and defended. The premises of its emergence were to determine the problems of its survival.[4]

These words bring us straight to the authorial interventions of medieval romance, not only those found in prologues and epilogues, where they are most often sought today, but all those passages where the author, narrator, or scribe tells us what he or she is doing as author, narrator, or scribe.[5] These are "recorded statements" about medieval romance — fragments from a time that has left no theoretical disquisition on the art of romance except in those fragments, or in praise and censure by medieval friends and foes of romance.

The emergence of romance is evident not only as a sequence of texts; it is also evident — and reflected (in both senses of the word) — in "recorded statements" about them.[6] Such statements impressed on the minds of medieval readers and audiences a sense for a group or family of works — a genre.[7] Since recorded statements document the emergence of romance in the minds of authors and publics, they are potentially of heuristic value, as guides toward understanding what medieval romance was, how and why it was written, and how it was received.

Modern criticism has made us acutely aware of the fact that recorded statements as authorial interventions are, more properly speaking, narrator's interventions, with all that this suggests as to implied author, narrative point of view, and narrator stance.[8] I do not believe that — *as literary historians* — we must always attribute such statements to a narrator totally divorced from the author. When we read in the *Charrette,* for example, that the countess of Champagne gave Chrétien the *matiere, san,* and commission to write the romance, we may regard the statement as a historical document and treat it as an archivist might: it is a credible statement about how the work came to be written. On the other hand, when, in the course of the *Charrette* narrative, we come upon the amusing intervention addressed to the audience about Lancelot's pretended drowsiness on the evening of his assignation with Guenevere — "Bien poez antendre et gloser, / Vos qui avez fet autretel" (4550–51)[9] [you can well understand and gloss, you who have done likewise] — when we read such a statement, it is entirely proper to regard it as the voice of the narrator rather than of a historical author about whom we may draw reliable conclusions.

This is a theoretical problem. We must confront it each time we analyze an authorial intervention. A narrator's words tell us something about how the romance is to be read and understood, and thus about the art that would produce such a reading. First and foremost, we see that Chrétien's art includes a narrator figure and an implied audience. The narrator and implied audience, whenever and however they may appear in discrete romances, open the reading to possible irony, deliberate prevarication, misrepresentation, or obfuscation that narrator's interventions *may* intend.[10] Such readings are not lacking in critical studies of the *Charrette* Prologue. A romancer's relation to audiences could be problematical, the role of the author and narrator nuanced and complex, as when, in the *Yvain* preliminaries, the author-narrator asserts that he, "Chrétien," is distancing himself from his audience.[11] Yet even in these cases a serious auctorial purpose is discernible beneath the narrator's stance. In *Yvain,* the humorous preliminaries mask critical commentary that may also control and justify writing the romance, going well beyond deference to patronage like that with which the *Charrette* and the *Conte du graal* begin.

There are also statements bordering on fancy or fiction that modern terminology may be at a loss to explain adequately. In the prose *Estoire del saint graal,* the scribal narrator tells how he was lifted into heaven, where he received from Christ's own hand a book he was to copy. Although this "event" is not historical like that referred to in the *Charrette* Prologue, its fictionality may still tell us something about the writing of the *Estoire.*[12] We may discover behind the event—the prevarication, hallucination, image, or mystical experience—something important about the medieval art of invention. Recent discussion among historians about medieval falsifications shows how these documents, among which we may include the *Estoire* Prologue, pose a very difficult if not baffling problem for modern readers.[13]

In the last analysis, the modern critic is confronted with two quandaries around and with which he or she must construe the meaning of a given medieval text: "documentary insufficiency" and "the remoteness of the linguistic and referential frameworks supporting the literary production of the period."[14] An author wrote a text of which our manuscripts are approximate reproductions. The reproduction is the work of scribes. A narrator's voice reads the story to us, much as medieval audiences listened to readers. Where the distinction between author, narrator, or scribe is not obvious.[15] I have used the term *auctorial* to identify interventions. Author in the sense implied by "auctorial" assumes in the vernacular the voice of authority implied in the Latin *auctor:*

> Vous qui avés oï d'Amours,
> Selonc le conte des auctours
> Et en latin et en roumans. . . .
> *(Amadas 5–7)*[16]

[You who have heard tell of Love, according to the tale told by authors in both Latin and French. . . .]

That authority may apply to a first author as source, to the author of the text, to the scribe copying it, or to the internal or external narrator producing the text for a reader or listening audience.

The modes of intervention suggested by these "authorities" need to be understood. Although romance prologues are not systematic disquisitions on the art of romance,[17] their words suggest that there existed an art which was readily comprehensible in its broad outlines, even to nonclerical audiences.[18] Might we not retrieve that art in its main outlines and processes by studying the recorded statements found in the romances and elsewhere?

Elsewhere the evidence of medieval Latin poetics, rhetoric, and historiography must be taken into account to complement and complete our interpretation of the recorded statements in romance. The art of romance presupposes reflection on the art when writing. Such reflection would use language, and therefore preconceptions, available in the twelfth and thirteenth centuries. The vernacular authors brought Latin techniques into the secular world, using them for adaptations from Latin and other languages. The aristocratic publics they wrote for seem to have been discriminating enough to understand the romancers' references to their art and to appreciate its adaptation to their own tastes and ideologies.[19]

There has been a great deal of discussion about how medieval authors conceived of composition, and how their conception, or conceptions, may have influenced their writing. Some words and expressions are very common, suggesting general agreement on their meaning and application to composition: *matiere, conte, vers, sans* and *san, antancion* and *antandre.* Others appear but once or twice, and are all the more perplexing because no one took the trouble to explain how such apparently rare or recondite words were used or understood: *conjointure, en uni dire, ambages.*

The fact that Latin equivalents for a number of these terms occur in medieval poetics and commentaries suggests that they did have recognizable technical meanings, at least for the educated. Yet, whether in Latin or in French, even technical terms may vary in definition or usage in different contexts and in different times and places.[20] For example, Hugh of Saint Victor defines *sententia* as the hidden or deeper meaning of a text, whereas Matthew of Vendôme uses *sententia* to refer in turn to the ideas an author wishes to bring out literally, to a proverb, or to the sentence made up of words.[21] In one place, Matthew uses the term *sensus* in a way that approximates the usual definition of *materia.*[22] Even the common word *materia* does not always convey the same meaning. Conrad of Mure, in a thirteenth-century art of writing, distinguishes between *thema* and *materia,* yet, in the same place, he admits that *materia* and *thema* may be synonymous.[23]

Similar problems crop up in French terminology. In the *Charrette* Prologue we are told that *matiere* and *san* come from the countess of Champagne (26–27); but Chrétien also refers to the contributions of his own *sans* (23). Is he contradicting himself? Or does his *sans* represent additions to Marie's *san?* Are *san* and *sans* only orthographic variants, or is there a different meaning implied for each instance? The Prologue to Marie's *Lais* poses the same orthographic problem.[24] We shall have to confront these ambiguities in recorded statements while delineating the art of medieval romance.

A word may have several denotations, depending on the branch of knowledge in which it is applied. Therefore, usage may vary, meanings overlap or diverge, to a greater or lesser extent in diverse contexts.

> Quelibet enim conditio, professio, facultas, dignitas habet et habere debet verba specialia et modum loquendi specialem. Nam verba et vocabula, quibus phisici in sua facultate solent uti, alium in aliis facultatibus sensum habent et intellectum, verbi gratia cum dicitur: Ista res est innaturalis vel non naturalis, vel extra vel ultra vel contra naturam.
>
> Ista locutio longe alium sensum habet in phisica quam in alia facultate, et sic de similibus. (*Summa* p. 100)[25]

> [Each and every condition, profession, discipline, and office has and must have a specialized terminology and language. For the terms used by the natural philosopher in his discipline have a different sense and meaning in other disciplines. For example, when one says: "This thing is unnatural" or "not natural" or "outside, above, or against nature." This expression has a sense in natural philosophy far different from that which it would have in another discipline, and the same is true for similar terms.]

There are terms whose meanings obviously changed with time, place, and context, in both Latin and the vernacular, or in passing from Latin to the vernacular. *Iunctura* did not have the same sense in Roman rhetoric as in poetics, and its range of application grew and its meaning conflated as it passed into the Middle Ages.[26] The failure to take into account specialized or historical distinctions explains much of the controversy about hidden or allegorical meanings in vernacular poetry.

The Medieval Art of Poetry and Prose

The medieval Latin art of poetry, reduced to the twelfth- and thirteenth-century arts of poetry and prose known today, has been deemed of dubious value for the interpretation of medieval literature, especially vernacular romance,[27] although it is obvious that the art of medieval romance is indebted to the traditions these treatises represent.[28] The principal difficulty has been twofold. First, the instructional intent of the treatises distances them from the masterpieces. Like elementary grammars, they are propaedeutic to spoken or written fluency. Second, other sources not obviously related to poetics like medieval historiography, hagiography, and oral traditions also contributed to the art of romance as it emerged and acquired integrity; they must therefore be examined as well for their contributions to the art of romance.

Some argue that we cannot today understand medieval narratives as they were written, that we would do better to confine ourselves to evaluating them by modern canons of criticism. I see no objection to the illustration of modern critical methodologies with medieval writings, as long as it is carried on with due care for philological accuracy and for the integrity of the medieval text. For example, Freudian and Jungian readings of romance are interesting approaches from a modern perspective. But they are no more historically valid than were readings of Ovid in medieval mythographies. As a general rule, we may posit that medieval writers were conscious of our critical expectations if they could verbalize those expectations. It behooves us to find those words.

This is crucial. It implies that recorded statements in and about medieval romance are meaningful. Repeated statements imply consensus and habit of conception, both among writers and in their publics.

But what of those instances where medieval writers do not use language corresponding to ours? Three explanations suggest themselves: what we esteem germane to the literary art was unknown to them or irrelevant; they concerned themselves with literary matters we ignore or reject; or, finally, we have not yet identified the language they used to speak of the expectations we share with them.

> Where rhetorical treatises and arts of versification seem to provide no key with which to unlock certain secrets in medieval texts, it is indeed possible to introduce concepts that have no historical justification. Possible—but is it always necessary? Should one perhaps not search again, in a different range of medieval writings, for a conceptual equipment of the time that might be profound and flexible enough to meet some of our own theoretical and critical demands?[29]

We must be fair to the medieval work itself. It may be more difficult to understand and appreciate a medieval writer than a modern one, but one can still try and thereby come a little closer to what Chrétien de Troyes and his contemporaries were about in the twelfth and thirteenth centuries. The effort is for that reason legitimate critical scholarship.

Despite the reservations expressed by some scholars as to the utility of or the need for considering rhetoric in relation to vernacular composition, that relation is a historical fact which, in a work of historical criticism, cannot be slighted or gainsaid. The happy progress made in recent years in study of the history of rhetoric lays to rest the narrow view that its contribution was merely formal, confined by and large to ornamentation by superficially imposed tropes and figures. This is not to say that rhetorical theory of the twelfth and thirteenth centuries explains medieval romance.[30] But given the demonstrable historical impact of rhetoric on the composition of romance, knowledge of that art is a prerequisite to modern understanding of its literary applications. Historical consciousness requires sympathy for an artistry which has a right to our scholarly and critical attention because it once existed, and which, by its very existence, counterbalances our own methodologies except in the minds of the most confirmed believers in continual progress. It is legitimate to explain an earlier art in its own terms, then translate that explanation into suitable modern terminology in order to evaluate and assimilate it.[31]

Methodology

I have collected recorded statements about the art of romance to draw from them the artistic conceptions and methods of composition the statements articulate. The evidence includes not only terminology, but also general statements regarding composition, even when they contain no particularly striking term or phrase. For example Godefroi de Lagni's Epilogue to the *Charrette* states why the narrative stops at that point: "Tant en a fet, n'i vialt plus metre / Ne moins, por le conte mal metre" (7111–12) [he has done that much, and will add no more nor less, lest he undo the tale]. Statements like these may be usefully juxtaposed with those found elsewhere, like "pars si qua sedebit inepte, / Tota trahet series ex illa parte pudorem" (*Poetria nova* 66–67) [if any part is ill-groomed, the work as a whole incurs censure from that one part], or "Omni parte sui modus omnis carmen honoret, / Ne qua parte labet, ne quam patiatur eclipsim" (*Poetria nova* 75–76) [in all of its parts, let the whole method of presentation bring credit upon the poem, lest it falter in any section, lest its brightness suffer eclipse].

In gathering auctorial interventions and other recorded statements, we must cast a wide but finely meshed net. The very frequency of banalities may be significant, if only to indicate their widespread acceptance. More important, further analysis of them in context may uncover unexpected meaning that contributes to the resolution of difficult problems.[32] The countless junctures that mark the interlacing branches in prose romance point to the *ambages pulcerrime,* the "long and winding paths" of narrative amplification that provoked Dante's admiration.[33]

There is a real danger of imposing one's own interpretation onto terms or expressions that may have had special technical meanings at the time they were written. To obviate this danger we must cull as many examples as possible from the texts, pay special attention to their context, and endeavor to locate them in the larger framework of medieval French and Latin criticism and composition. We must strive to survey the whole development of an idea or technique, as well as to determine its meanings and applications in different times and in different contexts. This is what Nitze failed to do when he linked Chrétien's *conjointure* to Horace's *iunctura* without taking into account obvious differences in the way each author applies these terms.[34]

Nonetheless it is often necessary to trace the evolution of a term or concept back to its origins. We have known for a long time, for example, that the conception of the three styles and that of natural and artificial order changed from the time of Cicero and Horace down into the twelfth and thirteenth centuries; the same may be true for other ancient terms used to refer to features of romance composition or medieval poetics.

As touched upon briefly, the relation of ideas on composition shared by French authors to the instruction given in medieval schools is a fundamental problem. Posing that problem concretely: if the methods of theology or biblical exegesis are applicable to the liberal arts and to what Hugh of Saint Victor calls the appendages of the arts—literature in Latin or, by extension, the vernaculars—then the arts of poetry should explain how they were to be applied. The relevance of the exegetical methods of composition can be demonstrated only after we have analyzed the pertinent, albeit often more pedestrian, instruction on composition and explication given in the trivium. That is, one must also focus on even elementary instruction in grammar, rhetoric, logic, and poetics before turning to medieval philosophy or theology for interpretative contexts. It is far more likely that the romancers went through the rudiments than that they pursued their studies beyond the arts courses in the universities. Errors in biblical references, if nothing else, suggest limitations in their knowledge of those disciplines.

The validity of the art of medieval romance described here lies in its heuristic value for the interpretation of texts. If composition and theory of composition are complementary, poetic practice should illuminate theory. It is one thing for an author to mouth a learned terminology, quite another to apply skillfully and meaningfully to the writing of romance the principles his or her words enunciate. This study of the art of romance aims at providing a framework to assist in such interpretation.

The Scope of the Art of Romance: Genre

What works will represent romance in this study? Jauss's theory of genre permits us to recognize groups or families of works possessing common characteristics and sharing a common history.[35] Genre identifies and defines a group of works through characteristics which, by virtue of their appearance and recurrence, constitute a tradition and reveal the expectations of audiences familiar with those works. The tradition is subject to correction and change in the light of past performances, audience demands, criticism, and recognition of new works. Genre in this sense describes and classifies historical phenomena. The historical fact of the emergence of romance conforms to the empirically derived genres Jauss and Köhler have proposed for medieval writings.[36]

The point is crucial to the issue of medieval versus modern critical expectations regarding the art of romance. How did medieval authors, scribes, and publics comprehend and speak of postmedieval notions of genre? That Jauss's theory of genre is, in its broad features, historically valid is apparent both in the generic awareness suggested by medieval use of the word *roman,* and in modern agreement as to which works, by and large, we classify as romance in bibliographies and histories of literature. Common features— *die systemprägenden Dominante*[37]—identify the genre. This does not preclude variation, expansion, correction, or independent developments.[38] The historical record of this process is not only the history of the emergence of romance as a genre. It also comprises the recorded statements of the art of romance that punctuate the process.[39] These are as instructive as the interpretation of texts.[40] The genre of romance, as a heuristic referent, is not monolithic, which accounts for the originality and dynamism of medieval romance as it emerged.

To be sure, there was lip service—deference to a tradition ignored, misunderstood, scorned, or unacceptable to some.

> De la richesce, et des vitailles,
> Et de la joie, et del deduit,
> Ne savroit nus dire, ce cuit,
> Tant qu'as noces plus n'en eüst.
> Por tant qu'as plusors despleüst,
> Ne vuel parole user ne perdre,
> Qu'a mialz dire me vuel aerdre.
> (*Cligés* 2316–22)

[I don't think anyone could tell the abundance and the food, the joy and the pleasure but that there was still more during the marriage celebration.

But since such a description would displease a lot of people, I won't waste
my words—for I intend to strive to improve my style.]

Modern taste tends to agree with the narrator's deference to his audiences
on this score. Yet *Cligés* is certainly Chrétien's most "rhetorical" romance.
Given its European reputation, the *Cligés*'s adherence to rhetoric's more formal prescriptions suggests that the romance was honored more than it was
scorned for its rhetorical glister.[41] As in most romances, auctorial interventions in *Cligés* frequently relate statements about the art of romance to the
text, thus making it an illustration of the art. Chrétien's proclivity for standard descriptive techniques in highly stylized portraits shows that he himself
came down in favor of that style.

> Por la biauté Clygés retreire
> Vuel une description feire,
> Don molt sera bries li passages.
> (*Cligés* 2721–23)

[To relate Cligés' beauty I wish to make a description, but one which will
be very short.]

As the arts of poetry point out: "Plerumque descriptio persone est tempestiva, plerumque superflua" (*Ars vers* 1.38)[42] [in many cases a description of
the person is fitting, in many superfluous]. The same can be said of the suppressed *Cligés* marriage ceremony: the "artful dodge" Chrétien uses to avoid
it is good medieval rhetoric.
  Chrétien also learned his art from other authors.

> Lisant trovomes an l'estoire
> La description de la robe,
> Si en trai a garant Macrobe,
> Qui au descrivre mist s'antante,
> Que l'an ne die que je mante.
> Macrobes m'ansaingne a descrivre,
> Si con je l'ai trové el livre,
> L'uevre del drap et le portret.
> (*Erec* 6736–43)[43]

[While reading in the *estoire* we came upon the description of the robe.
And, lest I be accused of lying, I call upon Macrobius to vouchsafe its
quality, he who applied himself to the art of description. Macrobius

teaches us how to describe the workmanship of the cloth and the portraiture, just as I have found that art set forth in the book.]

Chrétien's reference to Macrobius combines the work of fays and rhetoric[44] as an image of the art of romance itself—the artful interweaving or *conjointure* of the *merveilles* found in sources with a topical *vérité* expressed in descriptions and other amplifications. With Celtic legend and Latin rhetoric as the twelfth century understood it Chrétien invented romance. Many contemporaries followed his lead in the matter and art of their own works. They all wove diverse materials into narrative *conjointures*. *Conjointure*, as we shall see, defines vernacular *roman* as romance.

The following chapters attempt to determine how *bele conjointure* defines romance and, implicitly, the art of romance invention. First, there is an examination of the semantic range of *conjointure* and *jointure*, together with analogous terms in ancient and medieval Latin. This preliminary discussion points to the two arts that influenced the art of romance in its beginnings and evolution: the art of invention as the Latin Middle Ages inherited it from ancient rhetoric and poetics, and medieval historiography, especially as practiced in the vernacular chronicles and saint's lives that immediately preceded or were contemporary with the emergence and rise of twelfth-century romance. The art of invention and the techniques of medieval historiography offered what Trimpi calls the premises of the emergence of an art, in this case, of the art of romance invention and of the kind of writing we call romance today. They provided paradigms for composition that romancers used to treat the matter of their narratives.

Romance statements suggest that authors applied the acquired techniques to their own writings. This entailed initially the identification of material *(matiere)* to be adapted to the expression of an intended signification *(san)*. The matter chosen tended, like the illustrations in manuals on rhetoric, to be extraordinary: romancers chose marvelous adventures from which they drew a striking truth acceptable to the author and his or her implied audience or explicit patron. The rhetoric of romance, like traditional rhetoric, used extraordinary events as data for interpretation in the contexts fostered by medieval nobility: prowess, love, and rectitude. The resultant story *(conte* has become *estoire)* finally yields romance as a *bele conjointure* of narrative parts suitably arrayed—*ordre*.

The analysis covers the time from about 1150–70 to the end of the Middle Ages, during which high medieval romance emerged and acquired generic integrity. Auctorial interventions suggest a common conception of the art of romance invention that remained remarkably stable as a variety of traditional medieval poetics, itself very stable from the twelfth century on. Romance emerges quite rapidly in the time of Chrétien de Troyes as a discrete kind of writing, despite the plethora of narrative adventures, truths, and matters the romances illustrate. The study of auctorial statements reveals therefore historical standards by which we may today evaluate in medieval terms romances written during the high and late Middle Ages.

Conjointure

"What matter? There's more where that came from. . . . I have only to turn it on or off. . . . I'm a prestidigitator, I am." And from the lie I would make a truth. I'd spool it off (my unfinished opus) like a man possessed — themes, subthemes, variations, detours, parentheses — as if the only thing I thought about the livelong day was creation. With this of course went considerable clowning.
— H. Miller

The word *conjointure* is as ubiquitous in modern scholarship as it is rare in romance prologues and epilogues. Yet modern fascination with the word masks a startling, even disturbing variety of meanings that are attributed to it.[1] In reference to romance, the noun appears to be a hapax in the Middle Ages, occurring only in verse 14 of Chrétien's *Erec*. In fact, it is probably a nonce word, appearing at a time when *estoire* and *roman* were acquiring the specific generic senses of romance in the late twelfth century. That is, *estoire* as any kind of narrative was becoming *roman* as a specific narrative genre. That may be why, in the Prologue to the *Bel inconnu*, Renaut de Beaujeu adapts Chrétien's statement, replacing *conjointure* by *roman*: "Veul un roumant estraire / D'un molt biel conte d'aventure" (4–5) [I wish to draw a romance out from a very beautiful tale of adventure]. *Roman* as *conjointure* will therefore serve as a point of departure for this study of the art of romance as the art of *bele conjointure*.

French Lexicography: *Jointure*

The word *conjointure* was not unusual. It was used to refer to any combination of elements, however unwieldy, untidy, or heterogeneous. The expression *bele conjointure* itself, which Chrétien may have coined, allows for a *conjointure* that is not *bele,* like the rent and mutilated *conte d'avanture* Chrétien contrasts his *Erec* with. However, *conjointure* appears not only as a noun, but also as a verb, a modifier, and, without the prefix, as *jointure* in its various parts of speech.[2] For example, it could describe structural design.

> La sepolture si assist
> Que nule autre chose n'i ot;
> Bien la seele, et *joint,* et clot.
> Et lors se poïst bien prisier
> Qui sanz malmetre et sanz brisier
> Ovrir ne *desjoindre* seüst
> Rien que Jehanz fet i eüst.
> (*Cligés* 6072–78; emphasis mine)

[He constructed the sepulchre and nothing else. He seals, joints, and closes it well. He or she could indeed be proud who would succeed in removing or unjointing without mutilation or break anything Jehan had made in it.]

The description recalls language Godefroi de Leigni and Chrétien use to describe narrative closure: so well jointed and complete that nothing is lacking, nothing is mutilated, nothing superfluous.[3] It follows that *jointure,* as "jointing,"[4] brings together two or more parts and makes a whole out of them.

> Par tel engin et par tel art
> Est fez li huis de pierre dure
> Que ja n'i troveroiz jointure.
> (*Cligés* 5524–26)

[The hard-stone door is made so subtly and skillfully that you will never find any jointing in it.]

In the *Queste del saint graal* a description of David's sword includes similar language: "un pont de pierres precieuses si soutilment jointes qu'il n'ait . . . regart terrien qui poïst conoistre l'une de l'autre, ainz quit chascuns qui le verra que ce soit une meisme chose" (p. 223.8–12)[5] [a pommel of precious stones so finely joined that no human eye could distinguish the one from the other, but rather every observer will presume it to be all of one piece]. Subtle "jointing" seems therefore to distinguish the *conjointure* that is *bele.*

Subtle jointing fits the senses "attractive, well proportioned, shapely," the pleasing disposition of parts in human beauty. The combination of members extending from the part in the hair to the neck, the waist, or the feet is adorned with a pleasing array of noble and ideal social and intellectual components. The beautiful object of description is *joint:* all parts make a whole.

> Et la pucele vint plus cointe
> Et plus acesmee et plus *jointe*
> Que espreviers ne papegauz.
> (*Perceval* 1795–97; my emphasis)[6]

[And the maiden arrived appearing more elegant, gorgeous, and shapely than a sparrow hawk or a bird of paradise.]

The examples found in dictionaries illustrate a number of contexts for *jointure* and *conjointure* distinct from, but analogous to, the specifically literary sense found in Chrétien: the union of body and soul;[7] human relationships (conjugal, sexual, feudal, genealogical);[8] architecture (particularly interesting because of the frequency with which architecture is a model for poetic craft in the Middle Ages);[9] carpentry, stonemasonry, and other mechanical arts;[10] pharmaceutical and other chemical mixtures;[11] and, in general, any "assemblage des parties dont le corps est composé."[12] Such "assemblages" may be literary compositions, even mathematical structures,[13] or, on the other hand, an alloy, an admixture, even a hodgepodge of disparate elements.

Chrétien combines diverse *contes* and *aventures* into a new whole. The first part of *Erec* joins the White Stag adventure—the *premiers vers* (1796)—to the Sparrow Hawk tale,[14] just as the first part of *Yvain* conjoins a tale about a fountain giant to another about a fountain fay.[15] So subtly are the two tales conjoined in *Erec* that almost no one has perceived the joints, even though, in his reference to the "first verse," Chrétien points out one of them as clearly as Jehan does his in the *Cligés* tower. Of course, the end of the first *vers* does not terminate the first *part* of the romance, which is marked by the marriage of Erec and Enide. That marriage concludes what we may call the *altre vers*—the Sparrow Hawk adventure.

The converse of *conjointure* is *desjointure*. The concept is found in the description of Fenice's tomb (*Cligés* 6077). Elsewhere one finds: "Veés vous la cel tertre a cele desjointure? / Tres en mi ces desers a une grant couture" (*Alex* APar III.1163–64)[16] [do you see that hillock there at the point of separation? Right in the midst of those wastes there lies a large cultivated field]. The dictionaries define *desjointure* and its derivatives as a rent, tear, or break—a *faille.*[17] In narrative a *faille* may occur at a break in a story, as in interlace. This may produce a *bele desjointure.*[18] Or it may be a gap like the rents or lacunae in the storytellers' *contes* criticized in the *Erec* Prologue. Like *conjointure,* therefore, a *desjointure* may or may not be beautiful.

The definition of *jointure* as artful *conjointure* and *desjointure* is elaborately illustrated apropos of digression in Baudouin de Condé's fourteenth-century *Le prison d'amour.*

> Pour çou me couvient de mon preu
> Parler aucune fois un peu,
> Et ma parolle entrecoper.
> Mais cil ne doit mie coper
> Qui enter ne set et ajoindre:
> Or m'i laist Dex isi rajoindre
> Ma matere et si ranoer
> Que on ne le puist desnoer
> Ne de routure ne de neut.
> Mais il est drois que on reneut
> La corde quant elle est desroute;
> Ausi quant aurai entreroute
> Ma matere, g'i repairrai
> Toudis la ou jou le lairrai,
> Et ranoerai tout a point.
>   (187–201)[19]

[Wherefore it behooves me at times to say something on my own behalf, interrupting my discourse. But one should not cut off without knowing how to graft and adjoin. God grant that I may once again link and tie together my matter so that it cannot be unraveled by breaking or undoing (?) the knot. But it is fitting to tie again a broken cord. Just so, when I have interrupted my matter, I shall always return to it there where I left it, and tie it up again properly.]

Chrétien implies that he too is tying material together by *conjointure.*

> . . . tret d'un conte d'avanture
> Une molt bele conjointure
>
> .   .   .   .
> D'Erec, le fil Lac, est li contes
> Que devant rois et devant contes
> Depecier et corronpre suelent
> Cil qui de conter vivre vuelent.
>   (*Erec* 13–14, 19–22)[20]

[He draws from a tale of adventure a very beautiful *conjointure*. . . . The story is about Erec, son of Lac, which those who strive to gain their living by storytelling are wont to rend and mutilate when telling it before kings and counts.]

But it is also possible to delete material in order to effect a new narrative combination. Thomas d'Angleterre does so by excluding Governal's visit to Marc's court in search of Iseut, rejecting this *matiere* in favor of another version:[21] not all stones are suitable in a well-built house, nor do all houses realize the same plan or style.

Jointure permits incremental as much as interstitial linking. It may result from synthesis or analysis, from conflation and fusion as *conjointure,* or from accession, annexation, contamination, or augmentation[22] by *desjointure*. To put this into medieval terminology, we may say that *iunctura* in *narratio continua* produces either *perpetuus contextus* or *narratio partilis* with *interruptiones*.[23]

Therefore, both *conjointure* and *desjointure* may refer to the meshing of several *contes* into one, or to expansion by juxtaposing any number of separate tales. The prose romances utilize the latter to amplify, add to, and correct their sources.[24] The process entails not only elaboration of episodic romances, as when Chrétien's *Charrette* is expanded into the Lancelot-Grail cycle; it also permits elaborate interlacing, imbrication, and gradation of separate narrative branches.

> Si mistrent en escript lez aventures mon seignor Gauvain tout avant, por ce que c'estoit li commenchemens de la queste de Lancelot, et puis les Hector, por chou que de cel conte estoient branche, et puis lez aventures a tous lez .XVIII. autres compaignons, et tout ce fu del conte Lancelot, et tout cil autre furent branche de chestui, et li contes Lancelot fu branche del Graal, si com il y fu ajoustés.
>
> (*Lancelot* VIII.lxxia.48)[25]

> [And they wrote down first the adventures of my lord Gauvain, because he was the source of the quest for Lancelot; then came the adventures of Hector, since his was a branch of that tale, and finally the adventures of the eighteen other companions. And all of this was part of the Lancelot story, and all the others were branches of it. And the Lancelot tale was itself a branch of the Grail, just as it was joined to it.]

Intertwining branches are an image that captures the essence of prose romance interlace. They adorn the main branch they are grafted onto. That "grail trunk" rises up to the sky literally and figuratively at the beginning of the *Estoire del saint graal* and at the end of the *Queste*.[26]

Chrétien adapts another horticultural metaphor to romance composition in the *Perceval* Prologue. There he likens sowing fertile ground to beginning a new romance.

> Crestiiens seme et fet semance
> D'un romanz que il ancomance,
> Et si le seme an si bon leu
> Qu'il ne puet estre sanz grant preu.
>   (7–10)

[Chrétien sows and seeds down a romance which he begins; and he sows it in such fertile ground that it cannot but produce plentiful growth.]

The "fertile ground" is the book Chrétien says Philippe d'Alsace gave him for the *Conte del graal.* His contribution, the "seeds," will blossom and flourish, growing from the rich soil as the plots of Chrétien's adaptation. A text is thus generated from the careful arrangement and elaboration of one or more plots.

Most romances seem to join various plots. "Seignor, qui matere encomence, / En plusors leus met sa semence" (*Claris* 5659–60) [my lords, whoever begins a *matiere* sows in several plots]. The anonymous author of *Claris et Laris* combines a variety of plots which may each be the source of narrative.

> Toute li couvient recoillir,
> S'a matiere ne veult faillir;
> Mes c'est trop mauvese manire,
> Quant li hons faut a sa matire,
> Molt l'en doit por musart tenir;
> Si vueill a la moie venir.
>   (*Claris* 5661–66)[27]

[He must harvest all of it if he does not wish to lack *matiere.* But that writer is quite reprehensible and should be considered a dawdler who runs out of *matiere.* And so I intend to return to mine.]

Such preparation was traditionally a source of narrative elaboration and elucidation: *semina spargere* [sowing seeds] produces *narratio praestructiva.*[28] The *Claris* romancer has sown several plots, in both the agricultural and the narrative senses of the metaphor, and can, as it were, replenish his work by, in effect, harvesting different plots. Immediately after this intervention, for example, he introduces a wholly new plot: the Romans invade Arthur's realm.

Chrétien's use of *conjointure* permits two applications, the one material and the other formal. It denotes, first, a combination of elements drawn from a *conte d'avanture*—his *matiere*—and, second, his own arrangement of those elements, which is *bele.*[29] *Conjointure* brings out and enhances the quality of the source *matiere,* like the sower's seed in good ground.

> Crestïiens . . . antant et painne
> A rimoiier le meillor conte
> Par le comandemant le conte
> Qui soit contez an cort real:
> Ce est li contes del Graal,
> Don li cuens li bailla le livre.
> *(Perceval* 62–67)[30]

[Chrétien . . . applies himself and strives to versify the best story told in royal court, and he does so at the Count's behest. It is the story of the Grail, the book of which the Count gave him.]

It is a kind of amplification or abbreviation that brings out the qualities of a good plot.

Latin Terminology: *Iunctura*

Iunctura as both weave *(contextus)* and break *(interruptio)* is implicit in Hugh of Saint Victor's description of the artist's tasks: *disgregata coniungere* and *coniuncta segregare*.[31] *Iunctura* was a term in Roman poetic theory, perhaps invented by Horace.[32] Its most prominent occurrence is in his art of poetry, *Ad Pisones,* where it appears twice as a noun.[33] The first instance treats the shrewd conjunction of words when they are carefully sewn and sown together *(serendis),*[34] and thus interlaced. The sense of interlace associated with *iunctura* was enhanced by the word's connection with *serere* and *series*.[35] "Sowing" as "production" (cf. *iunctura pollet, Ad Pisones* 242)[36] evokes the garden sown with seeds that blossom in striking patterns and color combinations in the *Conte del graal* and *Claris et Laris*. The sense of "sewing" combines with *series,* a nominal instance of *serere* as "serial combination," by which Horace meant an artful arrangement of syllables, words, and short phrases in the sentence in order to effect an original or new and beautiful expression. But the verbs *serere* and *pollere* also connote *iunctura* in "plotting," or the achievement of what one medieval commentator on Horace calls "uniformem materiam," that is, *materia* without the patchwork of those who "interserunt diversas materias"[37] [interweave and intersperse disparate matters]. For Horace, such combination may result from both the invention of new words from the Greek and the revelation of new potential in common words. Chrétien saw his task, on the level of narrative invention, as discerning things "hidden"—Horace's *abdita*—in his foreign sources and drawing them out by adroit narrative arrangement and elaboration.

Materia uniformis was not always the goal of *iunctura* and *series*. After

Horace, use of *iunctura* attests to an extension of the word's semantic range beyond words and syntax, anticipating Chrétien's use of it in the *Erec* Prologue to describe narrative arrangement. By Quintilian's time, for example, it had absorbed the general sense of *iunctio* / *coniunctio* as "assemblage des mots dans la phrase";[38] in Porphyry, it is synonymous with *compositio* or elegant sentence composition.[39] In the Middle Ages, *series* and *iunctura* may describe sentence style. For example, the conversion of words from one part of speech to another allows for more suitable expression of thought or sentiment.

> et cuilibet aptes
> Talem juncturae seriem quae serviat apte
> Proposito.
> *(Poetria nova* 1612–14)

[And adapt to it (i.e., *iunctura*), in each of its cases, a related series of words which may adequately express the proposed statement.]

The semantic extension of *iunctura* from *compositio* as artful syntax to *compositio* as artful arrangement of parts is complete by the time of the medieval *accessus ad auctores*.[40] *Iunctura* could refer to the linking of parts in any phase of composition: "ordo rerum, diuisio operis, ordo uerborum, oikonomia, compositio uerborum . . . "[41] [order of parts, division of the work, order of words, narrative economy, syntax]. According to John of Salisbury, Bernard of Chartres taught the widely applicable principle to his pupils.[42] In Alain de Lille and Chrétien de Troyes, it refers to narrative arrangement and linking.[43] Clearly, *conjointure* has become something akin to modern *écriture* in its range of applications.[44]

Iunctura could also refer to rearrangement of material so that parts cohered in new ways. Hugh of Saint Victor notes that the Bible uses alternately natural and artificial order—what Bernard of Utrecht terms *communis ordo*.[45] This happens when events quite separate in time "quasi mox sibi succedentia, connectit, ut videatur nullum disiunxisse spatium temporis illa quae non discernit ullum intervallum sermonis"[46] [are linked so as to follow immediately on one another without any temporal interval seemingly separating events which are not separated by any interval in discourse]. *Conjointure* appears here to subtend *desjointure* (cf. *disiunxisse*).

Iunctura could apply to metaphor as well. Geoffrey of Vinsauf, for example, uses the expressions *iunctura occulta* and *iunctura aperta* (*Poetria nova* 241–63) to designate two kinds of metaphor.[47] In *iunctura aperta*, "quaedam signa revelant / Nodum iuncturae" (243–44) [certain signs reveal the point of juncture]. *Iunctura occulta* recalls the kind of narrative *conjointure*

Chrétien usually practices as well as those noted by Hugh of Saint Victor in the Bible:

> res ubi junctae
> Sic coeunt et sic se contingunt, quasi non sint
> Contiguae, *sed* continuae.
>
> (259–61)

[The elements joined flow together and touch each other as if they were not contiguous but continuous.]

This is *narratio continua*. The "hidden" link does not betray its function; rather "sic sedet in serie quasi sit de themate nata" (251) [the new element fits as securely into the context as if it were born of the theme]. It is an addition to the *materia*, but one which, like the hidden door in Jehan's tower in *Cligés*, conjoins separate material so precisely as to leave no sign of the juncture.

Continuatio was a desideratum: "in serie . . . continuationes, id est ut precedentia conveniant sequentibus" (*Comm* Utrecht p. 68.253–54) [in narrative sequence . . . *continuationes*, that is, let what precedes cohere with what follows]. *Continuatio* refers to the way different parts are joined together to produce a whole and complete *series*.[48] Horace's use of *iunctura* became a prescription for *continuatio*: "tantum pollet in illo carmine series, idest ordinatio materiae, et iunctura, idest copulatio. Et tantum honoris accedit rebus sumptis de medio, idest tantam seriem in ordinanda materia et tantam iuncturam in *continuationem* illorum et tantum honorem et ornatum orationis dabo saturae quam facio de communi materia"[49] [thus do *series*, or the arrangement of *materia*, and *iunctura*, or its combination, grow firm. And so much does it redound to the excellence of ordinary matter, that is, as much *series* as I make in ordering *materia* and as much *iunctura* in providing unbroken sequence or succession, by that much does the value and elegance of the satire grow that I put together using ordinary matter]. Horace's "ordinary matter" became an excellent poem by *series* and *iunctura*, much as Chrétien's *conte d'avanture* became romance by the *bele conjointure* of narrative parts.

If *iunctura occulta* suggests the blending of diverse *contes*, *iunctura aperta* makes for *narratio partilis*. *Disiunctum (disiunctio, disiungere)—disiunctura* appears in the dictionaries only as a medical term[50]—describes both inelegant parataxis and the artful collocation of words.[51] This is the explicit juxtaposition of narrative branches or *contes* and digressions.[52] For example, in the *Queste del saint graal*, the history of the colored wood from the Tree of Life is inserted into the description of the bed in the Ship of Solomon, which is part of the *conte* of Galaad, itself interlaced, as part of the Grail story, with the tales of other questing knights. These narrative branches are linked, broken off, returned to at a later juncture in an obvious, "open" way: "Mes a tant lesse ores li contes a parler d'aux et retorne a monseignor Boort de Gaunes. Or dit li contes que quant Boorz se fu partiz de Lancelot si come li contes a devisé, qu'il chevaucha jusq'a hore de none" (*Queste* pp. 161.33–162.5) [but with that the story leaves them to return to my lord Boort of Gaunes. Now, the story reports that upon taking leave of Lancelot, as related above, Boort rode on until nones]. By contrast, the effectiveness of Chrétien's use of *iuncturae occultae,* in the sense suggested above, depends on masking breaks. For, as Geoffrey of Vinsauf notes, "hidden" jointing creates the impression not of contiguity, but of continuity.

There are problems in equating Horace's and Chrétien's terminology. The first passage containing *iunctura,* in Horace, may be corrupt.[53] But since there is no evidence that the Middle Ages knew it other than as it has come down to us in the extant manuscripts, we may take that version and the medieval readings of it as authoritative for Chrétien and his contemporaries. A more serious problem is the fact that Horace is discussing choice of words and syntax rather than the elements of composition that his commentators read into the word. Closer to Chrétien's sense of continuous, unbroken narrative sequence is the discussion of inept combinations at the beginning of the *Ad Pisones.*

> Velut aegri somnia, vanae
> Fingentur species, ut nec pes nec caput uni
> Reddatur formae.
>
> (7–9)[54]

[As in the dreams of a sick person, fantastic forms are invented, wherein top and bottom do not cohere.]

These passages suggest that for Horace *iunctura* (note *iungere* in v. 2) could refer to a wide range of activities: letters in the word, words in the sentence or phrase, sentences in longer segments, parts in a description, or the whole work. In Chrétien's time, Alain de Lille uses the term to refer to narrative junctures: "Poete tamen aliquando hystoriales euentus ioculationibus fabulosis quadam eleganti sutura confederant, ut ex diuersorum competenti iunctura ipsius narrationis elegantior pictura resultet" (*De planctu* VIII.137–39)[55] [sometimes poets combine historical events and imaginative fancies, as it were in a splendid structure, to the end that from the harmonious joining of diversities a finer image of the story may result (p. 40.214–17)]. The joining of diverse matters suggests the *concors discordia* [harmonious discord] that Geoffrey of Vinsauf prizes in good style (*Poetria nova* 843), and that Thomas d'Angleterre tried to achieve in his *Tristan*.

> Seignurs, cest cunte est mult divers,
> E pur ço l'uni par mes vers
> E di en tant cum est mester
> E le surplus voil relesser.
> Ne vol pas trop en uni dire.
> (*Tristan* Th Douce 835–39)

[My lords, this tale is highly disparate; therefore, I have brought the different parts together through my verse; and I am telling as much of it as is necessary, omitting the rest. I have no desire to combine too much in my narrative.]

Here what is scattered and disparate is gathered together, linking originally separate elements in a new combination to achieve a more pleasing whole — "ex diuersorum competenti iunctura," in Alain's words.

Medievalists, following Alain's and Chrétien's usage, have taken the terms *coniunctura* and *conjointure* to refer either to a story pattern found in a source and redeployed in a new work or to a new structure or disposition the author gives to the source.[56] Auctorial statements support the latter sense. But the first reading is implicit in the special sense of archetypal conception of *materia* common in medieval descriptions of invention.

> Si quis habet fundare domum, non currit ad actum
> Impetuosa manus: intrinseca linea cordis
> Praemetitur opus, seriemque sub ordine certo
> Interior praescribit homo. . . .
> (*Poetria nova* 43–46)[57]

[If a man has a house to build, his impetuous hand does not rush into action. The measuring line of his mind first lays out the work, and he mentally outlines the successive steps in a definite order.]

Archetypal conception was likened to architectural planning. The mental ordering of parts in a coherent and cohesive structure (*narratio praestructiva*) conveyed the author's meaning and intention.

The invention of *conjointure* is thus part of "archetypal" invention as Geoffrey of Vinsauf describes it in the *Poetria nova*: "Circinus interior mentis praecircinet omne / Materiae spatium" (55–56) [let the mind's interior compass first circle the whole extent of the material]. In the mind, Geoffrey's compass, like Horace's square (*Ad Pisones* 72),[58] measures the work's parts and fits them by jointing in the whole. The process patterns all subsequent phases of composition: order, topical amplification, ornamentation, syntax, versification.

> Sic simul ergo
> Omnia concurrant, inventio commoda, sermo
> Continuus, series urbana. . . .
> *(Poetria nova* 2061–63)

[So, then, let all be in harmony: suitable invention, flowing expression, polished development. . . .]

The *conte d'avanture* was a work whose *iuncturae* were stitches in a patchwork quilt, *paniaus* sewn together helter-skelter,[59] with holes and tears that made not for *series* "intacta" (*Poetria nova* 127), but rather for discontinuous, patchwork scraps—the result of the *depecier* and *corronpre* castigated in the *Erec* Prologue.

Parts and Variants in *Conjointure: Vers* and *Divers*

Vers as a part in Chrétien's *Erec* and *divers* as the combined *matiere* in Thomas' *Tristan* describe features of *conjointure*. In Thomas d'Angleterre's *Tristan,* "unir" and its cognate "en uni dire" mean to "collect," "gather together" a "diverse" story, without implying anything about the quality of the resultant "collection."[60] It is a *conjointure,* whether *bele* or not. At this stage, the collection included Governal's visit to Marc's court, which Thomas then rejected as mendacious. Similarly, Albéric de Pisançon castigates the lying "estrobatour" (*Alex* AdeP 27) for telling the story of Alexander's murder of Nectanabus; like Thomas rejecting the Governal episode, Albéric deems the murder of Alexander's alleged father inappropriate and incredible. Wace too rejected incredible *matiere.*

> Tant unt li cunteür cunté
> E li fableür tant flablé
> Pur lur cuntes enbeleter,
> Que tut unt fait fable sembler.
> *(Brut* 9795–98)

[The storytellers have told so much, and the narrators narrated so much, in order to embellish their stories that they have made everything seem quite fictitious.]

It is curious that Wace faults the storytellers for attempting to "enbeleter." Chrétien distinguishes his *Erec* "conjointure" precisely because it is "bele." But in Wace's chronicle "enbeleter" means turning truth to fable;[61] for Chrétien the quality of the additions and the manner in which they are conjoined distinguish his romance as *conjointure* from fable or *conte d'avanture*. For Chrétien the disruption of *series* or coherent narrative development dismembers the tale. Elsewhere we find:

> Grans vilonie est ct grans honte
> De si bon conte desmenbrer
> Fors ensi com il doit aler.
> (*Elucidation* 320–22)

[It's a great wrong and shame to dismember such a fine story, which ought to proceed only as it is meant to do.]

Formal demands are meant to serve narrative coherence, even if the attempt is an apparent failure, as in the *Elucidation*.

Diversité is not necessarily to be eschewed in *conjointure,* as we observed regarding the passages on sowing different plots. The notion of *concors discordia* that passed from the Chartrain poets into the twelfth- and thirteenth-century arts of poetry and prose[62] aptly describes the union of disparate *matiere* in medieval romance.[63] Thomas d'Angleterre tried to retain as much as he could of the "diverse" versions of the Tristan legend.[64] He required only that the parts be congruent, that they preserve narrative continuity, consistency, and verisimilitude. This requirement still holds for Adenet le Roi toward the end of the thirteenth century.

> Ai un autre livre rempris
> Mout merveilleus et mout divers.
> Dieus doinst que teus soit chascuns vers
> Que blasmés n'en soie et repris!
> Mout est l'estoire de grant pris
> Et a oÿr moult gracïeuse;
> Tant est diverse et merveilleuse
> Que je croi c'onques nus n'oÿ
> Si diverse comme cesti.
> (*Cleomadés* 8–16)

[I have begun yet another book, one that is more marvelous and varied. God grant that each *vers* be above reproach and blame! The tale is of great worth and most pleasing to hear. It is so diversified and marvelous that I believe that no one ever heard one so unusual as this.]

Adenet le Roi is not unaware of the pejorative sense of *divers:* an African
king is ugly, among other reasons, because of his "si diverse taille" (1927)
[so strange shape]. This makes the attribute an antonym of *joint.* But it also
has the positive sense of *merveilleux,* as verse 14 in *Cleomadés* suggests. Referring to narratives, Marie de France states that "Ki divers cuntes veut trai-
tier / Diversement deit comencier" (*Lais* Mi 1–2)[65] [whoever wishes to treat
various stories must begin in varied ways]. Prudence and art keep diversity
in order. Each of her lays arranges events in a clear sequence of beginning,
middle, and end; the author remains attentive to the art of composition ("Ki
de bone mateire traite, / Mult li peise si bien n'est faite" [*Lais* Gui 1–2] [who-
ever treats a good *matiere* is displeased when it is not well done]) and to
the expectations of the audience ("parler si rainablement / K'il seit pleisibles
a la gent" [*Lais* Mi 3–4] [speak so reasonably as to please people]). Thus
auctorial control brings order to diversity. Chrétien thinks his "conjointure"
is "bele" not only because it corrects material faults and formal defects by
articulate jointing, but also because it expresses the truth of the *matiere*—a
notion consonant with medieval conceptions of the beautiful, and thus of
the *bele conjointure.*[66]

The *divers* as disparate combination includes different *vers* as parts of the
whole. Adenet le Roi's words in *Cleomadés* proclaim that each *vers* should
be faultless. *Vers* in Old French means not only a line of verse but also stan-
zaic, episodic, and narrative units.[67] As narrative it corresponds to words
like *branche, laisse,* some uses of *conte,* and other words and expressions
used to refer to parts of a plot.[68] We have shown that Chrétien's reference
in *Erec* to the "premiers vers" is an explicit designation of a narrative segment drawn from one or more sources and fit into the plot of the first part
of the romance.

> Li rois par itele avanture,
> Randi l'usage et la droiture
> Qu'a sa cort devoit li blans cers:
> Ici fenist li premiers vers.
> (*Erec* 1793–96)

[By this very adventure the king observed the practice and the principle of
right which was due his court by the white stag. Here ends the first
"verse."]

Alixandre de Paris' *Alexandre* offers a reading that may well be synonymous
with Chrétien's.

Qui vers de riche istoire veut entendre et oïr,
Pour prendre bon example de prouece acueillir

. . . .

Oëz dont *le premier* [= vers] bonnement a loisir.
Ne l'orra guieres hom qui ne doie pleisir;
Ce est du meilleur roi que Dieus laissast morir.
  (*Alex* APar I.1–2, 8–10; emphasis mine)

[Whoever wishes to hear "verse" from a noble story in order to have a
good example of how to acquire prowess . . . , listen to the first one
quietly and at your leisure. Scarcely anyone will hear it without pleasure.
It is about the best king whom God let suffer death.]

The singular in syntactic combination with *premier* in verse 8 is striking.
Do we not have in it a reference to the first branch of the Alexander romance,
or at least a first segment—childhood and *enfances,* for example—to which
others will be added? "L'estoire d'Alixandre vous voeil par vers tretier / En
romans qu'a gent laie doie auques profitier" (*Alex* APar I.30–31) [I wish to
relate the story of Alexander in "verse" (or "verses"?), in French, so that lay
persons might profit from it.]. A similar passage occurs in Geffrei Gaimar's
Engleis.

Ele en fist fere un livere grant,
Le primer vers noter par chant.
Bien dit Davit e bien trovat
E la chançon bien asemblat.
  (6485–88)[69]

[She had a book prepared about it, and the first "verse" set to music.
David spoke and invented well and put the song together aptly.]

The denotations of *vers, branche,* and *laisse* reflect the same correlation between units of discourse, both large and small, that we have found in *iunctura* and *coniunctura*—word, sentence, line, stanza, paragraph, amplification,
episode, plot, branch, and whole romance or even groups of romances in
cyclical or "incidental" conjunction like the Vulgate and post-Vulgate Arthurian cycles or the Guillaume cycles—as well as spatial and temporal in-
terlocking like that between Chrétien's *Charrette* and *Yvain.* In all cases,
diverse or varied segments *(vers)* are linked by *jointures* to fit into the plan
and conception of the work.[70] The result is a satisfactory array of parts appropriately conjoined.

To bring together a great deal of *matiere,* as well as to introduce amplifications at appropriate places, requires careful attention to plotting and narrative texture, to its coherence and the points where *matieres* and developments are conjoined. Hence the pertinence for *jointure* of words like *adjoindre, enter, coper, rompre, tourner* (together with complements like *point, pli, ploi*), *agenser, attacher, desmembrer, assembler, asseoir, entrelaissier, departir, desconfire, composer, forvoier, lignier, afaitier, adrescer, compasser.* These words denote combinations of parts in the *(es)traire* and *mettre* process used to describe romance composition.[71] *Jointure* in such composition, as *translatio,*[72] or the passage from source to work, comprehends rearrangement and new combinations.

> Et cel anelet li avoit douné la damoisiele del lac, si coume la grant hystore de Lanscelot le devise, cele meisme ystoire qui doit estre departie de mon livre, ne mie pour chou qu'il n'i apartiegne et que elle n'en soit traite, mais pour chou qu'il couvient que les trois parties de mon livre soient ingaus, l'une aussi grant coume l'autre, et se je ajoustaisse cele grant ystore la moiene partie de mon livre fust au tresble plus grant que les autres deus. (Huth *Merlin* II, 57)

> [The Maid of the Lake gave him that ring, just as the great story of Lancelot relates, the very story which should be separated from my book, not because it doesn't belong to mine or isn't drawn from it, but because the three parts of my book should be of equal length, the one as long as the other; and if I were to add that great story [of Lancelot], the middle part of my book would be three times as long as the other two.]

The post-Vulgate's use of *traire-estraire* is analogous to that in Chrétien's *Erec* and Renaut de Beaujeu's *Bel inconnu.* Renaut wishes to "un roumant estraire / D'un molt biel conte d'aventure" (4–5) [extract a romance from a most beautiful tale of adventure].[73] All these writers drew from their *matiere* something beautiful, whatever they may have understood that beauty to consist of. This is consistent with the passage from the post-Vulgate *Merlin* about the *Lancelot* Proper which was "drawn" or "branched" from it.[74]

Similarly, *traire a fin* or *a chief* tells how the narrative is brought to a conclusion: "Je ne vous puis pas tout retraire, / Ma matere voel a fin traire" (*Couci* 5438–39)[75] [I can't relate everything; I wish to draw my *matiere* to a conclusion]. Exclusion and stress influence choice, treatment, and disposition.

> Qui en rimer velt painne metre,
> Soutilment se doit entremetre
> De cele matire avant trere,
> Qui puist toute bone gent plere.
>   (*Claris* 1–4)

[Whoever wishes to strive to rhyme ought to undertake to set forth skillfully that matter which can please all worthy people.]

Ultimately, for Chrétien as well as the other romancers, it was the "right"
combination and adroit "jointing" that brought out the significance of heterogeneous *matieres*. They retained thereby the original Horatian intent to
use *iuncturae* in order to show beauty hidden in things.[76] Failure branded
the would-be authors: "ad tantam eciam stulticiam deuenerunt, et quibus-
dam monstruosarum fabularum laruis repertis diuersas partes sibique repug-
nantes coniungere niterentur monstrisque libros suos replentes monstruosam
larualemque paginam hominibus traderent" (*Dolopathos* lat p. 3.7–10) [they
lapsed into such nonsense that they invented the shapes of monstrous fables
and strove to conjoin diverse, mutually incompatible parts and, filling their
books with these, produced an unnatural, weird folio].

    Conjointure integrates[77] by apposite *iuncturae* diverse, seemingly incom-
patible material. But the purpose is not to produce a *monstrosum* like Horace's
mermaid, but rather to *monstrare abdita rerum*. Horace showed how "series" and "iunctura" permit the writer to draw from his or her "materia" the
"abdita rerum" (*Ad Pisones* 49), that is, the heretofore obscure sense of words.
Concors discordia replaced Horatian ideas of harmony by a more medieval
sense of mystery and hidden signification. For, as the Latin *Dolopathos* concludes, proper arrangement of the "strange" or monstrous could acquire significance, and thereby exemplify truth through the fabulous (pp. 2.35–3.16).
Romancers thought that such combinations, at once inspired, penetrating,
and judicious, could "dévoiler le mystère des choses."[78] The fundamental concern at every stage in the composition of a romance, from sentence and line
of verse to combinations of narrative *vers,* was the invention of *matieres* in
all the broad array of senses that this word had for medieval writers.

    Such composition involves *dispositio* as the arrangement of suitable parts.
As Nitze pointed out, there is an arrangement in each source of a romance
and another arrangement in the completed new work. The transition from
the former to the latter depends for medieval romancers on two paradigms
for artistic invention: the scholastic paradigm drawn from rhetoric and the
historiographical paradigm drawn from the writing of history. As we shall
see, both are concerned with narrative as a satisfactory array of parts — as
a *bele conjointure*.

2

Antecedent Paradigms of Invention: Literary Paradigm

Ut enim faber, volens aliquid fabricare, prius illud in mente disponit, postea, quesita materia, iuxta mentem suam operatur.
—*Glosae §32*

[Just as the artist who wishes to fashion something first sets it out in his mind, then, having looked for material, fashions it to fit his mental conception.]

The art of romance did not spring full-blown from the head of Chrétien de Troyes and his peers. They had a frame of reference, a paradigm for invention. That paradigm may be reconstructed from the medieval arts of poetry and prose and related documents. The fact that these works are not well understood by most students of romance requires an inquiry into their instruction on invention in order to anticipate its application to the art of romance.

Art of Invention

The medieval arts of poetry and prose draw on learned and scholastic traditions of ancient, especially Roman, origin.[1] These traditions linked poetics to one or more of the liberal arts, especially grammar and rhetoric.[2] Grammar and rhetoric occupied a place on the tree of knowledge that rose from humble techniques and crafts like poetry upward through the seven liberal arts and the sciences to, ultimately, philosophy and theology. The hierarchy of arts and sciences was based on distinctions among the different branches of the tree of knowledge, and on attention to the right and wrong uses of learning.[3] The best writing was supposed to illustrate the Ciceronian ideal of *sapientia* and *eloquentia*. The ideal, which became traditional in Christianity after Augustine, was given special emphasis by medieval writers.[4]

But there was no universal agreement on the value of the art of poetry.[5] Hugh of Saint Victor's dismissal of poetry as an unnecessary, even dangerous appendage to the liberal arts, Alain de Lille's distinction between the "poet" and the "philosopher," as well as Bernardus Silvestris' defense of poetry as a mode suitable to the expression of truth illustrate the problematic status of the art in medieval thought at the time romance began to emerge and blossom.[6]

The twelfth- and thirteenth-century arts of poetry and prose teach "Chartrain" or Platonic poetics, as set forth or practiced by figures like Bernard of Chartres, Bernardus Silvestris, John of Salisbury, Alain de Lille, Jean de Hauville, Gautier de Châtillon, and Joseph of Exeter.[7] The poets were the authorities and examples from whom Matthew of Vendôme, Geoffrey of Vinsauf, and others distilled the poetic art as it was taught and practiced in medieval schools.[8] The teaching contained in their treatises figured prominently in the emergence of romance in the twelfth century.[9] Although romance tended to form its own tradition as time passed, the influence of medieval Latin poetics on the genre while it was emerging obliges us to identify the salient features of the medieval treatises on poetry and prose.

Grammar traditionally gave instruction on correct writing in prose and verse, and included the study of "good literature." Analysis of the parts of speech, close textual commentary, and practice in correct writing were its principal assignments. The immediate fruits of this training may be seen in *accessus ad auctores,* commentaries, florilegia, and classroom exercises in composition *(praeexercitamina, progymnasmata)*. In these exercises pupils treated set themes narrow in scope and specific in the devices illustrated or recommended.[10] They show grammar as the *ars recte dicendi*—the art of correct speech.

Rhetoric "assumes many forms and uses in the twelfth century"[11] and after as an *ars bene dicendi*. It teaches how to move an audience. The means to achieve this end are set forth within a traditional scheme from which the arts of poetry and prose borrow their own arrangement and emphases:[12] invention, disposition, ornamentation, memory, and delivery. The *accessus ad auctores* introduce some of the main concerns in invention: *materia, intentio, utilitas, titulus, ordo,* etc.[13] They provide insight into how these subjects were understood and applied in the arts of poetry and prose and in contemporary writings.

There were three prerequisites to the mastery of the art: *ingenium, ars,* and *exercitatio*. *Ingenium* was inborn or natural talent, the capacity, intelligence, and insight necessary to invent a work; it governed the cognitive faculty called imagination, or the invention of identifiable images.[14] *Ars* was systematic instruction on all or part of the techniques whereby the conception and imagination achieved expression in a suitable medium.[15] It included the study of earlier works that illustrated or were thought to illustrate the art, as well as commentaries which showed how they were read and imitated.[16] Mastery came by *exercitatio* — practice in the various techniques of the art, imitation of the masterpieces, and, ultimately, the realization of a masterpiece or opus which might itself serve as a model for future writers. One read and studied the authors while imitating them in set compositions.[17]

As textbooks, the treatises on literary composition offer basic formal instruction, with systematic reduction to a didactic, often elementary level. The essentials are introduced and illustrated in an objective, fairly systematic (though not always thorough) way. They emphasize techniques to be used in classroom compositions rather than *ingenium* as such. This is not surprising. In the classroom, all must learn, no matter what their capacities. The worst will fail or be beaten into learning; others will progress further;[18] the very best (by the standards of the classroom) will go on to become Bernardus Silvestris, Alain de Lille, and Gautier de Châtillon. Others, like Benoît de Sainte Maure and Chrétien de Troyes, will apply their skills to writing in the vernacular.[19]

Now, Donatus' and Cicero's elementary treatises on rhetoric bear about the same relation to Cicero and Vergil as Geoffrey of Vinsauf and Matthew of Vendôme do to Gautier de Châtillon, Chrétien de Troyes, and the *Roman de la rose*. That is, they mark the authors' entrance into a pedagogical tradition that brings them from elementary composition to the masterpiece. The span separating the child and the master is a bridge, not an abyss.[20] Gervase of Melkley sees the *Architrenius* as useful for untrained but intelligent pupils.

Magister Iohannes de Hanvilla, cuius ubera discipline rudem adhuc mihi lactaverunt infantiam, multas quidem elegantias adinvenit, plures auditoribus suis tradidit. In libello vero suo de peregrino philosopho, quem Architrenium vocat, plurimas observavit. Cuius quidem libelli sola sufficit inspectio studiosa rudem animum informare. (*Ars poet* p. 3.20–25)[21]

[Master Jean de Hauville, whose bountiful learning nourished my still unformed youth, devised many fine ornaments, and he taught more of them to his pupils. Indeed, in his book on the wandering philosopher, called *Architrenius,* he observed most of them. The careful study of this book is sufficient in itself to form the untrained mind.]

Gervase also recommends the *Anticlaudianus,* Joseph of Exeter, Bernardus Silvestris, Lucan, Statius, Vergil, and Ovid as equally instructive.[22] All the authors named by Gervase evince the art of poetry and prose enunciated in the treatises. Gervase classifies the treatises themselves according to the scope of their instruction in literary composition. "Scripserunt autem hanc artem Matheus Vindocinensis plene, Gaufroi Vinesauf plenius, plenissime vero Bernardus Silvestris, in prosaico psitacus, in metrico philomena"[23] [Matthew of Vendôme wrote fully on this art, Geoffrey of Vinsauf even more so, and Bernardus Silvestris most thoroughly—he who was a parrot[24] in prose, in verse a nightingale]. Is this not a clue that Bernardus Silvestris' *prosimetrum,* itself a *conjointure,*[25] was the very art of poetry and prose which Gervase deemed most complete, rather than the brief, perfunctory treatises that have on occasion been proposed as containing it?

The *accessus ad auctores* identify three major considerations in the invention of the work: *materia, intentio,* and ethical character.[26] In the most general sense, *materia* is the subject matter, *intentio* the end the subject matter is made to serve, ethics the work's context. The *accessus* reduce the subject matter to a one- or two-sentence resumé.[27] For example, Conrad of Hirsau gives as *materia* for Lucan's *Pharsalia* both a general and a more circumstantial summary. "Si nosti civilis belli historiam, libri huius habes materiam: est enim auctoris huius materia bellum quod erat inter Cesarem et Pompeium et eorum consanguineos, inter quos post mortem istorum principum duorum, Cesaris et Pompeii, bellum incertum multo tempore fuit et varium" (*Dialogus* 1223–27) [if you knew the history of the civil war, you would possess the *materia* of this book; for this author's *materia* is the war between Caesar and Pompey and their kindred, between whom an uncertain and varied conflict waged for a long time after the deaths of the two aforementioned princes Caesar and Pompey]. The material gathered and put together had to fall within the scope of the initial conception: *ciuilis belli historia.* The subsequent resumé of the history's course is the *materia* proper.

Allegorical narrative also derives from a mental conception. For example, in Prudentius' *Psychomachia* "materia . . . psichomachia est, id est animae pugna, unde totum libri corpus[28] confectum est: ipsam enim concupiscentiam carnis adversus spiritum . . . , quam experimento propriae naturae, etiam se deessent verba vel exempla, in se recognovit" (*Dialogus* 833–37) [the *materia* . . . is a *psychomachia,* that is, a battle in the soul, from which the whole book is drawn together. He knew from personal experience lust's enmity toward the spirit, even if he lacked words and examples for it]. Every author distinguishes between the scattered material which may or may not be ultimately collected in his or her work, and the actual subject matter of which the work is finally composed, that is, the so-called *corpus* of the opus.[29]

There is a medieval terminology for these stages in the elaboration of
materia. Conrad of Mure's distinction between *materia remota* and *materia
propinqua* fits the general and the special senses of *materia* in the *accessus*.
"Materia remota sunt rudes lapides et inexpoliti et ligna nondum dolata, nondum levigata. Set materia propinqua sunt lapides et ligna bene preparata,
ut in structura domus, prout expedit, componantur" (*Summa* pp. 66–67)
[*materia remota* is represented by rough, unhewn stones and wood as yet
unplaned or unpolished. But *materia propinqua* is composed of stones and
wood fashioned so as to fit exactly into the frame of the house]. *Materia*
is indeed "the mother" — "quasi mater rei"[30] — out of which the work is born.
But it is also the goal of invention. John of Garland's distinction between
invention of *materia* as source and eliciting from that *materia* what will go
into the new work refers to the passage from *materia remota* to *materia
propinqua*.[31] For *materia propinqua* or *inventa* is not only source material;
it is also the material collected in a coherent whole. The author in quest of
suitable *materia* "materiam queret, quesitam inveniet, inventam ordinabit,
ordinatam exornabit, exornatam in publicum proponet et in lucem" (*Summa*
p. 67) [seeks matter, finds what he seeks, arranges what he finds, embel-
lishes what he arranges, and publishes what he has embellished]. There is
a potential here for further stages in the elaboration of *materia*.

The *accessus* illustrate these stages. An *accessus* to Prudentius distinguishes
the *materia* of the first part of the poem on Abraham's sacrifice of Isaac from
that of the second on the battle between the virtues and vices: "principalis
materia est Abram, secundaria omne quod introducitur" (*Accessus* p.
19.10–11) [the initial *materia* is on Abraham, the second includes everything
which is introduced into the work]. Stages are evident in "historical" as well
as allegorical narrative. We observed that the principal *materia* of Lucan's
Pharsalia is Pompey and Caesar, as secondary matter the Roman civil war —
and this information is introduced by a long summary of the poem up to
Nero's time.[32] Personages themselves have stories which could be drawn out
from their names and the identities attributed to them. The comedy *Pamphilus* has as *materia* three persons, Pamphilus, Galathea, and an *anus*. The
accessus continues: "Pamphilus fuit quidam qui quandam puellam, scilicet
Galatheam, valde diligebat et eam nullo modo habere poterat. Tandem ivit
ad Venerem, cuius consilio acquisivit sibi interpretem eiusque auxilio habuit
eam. Unde compositus est liber iste" (*Accessus* p. 53.11–15) [Pamphilus was
a certain person who very much desired a girl named Galatea, but he could
in no way possess her. At length he besought Venus; by her counsel he acquired a go-between who helped him win the girl. This book is put together
from this material]. The pupil reading these *accessus* could perceive a work's
transition from the smallest *materia* to its full elaboration in the completed

work.[33] The *accessus* confirms the derivation of *materia* both from the *ingenium* and from antecedent sources.[34]

The second major subject of the *accessus, intentio,* identifies the author's purpose in selecting *materia:* "Intentio est quid auctor intendat, quid, quantum, de quo scribere proponat" (*Dialogus* 226–27)[35] [*intentio* is authorial intention, what, to what extent, and about whom or what he or she proposes to write]. The definition recalls the loci of topical invention, as summarized in the mnemonic device "Quis, quid, ubi, quibus auxiliis, cur, quomodo, quando" (*Ars vers* 1.116)[36] [who, what, where, with what aid, why, when, in what manner]. These predicables are the "genus et species et cetera quibus opus perficitur quod auctor agendum aggreditur" (*Dialogus* 224–26)[37] [genus, species, and other things by which the author completes the work he undertakes to write]. They too furnish *materia* for the attributes of persons, things, and their actions that conform to auctorial conception of the *materia*. What is invented in the mind is also *materia propinqua* that fits an ethical, that is, moral or social context.[38]

The author invents the *materia* conforming to the *intentio:* "liber dicitur a liberando vel a librando, liberando quia nos legendo liberat ab errore, librando quia intentionem cum materia librat et materiam cum intentione" (*Accessus* p. 19.18–20) [the word *book* derives from the words *liberation* and *balance:* it derives from *liberation* because by reading we free ourselves from error, and from *balance* because it balances the *intentio* with the *materia* and the *materia* with the *intentio*]. The balance between *materia* and *intentio* discloses the ethical truth of the *materia*. The writer's conception of the work is the discovery of that truth. *Intentio* therefore controls selection of *materia propinqua*. The *accessus* to Prudentius' *Psychomachia,* for example, suggests the winnowing and sifting this entailed: "Si scriberet [scil. Prudentius] de monte vel huiusmodi, nihil esset ad hanc rem" (p. 19.20–21) [if he were to write about a mountain or something similar, it would not pertain to his subject]. That is, it would not pertain to the battle between the vices and virtues. This is precisely what Horace meant by the "inappropriate cypress."

> Et fortasse cupressum
> Scis simulare: quid hoc, si fractis enatat exspes
> Navibus aere dato qui pingitur?
> (*Ad Pisones* 19–21)

[And perhaps you can reproduce a cypress tree; but to what purpose would you depict it in bronze while showing a man hopelessly swimming after shipwreck?]

Rather the image selected must fit and express the intention behind the author's conception of the work. "L'image allégorique médiévale, toute pénétrée de raison et d'intention, organisée et comme traduite par celui qui la crée ou la transforme, contient presque toujours plus que sa traduction en idées; la traduction faite, reste l'image, dont la présence répond à quelque exigence du sujet."[39] The *materia propinqua* must be pertinent to the subject, that is, to authorial intention.[40]

In ancient rhetoric *intentio* expresses motive. The motive was a matter of contention *(quaestio)* within the accepted definition of the case or the issue *(status)*.[41] Judgment *(iudicium)* followed the identification, collection, and interpretation of the evidence in the context of the motive. The procedure was carried into the Middle Ages and applied to composition. "Intentio est affectus animi circa materiam vel oratio quae animum maxime intendit libro legendo" *(Comm* Utrecht p. 67.223–24)[42] [*intentio* represents one's feelings about a subject, or the words that direct one's feelings while reading a book]. It corresponds to a thesis, a principle of order that organizes the narrative and makes it coherent. The application of the principle, as the hypothesis, works out the thesis in a specific *materia* so as to make the latter credible and comprehensible.[43] The rhetorical potential of motive had profound implications for the medieval propensity to adapt and reinterpret by replacing one *intentio* with another.

Invention of the Work

There are three primary stages in invention. First, the author has an idea or mental conception of a subject. Second, material is sought and identified through which the initial conception may find appropriate statement and elaboration. Third, the mental conception and the *materia* are meshed as the subject matter of the work. From the moment of conception to the time of composition, *intentio* is the authority to which selection and elaboration of subject matter refer.

Conception of the Model for the Work: Status archetypus

Both Matthew of Vendôme and Geoffrey of Vinsauf adapt a paradigmatic conception of divine creation to the invention of the literary work of art.[44] The paradigm requires, first, a mental conception drawn up in the mind *(mens, ingenium)* or the "heart" *(cor, pectus)*. Geoffrey describes this stage *(status)* as "archetypal" *(archetypus)*. Next the author advances from a subject *(thema)* to the delimitation of the scope or *corpus* of the entire subject matter *(compendium)* in a specific sequence *(ordo)* and with a specific content *(omne materiae spatium)*. This completes the conception of the work, and the author may proceed to write it down *(Poetria nova* 43–70).[45] The same process is apparent in Matthew of Vendôme's description of invention from imagination through verbalization to arrangement.[46]

The three stages are suitable for all arts, and indeed all crafts. From God's creation to the mechanical arts, one perceives the same "dualité de l'esprit déterminant et de la *hylé* déterminable."[47] Geoffrey's comparison of poetic invention to architectural planning[48] parallels Matthew's likening it to breathing the spirit of life — "vitalis spiritus" *(Ars vers* 3.50) — into creatures. The spirit of life, breathed into man by God, stamps each human being with the human archetype.[49] Just so, the artist impresses a preconceived model or pattern onto disparate matter. This accounts for *archetypus* as attribute rather than substantive in line 48 of the *Poetria nova:* "et status ejus / Est prius archetypus quam sensilis" (47–48) [Its mode of being is archetypal before it is actual]. The artist's mental conception is not in itself an archetype, but rather is like an archetype insofar as it is a mental conception.[50] The archetype of Platonic or Neoplatonic thought is rarely directly accessible to human perception, nor can it be created by human minds. God alone conceives archetypes; His agent Nature mirrors them in matter on different levels of the universe.[51] The poet's language is archetypal because it reproduces the shape of ideas in his or her verbal inventions. Alain de Lille explains it in this way. Nature "mentales intellectus materialis uocis michi depinxit imagine, et quasi archetipa uerba idealiter preconcepta uocaliter produxit in actum" *(De planctu* VI.11–13)[52] [depicted for my mental perception the image of a real voice, and by this brought into actual being words which had been, so to speak, archetypes ideally preconceived (p.24.17–20)]. Since only God could create, the medieval author could do no more than "recreate" what already existed. "Quis partus Troie, cuius ruit illa ruina, / quomodo, quoque dolo, me recreare iuuat" *(Anth* §6.1–2) [it behooves me to recreate the birth and destruction of Troy, detailing how she fell and with what grief]. A creator creates something out of nothing, and "il n'est nus qui ce poisse faire fors que Cil seulement qui fist le ciel et la terre" *(St-Louis* §778)[53] [no one could do this except Him alone Who made heaven and earth]. This does not preclude divine inspiration.[54] But the artist's own infusion of the "life's breath" into the opus is only analogous to, not identical with, God's activity and that of His agents.

The artist's first step is "archetypal" in its likeness to divine creation and natural reproduction. Both Bernardus Silvestris and Alain de Lille model their inventions on Nature's, whereas Nature, as a personification, looks finally to God for her ideas. Of course, distortions may falsify or pervert Nature's handiwork.[55] Such defects are analogous to those produced by human impotence or perversity. Alain de Lille likens them to the inventions of unskilled poets — a group he distinguishes from philosophers who do indeed write in verse, but do so correctly and thus represent in their inventions a vital truth.[56] His distinction between poets and philosophers reflects Matthew of Vendôme's between hack writers and those whose verse is both artful and substantial (*Ars vers* 1.1). Distinctive writing requires the extraction of truth from falsehood by invention. The art of poetry and prose, learned in youth, provides the start and impetus for the discipline that flowers when nurtured by philosophy.[57]

Hugh of Saint Victor likened God, nature, and the artist to three *fabri*. "Opus Dei est, quod non erat creare. . . . Opus naturae, quod latuit ad actum producere. . . . Opus artificis est disgregata coniungere vel coniuncta segregare" (*Didascalicon* p. 16.8–12) [the work of God is to create that which was not . . . ; the work of nature is to bring forth into actuality that which lay hidden . . . ; the work of the artificer is to put together things disjoined or to disjoin those put together (p. 55)]. God conceives the archetype in its essential simplicity and wholeness. Nature stamps this model into matter. The artist perceives the model in nature and then invents material so as to imitate it.[58] The beginning is a mental image. The *ingenium* draws upon the source and the repository of images in memory. Images are human counterparts to divine archetypes perceived in nature.[59]

Just as the architect cannot construct without wood, stones, and mortar, the writer must select material *(electio)* suitable for the realization of the mental image — gather the *ligna* and *lapides* of *materia remota*.[60] For example, when the architect desires to provide protection against inclement weather *(intentio)* he considers the mountain. The mountain's slope permits runoff, and its hollows and caverns offer shelter; the roof's incline will achieve both ends. This satisfies the architect's intention and provides an "archetypal" image of a house drawn from the image of a similar form in nature. The actual house will be put together in conformity with that image. A mountain is broken down *(coniuncta segregare)* and put together again *(disgregata coniungere)* in a little mountain that preserves the original's slope, while leaving space for those who seek shelter in it. As Hugh of Saint Victor said, disjunction and conjunction are the fundamental techniques.[61]

In this analysis, raw material, such as wood or stone, is the original referent of *materia*. This sense is never lost; such *materia* is chosen if it is suitable for the realization of a work "où des éléments préexistants se combinent par la coopération de la pensée, de la mémoire et de l'imagination."[62] Invention discovers the lineaments[63] of the idea that inspires the invention (*De planctu* XVIII.68–72), which is a kind of *imitatio*.[64] Now, Alain de Lille was suspicious of some poetic inventions, probably those by Gautier de Châtillon and Joseph of Exeter.[65] This may be because of disagreement as to the validity of the ideas they set forth, a type of disagreement that accounts in part for the importance of corrective adaptation in medieval writing.[66] But it can also be because the invention is poorly executed or not clearly conceived. The author must have a clear, precise idea of what the work will be in order to express that idea effectively and artfully.

Statement of the Work's Contents: Thema *and* Materia

In forensic oratory, evidence is the "raw material" of a case. When reduced to a summary statement, it is made to conform to the speaker's conception and thus constitutes his or her *thema*. In classroom instruction in rhetoric and poetics such *themata* were given to pupils for elaboration.[67] Geoffrey of Vinsauf's use of *thema* illustrates this.

> sed mens discreta praeambula facti
> . . . tractetque diu de themate secum.
> Circinus interior mentis praecircinet omne
> Materiae spatium.
> (*Poetria nova* 52–56)

[Let the discriminating mind, as a prelude to action . . . , ponder long on the subject matter *(thema)*. Let the mind's interior compass first circle the whole extent of the material *(materia)*.]

Conrad of Mure, whose *Summa de arte prosandi* shows the influence of Geoffrey's *Poetria nova,* says that *thema* and *materia* may be synonymous, or may refer to the successive stages in the conception and elaboration of the work.[68]

> Aliud est thema, aliud materia. Thema est factum in genere propositum, vel est brevis oratio vel apertio dictorum, per quam auditor loquentis intelligit voluntatem. Exemplum: Scias quod Thuricenses contra Basilienses exercitum conduxerunt.
> Vel thema sit idem quod materia. . . . [69]
> Materia est plena verborum et sententiarum artificiosa ordinatio ex hiis, que in themate sumuntur. Exemplum: Scias, quod Thuricenses, amicorum consilio et auxilio freti, multitudine gravi collecta cum suo carrochio contra Basilienses venerunt et castrum eorundem cinxerunt obsidione. Tandem castrum inexpugnabile videntes, nulla victoria potiti tamen sani et incolomes ad propria sunt reversi.
> Vel materia est id, ex quo aliquid fit, sicut ligna et lapides materia domus construende. (*Summa* p. 66)

[*Thema* and *materia* differ from one another. The *thema* is a deed set forth in its generality, or it is a brief discourse or explanation by which the auditor understands the speaker's intent. For example: "Know that Zürich has led an army against Basel." Or the *thema* may be the same as the *materia*. . . . *Materia* is a complete, artful arrangement of words and sentences drawn from what is summarily set forth in the *thema*. For example: "Know that Zürich, supported by the aid and counsel of its allies, marched against Basel with great host and baggage and besieged the citadel there. However, finding it impregnable, they returned home safe and sound, but having gained no victory." Or *materia* is what something is made of, like the wood and stones used for the construction of a house.]

Thema and *materia* overlap in meaning, but they are not identical in practice. Rather their range of meaning suggests the invention of complex *materia* drawn from succinct ideas.

How brief the *thema* or *materia* may be depends on the kind of subject treated. A historical subject like that in Gautier de Châtillon's *Alexandreis* would be comparable to Conrad of Mure's examples; its *materia,* as distinguished from its *thema,* would have been even longer and the parts and subdivisions more complex than those which Alain de Lille amplified in the *De planctu Naturae* and the *Anticlaudianus*. "Notandum . . . quod partes hystorie non sunt certe et determinate, quia per uoluntatem [= *intentio*] hystoriographi et secundum ipsa gesta [= *materia*] distinguitur hystoria" (*Parisiana Poetria* 4.475–77)[70] [it is to be noted . . . that the parts of a *historia* are not certain and fixed, because a *historia* is distinguished by the historiographer's intent and the deeds themselves that are related]. But the *thema,* or subject, as distinguished from the *materia,* or subject matter, remained quite simple, as in the first line of Gautier's *Alexandreis*: "Gesta ducis Macedum totum digesta per orbem" (I.1) [the deeds of the Macedonian leader known throughout the whole world]. As early as Servius we read: "sicut nunc dicturi thema proponimus, ita veteres incipiebant carmen a titulo carminis sui, ut puta *Arma virumque cano,* Lucanus *Bella per Emathios,* Statius *Fraternas acies alternaque regna profanis*" (*Comm Serv* II, 5.101–4) [just as we now state the *thema* we are going to relate, so did our predecessors begin a poem with the poem's title, as, for example, "Arma virumque cano," or in Lucan "Bella per Emathios," and Statius "Fraternas acies alternaque regna profanis"]. Each author is seen expressing the poem's *thema* in the first line, which is also its title. The brief statement of the work is the seed out of which will be drawn the entire opus.

The *accessus* show how this brief, "thematic" material generates ideas, principal personages, places, animals, and events from the *materia*. Like the philosophers who admired the simple numbers that were the source of complex equations, poets valued the word and even the letters of the alphabet as sources of *materia,* which like a seed, they could germinate and grow. The process finally yields the vast and deep forests implicit in the word's brief compression.[71] The source of *materia* could indeed be simple and brief, compact and even compressed, as the *accessus* demonstrate when they equate it with the work's title or first line.[72] The arts of poetry and prose emphasize the *thema* as the "small unit of discourse."[73] In the *Documentum,* for example, Geoffrey of Vinsauf illustrates amplification with *materia* of one word: *lego* and *doceo.*[74]

The brief, even compact *materia* from which the work is drawn can be construed as the author's original conception of the work.[75] The procedure as Geoffrey describes it for drawing *materia* from *thema* is analogous to the preacher's who draws a sermon from a biblical *thema* or verse.[76] Such composition instilled "la joie d'une vision compréhensive à la lumière de quelques principes simples, de quelques notions très générales, des causes fondamentales et de certains rapports premiers"[77] that de Bruyne sees as characteristic of twelfth-century aesthetics. As the *thema* becomes *materia,* one perceives the consistent expansion, elaboration, diversification, and illustration of a simple idea. Theoretically, conception precedes the search for suitable material to represent or illustrate it, and the material chosen serves to express the original conception. "Quidquid enim est in opere, ante est in artificis mente"[78] [for everything in the work is beforehand in the artist's mind].

The question as to whether the arts of literary composition offer instruction on sentence composition or on larger units of discourse evaporates when one perceives that the same paradigm is suitable in all phases of composition and in works of diverse length and complexity.[79] Geoffrey of Vinsauf explicitly applies the paradigm for invention to amplification and abbreviation (*Poetria nova* 217–18), ornamentation (*Documentum* II.3.2), and conversions (*Documentum* II.3.121–23). Matthew of Vendôme likens the well-turned phrase or line of verse to the order of the entire work (*Ars vers* 3.50–52). The distinction between natural and artificial order was applied to the parts of speech as well as to narrative sequence.[80] In the sentence as well, "cogitandum igitur prius est de sententia quam cogitemus de verborum junctura. Mortua enim sunt verba si non incolumi nitantur sententia, quae quodam modo anima est verbi. Cum constiterit de sententia, procedendum est ad verba, diligentiam adhibendo, ut series verborum sit ornata" (*Documentum* II.3.2) [one must first determine the meaning before inventing the combination of words. Words are dead if they do not rest on a firm meaning, which is in a sense the soul of the word. Once the meaning has been established, one must proceed to the words, taking care that the sequence of words be ornate]. This passage sums up the paradigm for the invention, elaboration, and disposition of *materia*. It describes ornamentation in Horatian terms, that is, how "series iuncturaque pollet." The process is the same in the sentence, as here, or in narrative invention when passing from the mental conception to the finished opus.[81] One reduces the source material to a *thema*. "Sic enim gradatim descendendum est, donec inveniat animus in quo resideat et in quo complaceat" (*Documentum* II.3.123) [thus one descends by stages until the mind invents where it may rest and where it is content]. Afterward the work is drawn out of the *thema* by the elaboration of smaller parts and of the whole work.

The terminology used in the poetic manuals permits us to integrate the stages in invention with each other in summary form. The work begins as a mental or "archetypal" conception, a brief *thema* which will then be expanded into a lengthier, more complex *materia*. The collection of *materia* to fill out and complete the *thema* provides *materia remota*. The adaptation to auctorial intention fixes the subject matter, that is, the *materia propinqua*. The *materia* assumes the content and shape, the very vocabulary, prescribed by mental conception as informing idea.[82] Invention informs every stage of composition, from word to work.

Contents and Model as Image: *Materia propinqua*

The source(s) or *materia remota* and auctorial conception coalesce in the subject matter or *materia propinqua*. As we have seen, the auctorial conception arises in the mind as the seat of images. Through imitation of the mental conception the author gives substance and shape to *materia*. This is what Brian Stock has called the accommodation of myth to model.[83] The model is the archetypal conception, while the myth is the *materia* chosen for the work. Stock's "myth" and "model" are basic to *conjointure* in *materia propinqua*. He equates myth and model with the medieval terms *historia* and *figura*. The *historia* as *res gestae* transpires as narrative in time and space, whether these coordinates represent a literal historical chronology or a topical sequence like a *gradus amoris*. Within such temporal and topographic sequences the author's conception of the work stamps the *materia* as *figura* or representation of the conceptual model.

In and of itself, the model gives to narrative topical features that order narrative sequence and determine the place, content, and form of amplifications. For example, a mental conception of the human being is the model for the content and arrangement of the second part of Bernardus Silvestris' *Cosmographia;* the perversion of that figure models Alain de Lille's *De planctu*

Naturae. All Bernardus' works represent his conception of the relationship between man's free will and his destiny. Peter Dronke has shown how this difficult dichotomy—a *figura*—achieves diverse but complementary expression in each of Bernardus' works: dream vision in the *Cosmographia,* declamatory narrative in the *Mathematicus,* and discursive treatise in the *Experimentarius;* according to the commentary attributed to Bernardus, Vergil's *Aeneid* expresses the same *figura* one finds in his other works.[84] By changing the mode and *materia* in each work there emerges a more nearly total vision of the human condition in God's universe.

In Gautier de Châtillon's *Alexandreis* Judeo-Christian typology based on Ezekiel provides a model by which to measure and evaluate the career of Alexander the Great.[85] For example, the model informs the admonitions addressed to Alexander by various personages in the narrative; the substance of the auctorial interventions interpreting the import of Alexander's decisions; and, finally, Nature's descent into hell to plot his destruction. While Alexander plans to explore the underworld, his own nature, revolted at Alexander's plot, precedes him into hell and works to destroy him. For man to exceed God's imposed limits is a revolt that human nature cannot endure. This "logical pattern, a harmonious arrangement of discrete elements,"[86] gives meaning to Gautier's disparate *materia remota* and determines his selection from it of the *materia propinqua* of the *Alexandreis.*

Rupprecht Rohr's study of the elaboration of abstract models in French and Occitan lyric and romance shows how amplification functions as a kind of emanation.[87] The generation of amplifications expresses the initial conception of and model for the *materia remota.* The technique is analytic. Variations on the model derive their particular meaning or application from their place in the whole work. Such "poetic emanation" mirrors the parallel functions of God and Nature, the creative and procreative agents who transmit archetypes into matter by emanation.

Gautier's model for Alexander's career determines his use and choice of amplifications. For example, two topographies introduce Alexander's Asian conquests. Both are descriptions of Asia, the one drawn from above, as on a medieval map, the other from Alexander's own perspective as he nears the Ionian coast.[88] The first description illuminates the vast expanse and variety of the continent stretching away, nation after nation, to the great ocean at the edge of the world. The vast horizon encircles two foci: the one where Alexander himself stands, the other in Jerusalem. But the world is no ellipse with two foci. It is round and Jerusalem is its center. It is obvious how distorted the topography is, as Alexander gazes from his own perspective on the Asian continent. He perceives the world as if he were its center and his will decisive. The reference to Jerusalem in the first topography alludes obliquely to Alexander's distorted view.

> Inde Palestinae cunctis supereminet una
> Vnius Iudea Dei. Iherosolima terrae
> In centro posita est, ubi uirginis edita partu
> Vita obiit, nec stare Deo moriente renatus
> Sustinuit sed contremuit perterritus orbis.
>
> (I.420–24)

[Hence, the one Judah of the one God stands out over all of Palestine. Jerusalem is located at the center of the world, where the life born of the Virgin died; nor was the world, reborn through God's death, able to remain still, but rather it shook with fright.]

Alexander's moral view is distorted. This becomes apparent as he relinquishes Europe for Asia.

> "Iam satis est," inquit "socii, michi sufficit una
> Hec regio. Europam uobis patriamque relinquo."
> Sic ait et patrium ducibus subdiuidit orbem.
>
> (I.440–42)

["This is sufficient for me, companions," he said, "this region is all I need. I leave Europe and our fatherland to you." Thus he spoke, and divided the world of his forefathers among his generals.]

Ironically, Alexander's "sufficiency" betrays his greed for conquest.[89] He relinquishes homeland for "exile"—a Boethian vice. The decision foreshadows his project to leave the world and descend into hell.

The irony of Alexander's "Iam satis est" becomes profoundly serious in recurring admonitions that he shun excess and open his eyes to himself and the world he is vainly trying to dominate. Aristotle, the high priest of Jerusalem, the condemned soldier Polystratus, and the Scythian captive all address themselves insistently, yet ominously, to this theme *(thema)* as the narrative advances and Alexander's conquests extend farther toward the east. His career comes to a climax when Nature intervenes to thwart Alexander's Harrowing of Hell (book X). Alexander is betrayed from below by Proditio, on earth by the serfs he lifted to power. The final irony falls again on the theme "Iam satis est." One leader, Craterus, puts it pointedly to Alexander: "esuries mentis, cui maximus iste / Non satis est orbis" (IX.515–16) [a mind hungry, for whom this immense world is not enough]. Alexander's own words echo the condemnation of his excesses.

> Tracas Asiamque subegi.
> Proximus est mundi michi finis, et absque deorum

> Vt loquar inuidia, nimis est angustus et orbis,
> Et terrae tractus domino non sifficit uni.
>
> (IX.562–65)

[I have subdued Thrace and Asia, and the edge of the world is nearby;
and—may my words not incite the gods' envy—this world is too narrow,
and the width and breadth of the earth are not enough for one master.]

And so it ends.

> Magnus in exemplo est. cui non suffeceret orbis,
> Sufficit exciso defossa marmore terra
> Quinque pedum fabricata domus.
>
> (X.448–50)

[Alexander is an example: he for whom the whole world was insufficient
is now content with a small dwelling five feet down.]

Alexander's largess is proverbial. Here it is exemplified by his burning precious booty in order to press on more easily and unencumbered to the ends
of the earth. But we soon discover that his largess and indifference to wealth
serve a deeper avarice for conquest. Avarice is his excess and his vice, and
because of it Nature destroys him. Alexander's proverbial largess is a by-
product of greed!

> Quo tendit tua, Magne, fames? quis finis habendi,
> Querendi quis erit modus aut que meta laborum?
> Nil agis, o demens. licet omnia clauseris uno
> Regna sub imperio totumque subegeris orbem,
> Semper egenus eris. animum nullius egentem
> Non res efficiunt sed sufficientia.
>
> (X.191–96)

[Whither your hunger, Alexander? What limits are there to your greed?
What will be the end and goal of your quest? You achieve nothing, you
fool! Even if you were to enclose all kingdoms in one empire and subdue
the whole world, yet will you be driven by hunger. Things do not make a
soul content—only sufficiency can achieve that.]

Just as a single idea informs the representation of abstract notions personified or otherwise exemplified in visionary epic, so does the Boethian theme
of *sufficientia* and its distortion model and shape, in a typological scheme
of history, the choice and elaboration of Gautier's *materia propinqua* for the
story of Alexander.

Correction of Contents: Executio materiae remotae

Under the general heading of *executio materiae* Matthew of Vendôme defines choice and elaboration of *materia* as correction (*Ars vers* 4.1–31). *Materia remota* requires correction when it contains superfluities, lacunae, or errors which do not serve the principal intention of the new author. Although Matthew is concerned with the small unit of discourse, the faults he refers to may occur in all kinds of discourse. Lacunae, for example, may appear in the sentence or in episodic sequences: "actionum gradus expresso debemus imitari vestigio, ut narrationis nulla sit intercisio" (4.13) [we ought certainly to copy the steps of the action straightforwardly so that there is no interruption in the account]. Matthew treats these faults under *materia executa* or *pertractata* and *materia illibata*. He defines *materia executa* as a source in verse, *materia illibata* as a source in prose. One may generalize the two expressions to refer, respectively, to source material already written according to the art of poetry and prose and to source material not so written. This is the import of Matthew's actual instruction, and it fits the practice of accomplished and representative writers of his time in both Latin and French.[90] *Materia illibata* describes sources such as those Chrétien de Troyes alludes to in the *Erec* prologue, whereas *materia executa* is Chrétien himself for Hartmann von Aue and the Prose *Charrette*.

Both kinds of source must be made complete and clear by adaptation to a new or more accurately delineated model. This requires the removal of everything in the *materia* that may be unnecessary or otiose, including barbarisms and solipsisms, superfluous repetitions, ambiguities, lacunae in the ordinary sequence of human actions, and obscurities (4.3–15). For example, Matthew corrects *materia executa* by adding the "missing" stages to the *gradus amoris* in Ovid's version of Jupiter and Io because Ovid "actionum ordinem intercidere vel sincopare videtur" (4.13)[91] [seems to interrupt or telescope the order of the action]. Matthew recommends correction of similar faults which he identifies in Vergil, Lucan, and Statius.[92] *Materia illibata* should be adapted to fit the ordinary sequence of actions and typical representation of persons and events. The *gradus amoris* and similar topical models prepare the young writer to invent works composed according to more profound models such as that of Boethian sufficiency in the *Alexandreis* or man's destiny in Bernardus Silvestris' works. In fact, such elementary adaptation is preliminary to the more advanced kinds one recognizes everywhere in literary use of sources in the Middle Ages, and even in commentaries like that on the *Aeneid* attributed to Bernardus Silvestris. A given *materia* may acquire a variety of meanings appropriate to different models, or there may be different versions of it within the same context, as in the moralizations of Ovid.[93]

Involution as Topical Invention: *Informatio*

In rhetoric, *narratio* is one of the principal parts of oration: *exordium, narratio, conclusio*. However, *narratio* as such is not a prominent topic in the medieval treatises on composition. Traditionally *narratio* was a given *(materia remota)*, since the data of a case are the *materia* the orator must interpret. But the *narratio* may be read in different ways. The orator interprets narrative by determining its *status (constitutio)* or "type of issue," that is, "the conjoining of two conflicting statements, thus forming the centre of the argument and determining the character of the case."[94] In poetics the resolution of the conflict in *status* or issue identifies the prominent and appropriate quality or character of the *materia* by a hypothesis which interprets the facts of the case.[95] This makes the hypothesis a model for motive. It reveals how the author construes the *materia*.

The work will model the data by "involution," that is, by molding the *materia* to fit the model which is perceived to be more or less grossly adumbrated in it.[96] In rhetoric and, as we shall see, in medieval poetics, "the discrimination of *status* is not just that of kinds of arguments about action but of ways of seeing the action itself. . . . In precisely defining the *status,* he [the author] is focusing, as finely as possible, the picture he wishes to expose on the imagination of his audience."[97] Hence, "the interpretation of poetry, like that of all things, is an exercise of reason in the discernment of stages and divisions within a clearly delimited field of inquiry."[98] The interpretation of narrative is either open or by insinuation.[99] That is, the writer may state his or her conception of the narrative straightforwardly; or he or she may resort to artificial order, descriptions, digressions, and intentionally chosen qualifiers in order to "insinuate" it. The reading of the evidence in forensic oratory is analogous to the reading of the *materia* in Latin epic and in romance.

Both open statement and insinuation conform to the way the author construes persons and actions. *Personae* and *negotia* are primary elements in ancient definitions of *narratio*.[100] The emphasis on the division between persons and things in the *Ad Herennium* and the *De inventione*[101] was adopted by the medieval arts of poetry and prose.[102] Matthew of Vendôme's instruction on *descriptio* of *personae* and *descriptio* of *negotia* is typical.

Descriptio is not mere "description." It is more precisely "elucidation."[103] Invention itself is "excogitatio rerum verarum aut verisimilium, quae causam probabilem reddant" *(Ad Her* I.ii.3)[104] [the devising of matter, true or plausible, that would make the case convincing]. The *res* are, as it were, implicit in the *materia*. It is the office of the author to elicit or extract them from it. In practice, this is *informatio,* the involution that realizes the *materia*'s potential for topical statement. The author considers the *materia,* the persons, things, and actions contained in it, then models them according to his or her conception of the work. The technique was widespread in the Middle Ages.[105]

Matthew envisages *descriptio* as elementary topical invention. By practice it becomes a habitual manner of conception,[106] for "informari aliqua proprietate ex diutina mentis applicatione ad habitum pertinet" (*Ars vers* 1.85)[107] [*a habitual manner of expression* indicates a lasting property of mind]. Persons and their actions are set forth according to an exemplary model as perceived and reconstituted in the artist's mind *(ingenium)*; the conception is then put into words in the new *materia* by amplificatory devices like those named by Geoffrey of Vinsauf: paraphrase, conversion, description, *interpretatio,* etc. The process is called "informing" the *materia* by inference *(conjecturaliter)* and involution or *informatio. Informatio* is topical invention because it molds *materia* according to a shape and meaning deemed inherent in it.[108]

By amplification, special or idealized representations led to "exaggeration" by enhancement, exaltation, overstatement, emphasis on one attribute to the exclusion or subordination of others. This sometimes produced a real discrepancy between persons and objects in description and narrative—a discrepancy often remarked upon, but rarely properly explained. It is important to note that such "exaggeration" *(exaggeratio)* did not mean exaggeration, that is, overstatement beyond what is credible. Rather it had the meaning of the French word when it first appeared in the sixteenth century: "porter qch au plus haut point,"[109] that is, to exalt. This fits Matthew of Vendôme's sense of *descriptio.* Since *exaggeratio* and its derivatives in ancient and medieval rhetoric are amplification,[110] it is related to hyperbole and *interpretatio,* or what we might call "exaggeration not meant to deceive" and overstatement. According to Priscian, "locus communis exaggerationem habet manifestae rei"[111] [a commonplace contains the enhancement of something evident]. It serves to clarify, explain, make obvious, embellish, and impress. It accounts for both mannerist and marvelous features in topical inventions in the Middle Ages.

Topical invention contains three stages: (1) identification of the *locus,* (2) invention of *argumenta* for the *locus,* (3) amplification of the *argumenta* in the *locus.* Although there was variation in usage, *locus* and *argumentum* may stand as discrete terms referring to two stages in invention. The former refers to a place in the *materia* suitable for amplification in conformity with the author's mental conception of the work and within the limits of the definition of the *locus;* it is the "grounds, or 'topics,' " to hypothesize *status*[112] that requires clarification, adaptation, or correction. The result is a true, verisimilar, or at least coherent elaboration modeled on normal human expectation at the time of writing, as defined by audience, auctorial conception of the work, and his, her, or a patron's intention with it. Such inventions should therefore be appropriate to the model. "Plerumque descriptio [= topical invention] persone est tempestiva, plerumque superflua" (*Ars vers* 1.38)[113] [in many cases a description of the person (by topical invention) is fitting, in many superfluous].

The material invented in and for each *locus* constitutes the *argumenta* (4.18). If the *argumenta* seem perfunctory, they are faulty or inappropriate — like Horace's misplaced cypress. They should give credible, appropriate expression to auctorial conception of the work's model.

Within a given context like prowess, love, or rectitude, topical invention was eminently suitable for what Eugène Vinaver called "the 'thematic' mode," which "is above all a questioning mode."[114] It was adapted to French romance by clerics trained in the tradition to which contemporary Latin writings and arts of poetry and prose bear witness. "To such minds an event in a work of narrative art could not be expressed merely by a significant gesture or scene: it called for description and elaboration, it had to be related to its context and given its proper place in a sequence of co-ordinate occurrences."[115] Traditions and habits will determine what *loci* admit or require specificity and what arguments may suitably express the model as well as please the author or his or her projected audience. The storehouse of such arguments is memory, and the agent whereby memory's contents may be recalled and selected from, the *ingenium*.[116] The use of images in traditional rhetorical instruction on memory gives further substance to Matthew of Vendôme's own use of the expression *imaginatio sensus* for auctorial conceptions drawn from memory.[117]

Memory as a source of *loci* and *argumenta* meant that rather specific, conventional sequences like the *gradus amoris* were models for invention. Such inventions could be striking, original, and diversified, as the standard rhetorics and poetics show.[118] But "when teaching [such] 'introductions' . . . one does not draft a thousand set introductions and give them to the student to learn by heart; one teaches him the method and then leaves him to his own inventiveness."[119] This accounts for the way in which narrative in medieval texts exhibits variations on basic patterns like *gradus amoris,* stages in combat, hospitality, quest, and the other patterned actions which inform the medieval imagination, and according to which the authors elaborated their *materia.* "Ainsi, dans *Lancelot,* Chrétien énonce comme un code d'honneur ce qui est en vérité un code narratif qui détermine ce qu'on pourrait appeler le récit minimum (mais infiniment expansible)."[120] In fact, the predilection in ancient treatises on rhetoric for strange or unusual images to assist memory may well have fostered the emphasis on marvels in epic and romance. *Descriptio* as topical invention is the technique for elucidating strange or problematic *materia.*

Matthew's instruction on *descriptio* falls under three heads: (1) appropriateness, (2) selection of attributes, (3) *loci* of invention for *personae* and *negotia*.[121] Description of both *personae* and *negotia* requires delineation of what is characteristic for the model of the opus, that is, within its context or auctorial conception. It must serve the coherent elaboration of narrative within a whole and complete sequence of customary actions (*Ars vers* 1.38–40). The identification of suitable attributes for persons, things, and actions must also conform to the expectations one may have of them in the context and narrative chosen. They should be diverse, but still correlate with the given type's dominant trait, of which they are, in effect, the emanation. This is invention by inference of what appears of be true, verisimilar, or customary. To assist the student, Matthew lists *loci* that may demand topical invention. His instruction parallels medieval readings of Horace on the representation of suitable persons and actions, adapted to Ciceronian traditions on topical invention derived from the *De inventione,* the pseudo-Ciceronian *Ad Herennium,* as well as from other sources of rhetorical doctrine used in the Middle Ages: Quintilian's *Institutiones,* Cicero's *Topica,* Macrobius' *Saturnalia,* book V of Martianus Capella's *De nuptiis,* and book IV of Boethius' *De differentiis topicis.*[122]

The distinction between topical invention and the modern study of historical topics, both justifiable within their own spheres, must be maintained in historical criticism.[123] One distorts and truncates topical invention by reading the modern notion of historical topics into it. Topical invention was freer, especially in the vernacular languages.[124] Some topics tend not to change, like *translatio imperii,* the topsy-turvy world, or the *puer senex* which Curtius chose for special emphasis.[125] Yet if only the latter are considered, the real importance of topical invention in medieval writing is obscured. Topical invention was a mnemotechnic art used to develop certain subjects in context, according to auctorial intention. The preference for or popularity of specific topics or *argumenta* is only a part of that process, interesting in itself, but inadequate for appreciation of the technique. Attention to topical invention rather than historical topics would eliminate much controversy regarding the transmission of topics like the *translatio imperii et studii* or the *locus amoenus,* and make us "ready to see the topoi for what they really are: not the domain of mediocrity, but the places of dramatic tension between opposite extremes; places where to simplify does not necessarily mean to water down—rather, it often means to heighten the contrasts."[126]

Material Style: *Qualitas*

To refer to the characteristic quality of persons and actions, Matthew of Vendôme uses the Horatian expression *colores operum* (*Ars vers* 1.46, 1.75) and the medieval one *maneries* (1.60). Both terms imply an emphasis on the general and typical rather than the unique and individual. Even personal names are topical. Matthew describes a Caesar, a Helen; that is, he shows what they represent as types, not the particular Julius Caesar or Helen of Troy. In effect, the work is "colored," it acquires its topical sheen or manner, from the types it represents.[127] This conception of style emerged in late antiquity from Horatian and Ciceronian sources and was widespread in the twelfth and thirteenth centuries. It is material style.[128]

Material style was illustrated by the so-called Wheel of Vergil. The model for the Wheel was the three principal social orders, that is, the aristocracy both ecclesiastical and secular, the bourgeoisie, and the workers and peasantry. These orders were said to be illustrated by, respectively, Vergil's *Aeneid, Georgics,* and *Bucolics.* The parallel is obviously inaccurate, and, as such, a gross simplification and even distortion. The principle is nonetheless important.[129] The three styles *(genera dicendi)* began as the three levels of discourse recognized in classical eloquence: the grand style which employed tropical language to achieve pathos; the middle style which used figural devices for effective communication and persuasion; and the low style which relied on simple, even colloquial speech and slang to achieve effect.[130] However, the elocutionary distinction among the three styles disappeared as the quality of Roman education and latinity declined.[131] Moreover, the Bible upset the stylistic hierarchy, leading Augustine to value a *sermo humilis* in moral and ecclesiastical discourse.[132] The Bible uses simple language to speak of the most elevated subjects; its style, not Cicero's, best served the preacher intent upon moving his congregation to repentance, moral betterment, and an at least rudimentary understanding of dogma and the articles of faith.[133] The Bible, by justifying and even sanctifying low style, abetted the adaptation of the notion of quality to *materia.* For the medieval preacher, letter writer, and poet, style conformed to social and cultural language. Therefore, the representation of persons and things had to take into account greater social and professional distinctions than those suggested by the Wheel of Vergil. The concept of material style came to express these distinctions.

The beginnings of material style are apparent in Horace's influential *Art of Poetry.*[134] For Horace, *colores operum* refer to careful and appropriate depiction of social classes and types.[135] Each personage should be made to conform to what may be expected of, or what may be appropriate to, his or her type.[136] Tradition might provide the substance of such descriptions, especially for prominent figures: "sit Medea ferox, invictaque, flebilis Ino, / perfidus Ixion, Io vaga, tristis Orestes" (*Ad Pisones* 123–24)[137] [let Medea be ferocious and indomitable, Ino prone to tears, Ixion treacherous, Io unsteady, Orestes sad]. Or if the personage introduced were unknown, he or she should be made verisimilar in context and station in life, and remain consistent with the type chosen (125–30, 156–78). These desiderata anticipate material style. "The 'colors' were 'glosses' upon the events stipulated in the theme which offered particular interpretations of the actions. . . . "[138] For John of Garland Vergil's works illustrate the technique rather than pattern it or provide its rationale. No doubt there were three orders in human society. But there were also divisions within those orders, like shepherds and farmers among the people. John reminds us of this in his discussion of memory, the ultimate source of topical description.[139] New and original adaptations were not precluded, especially where traditions conflicted.[140] In fact, they often created an implicit *status* or issue: the new work was needed when the original's model of type or hierarchy conflicted with that of the public or of a new author, adaptor, or patron. Duby has related the history of such divergence during the time of the emergence of medieval romance; he has also shown the extent to which conflict arose between ecclesiastical and aristocratic views of quality and procedure[141] — the potential *status* for the recreation of Chrétien's *Charrette* in the Prose *Lancelot* or of Jean de Meun's continuation of the *Rose*.

Material style is concerned with *qualitas*. *Qualitas* comes from careful and consistent delineation of character in persons, things, and actions in the elaboration of *materia;*[142] it influenced profoundly the amalgamation of auctorial conception and source. According to Horace and his commentators, *qualitas* determined topical elaboration by insistence on selection of attributes that conform to a model for the type chosen for representation. Thus, a given work's *qualitas* is apparent in the kinds of persons represented and their actions, when they are inserted in a coherent and complementary way into the narrative. *Qualitas* in material style was very important in formal letter writing, which gave impetus to its extension to the arts of poetry and prose,[143] as in this example from John of Garland's treatise on the epistolary and poetic arts: "In hoc . . . dictamine inuenitur materia et qualitas carminis a persona infirmi et a personis amicorum" (*Parisiana Poetria* 1.122–23) [in this . . . work the *materia* and quality of the poem are invented in such a way as to fit a person who is ill or persons who are friends]. Selection relies on memory: "Set quia dicitur Electio, quasi extra multa aliquorum lectio, debemus eligere dicenda adminiculo artis memorandi, que poetis materiam ordinantibus est necessaria" (2.87–89) [but it is called selection as if in the choice from among many things we would select what is to be said with the assistance of the art of memory, which art is essential to poets when arranging their *materia*]. The art of memory is both the source for and a stage in topical invention.[144]

Matthew of Vendôme shows special concern for qualitative adaptation by his stress on "ordinatio in qualitate tractatus" (*Ars vers* 3.52) [orderly arrangement of the treatment]. This accounts for his emphasis on *medi-*

ocritas.[145] *Mediocritas,* as golden mean, requires representation of persons without undue diversity. "Sed, observata personarum proprietate, executio materie 'servetur ad imum / Qualis ab incepto processerit et sibi constet,' videlicet ut nichil in se diminutum, nichil inveniatur ociosum" (*Ars vers* 1.34)[146] [but while observing propriety in the delineation of character, let the material as it is worked out "remain to the end even as it came forth / At the first and have it self-consistent." Let the writing be neither scanty nor prolix]. This phrase expresses the correlation of all properties to one essential quality from which they emanate, a quality which defines the representative by fitting the particular person or thing to its mental model: "c'est . . . l'acte par lequel l'individu tend à égaler de plus en plus profondément l'égalité de l'espèce: 'Humanitas aequalitas quaedam et integritas essendi hominum est' . . . : mieux un individu humain réalise la stabilité, la norme, la perfection de l'Espèce, et plus il est égal à soi."[147] According to this scheme, the individualist is deformed or degenerate—Judas among the disciples, Cain among brothers, Lucifer among angels. Such deformity or perversity is condemned by Alain de Lille in favor of unique excellence, the consummate realization of *homo sapiens* exemplified by the New Man in the *Anticlaudianus* as well as in other twelfth-century versions of a "new" creation.[148] Man achieves human perfection as a unique exemplar of the species. As we shall see, this conception of character had a profound influence on character representation and selection of attributes in the romances.[149]

When Geoffrey of Vinsauf compares the three styles to Vergil's works, he stresses their relation to *descriptio* as consistent and credible delineation of properties (*Documentum* II.3.138–39, 145–51, 157–61). The technique was called Determination.

> Si bene dicta notes et rebus verba coaptes,
> Sic proprie dices. Si mentio namque sit orta
> Forte rei, sexus, aetatis, conditionis,
> Eventus, si forte loci vel temporis: haec est
> Debita proprietas, quam vult res, sexus vel aetas,
> Conditio, eventus, tempus, locus. Ista venustas
> Est electa,[150] quia bene cum determino[151] totum
> Termino sub tali forma.
>
> (*Poetria nova* 1842–49)

[If you heed the directives carefully and suit words to content, you will speak with precise appropriateness in this way. If mention has perhaps arisen of an object, sex, age, condition, event, place, or time, it is regard for its distinctive quality that the object, sex, age, condition, event, time, or place claims as its due. Felicity in this matter is an admirable thing, for when I make an apt use of qualifying words I give the whole theme a finished completeness.]

Matthew's and Geoffrey's examples indicate the true import of the Wheel of Vergil as an illustration of material style and topical invention: consistency in selection of attributes, accessories, and actions representative of the type or types depicted in the narrative. Since John of Garland himself associates the Wheel not only with the three orders, but also with the division into types and categories within orders, it belongs, as invention, to the conception of a model for the work and the expression of that model in the details of textual elaboration.

Conception and Interpretation

Interpretatio/expolitio refer to elaboration by repetitive or incremental statement.[152] The beauty of a lady shines forth through the inventory of her parts, costume, intellectual and moral qualities, and actions. Or the multifarious pleasures of a banquet are gathered into a composite whole and enumerated. Matthew enjoins syntagmatic multiplication of attributes, since incremental repetition makes the object of description readily comprehensible. But he also insists on paradigmatic conformity of descriptive attributes to the mental model for the description. A beautiful woman must be both physically and morally beautiful. The characteristic is imbedded in the *materia* by such descriptions.

The attributes chosen may identify species within genera. But the species are not particulars; according to the principle of material style, they are types within a given class.[153]

> Igitur quod dictum est de summo pontifice vel de Cesare vel de aliis personis que sequuntur [in Matthew's exemplary illustrations of *descriptio*], ne nomen proprium preponderet, ceteris personis eiusdem conditionis vel etatis vel dignitatis vel officii vel sexus intelligatur attributum, ut nomen speciale generalis nominis vicarium ad maneriem rei, non ad rem maneriei reducatur. (*Ars vers* 1.60)

> [Therefore, those characteristics which are attributed to the Pope, or to Caesar, or to various persons who are described should be understood, not as peculiar characteristics of those particular persons, but as characteristics that may apply to other persons of the same social order, age, rank, office, or sex. Names of specific persons are thus used to represent a general class of persons and not to indicate special qualities belonging alone to those persons who are named.]

The procedure provides for consistent, verisimilar *descriptio*.

This point cannot be stressed too much. No matter how vapid, jejune, or perfunctory Matthew's and Geoffrey's examples of *descriptio* may seem, the principle they illustrate is fundamental, even profound.[154] They illustrate how auctorial conception finds expression in words. Now, auctorial conception is not construed as imposition; rather it is thought to elicit from the *materia* possibilities deemed inherent and thus potential in it (*Ars vers* 1.45). Matthew faulted Ovid's incomplete version of Jupiter's rape of Io because it ignored certain essential elements implicit in the usual stages by which one consummates a love (4.13). But the potential for their inclusion was in Ovid. They needed only to be elicited from the source and made plain.

Conception is a kind of exegesis. The author as critical reader is like the apprentice writer practicing the three kinds of study: explication, study of the art, and composition. Exegetical probing of *materia* "instilled in the pupil's mind the habit of bringing out the significance of whatever he found not fully explained in his *auctores* — a habit of mind which in a writer could easily become a habit of conception."[155] This sort of invention is analogous to the discovery of meaning by etymology in Isidore of Seville. Every word is susceptible of a variety of meanings; one need only open a dictionary to appreciate this fact. But, what is more significant for Isidore, meanings can be discovered by inventive techniques often quite foreign to scientific etymology.[156] Words may become virtual allegories whose meanings emerge from a study of their hidden origin. "Etymologia est origo vocabulorum, cum vis verbi vel nominis per interpretationem colligitur" (*Etymologiae* I.xxix.1) [etymology gives the origin of words whereby the import of the verb or noun is inferred by *interpretatio*]. *Interpretatio* includes etymological wordplay as a means to delineate the properties of a subject.[157]

Genius, as the personification of *ingenium,* shapes *materia* to fit an authorial conception of it. The Middle Ages called this activity imagination. Genius

> uero calamum papiree fragilitatis germanum numquam a sue inscriptionis ministerio feriantem, manu gerebat in dextra:[158] in sinistra uero morticini pellem nouacule demorsione pilorum cesarie denudatam, in qua stili obsequentis subsidio imagines rerum ab umbra picture ad ueritatem sue essentie transmigrantes, uita sui generis munerabat.
>
> Quibus delectionis morte sopitis, noue natiuitatis ortu alias reuocabat in uitam. (*De planctu* XVIII.68–74)
>
> [carried in his right hand a reed of frail papyrus, which never rested from its occupation of writing; and in his left he bore an animal's skin from which a knife had cut and bared the shock of hair, and on this, by means of his compliant pen, he gave to images, which passed from the shadow of a sketch to the truth of very being, the life of their kind. And when these slumbered in the death of deletion, others were called to life in a new rising and birth (p. 91.100–109).]

Alain also describes a left-handed Genius, which allows for misrepresentation. The good and bad Genii are therefore analogous to and complement

Alain de Lille's own distinction, noted above (pp. 39–40), between the *iunctura* of the philosopher, which expresses truth, and that of the mere poet which, though artful, is mendacious or otiose.

Materia can never express an idea in its pristine or archetypal essence; nor is any particular expression final. The inherent inadequacy of any art or artifact makes each work implicitly susceptible of further elaboration, clarification, or correction. "This means that any work of adaptation — which, in medieval terms, is to all intents and purposes synonymous with any work of literature — depends for its success on a judicious use of two devices: the discovery of the meaning implicit in the matter and the insertion of such thoughts . . . as might adorn, or be read into, the matter."[159] Adaptation is never final because the expression of thought or meaning in the literary work of art is partial and selective.

In the realm of ideas, conceptualization and definition may not be sufficient for the work of art, although they may contribute to its elucidation. Abstractions usually resist all-inclusive definition in medieval literature.[160] They are not concepts but rather notions analogous to ideas in Neoplatonic speculation. An idea reveals itself in the configuration of conceptual and material representations[161] that interpret it as a model. In effect, interpretation states the significance of the work's interrelations, whether those interrelations are established by description or by plot. This means that there is lighting, but lighting through particular, specially chosen filters and prisms. This elucidation reveals relationships among elements in the narrative and makes it exemplary. Narrative elaboration of this kind is topical. The narrative subject is described from the model and point of view that the author deems appropriate to his or her intention. "Contemplandus est non effectus sermonis sed affectus sermocinantis" (*Ars vers* 1.60) [listeners should concentrate, not on what is said, but on the manner in which it is said]. Whether a meaning is construed as imposed on meaningless *materia* or elicited from its obscurity, the commentator does no more than interpret, that is, amplify upon that meaning. He or she may, of course, revise some or all of it, as does, for example, the commentary on the *Aeneid* attributed to Bernardus Silvestris. So does Jean de Meun with Guillaume de Lorris, as well as the Prose *Lancelot* with Chrétien de Troyes' *Charrette*.

Form and Modes of Amplification and Abbreviation: *Ornatus*

Tropes and figures enter into invention as amplifications and abbreviations.[162] The medieval treatises on poctics devote a large amount of space to these devices because they are relatively elementary manuals on composition,[163] and must therefore provide adequate instruction in the rudiments: the use

of the very tropes and figures encountered so often in grammatical and rhetorical treatises, versification exercises, and the interpretation of literature.
Amplification and abbreviation are the final stage in topical invention. They
constitute the form or mode of expression of the work's *qualitas*.[164] They
give access to the formal and conceptual intentions of the author, like God's
designs discovered in the world's *ornatus*.[165]

Eugène Vinaver has taught us to recognize certain formal devices as structural models for medieval narrative: parataxis in the *chansons de geste,* and
enumerative and incremental sequences (polysyndeton) in cyclic romance.[166]
Moreover, allegory, irony, and metonymy are common amplificatory modes
in medieval narrative. One could easily extend the list to include most common tropical and figural devices that, as amplifications and abbreviations,
are the *ornatus* of *materia*.[167] For example, paraphrase may embrace a vast
and coherent narrative design. According to the *Documentum,* the trope *cir-
cuitio* names the property for the object the property is attributed to
(II.3.28–30). In paraphrase as amplification,

> fit sermo vicarius ejus
> In serie vocum longa serieque morosa.
> Longius ut sit opus, ne ponas nomina rerum:
> Pone notas alias; nec plane detege, sed rem
> Innue per notulas; nec sermo perambulet in re,
> Sed rem circuiens longis ambagibus ambi
> Quod breviter dicturus eras, et tempora tardes,
> Dans ita crementum verbis.
> (*Poetria nova* 227–34)

[An expression made up of a long and leisurely sequence of sounds is sub-
stituted for a word. In order to amplify the poem, avoid calling things by
their names; use other designations for them. Do not unveil the thing fully
but suggest it by hints. Do not let your words move straight onward
through the subject, but, circling it, take a long and winding path around
what you were going to say briefly. Retard the tempo by thus increasing
the number of words.]

That *crementum* is precisely what Dante admired in the *ambages pulcerrime*
of Arthurian romance.[168] Tropes and figures are structural principles. Amplification and abbreviation extend them to larger units of discourse, and,
in some cases, to the entire work.

Training in amplification took place in the classroom exercises termed
praeexercitamina or *progymnasmata*.[169] Given themes were assigned for
elaboration by means of specific devices, including those borrowed from

among the tropes and figures for amplification and abbreviation. Since the
devices chosen had to suit auctorial intention and enhance the *materia*'s significance, the pupil had to reflect on the suitability of particular devices to
the given subject matter.[170] The technique is also apparent in *declamationes*
like Bernardus Silvestris' *Mathematicus*. In it, "authentic imaginative purpose" adapts a "demonstration piece" to the problem of man in his world.[171]
The preference for certain devices over others, especially in the classroom,
may betray tradition in a rut. But mentalities and psychologies as well as
political and social circumstances may also explain the attraction of certain
manners or modes of rhetorical amplification.

Geoffrey of Vinsauf's instruction is based on writers he thought exemplary:
Sidonius Apollinaris in prose and the Chartrain poets in verse were his
masters.[172] Their works favor the devices singled out by Geoffrey: *interpretatio*
and *expolitio,* with the varieties *frequentatio* and *imago;* paraphrase; comparison, including simile, allegory, and personification; description; digression, including flashback, foreshadowing, and excursus[173]; apostrophe;
prosopopeia; and opposition.

Alain de Lille's criticism of Joseph of Exeter and Gautier de Châtillon suggests the qualities expected of a writer amplifying by tropical and figural
devices. Alain attacks two faults. The first is patchwork combination and
lack of distinction in conception: "pannoso plebescit carmine" (*Anticlaudianus* I.165) [in a patch-work poem (he) writes for the mob (p. 51)]. Alain,
like Chrétien in the *Erec* Prologue, castigates faulty composition that results
when appropriate arrangement and credible material style are lacking. This
corresponds to inartistic *coniunctura*. The second major fault he perceives
in the two authors is that, lacking true eloquence ("os . . . mutum" [I.167]
[dumb mouth (p. 51)]), they strive to write about what they cannot make
clear ("tenebrosi carminis umbra / Pingere" [I.168–69] [to portray . . . in
a dark and shadowy ode (p. 52)]). These poets fail to delineate their model
in composition. They are allegedly unable to give substance to their rhetorical flashes and amplificatory colors, and the result is a vapid, gaudy
showpiece—"pictura suo languens pallescat in auro" (I.164) [the painting . . . growing dull and pale amidst its gold (p. 51)]. Faults like these are
roundly condemned in the arts of poetry and prose, where the writer is en-
joined to leave no obscurities or blemishes in the completed opus, but rather
to adorn it with well-shaped expression and solid substance.[174]

> Se nisi conformet color intimus exteriori,
> Sordet ibi ratio: faciem depingere verbi
> Est pictura luti, res est falsaria, ficta

> Forma, dealbatus paries et hypocrita verbum
> Se simulans aliquid, cum sit nihil. Haec sua forma
> Dissimulat deforme suum.
>
> *(Poetria nova* 741–46)

[If internal ornament is not in harmony with external, a sense of propriety is lacking. Adorning the face of a word is painting a worthless picture: it is a false thing, its beauty fictitious; the word is a whitewashed wall and a hypocrite, pretending to be something whereas it is nothing. Its fair form conceals its deformity.]

Accordingly, when Matthew of Vendôme completed a topical *gradus amoris* in Ovid,[175] he used amplification. Gautier de Châtillon's faults, then, would seem to stem from amplification allegedly obscure and without substance rather than from any inherent defect in amplification as such. Whether Alain's judgment is correct or not does not matter here; his standards do.

Matthew makes distinctive language, choice of words, and manner of expression depend on substance; "ut venustas significatorum in ipsa significantia redundare perpendatur" (*Ars vers* 2.10) [thus the beauty of what the words signify overflows to grace the very words themselves]. These features make for clarity, ease of understanding, and pleasure. They are underscored by Geoffrey of Vinsauf; for him, amplification and abbreviation through *ornatus* correct the faults Alain de Lille found in Gautier de Châtillon, obscurity giving way to illumination, sharp contrast, and clarity. *Conformatio,* or the accommodation of expression to thought, is achieved by amplification, the final stage in topical invention; this is true in both verse and prose (*Poetria nova* 1943–68; *Documentum* II.3.91–101 and 110–12). Eberhard the German extols these features in Geoffrey's instruction: "Ars nova scribendi speciali fulget honore, / Rebus cum verbis deliciosa suis" (*Laborintus* 665–66) [a new art of writing shines with splendid distinction, delightful in its combination of substance and words]. The tropes and figures, and the complementary techniques of Determination and Conversion, are principles of enunciation. They complete topical invention.

Disposition of the Work: Figura

The work's *figura* is the stamp of auctorial conception on the work's *materia.* It is mirrored in every step of composition. The entire opus is accordingly the image of the *figura* originally conceived in the artist's mind.[176] *Figura* not only forms, it combines into a configuration. Horace taught that the poet must attend to the locus, the "place" where invention is appropriate (*Ad Pi-*

sones 14–21).[177] Porphyry elaborates on "naturam quorundam poetarum . . . pessimam, qui incipiant grandia describere, deinde in locos
communes exeant, qui licet boni sint, tamen ridentur ac supervacui haben-
tur, nisi loco positi sint" (*Porphyry* p. 345.8–11) [the reprehensible habit
of some poets who begin by describing great matters, then decline into commonplaces which may well be very fine, but are deemed ridiculous and su-
percilious unless they are properly located]. What Horace understands as
series and *iunctura* require, respectively, proper sequence and proper linking; otherwise "vanae Fingentur species" (see p. 24). The jointing and conjoining, the relocation and disjunction this involves became basic features
of the medieval art of poetry and prose, as we have seen in Chapter 1. Narrative required not only proper sequence, but also accommodation of sequence
to sense so that its parts might assume topical significance. *Series* includes
personae, negotia, tempus, and *locus* in narrative. Topical invention, relying on all four, identified topoi for invention and gave quality to *series.* For
medieval authors, narrative texture comes from observation of *qualitas* or
material style, and in particular of the properties suitable to the four elements just named as they are interwoven in the fabric of the text.

As with many other features of classical rhetoric and poetics—natural and
artificial order, amplification and abbreviation—so with description, the Middle Ages made changes which, however wrongheaded they may have been
to begin with, came to define and determine an art of poetry and prose in
important and productive ways. Horace insisted that description be apposite, and the medieval treatises agreed; otherwise the work becomes fantastic or nightmarish. But what of works—dream visions, romance with its
failles—where there is a deliberate attempt to represent dreamlike or truncated narrative? Here the "useless" or "vain" becomes paramount. Medieval
commentaries classify such features under *digressio inutilis:* additions to the
matter that went off from it, but did not terminate or even bring anything
concrete back to the principal subject matter.[178] Such vain and empty digressions were appropriate in historical and poetic writing.

Now, such excursus could have their own design, reflecting directly or as
in a vision, darkly or clearly, the thematic patterns of the principal *materia.*
The analogies could be highly suggestive; commentators were alert to analogical possibilities when reading antique and late antique authors. Ovid
provided a casebook illustration, especially after the mythographers had begun to draw diverse allegorical readings—discrete digressions—from his writings. School exercises themselves practiced topical elaboration of Ovidian
themes. This was done for the vernacular when the *Philomela* attributed to
Chrétien de Troyes was included in the *Ovide moralisé.* Once the work was
conceived—including both matter and signification—it was a meaningful

combination of diverse elements conjoined in conformity with an overall informing conception: it was a *figura*.

Figura in narrative was termed *narratio fabulosa* in Chartrain poetics and exegesis on the authority of Macrobius.[179] Such narrative served to express the mysteries and workings of nature, especially human nature where moral and ethically related psychological factors offered a fruitful field for allegorical digression.[180] Exegetical probing produced glosses like that on the *Aeneid* attributed to Bernardus Silvestris and poems like Gautier de Châtillon's reading of Alexander's life in the light of providential history and Boethian moral imperatives. The writings of the great twelfth-century Latin authors became exemplars for the art of poetry and prose that the early vernacular romancers learned. In applying that art and the principle of *narratio fabulosa* to secular subject matters, they invented narratives that express the ideals, the social, moral, and psychological predilections, of their patrons and the aristocratic publics for which they wrote. Old *materia* underwent reevaluation, probing reevaluation that identified truths relevant to the aristocracy. The artist, by separating and conjoining, uncovered in the superficial order of narrative events — *histoire événementielle* — a deeper order explaining those events. That order is the work's *figura*.

The notion of *narratio fabulosa* led to renewed emphasis on natural and artificial order and especially the imbrication of both orders in narrative at once syntagmatic and paradigmatic. Temporal succession, erratic and haphazard as it may have been, could nonetheless be made to reveal the working out of principles of order as invisible to direct human scrutiny as the workings of nature and of God. Topics like noble birth, chivalry, love, the *translatio imperii et studii* were discovered beneath marvelous plots. Plot could have a temporal and a topical order, according to the Bernardus commentary on the *Aeneid*. Both orders have a *series* and a *coniunctura*. Analogical relations established by topical invention express the *figura* that links the diverse parts of the opus in that *coniunctura*.

Restatement of a topical theme could be straightforward or diversified.

> Sententia cum sit
> Unica, non uno veniat contenta paratu,
> Sed variet vestes et mutatoria sumat;
> Sed verbis aliis praesumpta resume; repone
> Pluribus in clausis unum; multiplice forma
> Dissimuletur idem; varius sis et tamen idem.
> (*Poetria nova* 220–25)

[Although the meaning is one, let it not come content with one set of apparel. Let it vary its robes and assume different raiment. Let it take up again in other words what has already been said; let it reiterate, in a number of clauses, a single thought. Let one and the same thing be concealed under multiple forms — be varied and yet the same.]

We have suggested above how this patterning of diversity informs the design of Gautier de Châtillon's *Alexandreis;* it will be apparent as well in the elaboration of diverse adventures and marvels in romance. The technique of *interpretatio* and *expolitio* evoked in the lines just cited from Geoffrey of Vinsauf relies on a principle valid for all forms of amplification and abbreviation and of topical and figural ornamentation: the adaptation, by obvious or subtle means, of matter to context. Circumlocution, comparison, apostrophe, and other kinds of amplification and abbreviation establish analogies, contrasts, restatements, or variations of a work's *thema.* Even abbreviation reflects the principle, and indeed makes explicit what amplification often obscures to all but the discerning eye: where abbreviation may set forth the *thema* with the brevity and clarity we perceived in Conrad of Mure's example of the siege of Basel, amplification may wind about the subject, varying the language, the image, contrasting and comparing, but ever with a view to expressing the *thema* through narrative diversity, as in the conclusion to the *Alexandreis* where Nature personified plots with Proditio in hell while the two serfs elevated to high station by Alexander plan his assassination.

As the *thema* expands into *materia,* it acquires meaning beyond that of mere events. The work passes from school exercise to vision of truth. The truth is discernible through the author's analysis of disparate matter, analysis informed by the mental conception or *status archetypus.* Analogy is an important instrument.

> Analogy so informs the entire work that it is rarely possible to define its limits and distinguish between a deliberate recasting of a motif and an incidental reflection of it. Once the work's themes and motifs are established, they appear to generate around themselves numerous episodes which incorporate them or reflect them in a variety of ways. Analogy is definite and obvious in some places, but it also consists of numerous and brief echoes in others. In the latter case, it functions merely as an *evocative* means of amplification, rather than as a precise and organized system of correspondences on a one-to-one basis. Few of these echoes bear an essential relation to the work's meaning, but the more of them we perceive, the fuller and richer the work becomes.[181]

What Norris Lacy has discerned in Chrétien de Troyes' romances is an art of composition that has its beginnings in Chartrain poetics. Even fleeting analogies, like those evoked by the *digressiones inutiles* of seemingly disparate episodes, have a rationale within the conception of the opus. That conception implies the selection and arrangement of *materia,* including the disposition of thematic and other topical developments.

Now, there is a terminological distinction between *ordo* as the arrangement of *materia propinqua* and as the work's disposition of that *ordo.* The medieval arts of poetry and prose discriminate between *dispositio* in the *materia propinqua* and *ordo* in the opus. But sources and topical patterns fit into either economy by "plotting."[182] The work itself may preserve that arrangement, or it may reorder it in whole or in part, that is, it may follow natural or artificial order.[183]

Natural and artificial order are not principles only for the disposition of the entire work. The terms were first used to refer to arrangement of words in the sentence; like *iunctura,* they were originally conceived with reference to Latin syntax and periodic style, or the small unit of discourse in latinity.[184] But the principle was extended so that, after Servius and by the time of the Vienna scholiast, natural and artificial order were being used to refer to disposition of *narratio* as well.[185] The Vienna scholiast justifies the *Aeneid*'s use of artificial order as deflection from chronological order in the recounting of events. Vergil, we are told, wanted to relate the destruction of Troy and the flight of the Trojans in order to enhance the dramatic immediacy of the tragedy.[186] Later the two orders are identified in the Commentary on the *Aeneid* attributed to Bernardus Silvestris, where a natural allegorical order is perceived as a *figura* of Man's rise to virtue from sin and darkness.[187] The *Aeneid*'s literal order is thereby made to conform to man's fate in this life.[188] The Commentator conceives of man's moral development as Matthew of Vendôme construed the *gradus amoris:* "in humanis actionibus quaedam est ordinaria successio" (*Ars vers* 4.13) [in human actions there is a certain usual succession]. The gradual working out of an "archetypal" pattern in the work, "the structured unfolding of the contents . . . in an ordered design,"[189] is the work's *ordo discretus* (*Poetria nova* 739)—"the imaginatively organized design of the whole work."[190] That "design" was perceptible to those trained like the author, or accustomed like the audience, to seek hidden meaning in the literal text. In effect, the art of poetry and prose taught the poetics of the Chartrain tradition evident in both ancient scientific and philosophical writings and rhetorical and literary texts.[191]

The allegorical reading of the *Aeneid* identifies an archetypal pattern which, as a structural model for the work, is a topical series or gradation. Such patterns may be represented not only by static topical *descriptio* or elucidation, but also by sequence and conjunction of stages in narrative. For, as Matthew of Vendôme notes, in the usual order of human actions, "quedam enim . . . aliarum sunt preambule, quedam aliarum sunt consecutive" (*Ars vers* 4.13)[192] [certain actions are preludes to others and certain ones are consequences of others]. Unless this is observed, texture ("contextus," *ibid.*) is not achieved. All human actions have a proper order. It is the author's task to identify — to invent — that order (4.18–19): whether in love, combat, hospitality, coronation, navigation, siege, or whatever — in short, in the "great public images"[193] of romance.

Shape and Conception of the Work: Figura and Status archetypus

Excogitation of the *figura* precedes excogitation of narrative. The *figura* is elicited from *rudis materia*. It makes source material meaningful and elegant. The original *materia* may be as simple as a one-word *thema*, or it may be complex, like that for historical or pseudohistorical narrative. Such "rough" *materia* undergoes painstaking and extensive rearrangement and embellishment. The resultant *figura* should express auctorial conception of the work in every detail of its shape and sheen.

The selection and rearrangement of *materia* may be usefully likened to the practice of medieval cartography. Benoît de Sainte-Maure himself once saw his work as a fragmentary *mappa mundi*.[194] Indeed, we have observed that the *Alexandreis* describes the world as God's creation and thus as the expression of the divine in human history and geography. The world center is at Jerusalem because that is where Christ's life and death occur. The rest of the world and the rest of history are located so as to center on and give expression to that event. Medieval maps are thus a *figura*. Their principles of order and representation are analogous to those we have been describing for poetic invention.

Geoffrey of Vinsauf evokes the cartographer alongside the architect to illustrate the organization and centering of the *Poetria nova* itself.[195] In the beginning the poet sets his course as the cartographer maps out his voyage — "ubi Gades / Figat" (*Poetria nova* 57–58) [where it will fix its Cadiz]. And the final product realizes just that intention: "Jam mare transcurri, Gades in littore fixi" (2066) [now I have crossed the sea; I have fixed my Cadiz on the shore]. But Cadiz is marked not by its geographical coordinates, but rather by its topical and tropical midpoints. Innocent III, the pope standing between God and man, to whom Geoffrey dedicated his treatise, becomes a beacon that illuminates the master artist teaching the principles of invention and order that derive by analogy from divine archetypes: "Et mihi te portum statuo, qui, maxima rerum, / Non Deus es nec homo: quasi neuter es inter utrumque" (2067–68) [and I resolve upon you as my goal, you who, greatest of creatures, are neither God nor yet man. You are neither — yet somewhere between the two]. "Neuter . . . inter utrumque" brings us to the midpoint, between the beginning and end of his treatise and between the opening and closing praise of the papal patron: "Hunc portum teneas, hic fixa sit anchora mentis" (1062) [occupy this harbour, cast the mind's anchor here].

This admonition lies, appropriately enough, between instruction on transposition, which separates artificially what is normally conjoined, and counsel against obscurity.

The medieval artist begins with a specific work in mind, a *status archetypus.* The verbal statement of that work, its *thema,* expands to emanate, as
a structure rising up from its base, until it achieves a whole and complete
figura. The entire construction arises in conformity with a mental conception that is built into carefully hewn and arranged blocks of matter. Walter
Benjamin has expressed the idea in modern critical terms. "Die Ideen verhalten
sich zu den Dingen wie die Sternbilder zu den Sternen. Das besagt zunächst:
sie sind weder deren Begriffe noch deren Gesetze. . . . Die Ideen sind ewige
Konstellationen und indem die Elemente als Punkte in derartigen Konstellationen erfaßt werden, sind die Phänomene aufgeteilt und gerettet zugleich"[196]
[ideas have the same relation to things as constellations do to the stars. This
means first and foremost that they are neither their concepts nor the laws
that govern them. . . . Ideas are eternal constellations, and insofar as the
elements are construed as points in such constellations, the material
phenomena are completely partitioned and preserved at one and the same
time]. In one sense, stars have no *materia,* we perceive only their light. But,
together, they form patterns that become constellations—potential *materia*—
in a mental image. The technique is the same in mundane arts—the architect
and the cartographer use the interior as well as the exterior compass to chart
their work—as in other, higher spheres, where God and Nature (*Poetria nova*
563) design their creations and creatures. In each and every case the mind
moves from idea to matter.

Hence, the pyramidal conception of invention extends from the imagination of the work in the *ingenium* through verbalization to arrangement,
characterization by context, and ornamentation as amplification and abbreviation. The process was adapted to medieval romance as it emerged in twelfth-
century France. It remained essentially intact down to the end of the Middle
Ages, when scribes like Michot Gonnot were still adapting prose romance
for aristocratic audiences. The principal compositional concerns expressed
by the romancers parallel those taught in the arts of poetry and prose; the
first romancers passed those concerns on to succeeding generations of imita-
tors and adapters. They established the romance tradition upon the most
conservative foundations. The paradigm for invention is apparent in the
romancers' statements about their art and in their *conjointures.* And it fits
the use of the term *(con)iunctura* - a narrative construction assembled from
sources and inventions. The new combination displays a preconceived *figura*
which makes the narrative true. The new *narratio fabulosa* of romance expresses truth through marvels and topical *ornatus.*

3

Antecedent Paradigms of Invention: Historiographic Paradigm

Tum genitor ueterum uoluens monimenta uirorum
"Audite, o proceres," ait "et spes discite uestras."
—Aeneid III.102–3

[Then the father, after pondering the records of the ancestors, said:
"Heed me, o princes, and learn what you may hope."]

Des or comancerai l'estoire
Qui toz jorz mes iert an mimoire.
—Erec 23–24

[Herewith I shall begin the story that will ever be remembered.]

Sources of Medieval Works

The paradigm for invention discussed in Chapter 2 was applied in the schools of the eleventh and twelfth centuries. The romancers who wrote between 1150 and 1200 appear to have learned the art of composition in those schools before adapting it to the vernacular language and its *matieres*.[1] Now, the typical romancer "n'était ni un philologue classique ni un celtologue, mais un conteur doué d'ironie, expert dans l'art de manipuler en les racontant les sujets qu'il empruntait, de façon à leur permettre, certes de faire la place à l'enseignement courtois requis *(sen)*, mais d'abord de satisfaire le désir de son public pour l'extraordinaire, le mystérieux, l'onirique . . . ,"[2] in short, for the *merveilleux*.[3] The romancers were perhaps not constrained by scho-

lastic standards to the extent that Latin writers were. The less literary vernacular[4] gave them more freedom to fashion the new genre of romance with
an art derived from the traditional scholastic paradigm.[5] The new romance
tradition would continue to evolve, in verse and prose, through the innova-
tions and continuations of new authors, adapters, and scribes, until the end
of the medieval period. The twelfth-century romancers reconstituted the paradigm for invention to make it fit what medieval historiography taught them
about handling sources—the *matieres* of Britain, France, and Rome.[6]

The first romancers practiced their art for the royalty and the high
aristocracy, where advancement, preferment, or payment might reward their
talent and efforts. They wrote to foster aristocratic ideals and ambitions,
presumably as they satisfied their own. The emergence of romance was not
unrelated to the crises in the nobility, and especially among the *iuvenes*—
sons who could not inherit by right of primogeniture. Duby identified this
group in twelfth-century France, and Köhler discerned its presence in early
romance. But romance also mirrors the conflict between royalty and the
church epitomized by the struggle of Thomas à Becket against Henry II. Thus,
romance could be made to serve royal aims and propaganda.[7] New, more
secular emphases—the French language, a secular audience with aristocratic
ideals and predilections, the *merveilleux* in the sources—did not alter its basic framework. Romance invention emerges from traditional invention.[8]

> Cil clerc dïent que n'est pas sens
> D'escrire estoire d'antif tens
> Quant jo nes escris en latin,
> Et que je pert mon tans enfin.
> (*Partonopeu* 77–80)

[The clerics say that it is unreasonable to write an *estoire* of olden days if
I don't do so in Latin, and that in the long run I am wasting my time.]

The *Partonopeu* Prologue goes on to cite authorities and examples illustrating how good *matiere* may be drawn from bad in French and other languages
while still providing examples of conduct in tales of marvelous beauty. "Ce
puet en cest escrit aprendre / Qui ot et set e wet entendre" (133–34) [he who
hears, knows, and wishes to attend can learn from what I have written here.]
The language has changed, but not the technique and intentions.

The arts of poetry and prose, interpretations of literature by commentary
and gloss, and exercises in composition deal only briefly and abstractly with
the identification of sources. In classroom exercises, the source seems to have
been given, so that the new version was a topical adaptation rather than a
combination or *conjointure*. Interpretation of texts did not concern itself with

the reconstruction of sources; at most, sources were identified if they were prominent.

Still, there is some awareness of the complexity of the problem of multiple sources. Thus, while Matthew of Vendôme speaks of only one source under *executio materiae,* John of Garland recognized that more than one was possible, especially in historical writing, and that a combination of sources presented unique and difficult problems of arrangement: "Notandum . . . quod partes hystorie non sunt certe et determinate, quia per uoluntatem hystoriographi et secundum ipsa gesta distinguitur hystoria" (*Parisiana Poetria* 4.475–77) [note that the parts of a *historia* are neither fixed nor established; for *historia* is distinguished according to the intention of the author and the events themselves that are to be related]. But there is nothing on what is meant by "parts," nor on the technique for combining or amalgamating them. Only more advanced theoretical disquisitions like Macrobius' *Saturnalia* deal with the combination of sources in invention. Still, historians had faced the problem long before vernacular romances were written. Their example is important in the emergence of romance and the art of romance.

Historical writing often required the selection and correlation of material from multiple sources. Since histories were studied and commented upon in medieval education, the student would have come to know the problem of sources by auctorial references to them. What was valid for *historia* as *res gestae* was valid for *historia* as *res ut gestae* or even as *fabula*. For *historia,* like *estoire* and modern *histoire,* may relate real or imaginary events. Moreover, commentaries distinguish between *historicus* and *poeta*. If the narrative was straightforward and factual (even when it included topical amplifications), the author was a *historicus* and wrote *historia;* if it was not straightforward but relied on artificial arrangement and reinterpretation of *materia,* the work was a *poema* and the author a *poeta*.[9]

This Latin distinction came late to French.[10] At the time the first works we usually call romance were written—the *romans d'antiquité*—there seems to have been little distinction made between them and contemporary *estoires* like the *Rou,* the *Chronique des ducs de Normandie,* and the *Brut*. All these works were *estoires;* when they were on occasion called *romans,*[11] it was to distinguish them from Latin-language works. Later, when French narrative began to use Celtic *matieres,* the word *roman* became more specialized in meaning, in order to distinguish such narrative from the more nearly factual records assumed to be found in the *romans d'antiquité*.[12]

These developments oblige us to consider the emergence of romance both from specific sources and, more generally, from more historical writing characteristic of French literary production in the Angevin world between about 1140 and 1170. Some knowledge of medieval historiography, especially in the vernacular, provides insight into how the first romancers or proto-romancers like Wace and Benoît de Sainte-Maure understood the amalga-mation and elaboration of sources. But first we must review modern source study.

Source Scholarship and Romance

When no obvious source is extant today, references to putative sources are usually set aside as a widespread effort by medieval romancers to give authority and credibility to their own inventions.[13] Were medieval patrons and audiences that gullible? A casual perusal of any comprehensive survey of Middle High German romance shows that virtually every title refers to a French or Latin source, most of which are either extant, attested to in con-temporary documents, or alluded to in the French romances. The few ex-ceptions, like Ulrich von Zatzikhoven's *Lanzelet* or the *Moriz von Craûn,* contain plausible indications of a lost French original. The German refer-ences to sources are therefore consistent and widespread.[14] It would repre-sent a singular reversal of French practice if German romancers insisted on and made regular use of source material, while their French counterparts said they did so only to dupe audiences or to mouth a meaningless commonplace.

Several complementary explanations account for the missing sources for much of French romance. First, they were oral; that is, they were either related by mouth to the author, who recorded the words and eventually composed a romance following what he or she had heard, or else they belonged to an oral tradition like that for the *chansons de geste* or that attributed to foreign jongleurs relating Celtic stories.[15] Second, the original sources were destroyed or removed prior to the composition of the romance, so that the author had to work from memory or derivative materials. Third, the sources are lost today. Fourth, the sources may have been construed as an ideal representa-tion in the author's mind. Fifth, the source references are a prevarication. There is evidence for all these possibilities.

An oral source may come from a specific individual or from a tradition. Like Wace recalling his father's account of the embarkation for the Battle of Hastings, Jehan Maillart says that he heard the story of the *Comte d'An-jou* told by a trustworthy nobleman who claimed to have witnessed the events related in the romance (*Anjou* 47–52, 82–86).[16] Jongleurs and other oral sources also existed, although their reports were suspect.

> En cele grant pais ke jo di,
> Ne sai si vus l'avez oï,
> Furent les merveilles pruvees

> E les aventures truvees
> Ki d'Artur sunt tant recuntees
> Ke a fable sunt aturnees.
> (*Brut* 9787–92)[17]

[In that great peacetime I am telling you about—I don't know if you have heard this—the marvels were experienced and the adventures found which have been told about Arthur so often that they have become fables.]

Wace did not ignore the reports of jongleurs; but he insisted on verification of their contents.[18]

Most romancers were less charitable than Wace. Chrétien castigates their performances in *Erec*. Jehan Bodel is downright truculent.

> Cil bastart jongleour qui vont par ces viliaus
> A ces longues vïeles a depeciés forriaus
> Chantent de Guiteclin si con parasseniaus.
> (*Saisnes* 27–29)

[Those bastard jongleurs who go from town to town with their long viols and patched capes sing about Guiteclin like perfect asses.]

It is not surprising, then, that after 1200 *chansons de geste* like the *Saisnes* used romance models rather than oral techniques.[19] Jehan Bodel says his best source was preserved in writing: "Tout si con li drois contes len fu dis et espiaus / Dont encor est l'estore a Saint-Faron a Miaus" (33–34)[20] [just as the correct story relates and sets it forth to him—the *estoire* of which is still at Saint Faron's in Meaux].

From what we know of the oral tradition represented in the early *chansons de geste,* it is no paradox to assert that the *chanson de geste* is a genre without any surviving example: all disappeared at the moment of performance—*in ventos vita recessit.* Nor was there any way, at the beginning of a performance, to assure how it would end; the performer read in the faces of the audience what to relate.[21] "Ensi que son voloir pour plaire li endite, / De parler s'apresta car chascun li encite" (*Restor* 1530–31) [just as he is moved to please, he prepared to speak, for everyone encourages him to do so]. Yet, to turn utterance into the written word required some documentation.

> De l'autre part, fut dan Gontier,
> Celui qui fut ja sun esquier,
> Fiz de sa sor, si ert ses niez:
> Ceo dit la geste a Seint Richier.
> (*Gormont* 327–30)[22]

[On the other side was lord Gontier. His (= Hue, Gontier's uncle) squire he was in fact, his sister's son and his nephew. This the *geste* at Saint Riquier's relates.]

Emphasis on documentation is a concern of writing, not of improvisation. In this sense, any *written chanson de geste,* even when pre-romance, is *estoire.*[23]

The thirteenth-century *Abladane* claims the actual loss of a source, an original Latin version allegedly burned in a fire at Amiens. The author supports the claim by citing those who had seen and read it before the fire. One cleric had taken it upon himself to draw up a French version "sans nulle mensonce aconcueiller" (*Abladane* p. 475.7–8) [without including any falsehood]. No less an authority than Richart de Fornival, chancellor of Notre Dame of Amiens (p. 475.1–2), is invoked to validate the French version. "Et quant le matere fut ainsi en romant, tesmoigna le bons chanchelier qu'il avoit veue la matiere et lute en ung livre qui fut ars trente ans aprés; le peuvent tesmoigner lé clers d'Amiens" (p. 475.8–10) [and when the *matiere* was rendered into French in this way, the good chancellor testified that he had seen and read the *matiere* in a book which had burned thirty years later. And the clerics at Amiens can attest to this fact].

The care taken by the anonymous *Abladane* redactor to authenticate the Latin and French versions reflects the concern evinced by many romancers to identify their sources under *accessus*-like heads: title, location, and circumstances of composition. References to sources were subject to verification should any doubts arise. In fact, "on ne voit pas pourquoi ils [the authors] auraient si effrontément menti, puisque n'importe lequel de leurs auditeurs pouvait toujours demander à prendre connaissance du *livre,* et, au surplus . . . , un Philippe d'Alsace [among others!] aurait trouvé d'assez mauvais goût que son romancier se targue d'une commande qu'il ne lui aurait jamais passée ou d'un intérêt qu'il ne lui aurait pas témoigné."[24]

Pierre Gallais does not deny the obscurity of many assertions about putative sources, nor that there may be special problems in specific cases like the Latin grail book referred to in the thirteenth and fourteenth centuries, Wolfram von Eschenbach's Kyôt, or Chaucer's Lollius. These instances are, first and foremost, mysteries today. We cannot assume out of hand that this was so for contemporary audiences. For example, they may illustrate the ironic or comic voice of the narrator, not of the author. But even if these authors project a nonexistent source, such a mystification would hardly have succeeded easily except in a milieu accustomed to the use of sources.[25] Citation, adaptation, and play with sources were common practices and could be appreciated for their own sake.[26]

Until about 1950, scholarship concentrated on the identification or the reconstruction of presumed sources. However, several recent developments have disturbed the apparent conformity, simple and comfortable, between the focus of early romance scholarship and the preoccupation with sources expressed in the recorded statements of romance.[27] First, we have learned that use of sources does not preclude adaptation and even originality in retelling. Auctorial statements frequently claim that the new version is an improvement on its source. The German romancers saw their adaptations as original and worthwhile, and comparative studies substantiate their claims. The same is true in French romances. Adaptation is evident where sources are extant, as in the *romans d'antiquité* or the prose romances.[28] Most writers were anxious to attempt something original.

> Començai a penser
> D'aukune bone estoire faire
> E de latin en romaunz traire;
> Mais ne me fust guaires de pris:
> Itant s'en sunt altre entremis!
> (*Lais* Pro 28–32)[29]

[I began to think about writing some good story, turning it from Latin into French. But that would hardly have redounded to my credit: so many others have done the same thing.]

A generation later Huon de Mery despairs of rivaling Chrétien de Troyes and Raoul de Houdenc (*Tornoiement* 3526–44) who got to the best stories before him: "qui bien trueve pleins est d'ire, / Quant il n'a de matire point" (4–5) [he who writes well is vexed when he has no *matiere*]. Like Marie de France, Huon decided to write something new. He put together a psychomachia combining features drawn from earlier works like Chrétien's romances and Raoul's allegorical poems on the moral and courtly vices and virtues.[30] Later in the century the anonymous author of *Kanor,* the last branch of the *Sept sages de Rome* prose cycle, adapted Huon's *Tornoiement* for his own rendition of the tournament in the *Forest perilleuse* of Broceliande, pitting "historical" knights against personified vices.[31] Guillaume de Lorris obviously relied more on his own invention than on previous sources; but those he did use, like Ovid, are rearranged and reinterpreted, in conformity with the art of the topical integument.[32] The reconciliation between fidelity to source and auctorial originality takes place in the framework of the paradigm for invention. It uses memory, a theory of transmission, and the techniques of medieval historiography.

Sources as Memory

Both Chrétien de Troyes and Marie de France refer to past records as memory. Chrétien saw books as the principal repositories of memorable events (*Cligés* 25–27), although he also seems to have used oral traditions as necessary, albeit imperfect sources (*Erec* 19–22). Marie de France cites both oral and written sources of past adventures.

> Plusur le m'unt cunté e dit
> E jeo l'ai trové en escrit
> De Tristram e de la reïne.
> (*Lais* Chiev 5–7)[33]

[Several have related and told me of Tristan and the queen, and I have found the story in writing.]

Both Chrétien and Marie saw themselves as preserving and passing on the memory of the past. In a still later work, *Guiron le courtois,* an event is recorded "en memoire et registre" (§268)[34] lest it be forgotten. The claim is common to both written and oral traditions.[35] Numerous passages refer to customs, names, and circumstances that no longer obtain at the time the new work is written.[36] Memory supported the topic of the transmission of knowledge and learning from the past, and fostered the survival and enrichment of a certain conception of civilization.[37]

In romance, *chevalerie* depends on *clergie* to preserve the memory of its deeds. Memory was fixed in the word. Indeed, *memoire* had the sense of the written record of a past event, just as it did that of mental recall.[38] Historians and romancers alike adopted the notion that, like architectural remains, the written word—*aere perennius*—immortalizes *gesta.*

> Si escripture ne fust feite
> E puis par clers litte e retraite,
> Mult fussent choses ublïees.
> (*Rou* III.7–9)[39]

[If there were no writings which were subsequently read and related by clerics, many things would have been forgotten.]

In the *Escoufle,* commission to memory turns a forgotten tale into one remembered as literature.[40]

> Mais qui en tans et en saison
> Puet metre .j. bel conte en memoire
> Et faire .j. dit de boune estoire
> Et ml't bien fait cil qui s'en paine,
> Ki vertés soit, c'est bele paine.
>   (26–30)[41]

[But he who can, in due time and season, record a worthy tale and make
a work out of a good story — and he does well who makes the effort — in
truth, that is a worthy task.]

For what historical event really existed after it had been forgotten, what fabulous event is not part of history once it has been written down?[42] Marie
de France committed to writing an obscure memory allegedly passed on by
word of mouth and song. The *covert* and *oscur* became thereby *apert*:[43] "si
cum l'estoire a descovert" (*Ducs* 43872) [as the *estoire* revealed]. In doing
so, historians and romancers satisfied the aristocracy's desire to establish its
civilization for all times past and future.[44]

The best historian is, like Dares and Dictys, the eyewitness capable of re-
taining, ordering, and understanding the events he or she witnesses.[45]

> Riches chevaliers fu Ditis
> E clers sages e bien apris
> E sciëntos de grant memoire:
> Contre Daire rescrist l'Estoire.
>   (*Troie* 24397–400)

[Dictys was a noble knight, a wise and learned cleric, knowledgeable and
possessed of a good memory. He wrote the *estoire* in opposition to
Dares.]

Similarly Dares:

> En lui aveit clerc merveillos
> E des set arz esciëntos:
> Por ço qu'il vit si grant l'afaire
> Que ainz ne puis ne fu nus maire,
> Si voust les faiz metre en memoire.
>   (*Troie* 99–103)

[He was a wondrous cleric, knowledgeable in the seven arts. Because he
saw that the matter was of such importance that none had ever been more
so, neither before nor after, he wanted to record the deeds.]

Commission to memory gives back to "author" its sense of authority, and
confers that authority on the romance.

Et me doinst [Dieus] par sa volenté
Que je puisse venir a chief
De recorder de chief en chief
La tres plus merveilleuse estoire
Qui onques fust mise en memoire!
Bien doit estre en autorité,
Pour ce qu'ele est de verité
Estraite, dou tans ancïen.
(*Cleomadés* 86–93)[46]

[And may He grant that I complete from beginning to end the most wondrous *estoire* ever recorded! It ought to be authoritative, since it is drawn
from the truth of the distant past.]

The Huth *Merlin* makes a distinction between the Gospel and Blaise's transcription of Merlin's words: the former is "en autorité" because recorded by
eyewitnesses, while Blaise's is only the second-hand report of eyewitness accounts (I, 32–33).[47] Arthur's knights as eyewitnesses were bound to report
their adventures fully and accurately upon returning to court.[48]

These passages rehearse various features of romance as memory: record,
authority, memorandum, *matiere,* as well as misremembrance and oblivion.[49]
They evoke a variety of authors and authorities stretching back into the past.
In many cases, such projections are obviously erroneous: Blaise in the prose
romances as Merlin's amanuensis, Tristan composing the lay of the
Chievrefoil, and others. Dares and Dictys, as first authors, are more credible as eyewitnesses to the Trojan War. The compiler of the *Ovide moralisé*
is fully aware of Ovid's place as the first author, and of the fact that subsequent writers added their *surplus de sen* to both letter and glosses; Ovid himself was merely "li premerain / Auctors et li plus ancien" (I.1140–41) [the
first and oldest author].

All these authors vouchsafe a theory of memory and transition that influences the medieval conception of historiography. How can we today fit
the written transmission of memorable events into a historical paradigm valid
for critical interpretation of medieval history and romance? How can we relate the paradigm to the actual origins and transmission of sources? Jehan
Bodel's classification of the three kinds of *matieres* treats matter as both specific antecedents to be used or rejected, like the versions and sources of
Charlemagne's Saxon wars related by jongleurs and in written records,[50] and
as the three broad species of *matiere* common in romance narrative: French,
Roman, and British. Despite some general differences between the two notions of *matiere,* especially formal and contextual differences,[51] it is more
useful to keep them together in discussion of *matiere* as *estoire.* To do so
conforms to medieval practice, without denying important subsidiary dis-

tinctions between them which we shall take up later. The grouping fits the common conception of the invention of *matiere* both in the mind and in antecedent records.[52] The distinction between oral and written sources, made in the *Saisnes* Prologue, as well as the topical evaluation of those sources as true, instructive, or vain, embraces implicitly the entire problem of source adaptation for French romance.

Tradition and Transmission of Sources

As French romance emerged in the twelfth and early thirteenth centuries it drew on various streams of transmission. Three stand out. A learned, superimposed tradition in the Latin language of Christian and classical origins was transmitted by clerics.[53] At the same time there existed an oral tradition which was partly indigenous and partly imported.[54] The indigenous component survives in the early *chansons de geste* — what Jehan Bodel calls French *matiere*.[55] The foreign component flows through various channels of transmission into France from outside. Their audience was very broad,[56] although the performances for the aristocracy had the largest impact.[57] Medieval evidence and the example of similar civilizations today, especially in Africa, suggest great diversity in the quality and historical reliability of such performances.[58] In both medieval France and contemporary Africa two or more different cultures meshed in one society. Like the Mohammedan and Christian religions, with their foreign languages and education superimposed upon native societies in Africa, Latin and Christian culture overspread an indigenous aristocratic civilization in twelfth-century France.[59] This mixing of cultures posed problems of assimilation that are apparent as early as 813, when the Council of Tours admitted the vernaculars into certain parts of the mass, notably for the use of *exempla*.[60] Vernacular literature achieved prominence in the twelfth century, but its early style must have seemed inelegant by Latin standards.[61] Some authors complain of the difficulty of translating from one language into another.[62]

The vernacular epic tradition of the early *chansons de geste* dealt traditionally with established Christian creeds and a martial aristocracy.[63] The imported "British" material had to be not only translated, but adapted to a new culture; first, for the sake of comprehension, and, second, out of perhaps a certain embarrassment because of the apparently widespread scorn felt toward the "Welsh" and their fantastic tales.[64] The vituperation heaped upon the jongleurs' art by Jehan Bodel shows that such distaste could extend to French *matiere* that did not use "riches vers nouviaus" (*Saisnes* 31) like those in which he couches his own literary amplifications on love and chivalry during Charlemagne's Saxon wars. French had acquired levels of style attuned to subject matter by 1200.

Oral sources enjoyed degrees of authority depending on whether they were respectable eyewitnesses of unquestionable integrity or roving storytellers reporting fabulous adventures from bygone days.[65] The jongleurs themselves were not all alike.[66] Besides musicians, dancers, and acrobats, there were those who improvised or recited tales and those who read them for audiences—"Cil list romanz et cist dist fables" (*Chev epee* 803) [that one reads romances and this one tells tales]. The lengthiest display of their activities is in *Flamenca* (592–709). It suggests that oral tradition was not confined to the *chansons de geste* and Arthurian material, but that it included Roman and other subjects originally dependent on learned or scholastic writing (*Flamenca* 621–60), like Roman epic, Ovidian tales, and saint's lives:

> Qui volc ausir diverses comtes
> De reis, de marques e de comtes,
> Auzir ne poc tan can si volc.
> (*Flamenca* 617–19)[67]

[Whoever wishes to hear diverse stories about kings, marquesses, and counts can hear as many as he or she wishes.]

The ambiguous *comtar* used to describe performances could comprehend readings, improvisations conforming to the techniques of oral formulaic tradition, recitation from memory,[68] and plain, straightforward storytelling in prose. The clerical training of many jongleurs may account for their knowledge of classical and biblical subjects as well as for their often highly diversified talents, styles, and repertory.[69]

There is disagreement regarding the chronology and modalities of the passage from oral to written tradition, "given the possibility that oral features may survive the conditions that produced them, at least for a time."[70] The extant documents are all, of course, written. And the evidence shows a gradual, if uneven, evolution from obviously jongleuresque to clearly scribal features; one must also distinguish between an author's original intention and subsequent practice.[71] The rejection of most oral features in favor of written sources[72] permits Jehan Bodel to place the *Saisnes* and French *matiere* together with Roman and British romances. These three *matieres*—French, Roman, and British—represent the principal *matieres* about 1200. In Bodel's time authors in the *matiere de France* tradition distinguished their works, based on "historical" documentation, from those springing directly from the "formulaic" memories of the jongleurs;[73] and they were beginning to employ *geste* to refer to coherent cycles of French families as subspecies of the *matiere de France*.[74]

All streams of transmission exploited by romancers are unstable. Much appears to be lost today, like the lays which may have been early sources for Arthurian romance.[75] Moreover, the *matiere* of one channel of transmission may flow over into another. Thus the tale of Narcissus could appear in philosophical adaptations of Ovid and mythographies, in classroom and literary adaptations in Latin, in French romances or lays, and in the performances of jongleurs and minstrels. Arthurian legends could be transmitted both orally and in writing.[76] *Beaudous* refers to a Latin version of the lay extant at Saint Martin's of Tours (283–86), just as Chrétien's *Cligés* had a source in the library of Saint Pierre's of Beauvais (18–22).[77] The anonymous *Lai de Tyolet* asserts that the Bretons invented their lays in early times, but that contemporary lays are based on Latin versions which were turned into French (27–36).[78] The Breton lays Marie de France knew represent a different line of transmission if, as she claims, they were mostly oral.

Despite the harsh criticism we have noted of oral traditions by some romancers, they were mined and adapted. Chrétien's *Erec* is an obvious example of the accommodation of patchwork oral material to narrative composition. Word-of-mouth may indeed serve as a source, from the "dit d'un abé" [an abbot's word] for *Cor* (591–92)[79] to that of peasants for the Oxford *Folie* Ox (135–40).[80] As late as *Meliador* Froissart claims to use oral traditions: "Cilz me dist, qui bien le perçut / Ferir dessus Melyador" (23512–13; cf. 30663–66) [he told me who saw him strike Meliador]. Professor Diverres' discovery of links between the romance events and contemporary history makes Froissart's allegations seem more likely.[81] As roman à clef it is almost a historical allegory. Occasionally, some monument or ruins, or a geographical peculiarity, is pointed to by the author as evidence for the deeds related.[82]

Geoffrey of Monmouth may have inspired enthusiasm for Arthuriana as much as Chrétien de Troyes did, but he inspired far less direct imitation and adaptation.[83] Wace and a few anonymous *Bruts* stand alone and relatively isolated in the transmission of *matieres*. Geoffrey's influence seems otherwise confined to Arthur's Roman and Saxon wars and the destruction of the Arthurian kingdom in thirteenth-century romances.[84] The rest of early Arthurian romance claims to rely on jongleuresque traditions or written sources lost today. Several routes of transmission seem to have been available for the Arthurian tales. There are credible theories of Anglo-Norman contacts and Latin transcriptions.[85] Multilingual Welsh and Breton intermediaries may have transcribed or inspired the transcription of brief plot summaries in prose into Latin or vernacular.[86] Native Welsh poets like Breri may have introduced

complete poems or cycles into southwestern and especially Poitevin France.[87]
These theories are not incompatible.[88] Knowledge of the ways of oral tradition and of the habits of jongleurs and other storytellers offers useful information on the modalities of oral transmission in twelfth-century Europe.

Many early romancers allude to both written and oral transmission: "La
vie d'Alixandre, si comme elle est trouvee / En pluseurs leus escrite et par
bouche contee" (*Alex* APar I.62–63) [the life of Alexander as it is found written in several places and related by word of mouth]. Alexandre de Paris may
have derived some details from oral traditions, as did Aimon de Varennes
for the *Florimont,* a romance about Alexander the Great's grandfather.[89] The
author of the prose *Berinus,* perhaps following a verse model, attributes one
episode to oral tradition.

> Li lieux ou celle avanture avint, que la nef fu perie, est orendroit appellez de
> toute gent qui vont par mer, gouffre de Sathanie, et lui mist l'en ce nom pour
> la raison de ce que gouffres en grieu vault autant a dire en françois que "ven-
> gence"; et la meschine qui la fu murdrie de son frere ot a nom Sathania, c'est
> a dire "vengance de Sathanie." Et en ce lieu est encores un grant peril de mer
> e y sont mainte gent pery. (§151)[90]

> [The place where that adventure occurred, that is, where the boat sank, is now
> called the gulf of Sathanie by all seafaring folk. It acquired this name because
> "gulf" in Greek is French "vengeance." The girl whose brother murdered her
> there was Sathanie, which makes the place name equivalent to "vengeance of
> Sathanie." And that site is still very dangerous for shipwreck, and many have
> drowned there.]

On the other hand, a passage in *Florence de Rome* suggests that jongleurs,
whose accounts are taken from allegedly reliable and authoritative sources,
were perfectly acceptable.

> Nostre chanson commence imès a esforsier;
> Juglaor que la chante ne fet a mesprisier,
> Ains le doit l'en forment loer et essaucier.
> La chanson est d'estoire, ce vos vuel acointier;
> Ainz ne fu tel trovee dès le tens Dessier.
> (5245–49)[91]

> [Our song here begins to improve. The jongleur who sings it should not
> be scorned; rather he ought to be praised and glorified. It is a song based
> on a historical subject, that I want you to know. None like it has been in-
> vented since the time of Dessier.]

Such esteem extends to all tales of past glory, according to *Floriant et Florete.*

D'autre part sont cil conteour,
La est des chevaliers la flour,
Quar volentiers les escoutoient
Que les ancïens faits contoient
Des preudomes qui jadis furent
Qui se maintinrent, si com durent,
Des grant batailles que il firent
Et comment lor terre conquirent;
Tout ce li conteeur contoient.
(6231–39)[92]

[On the other side were the storytellers. There was the flower of knight-hood, who gladly listened to them because they related the bygone deeds of former worthies who acted duly, the great battles they fought, and how they conquered their land. All these things the storytellers told.]

Although the romancers are critical or suspicious of jongleuresque sources, they are clearly less circumspect than historians in utilizing them.[93]

Instability in Transmission: *Mouvance*

We have identified above the principal modes for the transmission of tradi-tional *matieres* as formulaic oral, free oral,[94] and written. The formulaic oral tradition, identified in French by Jean Rychner, admits an especially demand-ing variety he does not discuss and which does not seem to have been promi-nent in the French tradition: exact memorization.[95] The free oral may correspond to the prose tales attributed to Breton or British jongleurs, who may have taken great liberties in inventing, expanding, or reinterpreting tradi-tional semimythic legends. Finally, the written tradition, handed down in Latin or the vernacular in manuscripts, was subject to the deliberate or in-advertent changes common in manuscript transmission.[96] None of these in-clude orality as reading out loud, which seems to have predominated throughout the Middle Ages.[97]

Paul Zumthor coined the term *mouvance* to broaden the conception of what Jean Rychner termed the "caractère mouvant" of oral traditions. *Mou-vance* is any deliberate alteration that may arise in the course of transmis-sion, whether oral or written.[98] Such *mouvance*—"une mobilité essentielle du texte médiéval"[99]—is "le caractère de l'œuvre qui, comme telle, avant l'âge du livre, ressort d'une quasi-abstraction,[100] les textes concrets qui la réalisent présentant, par le jeu des variantes et remaniements, comme une incessante vibration et une instabilité fondamentale."[101] No secular tradition in the Middle Ages is notable for textual editing in any modern sense; indeed, the text was generally presumed, or feared, to be subject to critical review and clarification, to reinterpretation in the light of new *matiere,* new understanding, new intentions, or a new audience or patron. The work "may survive in the sympathetic hands of later artists who reinterpret it for a continuing present whose duration it is always rash to underestimate."[102] Less stupendous but no less significant changes occur through scribal intervention.

Scribal adaptation is a fact of medieval writing. The implications of this fact have been recognized and acted upon by recent textual critics.[103] Roques' edition of the scribe Guiot's copy of Chrétien de Troyes evinces a certain respect for textual mutability: his is a Guiot Chrétien.[104] Such mutability is in part equivalent to printing errors.[105] But not only. Löseth's presentation of the variants in the Prose *Tristan,* Lathuillère's of those in *Guiron le courtois,* to some extent Flutre's summary of the *Perceforest,* are veritable laboratory reports on *mouvance.*[106] By his interventions, Gui de Mori altered and interpreted the *Roman de la rose.*[107] Gautier d'Arras' *Ille et Galeron* seems to have gone through two versions, a long and a short; perhaps each is by Gautier himself.[108]

The authors were well aware of scribal interventions to correct, alter, complete, or even reduce what they had written. Chrétien warns against it.

> Del *Chevalier au lyeon* fine
> Crestïens son romans einsi;
> N'onques plus conter n'en oï
> Ne ja plus n'en orroiz conter
> S'an n'i vialt mançonge ajoster.
> (*Yvain* 6804–8)[109]

[Chrétien completes his romance of the *Knight of the Lion;* for I heard no more told about him, nor will you unless someone decides to add falsehoods to it.]

Elspeth Kennedy has concluded from her study of the *Lancelot* Proper manuscripts that:

> The history of the . . . text is, therefore, not one of passive transmission. While . . . they have not fundamentally remodelled the text, the scribes were often "editors" in the sense that they . . . felt free to make any alterations which would in their eyes improve the text. Many of them were prepared to make certain corrections in order to make sense of corrupt passages, to modernize the language and to add and eliminate details to bring the romance more into line with current demands. According to their own or their patron's tastes they might enlarge upon certain aspects or abbreviate and condense. They were,

of course, able to use far greater freedom than a modern editor in ornament-
ing or elucidating their text. If they discovered a factual inconsistency within
the cycle or with some other well-known text, they would not, as a modern
editor, draw attention to it in some comment but would alter the actual text.
Some of the alterations may be the result of reader's marginal comments, but
many seem to have been made on the initiative of the men actually writing the
MSS. Nevertheless, the scribes did work within a certain framework, and it
would seem that the hypothesis of scribal interpolation to explain internal contradictions should be used with very great caution, as the whole trend of scribal
intervention is towards the smoothing away of difficulties and contradictions,
not the creation of them.[110]

A review of the manuscript descriptions for the major romances reveals the
pervasive intervention of scribes. Pierre Gallais has concluded from a study
of the auctorial interventions in the *Gauvain* or First Continuation to Chrétien's *Perceval* that they represent "l'intervention d'une volonté consciente,"[111]
and that, in general, "un certain nombre de ces interventions sont le fait de
tel ou tel rédacteur. Au moins trois copistes-remanieurs-interpolateurs ont
remis sur le métier la première suite du *Perceval* et leur travail ne s'est pas du
tout exercé de façon régulière, mais intermittente et très variable d'une branche
à l'autre."[112] Such interventions may be so extensive as, in effect, to produce
a new work, or they may be the more or less occasional or systematic, even
humble adaptation of a "corrupt," incomplete, or ostensibly wordy source
manuscript to new times, places, and tastes.[113] Scribal interventions may thus
approximate to topical invention.

Until recently, only changes effected in passing from one language to another have received serious attention. But textual integrity, understood as
the restoration of the original version by critical editing, may ignore manuscript integrity. Scribal intervention occurs when the work is construed as
the reflection of a mental conception. The copiest who did not understand
the "source" he or she was copying, or whose originals diverged from one
another, or whose understanding of the subject differed from the preceding
author's, could correct presumed or real deficiencies by inventing a new version corresponding to his or her conception of the narrative or its meaning.
No doubt, the scholastic practice of adapting set pieces lent respectability
and conventionality to such interventions. Some authors even invited additions or improvements, where appropriate, to what they produced. Jean Maillart anticipates them in the *Anjou* (8076–8104) by deft use of the humility
topic.[114] Adenet le Roi envisaged the possibility for *Cleomadés* (18505–35).
Jean de Meun asserts that the practice is common among poets.

> Je n'i faz riens fors reciter,
> Se par mon jeu, qui po vous couste,
> Quelque parole n'i ajouste,
> Si con font entr'aus li poete,
> Quant chascuns la matire traite
> Don il li plaist a entremetre.
> (Rose 15234–39/15204–9)

[All I do is recite, except when by my skill, which costs you little, I add a word or so, as poets are wont to do when each treats the matter it pleases him to take up.]

It appears that the author of the post-Vulgate cycle made a special — and vain! — effort to guarantee the 'completeness' and integrity of his romance, both by cross-references and by tripartite division into sections of equal length.[115]

Twelfth- and early thirteenth-century *mouvance* shows therefore a diversity of traditions and techniques of transmission.[116] A dominant learned language had imposed an art of writing through the schools. But there survive as well from former indigenous traditions the legendary heroes — saints and aristocratic forebears — sung in traditional oral modes. And storytellers whose native language was not French spread by music and song, epic and tale, the exploits recounted in Celtic and other legends. Finally, scribes were active, making the written word not only available, but also "clear," "open," and readily understandable. Within this wide play of artistic purposes and cross-purposes, medieval romancers forged an art of invention and adaptation.[117] The continual review of past records shows that a given romance may well be clear and precise, original and inspired — yet false or defective in the eyes of others. Medieval romance is a great dialectic between idealism and human perception. Expressing that perception in *matiere* is the art of bringing the unknown past into a meaningful present context. It is the invention and redintegration of presumed historical origins.

Medieval Historiography as an Art of Writing

The close relation between emergent romance and contemporary vernacular and Latin historical writing is reflected in the relation between medieval historiography and the art of romance.[118] Both history and romance claim to preserve the memory of the past. Historical writing required the identifi-

cation, evaluation, selection, and amalgamation of sources. Similar to medieval histories, romance projects behind the extant *conte* a line of
transmission back to real or presumed events in the past. This historical paradigm, although by and large an illusion, was apparently taken quite seriously by medieval writers and audiences. It contributed to the romancer's
conception of *conte,* and thus to the art of inventing *matiere* and *san.*[119]

The notion of transmission was paramount in the minds of those who wrote
vernacular histories in the twelfth century. It is therefore necessary to determine how medieval historiography construes the link between past event and
present composition; how it determines the significance of past events for
a context imposed by audience expectation or auctorial intention;[120] how
it evaluates and reconciles divergent sources, including oral traditions; and,
last, how it faces the practical problem of scribal intervention, both because
scribes made adaptations and because they sought to harmonize variant
sources.

Medieval historiography has been a growing preoccupation of twentieth-
century historical research. Study has focused on criteria for validity; terminology; the relation between historical writing and grammar, rhetoric, and
poetics; the differences between the medieval historical mentality and the modern science; and patronage.[121] The findings are instructive for the study of
romance, given the indistinct boundaries dividing historical from literary or
fabulous narrative in the twelfth century.[122] Moreover, historical writing again
influenced the forms and styles of romance when it turned from verse to prose
in the thirteenth century.[123] Authenticity, critical standards, auctorial conception and intention, and the evaluation of sources are subjects which have
not yet been fully elucidated for medieval historiography, but which are relevant to romance invention.

Four kinds of historical documents have been identified in medieval terms:
annals, chronicle, biography, and hagiography.[124] The medieval term
historia/estoire is very broad. "Du VIᵉ au XVIᵉ siècle, la mode a pu faire
passagèrement préférer un mot à un autre. Il reste que, tout au long de ce
millénaire, beaucoup ont pris *histoires, annales, chroniques* pour de parfaits
synonymes et ont, sans plus de réflexion, utilisé l'un ou l'autre pour désigner
tout ouvrage dont l'auteur avait entendu relater des faits qui s'étaient réelle-
ment passés."[125] Since romance also claims to relate past history, as *estoire,*
it too belongs to the "historical" mode.[126] By its interpretative side, romance
parallels the special sense of *historia* not only as the account, but also the
explanation, of past events.[127] This includes allegorical and typological explanation and adaptation, as in Gautier de Châtillon's *Alexandreis,* the *Queste
del saint graal,* and even Guillaume de Lorris' *Rose.*

> Mais en cel songe onques rien n'ot
> Qui trestot avenu ne soit
> Si con li songes recensoit.
>
> (*Rose* 28–30)

[But there was nothing at all in that dream which did not happen entirely as the dream depicted.]

Guillaume de Lorris calls his work both a *roman* (37) and an *estoire*: "Toute l'estoire vueil porsivre" (3505/3487) [I wish to follow through the whole *estoire*]. In the latter half of the fourteenth century, Guillaume de Machaut commences the biographical *Prise d'Alexandrie* with a mythographic involution of Venus and Mars' love into the birth of Pierre de Lusignan.

Vernacular histories have a special place in defining the aristocratic view of the world that one also finds in romance. This view does not deny the sacramental conception of history, but, by focusing on the great princely families, it puts the nobility clearly at center stage.[128] The new topical focus anticipates and, in some ways, prepares for romance,[129] which emerged with vernacular history, especially historical works written for the Anglo-Norman court.[130] The vernacular histories that appear at about the same time as the first romances were authored by romancers, notably Wace and Benoît de Sainte-Maure. They all show how *matiere, estoire,* and *conte* could construe sources as mental, oral, or documentary. In effect, romance adopted the techniques of historiography for identifying sources, amassing as much pertinent material as possible *(materia remota)* and collecting what seemed pertinent *(materia propinqua)* into an amalgam, then expanding on that material through topical amplifications that conform to the auctorial conception of and intention with the work.[131]

To understand the medieval historian's art, it behooves us to identify both the rhetorical presuppositions and techniques appropriate to the handling of sources, and, insofar as possible, each author's own interests as adaptor, renovator, or copyist when selecting *materia propinqua* from sources. Modern "editorial introductions have always included comments on the chronicler's use of written sources." This is also true in editions of romance—at least early editions.

> But this practice now needs reconsideration with interest not in evidence of factual criticism but in narrative strategies. . . . One begins to discover the substance of narrative by looking both for explicit statements of what interests the historian and for less direct indicators that often lie in his handling of sources. If an author is not simply copying from his source, then what he selects, passes over, or interpolates may tell much about the true bearing of his narrative.[132]

Recorded statements are the key to the historian's and the romancer's narrative strategies. In them *historia* recovers both the *materia* and the *intentio* of the *accessus ad auctores*. Auctorial interventions, taken as a whole, and when compared with the context they derive from, can yield useful general and specific information on treatment of sources and "narrative strategies" deployed in the invention of history and, by extension, romance — what Fanni Bogdanow has aptly described as the "tendency to combine in coherent groups."[133]

From about 1135 until 1170 or after, *estoire* refers to works as diverse as the *Saint Brendan* and Guernes de Pont-Sainte-Maxence's *Thomas Becket,* the *Brut* and the *Rou, Troie* and the *Chronique des ducs de Normandie.* As a genre, and as an art, romance for Chrétien, Gautier d'Arras, and the *Partonopeu de Blois* author derives from vernacular chronicles and saints' lives rather than from either the *chansons de geste* or medieval Latin narratives (although the influence of the latter is not negligible).[134] Medieval historical writing and historiography were influenced by the paradigm for invention. Grammar and especially rhetoric were the disciplines in which historical as well as literary narrative was studied, evaluated, and imitated.[135] The juxtaposition of study of Lucan, usually considered a historian during the Middle Ages,[136] and Vergil and Statius would make it seem perfectly normal to associate Norman chronicles with vernacular adaptations of Latin epic like the *Thèbes* and *Eneas.* The *Troie* itself is based on bona fide historians, as far as the Middle Ages was concerned.[137]

Romances and histories were written for future audiences.[138] The desire to preserve and transmit the memory of the past, as outspoken in Marie de France as in Geoffrey Gaimar, Wace, and Benoît de Sainte-Maure, is the immediate intention of all these works. The subject was the exemplary figure, whether saint or knight, family, nation, or people — Thomas à Becket or Arthur, Oedipus' or Rollo's families, the Trojan, British, English, or Norman peoples and nations. The combination of idea and personages in *estoire* makes past deeds exemplary.

Almost all the relevant texts evince a desire and an effort to gather as much material as possible on the given subject.

> Il purchaça maint essamplaire,
> Liveres engleis e par gramaire,
> E en romanz e en latin,
> Ainz k'en pust traire a la fin.
> (*Engleis* 6435–38)[139]

[He acquired many sources, in English and by learned writers, in French and in Latin, before he was able to bring it to a conclusion.]

But in seeking out material, the authors tended to identify and give priority to one or more authoritative sources, either because they were more nearly complete or because they seemed for some special reason more reliable. The eyewitness account was decisive in Benoît de Sainte-Maure's preference for Dares and Dictys over "Omer" as sources for the *Troie* (93–116, 24397–404). Guernes de Pont-Sainte-Maxence founds the authority of the second version[140] of his *Becket* on the addition of material from eyewitnesses whom he interviewed (146–50) and on the examination of primary documents, like the Constitutions of Clarendon (2391–562). There were, of course, obscurities, uncertainties, contradictions, and lacunae found in and among the sources. The authors dealt with these in different ways: reporting all divergent accounts, choosing among them, rejecting the problem outright as foreign to the subject being treated, making reasonable judgments, or admitting ignorance.[141]

Exclusions are important indicators of how the early authors conceived of their matter and the intention they had when putting it into French verse. For example, Gaimar excludes the life of a martyr both because it is already available and because it is hagiography, and thus different from secular chronicle (*Engleis* 2921–26).[142] A cross-reference is justified by something akin to the principle of material style in that it separates types and, as here, genres.[143] *Guillaume le maréchal* excludes William Marshall's exploits in the Third Crusade for similar reasons (7275–88).[144] In the *Ducs* Benoît de Sainte-Maure passes over the mysterious mutation of the Moors' skin color to white when they were slain, "quer n'afiert mie / A l'estoire de Normendie" (*Ducs* 26921–22) [since it is not pertinent to the history of Normandy]. Moorish history is no more a Norman subject than hagiography is a part of heroic adventures.

The vernacular historians may rely on written or eyewitness reports.[145] Now, even early *chansons de geste* claim to report reliable eyewitnesses and documents.

> Çeo dit la Geste e cil ki el camp fut:
> Li ber Gilie, por qui Deus fait vertuz,
> E fist la chartre el muster de Loüm.
> Ki tant ne set ne l'ad prod entendut.
> (*Roland* I, 2095–98)

[This the *geste* relates and those who were present on the field of battle— notably the worthy Giles, who wrote the document preserved in the monastery in Laon. Whoever doesn't know that much has not understood the matter rightly.]

Most *chansons de geste* have a historical kernel.[146] The kernel is precisely the kind of information that could have been gleaned from genealogies, paschal calendars, cartularies, and primitive annals—or the memory of eye-witnesses. But the art applied to the elaboration of that kernel was oral for-mulaic, a technique which moved from historical fact toward "myth"—a myth perhaps more credible to contemporary audiences than the forgotten or ob-scured facts,[147] but not to chroniclers.[148]

> A jugleours oï en m'effance chanter
> Que Guillaume fist jadiz Osmont essorber,
> E au conte Riouf les deus oilz crever,
> E Anquetil le prouz fist par enging tuer,
> E Baute d'Espaingne o un escu garder;
> Ne sai noient de ceu, n'en puiz noient trover,
> Quant je n'en ai garant n'en voil noient conter.
> De la mort Anquetil ai ge oï parler,
> Ochiz fu, ce soit on, n'en quier homme escouter,
> Mez je ne sai comment, ne qui face a blasmer;
> N'en voil por verité la menchonge affermer
> Ne le voir, se jel sai, ne voil ge pas celer.
>   (*Rou* II.1361–72)

[When I was young, I heard jongleurs relate that Guillaume had Osmont blinded in olden days, Riouf's eyes put out, the worthy Anquetil put to death treacherously, and Baute of Spain held with a shield. I don't know anything about that, nor can I find any confirmation of it; and without evidence I refuse to relate anything on it. I've heard tell of Anquetil's death—he was killed, that's known, and I don't believe anything to the contrary; but I don't know how, nor whom to blame. I don't intend to claim a lie as truth, nor hide the truth if I know it.]

Wace was just as perplexed by tales about Arthur; like Chrétien de Troyes later, he lamented the jongleurs' distortions and falsifications of the "histori-cal Arthur."

> Tant unt li cunteür cunté
> Et li fableür tant flablé
> Pur lur cuntes enbeleter,
> Que tut unt fait fable sembler.
>   (*Brut* 9795–98)[149]

[The storytellers have told stories and the fabulists spun yarns to embellish their accounts to such an extent that it all seems fantastic.]

Wace was obviously prepared to give credence to those tales, given his foray into Broceliande to investigate the marvels reputed to occur at the fountain of Berenton: "Merveilles quis, mais nes trovai" (*Rou* III.6395) [I sought marvels, but found none].

Marvels are a staple of medieval history, and they could be taken quite seriously.[150] Hagiography related them; the wonders of the ancient world account for much of the appeal of the *romans d'antiquité*.[151] Since marvels were deemed possible, it behooved the historian to seek them out, confirm their reality, or where that was impossible, their verisimilitude. But there was no generally received standard. Gaimar retained the Havelock episode in his *Engleis,* but Benoît de Sainte-Maure rejected the combats between gods and men related by "Omer."

Another important factor in the validation of sources, whether marvelous or not, was the suitability of *materia remota* for topical involution. Jehan Bodel's distinction among the matters of France, Rome, and Britain is founded on such topical credibility.

> La coronne de France doit estre si avant,
> Que tout autre roi doivent estre a li apendant
> De la loi chrestïenne qui en dieu sont creant.
> (*Saisnes* 13–15)[152]

[The French crown should take precedence, and all others in Christendom be subject to it.]

Similarly Benoît de Sainte-Maure places the Norman nation before all others (*Ducs* 33590–600, 39873–84). The claim is not patriotic; it is founded on a dynastic hierarchy analogous in principle to that implicit in material style.[153] The credibility of *estoire* depends on topical developments that explain historical narrative and make it exemplary.[154] For the evaluation of what happened as exemplary conduct was at least as important as the pleasure of hearing diverse stories of past events: "Historiam præcipue, quæ, jocunda quadam gestorum notitia mores condiens, ad bona sequenda vel mala cavenda legentes exemplis irritat" (*De gestis* Pro p. 103)[155] [especially history which, by exemplary accounts, incites its readers to persevere in what is good or eschew evil, seasoning good conduct with entertaining narrative].

Now, topical invention of historical *matiere* is not incompatible with the adaptation of written or oral Roman and Arthurian sources.[156] Both learned and popular traditions allowed for inventive adaptation. Marie de France knew that Priscien taught topical invention as a technique for drawing the truth out of fable,[157] and she applied it in her lays.[158] Chrétien de Troyes did so as well, with Macrobius as guide.[159] Hagiography had long patterned its narratives on paradigmatic sequences.[160]

It is therefore of major significance for the emergence of romance that Chrétien began his first romance with the very *conteurs* whose productions Wace could make nothing of. Chrétien was aware of the faults Wace attributes to jongleurs. But he saw more in the fountain of Berenton than Wace did. His topical involution of Breton *matiere* permitted the real marvels to take on the form and significance of current ideals and ideas.[161] This is what finally distinguishes romance from history: the supplanting of documentary evidence by topical evidence. That is, the interpretation of the past as exemplary of current moral, social, or feudal credos replaces the mere recording of glorious past deeds.

The Chain of Authorship from First to Latest Version

We shall have occasion to refer often to the place of the historical paradigm in the emergence of romance. To facilitate the ensuing analysis of romance invention, I shall anticipate my conclusions by proposing at the outset a paradigm for medieval historiography that is valid for romance as well. We shall see afterward that this paradigm synthesizes the romancers' conception of their art in relation both to the origins of *matiere* in specific (pseudo) historical events and to the paradigm for invention we discerned in the learned Latin tradition represented by the arts of poetry and prose.

   I. Original oral/written version contemporary or nearly contemporary with the events narrated.[162]
   II. Intermediate oral/written version or versions between original (I) and the immediate source or sources of the romance (IIIb).
   III. (a) Mental conception *(status archetypus)* followed by
        (b) Collection of written and/or oral sources *(materia remota)*.
   IV. The romance *matiere (materia propinqua),* including places for topical amplifications in (IIIa) and (IIIb).
   V. The opus, including arrangement *(ordo)*.

In stage III, a distinction must be made between theory and practice. Theory, or the art of poetry and prose, places the mental conception prior to the identification of source material. However, the practice of writing *historia* suggests that the actual stages in composition did not necessarily conform to the paradigm. For example, Chrétien de Troyes received a book from Philippe d'Alsace which he says he used as source for the *Conte du graal (Perceval* 61–68). Whatever Chrétien's conception of his source, his own contribution—the invention of the new work—began after his discovery, through Philippe d'Alsace, of that source. Similarly, Raoul de Houdenc insisted on the quality of the *conte* chosen for *Meraugis de Portlesguez* (1–16). However, unless the author makes *no* changes on the source, but merely transcribes it, both medieval poetics and romance practice assume the adaptation of the source or sources. Adaptation began as thought—the invention of the mental conception or *status archetypus*. With that thought, the new work supersedes the source. In this sense, the order of the paradigm remains intact in both theory and practice.

We have now surveyed the background and sources for the art of romance. Both scholastic theory of composition based on a paradigm for invention and the historiographical evaluation of sources permitted us to propose a paradigm that is an art of invention for twelfth-century romancers. The amalgamation of the models of poetics and historiography established a tradition that continued and evolved from the twelfth into the fourteenth century and beyond. We may now attempt to identify the principal features of the art of romance from auctorial interventions and, using the evidence from the medieval art of poetry and prose and from historiography, describe the art of medieval romance discernible in the genre's recorded statements.

4

Conte: Matiere and San

Ut etiam si quid apparuerit unde sumptum sit, aliud tamen esse quam unde
sumptum noscetur appareat.
— Saturnalia I.Praef.6

[So that if anything should reveal where it was taken from, it would nonetheless
appear to be different from that from which it was known to be taken.]

Conte: Lexicography, Terminology, and the Problem of Semantic Range and Specificity

Auctorial commentary on sources and adaptation is, of course, difficult to interpret and evaluate. Scholars have tended to explain such commentary with their own hypotheses on the relation between the extant medieval text and its alleged sources. This is so, for example, for Bédier's reconstruction of the archetype of Thomas' *Tristan,* a reconstruction whose presuppositions have been called into question by new theories of romance composition.[1]

To elucidate as effectively as possible the process of romance invention, auctorial statements about sources where none is extant must be assessed in the light of three factors: (1) the auctorial statements in the romance itself and, sometimes, those of contemporaries about it; (2) the conception of writing in the scholastic tradition from which the romancers' art may derive and evolve; and (3) the relation between auctorial statements and the completed romance. This means that we must take into account the same historical context historians do in dealing with social and political vocabulary in their documents.[2]

Interpreting commentary occurs on various levels. Apparent allusions to sources, for example, require close scrutiny in order to distinguish when they refer to actual sources and when they refer to the romance itself.[3] An obvious and unequivocal example of the latter, but in language that could be construed as the former, is found in Villehardouin: "maintes hautres bonnes gens dont li livres ne fait mie mention" (*Conquête* §5) [many other worthy persons which the book does not mention]. As Faral points out, "Non pas un livre que Villehardouin aurait consulté et exploité, mais le livre même qu'il composait: façon de parler habituelle des auteurs du moyen âge."[4] Although Benoît de Sainte-Maure refers to his sources: "Ne sai s'ert reis o cuens o dus, / Quar li Livres ne m'en dit plus" (*Troie* 725–26) [I don't know whether he was king, count, or duke, for the Book tells me no more about it], this does not preclude Benoît's referring to his own book in allusions like: "Li dozime bataille iert grant, / Que li Livres retrait avant" (*Troie* 493–94)[5] [the twelfth battle was a big one, and the Book relates it first].

Other cases are not so straightforward. For example, in Alexandre de Paris' *Alexandre* one reads: "Ce conte l'escripture, se la letre ne ment" (I.327)[6] [this is what the written word relates, if the letter is truthful]. Does this mean that the French romance, or "l'escripture," follows a source, or "letre," or that "l'escripture" and "la letre" are synonymous for either the source or the romance itself? Any of the three readings is possible. Similarly, Marie de France provides a puzzle in the following lines:

> El chief de cest comencement,
> Sulunc la lettre e l'escriture,
> Vos mosterai une aventure.
> (*Lais* Gui 22–24)

[At the outset I shall show you an adventure according to the letter and the writing.]

The third-person subject may lead to the virtual personification of the text as the self-referential *liber auctor*,[7] which may in fact reflect the transition from an oral narrator's voice to that of the narrator in a book.[8] Thus, the phrase "conte d'avanture" in the Prologue to Chrétien's *Erec* refers to potentially all versions, good or bad, of the Erec story. Chrétien's own is distinguished from all the others by being a *bele conjointure*. Similarly, the Prologue to Chrétien's *Cligés* uses "conte" (8) and "estoire" (18, 23) in the general sense of "tale" or "story." Further on, it states that this "roman" (see 22 note [p. 208]) is one version of a "conte," (43) while the Beauvais "livre" (20, 44) he allegedly got it from is another;[9] the romance—"son conte" (43)—is drawn from the Beauvais *conte*, which in turn follows the *estoire*, or "story," whose truth is vouchsafed by the source book.

> De la fu li contes estrez
> Don cest romanz fist Crestïens.
> Li livres est molt ancïens
> Qui tesmoingne l'estoire a voire:
> Por ce fet ele mialz a croire.
>   (*Cligés* 22–24 and p. 208)

[From there was drawn the story out of which Chrétien made his romance. The book is very old, which vouchsafes the story's veracity; this makes it more credible.]

Passages like this anticipate the *Escoufle*'s distinction between the actual romance and the tale upon which it is based.

> Mais je ne cuit que li desplaise
> Fors li nons, c'on en tient a lait.
> Mais c'est drois que li roumans ait
> Autretel non comme li contes.
>   (9072–75)

[But I don't believe that anything except the name will displease him, for the title is deemed ugly. But it is proper to give the romance the same title as the story.]

Of course, some references may not be true allusions, but merely lifted from the sources, as those works demonstrate whose sources are extant.[10]

Thus, context and circumstances as much or even more than common terminology determine whether a specific word like *conte* is used to refer to a source or sources, a tale in the abstract, an actual romance, or any combination of these states of the potential, incipient, or actual work: "Bien devisent toute leur oevre, / Si com l'estoire me descoeuvre" (*Amadas* 3891–92) [it does relate all their deeds, just as the *estoire* reveals them to me]. This passage may refer to an actual source, whether oral or written, the author's own conception of the story, and/or a narrator's interpolated remark on the romance he or she is relating.

The ambiguity is compounded by the fact that, in the Middle Ages, generic definitions are not remarkable for their consistency nor even for a genuine desire to classify and conceptualize.[11] One rather tends to find descriptions fitting some obvious mark or tag: "Poesis dicitur Graeco nomine opus multorum librorum, poema unius, idyllion paucorum versuum, distichon duorum, monostichon unius" (*Etymologiae* I.xxxix.21) [*poesis* is in Greek a work of many books, *poema* of one, *idyllion* of a few verses, *distichon* of two, *monostichon* of one]. Such descriptions permit ready identification of the designated work, but do not in practice evince consistency or universal agreement on usage.

Yet the modern demand for consistent usage seems ineradicable. For example, Jean Frappier accepts Ernest Hoepffner's correction of Marie de France. Although Marie calls her *Chaitivel* a lay five times (2, 203, 207, 225, 231), he asks: "Peut-on vraiment encore traiter ce poème de 'lai'?"[12] But, as Frappier observes elsewhere in the same article, the medieval author "devait savoir ce qu'il voulait dire"[13] when calling a work a lay or a fabliau. One can understand why the *Vair palefroi, Ille et Galeron,* the *Lai de l'ombre,* the lays of Marie de France, and the anonymous lays, Ovidian lays, or works like the *Lai de l'oiselet* were called *lais* in the Middle Ages, even if usage varies from work to work and no specific attribute or group of attributes fits all of them.[14] Are authors (rather than scholars or critics) any more precise or consistent with their terminology nowadays, when, for example, they refer to a "short story," an "epic," a "novel"?

The ambiguity of medieval literary terminology needs to be accounted for before it is deplored. One obvious explanation is that a given word meant different things to different authors. Although this explanation may account for the heterogeneous use of lay,[15] it seems less satisfactory for *matiere* and *conte.* These words are used to express a broad range of phases in composition. It is frequently possible to detect several specific senses even in the same work.[16] For example, *roman* may refer to romance, the Romance language (i.e., French), or both, in the same passage.[17] Similarly, *matiere* and *conte* may, in a given instance, express the entire paradigm for invention. They may, therefore, refer to any or all of its phases, from mental conception through identification and description of source and source history, to elaboration and adaptation of actual sources in the finished romance by topical invention, embellishment, and versification or *mise en prose.*

The romancers tend to make practical rather than theoretical or generic distinctions with their terminology.

> Ci fine l'ystoire et li conte;
> Mainte gent le prisent et loent
> Et mout volentiers dire l'oënt.
> (*Durmart* 15980–82)

[Here the *ystoire* and the *conte* end; many prize and praise it, and very gladly hear it told.]

One may construe these lines as advertisement for the author's own romance, or as a reference to the popularity of the tale or tales about Durmart prior to the new version. In addition, there are hints that not everything is being

told about Durmart, perhaps for the benefit of those in the audience familiar with other versions (1569–74, 6073–76, 9097–9100). One allusion to
the jongleurs suggests the popularity of earlier versions in spite of their alleged inferiority (15084–126). The paradigm delineated at the end of Chapter 3 as a kind of *translatio studii* provides a meaningful context for passages
like these. Since the *conte* is transmitted from the past to the present, and
since that transmission entails the elucidation of obscurities that hinder appreciation of the *conte,* and, finally, since this paradigm assumes a mental
conception of the *matiere* prior to its *mise en roman,* authors need not always specialize words and expressions that actually refer to a complex of
phenomena indicated by *matiere* and *conte* in their various phases of
realization.

A passage in the *Merlin* will illustrate the point. "Einsis departi Merlins
de Uiterpandragon et vint au Norhumbellande a Blaise, si li dist ces choses
et les establissemenz de ceste table et maintes autres choses que vous orroiz
en son livre" (M 50.1–4/S 56.15–17)[18] [thus did Merlin leave Uterpendra-
gon and come to Blaise in Northumberland. And he told him these things,
including the establishment of the table, and many other things that you will
hear in his book]. Blaise's *livre* is the *estoire* the romancer has written, and
it is also the text we read or listen to as transcribed from the romancer's original. The book the *Merlin* narrator transcribes from the "Latin" into French
is also Blaise's.[19] Just so, *Cligés* is both Chrétien's romance and the Beauvais
conte. All of this would have been readily comprehensible to a medieval audience familiar with the ways of patrons, authors, and scribes.

Less clear, perhaps, but nevertheless accessible to medieval audiences, another *Durmart* passage shows how terminology is made to fit practical circumstances within a single work. In it *conte* includes a topical description.

> Li rois Durmars que sages fist,
> Car ensi com li contes dist,
> Largece et cortoisie ama
> Tant cum il vesqui et dura.
>   (15917–20)

[King Durmart acted wisely, for, according to the *conte,* he loved largess
and courtesy as long as he lived.]

In fact, the romance adapts the description to material style. Durmart is a
prince who becomes a king. This transition permits the author to invent from
his or her *matiere* the topical qualities of *prouesse, largesse,* and *cortoisie*
characteristic of kings (15896–979) and then work them into the narrative
by involution. Even Durmart's youthful *folie* fits this elaboration through

the structuring device of *oppositio,* also exemplified in Shakespeare's Prince
Hal before the death of Henry IV. The quest for a new love, the queen of
Ireland, allows Durmart to correct himself, to assume the role and style that
behoove his royal station. This fact stamps the entire *conte* as "royal" (*Durmart* 14).[20] Insofar as such invention refers to an original—either the actual
source, or the source as conceived in some pristine, archetypal wholeness—
that original is part of the *matiere* and enters into the amalgam known as
materia propinqua.

Amalgam and Composition of Romance *Matiere*

De Bruyne translates Alain de Lille's *(con)iunctura* by "amalgame."[21] The
modern editors of the Alexander romances termed the combination of sources
in the various twelfth-century compilations of the *Roman d'Alexandre
décasyllabique* an "Amalgam."[22] This term is useful. It fits the language
romancers use to tell how they combine source material. The amalgam can
refer to the collection of narrative material in a single manuscript: "M'entremis
des lais assembler, / Par rime faire e reconter" (*Lais* Pro 47–48)[23] [I undertook to collect, versify, and narrate lays]. But, as Marie also points out, an
amalgam may refer to the meshing of more than one version in one work.[24]
Thus each of Marie's lays is also an amalgam, a composite. Furthermore,
numerous lays suggest auctorial additions that complete, explain, or interpret them.[25] Amalgam is therefore an appropriate term for the result of bringing together source material. Although this seems obvious enough, it is
important to know how the sources are construed and how they are combined into an amalgam. Furthermore, this interaction demands an investigation into the relation between amalgam and *bele conjointure.*

Conception of the Model for Romance: Pensers

In the *Saisnes,* Jehan Bodel contrasts the "vain" and "plesant" in Arthurian
matiere with the truth and meaning found in, respectively, French and Roman *matieres.* Yet contextualizing Bodel, we know that by 1200 even Arthurian marvels had become the object of careful scrutiny by serious
romancers intent upon drawing truth and meaning from what Marie de
France calls their "obscurity."[26] Further, their art is little different from that
of the *Saisnes.* Indeed, we have seen that Bodel's preference for French and
Roman subjects stems more from rhetorical parameters than from historical
accuracy and thus seems to be essentially encomiastic.

One source of obscurity in the *materia remota* elicited surprise, even con-

sternation: its strangeness, its *estrangeté*.[27] This was in part due to the fact
that all three *matieres*—French, Roman, Arthurian—came to twelfth-century
writers as relics from the past; very few could be called products of recent
history. The *matieres* also elicited strong reactions because they recount extraordinary events.[28] The content of most could be described as incredible,
plesant but *vain*. The "credo" or system of belief which informed the original *matiere* and made it comprehensible and acceptable in earlier times and
places had been lost.[29] Thus, Homer's Troy and Vergil's Carthage, the
wonders of Broceliande, even the exploits of Guillaume au cort nez,
Charlemagne, and Baudouin were incredible. However, the strange, the novel,
the disreputable may elicit curiosity, fascination, or even reflective thought
and a desire to emulate or to reject.[30]

The technique for drawing from strange *matiere* a seemingly inherent but
obscure significance, the "ceo k'i ert" of Marie de France's lays, is topical
invention. This technique could make *matiere* yield meaning without sacrificing any of its fascination. In fact, topical invention permitted the rediscov-
ery of apparent meaning through an inherent faith in the continuity of the
aristocracy and the transmission of its civilization by the written word. Topical invention restored meaning through a new "credo" that made the *matiere*
again coherent, credible, and useful.[31] The "plesant" and "vain" of Jehan Bodel
became the "plaisans" and "voire" of *Guillaume d'Angleterre* (14).[32]

Romance therefore begins with *pensers*. "Pur ceo començai a penser / D'au-
kune bone estoire faire" (*Lais* Pro 28–29)[33] [for this reason I began to think
of writing a good story]. Casting about for new material to which she might
apply her *pensers*, Marie de France hit upon the lays: "Des lais pensai, k'oïz
aveie" (*Lais* Pro 33) [I thought of the lays I had heard]. *Pensers* discovers
suitable *matiere*. As Chrétien makes clear, it also presides over adaptation.

> Matiere et san li done et livre
> La contesse, et il s'antremet
> De panser, que gueres n'i met
> Fors sa painne et s'antancïon.
> (*Charrette* 26–29)[34]

[The countess gives and furnishes him with *matiere* and *san*, and he undertakes to think; for he adds scarcely more than his effort and *antancion*
to them.]

These examples suggest that *pensers* subsumes the conception, invention,
and composition of the completed work—the entire paradigm for invention.[35]

Aimon de Varennes identifies these stages of topical invention in the composition of his *Florimont*. He proceeded from an oral report to a written

Latin version to the French romance. That is, a Greek story was told to Aimon during a sojourn at Philippopolis; he then drew up a Latin version of
the story in prose before returning to France, a version which included various additions apparently garnered from Greek folklore; and finally he composed the French romance in France after his return there.[36] In other words,
the *materia remota* was Aimon's Greek story or stories. When he had collected and combined this *materia* with secondary sources and his own conception of the work expressed through various real or potential amplifications,
he had the *materia propinqua* in a Latin version. The conversion of this
materia into French verse produced the romance.[37]

The invention began in the passage from *remota* to *propinqua*, when Aimon conceived his own version of the source material. It is this stage that
Geoffrey of Vinsauf describes as the *status archetypus*. Aimon was not merely
a translator. The phrase "the best of tales" — "la flour / Des contes"
(115–16) — expresses abstract notions idealized by a given society, like
aristocratic French predilections for love and chivalry, adventure and courtesy,
and largess and nobility (117–19, 9263–72). Aimon's adaptation of *Florimont*
required *pensers*, just as did the works of his contemporaries Marie de France
and Chrétien de Troyes.

> Lortz a sejour a Chastillon
> Estoit Aimes une saison
> Et porpansait soi de l'istoire
> Qu'il avoit eü en memoire.
> (*Florimont* 27–30)

[Then Aimon sojourned a time in Châtillon, thinking through the *estoire*
he had in his Latin version.]

Porpanser is reflective thought.[38] Aimon uses the word to suggest that he
perceived the latent sense of his Greek sources from which he fashioned an
examplary and meaningful romance.[39]

Aimon's account of the composition of the *Florimont* complements Chrétien's contrast between the *conte d'avanture,* dismembered and mutilated by
"Cil qui de conter vivre vuelent" (*Erec* 22) [those who wish to support themselves by telling tales], and his own *conjointure,* and also Thomas d'Angleterre's attempt to bring together coherently the diverse *matieres* he had
found on Tristan.

> Entre ceus qui solent cunter
> E del cunte Tristran parler,
> Il en cuntent diversement:

Oï en ai de plusur gent.
Asez sai que chescun en dit
E ço que il unt mis en escrit,
Mes sulun ço que j'ai oï,
Nel dient pas sulun Breri.
(*Tristan* Th Douce 841–48)[40]

[Those who are wont to tell stories and relate tales about Tristan tell it in a variety of ways. I have heard many versions, and I know well what each one says and what each one has written; but of those which I have heard, none relates it in the same way that Breri does.]

Thomas' words suggest that he seeks to realize a *Tristan archetypus* in his opus. Schematically this may be represented as shown in Figure 1.

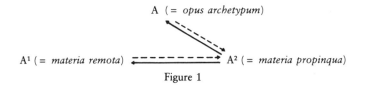

$$A \ (= opus\ archetypum)$$

$$A^1 \ (= materia\ remota) \qquad A^2 \ (= materia\ propinqua)$$

Figure 1

The broken arrows represent the direction of borrowing, the unbroken arrows the direction of *pensers*. The romancer's discovery of defects in the sources follows on the comparison of the multifarious versions he or she collects with his or her conception of the *materia,* perceived, as it were, in the mind's eye. The *materia propinqua* remedies the inadequacies so that it corresponds to the "archetypal idea" of the work.[41] Further, Thomas mentions numerous versions of the Tristan legend which he says he attempted to bring together in a consistent, coherent, credible amalgam. This additional information modifies the above diagram as shown in Figure 2:

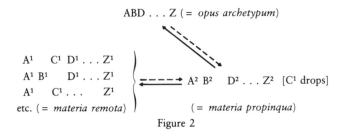

$$ABD \ldots Z \ (= opus\ archetypum)$$

$$A^1 \quad C^1\ D^1 \ldots Z^1$$
$$A^1\ B^1 \qquad D^1 \ldots Z^1$$
$$A^1 \quad C^1 \ldots \qquad Z^1$$
$$\text{etc. } (= materia\ remota) \qquad A^2\ B^2 \quad D^2 \ldots Z^2 \ [C^1\ drops]$$
$$(= materia\ propinqua)$$

Figure 2

Taking the sequence $A^1\ B^1\ D^1 \ldots Z^1$ to represent Breri, C^1 is analogous to works that contain Governal's visit to Marc's court, which Thomas says is missing in Breri and is incompatible with his own sense of the narrative,

i.e., the archetypal ABD . . . Z. He therefore drops it from his romance: A²
B² D² . . . Z².

Such auctorial conception of the work justifies other striking choices among
sources. Benoît de Sainte-Maure rejects "Omer" as a source for the Trojan
War (*Troie* 71–74) because "Omer" — probably the *Ilias latina* — relates the,
for Benoît, improbable combats between mortals and the gods and goddesses
(61–70). There are, moreover, other accounts of the Trojan War.

> En maint sen avra l'om retrait,
> Saveir com Troie fu perie,
> Mais la verté est poi oïe.
>   (42–44)[42]

[There have been many versions of the destruction of Troy, but the truth
of the matter is rarely heard.]

The validity of Benoît's version, like Thomas', derives from what he considered the most reliable sources, Dares and Dictys. Their authority seemed
unimpeachable because they were eyewitnesses. Therefore, Benoît rendered
them into French for those who did not know Latin (37–39). The assumed
passage from Dares' and Dictys' Greek texts[43] through the Latin versions of
Sallust's brother, Cornelius, to Benoît's own French version (75–141) anticipates Aimon de Varennes' *matiere* which also passed from a Greek tale
through his Latin *memoire* to the French verse romance.[44] The use of source
material is apparent in all these stages of composition, but it is most cru-
cially centered in the writer's initial conception or vision of the work to be
written — that is, in auctorial *pensers*.

It is difficult to obtain a precise idea as to how the archetypal "vision" of
the opus was construed by medieval writers. The arts of poetry and prose
are too brief and sketchy to provide help; the philosophical poetry of the
twelfth century is more pertinent to works dealing with divine creation than
to romance subjects. Still, the notion of the artist attempting to imitate God's
handiwork provides a starting point. It is widespread in romance, notably
in descriptions of beauty that nature could not duplicate, or that was equal
to God's own creation.

> Onques Dieus ne fist chose, s'il s'en met an labor,
> Que il [= the artist] ne contreface autresi ou gençor
> La façon et la forme, ja mar querrés mellor.
>   (*Alex* APar III.4461–63)[45]

[God never made anything the shape and form of which he (= the artist)
could not reproduce as well or even better if he set himself to it — none
better could be found.]

Contrefaçon or *re-creatio* of God's opus by the writer is also apparent in the account of the mysterious beginnings claimed for the thirteenth-century *Estoire del saint graal.* The anonymous redactor received from Christ a small book in which he found the *matiere* for the entire romance. But size is not the only difference between the archetypal and the verbal opus. The former had a perfection which, contrary to the sentiments expressed in the passage from the *Roman d'Alexandre,* the latter could not emulate.

> Mais se plus i avoit, pour çou, n'en ment mie li contes. Kar il ne garandist ses paroles de nule plus, mais del mains tout; kar chou tiesmongne li contes, si comme vous orrés deviser cha avant, que toutes les aventures dou Graal ne seroit ja seues par nul houme mortel; assés en couvient trespasser; mais en la sainte estoire qui fu envoié en tiere par la bouce de la veritet, chou est de Jhesu-Crist, en celui ne trouvera on ja vn mot de faussetet, kar chil seroit de trop forsenet hardement plains, qui oseroit ajoindre menchongne en si haute estoire com est l'estoire que li vrais crucifis a escrist de la soie propre main. (*Estoire* II, 439/I.119.7–14)[46]

> [But even if there were more, my story does not lie. For it in no way vouch-safes the truth of most of the words — quite the contrary. For the story bears witness, as you will hear below, that all the adventures of the Grail will never be fully known by any mortal. Rather a lot will be passed over. But the sacred *estoire* which was brought to earth through the mouth of the truth, that is, of Jesus Christ, will never be shown to contain a false word. For he would truly be mad with affrontery who would dare add mendacious material to an *estoire* as high and holy as is that which the true victim of crucifixion wrote with his own hand.]

The archetypal state of the work evoked in this passage may be approximated; it may not be reproduced in human language because it is the very word of God. The passage is important here because it implies and fits the notion of composition whereby the idea of the work may find expression, however unsatisfactorily, through amplification of a small amount of matter. That amplification is, therefore, only the image, the semblance of the idea. In amplifying a source, the author draws on "archetypal" material by thought *(pensers).* The amplification translates the thought into the work or, in medieval language, draws it out of the *materia remota.* The amalgam of mental and literal source material is as active in the composition of prose romances as in their twelfth-century verse predecessors.

The process of blending mental and actual written sources makes previously obscure *matiere* clear. Merlin says as much when he tells Blaise how the union of his story and Josephes' makes a new whole which is comprehensible because of the combination. "Et ensi comme je sui oscurs et serai enviers chiaus ou je ne me vaurrai esclairier, ensi sera tous li livres celés. . . . Si sera Joseph et li livres des lignies que je t'ai amenteues avec le tien et le mien. . . . Et quant li doi livre seront assemblé, si i avra un biel livre" (Huth *Merlin* I, 32–33) [and just as I am obscure, and shall be for those I refuse to reveal myself to, so will the whole book be hidden. . . . And Josephes and the book of genealogies which I named to you will be with your descendents and mine. . . . And when the two books are brought together, it will make a beautiful book]. That is, it will be a handsome amalgam. Here it is whole and complete in conception, even though that conception seems obscure and partial before the realization of the amalgam. If some of the *matiere* is missing, and perhaps ineffable, this will prove unimportant: "li doi seront une meesme chose fors tant que je ne puis dire, ne drois n'est, les privees paroles de Joseph et de Jesucrist" (Huth *Merlin* I, 33) [the two will be one, except that I cannot express, nor would it be right to do so, the private words exchanged between Josephes and Jesus Christ]. Similarly, the amalgam of the *Queste* and the *Lancelot* Proper, including the latter's material and topical adaptations of Chrétien's *Charrette,* gave to the story of Lancelot a meaning that had beforehand been obscure. As Eugène Vinaver astutely observed regarding the *Balain* interpolation, "the process [of writing romance] is not one of indiscriminate accumulation or gradual 'decomposition,' but of continuous development from simple and incomplete patterns to more elaborate and consistent designs."[47] The process may be reversed, if complex structures are broken up into shorter wholes, as in late medieval romance.[48]

Thus romance combines the two models of invention current in Chartrain conceptions of the literary art. The first, a historical vision based on the world of time, space, and sequential events, is the story of the creation of the world and man set forth in Genesis. This is the narrative model. The second used the archetypal, ahistorical framework of the *Timaeus* to describe creation and invention.[49] This latter type is the model for the topical invention of narrative significance. The former provided the pattern for medieval historiography and the historical paradigm; whether in terms of sacred or secular history, it was always at least implicitly typological.[50] The latter was the model for allegorical dream visions and *involucra.* The two paradigms came together in romance composition.[51] *Matiere* is submitted to topical amplification that conforms to a given context, sacred or secular; as auctorial conception, that context informs and qualifies the *estoire* derived from a combination of sources in an amalgam. The amalgam is the product of the transition from *materia remota* to *materia propinqua,* a transition possible because of *pensers. Pensers* is the use of *sans* to invent *san.*

Signification of Romance and the Genius of the Author

Critical discussion of *san* and *sans* has focused on the use of the word (or words) in the Prologues to Chrétien's *Charrette* and Marie de France's *Lais*. Both prologues use *san* and *sans*, distinguishing semantically between them, in some of the manuscripts, by orthography.

The Prologue to Chrétien de Troyes' *Charrette: San* and *Sans*

> Mes tant dirai ge que mialz oevre
> Ses [= Marie de Champagne's] comandemanz an
>   ceste oevre
> Que *sans* ne painne que g'i mete.
> Del *Chevalier de la charrete*
> Comance Crestïens son livre;
> Matiere et *san* li done et livre
> La contesse, et il s'antremet
> De panser, que gueres n'i met
> Fors sa painne et s'antancïon.
> (*Charrette* 21–29; emphasis in 23 and 26 mine)

[But I will say this much: her (Marie de Champagne's) command is more effective in the realization of this work than any *sans* or effort I bring to the task. Chrétien begins his book about the Knight of the Cart. The countess provides him with *matiere* and *san,* and he undertakes to think, for he scarcely adds any more to it than his effort and his *antacion.*]

The countess's "san"[52] is conveyed to Chrétien with the *matiere* of the work to be written. Chrétien's "sans"—a feature of *panser* in the *Charrette* Prologue—is allied to his effort or "painne," an alliance which recurs at the end of the Prologue as both effort and intention or purpose: "sa painne et s'antancïon."[53] The word *sans* seems to refer to the romancer's artistry, *san* to the donor's conception of the projected work.[54]

This interpretation of the *Charrette* Prologue prevailed by and large until Jean Rychner contested the traditional reading: "je ne pense pas que, dans le prologue de la *Charrette, sans* puisse signifier à la fois 'signification' et 'intelligence capable de dégager la signification de la matière.' "[55] *San* and *sans* are, for Rychner, the same word. Now, the two meanings do exist in the twelfth century. For example, the meaning "signification" occurs in the following passage from Benoît de Sainte-Maure concerning the interpretation of the name Jumièges: "Gemeges de gemissemenz, / Tex en ert la glose e li senz" (*Ducs* 911–12) [Jumièges means lamentations; that was its gloss and its signification]. Moreover, in the same work, Benoît de Sainte-Maure counts

on the Holy Spirit to give him the "intelligence capable de dégager la signification de la matière":

> Se mi senz est humle e petiz,
> Je crei que li Sainz Esperiz
> I overra ensemble od mei.
> (*Ducs* 2127–29)

[Although my ability to perceive the signification of what I write be mean
and small, I believe that I shall have the assistance of the Holy Spirit.]

Further, Benoît goes on to relate how "Sen ne naist pas es cuers humains
/ . . . / Com fait un arbre en un verjer" (*Ducs* 2739–41) [the ability to
understand is not born in the human breast . . . like a tree in an orchard],
but is acquired by learning and training in the art of writing, through acqui-
sition of the "doctrine" and "discrecion" necessary first to understand and
then to express what is profitable and beautiful in a given *matiere* (*Ducs*
2730–64). From these clear examples, it is possible to perceive analogous
pairings in the *Charrette* Prologue, referring to, first, the *san* of the patron
and, second, the author's own *sans*. Chrétien insists on a distinction of meanings both orthographically and by the juxtaposition of complementary or
synonymous words that reinforce the intended distinction between *san* and
sans.

In Chrétien's Prologue, *san* complements *matiere*. Thus, Marie de Champagne's *san* suggests how the *matiere* of the *Charrette* was to be understood,
or, more specifically, how knighthood and love may be conjoined in a
meaningful way in the persons and actions of Lancelot and Guenevere. Marie
gave Chrétien, in rhetorical terms, a hypothesis by which certain persons and
actions may be explained and exemplified (see above, p. 49). This interpretation is close to Gaston Paris' translation of *san* in verse 26 by "esprit," a
reading accepted and refined upon by Jean Frappier as "idée maîtresse,"
"l'esprit dans lequel elle souhaitait qu'il fût traité," "signification":[56] Marie
de Champagne gave Chrétien *matiere* and *san*, that is, "le sujet . . . et l'esprit
du roman."[57] In the *Charrette*, the "sujet" is the antecedent source or amalgam of sources, the "esprit," "l'esprit nouveau de la *fine amor*."[58] And Frappier suggests that the adaptation of the *matiere* to the new *san* involved an
adaptation by Chrétien in the characters of Arthur, Guenevere, and especially Lancelot.[59]

This double use of *san/sans* may be glossed by a judicious observation
once made by Hans-Robert Jauss: "le choix du héros implique une conception définie de l'action. On ne peut pas prendre n'importe quel héros pour
le mettre dans n'importe quel genre."[60] And he continues: "Je ne veux pas

dire que le choix d'un héros détermine le genre. . . . Il y a pour chaque genre une conception de l'action en rapport avec la conception du héros: un héros antique ne peut être placé dans la situation d'Erec ou de Roland."[61] In fact, such "incongruities" were to occur in some romance and epic combinations of *matieres;* Chrétien himself seems to make an analogy between Mabonagrain's *amie* and Lavine in his *Erec.*[62] But such incidences do not alter the validity of Jauss' observation for the composition of the *Charrette* and its distinction between *san* as the idea for the work—its context and material style—and *sans* as the capacity to elaborate that idea in the romance; that is, for Marie de Champagne's and Chrétien de Troyes' complementary roles in the delineation of the characters of Lancelot and Guenevere and their actions in the *Chevalier de la charrette.* Rychner himself comes close to this reading in his reply to Frappier: "la comtesse lui donne le sujet et la façon de l'interpréter";[63] and Chrétien contributed his *sans*—his *painne* and *antancion*—that is, his physical exertion and mental application to the realization of Marie de Champagne's command.[64]

For Jauss, a genre is formed by the interplay between a tradition that fashions audience expectation and modernization effected by auctorial intention.[65] The technique by which the *conte* is modernized is topical invention. Such topical clarification transformed one kind of story into another—what might have been a fabliau, for example, into a romance.[66] Topical adjustments of a generic nature are evident in the differences between Chrétien's *Cligés* and the *Marques de Rome* version of the Cligés *conte*[67] or in the moralization of Henri d'Andeli's *Lai d'Aristote* (38–59).[68]

Since *materia propinqua* includes the conceptual source, narrative elaboration follows a conceptual model, both in the representation of the principal personages and in the topical characterization of their actions. One of the extant prologues to *Guiron le courtois* will serve to illustrate the relation between material source *(matiere)* and mental source *(san)*, which is, in this case, courtesy, as articulated in the alternate title, *Palamede,* of the work.

> Autre proposement je n'ai fors a parler de courtoisie; et quant courtoisie est li chiés de mon livre, or seroit bien raison et drois que je de courtois chevaliers commençasse ma matere et je si ferai se je puis. . . . Quel non li porrai je donner? Tel comme il plera a mon seigneur le roy Henri. Il vuelt que cestui mien livre, qui de courtoisie doit nestre, soit apelés Palamedes pour ce que si courtois fu toutesvoies Palamedes que nus plus courtois chevalier ne fu au temps le roy Artus. (*Guiron* pp. 179–80)[69]

> [My sole purpose is to speak about courtesy. And since courtesy is the fountainhead of my book, it would be reasonable and correct for me to begin with a courteous knight, and I shall if I may. . . . What name shall I give it? One

that will please my lord king Henry. He wants my book, which is to be born of courtesy, to be called *Palamedes,* since Palamedes was always so courteous that there was no more courteous knight in King Arthur's time.]

Knights like Palamede serve as examples for the anonymous redactor's audience (p. 179),[70] who will know courtesy by heeding the romance narrative and the informative *san* suggested by its title. Henry's alleged imposition of a title may be intended to make just that point, especially since the second title, *Guiron le courtois,* is not precluded by the first. Palamede does not have the prominence in his romance that, say, Lancelot or Tristan does in the prose cycles named for them.[71]

It is not unusual for medieval romances and lays to have more than one title—*Guillaume de Dole* and *Roman de la rose, Perceval* and *Conte du graal, Chaitivel* and *Les quatre deuils,* Coudrette's *Melusine* as the *Roman de Parthenay* and the *Roman de Lusignan.* The importance attributed to titles in the *accessus* reveals the close correlation between title and both *matiere* and *san.* Jean Renart elucidates the title of *Escoufle,* for example, by contrasting the *matiere* as the ignoble bird and the noble *san* or subject matter of the romance (*Escoufle* 9072–101). Similarly, the *Palamede* or *Guiron le courtois* Prologue derives the first title, *Palamade,* from the *san* which is courtesy; the second comes from the *matiere* which relates the adventures of Guiron, the most prominent knight in the narrative.

Jauss' identification of character as a generic marker in romance reflects the notion of material style. The auctorial conception of topical abstractions may be represented in the attributes and actions of exemplary characters.

> Car en tous lius si le faisoit
> Qu'as autres examplaire estoit
> De sens et de cevalerie,
> D'ensegnement, de courtoisie,
> Et de francise et de largece;
> De lui et de sa grant prouece
> Est la renoumee si ample
> Que tous li mons i prent example.
> (*Amadas* 1419–26)[72]

[For he performed everywhere so as to be for others an example of right thinking *(sens),* chivalry, breeding, courtesy, nobility, and largess. His fame and that of his prowess were so widespread that everyone takes him as a model.]

Amadas is also a narrative model, developed and illustrated through his narrative adventures. This is the purpose of *estoire.*[73] Thus, in *Amadas* 1421, *sens* connotes, together with the other abstractions, an ability, a *prouesse*, that will receive more concrete exemplification in the actions and sentiments of Amadas.[74] Similarly, this is the way Thomas d'Angleterre construed the exemplariness of his *Tristan:* lovers would rediscover themselves and understand the love they knew through sympathetic identification (*Tristan* Th Douce 831–39).

The Prologue to Marie de France's *Lais: San* and *Sans*

Most of the discussion of Marie's Prologue has centered on the passage in Priscian she refers to in order to explain the art of invention in the *Lais*.

> Custume fu as ancïens,
> Ceo testimoine Precïens,
> Es livres ke jadis feseient,
> Assez oscurement diseient
> Pur ceus ki a venir esteient
> E ki aprendre les deveient,
> K'i peüssent gloser la lettre
> E de lur *sen* le surplus mettre.
> (*Lais* Pro 9–16; emphasis mine)

Alfred Foulet and Karl D. Uitti have proposed the following reading of these lines: "The Ancients were wont, so says Priscian, in the books they wrote to express themselves somewhat obscurely so that future writers who would learn from them might explicate their words and complete the meaning of what they said."[75] They go on to distinguish between the use of *sen* in verse 16 and *sens* in verse 20:

> Li philesophe le saveient,
> Par eus meïsmes entendeient,
> Cum plus trespassereit li tens,
> Plus serreient sutil de *sens*
> E plus se savreient garder
> De ceo k'i ert a trespasser.
> (Pro 17–22; emphasis mine)[76]

[The philosophers knew, and through their own experience understood, that, as time passed, men would grow more subtle of wit and better able to avoid missing the contents.]

Here *sens* is the mind capable of discerning the signification or *idée maîtresse* of *matiere* and drawing out this *surplus de sen*. As Foulet and Uitti point out, Marie de France utilizes in her Prologue the same senses of *sen* and *sens* that Chrétien does in the *Charrette* Prologue.[77] The trained mind uses his or her acquired art to discern the signification of old *matiere*.

It is the particular ability of the *philosophes* to extract *san* from various sources. "L'œil et l'esprit le lisent, grâce à une vision spéciale, longuement acquise et transmise, sensible aux moindres inflexions de ce discours; aux spécialistes d'interpréter: du moins chacun spontanément déchiffre le bout de page qu'il a sous les yeux."[78] The work of Zumthor's "specialist" is also, mutatis mutandis, that of Marie and Chrétien. Marie's allusion to the "philosophers" recalls Alain de Lille's distinction between the "philosopher" and the "poet."[79] Philosophers covered and uncovered mysteries, as an epitaph for Thierry de Chartres testifies: "Quod Plato, quod Socrates clausere sub integumentis / Hic reserans docuit disseruitque palam"[80] [uncovering what Plato and Socrates had wrapped in *integumenta,* he taught and discoursed on it openly]. The *surplus de sen,* the contribution of each "specialist," is the uncovering of "ceo k'i ert." The author of the new work is the authoritative and critical interpreter of traditional source *matiere.*[81]

The study of the authors was included in the art of invention mastered in grammar and rhetoric. "Pour ce ot non Astarus que il sot touz les cors / Des estoiles du ciel et du sens des auctours" (*Alex* APar I.280–81) [he was called Astarus because he knew the course of the stars and the meaning of the authors]. That is, study of the authors had a place alongside *exercitatio* in grammar and rhetoric. *Savoir le sens* is to have learned and assimilated what the authors teach, even if, as Marie de France avers, that teaching may be buried in obscurity.

But did Marie understand the *surplus de sen* the author brings out of the source to have been deliberately obscured by the ancients? Or did she think that they were unable in their time to pierce the *matiere*'s obscurities before passing it on to more enlightened generations?[82] The former seems more likely. The ancients hid their understanding of what they wrote so that subsequent generations might extract it from their writings—"*Pur* ceus ki a venir esteient / E ki aprendre les deveient" (*Lais* Pro 13–14; emphasis mine) [*for the sake of* those who were to follow and would have to construe what they had written]. The intent to obscure makes the *matiere* a pensum which subsequent "glossators" like Marie de France would elucidate with their *pensers* and *sens* (Pro 19–30). They would not pass over "ceo k'i ert."[83]

It is necessary to remark, parenthetically, that an absolutely correct reading of these lines is not essential to understanding the technique of topical invention about which Marie is speaking. The glossing Marie envisages is not that of an *Ovide moralisé*. Rather, it is clearly involution (see above, pp. 49–52), the elucidation of *matiere* by topical investment that expresses "ceo k'i ert," whether she thought the ancients were actually aware of the latter or not. Consequently, her technique is ultimately instructive and ethical in intent (*Lais* Pro 23–30).

Hence, the *sens* of the receiving audience is as important as that of the authors and donors: it too must discern the signification of the romances and lays. Benoît de Sainte-Maure, for example, was aware of the value of the written word for qualified audiences.

> Quer ne connois ne je ne vei
> Qu'en l'estoire ait rien si bien non
> E doctrine e cognicion
> A ceus qui i voudront entendre;
> Maint buen essample i porront prendre.
> (*Ducs* 2130–34)

[For I neither know nor perceive anything in the *estoire* that is not good, contributing to both the edification and the understanding of those who are willing to apply themselves to it. They can draw many a good example from it.]

I entendre is to use one's own *sens* to understand, just as, reciprocally, the artist's *sens* is the application of his or her *antancion,* as in the *Charrette* Prologue. As another romancer suggests, the audience's *antancion* became a topic in romance prologues.[84]

> Or entendés, et roi et conte,
> Çou que Jehans nos dist et conte
> D'un Romans que en escrit mist
> Au tans que il s'en entremist,
> Des aventures et des lais
> Biaus et plaisans, et le plus lais;[85]
> Mais sour tout ço son sens i mist
> Cil Jehans qui s'en entremist;
> Car il nos dist tante aventure,
> Qui bien i meteroit sa cure
> En escouter et en entendre,
> Mout grant sens i poroit aprendre.
> (*Rigomer* 6429–40)

[Now harken, kings and counts, to what Jehan tells and relates to us about a romance he put into writing, in which he undertook to describe the adventures and lays which are beautiful and pleasing—and I leave out most of them; this is what Jehan applied himself to most assiduously, he who undertook the task. For he relates so many adventures that one would learn a great deal from them by listening attentively.]

Since *san* comprehended the signification of what was written, audiences en-dowed with a noble mind — like Amadas' *sens* — would be able to understand and appreciate it.

San/sans, then, like *conte, matiere,* and *estoire,* is susceptible of a wide range of general and specific meanings in romance composition. It commonly designates Latin words of similar application — *sensus, sententia, significatio, scientia,* as well as *ingenium, intentio,* and *imaginatio.* We have already noted the importance of these words in the paradigm for topical invention. Their use evinces the concern found in romance prologues for literal or alle-gorical meaning; the artistic mind trained to express that meaning; and a public able to discern it.

The use of *san/sans* in romance falls therefore under three broad heads.[86] First, *sans* designates the mind possessing the three traditional prerequisites for the practice of an art: genius in the sense of natural endowments *(ingenium),* art as technique *(ars),* and training in the art *(exercitatio).*[87] Second, *san* refers to the meaning, signification, or context the author or patron gives to the romance, and, accordingly, the profit to be derived from reading it or hearing it read.[88] Finally, *sans* also refers to the critical acumen or the mentality of the proposed audience, an audience which may inspire, autho-rize, appreciate, or return the work to the workbench for correction or im-provement.[89] The broad semantic range of *san/sans* allows it to accommodate these divergent, but complementary, even graded applications in romance.[90]

For purposes of clarity, we shall adopt the distinctions suggested by the *Charrette* and *Lais* Prologues and use *san* to refer to the subject matter, while *sans* will refer to the capacity to express and understand significant subject matter. Where the orthographical distinction does not hold, the precise sense or senses of these terms will be based on the evidence of the passage cited. For more than one meaning may be intended, as when Raoul de Houdenc combines both the *san* and the *sans* of Chrétien's *Charrette* Prologue in his own *Meraugis.*

> Contrediseor sont, ne dïent
> Point de lor sens, ainz sont de ceus
> Qui tot boivent lor sens par eus.
> Por ce Raous de Hodenc dit
> Qu'il veut de son sens qui est petit
> Un novel conte comencier.
> (*Meraugis* 14–19)[91]

[They are liars, speaking not with their own wits/ideas, but rather draw-ing their wits/ideas in with their eyes. Therefore Raoul de Houdenc says he wishes to begin a new story with what little wit/ideas he has.]

In this passage *sans* clearly combines not only the ability to write well but also the sense or meaning—"ideas"—intended for the work.

Exercise of *Sans* as Imagination

The common meanings of *san/sans* as the artist's mind, the meaning of the work, and the profit to be drawn from it are suggested by Chrétien's and Marie's Prologues. They refer to the processes of both invention and retention; that is, they represent the activation of the related faculties of imagination and memory.[92] Both Marie de France and Chrétien de Troyes emphasize the role each faculty plays in preserving the past and in realizing the perceived intentions of first authors. In this they follow their predecessors who adapted French and Greco-Roman history in the vernacular.[93] The memory preserved from the past requires interpretation in order to be understood by contemporary audiences. Imagination is the faculty that makes understanding possible by giving a meaningful shape and context to earlier matter, thus making it credible to vernacular audiences. The obscure becomes clear, the disordered and incomplete becomes coherent and whole, as past authority acquires contemporary legitimacy.

Adaptation of *matiere* in French romance usually meant adaptation to contemporary aristocratic ideals and worldviews. It is analogous to the early Christian assimilation and accommodation of "Egyptian spoils."[94] Such adaptation precludes neither aristocratic admiration for the protagonists of Latin epic and history, nor horror before their downfall when trapped by fate and blind to or ignorant of redemption. Just as pagans in the *chansons de geste* could inspire admiration—"Deus! quel baron, s'oüst chrestientet!" (*Roland* I, 3164)[95] [God! what a baron had he been a Christian!]—so Christian knights might descend to villainy: "Nus ne fust miaudres chevaliers, / Se fel et deslëaus ne fust" (*Charrette* 3164–65) [none would have been a better knight if he had not been felonious and disloyal]. Aristocratic ideals also included "the kindling of love"—Dante's *accensio amoris*[96]—which constitutes, with prowess in arms and moral rectitude, a noble context for romance as well as for lyric.[97] These are the simple, basic ideas that romancers elucidate and gloss in their narratives.

To understand and appreciate these ideas required an aristocratic *sans,* which is mirrored or distorted in the exemplary figures lauded or vituperated in romances and vernacular chronicles. That *sans* includes artistic abilities.

> Tex sunt afaitié e corteis
> E maistre des arz e des leis
> Si ne fust buen enseignemenz,

Doctrine, oïrs, retenemenz,
Qui fussent sanz discrecion,
Vilain, sanz sen e sanz raison.
(*Ducs* 2147–52)[98]

[There are those who are elegant, courteous, and masters of the arts and of dogma, who, were it not for instruction, learning, attention, and retention, would lack discretion, and would be villains, deprived of wit and reason.]

In the *Partonopeu* African kings

sevent de rectorique
Por les grans sens bien deviser
Et por bele raison mostrer,
Et sunt bon clerc et bien letré
Et de parfons sens renomé;
Et trestuit sont bon chevalier,
Sage et artoz de lor mestier.
(7366–72)[99]

[know rhetoric by which they can discourse on the great ideas and set forth their thought eloquently; and they are good clerics, trained in letters, and renowned for their deep mind. And all of them are good knights, prudent and skilled in the exercise of their art.]

In other words, the capacity of such sages includes ability and training *(sans)* which permit them to communicate eloquently their thought and understanding *(san)*. These meanings come together in a description of the Seven Sages.

come Dex les aorèrent
Por le grant sens q'en aus trovèrent.
Saige clerc furent et sené.
(*Dolopathos* fr p. 5)

[They adored them as gods because of the great minds they found in them. They were wise and prudent clerics.]

Clerics like Helie de Toulouse in the *Lancelot* Proper and the hermits in the *Queste* use *sans* to interpret visions and dreams.[100] Like Chrétien and Marie, they use their *sans* to discern and elucidate the truth of the adventures related to them by knights and kings.

As adapted from the Latin *sapientia* topic,[101] the obligation to use one's *sans* to transmit knowledge is widespread from the earliest romances on.[102]

> Qui sages est nel doit celer,
> ainz doit por ce son senz moutrer
> que quant il ert du siecle alez
> touz jors en soit mes ramenbrez.
> . . . .
> Pour ce n'en veul mon senz tesir,
> ma sapïence retenir,
> ainz me delite a raconter
> chose digne por ramenbrer.
>   (*Thèbes* 1–4, 9–12)[103]

[The wise should not hide their wisdom, but rather reveal it in order to
assure fame after death. . . . Therefore I won't silence my thought or keep
my learning to myself. Rather I take pleasure in recounting something
memorable.]

The tendency to combine the different meanings of *san/sans* derives from
their common origin in *pensers*. Since the opus is originally a mental construction, the imagination and the meaning of the work to be written merge
in the conception of the work and its realization. For the audience, reading
or attentive listening permits apprehension of the work's meaning in the mind
of each reader or listener.

The union of source and interpretation is construed as an act of memory;
the author recalls and clarifies something more or less forgotten. The source
as repository of that memory is passed on to an audience otherwise ignorant
of it,[104] because the source is in a foreign language,[105] because it has heretofore been unavailable,[106] or because it has seemed incomprehensible.[107] The
art of writing such works was acquired in the schools. Exercises developed
the ability to discern and elaborate upon a given subject matter. Marie de
France, as we have seen, cites Priscian as authority in this art. Chrétien shows
that he too knew the technique, probably in part from study of Macrobius'
Saturnalia,[108] a work which is a veritable case study in topical adaptation
of old *materia* to a new language and audience. Chrétien deftly applies the
skill to Arthurian matter when he unites the fays of Celtic legend and the
art of topical invention acquired by study and imitation of the authors.

We have observed that instruction on grammar and rhetoric in the Middle Ages included what today would be called the study of literature. Such
study ranged from reading and simple glossing to exercises in imitation, adaptation, and original invention like those illustrated in the examples found
in the *Saturnalia*.[109] The author of *Athis et Prophilias* seems to have had such
study in mind; his words recall the *accessus ad auctores* and the *vitae
vergilianae*.

> Oëz del savoir Alixandre [de Paris]
> . . .
> Ne fu pas saiges de clergie,
> Mes des auctors oï la vie;
> Mout retint bien an son memoire.
> 　　　　(*Athis* 5, 9–11)[110]

[Hear Alexander's learning. . . . He was not knowledgeable in the arts, but he did know the life of the authors. He had a good memory.]

The notion of *clergie* as the sum and total of traditional knowledge and learning is evident in his references to Rome's *chevalerie* and Athens' *clergie* (*Athis* 171–88). Rome and Athens represent not only transmitted *savoir,* but also two poles of the same *savoir* distinguished by different emphases, yet linked by a common goal: the education of the complete nobleman.[111]

> Or vos dirai des .II. citez,
> Comant li pleiz est devisez:
> Athene est pleinne de clergie
> Et Rome de chevalerie.
> Pröesce por savoir chanjoient,
> Sifeitemant s'entr'aprenoient:
> En Athene n'avoit riche home
> Qui n'envëast son fil a Rome,
> Quant il ert saiges de clergie,
> Por aprandre chevalerie;
> Et cil de Rome espessemant
> R'anvëoient lor filz sovant
> A Athene, por bien antendre
> Le san et la clergie aprandre.
> 　　　　(*Athis* 189–202)[112]

[Now I will tell you about the two cities and how they divided their tasks. Athens is great with learning and Rome with knighthood. They exchanged prowess for knowledge, and in this way taught one another. No Athenian nobleman failed to send his son to Rome, when the latter had completed his schooling, to learn how to be a knight; and Roman fathers often sent their sons to Athens to acquire knowledge and learning.]

Such *san* was said to be either possessed perfectly by certain sages,[113] or only partially attainable by any one person.[114] It could also embrace the theological sciences, which of and by themselves give the complete "sens du monde"[115] found in the Old and New Testaments, as well as knowledge of God, which is the highest knowledge;[116] morals and courtesy;[117] magic;[118] and skill in in-

terpreting allegories.[119] It furthermore includes secular as distinguished from
divine or supernatural knowledge and skills,[120] including *chevalerie*.[121] Finally *san* descended through grammar and rhetoric[122] to composition[123] and
to romance itself, which in turn opened to comprehend almost "tot le sens
du monde":

> Et qui vos verroit demander,
> S'en puet riens en romanz aprendre,
> Et je diroie sanz mesprendre,
> Qu'il i gist tout li sens du monde,
> Tant come il dure a la roonde,
> Car se les estoires ne fussent,
> Les genz de droit riens ne seussent;
> Li philosophe les escrisent,
> Qui tout le sens du monde lisent,
> Qu'en Ebreu furent premier fetes
> Et de l'Ebreu en Latin tretes,
> Ou molt bien furent tranlatees,
> De Latin en Romanz portees
> Fors que li sacres de la loy.
> (*Claris* 29623–36)

[And were someone to ask you if one can learn anything from romances, I
would answer without fear of error that they contain all the wide world's
learning. For were it not for *estoires,* people would know nothing right.
The philosophers wrote them, they who read the world's learning. For the
estoires were first written in Hebrew, and then translated into Latin—and
very well translated they were—and then rendered from Latin into French,
with the exception of the mysteries of the faith.]

Could this claim be preposterous hyperbole or, rather, a sign of ignorance?
What is "tout li sens du monde" in romance?[124]

Various sources like these ascribe all knowledge and all disciplines to some
agent or other. John of Salisbury viewed the works of the ancients in this
way.[125] The artist who mined the truth embedded in obscure sources for
aristocratic audiences needed keen eyesight. Art provided the technique to
train artistic vision to penetrate the obscurities of *matiere* and uncover its
signification, as Marie de France saw her predecessors do, including those
who adapted Latin works into French (*Lais* Pro 30).[126] Composing a romance
requires a mind disciplined by training and practice, including a variety of
interrelated activities: *entreprendre; s'entremetre; metre paine, labour, travail, cure, estude, antancion; aprandre* as *san/sans* or *verité espondre;* and
others.[127] Past knowledge provides the art and the example.

> Pur ço deit l'om mult enquere
> E pener sei de ben faire,
> E des boens prendre esperemenz,
> Des faiz, des diz as anciens
> Qui devant nus esteient.
>
> (*Gui* 5–9)

[Wherefore one ought to strive and struggle to do well, taking example from the worthy, from the deeds and words of the ancients who came before us.]

Understanding is not based on discursive instruction alone. It takes place in the "heart," as the commonplace allusion to *cuers* and *oreilles* suggests,[128] as demonstrated by the following passage:

> Mais nus hom ne porroit manoir
> En vilenie longement,
> Pour qu'il prestast entierement
> A escouter cuer et oreilles
> Cest roumant et les grans merveilles
> Que cil dui fisent en enfance.
>
> (*Escoufle* 9052–57)[129]

[But no one could long remain a villain provided he or she lend heart and ears fully to listening to this romance, and to the great marvels those two performed in their youth.]

Both author and public have access to the same deep-lying significance. *Entendre* is as far from mere listening as the author's *matiere* is from mere transcription of a source.[130]

For twelfth-century and later romances, an aristocratic world of prowess in arms, noble love, and rectitude served as a context for narrative adventures. The eyes and heart were prisms of that world. Thus, the old source reached its intended audience as a reflection of the intended audience's vision projected onto the world as its meaning. Medieval theory of vision and optics provides a useful complement to the eyes and heart metaphor.

For much of medieval science, vision did not go in through the eyes (intromission), but came out from them, seizing and fusing with its own light (extramission)[131] the light emanating from the objects of vision. Vision thus joined its light with that emanating from those sources. The genius, the *engin* or *san* of the viewer, enhanced the source with its own light.

The comparison is helpful in describing the relation between matter and mind in the invention of medieval romance. For the audience had to understand the written word. Such understanding was founded on the quality of the audience's mind; some knowledge of the facts of the story—the myth, as it were[132]—so as to appreciate the given work's *surplus de sen;* and an attention to and concern for the ideals that provide the work's context.

Of course, the real quality of the audience varied. There is evidence, for example, that Chrétien's romances remained popular for their marvels more than for their *sen*.[133] Nonetheless, the different uses made of those marvels along with their new or different significance required some reflection on the story's possible meanings. As time went on, the audience's memory as the repository of the story and of its various truths assumed a very complex role in the reception of romances,[134] as increasing intertextual references to diverse legends demonstrate.[135] Such intertextual cross-referencing supposes a sophisticated audience, a public of veritable romance connoisseurs.[136]

The audience *sens* exemplified here expresses a topic prominent in romance: do not entrust power and authority—or romance narrative—to the ignoble, for they do not have the mind to use them right: "Je ne di pas qu'a totes gens / Doive li hom mostrer son sens" (*Durmart* 5–6)[137] [I don't say that one should reveal one's mind to everyone]. Noble aspirations should prevail over ignoble or villainous ones, a truth which the narrative of the *Durmart* itself illustrates.

The elitist notion of the audience becomes more specialized in some romances, depending on whether they stress prowess in arms, love, or rectitude. Thomas d'Angleterre, for example, presents his *Tristan* as a model of conduct by which lovers may recall their own experience, both happy and unhappy.[138]

> Le milz ai dit a mun poeir,
> E dit ai tute la verur,
> Si cum jo pramis al primur.
> E diz e vers i ai retrait:
> Pur essample issi ai fait
> Pur l'estorie embelir,
> Que as amanz deive plaisir,
> E que par lieus[139] poissent troveir
> Choses u se puissent recorder.
>   (*Tristan* Th Sneyd² 827–35)[140]

[I have spoken to the best of my ability, and have expressed the whole truth as I promised at the outset. I have recorded words and verse. I fashioned it as an exemplum, in order to embellish the *estoire,* so that it might please lovers and that they might discover in "places" things that recall their own experience.]

And indeed, Thomas' amalgam and elucidation of his diverse sources gave expression to a totally new, and courtly, conception of the love between Tristan and Iseut.[141] Here is the passage from the author's *sans* through the work's *san* to the *sans* of the public, all three of which ought to be commensurate because they are aristocratic. The passage to the romance public is possible because that public's own *sans* is not only aristocratic, as required of the first "Roman" romances, but more explicitly that of noble lovers. The latter's mind too required a disposition to love enhanced by reflection and experience. Reception, however, was not passive. Romance could raise problems for which no clear solution was evident, but about which reflection and individual response would have been appropriate.[142]

Chevalerie depends on clerical *san/sans* to know and understand its mission. The thirteenth century saw the emergence of great cycles dealing with universal mysteries of grace, love, and the meaning of life. In them, the *sens du monde* became the goal of interlaced quests. Dinadan echoes that goal in the prose *Tristan,* even while acknowledging failure: "je suis un chevalier errant qui chascun jor voiz aventures querant et le sens du monde; mes point n'en puis trouver, ne point n'en puis a mon oes retenir"[143] [I am a knight errant, and go ever seeking adventures and the meaning of the world. But I can't find or retain any meaning of use to me]. For Dinadan the grand ideas of chivalric society — prowess in arms, love, and even rectitude — lose their efficacy when they do not determine conduct. Like Wolfram von Eschenbach's Parzival, Dinadan despairs at the incomprehensibility of God's ways and the inconstancy of man's in the world.[144]

The elucidation of *matiere* may indeed reveal folly as well as wisdom;[145] even the sunlit tableau of Arthurian glory that brightens the *sens du monde* in *Claris et Laris* is set against a backdrop of avarice and villainy in the world contemporary with the composition of the romance.[146] Similarly, double-sided *san* rehearses Chrétien's despair and flight into *châteaux en Espagne* at the outset of *Yvain* (29–41). Thus, the limits of romance are discernible in the exclusion of the "sacres de la loy" in the *Claris* intervention. The example of divinity in the terrestrial paradise of *chevalerie* and *clergie* revealed the appalling failure not only of a civilization, but also of the art of romance that had tried since Chrétien de Troyes and Robert de Boron to integrate the secular mysteries of chivalry with the divine mysteries in the grail. The failure in *conjointure* is the failure of romance; for the *Claris'* exclusion of religious truths parallels a similar tendency in the prose *Tristan* and later romances.[147]

Two Aspects of Artistic Imagination: *Memoire* and *Engin*

Analogous to Chrétien's juxtaposition of *san* and *matiere* in the *Charrette* Prologue is the juxtaposition of *sans* and *memoire* elsewhere.[148] *Memoria* overlaps in meaning with *materia* as historical record. The modern semantic distinction by gender between *mémoire* as *memoria* and *mémoire* as *memorandum* did not exist in early French, which used both genders for both senses.[149] *Memoire* overlapped in meaning with *sans* as a mental and even cognitive faculty, the quality of which determined the authority and meaning of the auctorial word. Both senses might be implicit in a single passage: "Por ce me couvient a guanchir seur la moie oevre, dont il me preste sens et memoire" (*Joseph d'A* 31–32/23–25)[150] [wherefore I must turn aside from my work for which he gives me *sens* and *memoire*]. *Sens* and *memoire* can signify here both *san* and *matiere* (= *memoranda*) and *sans* and *engin,* or the ability to invent.

The pseudo-Robert de Boron uses *sen* and *memoire* as cognitive functions: "fist Diex home de la plus vile boue que il sot. Et quant il l'ot feit si bel com il fu et tel comme li plot, si li presta sen et mimoire et vie et clarté" (*Joseph d'A* 872–74/698–99) [God made man of the vilest mud he could. And when He had made him as beautiful as Himself, and in a manner pleasing to Him, He lent him *sen* and *memoire,* life and consciousness]. Merlin is especially remarkable for his *sens* and *memoire.* Because he had inherited an extraordinary *engin* from his satanic father,[151] he was able to pierce the mystery of marvels and discover their hidden truth.

Part of Merlin's *sans* is imagination,[152] that is, the capacity to foresee the future, interpret dreams, and appear in various shapes and guises. Thus he imposes his vision on matter by activities analogous to the three kinds of true dreams in Macrobius' classification, *visio, oraculum,* and *somnium.* Merlin's ability to assume various shapes, to impart to things seen by others a meaning he himself gives to the shapes he assumes, and to give meaning to obscure dreams, stems from his *sans* as *engin.* It parallels the artist's activity in the invention of topoi.

> Mais jamais n'orroiz miauz descrivre
> La verité de la matere
> Quant j'avrai espons le mistere.
> (*Rose* 1600–1602/1598–1600)[153]

[But you will never hear the truth of the *matiere* better set forth after I shall have explained its mystery.]

Bernardus Silvestris himself likened the poetic imagination to prestidigitation.[154] Merlin and writers, including romancers, practiced analogous arts.

As Chrétien suggests in the *Erec* Prologue, the medieval romancer must be guided by a higher wisdom.

> Por ce dist Crestïens de Troies
> Que reisons est que totevoies
> Doit chascuns panser et antandre[155]
> A bien dire et a bien aprandre;
> Et tret d'un conte d'avanture
> Une molt bele conjointure
> Par qu'an puet prover et savoir
> Que cil ne fet mie savoir
> Qui s'escïence n'abandone
> Tant con Dex la grasce l'an done.
> (*Erec* 9–18)

[For this reason Chrétien de Troyes says that it is right for each person ever to think and strive to speak eloquently and to teach effectively. And he draws a very beautiful *conjointure* from a *conte d'avanture,* by which it may be shown and made known that he does not act wisely who doesn't dispense his knowledge generously as long as God graces him with it.]

In this passage what is known ("s'escïence") is a familiar story ("conte") retold with the combined operation of "panser"and "antandre." In presenting the memorable, or in describing folly, the author teaches how to hold to the former and to eschew the latter, for "Soef se garde de folie / Qui d'autrui boche l'a oïe" (*Dolopathos* fr p. 6)[156] [one easily guards against folly who hears of it from another's mouth]. Copying the source, the *memorandum,* is scribal activity pure and simple; it is not invention as the cooperation of *san/sans* and *memoire.*[157] Copyists

> Noient dïent, qu'a noient vont
> Lor estude et lor mot qu'il dïent.
> Contrediseor sont, ne dïent
> Point de lor sens, ainz sont de ceus
> Qui tot boivent lor sens par eus.
> (*Meraugis* 12–16)[158]

[They say nothing, for their efforts and language are useless. They are contradictory, nor do they express their own thought, but are rather of those who drink in all they think from outside themselves.]

The distinction between *cordis oculi* and *capitis oculi* contrasts understanding and superficiality, whether the understanding is thought to come from original insight or from outside, even supernatural, sources. This was so in historical writing as well.[159] The deeds of the past that romance and history preserved as written memory *(memoranda)* serve an exemplary role in forming and informing successive generations, guiding them toward wisdom and away from folly.[160] *Memoire,* as the repository of images and the source of invention, required genius as *sans* to find suitable expression for its contents.

Thus, *ingenium* was rendered in French as both *sans* and *engin.*[161] *Engin,* however, may have both positive and negative connotations, depending on context. Solomon and his wife in the *Queste del saint graal* and the *Estoire del saint graal* illustrate this distinction within the context of *memoire.* Solomon desired to communicate with Galaad and, more explicitly, to provide him with the memory of his ancestor who foresaw his coming. But his *sans* was unable to discover a means to effect the communication. Solomon's wife, whose *engin* had always circumvented his *sans,* applied herself to his idea and invented the material and fashioned the objects—that is, the ship, bed, and sword—that were to bear her husband's message to Galaad.[162] *Sans* and *engin* work analogously in composition.

> Et Diex qui les biens donne et sans nombre et sans plois,
> M'a donné par sa grace engien, s'est biaus envois,
> De rimer les biaus fais des Contes et des roys.
> (*Restor* 6–8)[163]

[And God whose bounty is measureless gave me through his grace the capacity to invent; it is a fine gift, to be able to put into verse the fine deeds of counts and kings.]

If *sans* is deficient in *engin,* the listener may even be asked to correct the work.[164]

Soutileté[165] is a feature of *engin,* overlapping with the modern notion of finesse. Solomon's wife tells her husband: "Car il n'a ou monde chose de quoi je ne cuidasse venir a chief, au grant sens qui en vos est et a la grant subtilité qui est en moi" (*Queste* p. 222.1–3) [for there is nothing on earth which I don't think I could achieve by using your great *sans* and my great finesse]. In *Perceforest* it is in one place correlated with the marvelous.[166] The *Comte d'Anjou* concludes:

> Si n'est pas la subtilleté
> Molt grant, car avec rudeté[167]
> N'est pas subtilleté norrie,
> Ainz est sa rachine porrie,
> Ne grant senz n'ai pas aüsé:
> Si m'en aiéz pour escusé!
> (*Anjou* 8113–18)

[And the finesse is not very great; for finesse is not sustained by boorishness. Rather its root is rotted away by that defect. I haven't used great wit, wherefore I ask your indulgence.]

This example of the humility topic underscores the penetrating insight deemed essential to artistic invention.[168] In the *Ducs* Benoît de Sainte-Maure says that *sans* must include God-given nobility of mind (2123–39)[169] if one is to excel in an art. Nobility of mind was also deemed necessary to understand romance. In other words, *sans* may be attributed to the specifically noble audience the authors require for comprehension.[170]

Like Chrétien, who drew on Marie de Champagne's *san* and *matiere,* Benoît says he drew the *san* to write his Norman chronicle from both the Holy Spirit and Henry II.[171] Both patrons are efficacious in the conception of the work. Further, each *sans* is effective in its composition at the stage attributed in medieval scholastic poetics to the archetypal state of the work, which is distinguished from the author's *sans* that elaborates the original conception in writing. Marie de Champagne's role in the composition of the *Charrette* illustrates this, as does that of unknown ladies in the composition of romances written as a token of devotion or love service[172] (which is not to say that Marie de Champagne was Chrétien's secret love!).[173] Marie's role is analogous to Solomon's in the construction of the Ship of Solomon, while Chrétien's is comparable to Solomon's wife's in the invention of the *Charrette.* In these instances there is movement from idea to realization of the idea in matter, from *memoire* through *engin,* from *matiere* and *san* through *sans* to *opus.*

The Sources: Matiere

Faults in Sources: *Depecier* and *Corronpre*

Despite the scorn for jongleurs usually expressed in romances whose authors present themselves by and large as representative of a civilization of *chevalerie* and *clergie,*[174] Wace's summary critique of these *conteurs* and their *fablieus* is probably closest to widespread opinion: "Ne tut mençunge, ne tut veir, / Tut folie ne tut saveir" (*Brut* 9793–94)[175] [neither all false nor all true, all madness nor all wisdom]. Even Chrétien de Troyes started with their *contes* to write *Erec et Enide.* But he distinguishes his art from that of the jongleurs by giving to fable a *san* which is also "delitables."[176]

Most romancers, even when using written sources, express a certain circumspection in reporting what their *matiere* relates, as distinguished from the truth they construe in that *matiere.*

> Mès, si com je truis en l'ystoire,
> Que je pens bien k'ele soit voire,
> Cil font à l'enfant compaignie,
> Qui de sa science ont envie,

> Et bien sachiez certeinement,
> Se li escriture ne ment,
> Nule riens n'est si perilleuse,
> Si cruex ne si ennuieuse,
> Com familiers ennemis.
>   (*Dolopathos* fr pp. 54–55)[177]

[But as I find it in the *estoire*, which I believe to be true, the young man's companions are envious of his knowledge. And rest assured, if the text is true, that nothing is more dangerous, cruel, or vexing than an enemy who is also an intimate.]

Such circumspection need not be mere lip service. It is found in vernacular chronicles.

> Ne me fu dit ne jo nel di
> Ne jo n'ai mie tut oï
> Ne jo n'ai mie tut veü
> Ne jo n'ai pas tut entendu,
> E mult estovreit home entendre
> Ki de tut vuldreit raison rendre.
>   (*Brut* 1531–36)[178]

[It was not reported to me, nor do I relate it; I haven't heard, seen, or comprehended everything; and one would have to make a considerable effort if one wanted to account for everything.]

To these must be added the ever-present *m'est avis, si com j'entent,* etc., which may be used as fillers, but which also may reflect instances of careful reporting and evaluation of sources.

What faults do romancers attribute to their sources? Chrétien sums them up in the verbs *depecier* and *corronpre* (*Erec* 21). The vagaries of oral tradition made its productions "fable sembler" (*Brut* 9798).[179] Towards the end of the thirteenth century Adenet le Roi could still exclaim that

> Aprentiç jougleour et escrivain mari,
> Qui l'ont de lieus en lieus ça et la conqueilli,
> Ont l'estoire faussee.
>   (*Berte* 13–15)

[Apprentice jongleurs and wretched writers, who have put it together from material collected here and there, have falsified the *estoire*.]

"French" and "Roman" romances express the same criticism that one finds in Arthurian romance for indiscriminate patchwork, falsification, and lacunae.[180] The authors reject oral sources in favor of more reliable authorities: Geoffrey of Monmouth for Wace, the *estoire* preserved at Meaux for Jehan Bodel, a "livre as estoires" at Saint Denis for Adenet le Roi (*Berte* 7–11).[181] Perhaps these authors embellish their *matiere* from oral versions, much as the authors of *Thèbes, Eneas, Troie,* and *Alexandre* had recourse to Ovidian, pseudo-Ovidian, and other material to complete and decorate their primary sources.[182] But embellishment did not detract from a deeper *san*—indeed, it could enhance its significance.

Chrétien's *depecier le conte* is clearly synonymous with dismembering or fragmenting in sources.[183] Similarly, the combination of apparently *disiecta membra* produces the patchwork composition suggested in Adenet's expression "de lieus en lieus ça et la conqueilli." Less obviously, Chrétien's *corronpre le conte,* on the other hand, refers to producing a corrupt text in the technical sense, making distortions,[184] and keeping or making lacunae in the sources. Similarly: "Or vus ai fait ici mult grant digressiun, / Car ne voil en l'estoire fere corruptiun" (*Becket* 2561–62)[185] [now I have digressed extensively here, since I don't wish to introduce lacunae into the *estoire*]. That is, the digression on the Constitutions of Clarendon completes rather than "corrupts" Guernes' account of Thomas' life.

This interpretation of *corronpre* is borne out by the romancers.

> Si vos dirons d'un atre avant
> Dont li contes est conronpus,
> Que primes nen fut menteüs.
> (*Florimont* 1674–76)[186]

[And we shall speak about another first, on account of which the tale is incomplete because he was not mentioned beforehand.]

Similarly: "Ici se taist le contes de Perlesvaus, e revient au roi Artu la matiere vraie qui en nul liu n'est corrumpue, se li latin ne nos ment" (*Perlesvaus* ll. 6272–73) [here the story of Perlesvaus stops, and the true *matiere*, which is nowhere incomplete, if the Latin isn't false, reverts to King Arthur], and: "La teste de Lamorat remest leans en la court ne l'istoire ne devise pas que le roy en fist, ains s'en taist atant et retourne a compter comment Parceval ly virges vint a court, car de compter ceste branche ne nous povons nous souffrir que nostre livre n'en fust corrompuz" (*Folie Lanc* p. 81.416–20)[187] [Lamorat's head remained in the court, nor does the *estoire* relate what the king did with it; rather it stops at that and returns to relate how Perceval the virgin came to court. For we cannot leave that branch out without making the story incomplete]. The author of the post-Vulgate *Grail* attempted to insure the integrity of his romance against corruption by a tripartite division.

Et cest chose amentoit . . . pour chou que se l'estoire dou graal estoit *corrom-*
pue par auchuns translatours qui après lui venissent, tout li sage houme qui
meteroient lour entente a oir et a escouter porroient par ceste parole savoir
se elle lour seroit baillie entiere ou *corrompue,* et connisteroient bien combien
il i faurroit. (Huth *Merlin* I, 280; emphasis mine)[188]

[And he has called attention to this so that, if the *Estoire dou graal* were made
incomplete by any copyists who came after him, any prudent person who applied him- or herself to hearing and listening to it could know by what is said
whether it had been transmitted complete or incomplete, and would be able
to tell how much was missing.]

Similarly, Jewish interpretation of the Bible is false according to the *Ovide
moralisé* because it "vait le texte derrompant / Et la sentence corrompant"
(XIII.2183–84)[189] [rends the text and makes the meaning incomplete], that
is, it excises the Christian sense of the letter by *depecier* and *corronpre. Corronpre* here as in the post-Vulgate comprehends only deletions—"combien
il i faurroit"—not additions.

Nonetheless, abbreviation is not "corruption" when it still retains essentials. For example, in the *Perceval* Continuation I:

> La damoisele molt rioit
> Des merveilles que il disoit,
> Et l'ensaignoit qu'il devoit faire.
> Mais ne puis mie tout retraire,
> Que j'ai autre chose a cachier;
> Ce ne me weil plus delaier
> Ne la matiere trespasser.
> (*T* 13751–57)[190]

[The maiden laughed a lot at the marvels he told, and she told him what
he had to do. But I can't relate everything, for I have other matters to
pursue. I don't wish to linger on this subject anymore, nor omit any of
the *matiere.*]

The anonymous author of the Short *Perceval* Continuation I asserts that "Je
ne voel tere ne noier / La matire ne trespasser" (*A* 7930–31) [I don't want
to suppress, reject, or pass over the *matiere*]. MS *P* offers a variant to verse
7931: "Ne voel la matire fauser" [I don't wish to falsify the *matiere*]. Both
versions express the notion of *corronpre* in the technical sense of the preceding citations, underscoring by synonyms like *tere, noier, trespasser, fauser*
both *corronpre* and the completeness which is its opposite.

One perceives in the foregoing quotations processes parallel to Hugh of
Saint Victor's *coniuncta segregare* and *segregata coniungere.* From incomplete *materia remota,* the technique produces an amalgam, that is, a whole

and complete *materia propinqua*. The resultant work may be characterized in terms used to describe contemporary architecture: "In eadem vero ecclesia nulla scissura vel corruptio invenitur"[191] [in the same church one will discover no break or empty space]. No *depecier* or *corronpre*. Now, as Brugger once noted, every romancer practices, quite literally, *depecier* and *corronpre*.[192] Chrétien himself did so to produce his *Erec*. But his work achieved a *bele conjointure* of ornamental beauty and cultural or social significance; his is not the *embeleter* faulted by Wace in Breton fables, "beautification" that obscured the truth of history. The manner by which source material is selected and combined (*segregare* and *coniungere*) will therefore loom large as the romancers use their *sans* to fashion a *bele conjointure* that is whole and complete, not incomplete or corrupt.

Amalgam of Sources: *Unir*

In Thomas' *Tristan, unir* describes the collection and amalgamation of source *matiere*.

> Seignurs, cest cunte est mult divers,
> E pur ço l'uni par mes vers
> E di en tant cum est mester
> E le surplus voil relesser.
> (Douce 835–38)[193]

[My lords, this tale is highly disparate; I have therefore brought it together in my poem, saying as much as is appropriate, but leaving out the rest.]

We have observed above that all of Jehan Bodel's *matieres* may use one or more sources for a given work. Technically, if there is a single source, the *materia* is *simplex;* when there are two or more sources, it is *multiplex*.[194] In practice, however, romancers, like historians,[195] tend to compile *matieres*. Very few pretend to rely on only one source. The short prose *Abladane* is one of the few.[196] Heldris de Cornuälles' *Roman de Silence* uses an *estoire;* however, the wording does not preclude several Latin versions subsumed under the term *estoire*. The study of the romance's possible sources corroborates this.

> Si com l'estorie le nos livre,
> Qu'en latin escrite lizons,
> En romans si le vos disons.
> (*Silence* 1660–62)[197]

[Just as the *estoire* transmits it to us, which we read written in Latin, we are relating it to you in French.]

Like the historians, the romancers tend to use one primary source as authority, introducing developments or adaptations from other, secondary material.[198] The *matiere de Rome* illustrates the practice.[199] The *Thèbes* refers to Statius by name (2739, 8905), but the romance adapts other sources while making important changes in Statius.[200] The *Eneas* makes no explicit reference to Vergil, although his Middle High German adapter Heinrich von Veldeke refers to the Roman poet by name; but the *Aeneid* is obviously the primary source, and it has just as obviously been adapted.[201] Thomas d'Angleterre used Breri in this way. Like historians and his peers, he sought a single, reliable source on whose authority he based his own version; at the same time, he amassed as much pertinent material as could be found elsewhere, which the principal source may have "forgotten" to include or may not have known or understood.

Most romancers seem eager to seek out credible or serviceable versions of a given *conte*. For example, Gottfried von Straßburg followed Thomas' example by carefully searching through books in Latin and French until he discovered Thomas' version of the story of Tristan and Iseut. Not content with one authority, he consulted others as well, notably Eilhart von Oberg (or Eilhart's lost French source, since Gottfried mentions using works only in Latin and French).[202] This is also true for Benoît de Sainte Maure[203] whose principal source is the originally separate Dares and Dictys; at critical junctures Benoît identifies which author he is following.[204] Or he combines the two, as in the description of the burning of the Greek ships: "Volentiers i ont les feus mis, / Si com dit Daires et Ditis" (*Troie* 25987–88) [they eagerly set them on fire, as Dares and Dictys say]. But Benoît's Prologue proper refers only to Dares. Dictys is introduced as a secondary source at the point in the narrative where Benoît first meshes his account with that of Dares (24384–424).[205] When Dares fails him after the betrayal of Troy to the Greeks, Dictys becomes the principal source on the fall of Troy and the adventures of the returning Greeks (24405–16).

Exclusion of *materia remota* is an important feature in *unir*. It may occur for a number of reasons.[206] Many Alexander romances, for example, refuse to accept Nectanabus' paternity of Alexander the Great.[207] "Omers" belongs to the *Troie*'s *materia remota,* but its introduction of pagan deities fighting mortals and alleged date of composition a hundred years after the fall of Troy made it an unacceptable primary source for Benoît. Reduction or elimination of pagan deities was not uncommon in Roman *matiere,* contrary to the tendency in Arthurian romance to euhemerize mythological and supernatural figures rather than exclude them.[208] However, Benoît did not seek modern realism. Many of the extraordinary wonders he found in his *matiere* are retained; the adventures of the returning Greeks are as marvelous as those in Arthurian romance.[209]

Benoît also refers to sources other than Dares and Dictys.

> Ço vuelent dire li plusor,
> Mais jo nel truis mie en l'autor,[210]
> Que ço fu la premiere nef
> Ou onques ot sigle ne tref,
> Ne que primes corut par mer.
> Cil qu'i osa premiers entrer,
> Ço fu Jason, ço est cuidé,
> Mais n'en truis mie autorité.
> (*Troie* 913–20)

[Although I don't find it in my authority, most claim that this was the first ship ever to have a sail or tent, or the first to sail on the sea. Jason was the first man to dare to go on board, it is thought, but I don't find any authority for this allegation.]

Other obvious lacunae in sources are left to stand when no reliable authority is available.

> Antenor, ço me dit Ditis,
> Guerpi le regne e le païs;
> Mais il ne me reconte mie
> Ou il ala n'en quel partie.
> (*Troie* 27273–76)

[Antenor left the kingdom and the country, according to Dictys; but he doesn't tell me where he went or in what direction.]

Had Benoît forgotten Antenor's fate in the *Aeneid?* Of course, the *Eneas* ignores it too.[211] Benoît's treacherous Eneas fits neither Vergil nor the Old French romance. Yet Benoît obviously did use secondary sources on occasion, and he certainly could have consulted Vergil along with Solomon (1), Sallust (77), Pliny (16541), and others he does not name outright.[212]

Divergent accounts presented special problems. Benoît found conflicting versions of the fate of Orestes and Electra, but nothing in Dictys. Like many medieval historians,[213] he refused to opt for the one or the other.

> Si en distrent li auquant
> Que a sa mere en ert alee,
> Que ert, ne sai, deuesse o fee;
> L'autre, que de forsenement,
> D'angoissos duel, de marriment,
> S'esteit por son frere perie.
> (*Troie* 29580–85)

[Some say that she went to her mother who was a goddess or fay, I don't know which; others, that she died of madness, anguished grief, and dolor.]

But he cannot establish the truth of either version: "Onc verité n'en fu seüe, / Com la chose fu avenue" (*Troie* 29593–94) [never was the truth known regarding what happened].

Materia remota presents a special attraction for Benoît, who confesses a desire to expand his romance to include all nations in a vast encyclopedic panorama.[214]

> Tel uevre voudrai embracier
> E envaïr e comencier
> Qu'en tot le mont n'avra partie,
> Ou qu'ele seit, que jo ne die
> Quel est, com grant e com bien tient,
> Ne qu'il i a ne qu'i avient,
> Quel nature ont li element,
> Quel les contrees, quel la gent.
> Tot en dirai, se jol comenz,
> Qu'a ço sofist bien nostre engenz.
>   (*Troie* 23205–14)

[I want to take up, undertake, and begin a work such that there is no area of the world, wherever it may be, which I fail to describe in its size and population, its geography and history, its material wealth, provinces, and peoples. I'll tell everything if I once start, for I have the genius sufficient to the task.]

We have seen that he would partly achieve his aim by drawing a *mappa mundi* in the *Chronique des ducs de Normandie*. His desire for universality is characteristic of the elaboration required to move from annals to chronicles.[215] The potential expansion of *materia* to include not only all versions of a given subject, but also matters that do not belong to the original subject, at least in their literal senses, recurs as the tendency to material amplification in later prose romances.[216] Benoît's desire for universality was also realized in part when his *Troie* was inserted into a world history, itself included in an Old French adaptation of the Bible; similarly, Perot de Nesle made it one branch of a cycle containing seventeen other romances.[217]

Perhaps the most ambitious twelfth-century effort to amass material for a given romance is the immense and continually expanding cycle on Alexander the Great.[218] All in all, there are four principal stages in that expansion. First was the initial adaptation into French of Latin material. Then came the continued adaptation of the original version or versions as successive romancers and scribes introduced additional *matiere,* culminating about 1185 in Alexandre de Paris' amalgam. Later came adaptations into other languages, especially German and Spanish; these works were thereby cut loose from the French-language tradition and had no further influence on it. There were also certain episodic additions, like the *Vengeance* and *Paon* interpolations, intended to complete Alexandre de Paris' version.

The *matiere de France* offers examples of cyclic expansion by *unir.* Cycles of *chansons de geste* emerge in the late twelfth and early thirteenth centuries. They contain both extant *chansons* and new works written to fill out the cycles' genealogies.[219] As written *chansons* became more common, they tended to be grouped in families about specific knights. Three prominent cycles were recognized: that of the King, or Charlemagne; that of Guillaume, or Garin de Monglane; and that of the Insurgent Barons, or Doon de Mayence.[220] A fourth potential cycle dealing with the traitors as distinct from the insurgents did not materialize.[221] These cycles are an outgrowth of the oral tradition of the jongleurs, adapted to new tastes and new styles. Consistency of style, tone, or intention in the patchwork seems to have been sporadic and irregular—the epic cyclic amalgams, for example, evince a desire more for totality than for uniformity.[222] The pursuit of completeness began in earnest in the thirteenth century, when romances and epics were often literally sewn together, or manuscripts taken apart to insert new material *(incidences).*[223] A number of titles illustrate the history of amalgams in romance, some of which have been analyzed: *Huon de Bordeaux* and its continuations,[224] the Apollonius of Tyre legend and its ramifications,[225] and the elaboration of various prose and verse cycles beginning in the thirteenth century.[226]

Chrétien de Troyes' romances sometimes show *unir. Erec's* combination of *vers* shows that Chrétien's *conjointure* combined separate *contes.*[227] The *Charrette* in the Vulgate manuscripts illustrates various "reunifications."[228] The *Perceval* also illustrates the addition and deletion of material, not only in the continuations, *Elucidation,* and *Bliocadran,* but also in scribal interventions.[229] Adenet le Roi combined pseudo-Vergilian legends and a primary source in the *Cleomadés.*[230] Such adaptations betray the intent to effect a new combination of *matiere* analogous to the principle of *unir* in Thomas' *Tristan.*[231] Transmission other than by verbatim transcription or translation, which appears to have been rare,[232] aims—apart from inadvertent scribal errors—at a new amalgam of *matiere* that corrects former shredded *(depecier),* incomplete *(corronpre),* or irreconcilable *(divers)* sources.

Realization of the Romance: *Parfaire*

Parfaire refers to the attainment of an amalgam that is complete and whole. Any mental projection *(status archetypus)* into *matiere (status sensilis)* could achieve virtual "perfection" in the finished opus, just as the relative perfection of nature's creatures reflects their perfect archetypal *species* in God's mind.[233] This model patterns all kinds of invention. Medea promised Jason success in winning the Golden Fleece because

> Engin prendreie e bon conrei
> Com ceste chose parfereies,
> Que mort ne mahaing n'i prendreies.
>   (*Troie* 1414–16)[234]

[I would find the device and the means for you to complete this thing so that you would not be killed or wounded.]

We have seen how Solomon's wife used her *engin* to realize her husband's *san* by the invention of the Ship of Solomon.[235] *San* and *engin* cooperate in the art of invention. The same cooperation of faculties allowed for the *Paon* additions to Alexandre de Paris' *Alexandre*. In the last addition, *Le parfait du paon*, Jean de la Mote explains:

> Ensi est li paons parfais pour miex parfaire
> L'ouvrage de devant[236] qui miex plaist et doit
>   plaire
> Que ne fait le darrains qu'en rime ay volu traire.
>   (3900–3902)

[Thus the Peacock is complete in order better to complete the foregoing work, which should now be more pleasing, and ought to be so, than the last one which I have tried to put into verse.]

Jean de la Mote uses a variety of expressions—*acomplir, dire mot a mot, furnir*[237]—to tell how he made the addition, all of which signify the elimination of lacunae, the deletion of extraneous or erroneous material, and the realization of a whole work. This sense of *parfaire* also occurs in Marie de France's *Chaitivel:* "Issi fu li lais comenciez / E puis parfaiz e anunciez" (231–32)[238] [here the lay was begun, then completed and published]. Such "perfection" follows from the *painne* and *antancion* that Chrétien says he used to perfect Marie de Champagne's *matiere* and *san;* Godefroi de Leigni makes this explicit by his use of *parfiner* in the romance's epilogue.

> Godefroiz de Leigni, li clers,
> A parfinee la *Charrete*[239]
>
> . . . .
>
> Tant en a fet, n'i vialt plus metre
> Ne moins, por le conte mal metre.
> (7102–3, 7111–12)[240]

[Godefroi de Leigni, the cleric, has completed the *Charrette*. . . . He has written just this much; he refuses to add either more or less, lest he upset the story's balance.]

Several scholars have argued that chronological and geographical discrepancies in Godefroi de Leigni's part of the *Charrette* prove that he did not keep to Chrétien's intent and structure, that, therefore, he did not *parfiner* or *parfaire* the romance.[241] The geographical problems here, if they exist, are no more serious than the chronological discrepancies in *Yvain*,[242] a work Chrétien himself felt to be complete and whole (*Yvain* 6804–8). For present purposes, it is enough to note that Godefroi's intention reflects Chrétien's own art of romance. Godefroi's chronology is accurate.[243] The completion of the *Charrette*—"parfinee"—is analogous to that of Meleagant's tower: "An moins de cinquante et set jorz / Fu tote parfeite la torz" (6127–28) [the tower was completed in less than fifty-seven days]. The search for perfection in place of corruption completes the passage from *materia remota* to *materia propinqua* by the successive stages called *penser, unir, parfaire*.

Morton Bloomfield has shown that "perfection" was "the simple as opposed to the diverse, or completeness as opposed to incompleteness."[244] In fact, the collection of *materia remota* into *materia propinqua* often entailed excisions, as it does in histories.

> Qui voudroit estre racontans
> Des estours des hutins des guerres
> Et de l'essil des genz des terres
> Voisines, prouchaines, lointaignes,
> Des granz travauz et des granz painnes,
> Des granz mises et des granz fais,
> A piece ne seroit parfais.
> (*Claris* 60–66)[245]

[It would take a long time to complete if anyone tried to relate the fights, battles, wars, and devastation of neighboring, near, and distant peoples and lands; the great travail and suffering, the great undertakings and great deeds.]

But if a romance leaves out some of the "granz mises" and "granz fais," is it not as corrupt as the *contes* castigated by Chrétien in the *Erec?* In short, how may one reconcile "perfection" as the "simple" and "complete" in works like *Claris et Laris* that are obviously multifarious and even incomplete? Would there not, in such "incomplete" works, be a contradiction if the author, like Godefroi de Leigni, insists that the work is complete *(parfais),* but not simple? What are the possible meanings of "perfection" in medieval narrative?

The problem of perfection is particularly crucial for the apparently incomplete romances. For example, Chrétien's *Charrette* seems truncated, since it relates only one event in Lancelot's career, but with explicit allusions to antecedent material, like his upbringing by a fay (*Charrette* 2345–47), and hints of upcoming turns in the romance, like Guenevere's expectation of a clandestine meeting with Lancelot after he defeats Meleagant (*Charrette* 6848–53). Yet, as we have seen, Godefroi de Leigni is quite firm: his part of the work will not include any more of the story of Lancelot and Guenevere because additions would "upset" the romance's *conjointure*.[246] Chrétien himself is faulted in the *Chevalier a l'espee* for not having written a romance about Gauvain; yet this romance is itself brief and episodic, hardly relating more than the Gauvain section of the *Conte du graal*.[247] Elsewhere, one manuscript of the Didot *Perceval* notes an omission in Chrétien's *Conte du graal*.[248] The *Perlesvaus* itself seems to be corrupt because it lacks an obvious beginning and end.

A similar problem is raised by excisions. The noncyclic *Lancelot* identified by E. Kennedy stops *in medias res*. The post-Vulgate *Graal* is meant to complete the Vulgate cycle, yet the text refers to its own incompleteness. How does "perfection" square with the apparent "corruption" deliberately introduced in the post-Vulgate *Graal* to assure its three equal parts?

> Et sachés que messire Robers de Borron fait savoir pour verité a tous ceulx qui cest compte liront que de ceste forcenerie qui a Lancelot avint par tel maniere comme vous avez oÿ, conte la droicte histoire de latin assés greigneurs merveilles que le françois ne devise, car il ne puet mie tant demorer sur ceste chose comme il voulist, pour ce que trop a a compter de la Queste du Saint Graal. Mez qui parfaictement vouldra oïr les merveilles de ceste forcenerie, si voie l'istoire du Brait, car illec pourra il trouver appertement toutes les choses que messire Robert laissa a compter en son livre pour ce que li .iii. livrez soient tous d'ung grant, car pour autre chose ne fut translatee d'autre part l'istoire du Brait, fors pour ce que l'en meist ens les choses que en ce livre seroient obliees a mectre. (*Folie Lanc* p. 60.581–93)[249]

> [And know that my lord Robert de Boron declares as true to all who will read this story that the right Latin *istoire* relates even greater wonders than the French does regarding the madness that befell Lancelot in the way you have heard. For

he cannot linger over this subject as he would like, having much to relate from the *Queste del saint graal.* But if you wish to hear all the marvels about his madness, read the *Histoire du Brait,* for there you will find clearly set out all that my lord Robert failed to relate in his book so that the three books that make it up might all be of the same length; moreover, the *Histoire du Brait* was translated for no other reason than to put into it everything that has been left out of this one.]

This romancer's task was obviously more complex than Jean Maillart's, who, relying on the report of a single individual, could work on his *Comte d'Anjou* "Tant qu'il ot sa perfection" (8153) [until it had achieved perfection]. But since the *Folie Lancelot* insists on avoiding "corruption," we must return to the preceding question: how does this work distinguish between "excision" and "corruption?"

The post-Vulgate *Graal* seems to compromise between "excision" and "corruption" by means of cross-references to other works.[250] Cross-reference, a device borrowed from the historians, was practiced as early as Chrétien de Troyes, whose *Yvain* is linked to the *Charrette* much as the *Folie Lancelot* is to the so-called *Brait* and to the Prose *Lancelot*.[251] Similarly, since the mental conception precedes the written work, that conception could itself determine the retention or rejection of material, as in the deletion of Governal's visit to Marc's court in Thomas' *en uni dire* digression, or the rejection of Nectanabus' paternity in the Alexander romances. Thus completeness—the totality of the *materia propinqua* implied in Thomas' *en uni dire/unir* formula—meshed with the conceptual simplicity of the work's *san,* much as *courtoisie* explains the multifarious branches of *Guiron le courtois.* Conceptual simplicity dominated narrative diversity when amplification and abbreviation introduced topical commonplaces that expressed a common signification behind narrative diversity.

Abbreviation relates to conceptual simplicity in a figurative manner. A problematic passage in the long version of *Perceval* Continuation I illustrates *in nuce* this kind of abbreviation.

> A Caradoc grant joie fait.
> Je ne vos avroie hui retret,
> Ne ne porroient estre escristes,
> Les paroles que il ont dites.
> De la joie que il ont fete,
> Vos di bien qu'elle fu parfete;
> N'i ot conté perfescion,
> N'an faz autre discrescion,
> Mais que itant an sai je bien
> Qu'a raconter ne remest riens

De tot quanquë il onques firent
Puis celle ore qu'il s'antrevirent.
(*E* 12129–40)

[They joyfully received Caradoc. I could not have told you today, nor
could one write what they said to him. I assure you that the joy they
showed him was complete. Its totality has not been related; I describe no
more of it, but I do know for sure that nothing was left to relate of all
the joy they showed him from the moment they first saw one another.]

For verse 12135, *M* reads "N'i ot rien de inperfection," *Q* "N'i ot riens de
parfeccion." Lucien Foulet comments on 12135, s.v. *parfescion:* "ce dernier
vers n'est pas clair, plusieurs explications sont possibles, nous proposons celle
qui nous paraît la plus probable: la joie fut parfaite, mais on n'y conta pas
la perfection, c' à d. ce qu'on y conta, ce n'est pas du tout la perfection (allusion aux souffrances de Carados)? *M* et *Q* diffèrent entre eux et ont des textes
contradictoires et différents de celui de *E*."[252] Obviously, this interpretation
does not eliminate the contradictions between the two other manuscripts concerning this passage: the joy in *Q* cannot be "parfete" and yet fail to evince
"la perfection." *M*'s reading seems more sensible: there was no imperfection
in their joy. In this context, *E* and *Q* agree on the sense, if not the wording:
both deny "perfection" to the written account.

Roach renders "discrescion" in 12136 (common to all three manuscripts)
as "mod. Fr. *description.*"[253] If we take his reading of *discrescion* in the medieval sense of *descriptio* as topical amplification,[254] a meaningful reading
emerges for the problematic passage. The *thema* is joy, and that joy is "perfect," that is, simple and whole.[255] But the perfection, the fullness of that
joy cannot be recorded, nor will the author amplify further (12136). If perfect joy had been amplified, it would have contained all the actions and words
of Caradoc and his hosts from the moment they met (12137–40). An author
may, therefore, keep the simple *thema* of joy, but decline to amplify on its
"perfection" by means of a description.[256] Chrétien's *Charrette* itself is in some
ways incomplete, and yet, according to Godefroi de Leigni, it is *parfinee.*
This is because the essential quality of Lancelot and Guenevere's love has
been expressed, and no more is necessary to its statement, even though the
story of that love could be continued. Therefore, if the author of the *Perceval* Continuation had chosen to amplify on the theme of joy, both material elaboration of events during the reception of Caradoc and topical
amplification of their joyous character would have provided an elaborate,
detailed description of joy in all its perfection—a description analogous perhaps in subject and in scope to the *Joie de la cort* in *Erec.*[257]

Dilation often yields to succinct, slightly humorous statement.

> Se jou de cascun devisoie
> Chou que il fist, trop demourroie
> A revenir a ma matere.
> Autre mention n'estuet querre,
> Fors que de tant que bien le fist.
> *(Manekine* 2875–79)[258]

[If I were to relate what each one did, I would take too long to return to my *matiere*. It isn't necessary to say any more than that he did well.]

We have the *somme* of the *matiere*[259] when something is so well known as to require no elaboration,[260] or the matter is so "high" as to be ineffable.

> En cele oroison si ot
> Assez des nons nostre Seignor,
> Car il i furent li greignor
> Que nomer ne doit bouche d'ome,
> Se por paor de mort nes nome.
> *(Perceval* 6484–88)[261]

[A great many names of our Lord were in that prayer, for it contained the highest names, which man's tongue should not utter unless under pain of death.]

In circumstances like these, the romancers commonly invoke the inexpressibility topic: "Le tierc de ses prouesces ne vous diroit contere, / Fontaine de tous biens, la some et la matere" *(Prise* 494–95)[262] [no storyteller could relate a third of his deeds of prowess, he who was a fountain, the very sum and substance, of all good qualities].

If perfection is not explicit, it is clearly implicit and recognizable as such. This is the case for the long *ambages* of the *Lancelot-Grail,* which the anonymous author of the *Estoire* says he has spun out from a book no bigger than a man's palm.[263] The "language of the heart" was inscribed in it.[264] But written language is lengthier and less articulate about divine mysteries, making the inexpressibility topic also an instance for amplification. Hence the length and admitted incompleteness of the prose romances when expressing "ce que langue ne porroit descrire ne cuer penser" *(Queste* p. 278.4–5) [what tongue could not describe nor heart conceive].

The prose romances demonstrate narrative and even thematic incompleteness, an unavoidable *faille,* despite the extensive amplification of narrative and themes. One kind of amplification, digression, permits such *failles.*[265] Digression included not only the kinds treated explicitly in the medieval arts of poetry and prose: chronological rearrangement, interlace, and the departure into new but thematically or narratively related subjects. As we have observed, it also included the so-called *digressio inutilis*—the digression that is incomplete.[266] That incompleteness is justified because it is the *reprise* of a pattern found in the main plot, a *reprise* so important that, at times, it dominates the plot and gives the romance its title, as in the *Atre périlleux.* A similar *digressio* occurs in the *Chievrefoil.* The description of the union of honeysuckle and hazel tree—a "graft" never made in the plot—expresses the totality of the love of Tristan and Iseut, just as the narrative of the clandestine encounter does in a minor episode in their immense story. Two parallel episodes, that of the botanical union and that of the union of Tristan and Iseut, complete one another and, in so doing, express the quintessential constancy of the *fin'amor* (*Chiev* 8) of Tristan and Iseut that permeates the entire legend.

Many authors played with such forms of incompleteness[267] in continuations that never end or in *glissements* that turn the plot aside from the story that one may expect.[268] Such "digressive" games play on perfection. They in no way belie the importance of *parfaire,* nor deny its presence when topical patterns in narrative sequence are complete. This is so in the *Charrette* as well as in the Grail plot of the Vulgate cycle.[269] In each case, the incomplete narrative is made perfect by a complete and whole model *(status archetypus)* enunciated by topical involution in the narrative.

Of course, some romances are not abbreviated, but are really incomplete, like Chrétien's *Perceval,* the First and Second *Perceval* Continuations, and Wace's and Benoît de Sainte-Maure's chronicles. Such "involuntary" imperfection inspired additions and continuations, either as beginnings, conclusions, or interpolations. Or the author may, like Robert de Boron, indicate which parts of the romance he or she was unable to complete:

> Ausi cumme d'une partie
> Leisse, que je ne retrei mie,
> Ausi couvenra il conter
> La quinte, et les quatre oublïer,
> Tant que je puisse revenir
> Au retreire plus par loisir
> Et a ceste uuevre tout par moi,
> Et chascune mestre par soi.
> (*Estoire* RoB 3501–8)[270]

[Just as I leave out one part which I don't relate, so I must tell the fifth part, leaving out the others until I can return to relate them more at my leisure, and thus complete the whole work and each part of it.]

In this way no one will think the romance imperfect in its conception. Many romancers indicate lacunae in their sources,[271] treating them like medieval historians: "Aprés ceste parole dist pluseurs choses de quoi je ne sai la certaineté" (*Cassidorus* §404)[272] [after this he said several things which I am not certain of]. One relates the *certain*.[273] Of course, such passages may be merely a narrative ploy to avoid unnecessary amplification; or they may simply cause suspense. "Ge ne sai pas quant qu'il dist la, / Quar les plusors mos consilla" (*Durmart* 839–40) [I don't know all he said there, for he said many things in private]. The narrator here is playing the eyewitness reporter; the author is not speaking. For immediately after, in verses 844–45, we learn the gist of his words: that Durmart wishes to better himself by changing his life. The passage is therefore formally analogous to the abbreviation of joy in the description of Caradoc's reception discussed above; Durmart spoke of *bonté*, a general quality to be exemplified in the ensuing plot.

The notion of the complete or perfect romance recalls Jean Frappier's theory of the Vulgate architect.[274] The architect planned the work, but may not have seen it through to completion. The evidence for the introduction of Galaad in place of Perceval as the Grail knight, for example, suggests a radical revision in the original conception at some point in the realization of the work, a revision in conformity with the more hieratic idea of the grail and the Arthurian world developed in the *Queste del saint graal* and later in the *Estoire*.[275] The change is analogous to that made to include the front portal at Chartres, the only part of the original structure to survive in the new construction: "l'unité de structure n'a pas entraîné une identité d'art et d'esprit d'un bout à l'autre du *corpus*."[276] The work was not complete or even offered as complete. Similarly, the post-Vulgate was construed as a graft onto the Vulgate, not as an entirely separate or even opposing work, despite variations in *esprit* like those Frappier pointed to in the Vulgate. Romance, especially cyclic romances like those which emerge in the thirteenth century and after, may, in the author's or "architect's" mind—like Geoffrey of Vinsauf's *status archetypus*—contain "endless possibilities of further growth. Hence the part assigned to unrealized movements, to themes projected into the future—or into the past."[277] The multiple quests or elaborate genealogies in such romances may or may not be conveyed in their entirety[278]—indeed, they may not need to be. If enough is related, the work is perfect in conception and, implicitly, in expression, since enough is said to make the reader or listener aware of the work's intention or meaning. The continual invention of amalgams to achieve "greater" perfection, indeed a universally complete and whole work, dominates the writing and copying of romance to the time of the first printed versions, as one may observe in *Perceforest* and in Michot Gonnot's exemplary B. N. fr. 93 and 112.[279] As Vinaver suggests, the potential is infinite, or at least universal. In a sense, the ultimate romance would be Benoît de Sainte-Maure's *mappa mundi.*[280]

However, the given subject may serve by itself to delimit a *matiere* and save it from being lost in expansion, like rivers in the sea. Such expansion, however artful the interlace and jointing, becomes "perplexe," and "la trop longue perplixité n'est pas bonne" (*Berinus* §576, var.2)[281] [overly complex interlace is not good]. These words, from a late, printed version of the *Berinus,* reflect the growing complexity of late medieval prose romances, with their intricate, often perplexing narrative threads.[282] *Matiere* may be extensive. But mortals do not possess God's infinite mind; therefore romancers tend to contain their *materia propinqua* within imposed but meaningful and coherent boundaries: "Ci fenissent li livre, des or mais est mesure" (*Alex* APar IV.1690)[283] [here the books end, and that is enough]. Even the author of such an "ambagious" collection of *matieres* as *Claris et Laris* tried to find suitable limits.[284]

The romancers sought the *droite voie,* at once more simple and brief. "Ja autre conte ne prendra, / La plus droite voie tenra" (*Guil d'A* 7–8)[285] [he won't take up another story, but rather will keep to the straight way]. The interlacing of *contes* characteristic of longer romances relies on artificial order, digressions, and other devices recommended in the arts of poetry and prose to ramify a given *materia.*[286] But the authors kept to the *droite voie* by insisting on control of what was appropriate, that is, of *ço k'i afiert:* "Mais des aventures que il troverent ne des painnes que il orent ne vos puis je pas faire conte fors tant que au livre en monte, ne de Gavain ne de ses compagnons" (Didot *Perc E* ll. 250–52)[287] [but of the adventures they encountered and the pains they endured I can tell you nothing now, except inasmuch as it pertains to the book—and the same is true regarding Gauvain and his companions]. Interpolations were made from secondary sources when they contributed to the elucidation of the narrative.[288] In effect, they grafted new material onto the first *matiere.*[289] Otherwise they were excluded: "cele . . . fu apielee la damoisiele dou lac, cele qui norrist grant tans en son ostel Lanscelot dou lac, ensi comme la grant ystoire de Lanscelot le devise. Mais ceste ystoire del saint graal n'en parole pas grammrent, anchois tient une autre voie" (Huth *Merlin* II, 137)[290] [she . . . was called the Lady of the Lake, who for a long time cared for Lancelot of the Lake, as it is related in the *History of Lancelot.* But this *Histoire du Saint Graal* doesn't say much about that, but rather takes another path].

The *droite voie*, however, does not preclude interlacing other *contes* about other, even relatively secondary knights. C. E. Pickford's editions of *Erec* and *Alixandre l'orphelin* are examples of this kind of interlace. There is also a Lyonel *conte* anticipated and then related in some manuscripts of the *Lancelot* Proper.[291] Such additions were intended to be complete: "Ensi remest Lyoniaus avoc sa dame, ne plus ne parole cist contes de lui ne d'aventure qi li avenist, car il a son conte tot entier" (*Lancelot* III.iv.22*) [so Lionel stayed with his lady; and the story no longer deals with him, or with any adventure that befell him. For he has his own story]. The *conte* of Lionel is a part of the complete collection of *contes*[292] never actually realized except in the mind of their architect.[293]

Such narrative possibilities, like the description of the joy aroused by Caradoc's arrival, are implicit and simple, not explicitly defined or elaborated.[294] The summary version may be sufficient for the author's intention, as in Caradoc's case; or the full account may be left for another to complete. Perfection obtains for a whole and complete work. If for some reason that ideal is not achieved, because it was physically or humanly impossible, or even willfully suppressed by deliberate deletion or neglect,[295] the admission of imperfection betrays an awareness of the goal of potential perfection.

Clearly, the idea of perfection could also be applied heterogeneously, from brief, episodic lays through episodic biographical romances like the *Charrette* to the multifarious ramifications of the great prose romances. Adenet le Roi even distinguishes between true and fanciful tales on the grounds that the latter can omit matter, whereas the former cannot (*Cleomadés* 6592–98); his distinction conforms to that between the digressions allowed historians and the incomplete but "poetic" *digressio inutilis*. Also, there are many instances of the narrator's stance expressed by *ne sai mie*.[296] But this is not to say that the phrase always is a narrator's filler, for works whose sources are extant may confirm the expression of ignorance.

Now, there is another explanation for the incomplete but still not corrupt romance. Romances often make apparent allusion to other *contes,* like that to Lionel's mentioned above or that to the *Brait* in the *Folie Lancelot*.[297] For R.S. Loomis, these allusions refer to oral tales known to the author and his or her public, and therefore not in need of elaboration in order to be understood by contemporary audiences;[298] analogous references to antique and French tales also occur.

> Donc le dut bien Lanceloz faire,
> Qui plus ama que Piramus,
> S'onques nus hom pot amer plus.
> (*Charrette* 3802–4)[299]

[Therefore Lancelot should indeed perform well, he who loved more than Piramus, if any man could ever love more than he did.]

And there are the constant assurances of auctorial opinion about other *contes* typical of the narrator's stance in romance. Vinaver's hypothesis that such references are anticipatory would not be invalidated by the existence of the tales Loomis suggested. The extant romances show that these oral versions could also be adapted and incorporated into a new romance, just as written versions could.

Invention is a word with a broad range of meanings. When Loomis argues, for example, that Chrétien de Troyes "did not invent" the narrative of a given romance, and "that one must carefully distinguish the variants which are due to borrowing from Chrétien and those which sprang from the same roots,"[300] he may be right. But it is also correct to say that Chrétien, as *trouvère,* did "invent" the narratives he found in written or oral state, that the sources of his *conjointures* are as much mental as material, as much *san* as *matiere.* Perfection requires a conception of the work as whole and complete as the joy at Caradoc's arrival; it does not necessarily entail a whole and complete account, other than by implication. Conception also prepared for topical inventions drawn from appropriate *loci;* and it permitted the identification of suitable limits for the perfect expression of the *pensers* or "meditative probing"[301] of *materia remota.* The establishment of those limits provided "cut-off points." These could in fact be so drastic as to leave the narrative incomplete when it no longer expressed ideas the author was incorporating into the new work, or when that expression would be redundant.[302] Such *desjointure* in *conjointure* could still permit the narrative whole typical of Chrétien, or it could undermine the principle of *conjointure* as he understood it, as seen in the prose cycles. In either case, the incomplete adventure enhanced *émerveillement,* whereas the truth of what was related emerged from the configuration of topical elements that, by themselves, were sufficient to reveal the meaning of the narrative through *samblance*—the image its topical form made of narrative. Analogical *reprises* permitted the achievement of a "thematic unity"[303] that vouchsafed the perfection of the work, despite apparent literal corruption. Like Norris J. Lacy, "we could argue that, since diversity possesses positive value in . . . romance, an episode which presents only a tenuous relationship to the main theme is an essential element in making the romance what it is. Remove an episode: the theme and thesis remain the same, but the work is not quite what it was before. Rearrange the loose-knit episodes of the quest: the character of the poem changes."[304] As he points out, less well constructed romances do not always realize so desirable a "balance." Nonetheless, "analogical composition" provides a principle of organization that allows both for narrative diversity (the adventure) and "thematic unity" (the truth).

Conclusion

Examination of the principal *matieres* in French romance leads to the following conclusions about the use of sources, or *materia remota*. First, virtually no romance fails to claim one or more sources, whether oral or written, in Latin or a vernacular; this conforms to expectations enunciated in the arts of poetry and prose and to medieval conceptions of invention as distinct from creation. Second, romance narrators tend to prefer written authority, especially when it is taken or construed to be that of an eyewitness. Third, the *matiere* may or may not be considered complete; however, the authors seem inclined to add something even to simple *matiere*. Fourth, care was taken to amass as much *matiere* as possible that was appropriate to the work undertaken and to make of it an amalgam of *materia propinqua*. *Verité* emerges from the romancer's *pensers,* that is, the excogitation of the sense or meaning inherent or implicit in the source *matiere* as "ceo k'i ert." Romance derived its emphasis on *matiere* and topical truth from medieval historiography. The coordination of *aventure merveilleuse* and *verité* depends on the auctorial conception of the work, the *intentio* that plots the entire narrative in its perfection. The completed work is the perfect whole, with every part in its appropriate place; it is a *bele conjointure,* or *roman* in Renaut de Beaujeu's sense.

5

Estoire: Aventure merveilleuse

Mout ert sages des set arz:
Mainte merveille saveit faire.
— Troie 6898–99

[He was well versed in the seven arts:
he could produce many a marvel.]

Molt se merveilla Blaises . . . des merveilles que Mellins li disoit et toutes
voies ces merveilles li sembloient a estre vraies et boines et beles, si i entendoit
molt volentiers.
— Merlin M 16.81–84/S 19.25–27

[Blaise marveled greatly at the marvels Merlin related to him. And yet
these marvels seemed to be true, good, and beautiful, and he listened to them
very willingly.]

Introduction: Two Levels of Narrative Coherence

Estoire was a common designation for both vernacular history and romance
in the twelfth century.[1] It comprehended two levels of coherence. One was
marvelous and frequently enigmatic, unclear, or meaningless narrative
matiere; the other was the author's *san* or conception of that *matiere.*[2] *Matiere*
and *san* correspond to the two levels of coherence Jean Fourquet identified
in Chrétien de Troyes.[3] These levels represent the simultaneous presence and
operation of a "mythic" and a "courtly" coherence in the narrative. The mythic
coherence or *matiere* evokes wonder, the courtly coherence or *san* expresses
praise or blame.[4] In effect, the *estoire* as "text is not a story, it is a commentary on the story it tells."[5] It is necessary to distinguish between *matiere* and

146

san, the two *niveaux de cohérence* through which amplification functions as story and commentary.

Amplification, or the elaboration of *san* in *matiere,* is, properly speaking, topical commentary rather than mere glossing. The topical invention that allows for such elaboration is grounded in additions to the narrative and in narrative description. Descriptive topical commentary, as *excessus,* relies on emphasis and hyperbole, and tends to develop the extraordinary and the marvelous; additional topical commentary, as *usus,* tends to comment on the generalization and simplification that point toward the ideal or commonplace.[6]

Examples of these two features of narrative—marvels and interpretation of marvels—were inherited from antiquity by way of *praeexercitamina,* especially as exercises in *narratio.* For the *san* of an *estoire* to be credible, descriptions and additions were necessary, especially given the variety of human affections which narrative must treat, as well as of actions that call forth those affections or derive from them. A narrative's credibility depends on topical amplification. "Veri similis narratio erit si ut mos, ut opinio, ut natura postulat dicemus; si spatia temporum, personarum dignitates, consiliorum rationes, locorum opportunitates constabunt . . . " (*Ad Her* I.ix.16) [the *narratio* will be credible if we recount in such a way as to conform to custom, common belief, or what is natural or normal in human affairs, and if the length of time, the rank of the persons represented, the justification for decisions taken, the sensibility of the places introduced are consistent . . .]. These qualities apply even to *fabulae,*[7] since they too must represent action that is founded on a credible truth. The resultant work will both please and instruct. These rhetorically situated features of narrative were not lost on medieval romancers. Even when the character of their *matiere* made the *estoires* seem far removed from the verisimilar, *san* retained a verisimilar or credible context.

Therefore, the marvelous features of adventures drawn from heterogeneous sources were not new to romancers. The study of rhetoric familiarized them with the extraordinary cases that, because of doubtful issue, they had to interpret and rationalize as criminal or innocent, praiseworthy or blamable, in the light of accepted usage. The cases were often literary in origin. For example, the following illustration is the source of a number of explicit rhetorical interpretations in the *Ad Herennium:*

Aiax in silva, postquam resciit quae fecisset per insaniam, gladio incubuit. Ulixes intervenit, occisum conspicatur, corpore telum cruentum educit. Teucer intervenit, fratrem occisum, inimicum fratris cum gladio cruento videt. Capitis arcessit. (*Ad Her* I.xi.18)[8]

[In the forest Ajax, after realizing what in his madness he had done, fell on his sword. Ulysses appears, perceives that Ajax is dead, draws the bloody weapon from the corpse. Teucer appears, sees his brother dead, and his brother's enemy with bloody sword in hand. He accuses Ulysses of a capital crime.]

The illustration points to the *romans d'antiquité*. But similar circumstances lead to conjecture regarding Guenevere's adultery with Keu in the *Charrette* and murder in the *Mort Artu*.[9] Such cases were the subject of the exercises in declamation discussed above (pp. 59–60).

However, when romance *matiere* undergoes amplification, it also yields the wondrous, the marvelous, the mythic in the story, and not just the commentary derived from *san*. Romance *matiere,* then, is in itself a source of fascination as well as an object of scrutiny and invention. It provides on the one hand the fascination of romance *merveilles* and on the other the topoi from which is drawn its *verité*.

Jean Fourquet's conception of the *niveaux de cohérence* applies to the finished work. But it is also useful to relate it to the art whereby the work was put together—its *mise en roman,*[10] when "reasoned commentary," or the topical cause, and "lengthened narrative sequence," or narrative articulation of the marvelous, are conjoined.[11] The process, the adaptation of the source to context, the amalgamation of *matiere* and *san,* entails the union of marvels drawn from sources *(matiere)* and of a topical *verité (san)* the author descries and lays bare in those sources.[12]

There is clearly a correlation between the marvel and its imposed context. When the narrator speaks of the marvel shared by Lancelot and Guenevere in the *Charrette,* for example, it is both the joy of love known through carnal union *(matiere)* that is meant and the context *(san)* of that love.

> Il lor avint sanz mantir
> Une joie et une mervoille
> Tel c'onques ancor sa paroille
> Ne fu oïe ne seüe;
> Mes toz jorz iert par moi teüe,
> Qu'an conte ne doit estre dite.
> *(Charrette* 4676–81)[13]

[There befell them in truth a joy and a marvel the likes of which had never yet been heard or known. But I will never say what it was, for that is something that should not be told in a story.]

The narrator's suppression here—the "intermittence" in C. Dinshaw's words—is not merely a matter of propriety or taste. First and foremost, these lines acknowledge experiences the marvel of which no romancer can adequately communicate. Chrétien makes sure, however, that the character of their union is nonetheless unmistakably courtly. One need only contrast the adoration and joy which accompany it with the seamy intercourse Meleagant imagines between Keu and Guenevere to appreciate the distinction (*Charrette* 4878–80). Guenevere herself underscores the difference between villainous and courtly love.

> Je ne regiet mie an foire
> Mon cors, ne n'an faz livreison.
> Certes, Kex n'est mie tex hom
> Qu'il me requeïst tel outrage.
> (*Charrette* 4842–45)[14]

[I don't put my body up for sale or give it to anyone. Keu is hardly the man to ask such an outrageous thing of me.]

The marvel of their love and their lovemaking is also courtly and courteous.

The *san* discerned in *matiere* by the author identifies a context which qualifies the marvel, despite its essential inexpressibility. Initially, the reader or listener wonders who Lancelot is in Chrétien's *Charrette;* he or she discovers his intended qualities and the identity of the Queen's lover — his name — only after Chrétien has flashed before our eyes extraordinary adventures that yield some knowledge of Lancelot's love. All of this forms the proper context and determines how one understands the joyous marvel the two lovers share.

This characteristic union of context and the marvelous obtains in the *Perceval* as well, where we must distinguish between the experience of the grail procession which evokes wonder in Perceval and reader alike, and the hermit's matter-of-fact answers to the unspelling questions, which are quite distinct in mode from the experience. The distinction locates direct, even carnal sensual experience of the marvel in the context within which the marvel occurs, the context which the author may amplify more or less abstractly or conceptually as the topical *verité* of an *aventure merveilleuse*. From the paradigm of invention, then, the marvel is discovered in the sources, the *verité* in *pensers*. Both undergo elaboration in the telling of the tale that contains them.

As the examples from the *Charrette* and the *Conte du graal* make clear, the distinction between the two levels of coherence, that of *matiere* and that of *san,* does not usually appear so sharp in romance. Rather, the same indistinct boundaries found in the fairy tale between what is "real" and what is not hold *matiere* and *san* in balance.[15] But, for purposes of analysis, separate treatment is desirable, since it facilitates understanding the distinct qualities of *aventure merveilleuse* and *verité* in romance; furthermore, the distinction corresponds to the two-stage auctorial response to the *matiere* of romance: first, *émerveillement,* then inquiry. This play between *merveille* and *verité* in *aventures* that makes up the romance plot is based, as in *Yvain,* on a "jeu de la vérité" (6624) which solicits the mystery of marvels in order to draw from them a deeper signification.[16] This solicitation is at the heart of invention: growing *émerveillement* with a *matiere,* constant mining of its *surplus de san.*[17]

The beautiful, if complete or universal, is both a marvel and a truth, especially in the union of material wonders (whether persons, objects, or actions) and the ethical, social, or more specifically aristocratic significance of the wonders.[18] As the epigraph for this section suggests, the romance audiences found the good, true, and beautiful in the marvels they heard related to them.

Relation between Adventure and Marvel

The *aventure merveilleuse* in romance is not reducible to a simple definition. Indeed, both words in the expression are used to refer to phenomena so multifarious and diverse as to defy useful categorization.[19] To compound the problem, modern usage or expectations—notably, the *merveilleux* as the "supernatural" or "Celtic"—does not always correspond to explicit medieval usage and expectations.[20] "Le fantastique que nous attribuons au roman médiéval est le nôtre."[21] Mutatis mutandis, the problem of the fantastic holds for the *merveilleux* as well. This is in part a matter of definition; no doubt, if one cannot find the word, one can discover elements of the modern notion of the fantastic in the medieval marvelous.[22] Besides difficulties stemming from differences in epoch, there was also variation during the Middle Ages in the function and the representation of the marvelous in romance,[23] especially when it absorbed the miracle as such.[24]

In terms of the art of romance, however, we must regard the designations *merveille* and *aventure merveilleuse* as auctorial interventions of significance. But specifically in these two terms, more than for any other feature of that art, diversity makes generalization difficult. The manifold illustrations of the two terms impede generalization because of the very specific peculiarities in their content. However, if we bear in mind that such phenomena are the *matiere* of romance, and, further, that diversity is their principal characteristic and quality, it should be possible to identify, define, and illustrate the marvel and its adventure in the paradigm of romance invention.

The narrative elucidation or amplification of marvels is frequently partial, leaving something out and hence seeming, on the whole, inscrutable.

At times, such elucidation merely points in the direction our understanding should go.[25] This is especially obvious in grail romances. But even incidental, apparently complete episodes may be mysterious, partly because they serve as a pretext for action, partly because their significance depends upon a context chosen for the entire narrative but not yet made explicit. For example, we never learn from the narrator the why or the wherefore for the flaming lance in Chrétien's *Charrette* or, to take another example, for the talking doe in Marie de France's *Guigemar*.[26] Instead, the narrative may evince a certain ambiguity regarding the *merveille* that suggests supernatural intervention. The maiden who appears to Lanval in Marie de France's lay — who is a marvel of beauty (*Lais* Lan 579–84) — also possesses magic powers. Although she is frequently called a fay by modern readers, the designation has no explicit textual justification. In this way, she illustrates the tendency in French romance to euhemerize partially the marvels of Celtic *matiere,* in which Lanval's beloved may indeed have been a fay.[27] Such euhemerism here rehearses the correction or modification of the mythological in the *romans d'antiquité.* We find the same process at work in *Partonopeu de Blois* as well, where Melior is called both a fay (1125, 4369) and a princess (1335–41). Like the Maiden of the Hidden Isles in *Florimont* or Morgain and Viviane in the prose romances, she uses her magic power to gain love. All of these women are marvels because of their extraordinary, even supernatural qualities and skills.

But the extraordinary in marvels is not necessarily inhuman, supernatural, or divine. Great feats of arms, victory and defeat, blow and counterblow, are also continually designated as marvelous, unique, superhuman. Alexander's prodigious leap from a turret onto the walls of Tyre in the *Alexandre,* for example, is a marvel,[28] but it is not supernatural. The same is true when two men alone defeat and kill forty armed opponents.[29] Nor is the supernatural necessarily the same for the Middle Ages as it is for us. Today we can give scientific explanations for phenomena that were once mysterious, extraordinary, or unique, like an earthquake, a comet, or a heavy snowfall. To medieval audiences such phenomena were marvels like Arthur's decision to slay children, the great cities and monuments of Roman *matiere,* or cannibalism;[30] the boundaries separating the marvelous from the customary were ill defined, yet often different from what we might recognize today.[31]

Merveille is usually juxtaposed with *aventure,* as in the compound expression *aventure merveilleuse.* Although the two words are close in meaning and often interchangeable syntactically — *merveilles aventurables* is also possible (*Estoire* II, 311) — they do not entirely coincide in romance usage. The romancers rarely relate adventures that are not in some way marvelous. However, the following examples using the nexus of combat, illustrate the vari-

ety of what does or does not make an adventure marvelous: "si chevaucha
en tel maniere huit jours, si coume sa voie le menoit, sans aventure trouver
qui a conter fache" (Huth *Merlin* II, 31–32)[32] [he rode on thus for a week,
following his route without encountering any adventure worth telling]. Similarly, in Chrétien's *Conte du graal,* a span of five years separates the Hideous Damsel's announcement of Perceval's failure at the Grail castle and the
Easter spent with his uncle the hermit (*Perceval* 6220–37)—five years of adventures for Perceval, not one of which is singled out for report.[33] Those
adventures are combats and as such might have interested medieval audiences.
But Perceval has proven his ability in arms. His adventures are thus not marvelous but rather meaningless because he has forgotten God. Indeed, when
Perceval remembers God on Good Friday—a conventional experience, but
here for Perceval an extraordinary occurrence—Chrétien relates the marvelous
adventure at length. Similarly, Chrétien abbreviates Yvain's victories in tournaments, but amplifies his disgrace and madness as a great marvel. Finally,
other romances include adventures like those Chrétien omits, in part as
sources of excitement for audiences which took pleasure in the combats and
sieges of early epic. The *Troie* shows that description of combat could be
artfully varied, even diverse; and the amplification of battle motifs in the
Perceval Continuations, as well as in much thirteenth-century verse romance,[34]
shows that adventure as combat for its own sake was still appealing even
when not a marvel.

   To delineate the problems more satisfactorily, we may look again at several
historical works contemporary with the romances. *Guillaume le maréchal*
in particular helps clarify the distinction between *aventure* pure and simple—
the kind not recorded in Perceval's quest for the grail—and the *aventure merveilleuse.* In William Marshall's time, knights customarily wandered about,
like Calogrenant in *Yvain* (362–66), in search of adventure.[35] Adventure was
often sought in tournaments,[36] and the extraordinary could occur even in
them. For example, Prince Henry and his knights were often defeated in tournaments (*Guil maréchal* 2565–76), something unexpected, and thus marvelous, because they were the best equipped and trained knights.

   A similar action elsewhere shows the death of a knight as part of the way
of the world and thus among those unexceptional adventures "a
prendre . . . tout ensi comme eles avient ou siecle" [to be taken as they
happen here below]. In the Huth *Merlin,* however, the maiden who loves
a dead knight is revolted at the ordinary course of worldly events. She thinks
knightly adventures are unnatural misfortunes of extraordinary magnitude:
"ces aventures . . . sont plus hounies et plus mesaventureuses que autres, dont
li preudomme muerent par tel mesqueanche" (Huth *Merlin* II, 12–13) [those
adventures are more shameful and more sinister than others when worthy

men die from such mischief]. Elsewhere, the Morholt sorts matters out by distinguishing between death by spear and death by sword. The former is merely an adventure and therefore not surprising. The latter, however, is "autre chose" because good knights do not usually slay defeated opponents by sword; the adventure becomes marvelous (*Guiron* §14).[37] Similarly, a father's grief at the death of his son is no marvel per se; it is expected.

> quer cuers ne puet mentir;
> Nature nel velt consentir;
> Autrement en fust il blasmez.
> (*Guil maréchal* 6993–95)

[For a heart cannot lie—nature won't allow it. Otherwise he would have incurred blame.]

A marvel would rather consist in the grief of a person who killed the son. Of course, extraordinary grief could be marvelous, like Gauvain's at the death of Gaheriez in the *Mort Artu*.[38]

Foreseeable behavior produces no wonder in *Guiron le courtois*: "Ce ne seroit mie trop grant merveille s'il me delivroit, car en moi delivrer ne feroit il fors cortoisie; et cortoisie devroit il faire greignor que altres, car il est meillior chevalier que autres; por ce ne seroit mie grant merveillie s'il me faisoit ceste cortoisie" (§45) [it would be no great marvel if he were to set me free, for in doing so he would be demonstrating nothing but courtesy; and he ought to be more courteous than others, for he is a better knight than others. That's why it would be no great marvel if he showed me that courtesy]. On the other hand, the love Enide's father expresses for his daughter is extraordinary, because of the intensity and purity of the paternal affection upon which Chrétien amplifies.[39] But other excesses, as viewed in the Middle Ages, like incest, homosexuality, or women performing as knights are marvels because such occurrences were deemed unnatural.[40]

The marvelous is also a matter of insight. To Merlin, for example, there can be no marvels, since he has the gift to perceive what transpires in the future, in the hidden regions of the world, and in human hearts.[41] In one episode, Arthur relates to Merlin marvels he experienced both awake and asleep. The most marvelous was the appearance of a child who knew secrets which Arthur believed no one was privy to, including the closely guarded episode of the young king's incest. The youth's extraordinary knowledge is a mystery which provokes wonder at a truth still obscure and therefore unknown or not fully comprehended. It is therefore a marvel for Arthur. Merlin, however, explains the marvelous child to Arthur as, ultimately, no marvel: "de chou ne vous devés pas miervillier, que il n'est nule si celee chose que elle ne soit descouverte. Et se la chose estoit faite desous terre, si en seroit la verités seue deseure terre" (Huth *Merlin* I, 157) [this ought not make you marvel, for nothing is so hidden but that it might be revealed. And if the thing were done beneath the earth, yet would the truth surface and be known]. Further, Merlin does not even find Arthur's wonder incomprehensible, for Arthur sees only the surface of the marvel, not its hidden explanation. To comprehend the reason or cause of the marvel dissipates *émerveillement,* the mystery disappears, and the adventure ends.[42]

The marvelous provides the mystery and singularity fundamental to romance adventure. For this reason, in spite of Merlin and similar characters, mystery is not always entirely dispelled; many adventures remain only partially known and also at least apparently causally unmotivated. The origins and mystery of the Golden Fleece are nowhere related in the *Troie.*[43] The first adventure encountered in the *Atre périlleux* long eluded any clarification that would subordinate or centralize it in the narrative, and thus explain the romance's title, which otherwise can be explained only by the sheer marvel of the adventure.[44] A marvel persists as long as it is not understood. It becomes narrative through the adventure, the purpose of which is to know and understand the marvel. As we shall see below, this is the foundation for the exemplary character of romance adventures: "Car qui bien i voudroit entendre / Maint bon essample i porroit prendre" (*Epervier* 9–10) [for whoever would listen attentively would find many a fine, exemplary lesson in them]. The exemplariness of marvels is also found in medieval historiography.

Marvel from History to Romance

In medieval historiography[45] the marvel, "objet des plus tenaces traditions orales de l'époque," was always important, "avec cette précision importante qui remonte au moins à Saint Augustin, qu'on appelle *merveilleux,* non pas ce qui le serait effectivement mais — tradition orale encore — ce qui paraît être tel. Notons tout de suite que le moyen âge s'étonne aussi facilement qu'il croit, d'autant plus qu'il ignore les lois de la nature; le merveilleux court partout dans les textes de ses historiens, il va de la plus simple surprise jusqu'à l'absurde."[46] Or, in medieval words:

> Autre aventure, autre merveille,
> Dum nule a li ne s'apareille,
> Poez oïr deu duc vaillant,
> Aiceis que plus trespas avant.
> (*Ducs* 27593–96)[47]

[Before I go on, you may hear told another adventure about the valiant duke, another marvel, unlike any other.]

Hagiography as history facilitated the inclusion of wonders as miracles[48] anticipating the supernatural explanations of extraordinary actions in Gaimar's *Engleis,* where the truth of a marvel may reveal a saint (4049–62) just as skill in hurling a sword may reveal a king (5271–86). In *Guillaume le maréchal,* on the other hand, everything seems to evoke marvel and astonishment: largess (34–35), combat (1490–93), a stone throw (1830–34), a trick (2869–74), a theft (4100–4108), the anger in a king's face (13793–800), the French king's invasion of England (14491–97), a cow that strays into the midst of a battle (16945–52), and even a great desire to sing (18528–38).

Compilation changes to composition when arbitrary recording of marvelous events gives way to the organization of events around particular figures or actions. The disparate record of the annals becomes syntagma in chronicles;[49] then syntagmatic history becomes paradigmatic when organization of the material suggests its exemplariness or significance. In this structure, the marvel focuses attention, illuminating adventures that would not otherwise seem significant.[50] Finally, the difference between chronicle and romance does not rest alone on the verifiability or fictionality of its characters. Romance evinces a tendency to single out a particular marvel as the source of adventure. The narrative relates the quest for the marvel and its achievement.[51]

The Golden Fleece is the splendid but largely gratuitous account of the beginning of Greco-Trojan enmity: the destruction of Laomedon's Troy, the abduction of Helen, the Trojan War itself, the scattering of the returning Greek fleet, and the founding of Rome and other European nations, are incidental but marvelous consequences of its achievement. From this perspective, the Golden Fleece itself also figures importantly in the *matière de Rome,* and, through Brutus, in the *matière de Bretagne*—perhaps explicitly in the lost beginning of Gaimar's chronicle[52]—and through *Partonopeu de Blois,* in the *matière de France;*[53] indeed, it is just as important as is the grail in the Arthurian world. In the search for the Golden Fleece, for Helen in the siege, for their homeland in the return voyage of the Greeks, the common denominator is the questing structure. The quest for and actual assault on or confrontation with marvels effect a meaningful concatenation of adventures, however varied in content and manner of representation. Quest and conquest coalesce.[54]

Although both romance and history (including hagiography) relate adventures and marvels, they differ in how they validate or "certify"[55] them as *matiere,* as well as in how they correlate narrative economy and sequence with the marvels. Here is where the marvelous adventure enters. As stated above, romance tends to single out one marvel as the goal of narrative adventure, and to that marvelous adventure all other adventures and marvels are made subordinate. The author of the Lancelot-Grail cycle never forgot that all adventures in Logres are there because of, and ultimately lead to, the grail.[56] To center on the marvelous adventure is to subordinate the selection of additional material to that intention. But the marvel itself must acquire coherence within the narrative economy. Unless the marvel is achieved and known by author, protagonist, and public, the romance is incomplete.

In the Middle Ages, it was assumed that there is always a hidden explanation or rationale for wonders. "Mira vero hujusmodi, dicimus non tantum propter raritem [sic], sed etiam quia occultam habent rationem"[57] [wonders of this kind are so called in truth not only because of their rarity, but also because they have a hidden rationale]. *Raritas*—the extraordinary—is presumed to have an *occulta ratio* that can be uncovered. In sacred history and hagiography, marvels reveal divine action in history.[58] Similarly, the knight's quest in romance narrative rehearses the author's inquiry into sources; together the knight and author conjoin *chevalerie* and *clergie*. Both knightly quest *(matiere)* and authorial inquest *(san)* seek marvels.

Laetus horror,[59] the medieval response to the extraordinary, was emotional, aesthetic, often profound and indelible. There is much of Jung's notion of synchronicity in the medieval reports of encounters with such acroama: "Es scheint nämlich, als ob die Zeit nichts weniger als ein Abstraktum, sondern vielmehr ein konkretes Kontinuum sei, welches Qualitäten oder Grundbedingungen enthält, die sich in relativer Gleichzeitigkeit an verschiedenen Orten in kausal nicht zu erklärendem Parallelismus manifestieren können."[60] [it seems, indeed, as though time, far from being an abstraction, is a concrete continuum which contains qualities or basic conditions that manifest themselves simultaneously in different places through parallelisms that cannot be explained causally]. This mysterious but essential relation between disparate, unique, or strange events—what Walter Benjamin has termed "transcendental resemblance" *(unsinnliche Ähnlichkeit)*[61]—explains the often profound, certainly extraordinary and even comic (because disquieting) effect of marvels on the observer, an effect which is not that pursuant to mere simultaneity. Whether Jung's explanation for such experiences is correct is not at issue here. His words are useful because they describe marvelous phenomena as they are perceived not only in modern psychotherapy but also in romance adventures. One becomes unsettled and desires to understand why and wherefore.

The response to the coincidence of the comet of 1066 and the Battle of Hastings in medieval histories illustrates this sense of analogy or synchronicity in events.[62] William of Malmesbury details the comet's passing after the deaths of Emperor Heinrich III and King Henri I of France. He dwells upon the occurrence as a portent for change of empires, and recalls the fear and wonder it provoked by the example of a certain monk who, "viso coruscantis astri terrore" [having perceived the terrible burning star], exclaimed: "Venisti . . . , venisti, multis matribus lugende; dudum est quod te vidi, sed nunc multo terribiliorem te intueor, patriae hujus excidium vibrantem" (*De gestis* §225) [you have come . . . , you have come, thing to be wept by many mothers. I have seen you for a long time; but now I behold you more terrible, quivering with destruction for this land]. William is clearly willing to accept the synchronicity of events, as in his belief that a dream of Edward the Confessor came true on Hastings field (§§226–27). These historical examples show a sense of synchronicity like that in the romances, from Chrétien to the *Queste del saint graal* and the *Mort Artu.*

The comet of 1066 announced great adventures for the Normans, the English, and the French. Benoît de Sainte-Maure also gives it prominence in the *Ducs.*

> Dunc en ceus jorz si faitement
> Aparut sus, en firmament,
> Une clartez e un planete,
> Unne resplendissant comete,
> Dunt el eisseient trei grant rai.
> Ce lis e truis e vei e sai
> Que quinze nuiz durerent bien,
> Si distrent astronomien
> Que c'ert des rennes muemenz
> O de reis o de hautes jenz.
> (*Ducs* 39007–16)

[Then in those days there appeared in the heavens a brilliance and a planet, a resplendent comet from which there issued three great shafts of light. I read and find, see and know that it lasted for two full weeks. And astronomers said that it portended the change of kingdoms, kings, or highborn persons.]

As in William of Malmesbury, the first reaction in Benoît is astonishment and marvel,[63] the second is a tentative inquiry into the event's significance:[64] "admiratio quaestionem generat, quaestio investigationem, investigatio inventionem"[65] [marvel elicits inquiry, inquiry investigation, investigation invention]. Writers did the same with their *matiere,* which they regarded as the record of marvelous adventures in the distant past.

Aventure merveilleuse springs from a hidden source, an *occulta ratio.* Medieval imagination looks for forms inbedded in things and seeks out the rationale for marvels in the shapes possible in matter.[66] This form of inquiry can be described as methodologically scientific. William deems the monk who prophesied at the coming of the comet a learned, mature person. The same monk had once tried to emulate Daedalus' flight—"fabulam pro vero amplexus" (*De gestis* §225) [taking a fable for truth]—by binding feathers to his hands and feet and springing from a tower. Disabled for life, he explained his failure by saying that he forgot the tail feathers! Nevertheless, the hypothesis is essentially scientific in that it combines analysis with experimentation. William, however, disagreed with his explanation, and advanced a different one. The monk did indeed fly over two hundred meters ("spatio stadii et plus"). Only after wind and fright overcame him did he fall.

Essential here is that both the monk and William seek to reduce the wonder of flight to physical explanations and thus a scientific rationale. Their science is, of course, medieval science, perhaps even "popular" medieval science.[67] Similarly and significantly, the investigatory mode occurs in romance. The explanation of the flower maidens in the *Alexandre* by their "nature" (APar III.3530), for example, presumes a taxonomy in nature far more credulous than is usual today. But it does show that marvels, in romance as well as in history, are deemed to have a hidden rationale and a "natural" explanation.

Explanation of events entails the inclusion of fortune, which is a common factor in adventure. The alternation between good and bad fortune, between *bele aventure* and *aventure malaventureuse,* is a phenomenon of history; it also determines romance adventures, be they natural or unnatural.[68]

> Ensi qu'il poet aler si aille,
> Car ainsi vont les aventures,
> Qui à le fois viennent moult dures
> Et à le fois miex qu'à souhait.
> Ne moustrons samblant de dehait,
> Laissons fortunne couvenir
> De tout çou que poet avenir.
> (*Mance* 636–42)

[Let it happen as it will. For that's the way with adventures, which at times are grievous, at times happier than one could wish. Let's not appear displeased, but leave fortune to decide everything that may happen.]

In the *Troie* the Trojan War exemplifies history's ups and downs by both the adventure of battle and the scattering and destruction of the Greek navy at the end.[69] Put in the larger context of the *Troie* and also of the *Chronique,* the scattering of the Trojan survivors led to the foundation of all the major nations of Western Europe. The transferral or translation of civilization, when not an effect of divine will, is usually construed as subject to fortune.

Fortune, whether represented by haphazard ups and downs or regular cycles, is beyond human control: "Or advint que par la grace de Dieu que fortune se leva en la mer, et uns orages et tempeste si horrible . . . " (*Melusine* JdA p. 128.26–27) [now it happened by the grace of God that fortune rose up at sea together with a storm and frightful tempest]. But fortune's effects may be dealt with by concentration of purpose and the exercise of will.[70] Thus, in spite of fortune's rotations, the knight in Condé's narrative forces his lady's hand by his own constancy: he passes back and forth before her castle for two weeks, "Dont ses gens orent grant mierveille" (*Mance* 1795)[71] [whereat his retinue marveled greatly]. Repetition makes his act extraordinary, and his household marvels at such to them incomprehensible constancy. That constancy is the hidden rationale *(san)* of the marvel he acts out. Or, for example, in *Amadas et Ydoine,* Ydoine experiences two great adventures. One, abduction by a devil, comes about through the chance turn of fortune's wheel (7130–36). The other stems from a prevarication, but the actions of the victims indicate what is appropriate in such "misfortune." Ydoine predicts the death of her husband if he consummates their marriage; that "fate" is circumvented by dissolving the marriage.[72] In both cases, purposive action neutralizes fortune and resolves matters favorably.

Although common usage ascribes adventures to fortune and the adventurer's purposefulness,[73] they may also come about by the intervention of God, the devil, the gods, or some undefined force or agent in social or moral stasis. This kind of adventure is frequently termed *destinee,* a notion analogous to *fatum* in Latin, but broad enough to include Christian notions of divine intervention, intention, and foreknowledge.[74] In these cases, the record of such *destinee* is itself a narrative *aventure.* "Or sachiez que nos trovons en escrit que Blaise nos reconte, si come Mellins le fist mestre en aventure, que au jor que Percevaux se desparti de son oncle . . . " (Didot *Perc D* 1256–58) [know then that we find it written in what Blaise reports to us, just as Merlin had it written down as an adventure, that on the day Perceval left his uncle . . .]. Many romancers are quite explicit about narrative as a record of past adventure.[75] "Car après nos mors quant elle sera amenteue a nos hoirs, elle sera moult voulentiers escoutee et oie, car trop est mervilleuse" (Huth *Merlin* II,43) [for after our deaths when it will be mentioned to our heirs, it will be eagerly listened to and heard, for it is most marvelous]. Recording adventures for future generations upholds aristocratic civilization.[76]

Representation of the Marvelous Adventure: Exaggeration and Incongruity in the Rhetorical Tradition

Romance legend emphasizes the desire of the alleged "original" authors to record marvelous adventures so that succeeding generations might remember them. The topic, to be effective, requires amplification of the marvels found in the sources. This raises the problem of the representation of the marvelous adventure in written narrative. Historians and romancers alike relied on the traditional art of description and narrative amplification to represent the marvels in their sources and thus transmit them in a striking but "visible" manner.

Exaggeratio as overstatement[77] entails the selection of attributes that move the object out toward the marvelous. Like the stuff of dreams, the object of *exaggeratio* may sometimes seem to admit from the extreme limits of consciousness extraordinary shapes and forms that appear uniquely portentous and wondrous.

> Cum inter vigiliam et adultam quietem in quadam, ut aiunt, prima somni nebula adhuc se vigilare aestimans, qui dormire vix coepit, aspicere videtur irruentes in se vel passim vagantes formas a natura seu magnitudine seu specie discrepantes variasque tempestates rerum vel laetas vel turbulentas. (*Somnium* 1.3.7)[78]

> [As between waking and deep sleep, in a certain so-called first cloud of sleep we believe we are still awake when one who has scarcely begun to sleep, but thinks to be still awake, seems to perceive rushing in or wandering about shapes that differ in size or kind from their natural form, as well as the happy or unfortunate turn of events.]

Such fabulous descriptions induced critical medieval readers to liken "romanz de vanité"[79] to dreams.

> Cume de fable e de menceonge
> La matire resemble sounge,
> Kar iceo ne put unkes estre.
>   (*Edmund* 29–31)[80]

> [The *matiere* resembles a dream, as in fables or lies; for such a thing could never be.]

And yet, such "dreams" may, by *exaggeratio,* represent a truth despite their apparent unreality: "ut, audita loci venustate, coniecturale esset argumentum Verrem in loco *tante* pulchritudinis sibi a Cicerone deputatum licentius commisisse adulterium" (*Ars vers* 1.110; my emphasis) [so that when his readers understood the loveliness of the country, they would consider Verres, who committed adultery in the midst of *such great* beauty, to have even more unbridled lusts than Cicero had imputed to him]. The attraction of exaggerated description holds for the *Joie de la cort* in *Erec*. Like Cicero, Erec corrects the misuse of the *locus amoenus* by defeating Mabonagrain, an opponent of extraordinary size and strength—"granz a merevoilles" (5850) [wondrously big]. The ensuing joy is unparalleled.

> Onques tel joie ne fu feite;
> Ne porroit pas estre retreite
> Ne contee par boche d'ome,
> Mes je vos an dirai la some
> Briemant sanz trop longue parole.
> (*Erec* 6119–23)[81]

[Never was such great joy expressed—it could not be related in its totality by human tongue. But I'll tell you the sum of it briefly and in a few words.]

In rhetorical terminology, this is *exaggeratio,* or magnification.

At the same time, *exaggeratio* often produces a singular disparity between the description of romance marvels and their appearance in the narrative itself.[82] The beauty of Fenice and Cligés illuminates the hall at their first appearance in the romance, yet at night Fenice can be smuggled unnoticed out of the cemetery she was buried in after her false death. A knight may attack what is called a giant, and still, with both feet on the ground, cleave his head. The giant and Fenice's light belong to hyperbole, by which "Cursum sermonis mihi tendere convenit ultra / Quam poscit veri regula recta pati" (*Laborintus* 415–16) [my statement appropriately stretches the truth]. This sort of *exaggeratio* assured clarity in immediate representation while enhancing the marvelous quality of the description.

Hyperbole functions as a principle of organization and intensification in narrative, focusing while it magnifies.[83] In romance it served the adaptation of the marvelous adventure[84] from the *materia remota* to the auctorial conception of the sources. In effect, it streamlined the marvel, without sacrificing exuberant description.[85] This applies to marvelous events or to phenomena ranging in diversity from the natural to the supernatural. An extraordinarily heavy rain, snakes and beasts in the desert, maidens alone in the woods, automata that make music in splendid palaces set in the middle of nowhere, a fountain of youth, prophetic trees—these phenomena in the *Alexandre* are descriptive marvels set in Asia and faraway India.[86] Similarly, Alexander, like Xerxes, has his men punish the sea with whips because of a storm; in retaliation, Neptune sends a great serpent:

une semblance en guise de poisson
Errant par mi la mer, fendant a esperon;
La guele porte ouverte a guise de dragon
Et giete feu et flambe fierement a tençon,
Les nez et la cité aclot tout environ;
Adont leur recommence grant tribulacion,
Une ire, une tempeste, une confusion
Qui leur nez achanterent, et froissent li chevron;
Par un po que ne furent cueilli li paveillon
Quant en mer se refiert a guise de plunjon.
                                    (*Alex* APar I.2755–64)

[An appearance like a fish came through the sea at great speed. It held its mouth wide open like a dragon, spitting fire and flame fiercely and aggressively. It completely surrounded the boats and the city. Then began anew great travail, vexation, storm and disarray, the boats capsized and their rudders shattered. The tents themselves were on the verge of being engulfed, when it turned and plunged back into the sea.]

Yet Alexander continues to lash the waves. So another marvel occurs: the arrows forged by a blacksmith in the city begin to bleed, presaging the death of Alexander's soldiers. Nonetheless, the serpent withdraws, the walls are scaled, Alexander achieves the adventure, taking the city of Tyre despite Neptune's marvels by his own marvelous leap onto its walls. The elaborate hyperbole used to describe these marvels makes them explicit and clear as extraordinary adventures in which the hero prevails. But the intensification does not allow the description as such to be imposed on the narrative; rather it aids in organizing and focusing the narrative on the hero. The marvels evoke wonder before returning to the proportions of the story being told.

Hyperbole influences the audience's response to marvelous adventures in two ways. First, it provokes surprise and amazement, even comedy or irony; this tends, at first blush, to quiet critical judgment. Second, on reflection, hyperbole is exaggeration not meant to deceive.[87] Rhetoric and poetics saw in it a means to accommodate the extraordinary and the customary (*excessus* and *usus*);[88] it must therefore be understandable within the context of the romance.

Currat yperbolicus, sed non discurrat inepte
Sermo: refrenet eum ratio placeatque modestus
Finis.
                                    (*Poetria nova* 1013–15)

[Give hyperbole rein, but see that its discourse does not run ineptly hither and yon. Let reason keep it in check, and its moderate use be a source of pleasure.]

Medieval romance tends to thrust the marvel forward in its hyperbolic extremity and uniqueness, then gradually incorporate it into the narrative through the adventure. A concomitantly gradual deflation ensues, even while a sense of the extraordinary persists. In large measure the achievement of the adventure reduces the hyperbolic to extraordinary human achievement. Or, in other words, the author accommodates the marvel to the audience's narrative and idealistic sensibilities and expectations. Thus, for example, Yvain's first fountain adventure does not preclude his returning to the fountain; but emphasis passes from the supernatural to the comic.[89] The marvel itself has lost none of its attributes. It has merely been incorporated into a meaningful economy: the context of the Round Table and Chrétien's *san*.

"Exaggeration" as emphasis, an established technique for topical description in classroom compositions, served the representation of the marvelous but obscure sources of romance. Delineation of marvelous features made a link possible with the romance *san* if the marvel could be seen, confronted, and amplified upon with the usual devices of topical invention. This is true even if, independent of the narrative milieu in which it is placed,[90] it has only a tenuous link to the rest of the romance. The palace of Ysopet in the *Berinus,* the chamber of beauties in the *Troie,* the walls of Carthage in the *Eneas,* produce no adventure and require no narrative. The shipwrecked Trojans perceive the walls of Carthage in all their splendor, then pass unimpeded into the city; ironically, the defenses admit rather than close out the city's enemies. Similarly, Chrétien often builds suspense on a marvelous adventure, then bypasses it in the narrative to surprise us with a different, unexpected, but equally marvelous adventure.[91] Description as expression of *san* enhances marvels drawn from *materia remota* by amplifying on their wondrous parts and attributes in conformity with auctorial intention and narrative context.

To return to the initial problem of this section: Is it possible to define or otherwise characterize such extraordinary or incongruous phenomena, to find common features in such diversity? No single example is or can be typical; no definition based on it can be all-inclusive.[92] Marvels exhibit meanings, applications, and functions so various and often so subtle as to preclude useful synthesis or classification. "Le motif merveilleux . . . est complexe, il est plurivalent. . . . Il agit sur les sens, sur l'imagination, sur la volonté des personnages qui le contemplent dans sa forme réalisée, ou s'en servent, ou ne peuvent s'en servir; il agit directement ou indirectement. Il incite, il persuade, il commande, il console, il protège ou il punit."[93] The diversity, however, meets traditional expectations in narrative.

Narratio in classical rhetoric relied on variety and surprise in plots replete with adventures and marvels.[94]

> Hoc in genere narrationis multa debet inesse festivitas confecta ex rerum varietate, animorum dissimilitudine, gravitate, lenitate, spe, metu, suspicione, desiderio, dissimulatione, errore, misericordia, fortunae commutatione, insperato incommodo, subita laetitia, iucundo exitu rerum. (*De inv* I.xix.27)[95]

> [This form of narrative should possess great vivacity, resulting from fluctuations of fortune, contrast of characters, severity, gentleness, hope, fear, suspicion, desire, dissimulation, delusion, pity, sudden change of fortune, unexpected disaster, sudden pleasure, a happy ending to the story.]

Cicero's definition of *narratio* facilitated carrying the marvelous anecdotes from Greco-Roman narrative into the Middle Ages via the classroom, and helped establish emphases and predilections among romancers trained in that tradition.[96] It met contemporary fascination with the marvelous in the traditions and folklore of Eastern, Celtic, and French *matières*.

The marvelous phenomena of these sources range from the apparently incongruous (that is subsequently shown to be not really so), through the really incongruous (that can, however, be eliminated), to the unexplained (and ultimately inexplicable). Incongruity, for example, can perhaps best be illustrated by romances in which two *matieres* are meshed in one work, each with its own typical *merveilleux*. For objects of marvel in Roman *matiere* are often different from the Arthurian or French kinds, although to represent them romancers used the same techniques.[97] But by the thirteenth century Roman and French subjects were also absorbing motifs and themes from Arthurian romance and then amplifying them as in the first *romans d'antiquité*. This is particularly evident in the Seven Sages of Rome and the Huon de Bordeaux cycles.[98] While the trial motif of the early Seven Sages romances is dropped almost altogether in branches after *Marques*, Arthurian adventures come more to the fore, sometimes explicitly set in the Arthurian world (*Laurin*), sometimes merely emphasizing the quest as a pattern for the marvelous adventure (*Helcanus, Pelyarmenus, Kanor*).[99] The extraordinary in marvels made them welcome in all three of Bodel's *matieres*. For example, a setting that turns heroes into cowards and makes fearless the timid is found in a variety of works.[100] The transfer of adventures or marvels common in one *matiere* to another is usually striking and more or less incongruous. But whether blend or admixture, such themes, motifs, and descriptive amplifications—unexpected because characteristic of another kind of *matiere*—enhance the sense of *émerveillement.*[101]

Chrétien's *Cligés* is an early example of the successful amalgamation of Greco-Roman and Arthurian marvels. The first part, on the loves of Alexandre and Soredamors, contains extensive marvelous amplifications: the descriptions of Soredamors and the love monologues hark back to *Eneas,* while the descriptions of combat and siege are typical of all *romans d'antiquité.* Alexandre's trick to get into Angrés' castle at Windsor, like his namesake's leap onto the walls of Tyre, is "un hardemant molt perilleus / Et . . . un vice molt merveilleus" (*Cligés* 1803–4) [a most perilous act of courage and a most wondrous deception]. Further, as if the Romans had again invaded Britain, Eastern flowers bloom under an Arthurian sun.

> Tant fu preuz et de fier corage
> Que por pris et por los conquerre
> Ala de Grece an Engleterre,
> Qui lors estoit Bretaigne dite.
> (*Cligés* 14–17)

[He was so worthy and of awesome disposition that, in order to win renown and fame, he went from Greece to England, which was then called Britain.]

Similarly, intertextual play with motifs from the Tristan legend further diversifies the romance's marvelous features.[102] In the second or Cligés part of the romance, there are marvels drawn from both the Tristan legend and a tale about a *fausse morte,* probably derived from some version of the Seven Sages of Rome.[103]

> Il feront tele mervoille
> De li qu'ainz ne fu la paroille
> De nul cors de fame cheitive.
> (*Cligés* 5885–87)

[They will work a wonder on her the likes of which was never perpetrated on a wretched woman's body.]

Fenice herself confirms the fact that "Mervoille iert, se vive an eschap" (6190) [it will be a marvel if I come out of this alive]. Around this marvelous adventure (cf. 5938) (which is also found in *Marques de Rome, Amadas et Ydoine,* and elsewhere),[104] Chrétien groups amplified marvels like those in the first part of the romance as well as in the *romans d'antiquité:* descriptions of human beauty, combats, monologues and dialogues, marvelous architecture.

"Or oi mervoille" (*Cligés* 5527) [now I hear a marvel], exclaims Cligés when he learns of the secret tower Jehan is prepared to turn over to him and Fenice. Thus, the *Cligés* contrasts with and adapts the extraordinary Tristan legend with its love potion, a *Cligés* analogue, as well as the marvelous architectural phenomena of the *romans d'antiquité,* to the Arthurian ideals and conduct typical in Chrétien's other romances. The romance is an incongruous yet artistically successful amalgamation of marvels drawn from heterogeneous sources *(matiere)* and ingenious inventions *(san).*

Commonplace motifs are also potential marvels. In the second part of *Cligés,* both Cligés and Fenice receive a brief but hyperbolic description.

> Por la biauté Clygés retreire
> Vuel une description feire,
> Don molt sera bries li passages.
> (2721–23)[105]

[To relate Cligés' beauty I wish to make a description, but one which will be very brief.]

Later, when Cligés hears of Fenice's abduction by the duke of Saxony's men, his rage is unbounded (3654–67). But the real marvel is the self-control and deliberation he exercises in rescuing her: "Einz est mervoille qu'il n'enrage" (3657) [rather it's a wonder he doesn't go mad], explains the narrator. On their safe return, the Greeks extol and wonder at Cligés' prowess, as the Britons did before when Alexandre his father returned with Angrés as his prisoner.

> Cil qui l'oent
> Molt s'an mervoillent et molt loent
> Sa proesce et son vasselage.
> (3897–99)

[Those who hear it wonder greatly, and praise highly his prowess and knighthood.]

But Cligés' love produces another marvel, so extraordinary as to elicit the topsy-turvy topic: the valiant hero knows a lover's fear when alone with Fenice (3793–3812). The description of the single combat with the duke of Saxony enlarges upon the relation between love and prowess that explains the marvelous victory, a victory prefigured by Cligés' surpassing beauty. Such developments are founded on the marvels represented hyperbolically by the beauty and inner qualities of Fenice (2692–94) and Cligés (2752–59). Thus Chrétien makes exaggeration and incongruity fit the sense of the romance, demonstrating how the diversity of the marvelous *(matiere)* may be grasped through appropriate rhetorical tools.

Spectrum of Marvelous Adventures

In contrast to the often perfect combination of physical, social, or intellectual attributes that characterizes the idealized figures and courts of romance are the totally disparate but marvelous amalgamations and even conglomerations that make up their adventures. Typical of the latter are the *bestes diverses* of the prose romances: "Chele beste estoit tant diverse que nus hom tant l'avisast, ne seust a dire de quele maniere ele estoit, (ele avoit toutes diversites)" (*Estoire* II, 272/I.69.15–17)[106] [that beast was so diverse that no one, no matter how much he or she considered it, could say what manner of beast it was (it embodied all diversities)]. Another example is the beast that guides the narrator in the Prologue to the grail book he copies from: "com plus le regardoie, mains pooie savoir quex biestes chou estoit, et sachiés qu'ele estoit diverses en toutes coses: que ele avoit tieste et col de brebis et blanc comme nois negie; et si avoit pies de cien et jambes et quisses, et tout çou estoit noir comme carbons; et si avoit le pis et le cors et la crupe de goupil et keue de lyon. Ainsi estoit la beste de diverses semblances" (*Estoire* II, 25–26/I.9.2–7) [and the more I considered it, the less was I able to discern what kind of beast it was. For you can rest assured that it was exotic over all other beasts. For its head and neck were like those of a lamb and were whiter than new fallen snow; and it had the feet, legs, and thighs of a dog, and these were black as coal. And it had the chest, rump, and body of a fox and the tail of a lion. It was therefore a beast of diverse kinds]. The grail itself is no less diverse, both as "actual" object and as allegorized in the dreams, visions, adventures, and commentary it provokes. By contrast, the *maniere* of the Arthurian court, as well as of those who populate it, is like Lancelot: "che fu, che dist li contes, li plus biax enfes del monde et li miex tailliés de cors et de tous menbres; ne sa fachons ne fait pas a oublier en conte, mais a retraire oiant toute gent qui de grant biauté d'enfant voldront oïr parler" (*Lancelot* VII.ixa.3) [the story says that he was the most beautiful child in the world, the best shaped in body and in all his limbs; and his appearance should not be left out of the story, but rather told to all those who wish to hear tell of great beauty in the young]. Even certain "enormities" fit into Lancelot's *maniere,* just as they do into Arthur's court,[107] notably the great chest which holds a large and loving heart, and the tendency to folly when under severe emotional stress (*Lancelot* ixa.4–5). This ideal figure is extraordinary, unique, extreme in his removal from ordinary acts and feelings: "ne de sa maniere

ne fu onques enfes veus, car ja nus ne li veist faire malvais samblant, se droite
raison n'i eust, teile dont nus hom nel deust par droit blasmer" (*Lancelot*
ixa.7) [nor was there ever seen a young man of his kind, for no one ever
saw him put on a bad expression, unless he had good reason to do so, one
that no one rightly should blame him for].

Diversité in *maniere* ranges from the extraordinary to the extreme.[108] This
concors discordia (Geoffrey of Vinsauf) of disparate elements assumes a design that turns the representation into an image. "Sic se contraria miscent,
/ Sed pacem spondent hostesque morantur amici" (*Poetria nova* 834–35)
[thus contrary qualities mingle, but they promise peace, and, enemies once,
they stay on as friends]. The incongruous exists as such by removal from
a given locus, often identified with a court, a house, or a castle. By its own
qualities that locus represents the context the author idealizes or vituperates
in the knight or lady who ventures forth in search of "la plus mierveillouse
aventure del monde" (*Estoire* III, 11/I.164.16–17) [the most wondrous adventure in the world]. Such a range of marvels produces a spectrum of the
merveilleux extending from the topical marvel to enchantment and mystical
experiences, from the extraordinary to the unique, from dissemblance to the
extreme.

Of course, these categories in the spectrum blend into one another in the
examples. I have nevertheless categorized the range of marvels in romance
by illustrations that emphasize one of the three primary colors in the spectrum.

The Extraordinary

The extraordinary[109] designates the unusual and uncommon, the striking and
remarkable, the excessive. It may also suggest mystery or hidden significance,
the *ratio occulta* of the historians. For "un acte insolite . . . , la rupture de
l'ordre établi, tout cela constitue aux yeux du chroniqueur un fait merveilleux,
un prodige et, le plus souvent, ce prodige a la valeur d'un présage."[110] The
negation, *n'est merveille,* shows that the obvious is no marvel.

> Qu'il n'est merveille, ce m'est vis,
> S'en ne set che c'on n'a apris;
> Mais merveille est quant on n'aprent
> Ce que on ot et voit sovent.
>   (*Perceval* 523–26)

[For it seems to me no wonder not to know what one hasn't learned. But
it is a wonder not to learn what one hears or sees frequently.]

To deny the marvelous shows that the object under consideration is comprehensible or expected, that it elicits no astonishment because it has a

meaningful place in the world. As adventure, that which is not marvelous may in fact serve an eminently social function in and of itself.[111] Knights customarily seek adventures to test their mettle.[112] But when the expected fails to occur, something extraordinary may happen. "Toujours l'irruption de l'événement extraordinaire ouvre aux héros et aux héroïnes l'accès à un monde autre que celui où ils vivaient auparavant."[113] Jean Renart's use of *aventure* and *merveille* suggests the relation between the two phenomena in romance.

> "Sire, fet il, vos ne savez?
> Puis cele heure que Dex fu nez,
> Neïs au tens le roi Artur,
> Ne sai se c'est par vostre eür,
> N'avint ausi bele aventure,
> Ce cuit, de nule creature
> Com il a la fors avenu.
> —De qoi?—Quë il i a venu
> Une mervelle tote droite,
> La plus bele et la plus adroite.
> Ne sai se c'est ou fee ou fame,
> Mes ou marchié n'a remez ame,
> Ainz l'ont tuit a procession
> Amenee d'une meson
> Dusqu'en cest grant palés la hors."
> (*Dole* 4679–93)[114]

[He said: "My lord, you don't know? Since the birth of our Lord, and even in Arthurian times, such a beautiful adventure never befell anyone, methinks, as occurred outside—whether it be the result of your good fortune, I don't know." "An adventure involving whom?" "There came a real marvel, the most beautiful and most exquisite. I don't know if she be fay or woman, but not a soul remained in the marketplace, rather all conducted her from a house to just outside this great palace."]

In Marie de France's lay, the arrival of Lanval's mistress and her attendants at Arthur's court is no less remarkable, nor is the effect any less wonderful (*Lais* Lan 575–92). Indeed, she and Liénor in *Guillaume de Dole* are sisters: "Ne sai se c'est ou fee ou fame." The same ambiguous, half-fay half-human quality of the heroines in *Florimont* and *Partonopeu de Blois*[115] explains their ambiguous, extraordinary effect. Even the disappearance of the distinction between fay and woman, the supernatural and the natural, may leave the unnatural, or, again, the extraordinary as differentiated from the expected.

In romance, there is universal astonishment and fascination before the appearance, or apparition, of extraordinary human beauty like Liénor's. The

Guillaume de Dole passage uses her extraordinary features to elicit subjective, affective fascination. In it, the extraordinary is immediately incomprehensible, even mysterious, the marvel a *je ne sais quoi* that is experienced, but not expressed or understood in its totality.[116] When it does become known, the marvel becomes the ordinary or mundane, as the extraordinary is assimilated into an ordered world. This occurs with the marriage of Liénor and the emperor. The extraordinary, however, may not be assimilated into a known world, as in Lanval's departure for Avalon. Similarly, the dragon that calls forth Guinglain's quest in the *Bel inconnu* is transformed by the *fier baisier* into the beautiful Blonde Esmeree, who becomes thereby acceptable, with Guinglain himself, at Arthur's court. This assimilation into an ordered world contrasts with examples of nonassimilation like the traditional failure to integrate Tristan and Iseut, transformed by the potion, into Marc's court. The marvel of their love is not only extraordinary, its extraordinary nature cannot even be properly assimilated by the lovers themselves, even in Thomas' version;[117] it finally destroys them, not the court. The grail has a similar destructive effect in the Lancelot-Grail cycle, as does the Golden Fleece in Benoît's *Troie*.

The Unique

The marvel, whether supernatural or not, may be unique when it is totally different *(divers)* or outlandish, or when it is a consummate exemplar of its type or class.

> Molt estoit la pucele gente,
> Car tote i ot mise s'antante
> Nature qui fete l'avoit;
> Ele meïsmes s'an estoit
> Plus de .Vc. foiz mervelliee
> Comant une sole foiee
> Tant bele chose fere pot;
> Car puis tant pener ne se pot
> Qu'ele poïst son essanplaire
> An nule guise contrefaire.
>   (*Erec* 411–20)[118]

[The maid was very noble. For Nature who fashioned her had applied
herself totally to the task. Nature herself marveled five hundred times over
at her success in producing such a remarkable being. For she could never
again strive enough to be able to emulate in any way her exemplar.]

The marvel is thus implicitly unique, either by its extraordinary mythic origins or by its consummate exemplariness. The relative preponderance of the

one kind of marvel or the other—the mythic marvel or the topical marvel—
distinguishes between marvelous and exemplary romance.[119] The former is
most evident in Beroul or *Perceval* and its first two continuations, while the
latter dominates in *Cligés* and *romans roses* like Jean Renart's, where the
tension between marvel and truth manifests itself as "le résultat, infiniment
variable, de tensions contradictoires entre la faculté d'imagination et le souci
d'adhérence au réel."[120] Liénor in *Guillaume de Dole* is a marvel, but one
no more supernatural than Fenice; both display unique beauty. Both the
mythic and the conventional marvel attest to the expectation of the marvelous
as a component of *estoire*.

Despite the virtually infinite variety of phenomena that are designated marvel, some do, to be sure, recur in different works as analogues in the transmission of themes, motifs, and images.[121] Chrétien, for example, was well
aware of this *literary* propensity to repeat marvels. If Nature could not repli-
cate Enide's beauty, he could. In *Cligés*, Fenice is a unique exemplar of beauty
and virtue, despite the proclamation of Enide's unique excellence in *Erec*,
and, closer to Fenice, even after Cligés' mother, Soredamors, is praised for
her extraordinary—and unique—qualities (439–49, 762–849). Chrétien himself plays with the multiplicity of such uniqueness, which functions like the
phoenix, a continually resurrectable marvel.

> Fenyce ot la pucele a non:
> Ce ne fu mie sanz reison,
> Car si con fenix li oisiax
> Est sor toz les autres plus biax,
> Ne estre n'an pot c'uns ansanble,
> Ice Fenyce me resanble:
> N'ot de biauté nule paroille.
> Ce fu miracles et mervoille
> C'onques a sa paroille ovrer
> Ne pot Nature recovrer.
> (*Cligés* 2685–94)

[The maid was named Fenice, and not without reason. For just as the
phoenix is more beautiful than all other birds, and just as there can be no
more than one at a time, so Fenice, it seems to me, had no equal in
beauty. She was a miracle and a marvel, for Nature could not reproduce
her likes.]

Now, each of these beauties does have a distinguishing feature topically added to the perfect exemplar and paramount in the narrative: Enide's poverty
(a blemish that does not quite hide her beauty), Soredamors' disdain for love,
and Fenice's preoccupation with total sexual fidelity. Like Lancelot's large
heart in the Vulgate, these refining adaptations make the marvel unique.

Descriptions of marvelous beauty in Chrétien's subsequent romances—*Yvain* (1148–65, 1465–1510) and *Perceval* (1795–1829)—stress the same uniqueness in commonplace images.[122]

By *exaggeratio* the principal objects of medieval imagination—the lance, the woman, and the grail—serve successive meditations on commonplace persons and things made unique. The representation—as distinguished from the contextual elucidation—of marvel is often remarkably different from adaptation to adaptation, because some distinguishing marks provide in themselves for uniqueness, like the rose on Liénor's thigh in *Guillaume de Dole* or Laudine's self-inflicted laceration of her beauty in *Yvain*. Further, these distinctive marks play against the commonplace: we perceive Laudine's beauty through her grief, as we see Soradamors' beauty allowing her to be transformed into an arrow in Alexandre's mind. These refining adaptations allow the commonplace to become a unique re-creation.

Unlike the adapted commonplaces regarding the uniqueness of women's beauty, adventures, as the manifestation of fortune and passageway to marvels, may or may not be unique. Calogrenant's defeat at the fountain, for example, is not unique because most knights had or would have suffered the same fate (*Yvain* 404–7). A range of exceptionality from the ordinary adventure through the extraordinary to, finally, the unique encounter defines fortune's adventures.[123] Indeed, Chrétien allows the fountain to undergo multiple and differentiating representation, thereby mirroring what occurs when a commonplace marvel is adapted to a new romance. Thus the supernatural spring is encountered first in Calogrenant's adventure; then it is achieved by Yvain in an extraordinary way; next, Keu brings in the element of humor in comic distortion. Next, the fountain further becomes the focal point for Yvain's quest, as he rotates about and occasionally touches back at the fountain, signaling a shift in focus from the adventure itself to its hero; and the final unleashing of storms leads to Yvain's reunion with Laudine, a conclusion that brings together both the marvelous and the humorous features of the preceding fountain adventures.[124] Yvain is, in the last adventure, both defender and aggressor at the fountain, emphasizing the change of roles and hence the transferability of the marvelous adventure. In this way, Chrétien sustains the *aventure merveilleuse* that is supernatural and topical, unique and recurrent, one and diverse.

The kaleidoscopic sequence of objects designated as the grail in the various grail romances (a variation that betokens its mystery or ineffability, and borders on transmogrification in the *Queste*) is authenticated by the mysteries to which the grail is conjoined; they provide the hallucinatory, visionary ambience into which it finally disappears with its secrets. It is consistent with the marvel that the unsuccessful knights in the *Queste,* untouched by the grail's illumination, encounter no adventures, or, if they do, fail to understand them.

Their careers are also unique, terminologically distinguished from the grail adventures by words like *mescheance* and *mesaventure*.[125] The special status of a grail knight may be exemplified through Lancelot. Lancelot relies on the queen whose love, he believes, made possible his extraordinary achievements. When he learns, tragically, that Guenevere actually weakened rather than strengthened him, he realizes that his conduct must change to fit the new source of his worthiness, the grail. He accordingly sits down, much as he at times performed *au noauz* in Chrétien and in the *Lancelot* Proper. Henceforth boats and the winds, not horses and his own will, carry him on his travels. These marvelous adjustments mark his admission to the grail adventures.[126]

Given the mass of *materia remota* the romancer may have to sift through, uniqueness may function as criterion for inclusion or exclusion in the *materia propinqua*. Thus, for example, the conclusion to the Agravain section in the *Lancelot* Proper relates that thirty-two knights set out in quest of Lancelot. But only the adventures of Agloval are related[127] even though his adventures are as ordinary as those of the others who seek Lancelot. But his quest suddenly becomes unique and extraordinary when he visits his mother and finds his brother Perceval. In the *Alexandre,* on the other hand, Bucifal is a marvelous and unique horse; and so the adventure by which Alexander tames him must be unique. Bucifal required his master to assume his proper role (*Alex* APar I.484), just as Perceval allows Agloval some of his uniqueness.[128] The horse is just as much a portent of Alexander's glorious career as the snake which entered Alexander's cradle after his birth, only to die suddenly (*Alex* APar I.260–62). Later, the birth of a monstrous child signals his imminent death (*Alex* APar IV.4–14).[129]

Thus, sometimes heroes are revealed through their connection to the marvelous—a connection which may include unique heroes as well as unique monsters. Or, conversely, the adventure may also be unique because of a special combination of event (rather than person or monstrosity) and hero, as with Agloval's return home to find Perceval. Similarly, "Yder de la terre as norois a qui la bele auenture auint en la court le roy artu de .V. aniaus qu'il traist du doi de la main al cheualier mort qui demandoit vengance que onques cheualier qui en la cort le roy artu fust nel pot traire ne auoir" (*Merlin* S 218.12–15) [Yder of the land of the Norse, to whom befell the beautiful adventure in Arthur's court, the adventure of the five rings he drew from the finger of the hand of the dead knight who asked for vengeance; there never was a knight in King Arthur's court who could pull them off or have them]. Yder's adventure is a sign like the sword in the stone at Arthur's identification as king in the *Merlin* and at Galaad's coming at the beginning of the *Queste*. In these cases, however, prior selection is evident.

Similar signs precede Lancelot's arrival at Arthur's court. At the beginning of his career, he withdraws a spear stump from the body of an unknown but mortally wounded knight.[130] Lancelot's act is motivated by his qualities, and his own sense of his unique excellence. Given Lancelot's qualities, there is nothing extraordinary in his unique decision—no other knight will attempt the act—to remove the spear stump. However, those qualities are not yet manifest in the narrative. His youth and daring seem therefore incommensurate. Lancelot's first adventure at Arthur's court is on a par with Perceval's combat with the Red Knight in Chrétien's *Conte du graal* and Tristan's with the Morholt in Thomas. But Guenevere changes all that. Lancelot is not knighted by Arthur, as foreordained, but inadvertently by Guenevere herself; in the broad context of the Lancelot-Grail cycle, his uniqueness in the Guenevere-inspired turn of events is a revolt against divine planning and therefore a "wonderful sin."

As is the case with saints' lives, many romances relate the first accomplishments *(enfances)* of their protagonists in order to set them apart from their peers before relating more prodigious adventures. After precocious signs of prowess, the young knights may more credibly assume the unique role assigned to them in the rest of the narrative. The circumstances of the birth and childhood of Alexander, Lancelot, Perceval, Tristan, and others are uniquely marvelous. The same is true in other *matieres,* where the marvel precedes and announces its achiever in the finished narrative. It stands out as unique, makes the hero extraordinary, and elicits marvelous narrative as adventures that achieve or realize marvels.[131]

The Extreme

The extreme is the remote or distant that is removed from the human and humane, court and society. " 'Extremi Garamantes.' Extremi autem, quia saevi et a consortio humanitatis remoti." (*Etymologiae* IX.ii.125) [the "extreme Garamantes." "Extreme indeed, because they are wild, far removed from intercourse with humanity]. By extension the extreme may imply finality, the uttermost, the highest or most intense degree, or the radical, immoderate, and excessive. The outer world of the forest as well as the inner world of love inspires and compels the knight and generates narrative.

The heroes and heroines in romance are always extraordinary; their combination with the marvelous constitutes precisely the kind of juxtaposition that romancers seek to elucidate by *conjointure.* The *aventure merveilleuse* mediates *dépassement de soi,* not individual self-realization.[132] The achiever is not a mere individual, but, as it were, "merveille de Dieu" (*Guiron* §113)[133] [God's marvel]. The juxtaposition of extremes in the marvelous adventure allows for simple and sharp demarcation in the representation of the unique or extraordinary. The actor in the marvelous adventure assumes an essential *outrance*. The extreme may therefore refer to any experiential categories or topical attributes within time and space: distance, duration, size, artistry, strength, brilliance, weight, beauty, sanctity, etc. The marvel is most manifest at the utter confines of human experience and beyond, because there actions and things are least ordinary, like beasts in the bestiaries the further their habitat is from the familiar world. The overwrought, farfetched, or outlandish, the "exaggerated" features of romance marvels characterize the search for the extreme in representation.

Although the romance may modify the intensity, parts, or qualities of such phenomena, one may take them as source data, as found in *Märchen* and saga.[134] Myth, even as narrated in Ovid, falls into the same group.[135] The extreme may border on the paradoxical, as when the werewolf assumes human, even courteous traits in Marie de France's *Bisclavret*, or the incredible, as in Pallas' and Camille's tombs in the *Eneas*, for which the anonymous author accumulates artistic wonders in "merveillose" and unnatural "richece" (*Eneas* 6513)[136] [marvelous . . . abundance]. No doubt, such enormities in Arthurian *matiere* inspired Jehan Bodel's reference to its "pleasing" *vaniloquentia*.[137]

At the extreme also lies the borderline between adventure and enchantment. " 'Che sont des aventures de Bretaigne ou des enchantemens de ceste terre.' Et cil respont qu'il cuide bien que chou ait esté enchantement, car d'aventure se mervilleuse comme ceste fu n'oi onques parler ne près ne loing" (Huth *Merlin* II, 180) ["they are the adventures of Britain or the enchantments of this land." And he answered that he thought that this was indeed an enchantment, for he had never heard tell, anywhere, of an adventure as marvelous as this one]. Enchantment escapes human comprehension and becomes fantastic.[138] "Et Porrus fait tant d'armes au trenchant de l'espee, / Tant tue et tant abat c'oevre samble faee" (*Parfait* 2930–31)[139] [and Porrus performs so many feats of arms with his sword's cutting edge, he kills and strikes so many, that his accomplishments seem like magic]. The truth of the matter defies explanation, even as exaggeration. From enchantment we pass to another extreme, where the names of God may not be uttered out loud, but only whispered into Perceval's ear (*Perceval* 6484–91), or where the marvels and adventures of the grail, the direct vision of which permits Galaad to ascend into heaven, forever deny their mystery to the reader's scrutiny.[140] Mystical vision overwhelms human comprehension and faculties, undoing flesh and blood.[141] This ascension does not deny that such marvels are ultimately comprehensible, but not to ordinary men and women.

The foregoing shows the extent to which *conjointure* as *concors discordia* structures the representation of marvels. Not only do we perceive the union of *matiere* and *san* (which, as will be shown below, characterizes the combination of *aventure merveilleuse* with topical truth); it is also obvious that the marvelous adventure itself joins diverse *matieres* in new and striking combinations, ranging from images and descriptions to whole plots. Some combinations blend into a whole and complete amalgamation—a *coniunctura occulta*—as found in Chrétien's romances; or enter into abrupt juxtapositions, even "disjointed" combinations, in *iuncturae apertae,* as in the Seven Sages cycle.[142] All these features contribute to the aesthetic of romance, an aesthetic founded on wonder in both romance protagonists and romance audiences.[143]

> Çou le met en boine esperance
> Qu'Amadas l'ait pucele et pure,
> Par si merveilleuse aventure
> Que ja mais jor c'aiés a vivre,
> En fable n'en cançon n'en livre,
> N'orés ausi fiere controeve.
>   (*Amadas* 1994–99)

[This makes her hope that Amadas will possess her as a maiden undefiled, and do so by an adventure so marvelous that you will never hear such an extreme invention in fable, song, or book.]

These lines suggest that the *aventure merveilleuse* functions as the narrative proper of romance. One might say that *merveille aventureuse*[144] is the source of romance, functioning both within the narrative and also for the romancer, as a focus that aids in selecting from and arranging the *matiere*. The author's selection of marvels from the sources is therefore an essential step in romance invention. Of course, a marvel may make *materia* seem "confusa et inevidens nec satis artificiose expedita" (*Ars vers* 4.14)[145] [confused and obscure and . . . not handled with enough artfulness]. The romancers themselves refer to their sources in similar language—obscure, incomplete, disjointed—because the marvel's function is partly to provide an economy that by definition makes narrative at least initially neither clear nor comprehensible. Yet this is also an integral part of the extraordinary character of the marvel, its mystery—the mystery that elicits fascination when there is no ready, customary frame of reference, no context that gives significance to the extraordinary phenomenon which in its original rationale (based on a non-Christian mythology or an ignoble society) was not acceptable according to French aristocratic norms.[146]

Aesthetics of Marvelous Adventures: *Emerveillement*

A marvel exists through the experience of *émerveillement*.[147] "Li preudom a bien escouté, si s'en esmiervelle moult. Car il n'oi onques mais parler de tel merveille" (Huth *Merlin* I, 14) [the good man listened carefully and marveled much at what he heard. For he had never heard tell of such a marvel]. The dissipation of *émerveillement,* or disenchantment with the marvel, ranges from total to partial cognizance of its mystery. The validation of the marvelous adventure requires emphasis on its mystery — its apparently inexplicable, ineffable, even archetypal quality. It is the city to be taken or destroyed, the lady to be won or freed, the talisman to be gained or known, the potion to be drunk or avoided. Medieval romance is replete with marvels like these that serve as sources of adventure. The adventure narrates the realization or the loss of the marvel in the great actions of romance: quest, marriage, combat, celebration.[148] Personages in the narrative, narrators, and authors evince not only curiosity or fascination pure and simple before these marvels, but also disturbance, awe, and even humor.[149] It follows that marvels and their adventures contribute to the beauty of romance. "Le beau, c'est l'admirable. Mais l'admirable souvent ne s'exprime pas, ni se comprend."[150] *Admiratio* is endured in wonder, joy, stupor, or anxiety and pain,[151] which articulate varieties of *émerveillement.*

Marie de France's *Chievrefoil* offers a marvelous image of the love of Tristan and Iseut — the vital union of honeysuckle and hazel — which Tristan restates in these words: "Bele amie, si est de nus: / Ne vus sanz mei, ne jeo sanz vus" (*Lais* Chev 77–78) [Beloved, so it is with us: neither you without me, nor I without you]. The comparison and analogous leitmotifs in Thomas d'Angleterre and Gottfried von Straßburg[152] become a narrative in this lay, which tells the fate of the two lovers: continual separation that is continually overcome by clandestine encounters, an almost seasonal renewal. In the lay, Tristan makes his dolor known to Iseut by a sign and a reference — the "escrit" (Chev 61) [writing] and the hazel. The marvelous image (which takes the traditional comparison at least half literally) becomes the vehicle that elicits the adventure recounted in this lay: the encounter which is the *summe* of all the encounters between Tristan and Iseut since the potion: "Ceo fu la summe de l'escrit / Qu'il li aveit mandé e dit" (Chev 61–62)[153] [this was the sum of what he had communicated and expressed to her in writing]. To continue the marvel, the encounter becomes the origin and burden of the lay Tristan writes to commemorate the event (Chev 107–13). This single episode, a synecdoche, stands for the whole Tristan legend, as its botanic marvel is a metaphor for the union of Tristan and Iseut held in the love potion's ban. While Thomas d'Angleterre, Beroul, and others focused on the marvelous love potion which permeates the entire narrative with its poison, Marie de France centers on the "summe de l'escrit," suggesting Geoffrey of Vinsauf's description of "emphasis":

> Modicumque prematur in orbem
> Summula materiae, quam tali comprime lege:
> Plurima perstringat paucis expressa locutrix
> Emphasis.
>
> (*Poetria nova* 691–94)

[Let the entire theme be confined within narrow limits. Compress it in accordance with the following formula. Let *emphasis* be spokesman, saying much in few words.]

Abbreviation by emphasis in the *Chievrefoil* implies the wondrous, potentially mortal union that marks the legend. In all versions of the lovers' story, images form constellations about the mystery of a marvelous union teetering between the extremes of life and death.

The apparently numinous quality of many romance marvels implies for many educated moderns unconscious or archetypal origins. Extraordinary phenomena, whether scientifically explicable or not in our own times, disturb unconscious regions of the mind and utilize the emotions this disturbance evokes: fear, anxiety, joy, exhilaration, awe, a *laetus horror*. To cope with such emotions, which may well be overwhelming (as many a romance adventure suggests), the romancers were not averse to producing distance through humor—the narrator or some personage, or the very concatenation of events or topical amplifications in the narrative, may be arranged around the trickster and more or less comic antics. But it may be an unsettling comedy which results, like Keu's, Dinadan's, or Ipomedon's.

However, most romancers prefer to frame the marvelous in a conventional context that finally resolves mysteries and leads to a happy ending. Marie de France adapted the idea of the marvelous adventure found in "Latin" *matieres,* the possibilities of which she deemed exhausted by vernacular writers,[154] to the Celtic world of the *Lais.* In *Guigemar,* the hero's lovelessness foreshadows a nobler *destinee* (*Lais* Gui 108, 326, 607), to be achieved marvelously through the encounter with the horned doe and the lady in the castle who, like the doe, is said to suffer for his sake "Issi grant peine e tel dolur / K'unkes femme taunt ne suffri" (116–17) [such great pain and dolor that no woman ever endured so much]. Those who love will marvel at this lay:

> Dunt tuit cil s'esmerveillerunt
> Ki aiment e amé avrunt
> U ki pois amerunt aprés.
>
> (*Lais* Gui 119–21)

[Whence all those will marvel who love and have loved, and who will love in the future.]

Thus, adventures and marvels are not merely part of a temporal sequence. They flow, as it were, from, and yet focus on, the irrational. As a result, experiential knowledge through *émerveillement* is distinct from cognitive knowledge based on reflection and analysis after the experience and after the reading. We may observe this by comparing the death of Tristan and Iseut in Thomas d'Angleterre with that of Troilus in Chaucer. From this side of the love death, lovers may sympathize with a story that is their own (*Tristan* Th Sneyd² 831–39). Troilus' reflections on his love from beyond the grave suggest the view of those who would stop or have stopped loving.

A counterpart to Troilus' sardonic laughter at the world's folly is Merlin's hilarity at others' blindness or confusion when confronted by marvels.[155] There may be comfort in knowing what lies behind marvels, especially in dissolving those which are baneful. Just as clearly, anguish and fear may emerge when their meaning remains hidden or inaccessible, or when they threaten individuals or their societies. This occurs when chivalry loses its meaning during the siege of Troy or in the battle on Salisbury Plain. Troy is destroyed or the grail is borne away, as are those heroes and heroines who struggled for them. Their marvel is forever lost. Only *mescheance* remains for the survivors:[156] failure in the grail quest effects a return to meaningless or incomprehensible adventures. Of course, the loss of meaning may enhance *émerveillement:* "La bataille fu commenciee grans et merveilleuse . . . " (*Mort* §182.1–2) [the battle began great and marvelous]. Extraordinary events occur: the two companions Lancelot and Gauvain fight against one another; Arthur defeats the Roman emperor; finally, the focus shifts to Arthur's war with Mordred which ends when a ray of light darts through the wound caused by the father killing the son begot in incest, the destruction of the Round Table, and the mysterious end of Arthur and Excalibur. The battle whose outcome was repeatedly warned against in sign, vision, and dream becomes a reality and yet a meaningless one, because it was once avoidable. Excalibur retrieved by the hand in the lake, like the grail from above in the *Queste,* and the ambiguous fate of Arthur confound the understanding, and the end of the *Mort* is as awful and incomprehensible, and thus as marvelous, as the end of the *Queste.*

On the other hand, *émerveillement* before a marvelous adventure may provoke only idle amusement at trifles like the automata in the *romans d'antiquité*[157] or aesthetic enjoyment as expressed in the desire to possess or even merely see the object. An amazingly secure fortress is a sight to behold; "Alixandres la voit, si l'a aus Grieus mostree; / Pour veoir la merveille s'i est l'ost arrestee" (*Alex* APar I.2200–2201)[158] [Alexander sees it, and he showed it to the Greeks; the army stopped to look at the marvel]. One marvels at the walls of Carthage in the *Eneas,* but attacks the walls of Troy in the *Troie;* one gazes in wonder at the Ship of Solomon, or gets into the one destined for Guigemar.

One waits for adventure, or spurs on in search of it, as recalled in the eagerness with which Arthur's court waited for adventures at prominent festivals or before meals. After initial astonishment, the announced adventures evoke either attraction or repulsion. "Ne ceste chose n'est pas si merveilleuse que aussi merveilleuse ne soit aucunes fois avenue, et c'est une chose qui auques vous doit reconforter" (*Folie Lanc* p. 117.282–84) [nor is this so marvelous but that things just as marvelous have occasionally occurred, and that ought to console you somewhat.] The attraction of marvel leads to awareness of its initial inscrutability followed by a desire for the adventure necessary to discover and know it. Similarly, aversion to it causes fear or distress.

> Li rois respont qu'il li estuet
> Sofrir, s'amander ne le puet,
> Mes molt l'an poise duremant.
> (*Charrette* 61–63)

[The king answers that he would have to tolerate it if he can't change matters, but that it distresses him very much.]

There may even be an attempt to avoid the marvel's adventure. "Ne il n'a encor nul leans qui sache vraiement dont ceste merveille avient, fors qu'ilz dient que ce sont des merveilles de Logres. Et pour ce qu'ilz perdent ainsi de leurs amis charnelz toutes les fois que chevaliers errans y viennent, heent ilz tant les chevaliers errans comme vous savés" (*Folie Lanc* p. 117.746–50)[159] [nor is there yet anyone therein who truly knows the origin of that marvel; they only say that such are the marvels of Logres. And since they lose their beloved kin every time a knight errant comes that way, they hate knights errant, as you know.]

Similarly, knights on quest, as distinguished from mere globe-trotting knights errant like Calogrenant,[160] rarely wish to be deterred from their marvelous goal by intervening adventures.

> Se jel pooie refuser,
> Molt volantiers m'an sofferoie;
> Mes ainçois voir me conbatroie
> Que noauz feire m'esteüst.
> (*Charrette* 2646–49)

[If I could decline it, I would gladly pass it by. But I would in truth rather fight than be compelled to do something worse.]

Emerveillement produces a single-mindedness that is almost obsessive. Like Rimbaud's *bateau ivre,* the knights are relentless and undaunted, borne, like Rimbaud's ship, where one wants to go: "Moi, l'autre hiver, plus sourd que les cerveaux d'enfant, / Je courus." The response to the marvel may be contemplative or investigative, passive or active—or both. Lancelot sits down to wait for adventures to come to him: "il dist qu'il ne se remueroit d'ilec, ainz atendroit la merci Nostre Seignor" (*Queste* p. 246.12–14)[161] [he said that he wouldn't move from the spot, but would wait on Our Lord's mercy]. Mercy, as for Rimbaud, may take the shape of a boat.

This obsessiveness meets with appropriate responses. Arthur's court often receives reports from knights returned from adventures which they honorably or shamefully completed. "Je voeil," exclaims Merlin,

que .iiij. clerc soient establi chaiens qui ne s'entremetront d'autre chose fors de metre en escrit toutes les auentures qui auendront a vous & a uos compaignons si que apres nos mors soient amenteues les proeces des preudomes de chaiens. (*Merlin* S 321.37–40)[162]

[I want four clerks to be appointed herein who will do nothing but record all the adventures which occur to you and your companions, so that, after our deaths, the deeds of prowess performed by those who dwell here may be recalled.]

And all agree, because the Arthurian knights, and the romancers, share the desire that a permanent record of their deeds stand as marvels for all time. This is a romance commonplace: "De moi et de mes fais et de mon hardement / Veul je que se mervellent a tous jors mais la gent" (*Alex* APar III.4985–86) [I want people ever to marvel at me, my deeds, and my courage].

It is essential to appreciate *émerveillement* as an important characteristic of romance. *Emerveillement* further generates narrative in the *aventure merveilleuse.* Although adventure and marvel overlap in semantic range, the former is clearly dependent on the latter for its significance in romance.[163] If no marvel is linked to an adventure, it remains just another event caused by fortune. But there is an implicit sequence in adventure and marvel: to know the marvel, to experience *émerveillement,* one must seek it out and proceed toward it. The approach or *adventus* of the *nouvelle* reporting the marvel elicits the personage who sets out to know it as *eventus.*[164] Hence the scheme of quest and conquest in narrative generation.[165]

Narrative Generation from Marvel to Adventure

Suspense

At a time when audiences were not so familiar with how traditional tales
might end, suspense is a critical mode of narrative elaboration. Suspense in
romance is most commonly expressed by *se mervellier*.[166] The audience's interest in or anxiety as to what will happen, especially to the principal figures,
follows from the uncertainty of marvels and adventures, from hope for success and fear of failure, or it may derive from emotions of joy or dread before an announced or otherwise anticipated climax. The sequential form of
the adventures leading to a final encounter and the conclusion enhances suspense in increasing the expectancy of the audience. This is well known in
Arthurian romance.[167] But French and Roman romances also employ suspense as a by-product of narrative progression toward the achievement of
a marvel. For example, in the sieges of *Thèbes* and *Troie*, destiny ineluecta-
bly works itself out through a sequence of combats, yet seems to hover un-
certainly between progression toward or regression from the destruction of
Oedipe's sons or of the Trojans—"destruiement / Lait e estrange et mout
prochain" (*Troie* 25558–59)[168] [ugly, awful, imminent destruction]. Signs
not only announce the destruction of Troy; they also portend that of the
Greeks for their own excesses.

> Dès ore orreiz lor destinees:
> Quant jos vos avrai recontees,
> Ne direiz pas qu'a nule gent
> Avenist onc plus malement.
> Tuit alerent puis, ço lison,
> A duel et a perdicion.
>   (*Troie* 26597–602)[169]

[Now will you hear their destinies. When I shall have related them to you,
you will agree that no people ever suffered greater misfortune. As we
read, they all came eventually to grief and destruction.]

The conclusions to *Thèbes, Eneas* (for Turnus and Camille), and *Troie* parallel the *Mort Artu*'s. For example, Ulysse had been instrumental in devising
the capture of Troy, and he found his way home safe and sound. But there
he was to die by the hand of his own son—not Telemaque, but another, marvelous son born of the fay Circe. Not recognizing his father, that son fights
and kills him. "Tel merveille n'iert mais oïe" (*Troie* 29818) [such a marvel
will never again be heard]. But it had been heard before and would be again:
the event combines elements of both Oedipe and Mordred.

> Son pere fiert par mi le cors,
> Qui de maint peril ert estors
> Et de mainte bataille dure;
> Mais itel esteit s'aventure.
> 　　　　　(*Troie* 30151–54)

[He strikes his father through, the one who had escaped many a hard peril. But such was his adventure.]

The *Troie* relates that a marvelous dream foretold the *aventure* that initiated the suspense.

> A vis li ert qu'une semblance
> De tel beauté, de tel poissance
> Que forme, ymage ne peinture
> Ne chose d'umaine nature
> Ne pot estre de sa beauté,—
> Bien poëit estre entre home et dé;
> Nature humaine trespassot,
> Mais as deus ne s'apareillot;
> Meins beaus esteit, mais, ço sai bien,
> Forme d'ome n'i montot rien;
> Entre la nature devine
> E l'umaine ert la soë fine,
> Resplendissant plus a merveilles
> Que li soleiz ne les esteiles.
> 　　　　　(*Troie* 29827–40)[170]

[He thought he saw a semblance of such beauty and power that neither shape, image, nor painting, nor anything human could be so beautiful—it could well be half-human half-divine. He surpassed human nature yet was not comparable to the gods. He was less beautiful than they, but I do know for sure that human form could not attain such perfection. Between divine and human beings was his fair self, more marvelously resplendent than the sun or stars.]

Ulysse's son is a male counterpart to Liénor in *Guillaume de Dole* and to Lanval's fay-like mistress. But Ulysse's desire to embrace the dream image is interpreted as a fatal "conjoncion" (*Troie* 29861): he must avoid any contact with him. However, Ulysse misreads the warning as a reference to Telemaque.

Here the suspense derives less from uncertainty as to what will happen than from how the narrative will portray the fateful moment. The reader's privileged knowledge permits the concatenation of suspense and surprise, adventure and chance, that makes for increasing expectancy, that is, the kind of suspense based on the ineluctable occurrence of the anticipated. Much like the Trojans ignoring or not understanding prophecies on the destruction of Troy, Ulysse advances to death: "Mais ne poët estre autrement: / Itel esteit la destinee" (*Troie* 30228–29) [but it could not have been otherwise: such was destiny]. Suspense is therefore used to counterpoint the narration of the protagonist's destiny.

Longer works introduce parallel adventures leading to a common conclusion, like threads tying and untying by narrative lace and interlace, allowing for a variety of alternating fields of suspense.[171] Most resolve themselves in a concluding achievement or defeat. As in the great quest for the grail, the *merveilles de totes autres merveilles,* on which all Arthurian quests and, ultimately, all history converge, suspense finally transforms into awe and silence before the ineffable. It does not matter in romance whether an anticipated adventure actually retains its wondrous qualities to the end of the plot. Achievement of adventure usually dissipates both suspense and marvel because true achievement is knowledge of the adventure.[172] In cases of static representation, suspense may dissolve into awe, since there is no real challenge to be overcome, as with many of the architectural splendors in the *romans d'antiquité.* They are viewed, as it were, like museum pieces that enhance the glory of their inhabitants and their civilization while aesthetically satisfying as wonders. But they generate neither suspense nor narrative.

Narrative Emanation from Marvels

Concentration on the marvel shifts the adventure from disparate encounter to obstacle. As an obstacle, the adventure may be a necessary stage in progress toward the marvel, or an impediment to progress. Chrétien is a master welder of disparate adventures, utilizing surprise to introduce an unexpected adventure, or to eliminate or diminish an expected one. The knight's concentration on the marvel makes the choice coherent while transforming it into an obstacle. Further, his choice reflects auctorial organization of sources into a suitable *conjointure* on Fourquet's mythic level of coherence. Some romances—like Beroul's and Eilhart von Oberg's Tristan poems, the First and Second *Perceval* Continuations, and the *Lanzelet*—illustrate the chroniclers' tendency to compile adventures and marvels in more or less chronological sequence. But more important, they betray an implicit pattern fixed on a marvel: the love potion in the Tristan romances, the grail in the Continuations, Lanzelet's potential for love in the *Lanzelet.* Thus, even in sources unstructured or incoherent by Chrétien's standards, a marvel illuminates so to speak any matter conjoined to it.

The structural and narrative subordination of episode to marvel that may be implicit in the sources anticipates the romancer's selection or rejection, arrangement, and elucidation of the total marvelous adventure in the completed work.[173] Chrétien says he "drew" his *conjointure* in *Erec* from the *conte* he found told by others. His work is therefore dependent on the sources, however *depeciees, corronpues,* or *oscures* they may have seemed to him, because all contain marvels. Modern studies of narrative grammar and folktale morphology suggest a virtually archetypal pattern for oral traditions in folktale, saga, and myth.[174] The principle of organization around a central marvel carries over to written sources, like those of the *romans d'antiquité* and romances based on extant earlier writings that already contained a pattern or organization of contents, which the romancers retained, adapted, or replaced. The romances preserve original marvels for mystery, suspense, and structure in a new context.

The notion of marvel in romance poetics is analogous to creative emanation, whereby God radiates attributes and qualities as the world's adornment, or, in rhetorical terms, to repetition and multiplication of attributes, with all this implies.[175] But the marvelous source of the tale may be anonymous:

> Et si vos voel dire et conter
> *Les Mervelles de Rigomer,*
> Dont cis romanç muet et commence.
> (*Rigomer* 15–17)[176]

[And I want to tell and relate to you the *Marvels of Rigomer,* from which this romance springs and begins.]

The marvel generates adventure. The combination of marvel and adventure may itself be composed of adventures and marvels whose significance and place are made, explicitly or implicitly, to derive from the central marvel as if they emanate from it.

This conception of narrative elaboration from a marvel pregnant with great adventures leads to the Lancelot-Grail cycle. In the Prologue to the Vulgate *Estoire del saint graal* that begins the cycle in its final shape, the anonymous author/narrator asserts that he received the work directly from the hands of Jesus Christ, and that its contents are a marvel. "Chou est li livres u tu troveras dedens si grans merveilles, que nus cuers mortex ne poroit penser" (*Estoire* II, 9/I.5.3–4)[177] [this is the book in which you will find such great marvels that no mortal heart could conceive them]. The principle of emanation or elaboration from the small book is lineage (II, 12–13/5.24–35): the family tree and its branches are all in the kernel from which they spring. This entails a gradation of marvelous adventures that converge on the central grail marvel.

As an increasing number of knights participate in branching adventures and quests, it becomes impossible to relate everything.[178] By the time Galaad arrives at Arthur's court in the *Queste,* the desire to know the grail seems to sweep all else aside, as if its light were now so brilliant as to make details indiscernible, obscuring all adventures except that most extraordinary "començaille des granz hardemenz et . . . achoison des proeces . . . les merveilles de totes autres merveilles" (*Queste* p. 278.5–7)[179] [beginning of the great feats of courage and . . . the cause of the deeds of prowess . . . the marvels of all other marvels], without which derivative marvelous adventures have no meaning nor, indeed, could they exist. Intermediate adventures are reduced or eliminated entirely, like stars in the sunlight. Lancelot and Galaad "troverent aventures merveilleuses qu'il menerent a chief. . . . Si n'en fet mie li contes del saint Graal mencion, por ce que trop i covenist a demorer qui tout voldroit aconter qan qu'il lor avint" (*Queste* p. 251.26–30) [encountered and achieved marvelous adventures. . . . But the story of the grail does not relate them because it would take too much time to relate all their adventures]. The same is true for Galaad's five years of adventures with Perceval (p. 265.15–21), and for Boort's alone (p. 265.29–33). The grail completely reclaims the narrative (p. 266.8–9), like a black hole that swallows light, no longer permitting emanation.

The origins of the grail, that inexhaustible source of *émerveillement,* were probably a Celtic horn of plenty, and more certainly a humble, if perhaps rather unusual, low-bottomed bowl; adaptation moved the image far from both sources by the thirteenth century. But that adaptation, too complex to detail here,[180] shows the range of marvels uncovered in sources and of inventive elaboration of the mysteries suggested by *émerveillement.* The discovery and publication of *matiere* containing a suitable or potential marvel are both invention and transmission of the marvel.[181] Transmission provides a means to explore the marvel further and to experience its narrative emanation.

Morton Bloomfield aptly characterized romance marvels as "inexplicable events which seem to have their center above and beyond the poem,"[182] so that "meaning is often moved out of the realm of experience and put into the unknown."[183] Achievement of the extreme unknown is precisely what happens in the case of the grail at the end of the *Queste* (p. 279.2–7). The disappearance of the grail into heaven terminates the adventures it generated. Just as adventures emanate from the Golden Fleece or the grail, they are generated by any marvel in which the romancer discerns mystery and adventure. The way in which marvels are portents of future events in medieval chronicles translates as emanation in romance narrative.

When marvels bode ill, as in the *romans d'antiquité* or in the *Queste* and *Mort* of the Vulgate cycle, they produce *mesaventures* or *mescheances*. When in the *Queste* the grail removes from Corbenic to Sarras, and thence into heaven, the local Arthurian and, finally, the entire world reverts from providential order to chaos, and fortune reigns supreme.[184] As in the world of the *Roman de Troie,* great and awful tournaments and battles give rise to excesses, stupid errors, missed opportunities. Arthur's repeated warnings before the battle on Salisbury Plain mirror Hector's failing to heed Andromaque and Cassandre on the day of his death. Such *mescheance,* often foreseen and even avoidable, is inexplicably, totally mysterious and malignant, and thus marvelous in its workings. Even fortune's regular rotations do not bring order to the mindless interplay of chance and human impulse. In terms of the grail the old habit of seeking a coherent justification for events gives way to blame and conflict, as if the harm done in tournaments and battle, in the woods or at the dinner table, were the result of some malicious destiny for which individuals are responsible. The archer whose arrow happens to pierce Lancelot's thigh is at fault and must flee for his life, just as Guenevere herself is to be punished for inadvertently giving to Keherdin a poisoned apple someone else intended for Gauvain. Lancelot is held responsible for an equally uncontrollable act, unwittingly killing Gaheriez. All these events are *mescheances,* extraordinary yet incomprehensible mishaps turned into abominations by sudden human judgment, impulse, or ignorance, like fratricide and matricide as portrayed in the *romans antiques.*

When the boat bearing the body of the Maiden of Escalot arrives mysteriously below Camelot, Gauvain half believes himself again in the adventure world of pre-*Queste* days, and all marvel at the boat's extraordinary beauty (*Mort* §70.18–24). Indeed, one might wonder whether Guigemar could once again sail marvelously, yet happily, to his love. But the Maiden's letter found in the boat corrects Gauvain's surmise, reaffirming the context of *mescheance* with its own kind of marvels.

> Endementiers que il regardoient les letres et la damoisele, que il plaignoient sa mescheance, li haut home furent descendu del palés et venu au pié de la tour pour veoir qu'il avoit en la nacele. Et li rois fet meintenant la nacele descouvrir et prendre la damoisele et aporter la amont el palés; si s'assemblent li un et li autre por veoir cele merveille. (*Mort* §71.47–54)

> [While they were looking at the letter and the maiden, pitying her misfortune, the nobles had come down from the palace to the foot of the tower to see what

there was in the boat. And the king had the boat uncovered immediately, and
the maiden taken and borne up to the palace. And they gathered to look at
that marvel.]

The marvel is one link in a concatenation of events culminating, through
their own inertia, in the duel between Lancelot and Gauvain and the car-
nage on Salisbury Plain. These events generalize in the star-crossed knights
and vendettas of the post-Vulgate cycle, where the innocent unwittingly do
wrong and become guilty.[185] The prose romances in general contrast sharply with the rose-colored world that tends to characterize the marvels in the
so-called *roman rose* of thirteenth-century verse romance.[186]

The fascination with both the light and the dark sides of the marvel, its
meaning and meaninglessness, its mystery and obscurity, is fascination with
the unknown. The eruption of the extraordinary into an orderly world belongs to an order of phenomena that are seemingly acausal or coincidental,
or that fit into an unknown order of events. Objects or persons may defy
comprehension, and the romancers, in their efforts to represent extraordinary apparitions, evoke the intervention of fortune, nature, God, or the mind
of an exalted patron to explain the wonders. The dissipation of marvel may
be more or less total—the marvelous walls of Carthage still stand in the *Eneas,*
while those of Troy are brought down in the *Troie.* Supernatural figures become human and less extraordinary or more topically precise, like Melior
in *Partonopeu de Blois* and the Belle Esmeree in *Le bel inconnu.* But in all
these cases, romance achieves the reduction of marvelous phenomena by narrative order whether that order emanates from a beneficial or a malicious
source in this world or some other. Success measures the degree to which
the given romance expresses knowledge of the marvel. From the earthly paradise of Guillaume de Lorris' *Rose* to the incomprehensible lot of Balain, or,
on a more down-to-earth but still marvelous level, from the fate of the
Chasteleine de Vergy and of the Châtelain de Coucy on the one hand to that
of the knight and his lady in the *Lai de l'ombre* on the other, marvels are
seen to produce extraordinary adventures.

Inquiry into marvels was a crucial auctorial enterprise. Invention could
suggest ominous signs for the feudal and aristocratic world. The failure to
preserve the grail may well be emblematic of the aristocracy's failure to control its own destiny in the face of new, extraordinary forces erupting into
its ideal order.[187] Historically and psychologically, the obsession with marvels achieved or lost may well be indicative of a profound social malaise.
The evolution of romance in the thirteenth century suggests how critical the
malaise may have become.

Economy of the Marvelous Adventure

Since romance is a record of marvel and the adventure or adventures it generates, an adventure that leads to the discovery of the truth in a marvel is *chose qui face a ramentevoir en conte.* The marvel in the source is the source of narrative amplification,[188] and a total romance narrative may be termed an *aventure merveilleuse.* The *aventure merveilleuse* usually rests upon a literal or visionary separation in time and space, the narrative distance, between the agent (the "hero") and the marvel. The adventure and the marvel that mesh in the *aventure merveilleuse* produce by their correlation what Fourquet called "une ambiguïté créatrice de mystère."[189] In romance, the dénouement occurs when, through adventure, the marvel yields its truth.[190]

Episodic adventures and marvels are usually inserted between the announcement of the central marvel and its attainment.[191] But these are subordinate in the prime *aventure merveilleuse* which, accordingly, determines or explains their place and function.[192]

> Dans cette structure le rôle de l'*aventure,* de l'événement merveilleux ou singulier, est de permettre le passage du plan inférieur au plan supérieur. L'*aventure* se place aux moments critiques du récit, produisant un choc, une surprise, jouant comme une bascule, un déclic. Elle est aussi le noyau, le diamant brut et le centre de gravité autour duquel s'organise le récit, suivant de variables agencements dus à l'art du conteur. Plusieurs aventures peuvent d'ailleurs s'enchâsser dans un lai,[193]

and a fortiori in a romance. The fundamental structure implicit in the expression *aventure merveilleuse* ranges from simple and singular in most lays to expansive and multiple in the prose romances. The marvels and adventures that function as narrative stations effect the integration of the marvel into the narrative economy.

Aventure/merveille provides a structural, indeed, a virtually archetypal framework for the narrative. It makes a *conjointure* of adventures correlated thematically and contextually into a marvel.[194] The narrative focus on the marvel makes it a basic joint in the narrative correlation of episodic adventures and marvels. A marvel is at one and the same time the goal of romance protagonists, the core or focus of the narrative, and its *telos,* that is, the source of narrative signification. It functions as cause, whereas intervening adventures relate displacement or separation from a point of departure toward the marvel. Brief works like lays, which retain the skeletal marvel plus adventure that longer works develop, are potential parts of a romance, like the clandestine visit in the Tristan legend *(Chievrefoil, Laüstic),* or the bride or love testing in the Caradoc interpolation in the *Gauvain* Continuation (Biket's *Cor*).

Adventures are announced at court. But they usually transpire outside the court, sometimes in secrecy, as in those romances focusing on love.

> Ky aventures veut oïr e ver,
> Il ne puet touz jours demorer
> A ese ne a sojourn trere,
> Mès aler deit estrange tere
> Pur aprendre affetement
> Les maneres d'estrange gent.
> Ki plus loinz va plus verra
> E plus des aventures savra;
> Jeo le sai bien, car prové l'ai;
> En ma juvente m'en aloy
> En plusurs teres a oïr
> Aventures pur retenir.
> (*Melior* 1–12)

[He who wishes to hear and see adventures cannot always dwell in ease and repose. He has to go to foreign lands to learn properly the ways of foreign peoples. He who goes farther will see more and know more adventures. I know this for a fact, for I have experienced it. In my youth I went to several countries to hear adventures that I wanted to remember.]

The separation from the marvel evokes restlessness and curiosity in reader and protagonist alike.[195] The *conte* relates the great adventure, usually divided into units constituting shorter adventures. The relation of the entire sequence is the romance narrative. The return to the point of departure or to a state of rest after achieving the marvel is a return to order in knowledge of the marvel. This oscillation is actually what Gauvain defends when responding to Cador's condemnation of *uisdive* in Wace's *Brut* (which may be why one scribe inserted the romances of Chrétien as an illustration just before this narrative). The circle or cycle of withdrawal and return is the archetypal pattern of the folktale, saga, and myth,[196] which romancers preserve with the marvels drawn from their sources.

By the same token, much of thirteenth-century verse romance seems today—and, perhaps, did so in its own time—to have suffered from the failure to invent or select from sources or from the imagination marvels sufficient to organize the adventures leading to them, and subordinate those adventures to the marvel as a narrative goal. The problem is especially crucial in those that extend the narrative to two, three, even four times the length of Chrétien's romances. Even a structural organization as elaborate as that in *Claris et Laris* cannot artificially make up for the lack of a central marvel by multiplication of quests.[197] Chrétien de Troyes understood this when he contrasted the failure of the knight errant Calogrenant and the quester Yvain. The former fails at a marvelous adventure which was, for him, only one possible adventure among others; Yvain seeks and achieves that specific adventure, which becomes unique to him because it reveals Laudine, just as the White Stag and Sparrow Hawk adventures in *Erec* reveal Enide. Later verse romance sometimes seeks to make up for the loss of the central marvel by multiplying quests and specializing heroes and heroines within an arbitrary structure.

The Hero: Function and Name of the Achiever

The marvelous adventure is what one must look for in romance; it was what the romancers sought in their sources, and what the original protagonists allegedly wanted to have remembered about their deeds. " 'E sés tu,' dist li chevaliers, 'pour coi je t'ai ensi conté ceste aventure?' Pour che que je voel que elle soit mise en escrit. Car après nos mors quant elle sera amenteue a nos hoirs, elle sera moult voulentiers escoutee et oie, car trop est mervilleuse' " (Huth *Merlin* II, 43) [the knight said: "And do you know why I told you this adventure? Because I want it to be written down. For after our deaths, when it will be reported to our heirs, it will be eagerly listened to and heard, since it is so exceptionally marvelous."] Conversely, the shame of *recreantise*—sloth, fear, retreat from duty—is a negative response to marvelous adventures. It does not contribute to narrative, a fact made explicit for the Roman emperor Fastydorus in the Seven Sages prose cycle: "si n'a pas molt a faire d'aler en estrange paÿs; ainz li plaist trop miex a estre entre les barons de sa terre que il ne fait a aler hors du paÿs et li metre en aventure de mort"[198] [he doesn't concern himself much with going to foreign lands, but would rather be among the barons of his land than go abroad and expose himself to possible death]. Fastydorus is not unlike Arthur himself in this respect, as characterized in both Chrétien, the Vulgate cycle, and elsewhere,[199] at least after Arthur has passed his prime. Fastydorus' idleness is offset in Arthur's case by largess which draws knights to the court whence they go out in search of adventures and marvels. The great failure for Arthur is loss of largess, as in *Perlesvaus,* followed by dispersion of the Round Table, which means that knights are no longer available when the marvel announces an adventure. Narrative is not possible. The "adventurous courts" of romance draw knights and ladies by largess and festivity; the knights and ladies in turn attract marvels and adventures, to which they are especially responsive.

An adventure requires the right knight. Very often even the best of those present at the call to adventure fail to respond.[200] This is also true among ladies: Soredamors "desdaigneuse estoit d'amors" (*Cligés* 440) [was scornful of love], a kind of *recreantise,* before the arrival of Alexandre.[201] Among the knights good or bad who accept the call of the marvel, many are unfit, like Keu, Dinadan, and other secondary knights.[202] Now, as Vinaver first showed, Dinadan wanders the earth seeking in vain the meaning of adventures. Curiously, he is also the object of bemused tolerance and even laughter and ridicule, not unlike that frequently directed at Keu or even Chrétien's Perceval.[203] Some figures suggest incongruities in the scheme of things: the Beau Couard or the Laid Hardi. Others are merely ridiculous,[204] while still others are horrible, like the children of incest Mordred, Eteocles, and Polinices. Sometimes the incongruities are removed or corrected, as when Perceval restores the Beau Couard's courage.[205] Similarly, hermits effect a transformation in the character of Lancelot in the *Queste.*

Nonetheless, these cases remind us that the specter of a world deprived of meaning—the world of marvelous *mescheance*—hangs heavy over romance heroes.[206] In the *Mort Artu,* marvels are no longer a source of knowledge; all the knights die in the "bataille . . . grans et merveilleuse" (§182.1–2) [battle great and marvelous] that ends the Arthurian world. "Sire, ce sont li geu de Fortune; or poez veoir qu'ele vos vent chierement les granz biens et les granz honors que vos avez eü pieça, qu'ele vos tolt de voz meilleurs amis; or doint Dex que nos n'aions pis!" (*Mort* §190) [my lord, these are the games fortune plays. Now you can see that she makes you pay dearly for the great rewards and honors you have enjoyed up till now, for she has bereft you of all your friends. God grant that worse doesn't happen]. In Roman *matiere,* despair surfaces as knights blindly seek death. The Trojans go out to battle in spite of Cassandra's warnings, just as Gauvain does in pushing his personal vendetta against Lancelot in the *Mort Artu.* Despair in love propels Troilus to death in the *Troie;* despair of ambition does the same to Turnus in the *Eneas.* Temporary insanity follows love lost not only in *Yvain,* but also in *Partonopeu de Blois, Florimont,* and the prose romances.[207]

When a marvel seems to lose its significance or its accessibility, to escape from one's grasp and become a baleful source of destruction, the knight, unable to control fate, loses his sense of self and falls victim to madness, acting out an archetype of destruction. Perhaps nowhere does the excess, even the humor and cruelty, of such meaningless encounters appear more sharply delineated than in the two adventures Arthur falls victim to at the beginning and end of *Jaufre.* There Arthur insists adamantly on having an adventure.

Consequently, a necromancer-knight provides him and the court with one that reduces the king and the entire Round Table to pathetic impotence.

> Adoncs fo Galvains angoisos
> E sei compainos atresi,
> Qe cascus si rom e s'ausi,
> Els autres q'eron remasut,
> Ausit an dol e entendut.
> (*Jaufre* 350–54)[208]

[Then was Gauvain afraid, and his companions likewise; each one rips and tears at himself. And the others who remained behind heard and perceived their lamentations.]

The fright dissolves when the trickster-magician reveals the adventure to have been an illusion.

> El rei es se meravilatz,
> E es se be .c. ves seinatz
> D'aiso consi es avengut.
> (*Jaufre* 433–35)

[And the king marveled, crossing himself a good hundred times, at what happened.]

This "comic" adventure anticipates the great madness that later in *Jaufre* overwhelms the domain of the knight imprisoned by Taulat. Such madness seems to prevail, with more or less intensity, whenever a marvelous adventure occurs without a knight capable of achieving it and thus correlating it with romance *san*.

As in *Jaufre*, Arthur conventionally insists that no festival begin until an adventure has been announced.[209] As the principal motifs of romance, adventure and marvel are what knights and ladies encounter or seek, wherever that may be and whatever they may do otherwise.

> C'est cil qui sosteneit le fais,
> Qui les granz estors mainteneit
> E qui les granz esforz faiseit,
> Cui aveneient aventures.
> (*Troie* 20348–51)[210]

[He is the one who bore the weight, who waged the great battles, made the strenuous efforts—to whom adventures happened.]

Such are in fact the persons of history, whether those like kings most exposed to fortune's turns, or the chosen elite suitable to the achievement of a great social, moral, or religious task. As a given figure confounds fortune and, by his or her character or will, imposes a counterbalance that exposes the marvels, the concomitant adventure becomes meaningful. The hero, male or female, effects the integration of the marvel into a social or moral economy. The actor pushes his or her achievements to the limits of human capacities, moving beyond common or conventional experience while remaining exemplary by the unique excellence the marvel reveals.[211] As with his or her folktale counterpart, the hero brings back the prize.[212] Good order depends on those who uphold or realize it.

Subsequently, there occurs a metastatic exchange between the marvel and the person "chosen."[213] For example, Bucifal, a unique and marvelous horse, produces an adventure when brought together with Alexander; the horse's mad cry gives way to tame submission, a new marvel coloring the person of Alexander himself as he begins to take on the shape of Alexander the Great.[214] The agents of medieval romance are themselves elements of the marvel; their intervention — the adventure — contributes to its elucidation.

Paul Zumthor has noted how frequently psychological factors are ignored in marvelous adventures, even in as "realistic" a work as the *Chasteleine de Vergi*:

> Non par goût de l'absurde, mais parce que ces motifs ressortissent à l'ordre des évidences, existent par eux-mêmes, objectivement, ailleurs, dans un univers auquel on nous invite à participer. . . . L'intérêt se trouve ainsi concentré sur la situation plus que sur les personnages: ceux-ci rayonnent d'elle, la réalisent; ils la personnalisent (par leurs dialogues et leurs monologues) mais ne lui confèrent pas de dynamisme psychologique qui leur soit propre. Le récit, comme tout ouvrage narratif de cette époque, est conçu comme "enseignement"; c'est-à-dire, le plus souvent, comme la révélation de faits extraordinaires.[215]

In short, all elements involved in the representation of the marvel, including those who achieve or fail to achieve it, are expressive of the marvel. This provides for the *participation mystique* of the heroes, and, through catharsis and moral sympathies, that of the audience as well.

For example, the *Troie* begins with the Golden Fleece (*Troie* 763–80). The goal of the quest is the marvelous Fleece itself.

> Tote la gent de la contree
> I est venue e assemblee
> Por esguarder la grant merveille,
> Qu'onques ne vit nus sa pareille,
> Ne ja nen iert mais tel veüe:

> Fiere parole en ont tenue.
> La Toison ont mout esguardee:
> Diënt que c'est chose faee.
> Bien afichent veraiement,
> S'as deus ne venist a talent,
> Ne poüst pas estre engeignié.
>
> (*Troie* 1987–97)

[Everyone in the country assembled to view the great marvel, the likes of which none had ever seen, nor ever will. They say many extraordinary things about it. They gazed on the Fleece, saying that it was an enchanted thing. They affirm that in truth it would never have been won by any cunning had not the gods approved.]

Achieving the marvel therefore requires special privilege. Medee possesses the knowledge necessary to win it, knowledge which she shares with Jason. The achievement brings the adventure to an end. Even the Golden Fleece itself, once all have marveled at it, disappears from the narrative (*Troie* 1959–64). Jason momentarily takes its place as a new marvel, to win Medee, as it were in the Fleece's afterglow. He alone achieved the quest, which makes him extraordinary and, therefore, heroic.

The qualities that permit the hero to achieve an adventure mark his or her potential. In the Huth *Merlin,* a knight pursues the *beste glatissante* [yelping beast] with two purposes: "savoir la verité de li" and "savoir la verité de moi meesmes" (I, 151) [know the truth about it . . . and about myself]. This confirms the affinity between the extraordinary knight and the marvelous adventure.

> "Mais certes je ne di mie que che soit par vos oevres que vous soiiés si mescheans, ains le voit on toutdis par coustume que nostre sires envoie plus tost as preudoumes et as vassaus corous et anuis en cest monde qu'il ne fait as mauvais. . . . " "Certes, Merlins," che dist li rois Artus, "vous dites voir: cis consaus est boins et loiaus, car toute jour le voit on avenir coume vous le devisés."
>
> (Huth *Merlin* II, 128)

["But surely, I am not saying that you are so unfortunate because of anything you have done. Rather one ever sees that, as a rule, our Lord visits tribulation and vexation more swiftly upon worthy men and vassals than he does on the unworthy. . . . " "Indeed, Merlin," says King Arthur, "you are right. This word of wisdom is good and honest, for it is seen to happen every day just as you describe it."]

Similarly, Jason's qualities impel the envious Piné to send him in search of the Fleece, just as Hector's draw adventures, and ultimately his death, upon himself.

But it is also remarkable that both Jason and the Golden Fleece disappear from the narrative. The Fleece was a given, and it elicited an adventure because the qualities of a knight and a lady, Jason and Medee, made it possible for him to seize it. In all this, the Fleece remains as autonomous as the rose or the grail in their respective romances. Those who achieve these goals distinguish themselves by that achievement. Their actions, as marvels, are productive of other adventures and marvels that call forth other heroes and heroines, themselves extraordinary by their actions and sentiments. The distance between Greece and Colcas offers many adventures, first and foremost the adventure of Laomedon's Troy. We see here the principle for narrative continuation and cyclic expansion and digression that later prose romance sought to realize.

The spatial and temporal separation of marvel and seeker is not limited to the quest motif. The predominant theme of medieval French romance is love. The object of love is a person of marvelous, even enchanting beauty, and the "courtship" a marvelous adventure. The love of Floire and Blancheflor leads them into splendid Eastern gardens and palaces. Liénor in *Guillaume de Dole* elicits a courtship singled out by an extraordinary feature in her beauty: she possesses a *mystère* that must be known and understood before she can give herself to her love. The rose on her thigh is a highly ambivalent sign of her extraordinary self—the fault in a Chinese vase. The false sense of her rose is that perpetrated by the Emperor's deceitful seneschal when he implicates her in fornication. Conrad comes to know his lady's rose, that is, her true nature, and the knowledge is not only the undoing of the seneschal, but also the experience of the marvel that she is.[216] Similarly, Erec's adventure is the discovery of Enide and their marriage. Yet he knows only the adventure (*Erec* 1463), not the marvel of his lady until the wedding night. As wife, she too knows the change from *pucele* to *dame* (*Erec* 2052–54), and assumes for the first time in the narrative her real name.

Fascination with the lady's beauty impels the knight to love and know her. This love makes him unique. Chrétien's Lancelot is made known by name as he does battle for Guenevere. But what finally distinguishes Lancelot is his unique, privileged knowledge of Guenevere. Lancelot's experience is of the same kind as Perceval's when Blancheflor, a "passemerveille" (*Perceval* 1827), becomes a source of *émerveillement* during the night he spends with her. "Et s'estoit or merveille estrange" (*Perceval* 2631)[217] [and this was then an extraordinary marvel] because she inspired him to vanquish Anguingeron and Clamadeu. Her effect on Perceval is analogous to Enide's on Erec, Medee's on Jason, and Guenevere's on Lancelot.

But love is also long-lasting and complex. As Enide only gradually realizes the quality of the love she and Erec feel for one another, so Perceval's heart unlocks only gradually to the marvel of his love. When the three drops of blood in the snow remind him of love, Perceval realizes he has witnessed other marvels: the bleeding lance and rich grail in procession. The effects of Perceval's silence in this adventure are disastrous, indiscriminate, and uncanny—totally opposite to those in the Belrepaire episode.

> Dames en perdront lor maris,
> Terres en seront escillies
> Et puceles desconseillies,
> Qui orfenines remandront,
> Et maint chevalier en morront;
> Tot cist mal esteront par toi.
> (*Perceval* 4678–83)

[Because of this, ladies will lose their husbands, lands will be laid waste, maidens forlorn and orphaned, and many a knight will die. All these evils will come to pass because of you.]

It is a *mescheance,* a disaster that harms precisely those whom the knight is bound to protect: widows, orphans, maidens, and other knights. Thus, in the second part of the romance Perceval quests in search of this marvel he has neglected.

Curiously, Perceval's quest is different from the quests of those who set out at the same time he does in the *Conte du graal.*[218] Like Calogrenant (*Yvain* 173–77), most knights begin their quests by pursuing virtually any available adventure that presents itself[219].

> Et si creante
> Li uns a l'autre et dist et jure
> Que merveille ne aventure
> Ne savront qu'il ne l'aillent querre,
> Tant soit en felenesse terre.
> (*Perceval* 4742–46)

[And each one guarantees, maintains, and swears that, all together, they will hear of no marvel or adventure that they do not go in quest of, in however an evil land it may be found.]

But Perceval "redist tout el" (4727) [says something quite different]. His is the quest, like Yvain's, for a specific goal.[220] The goal orientation and the choice define him as different from the other questing knights.

Perceval's experience raises the issue of the right and wrong relation of the hero to adventure. In the *Queste,* Boort too must confront a beautiful woman, but one who is really the devil. However, he possesses the character, the inner worth as the *Queste* defines it, that allows him to resist unconsciously and instinctively, as we might say today, an attraction which he is able to understand only later (*Queste* pp. 181.29–182.1). Recognition is not the key to this marvelous adventure; rather, the attitude and conduct appropriate to its achievement single out and, in the event, name the successful knight.

Appellation, nomination, and election receive special attention in romance. Appellation becomes the designation or at least the identification of a given figure for a specific role. "Ele me dit . . . que moy ne aultruy ne le [her name] sçauroit jusques à ce que il y auroit ung chevalier en la Grant-Bretaigne qui metteroit à fin les malles adventures de la forest Darnant, lequel chevalier descouvrira le nom" (*Perceforest* 91:204) [she said to me . . . that neither I nor anyone else would learn (her name) until a knight would appear in Great Britain who would put an end to the evil adventures in Darnant forest, and that knight will discover the name]. The accommodation of hero to role is, of course, auctorial election. Election of the hero in this sense constitutes a unique elite. Achievement of the marvelous adventure bestows on the achiever a name that does not individualize in any modern sense; rather, the achiever typifies and distinguishes the name.[221] Melusine's name distinguishes and makes marvelous a family and its castle.

> quant basti fut le chasteau,
> Melusigne, qui le vit beau,
> De son droit nom le baptiza.
> Partie de son nom prins a,
> Lusignen lui donna en nom.
> Encore en est partout le nom
> Dont maint portent du fort le cry.
> Il est ainsi que je l'escry;
> Encor le bon roy ciprïen
> Si crye en son cry: Lusignen!
> Ainsi com orrez en l'istoire
> De quoy aprés feray memoire.
> "Melusigne" autant dire vault
> Com merveille qui ja ne fault.
> Ainsi cilz fors est merveilleux
> Plus qu'autres et aventureux.
> (*Melusine* Co 1331–46)[222]

[When the castle was completed and Melusine saw that it was beautiful, she christened it with her own name. It received part of her name, she called it Lusignan. The name is still widespread, and many use it as a battle cry. It is as I write it. The good king of Cypress still shouts it in his battle cry: "Lusignan!" That's how you will hear it in the story as I record it hereafter. Melusine means the same as "unending marvel." That is why this castle is more marvelous and adventurous than others.]

Lancelot's name appears in the *Charrette* narrative when Guenevere pronounces it; Perceval knows his name, "instinctively," after the grail castle adventure. But, in his case, the significance of the name is dependent on the adventure. We see this as *Perceval le Galois* becomes *Perceval le chaitis* (*Perceval* 3573–82) — the foolish Welsh lad becomes the wretched knight.[223]

Matthew of Vendôme refers to the topical use of names in the *Ars versificatoria* when he casts Helen of Troy as a generic Helen exemplifying feminine beauty.[224] The complexity which the modern novelist might seek in individual psychology is reserved in romance for the marvel and its adventures. Bestowal of name lends distinction in a social sense. Chrétien de Troyes seems to have been the first romancer to utilize this technique consistently.[225] The conclusion to the Sparrow Hawk episode is the naming of Enide, who thus realizes herself in marriage.

> Ancor ne savoit l'an son non,
> Mes ore primes le set l'on:
> Enyde ot non au baptestire.
> (*Erec* 1977–79)

[Her name was not yet known, but now it is for the first time. She received the name Enide in the baptistery.]

"Belle Enide" becomes "bonne Enide" through the quest.[226] A similar link between appellation and achievement occurs in the *Charrette*. Like Julius Caesar's name, which Matthew of Vendôme makes typical for emperor, Lancelot's name comes to designate the type of the courtly lover, assuming the marvel which was the goal of his quest and which indeed made his quest possible: an extraordinary love.

Other name scenes are more ambiguous. Perceval's discovery of his name is hardly auspicious, since it is associated with failure. In fact, by his own admission, and by the ostensible judgment of the narrator and of informed personages in the narrative like his niece, the Hideous Damsel, and his uncle, he is *malheureux* and his life has become an evil, a *mal*.[227] He forgets God, becoming, like Leviathan, a figure in a constellation with evil. The case is all the more compelling in that he, like Enide and Lancelot when they err, is guileless — he is innocently guilty. But he is redeemable, unlike Balain, "li plus mescheans chevaliers qui soit" (Huth *Merlin* II, 42) [the most unfortu-

nate of knights] in the post-Vulgate cycle. Similarly, the Lancelot-Grail cycle plays upon the connotations of the names Lancelot and Galaad as
expressive of evil and good, Guenevere and the grail or Satan and Christ.
Each knight in the *Queste* discovers the grail according to his "talents" —
that is, each provides for and achieves election according to his works, works
which realize inborn qualities through the achievement of adventures and
the knowledge of marvels.[228] Appellation demonstrates the election or rejection of the name bearer by the marvels he or she knows or fails to know
through adventures.

Mystery and the Marvelous

The romancers often stress the essential qualities of their figures by true or
false identities. Knights may hide their birth or sex under assumed names,
roles, or guises, as Fergus hides his low birth, Silence hides her womanhood,
or Ipomedon hides his love.[229] Pseudonyms or assumed names may clarify
(or obscure) a significant trait, like Chevalier au lion, Chevalier de la charrette, Chevalier à la manche, Chevalier aux deux épées, or Bel inconnu. Curiosity as to naming and significance of such appellatives moves mystery from
suspense to enigma,[230] from concern for what will happen (adventure) to the
source of the happening (marvel). Confusion and error, apperception and
intuitive apprehension in narrative figures and in the audience are common
effects of such curiosity.

Some mysteries are never entirely resolved.[231] Perceval seeks out "estranges
aventures" (6227) that go untold because he forgets God; yet when he is
reminded of God and told His mysterious names, we, as audience, are not
privy to this "sorplus" (6481–91). For Chrétien the mystery of God and the
mystery of love are marvels too great for tongue to express. In one sense,
what Perceval came to know — "reconut," relearned, recognized,
apprehended — every Christian is supposed to know.

> Issi Perchevaus reconnut
> Que Diex el vendredi rechut
> Mort et si fu crucefiiez.
> (*Perceval* 6509–11)

[Thus did Perceval come to know that God died and was crucified on that
Friday.]

But common knowledge is no longer superficial when acquired through the
experience of the marvel it communicates. The conventional words of love

exchanged during each encounter with Flamenca bring Guilhem gradually closer to the marvel which attracted him to Archambault's city in the first place.

> Amors ben pres de lui s'acointa
> E fes si mout gaia e cointa:
> Fort li promet et assegura
> Qu'il li dara tal aventura
> Que mout sera valent'e bona.
>
> . . . .
> "E tu sols deus la desliurar,
> Car tu es cavalliers e clercs."
> (*Flamenca* 1783–87, 1798–99)

[Love, grown gay and attractive, becomes his close confidant, promising insistently and guaranteeing to give him an adventure both very worthy and good. . . . "You alone must free her, for you are both knight and cleric."]

When he and Flamenca finally achieve their marvelous adventure, it is not only unsaid, it is inexpressible, as for Lancelot and Guenevere in the *Charrette*.[232]

> Que non es homs pogues notar
> Ni bocca dir ni cors pensar
> La benanansa c'usquex n'a;
> A negus homes meils non va;
> E quanc dic meilz—non jes tan be,
> Quan dic tan be—non lo mile.
> (*Flamenca* 5977–82)

[For no one could record nor tongue express or heart conceive the happiness that each enjoys from it. No one ever enjoyed it better. And when I say better, that is not good enough, nor in saying not good enough do I catch the thousandth part of it.]

Such hyperbole preserves something of the inscrutable or ineffable quality of marvels. Only Perceval, Galaad, Lancelot, and Guilhem attain full and complete experience. The audience only observes through the prism of language and whatever understanding and experience it may bring to the words. We do not know as they are described as knowing. Their understanding of mystery is our *émerveillement*.

Thus, a distinction exists between the narrative agent's alleged knowledge of the marvel and the audience's, a distinction which the authors deliberately use to evoke *émerveillement* and obscure the narrative separation between knowledge and mystery.[233] Knowledge rarely lends itself to conceptualization or didacticism, as in the hermits' explanations in the *Conte du graal* or in the *Queste:* "l'explication se réfère aux épisodes du récit lui-même [that is, to the adventures], et remplit une fonction dans son déroulement."[234] Zumthor goes on to identify the separation between the implicit medieval reader and the nonimplicit modern reader,[235] a separation analogous to the explicit class distinctions made in romances between those capable of understanding and thus knowing the context of the marvelous adventure on the one hand and those explicitly excluded and thus unable to know it on the other. Although there are diverse kinds of persons in audiences, ideally with respect to *senz* and *sapïence* (*Thèbes* 9–10) all are similar.[236] The personages chosen for the narrative adventures will be determined by social norms and prejudices.

> Ne parlerai de peletiers
> Ne de vilains ne de bouchiers,[237]
> Mes des deus freres parleré
> Et leur geste raconteré.
> (*Thèbes* 17–20)

[I won't speak of wool merchants, villeins, or butchers, but rather of two brothers; and I'll relate their history.]

The two are royal albeit perverse progeny.[238]

To the extremes of good and evil in the marvelous adventure correspond the extremes of good and evil through election which are opposed to condemnation and skepticism, as we see in the cases of Balain and Dinadan. How different these two are from Galaad! "Balain's Dolorous Stroke which inaugurated the fearsome adventures of Logres and destroyed three kingdoms . . . was not a deliberate outrage, but an unintentional fault, the culmination of a series of mischances which befell the unhappy knight."[239] Unintentional fault, but awful in its Old Testamental revenge.

> Ore comenchent lez aventurez et lez mervaillez du roialme aventurus, qui ne remanderont devant que chierement sera achaté che que la Seintim Lanche ont atouchez lez mains ordes et cunchiés et ont navré lez plus preudhome dez princez; si en prendra li Haus Maistres sa venjanche sor cheus qui ne l'ont pas deservi.[240]

[Now begin the adventures and marvels of the adventurous kingdom, which will not cease until it has been atoned for dearly that vile, filthy hands touched the most holy lance, and wounded the most worthy of princes. And the High Lord will take his vengeance on those who have not deserved it.]

The extension of *mescheances* from the Vulgate *Queste* and *Mort* to the entire cycle in the post-Vulgate effectively and mysteriously deprives the Arthurian world of the very significance the grail offered it in the Vulgate. Destiny works here as it does in the *Troie*: an incomprehensible force, it impels knights to disaster, and they destroy one another in marvelous adventures. Empty of meaning and even of redeeming opportunities, they participate in *mescheances* that, by the very adventure, assure guilt even in success. This was also Alexander the Great's fate in Alexandre de Paris' romance.[241] It is as if only adventures like those encountered in Perceval's five years of *errances* were left to relate in the thirteenth century. In the Second Version of the Prose *Tristan,* it is no wonder to find Dinadan ask in vain for adventures that give meaning to existence; there is no sense to prowess, love, or religion in *mescheance.* God's ways here are indeed mysterious. Subsequently romance tended to reject destructive marvels, returning to more pleasing adventures far removed from religious concerns, soul-searching, and doubt.[242] Romance had been a quest, an inquiry into marvels like the grail, the city, the woman, the heretofore indomitable other which can be achieved and known only by conquest. Now it tended merely to rehearse the same pattern of withdrawal and return separated by little more than the chivalric equivalent of prizefighting.

Since "memorable" events in history and romance stand out as extraordinary, their fascination elicits curiosity, a curiosity enhanced by their real, seeming, or provisional inscrutability. A knight typically sets out on a perilous adventure (*Claris* 24805–6). To know it, one seeks the marvel out, whatever and wherever it may be. The knight does so since he

> Forment desire l'aventure
> A savoir, qu'ele senefie;
> En son cuer pense et bien afie,
> Ja pour poor nel leissera,
> Tant que de verite savra,
> Quel aventure est, qu'il va querre.
> (*Claris* 24822–27)[243]

[desires very much to know what the adventure means. In his heart he thinks and affirms that he will never leave off out of fear until he knows in truth what that adventure is that he goes seeking.]

That achievement is the protagonist's adventure as *conte.*[244] All marvels possess some mystery that elicits inquiry. Adventure or a series of adventures provides the means to achieve the marvel.

Narrative adventures parallel the author's own inquest into the wonders of his or her sources. The peculiarity of the sources elicits fascination and the desire to understand them. Fascination is further enhanced by the marvel's coincidental rather than its causal character: *il avint que*. . . . The *aventure merveilleuse* is a pretext for the romance text, whereby the mysteries of the *matiere* are illuminated by authorial introspection until a *san* emerges.

Introspection is the right word. For if the marvel is found in the sources, its elucidation is a matter of invention. Invention is a mental process whereby the source and the understanding of the source coalesce before the mind's eye as a *status archetypus,* which is then fixed by involution in the *status sensilis* as *materia propinqua* and finished opus. The ineffable marvel is therefore not an impediment to good romance, it is its very essence. If to leave out the "surplus" was an established feature of the writing of the ancients, as Marie de France tells us, it was the task of the moderns to elucidate "ceo k'i ert." But her own *Lais* demonstrate the fact that *gloser la letre* is not necessarily to gloss as the *Ovide moralisé* glosses the tales of Ovid. *Ceo k'i ert,* in the *matiere,* includes marvelous adventures. They are what the ancient Bretons wanted to have remembered, precisely because they are marvelous. Similarly: "Des bons, dont auques sai la vie, les grans merveilles et les grans fais qu'il firent en l'ancien temps, vueil je metre en auctorité un livre grant et merveilleus tel comme je le voi en latin" (*Guiron* Pro p. 179) [I want to give authority to a great and marvelous book, as I find it in Latin, about the worthy, of whose lives I know something, and the great marvels and deeds which they performed in former times]. The "estranges choses et merveilleuses" (*Guiron* Pro p. 178) [strange and marvelous things] contained in it account for the romance's aesthetic appeal and its exemplary quality. No doubt, this explains the *Guiron* romancer's serial structure, which relates adventures within adventures and the knights' passing time during quests by relating their past achievement and encounters.[245] Such imbrication is precisely what we find in the graveyard adventure in the *Atre périlleux*.[246] The selection of marvelous adventures is part of the invention of *materia propinqua,* with as much marvelous material as narrative coherence will allow.

Coherence does not necessarily imply a sequence. But it does imply a context which makes the diverse *aventures merveilleuses* credible and comprehensible within narrative economy. *Conjointure* relies on a context wherein the marvelous—the *mirabilia*[247]—assumes significance as part of an orderly and comprehensible sequence of disparate events.

6

Estoire: Verité and *Senefiance*

> *Li mot fan de ver semblansa.*
> —Marcabru *XVIII.3*
>
> *The words produce the image of truth.*

Significance of Marvels

One striking feature of marvels is their apparent purpose or design.[1] When accommodated to a given context and audience,[2] intentionality *(antancion)* transforms the plot of the marvelous adventure into a significant illustration of chivalric life and mentalities. In the preceding chapter it was frequently difficult to distinguish between the marvel and its signification, since many marvels are no more than amplifications—*exaggerationes*—of topical images. Extraordinary descriptions of knights and ladies, of splendors architectural or mechanical, or of mystical states and visions are prominent examples. In them the marvel conveys an explicit message. "Par la lecture on communique non pas avec un monde féerique, mais avec le travail d'un écrivain"—the "painne" and "antancion" that Chrétien brought to the writing of the *Charrette*. "C'est ce travail qui définit le merveilleux."[3] Romance narrative translates the process of topical invention into the romance protagonist's discovery of meaning in confrontation with adventures and marvels.

> Cette quête incertaine et toujours continuée, que paraît commander, d'interrogation en interrogation et de réponse partielle en réponse partielle, une maïeutique des événements, signifie essentiellement la découverte progressive que le héros fait de lui-même et de ses virtualités, dont il prend peu à peu conscience et qu'il réalise dans l'action.[4]

Even those romances that seem to progress little beyond the repetitious statement of qualities continually revealed, but neither nuanced, elaborated upon,
nor magnified in encounters, serve to enhance those qualities *(interpretatio)*
and, through them, to provide some form of edification or assurance to the
audience that willingly suspends disbelief.

We may illustrate this insistence by miracles, the marvels of hagiography.
The Latin lives were written principally for a religious audience, more often
than not for monks.[5] They contain an implicit or explicit exhortation to strive
to emulate the saint and his or her exemplary life, to acquire his or her virtues, if not through torture and martyrdom, at least by strict adherence to
prescribed practices. This is the *sanctus imitabilis.* On the other hand, the
public for the vernacular lives is by and large lay; admonitions to imitate
the saint are, strictly speaking, inappropriate (except, of course, in the
representation of redeemable sinners like Theophile). The vernacular lives
emphasize hope for and trust in the intercession of the saint in favor of pardon for sins regretted with a contrite heart. They encourage prayer to the
sanctus adiutor.[6]

> Aiuns, seignors, cel saint home en memorie,
> Si li preiuns que de toz mals nos tolget.
> En icest siecle nus acat pais e goie,
> Ed en cel altra la plus durable glorie!
> *(Alexis* 621–24)[7]

[My lords, let us remember that holy man and pray to him to preserve us
from all harm. May he purchase peace and joy for us in this world and
enduring glory in the next.]

The marvels of the saint, the miracles performed in life or death, manifest
sanctity and vouchsafe the effectiveness of prayer. The written record
preserved the memory of the miraculous marvels, gave meaning to existence,
and confirmed faith; the stories edified.[8]

The *chanson de geste* took narrative cues from hagiography and raised
knightly prowess to the prominence of saints' miracles and their torments.
This is especially true for death in battle against pagans, a death tantamount
to martyrdom. But history as the record of achievements by noble families—
dynastic history[9]—became legendary history in the majority of *chansons de
geste,* which usually dwelt on heroism apart from holy wars, in the turbu-
lent relations between king or emperor and barons, or among the barons
themselves. French epic did not neglect marvels. We have observed that its
products were often so incredible as to preclude their being taken seriously
by chroniclers and other medieval historians.[10] The mighty blows of Roland

and Olivier, the marvelous encounters of Guillaume or Huon de Bordeaux
in Saracen lands are marvelous adventures like those of their Arthurian and
Greco-Roman peers. Epic heroes had a political and ethical immediacy for
the aristocracy that, by and large, their hagiographic counterparts could hold
only for those preferring the monastic life.

> Itel valor deit aveir chevaler
> Ki armes portet e en bon cheval set;
> En bataille deit estre forz e fiers,
> U altrement ne valt .IIII. deners;
> Einz deit monie estre en un de cez mustiers,
> Si prierat tuz jurz por noz peccez.
> (*Roland* I, 1877–82)

[Such should be the worth of a knight who bears arms and rides a good
horse: he should be strong and fierce in battle, otherwise he's not worth
four deniers, but should live as a monk in monasteries, praying daily for
our sins.]

Imitation of Roland, Olivier, Guillaume, and other barons defending their
rights against autocratic or stupid sovereigns was feasible for knights and
barons in twelfth- and thirteenth-century France. Excluded were members
of the lower classes.[11] For them, knighthood served in the secular realm a
role similar to that of sainthood in heaven: knights assured security, protection, and justice when they exercised their *dangier* correctly. Knighthood perhaps also provided cathartic consolation for the harsh existence of
commoners.[12]

To the ideals of epic—prowess and virtue or strength—the romances added the values of love as sung by the troubadours:[13] "cil ne doit en pris monter
/ Qui vers Amors n'a son corage" (*Bel inc* 3768–69) [he should not earn
renown who doesn't love]. The moral and feudal models defined the ideal
of love and lovers, made comprehensible its difficulties, and facilitated its
reception by the aristocracy.[14] Its beginnings are apparent in early vernacular histories;[15] historic romance as the *estoire* of past marvels and their concomitant adventures defines a class, its vocations, and ideals.[16]

> Pur remembrer des ancesurs
> Les feiz e les diz e les murs,
> Les felunies des feluns
> E les barnages des baruns,
> Deit l'um les livres e les gestes
> E les estoires lire a festes.
> (*Rou* III.1–6)

[In order to remember the deeds, works, and customs of our
forefathers—the felonies of the felonious, the noble deeds of the noble—
one should read books, records, and histories on festive occasions.]

The emphasis on *mores* classes such works as illustrations of noble and ignoble conduct. What that conduct would be depended on the didactic intent
of the author and the suitability of the narrative to the proposed audience.
There could, of course, be differences of opinion and variant intentions when
dealing with the same *matiere*. For example, Gaimar faults a contemporary
for not devoting more of a chronicle to love and sport as illustrative of vener-
able customs and the noble life (*Engleis* 6495–6502). No doubt he is following here the example of one of his major sources, Geoffrey of Monmouth.
But he is also anticipating the emergence of romance, which would evoke
past glory for contemporary edification in the context of chivalry, love, or,
eventually, Christian morality. These contexts evince the balance between
belligerent and peaceful activities Gaimar sought, suggesting debate like that
in Wace's *Brut* between Cador and Gauvain as to the relative worth of war,
or epic activities, and peacetime pursuits more typical of romance narrative.[17]

To accommodate marvels and the ideals of romance the romancers used
euhemerization and anachronism.[18] Sources handed down as marvels and
adventures from a presumed past underwent amalgamation with the ideals
"translated" out of them as empire, nation, class or social order, learning,
and love.[19] At the end of the thirteenth century, Dante identified those ideals
as prowess in arms, noble love, and rectitude.[20] He argues that these subjects should receive the most excellent representation in the best poetry and,
by implication, in romance. Each of the ideal themes identified by Dante
subsumes its opposite: *armorum probitas* implies life and death, *amoris accensio* implies love and lust, while *directio voluntatis* implies rectitude and
malevolence. Most romances pit the idealized knight and lady against willful culprits who seek to undermine what the idealized figures represent. That
representation is, however, more topical than it is discursive.

Truth of Narrative Matters

Romancers claim to possess a knowledge and a skill which they are duty
bound to put at the disposal of their audiences.[21] What they know they elicit
from the *matiere* they find, making it express and illustrate that knowledge.
How did they come by their skill? What vouchsafed the truth of what they
wrote?

Verité, in its simplest sense, is the empirical data of the matter at hand.
It states their physical or historical reality.

> Amix, digas me veritat,
> On lo laisset ni on lo vist?
> Era sanz?
>   (*Jaufre* 6370–72)²²

[Friend, tell me the truth. When did you leave him, where did you see him? was he well?]

Accordingly the *novas,* the *nouvelle,* is a true account of an *aventure.*

> "Sius plas, digas m'en veritat."
> E Jaufre a l'o tot comtat
> Del jaian con es avengut,
> Ni en cal guisa l'a vencut,
> Ni cos combatet am Taulat,
> C'al rei Artus l'a enviat,
> E del cavallier qu'era pres
> Col desliuret, ni col trames
> Al rei Artus ab los .v. cenz
> Si garnitz que res non es mens,
> Comtat loi a tot enaissi,
> Que anc de res non li menti,
> Con ieu vos ai denant comtat.
>   (*Jaufre* 6769–81)²³

["Pray tell me the truth." And Jaufre told all about what had happened with the giant and how he defeated him; how he fought with Taulat whom he had sent to King Arthur; and how he delivered the imprisoned knight and sent him to King Arthur with his five hundred men completely outfitted. He told it just so, without a lie, as I have told you before.]

However, as we have observed, the facts of the case may not be clear. This uncertainty produced the issue *(status)* in forensic rhetoric and required a trial to establish probable or credible truth. The trial entailed the selection, interpretation, and disposition of evidence. The technique, which included topical invention, is used in *Jaufre* as well. One need only peruse the text summarized in the above citation to appreciate to what extent topical interpretation has permeated Jaufre's adventures with credible or received ideas, commonplaces, and practices.²⁴ Similarly, Thomas of Kent conceives of truth in terms of topical *circumstantiae,* using truth and lie to enhance the figure of Alexander by contrast.

> Le roy Porrus li dit: "Donc dy moy la verité,
> Quels hom est Alisandre, cum grant e de quel é?"
> "Par foy, sire, frans est e larges e de grant bonté,

Mes petit est de corps e vielz e mult barbé.
Il ad, mien escient, plus de cent anz passé,
Si est freiz tant k'en mie esté
Ad il a son manger treis mantels affublé."
(*TChev* 5267–73)

[King Porrus said to him: "Tell me then the truth. What kind of man is
Alexander? How tall is he and how old?" "In faith, my lord, he is noble,
generous, and of great goodness; but he is short, old, and has a heavy
beard. He is, I know, over a hundred years old, and is so cold that in the
middle of summer he wears three mantels when he eats."]

Romances may elucidate several different kinds of truth in fictional garb.[25]
The representations of truth correspond to explicit auctorial concerns that
vary from romance to romance according to diverse topical involution in
sources. The real and apparent intertextuality and deconstruction this process suggests constitute the romance tradition—a tradition the romancers were
aware of, and within which they worked inventively. That tradition gave
relevance to marvelous tales of old.

Topical Invention of Narrative Significance

Transmission tended to strip marvels of their earlier rationale, usually a
mythological worldview that had become incomprehensible or unacceptable to the receiving civilization. The very obscurity, incomprehensibility, and
therefore seeming mendacity of the sources made them an object of wonder—
wonder that found meaning in new contexts. Topical invention was a technique to elicit context from a source, either by lifting through studious *pensers*
the veils of obscurity laid over the material by the "ancients," or by restoring
the work damaged by time and the vicissitudes of transmission.

Romancers insist on the truth of their *matiere,* and thus of the romance
and the marvels it relates. Adenet le Roi says that he has included in the *Cleomadés* only "certaine chose et voire" (18513)[26] [certain, true matter]. Before
him, Wace sought out reliable evidence for his own romance chronicles, even
when the search took him into the forest of Broceliande. He found nothing
true and certain there. What Breton or British *matiere* he did know seemed
dubious, so that he refused to include it in the *Brut* or the *Rou.* Like Gauvain and Hector in the Vulgate *Queste,* he encountered no adventures in
Broceliande. Wace could not see the grail, as it were, because he failed to
perceive that the marvels of Broceliande spring up in the mind as visions of
truth.[27] It took a Chrétien de Troyes to discover truth by the fountain of
Berenton. The scribe of B. N. fr. 1450 seems to have understood this, as
he inserted Chrétien's romances into the *Brut* after Wace's rejection of fabulous Breton tales.[28]

What Chrétien and his generation of romancers discovered was "literary truth."[29] They recognized the difference between a real or factual truth and an ideal or projected truth, the latter being translated through topical involution.[30] Marie de France recognized this genius among the ancients.[31] Were these inventions just so many castles in Spain? Or did they evince "the capacity for creating something that starts as a dream and ends by fashioning human life"? For, Eugène Vinaver continues, "It takes time before it [the dream] is ready to be translated into a reality."[32] That reality in the Spanish, and French, castles of medieval romance is love. This is what Chrétien seeks there, as the *Yvain* preliminaries suggest. Surely there was precious little love in the forest of Broceliande when Wace went there. Chrétien de Troyes found it by invention, invention which, in the author's mental conception, serves to "surmonter les contradictions du réel,"[33] like the stylistic and social contradictions found in the *vilain courtois.*

Erich Köhler has described courtly romance as first and foremost "a quest for truth" *(Wahrheitssuche).*[34] Jehan Bodel measures the quality of different kinds of romance by their relative approximation to truth. The *matière de Bretagne,* although "plesant," was also "vain." French material is "veror," more true even than Roman *matière,* wise and instructive as the latter may be (*Saisnes* 9–11). Yet Bodel's *Saisnes* is obviously not history by the standards even of Guernes de Pont-Sainte-Maxence's *Thomas Becket* or of the anonymous *Guillaume le maréchal.* The *Saisnes* includes amplificatory developments, especially on love, which preclude our taking Bodel's truth as fidelity to historic fact.

Romancers also stress the veracity of their sources.[35] Heldris de Cornuälle, for one, professes to retain what is "true" in his Latin source (*Silence* 1660–69), although he also confesses to having blended the true and the false.

> Jo ne di pas que n'i ajoigne
> Avoic le voir sovent mençoigne
> Por le conte miols acesmer.
> (*Silence* 1663–65)

[I don't deny inserting many a fable into the truth, in order to embellish the story.]

The mendacious additions fill in gaps or provide rhymes.[36] Heldris' words seem to justify Wace's rejection of Arthurian fables, embellished by the storytellers, as more false than true.

The emergence of Arthurian prose romance to correct Chrétien and his contemporaries would further seem to support Wace's judgment. Prose romance was allegedly written to preclude the distortions and falsifications necessitated by or inherent in verse history and romance.[37] Still, thirteenth-

century prose romance sometimes relies on the verse sources it condemns.[38]
In fact, the principal distinction between the two seems to reside in the truth
each espouses as ultimate and final[39] — Dante's arms and love in the verse
romances, but virtue and moral rectitude in the prose romances. This distinction does not depend on the medium of verse or prose, as hagiography
demonstrates by using both.

The prose romances themselves offer instructive indications as to how truth
and falsehood are perceived in romance. One of their methods is the adaptation of source to a new truth, or at least to a new conception of the truth
as expressed in earlier versions of the same romance. This adaptation can
be readily observed both in the prose romances' version of the love of Lancelot and Guenevere in Chrétien's *Charrette* and in the replacement of both
Lancelot and Perceval by Galaad as the best knight.[40] The post-Vulgate *Graal*
also effects adaptations on the Vulgate to which, nonetheless, it is related
much as Chrétien related his *Yvain* to the *Charrette:* by cross-references.[41]
The same is true in the Prose *Tristan* and subsequent prose romances.[42] Amplificatory additions reflect back on and thus show in a new light earlier
matieres to which they are adjoined, producing a new vision that conforms
more closely to the truth of the *matiere* as the new author or scribe perceives
it. Prior to such elucidation, the old matter is incomplete *(corronpue)* from
the new point of view; the additions complete its meaning.

The anonymous author of the Vulgate *Estoire* uses the technique to blend
a "scientific" and a "creationist" explanation of the Turning Island. The
"peasants" call it Turning Island because it rotates once each day with the
heavens. But this explanation is not enough.

> Quar dont seroit-il [= the tale] uns enlacemens de paroles, se il de cascune
> doutance dont il parleroit ne moustroit apiertement raison et couinssance,
> autressi comme font une maniere de gent qui dient maintes paroles et les
> vauroient affremer a voires, et si ne puent traire avant nul tesmong, fors que
> tout seulement que dire l'ont oï as autres. (*Estoire* II, 428)

> [For otherwise it would be a jumble of words if it didn't propose a clear expla-
> nation and interpretation for each dubious subject it treated, as does a certain
> kind of loquacious people who would assert the veracity of what they say, and
> yet offer no evidence except that they have heard it from others.]

Wace stopped short at unsubstantial reports. But Heldris de Cornuälle did
not, nor did Chrétien or the author of the *Estoire.* "De ceste maniere mau-
vaise se escuse chis contes, kar il ne traist auques parole nule avant, u il puisse
apiercevoir doutance, que il ne le face de tout en tout apert counoistre et
pour çou est-il a droit apielés l'estoire des estoires" (*Estoire* II, 428–29) [this

tale declines to avail itself of such devices, for it advances nothing that seems doubtful without making it completely comprehensible. And that is why it is rightly called *estoire* of *estoires*]. The author invents a plausible explanation for the island, relying on medieval notions of creation and science regarding what is credible and possible. The manner is not different from Chrétien's, except that the latter's truths are different from and, indeed, fundamentally alien or even opposed to those of the prose romances. The distinction recalls that made by Alain de Lille between the useless *coniuncturae* of poets and the valid ones of philosophers, or that in the Horace commentaries between *compilatores* and *compositores*. The specific informing truth, the one acceptable to author and audience, makes the difference between *enlacemens de paroles* and *tesmong*.

But what are the character and import of the additions romancers make? The example of the *Ovide moralisé,* although relatively late, is instructive. The glossators of mythological fables found a historical beginning for their sources. By euhemerization they reconstructed the historical core of the fables that had been "falsified" in pagan mythology and religious literature. Jupiter the god derived from Jupiter, king of Crete. Such "historical" readings of the fables explained the active participation of the gods in the affairs of men. Benoît de Sainte-Maure, for example, faults "Omer" for just such blending of human history and mythology. However, Benoît and the other authors of the *romans antiques* do not entirely suppress the gods and goddesses. Rather, they tend to retain, even enhance, the roles of those corresponding traditionally to forces active among men: Venus, Cupid, Minerva, Juno.[43] Benoît's suppression of the pagan pantheon is partly expressed in terms of material style: their conflict with mortals seemed preposterous to him. One is reminded of Beroul's reluctance to pit knights against villeins.

> Li contor dïent que Yvain
> Firent nïer, qui sont vilain;
> N'en sevent mie bien l'estoire,
> Berox l'a mex en sen memoire:
> Trop ert Tristran preuz et cortois
> A ocirre gent de tes lois.
> (*Tristan* Ber 1265–70)[44]

[The storytellers say they killed Yvain, but those storytellers are villeins. They don't have the story right. Beroul has a better version in his memory (writing?). Tristan was far too noble and worthy to kill people of such a social order.]

Beroul's words reflect material style that fits action to character and social order for the sake of decorum and verisimilitude. Additions or adaptations conforming to context in no way falsify the matter in the topical sense. Rather, they make the narrative conform to expectation and thus to what is credible. The goal of topical invention is ethical or social truth.

Benoît asserts that he will add to the *matiere* of Dares and Dictys, insisting, however, the he will be circumspect in making the additions. "Ne di mie qu'aucun bon dit / N'i mete, se faire le sai" (*Troie* 142–43)[45] [I don't deny that I put in a few additions, when I know how to do so]. He insists he will add no more nor less than what is necessary (132–37). A glance at the *Troie* might suggest that, for Benoît as for Voltaire, *le superflu, chose très nécessaire!*

But are Benoît's additions "superfluous"? Completeness and perfection explain some additions.[46] As we have seen, Heldris de Cornuälle argues that his own "mendacious" accretions enhance the quality of his romance, but do not subtract from the truth that is already in it (*Silence* 1666–67). Do these words not refer to the *colores operum* by which Horace and commentators like Matthew of Vendôme sought to enhance the truth of what they wrote?[47] A passage in *Perceforest* seems to refer to procedures analogous to those suggested by Benoît and Heldris while trying to strike a balance between excessive amplification and abbreviation.

> Pour ce que je ne vous puis pas tout recorder par parolles, — pour ce que je vous feroye ennuy et que la matiere n'a mestier à prolonger, — convient que je florisse les faitz et prolonge par parolles ung peu plus long que je ne les ay trouvees au latin, pour estre ung petit plus delectables à ouyr, sans rien adjouster aux faitz de nouvel; car se je disoye: "celluy tua celluy, et celluy navra l'autre," et m'en passasse aussi briefvement que fait le latin, on vous auroit tantost tout compté, et si n'y auriez plaisance à l'ouyr ne deduyt. Et se je floris les faiz par parolles plaisantes selon les faitz qui sont touchez en gros au latin, ce n'est pas de merveille, car tout aussi tost pourroit il ennuier par trop brief passer que par trop demourer. (*Perceforest* 74:89)[48]

> [Since I cannot report to you everything — because I would displease you and the matter doesn't need to be any longer — it behooves me to adorn the account, amplifying it somewhat more than I have found in the Latin version; this will make it more pleasing to hear without adding anything new to the account. For were I to say: "this one killed that one and that one wounded this one," and thus dispensed with it as briefly as the Latin does, you would soon have heard everything and there would be no pleasure or delight in hearing it. But if I embellish the deeds with pleasant language that fits the deeds which are touched more generally in the Latin, it's no wonder, for one could bore as quickly by excessive brevity as by inordinately dwelling on the topics.]

There had to be a correlation between the source material and the auctorial inventions: "aloignier ne voil ma matire / Ne faire fable de noient" (*Perceval*

Cont I *EMQU* 882–83)[49] [I don't wish to lengthen my *matiere* nor make a fable out of nothing]. Thomas of Kent is even more explicit about such amplification in translating a source.

> La verité ai estrait, si l'estorie[50] ne ment.
> N'ai sez faiz acreu, çoe vus di verreiement,
> Mes beles paroles i ai mis nequedent.
> N'i ai acreu l'estoire ne jo n'i ost nient;
> Pur plaisir as oianz est un atiffement;
> Home ne deit lange translater autrement;
> Qui direit mot por mot, trop irreit leidement.
>   (*TChev* P11–17 = p. 120)

[I have drawn out the truth, if the history is not false. I have not added to what it says, I assure you, but I have nevertheless embellished it. I have not added to the history or removed anything from it. There is ornamentation to please the audience. One should not translate a language in any other way. Whoever renders it word for word carries out the task in an ugly manner.]

Now, Thomas of Kent is not speaking about tropical or figural ornamentation.[51] Topical additions, or more properly amplifications, permit us to understand better Jehan Bodel's qualitative distinctions regarding the truth of the *matieres* of France, Rome, and Britain on the basis of relative majesty, as well as to perceive how euhemerization and the use of *integumenta* and glosses (as practiced in the *Ovide moralisé* and allegorical romance) could make obscure sources clear by expressing a new truth allegedly enclosed in the wonders found in the sources.

Jehan Bodel founds his assessment of French *matiere* on the preeminence of the French crown.[52] Surely, when Bodel wrote the *Saisnes,* just before 1200, Philippe Auguste, the legitimate heir of Charlemagne, seemed more credible, more real, more true, and thus better as king than did John Lackland, whose only support was the misty bond between his father, Henry II, and a marvelous Arthur found buried at Glastonbury. French *matiere* draws from the crown a preeminence extending from the Charlemagne of the Spanish and Saxon wars to the contemporary reigning monarch;[53] that preeminence is meaningful because of the qualities Jehan Bodel perceived in the French crown and which he amplified upon in his adaptation: "Seignor, ceste chançons ne muet pas de fabliaus, / Mais de chevalerie d'amours et de cembiaus" (*Saisnes* 25–26) [my lords, this song does not spring from fabliaux, but from knighthood, love, and jousts]. He still believes that those ideals are perceptible in his principal source, "Dont encor est l'estore a Saint-Faron a Miaus" (*Saisnes* 34)[54] [the *estoire* of which is still at Saint Faron's at Meaux], from which "naist de la chançon et racine et tuiaus / Dont li chans et li dis est raisnables et biaus" (*Saisnes* 41–42) [arises the root and trunk of the *chanson,* whose song and words are understandable and beautiful].

These words recall Geoffrey of Vinsauf's summary description of amplification: "Sic surgit permulta seges de semine pauco . . . " (*Poetria nova* 687) [in this way, plentiful harvest springs from a little seed . . .]. Benoît de Sainte-Maure's topical harvest was indeed plentiful, as the *Troie*'s lengthy amplifications show.[55] Amplification justifies the "mendacious" material Heldris de Cornuälle incorporated into *Silence.* Similarly, Guillaume de Lorris does not view his amplifications as detracting from the truth of the *Roman de la rose,* not only because he made the dream analogous to biography (*Rose* 28–30), but also because of the application of the dream's personified ego to the universal experience of love. It is true because it is credible, and it is credible because the ideas that inform the narrative, as well as their plotting, conform to audience ideals and expectations.[56]

Jehan Bodel's adaptation of Charlemagne to the ideals and ambitions of the French crown of around 1200 is not dissimilar to the euhemerization of mythology in mythographies. This kind of topical invention further corresponds to the adaptation of sources of Celtic provenience in Arthurian romance. These tales, like the Ovidian myths, are *vain* and *plesant,* [57] their matter allegedly as marvelous as that of Horace's *vanae species.* But like dreams, whose surface or letter is also *vain* and *plesant,* they may conceal truth, truth which may be descried by topical invention.

Adaptation reveals ethical stances in Arthurian romance as well. First, there are the alleged historical facts paralleling the euhemerization of Jupiter as the king of Crete in the mythographic Ovid or the historical Guillaume's appearance as a biographical source in the *Rose.* More important, a topical truth imbues the *matiere* with accepted ideals by euhemerization: *chevalerie, amours,* and *cembiaus* in Jehan Bodel,[58] *chevalerie* and *clergie* in Chrétien, *amours* in Guillaume de Lorris, the *fin'amours* of courtly *chansons* and a popular *conte* in *Guillaume de Dole.*[59] At issue are opposing or contrasting worldviews.[60] The validity of each truth depends on the faith of the audience and the author's success in convincingly comprehending that faith and expressing it in his or her romance.[61] "The affirmation of shared ideals within the context of public performance is a fact of great importance for any culture in which tradition is the prime element of law and in which the law is itself transmitted orally."[62] Law in Old French—*loi*—is of wide application, ranging from the legal system to the authority which established it: aristocratic court, the church, the lord, the king, and God—all could be made to claim authority in matters of war, love, and virtue.[63]

There was no general agreement regarding particular worldviews and the truths meant to validate them.[64] Jehan Bodel himself may not have escaped implicit, even, perhaps, explicit censure for "vanity," especially in hagiography and in the grail romances.

> Kar ge le vus di seurement,
> Meuz vaut oir ici entour
> Ke de la geste paenur,
> De Guercedin e de Saisons,
> Deu enemis e felons,
> E d'autre teus pur verité,
> U l'em vus ment a grant plenté;
> Ky aime e ot la vanité,
> Deu li en set mut de malgré.
> (*Osith* 88–96)[65]

[For I assure you that this sort of thing is better to listen to here than the pagan *gestes* of Guercedin and the Saxons, enemies of God and felons, as well as of others of the same ilk wherein there is an abundance of lies. God is angry with those who love and listen to vanity.]

All three *matieres* are exemplary rather than factual. Consequently, they are all alike in argument; the preference for one truth or the other may well depend on extraliterary circumstances.[66] In his preference for French over British matter, Bodel does not deny the pleasing features of Arthurian romance, but he does describe as vain the, for him, fictional superiority of the British over the French that such matter suggested. His is a dynastic argument comprehensible in the context of the *translatio imperii* commonplace. Similarly, the difference between the worldview implicit in Chrétien's romances and that in the prose romances ultimately rests on opposing aristocratic and religious morals.

Roles of Author, Narrator, Patron, and Audience in Topical Invention: Antancion

Romance *matieres* translate and express an intention.[67] Their *intentio,* as we have seen, can be that of author, narrator, patron, or audience. Ideally these coincide. Earlier scholarship tended to emphasize the author's *intentio* to such an extent that even formal or thematic patterns were explained by reference to the author's alleged personal opinions, as seen, for example, in the obsolete critical debasement of the *Charrette* because of Chrétien de Troyes' putative bourgeois aversion to adultery.[68] Of late, the audience's expectations, as well as the specific audience addressed in the text, have begun to receive more attention.[69] Medieval audiences may be as elusive as their authors.[70] But any author trained in the tradition of the paradigm for invention would be aware of *intentio* as the expression of auctorial conception and, as a corollary, the intended audience's ideas and expectations, including those of the specific person for whom the work was written.[71] There is explicit reference to these considerations in those romances which insist upon an audience composed only of nobility and clerics, or of lovers, capable of appreciating the ideals and subjects set forth. Understanding is thus essential to appreciation: it is not enough to know the simple meaning or to appreciate only the significance of what is related. One must be swayed by and seek to assimilate it. In this way, understanding would lead to conviction and commitment.

The invention of chivalric language—Marie de France's "surplus de sen"—in received *matiere* effected a union of *matiere* and *san* that served a specific intention. Vernacular histories illustrate this process in verisimilar, exemplary narrative, and romances followed their lead. But the eye of the heart, perusing the records of the past, read differently from the eyewitness, the most reliable authority in medieval historiography. The marvel of the *materia remota* took on the topics dictated by auctorial intention and became *materia propinqua*. That is, the mind of the artist scrutinized sources and identified in them those places *(loci)* suitable for amplification in conformity with auctorial intention. That context was deemed inherent in the source, but obscure prior to study—that is, study as "vehemens et assidua animi applicatio ad aliquid agendum cum summa voluntate"[72] [strenuous, assiduous application of the mind to realizing a specific intention with the utmost determination]. For the *accessus ad auctores*, such "study" realizes auctorial *intentio*: according to the *Charrette* Prologue, it is the "painne" that accompanies "antancion."

Auctorial intention may be narrative or contextual. Narrative intention reconstructs past events from surviving fragments. It satisfies the purely historical requirement to preserve the memory of the past by recording it in writing. Thus, the different authors who wrote romances about Alexander the Great wished to keep alive the memory of his deeds.[73] Similarly, the anonymous author of the *Dame a la lycorne* intended to recall the adventures of two lovers (*Lycorne* 8562–63); *Guiron le courtois* is written "pour ce donques que nus ne s'entremet d'escripre les fais des Bruns ne du bon chevalier Guron le courtois" (Pro p. 182) [because no one undertakes to relate the deeds of the Bruns or of the good knight Guiron le courtois]. Narrative intention is apparent even in details of plot organization, as when rubrics announce the progress of the work: "en cestui lieu proprement ou nous avons laisiez nos amyz en prison mon intention est de raconter . . . comment par la vaillance et prouesse de messire Lancelot du lac messire Guiron le courtois fut delivré de prison" (*Guiron* §132 n. 1) [at that very place where we left our friends in prison my intention is to relate . . . how the valiancy and prowess of my lord Lancelot du Lac delivered my lord Guiron from prison]. Or even more broadly: "Contar vos ey pleneyrament / Del Alexandre mandament" (*Alex* AdeP 25–26) [I shall relate to you fully Alexander's power]. Linking passages in interlaced adventures effects the same purpose as the rubric: to make known auctorial intention regarding narrative progress.

Contextual intention, on the other hand, is more fundamental to the truth of romance. Thus, the foregoing illustration stating the intention to relate Lancelot's liberation of Guiron includes topical allusions to *vaillance* and *prouesse* that make Lancelot's feat credible. The Alexander legend was also written to stand as an example for all times (*Alex* APar I.1–10, 30–31). The *Dame a la lycorne,* besides telling the story of two lovers, proposes to use their love for exemplary illustration, that is:

> pour moustrer ensengnement
> Que doivent fere li ament;
> Car qui d'amour bien voet joïr,
> A tout pechié il doit fuïr,
> Et qui ce visce bien esloingne,
> A boine fin vient sa besongne.
> (*Lycorne* 8564–69)

[to teach how lovers should conduct themselves. For he or she who wishes to delight in love should eschew all wrongdoing; and by acting accordingly, his or her undertaking will come to a good end.]

In *Meliador,* the fondest desire of the knights is to engage in combat with other knights: "Tele estoit li affection / D'yaus tous, selonch m'entention" (19096–97) [such was their common desire, according to my reading of the narrative]. Contextual *antancion* is a critical reading of the *matiere* that elucidates it according to the chosen context.

The articulation of *materia propinqua* to fit a given intention required careful consideration by a mind trained to provide a consistent reading: the author

> s'antremet
> De panser, que gueres n'i met
> Fors sa painne et s'antancïon.
> (*Charrette* 28–30)

[undertakes to think, for he provides little more than his effort and his *antancion.*]

As we have seen, auctorial *sans* is the trained mind of the artist which, made parallel and virtually synonymous with *antancion* in these lines, distinguishes the informing idea—Marie de Champagne's *san*—from the elaboration of that idea in a plot. The elaboration is the invention of the plot as the author alone conceives it,[74] that is, the operation whereby, through *painne* and *sans* as *antancion,* the author achieves a *bele conjointure.*[75] Adaptation, correction, or the reconciliation of differences entailed interpretation and clarification—the extraction of meaning from strange, marvelous, or perplexing sources. The artist's task *(coniuncta segregare* and *disgregata coniungere)* required thought on and selection of the material most suitable for an extraordinary, striking impact (the *aventure merveilleuse)* and for the potential significance of that material (its *verité).* In this phase of composition, the romancer effects the transition from what Geoffrey of Vinsauf terms the *status archetypus* to the *status sensilis.*

Such adaptation could be far-reaching. Jean de Meun's adaptation of Guillaume de Lorris first rereads and corrects Guillaume's narrative, then appends an elaborate conclusion that conclusively rejects and overwhelms his predecessor's courtly idealism.[76] To preclude precisely such revision, Chrétien de Troyes warned his readers against "mendacious" additions that might be introduced into *Yvain* by subsequent scribes, copyists, or authors (6804–8).[77]

Now, one writer's truth may be another's lie, as Jehan Bodel's evaluation of the *matière de Bretagne* suggests, and as the prose adaptations of Arthurian verse romance prove. In other words, corrections were made. The cemetery scene in Chrétien's *Charrette,* for example, shows Lancelot in possession of the qualities necessary for the liberation of the prisoners in Gorre, including Guenevere herself. Lancelot's unique role corresponds to his unique combination of love and prowess. But in the Vulgate prose cycle that combination not only anticipates Lancelot's successful liberation of the prisoners, as in Chrétien. More important, it also explains the eventual condemnation of his love for Guenevere in the *Queste,* a condemnation foreshadowed by the prose romance's introduction of a second tomb into the cemetery, a tomb which only a virgin and chaste knight may open. That knight will be Galaad. The reading of the love between Lancelot and Guenevere in Chrétien's *Charrette* was corrected in this way to conform to the intention of the Lancelot-Grail. The imposition is not mendacious; it supports a new truth from which it may be said to emanate by the topical technique of doubling.

Eleventh- and twelfth-century historiography once more provided a pattern for such techniques. Recent studies in this field suggest the importance of auctorial intention in the adaptation of historical narrative to secular ideals.[78] Modern perplexity about the character of historical truth is a problem that troubled medieval commentators as well, although for different reasons. Their search for historical validity in the chronological sequence of events, which seemed less causally determined than simply intermittent, was often founded on the identification of significant patterns connecting one event to another, integrating them in a common mode.[79] A pattern or model may provide formal arrangement and correlation of material evidence susceptible of discursive commentary and allegorization. In this scheme of things, both historical *gesta* and dream visions fall under the same heading as significant narrative *(narratio fabulosa),* whatever the mode of and model for representation; both underscore the exemplary or moral intention that defines narrative adventures and marvels.

Vernacular history coincides with romance in the operation of intention. But the pattern chosen for representation changes as romance distinguishes itself from history. The difference is most obvious in extreme cases. History in annals is the sequence of events that seemed important at a given time and place, but whose occurrences are essentially fortuitous, even random:[80] they evince no immediately perceptible organizing principle. Even the paschal calendar is closer to romance than such mere chronological lists of events: that is, it focuses on the elusive wonder of Easter. Romance similarly discloses a meaningful pattern in disparate material. The identification of the pattern is the discovery of the work's principle of organization; intention identifies the kind of pattern the author seeks.

There is in this intention something of the notion of the "mind-set," of which the most notorious examples in the Middle Ages are falsifications of documents.[81] History and, a fortiori, fiction are read according to a given model of historical, social, or moral significance; a writer's reading of a romance plot is rhetorical and preconceived. Chrétien de Troyes achieved formal organization of discrete "historical" elements by the use of patterned *reprises* that express an informing idea in diverse episodes.[82] The *Charrette* Prologue brings together all the major factors in romance composition: a patron's *matiere* and understanding *(san),* as well as an author's intention in the plotting of the romance. Chrétien's auctorial intention realized Marie's in the elaboration and writing down *(painne)* of the romance narrative. The skill in locating the *inventa* in meaningful patterns required discernment of how the *inventa* themselves may signify. The resultant configuration gave expression to the idea upon which the opus was modeled.

The notion of a context within which one may understand and appreciate romance narrative is not the same as that of the *Thesenroman* once applied to Chrétien de Troyes.[83] One can no doubt extract a coherent thesis from a romance by glossing and synthesis. But the text itself is not incoherent if the author has not devised a conceptual grid which molds the narrative into a virtual equation or treatise, such as Ovid's *Ars amatoria* and *Remedia.* The reason that only the aristocracy and the clericy could appreciate romance is that romance quite explicitly spoke their language, the language of prow-

ess, chivalry, and love set forth by applying medieval poetic theory in vernacular works; villeins, like the one in *Yvain,* did not understand that
language.[84] Similarly, when the cleric abdicates his dependence on the
aristocracy, the latter's language may survive in romance, but it also undergoes a reevaluation, as in the *Queste del saint graal* and Jean de Meun's *Rose.*
The cleric judges and dictates conduct in these latter works. He or she is
unlike the scribes at Arthur's court in the prose romances, who simply record the deeds of knight errantry in the knight's own language, or Chrétien
in the *Charrette,* who speaks of love with the *san* of a lady.

Language of Narrative Articulation: Raison

Raison refers to language, and, more specifically, language that explains the
causes of or the principles for actions and sentiments, as in the troubadours'
razos.[85] These two senses, distinct in classical Latin, came together in the
Middle Ages. In romance, *raison* could designate both narrative and the narrative's implied significance: "Par meïsmes ceste raisun / Pernum essample
del leün' (*Fables* XIV.33–34)[86] [by these words and actions let us make an
example of the lion]. Use of *raison* to refer to narrative allowed for ideas
assumed to be inherent in matter to be elicited from it by topical invention
so as to determine or explain action. *Raison* therefore refers not only to the
speech act but also to its contents.

> Mesire Bruns tot escouta
> Quanque li Galois li conta;
> Bien a sa raison entendue.
> (*Durmart* 3965–67)[87]

[My lord Brun listened to all the Welshman told him; he understood what
he said very well.]

As speech, the word may apply to the language of a specific social class or
audience, and, accordingly, express the attitudes that characterize that audience or the principles it takes to motivate conduct and validate narrative.
For example, the *Durmart* author concludes his "roial conte d'aventure" (14)
[royal tale of adventure] by admonishing his audience—royalty and high
nobility—to heed the tale and act on its exemplary narrative.

> Or entendés a ma raison
> Roi et duc et conte et baron,
> Vos qui les grans terres tenés
> Et qui povre vie menés;
> Menbre vos des bons anciens

> Qui jadis fisent les grans biens
> Dont il les grans honors conquisent.
> Faites ausi comme cil fisent
> Dont li grant bien sont raconté;
> Sovigne vos de lor bonté
> Que lor largece et cortoisie
> Soit renovelee et florie,
> Et que par vos soit rensaucie
> Onors qui trop est abaissie.
>   (*Durmart* 15957-70)[88]

[Attend to what I am going to relate, kings and dukes, counts and barons, you who hold the great lands while leading a mean life — remember those worthies of old who in bygone days performed the magnificent deeds whereby they won great honor and land. Do as they did whose good deeds are recounted. Remember their goodness, that their largess and courtesy may be renewed and flourish, that through you honor may be restored, which is now so demeaned.]

The author, story, and audience focus on the abstract qualities the contemporary nobility should perpetuate in imitation of forefathers represented in the romance, qualities which are topical. These qualities suppose auctorial comprehension, topical elaboration in the tale, and affirmative attention to their significance by the audience. "Ne veul que ma raisons soit de tel gent oïe / Qui bien ne sache entendre que ele senefie" (*Alex* APar IV.1621-22) [I don't want my words to be heard by people who are unable to understand their significance]; rather, "ceste raison devroient cil oïr / Qui sont de haut parage et ont terre a baillir" (*Alex* APar IV.1630-31)[89] [those ought to heed my words who are of high birth and possess lands]. The abstract qualities that make the *conte* a *raison* also characterize the mentality of the work's projected audience, which facilitates communication and comprehension. Further, *raison* removes the tale from the category of mendacious fable (*Alex* APar IV.1623).

Raison in these examples refers to narrative, speech, and reason as a mental faculty. As narrative, it is a coherent and orderly account of events.[90] As speech, it is the language peculiar to the social order represented by the implied audience, usually understood to be aristocratic and including clerical sympathizers. In the Middle Ages, when hierarchy and status were readily translated into material style, that translation was apparent in narrative emphases. Those emphases, and thus predilections, defined the audience by the qualities and ideals that audience as a social group associated with its own ethic. As reason, *raison* defined the authority of the author as the one who spoke an exemplary truth: what one praises or blames must be right — that is, *avoir raison*.[91]

The author of *Yder* thus includes the courteous and the noble in his audience.

> Cest livre falt ici e fine;
> Por rei fu fait e por reine
> E por clers e por chevaliers
> Qui bials diz oent volenters,
> Por dames e por damaiseles
> Qui mult sunt cortaises e beles,
> E nient pas por altre gent
> Ne fu fait le livre naient.
> (*Yder* 6762–69)[92]

[This book stops and ends here. It was written for king and queen, for clerics and knights who willingly listen to fine words. It was made for ladies and maidens who are very courteous and beautiful, and for no one else.]

Rhetoric traditionally taught that certain subjects are suitable only for certain audiences. Only the courteous can appreciate a romance intended to display courtesy. The most intimate audience is the loved one.[93] But the loved one herself is usually exemplary and thus part of a specific group of connoisseurs frequently described as lovers. From this perspective, Aimon de Varennes writes for both his lady and the ideals of courtesy.

> Aymes por amour anulli
> Fist le romant si saigemant
> Que tei l'orait que ne l'antant
> Por coy il fut et faitz et dis:
> Par cortoisie fut escris.
> (*Florimont* 8–12)

[Aimon wrote the romance for someone, and he did so with such prudence that one could hear it and not understand why it was made and published. It was written for the sake of courtesy.]

Similarly, the art of love in Guillaume's *Rose* corresponds to her for whom he undertook to write the romance. She is therefore analogous to the romance and "doit estre Rose clamee" (44) [ought to be called Rose]. The truth the adventures hold for "real life" makes the dream true (*Rose* 28–30).

The fictional examples of the trials in the various versions of the Seven Sages express truth in the same manner[94] as do Jean Renart's renditions of aristocratic marvels: by exemplary narrative.

> Et ki boune parole assenlle
> Por traire as gens en essamplaire,
> C'est une chose ki doit plaire
> A tos ciaus ki raison entendent.
> (*Escoufle* 6–9)[95]

[He who brings words together to provide people with exemplary material—this is something which should please all those who understand human speech-narrative-reason.]

Just so, Hue de Rotelande evokes the commonplace duty to give expression to truth and its appearance.

> Cil qui raison et bien entent
> Ne deit reposer longement,
> Ainz jorz et noiz et a tuz tens
> Ses ovres mustrer et son sens.
> (*Protheselaus* 3–6)

[He or she who understands human language-narrative-reason and the good should not long be idle, but rather should reveal his or her works and artistry both day and night and at all times.]

Medieval romance aims at both pleasure and moral or social utility, as the author comprehends the latter for the projected aristocratic audience. From it the narrative produces "fruit" (*Anjou* 40–44) rather than "trufles" (*Anjou* 19). "Li uns dit bourdes, l'autre voir" (*Anjou* 3) [the one tells jokes, the other truth], and it is the latter which is deemed proper to romance by its authors and its publics. Anything else is branded mendacious, idle social entertainment, or mercenary.[96] *Raison* is therefore communication which distinguishes not only human beings from brutes, but also the noble from the ignoble, the courteous from the villain, and lovers from fornicators.[97] Romance authors knew that material style required each part of society to be addressed in its own language. Specialized *raison* bears a message that the chosen audience will be able to appreciate because the language is already familiar to it.[98]

In addition to these meanings, *raison* can also signify interpretation: "Tout le songe leur conte et chascuns d'els se peine / De respondre par sens bonne reison certaine" (*Alex* APar I.275–76) [he relates the whole dream to them, and each of them strives to respond with good, assured speech founded on understanding]. If *sens* here is synonymous with *sans* in the *Charrette* Prologue, we have in this passage an analogue to Chrétien's description of the art of narrative invention.

Within even a single work, however, various interpretations may inter-
vene to conflict with or balance one another. Chrétien de Troyes is a master
at arranging such conflicts.[99] Numerous romances use staple or recurrent
figures to introduce diverse and conflicting interpretations of the narrative.
Keu [100] and Dinadan, [101] Gauvain, [102] and *puceles* who call to adventure [103] —
all these familiar figures are potential sources of discord and indirection, all
rely on the authority which their own exemplarity implies and which they
elevate to a rule of conduct.

Within these intertextual and infratextual references, the romancer weaves
his or her intention. He or she *atourne a bien* by charting a narrative path
that permits the harmonious counterbalancing of the different codes which
explain and determine conduct, rendering it exemplary; or, as in many prose
romances, the examples of one kind of *bien* are made to fail, as the narrative
sets forth the dissolution of order in the diverse codes and opposing *raisons*
of different figures.[104] The author, once subservient to the nobility whose
glory he or she proclaimed, points an accusing finger at that nobility and
its language. Intentions have changed, and so have the language and the
narrative.

That *raison* as the language of a class of people and as narrative has obvious affinities to the concept of material style does not preclude overlapping
or diversified classes in the single individual. In fact, Matthew of Vendôme's
awareness of such "individual" disparities accounts for his insistence on focusing a given description on a unique or at least primary trait.[105] In effect, the
same individual assumes different *personae* and *raisons* for different kinds
of writing. The nobleman of, say, 1225 saw himself differently exemplified
or differently addressed ethically in a *chanson de geste,* a romance like the
Charrette or the Vulgate Arthurian cycle, a *chanson* or a *sirventés,* a saint's
life or a fabliau. These "genres" distinguish the different *raisons* of the nobleman. And they exclude inappropriate *raison,* by author, work, and audience,
as emphatically as Guillaume de Lorris bars shepherds from the Garden of
Deduit or Love's kiss. Only *oppositio* allows the representation of that opposite, as in the devastation wrought by the villein admitted to the garden
in the *Lai de l'oiselet.* Careful typing of *raisons* that reduces — or raises — the
individual to the type reflects the "simplicity" of romance descriptions.

Unity of Romance Description: *Simplece*

Simplece is rarely mere naiveté, nor does it necessarily imply a defect or stupidity. Both meanings derive from its sense of "uncomplicated, open."[106] By
extension, it came to describe that which is not mixed, confused, or
obscure — that which hides nothing. A "simple" person is forthright or open;

an aristocrat, when *simple,* displays *franchise* and *largesse,* giving "goodness" from his or her rich and noble bounty.[107] A young, innocent person may, like Perceval *li nices,* be naive, ingenuous, or deprived without being stupid or retarded. For similar reasons, Tristan may call Iseut aux blanches mains "simple."

> Simple est s'ele ne l'aparceit
> Qu'altre aim plus e coveit   .
> E que milz volsisse culchier
> U plus me puisse delitier.
> (*Tristan* Th Sneyd[1] 511–14)

[She is naïve if she doesn't notice that I love and desire another more, and that I would rather bed down there where I can have more delight.]

By contrast, confusion shows a distraught, distracted — *divers* — state of mind, unable to choose reasonably among different impulses, like Tristan himself.

> Mais maint en sun cuer change
> E quide troveir en l'estrange
> Ço qu'il ne puet en sun privé:
> Ce lui diverse sun pensé,
> Ço qu'il n'ont volent assaier
> E enaprés lor aparer.
> (*Tristan* Th Sneyd[1] 281–86)[108]

[But many change their minds and presume to find in what is foreign what they cannot find in what is their own. This causes confusion in the mind, for they want to try what they don't have and be content with that henceforth.]

Simplece also contrasts with the artist's invention of an ostensibly obscure *matiere,* the hidden significance of which the new work uncovers and sets forth clearly and openly through its descriptions, hiding nothing.

"Simple" descriptions are, by and large, *gros* in Jean de Meun's sense of "clear," "readily comprehensible," and "exemplary." They are for

> gens lais, qui n'entendent letre,
> Car teus genz veulent grosse chose,
> Senz grant soutiveté de glose.
> (*Rose* 17394–96/17364–66) [109]

[unlettered laymen, for such people want something plain, without complicated glossing.]

Simplicity is thus a mode for a lay audience with limited capacity for intellectual discrimination. Jean is here concerned with rhetorical decorum, that is,
the accommodation of subject to audience by the interpretant.[110] The
aristocratic audience to which most romance addressed itself was, by and
large, unlettered, but not necessarily unintelligent.[111] Subtle glossing required
of the reader special knowledge or training. Jean cuts short his digression
on optics to get on with other, more obvious, matters: the distortions in the
mind of those in love.

> Car trop i ra longue matire,
> Et si serait grief chose a dire,
> Et mout serait fort a l'entendre,
> S'il iert qui le seüst aprendre
> A genz lais especiaument,
> Qui nou dirait generaument.
> (*Rose* 18273–78 / 18243–48)

[For the matter would be too long, and a hard subject to treat, and difficult to understand, even if there were someone who could teach it to lay
people, unless he or she were to speak in general terms.]

Based on this evidence, one could expect in an aristocratic public a sharp
eye for significant detail, but little appreciation for complex or systematic
thought; and familiarity with matters pertinent to the life of lord or lady,
knight or maiden, including even the broader social, geographical, and eco-
nomic differences this might entail, but little knowledge of or interest in
science except as *curiosa* or marvels: "billige Unterhaltung und Aufregung
mit religiösen Anregungen und Aussichten . . . —billige Existenzerweiterung,
die Funktion des Romans"[112] [easy entertainment and excitement, including
religious stimulation and outlooks . . . —a facile broadening of life, which
it is the function of romance to provide]. Jean de Meun's "grosse chose" suggests just such writing and its ethical purposes.

   On the other hand, the three most excellent subjects Dante perceived in
vernacular literature—prowess in arms, love, rectitude—provide an aristocratic context. But explicit systematic or theoretical analysis of any of them,
or any feature of them, is rare in romance.[113] Indeed, the passage from extended example to discursive argument characterizes, as we shall see, the
movement from romance to *Dit* illustrated in *Cristal et Clarie* and *Floris et
Liriopé*. Even Guillaume de Lorris' part of the *Rose* is far removed from the
headier discussions and analyses of a Guillaume de Machaut or a Christine
de Pizan. The only striking variations provided by romance are either a hierarchy within one or the other of the Dantesque contexts, or sharp didactic
opposition as suggested by idealization and vituperation or by happy and

unhappy endings.[114] But these extremes are essential features of topical invention and Ciceronian *narratio* — a narrative meant to conform to presumed standards of decorum or of customary conduct in the representation of persons.

> Dementres qu'il parole li dus Melcis cemine,
> Ensanble o lui amaine une *noble* mescine
> Qui *plus* est *bele* et *gente* c'onques ne fu Lavine;
> Sa fille iert, n'ot plus d'oirs, molt estoit *de cuer fine.*
>
> (*Prise* 575–78; emphasis mine)

[While he is speaking, Duke Melcis advances accompanied by a noble maiden more beautiful and noble than Lavine ever was. She was his daughter, he had no more heirs, and she had a very gentle heart.]

This "simple" description is a topical addition to the source. The hyperbole serves to clarify and simplify the source, and thus derives from *ceo k'i ert.* To introduce diverse amplifications that would individualize the daughter would have been unwarranted and undesirable in romance rhetoric, since then the marvel of her beauty would have no social signification: the maiden would have no *simplece.*

Hyperbole permitted the romancer to reduce a description to its essential elements, that is, in a sense, to abbreviate. Now, *brevitas* is "moins la brièveté matérielle qu'une concentration":[115] "Vel manus artificis multas ita conflet in unam, / Mentis ut intuitu multae videantur in una" (*Poetria nova* 700–701) [let the craftsman's skill effect a fusion of many concepts in one, so that many may be seen in a single glance of the mind]. Such concentration or *emphasis* preserves the extraordinary and essential features of a marvel while making all its attributes fit a specific, "simple" context and intention.

Simplification in its medieval sense thus makes something coherent. Principal personages exemplify fundamental ideas and ideals like courtliness, *fin'amours,* prowess, virtue, or providence through the qualities *(teches)* that make up their *maniere,* that is, the array of abstractions imminent in and elicited from the more general idea they exemplify or personify, thereby making the marvelous "other" both comprehensible and admirable.[116] Such writing can become subtle in execution, although in expression the ideas are often as simple and universal as in the psychomachiae of Prudentius, Alain de Lille, and Jean de Meun, or as in the episodic interventions of Nature in Gautier de Châtillon's *Alexandreis.* The subtlety derives from careful integration of abstract ideas in diversified, episodic adventures; the combination is indeed basic to romance *conjointure.* Allegorical personifications translate in romance into exemplary figures whose attributes exemplify the principles by which they act and which their acts realize in marvelous adventures.

The movement from idea to example is that from the general to the specific, from the topic to the case at issue, from the *san* to the *aventure merveilleuse*. The fact that the marvel is strange and extraordinary obliges the author to be cautious in the invention of *ceo k'i ert* while choosing and elaborating his or her sources. Apperception permits imitation of the mental conception of ideals like Dante's three noble subjects. The heterogeneity of the sources was viewed as only surface heterogeneity.

Of course, *materia remota* may contain virtually archetypal images apart from those ideals. They are relatively few in number, but have a universal, unconscious validity. Tuve has identified some of them as "quest, pilgrimage, marriage, death, birth, purgation"—that is, the "great public images" that are "too complex to state in full, though experienced by all of us."[117] The "great public images" as great narrative patterns and motifs represent the obscure rationale of the *materia remota,* incomplete *(corronpue)* until brought into conjunction with great contemporary ideals—or contexts—like those identified by Dante. This is essentially the way the Middle Ages conceived of imagination: the accommodation of archetypal images and comtemporary social, political, or moral ideas and ideals.[118]

Rhetorical instruction sharpened auctorial discernment. One learned how to ferret out simple motives from complexity and confusion. Abstraction is one of the modes for this process. In abstractions, distinctions were established by clear and simple oppositions, by appealing to abstract ideals and their opposites as they reveal themselves in the narrative—the evidence as it were for idealization or vituperation. Thus, Aristotle taught Alexander

> la vie du siecle et quanqu'a lui apent
> Et connoistre reison et savoir jugement,
> Si comme rethorique en fet devisement.
> (*Alex* APar I.340–42)

[secular life and all that pertains to it, and to recognize reason and know how to judge, as rhetoric sets forth.]

Following in the tradition of epideictic oratory, the artist chose a *matiere* suitable to a given or invented *san,* as when Marie chose antique or Breton stories suitable for retelling. The simple, unadulterated truth of the opus to be written was integrated into selected *matiere* after reflection and meditation, inquiry and "research," and, finally, topical invention. The author has translated the *status archetypus* into words. The results in the romance are most obvious in descriptions.

Rhetoric of Character and Description

Character is a problematic subject in medieval romance. Of late there has been a tendency to emphasize so-called individual rather than typical features in romance descriptions.[119] Romance protagonists do show unique excellence.[120] But the uniqueness is in the excellence, and the excellence is determined by an array of qualities that serve to explicate a general virtue or defect like courtesy or villainy. The agents of romance fit into a context that controls its exemplars as rigorously as dream-vision allegory controls the designation of personifications. The carolers in Guillaume de Lorris' Garden of Deduit are conventional stereotypes of corporeal beauty; their names inform conventional descriptive schemes with an appropriate context.[121] Although romance usually relies on more heterogeneous matter, the matter is nonetheless accommodated to the context represented by the agents in the adventures. Such accommodation fits a conception of identity as conformity to an ideal kind or type.[122]

It follows that these figures are special or even general in character rather than particular: they are described *generaument*, as Jean de Meun puts it.[123] The particular—today we would say the uniquely individual—seemed in the medieval view deformed, even comic; it was found in *fautures* like dwarfs, giants, madmen, villains and villeins, sinners, and otherwise defective creatures in romance.[124] For example, Meleagant's one major defect defines his moral character.

> Nus ne fust miaudres chevaliers,
> Se fel et deslëaus ne fust;
> Mes il avoit un cuer de fust
> Tot sanz dolçor et sanz pitié.
> (*Charrette* 3164–67)[125]

[No knight would have surpassed him were he not felonious and treacherous. But his heart was of wood, void of gentility and feeling.]

Similarly, Guigemar is imperfect until he loves; his defect is seen as a lamentable fault by family and friends (*Lais* Gui 57–68). Or again, Archambaut is perfect except when dominated by jealousy.

To perceive individuals in any modern sense in characters of medieval romance is anachronistic. Köhler has shown that such "distinction" as there is represents rather an imbalance between ideally perceived order and discordant reality, an imbalance removed in favor of the ideal through adventure.[126] In the medieval world of romance, *mesure* is the ideal.[127] But the individual who incarnates *mesure,* or, more properly, *maniere* (cf. ME *kynde,* "nature"), does strive for unique excellence. The Round Table is made up of equals in rank, but not in kind; ideally, their kind or *maniere* makes them exemplary representatives of a type socially desirable because it is suitable to the achievement of specific tasks in war, love, or moral conduct.[128] *Mesure* as *maniere* is in fact the *mediocritas* that Matthew of Vendôme valued in descriptions (*Ars vers* 1.31). *Maniere* expresses the special *(species)* or general *(genus).* It may connote both generic class and manners or civility, and thus polish, gentility, and refinement.[129]

> Molt estoient igal et per
> De corteisie et de biauté
> Et de grant debonereté.
> Si estoient d'une meniere,
> D'unes mors et d'une matiere.
> (*Erec* 1484–88)

[They were both of equal status and rank in courtesy, beauty, and birth; they were of one kind, one mold, one substance.]

This virtually Platonic affinity of Erec and Enide is "generic"; it reflects their nobility and qualifies their love and marriage.

In romance, the general may be found in prowess in arms, love, or rectitude. The hierarchy, like that in the Prose *Lancelot,* places rectitude higher than love, and love above knightly prowess. The narrative demonstration of excellence, however, usually takes place through armed conflict because knights are the typical protagonists of romance. The "general" figures in the Lancelot-Grail cycle, who incorporate most completely the unique excellence of knighthood, are, in ascending order, Gauvain, Lancelot, and Galaad. Within each category there are "special" representatives, complementary figures, species with comparable complexes of informing qualities or attributes. Thus, Bohort and Perceval are classed with Galaad as either chaste or virgin; the knights of the Round Table, of every kind and description, are best represented by Gauvain; and finally, the different loves in Arthurian romance are exemplified by Lancelot and Guenevere.[130] There is similar differentiation in the Seven Sages of Rome prose cycle [131] and among the sons of Priam in Benoît's *Troie.*[132] The categories are rarely systematic and classificatory, but they are normative in that they reflect an array of ideals and qualities that inform the text.

The characterization of each figure is achieved by topical amplification, both through the properties ascribed to him or her, and through the demonstration of those properties in adventures achieved or failed. When there are a number of similar representations, the achievement of the main *aventure merveilleuse* provides a distinguishing hierarchy by identifying the personage possessing unique excellence. That personage stands to other knights as the saint would to a community of monks—as exemplified by Saint Brenden, he or she serves to edify and to exemplify perfection.

Indeed, the idealism and exceptional qualities of romance protagonists tend toward the unique exemplar in marvels like Fenice.[133] In a similar way, uniqueness rather than individuality characterizes the representation of Galaad. There are several Galaads in the lineage of Joseph of Arimathea; Lancelot himself is so named. Yet the last Galaad, the finest exemplar of the name, is so thoroughly imbued with chastity and virginity as to admit no human idiosyncrasies. All these figures achieve, through their actions and thoughts, a distinct identity,[134] but, again, not identity in the sense of individuality, the *étrange,* or an aberration from the idealized norm.

Matthew of Vendôme formulated topical plans for general characterization in his instruction on description. For example, *nomen est omen,* the name implies the type. Galaad's name, like Lancelot's, Gauvain's, or Arthur's, becomes generic, as in a "Galaad," a "Lancelot," and so on, "ut nomen speciale generalis nominis vicarium ad maneriem rei, non ad rem maneriei reducatur"[135] [the particular designation should be taken to stand for a general designation according to the nature of the subject, and not according to the subject used to exemplify that nature]. *Maneries* is the object of this kind of descriptive representation of the protagonists and actions in marvelous adventures. The marvel as the extreme is closest to the abstraction, whatever sacrifice there may be thereby in "realism" or "individuality": "Se sa beaulté vouloie descripre, trop y pourroie mettre, car il n'est langue d'homme qui le sceust prononchier ne cuer penser"[136][if I wished to describe her beauty, I would have to say too much, for neither could human tongue express it nor heart conceive it]. The purpose of such representation—emphasis on the unique, prominent, and intended trait in character—is to show excellence. Every knight in a romance aspires to the prowess, love, or virtue of which Roland, Lancelot, and Galaad are exemplars. Appellation, so important in the identification of the hero, is topical identification as well.[137]

Excellence also determined choice and emphasis in narrative. Figures of base birth, like Fergus, are even rarer than knights who are women.[138] Most romances deal only with royalty or princely and noble families, passing over less high-born knights even when their achievements are said to outshine those of their betters.

Icilz Alis si estoit de grant renon, mais il n'estoit ne quens ne dus; mais il estoit parolé de lui sus trestouz autres chevaliers, mais ce ne puet mie dire le fait de chascun a part lui. Ainçoiz est drois et raisons que l'en raconte tretout avant des granz seigneurs: et pour la raison de ce voudrai je dire qui cilz furent de la table reonde qui le firent le miex et des autres me voudrai je taire. (*Laurin* ll. 2772–78)[139]

[This Alis was well known, but he was neither a count nor a duke. Yet people talked about him more than about all the other knights, but this work cannot relate what everyone did except for him. Rather it is proper and correct to relate first and foremost the deeds of the high nobility. Therefore I wish to recount who those of the Round Table were who performed best, and say nothing of the others.]

A similar preference appears in *Guillaume le maréchal,* whose anonymous author dwells on the tournaments of the Young King Henry despite the losses he sustained much to everyone's surprise.[140]

From another perspective, Lancelot's exceptional achievements set him apart in the records allegedly kept at Arthur's court (*Lancelot* lxxxiv.72). Of course, Lancelot's love for the Queen imposes upon him a character and actions that distinguish him among his fellows. But he is also a king's son. The post-Vulgate cycle gives a fuller account of Arthur and the other knights, particularly those in Gauvain's family, since Lancelot and his family dominate the Vulgate cycle.[141] These emphases achieve a virtual classification of branches and continuations according to material style.

Adaptation of *matiere* permitted topical changes at different stages in the composition of the same romance or in succeeding versions.[142] The successive reinterpretation of certain figures after Chrétien is a well-known phenomenon, although the artistic presuppositions of such modification have not always been appreciated. Middle High German and Dutch poets seem to have distinguished between the source which they were more or less bound to follow and the character of the principal figures, which was subject to their own intention.[143] For example, Chrétien and Hartmann von Aue display different conceptions of the character of Erec and Enide.[144] In the crisscross of accusations that produce the crisis in their marriage, the conflict between Erec and his companions, who are dismayed that their lord is no longer *ber,* runs as deep as the debate on *uisdive* between Cador and Gauvain in Wace's *Brut.* Chrétien's option for love over prowess in *Erec* is credible and characteristic of his romances. But Hartmann von Aue's condemnation of Erec's uxoriousness and harshness toward Enide provides a different reading of the story, one that accords more with Cador's view of the world than Chrétien's, as revealed in his exchanges with Gauvain.

Rhetorical tradition and the medieval propensity to debate encouraged the emphasis on contrasting and even antithetical models of conduct: good and bad, beautiful and ugly, true and false—in short, contrasting perfection to corruption.[145] Heroes and villains, the fortunate and unfortunate are all entangled in marvelous adventures. Topical dichotomies enhance the tendency: Christians are right, pagans are wrong; Bademagu is *preu,* Meleagant is *fel;* Aigres is wise, Berinus is foolish.[146] The foundation for topical dichotomy is rarely complex. Constituent attributes, as Matthew of Vendôme taught, are subordinate to the principal quality; if they are found in the source but do not fit the intended representation, they may be rejected out of hand. Even as "unschooled" a romancer as Beroul made descriptive epithets and actions fit the conception he had of what was appropriate to the principal figures.[147] Marc is, for all his sovereignty, unsteady and unresolved. This is not realism. Rather, it is inner alienation from role,[148] a sort of individuality that could produce distancing in an aristocratic public. The pagans for all their prowess are not Christian; Meleagant for all his strength is not courteous; Marc for all his royalty is not sovereign over himself or his subjects; all are ultimately undone. There is little sympathy or tolerance for such individualized idiosyncracies in romance.

There may of course be a time in the romance when the hero or villain hovers indecisively between good and evil. Prior to the decision, he or she is virtually unclassified and, consequently, possesses only potential attributes. Or there may be, as Nero showed, first one propensity, then another, opposite one dominating the episode (cf. *Rose* 6467–88/6437–58). The "epic" manner of treating conflicting sentiments—separating and compartmentalizing them by parataxis—was serviceable in romance,[149] where change may be sudden and decisive from one character type to another, as occurs for Durmart, Archambault, and Perceval. Cassidorus, Pelyarmenus, and Fastydorus in the Seven Sages prose cycle illustrate this method very well. Cassidorus incarnates a number of types in his long career, from divine and saintly *puer senex* through weak lover to a near saintly hermit. Pelyarmenus, on the other hand, opts early for *desmesure,* and finally succumbs, like the pagans and Meleagant, to his folly (but his career is as fascinating as that of Shakespeare's Richard III). Fastydorus, finally, never undertakes anything, and remains nondescript—he has no real description and no narrative![150]

Changes of character or type are possible either by the experience of a new context or attribute, or when a new author with a different conception of the narrative derives a new context from a given *matiere.* The transition from one type of personage to another may therefore be very sudden or even bewildering for the modern reader. It can occur in the process of falling in love, which usually begins with a *coup de foudre,*[151] probably the most common change of state in romance. The protagonists are usually perplexed, overwhelmed, and at a loss to explain their new character. This is because they have taken on an unfamiliar type, which time alone will allow them to integrate—if they do not disintegrate first. Not only are such sudden changes true of lovers, they also occur to Lancelot, Perceval, and Boort in the *Queste* as they advance from *chevaliers terrestres* to *chevaliers celestieux*.

The principles of representation in medieval romance have their origins in rhetoric.[152] Andreas Capellanus used them, for example, to adapt social hierarchy to ages, conditions, stations, inner qualities, and other topical places.[153] Romancers followed rhetorical categories to achieve more or less abrupt alterations in character by a new description. Passage through the "ages of man" may thus explain metamorphoses. Remarkable illustrations of such adaptations include Cassidorus in the Seven Sages cycle, Perceval in Chrétien and the Continuations, Lancelot from Chrétien through the prose romances, and Archambault in *Flamenca*.[154] Change or reevaluation of attributes follows from a new context, and thus different significations, for marvelous adventures. The change may be drastic and dramatic, yet still seem credible, like Lancelot's swift conversion in the *Queste* and his equally sudden backsliding in the *Mort Artu,* or, again in the latter work, Gauvain's swift hatred for, then instantaneous reconciliation with, Lancelot. There is a similar change in the post-Vulgate adaptation of the Arthurian world to a less idealized view of knighthood.[155] The knights' attributes tend to degenerate into vices, as one may observe in the amplification of Gauvain's and Gaheriez' violent, even murderous propensities, or of Lancelot's fits of madness. Galaad becomes less messianic; he may even be imprisoned, and the assistance of other knights replaces divine "reinforcement."[156] The meaninglessness of life is particularly striking in the sad fate of Balain, Pascalian in his awful failure to do what is right or even to comprehend his fate.[157] These adaptations are no less astonishing than the serial redescriptions of Helcana in *Cassidorus,* in turn a maiden capable of intrigue to win the one she loves from her own mother as rival, an empress, a saintly man, and again an empress before dying.[158]

Each stage has its appropriate epithets, and hence properties and topical responses to adventures and marvels. The individual is beneficiary or victim of the heterogeneous places assigned to him or her in the world. "The contrast and interaction between a hero, ideally vigorous and young, and a monarch, ideally older and wiser, forms a basic structural focal point in countless romances, around which narrative play is possible and meaningful; play of the narrative real against the societal and literary ideal further enlivens this interaction."[159] The "difference between traits and deeds suitable for certain ages and stations in life"[160] illustrates the accommodation of such play to character roles in amorous and chivalric situations, changes which may generate narrative branches and structure the entire work.[161] These are ways in which a received *matiere* may be, in Alfred Adler's sense, experimented with in order to discover potentialities for invention *(ausspekulieren).* [162]

Conflict within the character may be patterned by opposing abstractions. One identifies the predominant characteristic that determines actions, as when Lancelot chooses Love over Reason to be henceforth the lover of the Queen, rehearsing the original choice in numerous diverse adventures. [163] In *Yvain,* the narrator wonders that Love and Hate may dwell in the same body — that is, that companions like Yvain and Gauvain can fight one another. The incorporation of opposing characteristics in the same figure poses a rhetorical dilemma; neither quality predominates or is subordinate to its opposite, yet each is prominent enough to preclude the inactivity of a Fastydorus or a lover become *esbahiz:* "force enferme, enfermeté forz" (*Rose* 4322/4291) [of weak strength, strong infirmity]. The conflict between Yvain and Gauvain is resolved by transferring the locus from "leiautez la desleiaus" (*Rose* 4295/4265) [disloyal loyalty] to self-revelation that shows right and wrong. The companion supersedes the opponent; love supersedes hatred.

Raoul de Houdenc utilizes similar combinations in *Meraugis de Portlesguez* to define the relationship between beauty and prowess in men and women. The contrasts and combinations are illustrated by the handsome but villainous Outredoté, by an ugly but courteous dwarf of noble birth, [164] and by Meraugis and Gorvain Codruz' debate over the relative importance of beauty and worth in love. The encounters in the romance pit the different examplars against one another, which permits the author to show both qualities and defects as well as to establish a hierarchy of noble and ignoble abstractions. [165]

The irregularities and contrasts within typical representations illustrate the *concors discordia* that is fundamental to *conjointure.* The tension of opposites manifest in conflicts *(status)* is resolved within a hierarchy imposed on — and thus also dissolvable by — context, that is, auctorial intention and point of view. The dialectic is readily amenable to adaptation in romance *mouvance.* Although such variations may strain Horace's injunction against extreme character variation — but romance by the thirteenth century had already defied his strictures as much as it had those against cyclical narrative — adaptation does evince his concern for accommodation of person to age, station in life, and the world in which he or she appears.

A truly *callida iunctura* of antithetical properties also permits parody. Thus, Keu combines features of the *médisant,* the knight of the Round Table, and the efficient seneschal. [166] He becomes thereby a source of perplexity, consternation, anger, or farce. The comic pleasure derives, however, from nugacity rather than from human complexity or individual character study. There is nothing subtle about Keu; there is only a self-contradictory character to know and be amused by. Even a unique figure like Dinadan in the

Prose *Tristan,* in *Escanor,* and (as Dodinel) in *Claris et Laris* provokes only
laughter from his companions when he questions the efficacy of arms, love,
and religious zeal.[167] But he also raises legitimate questions about love and
knighthood as ideals in the violent world of prose romance or even in the
contemporary world of the romancer and his audience.[168] *Fergus* illustrates
another kind of incongruity. The son of a peasant father and a noble mother,
Fergus emerges as a kind of Perceval.[169] Similarly, in the post-Vulgate, Tor
son of Ares is made out to be half peasant through his father; yet he is the
first knight Arthur dubs (Huth *Merlin* II, 69–71). The romancer does has-
ten to explain that Tor's actual father was not the peasant who raised him,
but a noble, who illegitimately conceived him with his noble mother (II, 72).
(Tor thus realized Julien Sorel's dream to have been a noble bastard!)

On the other hand, figures like the Laid Hardi and the Beau Mauvais represent, as their pseudonyms indicate, the oxymoronic type. But the substantive predominates in each, thus maintaining a hierarchy beneath surface
incongruity. A similar incongruity is the love between the handsome, chival-
rous Girflet and the ugly Rose Espanie in the *Bel inconnu* (1723–35); or,
in the Second *Perceval* Continuation, that of the Beau Mauvais for Rosete,
a consummate exemplar of ugliness (23170–200).[170] In *Claris et Laris,* a Beau
Mauvais unwittingly does battle with women knights (27664–938). Finally,
the sons of Melusine portray a whole range of grotesque traits and qualities.[171]

These personages are comparable to the incongruous union of love and
hate in *Yvain*—a discordance paradigmatic in that romance, if one reflects
on the ambiguous sentiments of Laudine in both parts. They personify oppositions inherent in the moral or social evaluation of love and chivalry. The
fascination they evoke stems from their marvelous, extraordinary character.[172] Romancers usually reconcile opposites by eliminating or subordinat-
ing one quality to the other through topical amplification and clarification,
as is done for Tor and Fergus;[173] by exploiting the motif of the underdog
or misunderstood hero, as for Lanval or the Bel inconnu;[174] or by producing
some marvelous transformation like that of the ugly *amie* of the Beau Mauvais in the Second *Perceval* Continuation, who changes into the most beautiful maiden at Arthur's court:

> L'an ne savoit damoiselle
> De sa biauté an la contree.
> Ce ne sai ge s'elle iert faee.
> (*Perceval* Cont II 23530–32)

[A maiden of her beauty was not known in that country. I don't know
whether she was bewitched.]

Actually she is the result of a topical transformation, guaranteeing that like will cleave to like, or that some assimilation will occur. The radical transformation is fundamentally analogous to Enide's in Chrétien from the vavasor's poor daughter to princess and then queen. In *Flamenca* Guilhem, both cleric and knight, is brought through love to subordinate the religious functions of the former to the secular preoccupations of the latter; and Archambault undergoes a radical alteration in his descriptive attributes when he passes in and out of jealousy.[175] Here as elsewhere in romance descriptions, the principle of material style provides a technique for topical adaptation; role changing provides the rationale.

All these examples show how topical invention brings marvels and adventures into narrative context. Defects, conflicts, even contradictions are credible within a given context, as diverse topical developments play on narrative and narrator point of view.[176] They further suggest a more complex hierarchy and a wider range of species for the ideas that give meaning (that is, context) to the narrative through the descriptions of principal actors.

The incompatibility of real and ideal that Speer identified in the *Cassidorus* is, in a sense, built into the *descriptio/narratio* combination, whereby the former strives for simplicity and the latter for diversity. The resultant combination is uneven. For example, the Ugly Hag in *Jaufre* is, by description, a consummate exemplar of ugliness; but the narrative reduces her to more human appearances.[177] Hyperbole accounts for the formal differences, while context accounts for coherence. Such vacillation in appearance is common in the *somnium*. Philosophy in Boethius' *De consolatione* begins a long line of those who, "statura discretionis ambiguae" (*De cons* I Pr i.8) [her stature uncertain and doubtful], vacillate in description and narrative like Alice's rubber neck in Wonderland. This is credible in dreams; romances, although commonly located in a historical time and space, still reflect the aberrant vision common in dreams. Context makes both historical and visionary environments meaningful by clear, coherent, and simple topical amplifications.

Emphasis on and indeed laudation of a prominent or fundamental trait in character meshes with marvel as hyperbole. The romancers frequently avail themselves of the so-called "inexpressibility topic" to diminish incredulity before hyperbolic descriptions bordering on the marvelous. "Daphus et li emperes et leur compaignie, dont il avoient perdu les .x., faisoient d'armes, et avoient fait tant que touz esbahiz sui du recorder que por mençonge ne le doive on tenir" (*Helcanus* §43) [Daphus, the emperor, and those with them, of whom they had lost ten, fought and accomplished so much that I fear to report it lest my words be taken to be lies]. *Le vrai peut quelquefois être invraisemblable.* But in romance incredulity dissolves into *émerveillement*, thereby saving the figures from out-of-hand rejection. "Ainsi le merveilleux n'est pas, en fait, incompatible avec la crédibilité."[178] And, of course, coherent, consistent representation restores credibility as admiration.

> Signor, ce nen est mie fable,
> Ançois est cose veritable;
> N'a home en tout le mont si baut
> Qui l'oseroit si metre en haut,
> Se il de la verté nel savoit
> Et il des clers tesmoig n'avoit.
> Eracles a grignor vergoigne
> Que li livres nes ne tesmoigne.
> (*Eracle* 6173–80)

[My lords, this is no fable, but truth. No one in the whole world would be so brash as to advance it if he didn't know it to be true and if he didn't have clerical authentication. Eracle is even more ashamed than the book reports.]

By the same token, such auctorial *exaggeratio* as amplification of the extraordinary made romance exemplary by emphasis on the specific features or traits the author intended to illustrate. Eracle is ashamed because God has closed him out of Jerusalem when he lacked humility in a place where the Lord had been (*Eracle* 6219–32).

Rhetoric of Action and Custom

The medieval art of invention, often likened to architectural planning, was also a kind of archeological reconstruction. The discovery of custom in a marvelous adventure provided the marvel with a rationale according to which the work could be restored as the new author construed it to have been. Euhemerization of the marvel as custom is anachronism.[179] Anachronism is the imposition onto past material not only of medieval paraphernalia—jousts in ancient Rome—but also of medieval conceptions and ideals like feudal custom, chivalry, and courtly love.[180] There is not, however, any deliberate intention to shock by *Verfremdung* or alienation. Rather, what we construe as anachronism was for the romancers the adaptation of obscure or confused material to conventions and procedures deemed universal. Anachronistic adaptation attempts to make history comprehensible and instructive. Just as God's designs in history are obscure until elicited from historical sources by study and illumination, so the writings of the past are obscure before yielding the *surplus de sen* which is their hidden meaning.[181] The identification of the present in the past was the authentication of both past and present by universal, even atemporal customs, ideas, and ideals — *tot li sens du monde,* as the author of *Claris et Laris* puts it.

Concern for historical fact inspired great respect for transmitted *matiere,* as the foregoing example from *Eracle* illustrates (6177–78). The *translatio,* however, did not preclude a distinction between an ideal past and a real past, or even a real present.[182] Yet, in the final analysis, whether the invention was historically true mattered less than whether it was topically true. The belief that past history was understandable in the light of contemporary ideals opened *matiere* to the discovery of *ceo k'i ert,* that is, of that matter's topical truth as universal truth in a particular time and place.[183] For example, the description of fish Alexander observes in his underwater excursion in the *Roman d'Alexandre* is redone in *Perceforest* in terms of combat; this in turn inspires in Alexander the idea for the tournament which he then stages for the first time in England.[184]

Corruption, distortion, and interpolation in transmission were obvious when several versions conflicted or sharply diverged, or when *matiere* was incomprehensible or incredible.[185] This made such *matiere* especially open to topical interpretation. *Costume,* the adaptation in romance of a marvelous adventure, was the feudal rationalization of marvelous matter, illustrated by the euhemerization of the *geis* of Celtic legend. Originally, the *geis* expressed the will of benevolent or malevolent powers from the otherworld,[186] a meaning that was lost in transmission to French-speaking audiences. Romance *costume* imposed a new context on the *matiere* and its central marvel. For example, the Round Table acquired, in its progression from Wace's Breton fables to the great prose romances, many attributes and explanations that enhance its feudal and chivalric validity as the source of marvels and customs.[187]

Like the marvel, the *costume* is an extraordinary phenomenon; but unlike the marvel, *costume* offers clarification in contemporary language and contexts. Chrétien uses it to explain the significance of the cart Lancelot must ride in order to find Guenevere. A sign of shame in bygone days, it served to expose criminals to public disgrace and ridicule (*Charrette* 321–38). Since Chrétien's *matiere* would have been falsified if he had changed the cart into a pillory (the means, he reminds his audience, to punish wrongdoers in his own day and age), he effected a comparison and a credible interpretation based not on Celtic otherworld mythology, but rather on a current maxim.[188] Sententious commonplaces identify the customary in narrative diversity and strangeness.

> Por ce qu'a cel tens furent tex
> Les charretes, et si cruex,
> Fu premiers dit: "Quant tu verras

> Charrete et tu l'ancontreras,
> Fei croiz sor toi, et te sovaigne
> De Deu, que max ne t'an avaigne."
> (*Charrette* 339–44)[189]

[Because carts were such in those days, and so grievous, it was first said: "When you see a cart or come upon one, cross yourself and remember God, lest evil befall you."]

The technique is topical. For Chrétien links the cart to Lancelot by a psychomachia similar to the love-hate conflict developed in *Yvain:* the struggle in Lancelot's mind between reason and love (*Charrette* 365–77). The knight's encounter with the marvelous adventure becomes the encounter with an irrational but usually human impediment to love and chivalry. The custom, construed as an adventure, is understandable when topically amplified according to the context and deftly conjoined with the source *matiere.*

> Quasi non sit ibi collatio, sed nova quaedam
> Insita mirifice transsumptio, res ubi caute
> Sic sedet in serie quasi sit de themate nata.
> (*Poetria nova* 249–51)

[As if there were no comparison there at all, but the taking on, one might say, of a new form marvelously engrafted, where the new element fits as securely into the context as if it were born of the theme.]

The result is the paradoxical union of the extraordinary and the customary—a truly *callida iunctura* in *concors discordia.*[190]

The location of most romance adventures in the distant past facilitated the accommodation of the marvelous and of custom. As in the cart episode in the *Charrette,* an extraordinary occurrence could be reduced to a custom serving a comprehensible, if "foreign," function and enhancing chivalry, love, or some other universally admirable quality or ideal. Thus, Chrétien's audience understood the pillory and its purpose; the replacement of pillory by cart was facilitated by the maxim. The cart was demythologized and turned to a meaningful purpose in the context of the romance's *san.*[191] The custom of Logres protecting women traveling alone served much the same purposes, both by humanizing the wood fairies of Celtic legend, and by accounting for maidens alone in the Arthurian forests—no doubt as astonishing to medieval audiences as the flower maidens in the *Roman d'Alexandre*! The origin of this custom is adumbrated obscurely in the rape of the wood fairies by King Amangon in the *Elucidation.*[192] In each of these instances, we have fidelity to source *matiere* combined with topical elucidation of the *matiere*—the combination of *matiere* and *san.*

Custom varied from region to region.[193] Romance could thus vary custom from one adventure to the other; the irrationality or willfulness of those who impose customs accounts for their diversity in the feudal world of romance. For example, a passage in Guernes de Pont-Sainte-Maxence's *Becket* relates malevolent, willful custom to a meaningful, established scheme of things.

> Custume n'est pas dreiz, bien le poëz veeir.
> Kar chascuns riches hum qui Deu ne volt cremeir,
> Alieve sur sa gent custume a sun voleir.
> Une custume ad ci, la en vei altre aveir.
> Mais Deus n'aime custume, mes fundement de veir.
> E mult par est la vie del chaitif humme brieve;
> Or est chalz, or est freiz, cume cele eve tieve.
> Pur ço fait grant pechié cil qui custume alieve
> Dunt nuls huem ad damage u ki nul humme grieve:
> Kar nel puet pas oster la u li quers li crieve.
> *(Becket* 3571–80)[194]

[Custom is unjust, as you can plainly see. For every powerful nobleman who does not fear God capriciously imposes custom on his people. One custom prevails here, another I see yonder. But God loves not custom, but that which is founded on truth. And the life of the wretched is very short, now hot, now cold, like tepid water. Wherefore he who imposes a custom that causes harm or grief to any man does a great wrong; for the latter cannot remove it from there where it crushes his heart.]

Guernes was opposed to Henry II's imposition of secular authority onto ecclesiastical courts by the Constitutions of Clarendon, which were, in his eyes, sinful and wrong. Custom was nevertheless a powerful authority. Gautier d'Arras suggests that it cannot be easily undone.

> Vos savéz c'on claime droit
> En ce que li coustume doit,
> Car je vos di bien sans doutance
> Que grant cose est de coustumance.
> *(Eracle* 3409–12)

[You know that justice is founded on custom, for I tell you without any doubt that custom has great force.]

The authority of custom in romance can be attributed to its relation to aristocratic authority and prerogatives of romance audiences;[195] established or traditional custom enjoyed great authority as a guarantee of stability.

As an aristocratic prerogative, custom expresses the lord's *dangier*. In *Erec*,

Arthur restores the custom of the hunt for the white stag out of deference
to his father who established it.

> Et je ne voel pas que remaigne
> La costume ne li usages
> Que siaut maintenir mes lignages.
> De ce vos devroit il peser,
> Se je vos voloie alever
> Autre costume et autres lois
> Que ne tint mes peres li rois.
> L'usage Pandragon, mon pere,
> Qui rois estoit et emperere,
> Voel je garder et maintenir,
> Que que il m'an doie avenir.
>   (*Erec* 1760–70)

[I don't want the custom or the practice to die out which my lineage is
wont to maintain. It ought to grieve you if I sought to raise another custom or other laws than those which my father the king upheld. Whatever
may befall me in consequence, I want to keep and maintain the practices
of Uther Pendragon my father, who was king and emperor.]

Despite the initial chaos it will surely produce when the time comes to award
the kiss of the stag to the most beautiful woman, "Car parole que rois a dite
/ Ne doit puis estre contredite" (*Erec* 61–62) [for a king's word, once pro-
nounced, must not be gainsaid], Arthur affirms his *dangier*. On the other
hand, when Arthur abandons his customary largess in the *Perlesvaus,* the
kingdom falls into decline and the court disperses (ll. 67–566). He has
replaced customary royal largess by a new, wasting indifference; his *dangier*
has declined.

Dangier may refer to either benevolent or malevolent authority.[196] A kind
and just ruler could establish beneficial customs like that of protecting women
against rape when traveling alone in Logres;[197] on the other hand, the custom of Gorre virtually institutionalized a ritual for rape! Most references to
custom in romance, however, connote neither good nor bad; they evoke surprise and marvel because things were done in an unusual way in other times
or places, even when reduced to everyday objects or events.[198] Ceremonial
by nature, these customs are retained from, adapted to, or elicited from
materia remota as topical *argumenta* in a feudal vision of the world.

Past custom could therefore become exemplary, prescribing honorable
conduct.

Mes encontre ces vers doit la teste drecier
Qui veut de bonnes meurs son cuer asouploier
Et savoir qu'il doit fere et quel chose leissier,
Comme il doit ses amis et blandir et proier,
Ceus qu'il a fes tenir et autres pourchacier,
Et ceus qu'il ne connoist par oevres essaier,
Ses anemis grever et si estoutoier
Que uns seuls envers lui n'ost mostrer samblant fier.

(Alex APar I.42–49)

[But he ought to heed this verse who wishes to bend his heart to good conduct, to know what to do and what to avoid, how to win friends and make requests of them, those whom he ought to keep and those he ought to gain, how to test those he does not know, and how to harm his enemies and show such bravado that no one dares threaten him.]

Some customs attain topical value by continuation or repetition. The quality of customs alive in a given time and place may indicate the quality of its civilization. In Chrétien's *Yvain,* modern France is unfavorably contrasted with the happier world of Arthur's court, where better customs in love and chivalry prevailed (21–24). The *Queste del saint graal,* relating the nefarious influence of love in the Arthurian world, suddenly opens to a sweeping condemnation of chivalry's seemingly universal debasement of humanity and piety.[199]

Car il estoit un des chevaliers dou monde qui plus parfetement creoit en Nostre Seignor. Et neporquant ce ert contre la costume de la terre: car a cel tens estoient si desreez genz et si sanz mesure par tout le roiaume de Gales que se li filz trovast le pere gisant en son lit par achaison d'enfermeté, il le tresist hors par la teste ou par les braz et l'oceist erranment, car a viltance li fust atorné se ses peres moreust en son lit. Mes quant il avenoit que li filz ocioit le pere, ou li peres le filz, et toz il parentez moroit d'armes, lors disoient cil del païs qu'il estoient de haut lignage.

(Queste p. 95.13–22)

[For he was one of the world's knights who loved our Lord most perfectly. And yet this went against the prevailing custom of the land. For there were in those days such mad, unrestrained people abroad in the kingdom of Wales that, if the son found his father lying ill in his bed, he dragged him out by the head or arms, and killed him on the spot, for he would have been considered unworthy if his father had died in his bed. But when it happened that the son killed the father, or the father the son, and the whole family had died by armed combat, then did the inhabitants of that country say that they were of high birth.]

Perceval's own family is decimated by the chivalric customs of the time in the *Conte du graal* and its continuations and adaptations.[200]

By contrast, in the *Thèbes,* the new custom of the annual exchange of kingship in Thebes has the consent of Eteocles, Polinices, and their consellors, and begins in an orderly manner (*Thèbes* 585–98). But it is a new and unprecedented custom. Edipe's curse succeeds: "Nouveleté i treuvent tal / Qui leur revertira a mal" (*Thèbes* 559–60) [they found a novelty that will undo them]. For the brothers' own character is such that, like Henry II for Guernes de Pont-Sainte-Maxence, or Arthur in *Perlesvaus,* they cannot follow a good custom or law—in the *Thèbes,* the right of primogeniture.

The emphasis on custom in romance reflects that genre's aristocratic character. This is not undercut by the fact that many customs are as reprehensible as Guernes makes Henry II's out to be. The evil or unjust cases provide adventures that good knights achieve in order to terminate the customs.[201] The knight or lord who established the offensive custom is corrected and may even become a respectable knight by establishing benevolent customs. Good custom thereby becomes an admirable image of past glory. The translation of good custom to the present upholds aristocratic civilization and justifies its claims to a prominent place in world economy and order.

Modality and Narrative

The range of romance from (pseudo)historical narrative to dream vision, wherein marvel alternates with custom and marvelous images are interspersed with personifications, allows for two distinct, although often interpenetrating, even indistinguishable modes of representation. These are the exemplary mode based on metonymy and the allegorical mode based on metaphor.

Example: Narrative as Mirror

Vernacular history was exemplary.

> Bon sunt li fait a reconter
> E mult les fait bon esculter,
> Kar ceus en forment a bien faire
> Qui les oent sovent retraire.
> (*Ducs* 14833–36)[202]

[The deeds are worthy of being told, and it does one good to hear them, for they form good conduct in those who hear them related often.]

In Benoît de Sainte-Maure exemplarity provides a veritable program wherein *estoire* becomes a mirror of conduct for the audience.

> Autresi sunt cum mireors
> Les estoires des anceisors:
> Maintes choses i ot l'om dire
> U l'om mult cler se veit e mire.
> (*Ducs* 14837–40)[203]

[The tales of our ancestors are like mirrors. One hears many things told in them wherein one may see oneself clearly reflected.]

The intended audience is encouraged to measure its qualities against those of the great heroes and heroines of the past. The individual was to strive to become as exact an imitation or reflection as possible of those qualities. The audience for history, like the author, must seek out *ceo k'i ert* and profit from its exemplary lessons.

> Ausi cum cil, ceo m'est avis,
> Qui vait coillant les bons espis
> E ce laisse qui n'a valor,
> Deivent faire li oeor:
> Le bien retiengent des escriz,
> Quant il lor ert contez e diz,
> E sin vivront plus sagement
> E mieuz e plus honestement.
> (*Ducs* 14841–48)

[The listeners ought, in my opinion, to imitate those who glean the good grain, leaving what has no value; they retain what is profitable from the writings related and told to them, and will live more prudently, better, and properly on that account.]

Essentially, history serves as a mine of good and bad examples by which one may study and measure one's own worth and actions. The *Ducs'* references to topical abstractions show how historical examples were to be understood in context, and thus how they were to illuminate admirable or reprehensible shadings in historical figures and their actions.

> Par bons essamples, par bons faiz,
> Ceus qui orribles sunt e laiz
> En eschieve l'om mainte feiz.
> Amors e leautez e feiz
> Nos amonestent a tenir,

> Qu'avisunques se puet joïr
> Nus qui seit de faire deslei;
> Toz jorz torne e revert sor soi.
>
> (*Ducs* 14849–56)[204]

[By good examples, by good deeds, one frequently eschews those which are reprehensible and ugly. They admonish us to hold to love, fidelity, and trust, for one can hardly enjoy the fruits of wrongdoing: it always turns and comes back against its perpetrator.]

Examples inspired right conduct in audiences of the same social order and mind as the narrative protagonists. The achievements of past lords, and especially of actual ancestors, display qualities worthy of emulation.

But examples could also provoke admiration and wonder, as hagiography demonstrates.[205] The *Espurgatoire* attributed to Marie de France states:

> Li autors nus fet ci entendre
> Que nus devum essample prendre[206]
> Des granz tormenz qu'avez oï,
> Dunt li livre nus cunte ci,
> E des miseires ki ci sunt
> E des granz peines de cest munt.
>
> (1401–6)

[The author gives us to understand here that we ought to make an example of the great torment that you have heard told, and which the book relates to us now, and of the miseries found there and the great suffering of this world.]

Here, example is not a model for conduct but a consummate representation or vision of our fate and hope as shown through the knight. The typical French saint's life terminates not with an exhortation to change one's life and, in effect, to enter into a new order, but with a prayer—prayer founded on hope and trust that the saint's intercession will be effective because of the exemplarity of his or her life.[207] Similarly, according to his hagiographer, Saint Alexis did not inspire popular imitation; yet his life had a bearing on the fate of Rome and all Romans, both on earth and in the afterlife.

Hagiography, history, and romance include admonitions to avoid the devil's or the villain's snares. Similarly, the fable acquires moral authority by its exemplary truth.

> Plaist vous oïr bons dis et biaus
> Ki sont d'auctorité nouviaus?
> Essample sont tuit veritable;
> N'est mie mençoigne ne fable,

Anchois sont merveilles provees;
Plus fieres ne furent trouvees.
(*Sept sages* V 1–6)

[Would you like to hear the words good and fine which have recently
come into authority? They are all true examples; they contain neither lie
nor fable, rather they are proven wonders—more spectacular have never
been invented.]

The verse *Sept sages* is still close to hagiography, relying on strict morality
and misogyny to evaluate its principal figures. The validity of such exemplarity depends on a lay audience favorably disposed to the instruction (*Sept
sages* V 245–48).[208] For such an audience, romance serves the practical purpose of disseminating truth and useful instruction, as Benoît says in the *Troie*
(1–32).[209] This intention is the foundation for the *sapientia* topic with which
many romances begin.[210]

Most romances rely on exemplarity, albeit in contexts radically different
from those of hagiography, contexts suitable to the aristocracy that include
courtesy and love. Many romances, for example, presume an audience of
lovers. Thus, in the epilogue to *Tristan,* Thomas d'Angleterre calls upon them
to recognize their own experiences in Tristan's and Iseut's. One recalls the
Charrette's whimsical wink to the audience: "Bien poez antendre et gloser,
/ Vos qui avez fet autretel" (4550–51)[211] [you can well understand and gloss,
you who have done likewise], to explain Lancelot's conduct the evening before his rendez-vous with Guenevere. In brief, "la tradition transforme, dans
les éléments de langage mis en œuvre, les fragments d'information objective
qu'à l'état natif ils véhiculent, en une information subjective, engendrant,
non point une connaissance, mais une reconnaissance."[212] Such ad hominem
appeal achieved credibility through the topical investment of character, adventure, and marvel with exemplarity.

Examples were very persuasive, and rhetoric encouraged their use.[213] The
trials in the different versions of the Seven Sages of Rome legend, for example, are a frame for exemplary tales linked to the denouement of the frame.[214]
Topical amplifications controlled understanding of the narrative in accordance
with auctorial intention, while the kind of public anticipated precluded mis-
understanding or lack of understanding, and the universal expectation of exemplary significance guaranteed attention to exemplifying intentions.

Et ci dis est mout bel et gens
C'ancor i poront mainte gens
Example prendre et demander,
C'il i volent a droit penser.
(*Beaudous* 293–96)[215]

[And this work is very beautiful and noble, for many people can draw from and seek examples in it if they are willing to think rightly.]

The orthodox audience was a prerequisite to comprehension.

> Tout ce li conteeur contoient
> Et il [the knights in their audience] volentiers les ooient
> Et se miroient es biaus dis
> S'en devenoient mieux apris,
> Quar qui romanz velt escouter
> Et es biaus dis se velt mirer
> Merveil est s'il ne s'en amende,
> S'il est ensi qu'il i entende;
> Parole qui n'est entendue
> Vaut autretant comme perdue.
>
> (*Floriant* 6239–48)[216]

[And the storytellers told all these things, and they (the knights in their audience) willingly listened to them, mirroring themselves in the fine deeds and thereby becoming better informed; for if they are willing to listen to romances and mirror themselves in such fine words, it is a wonder if they don't improve, provided they apply themselves to doing so. A word unheeded is as good as lost.]

The mirror image permits the reflection of the marvelous adventure as example—like the *merveilleuses proves et fines* of the *Sept sages*—in the mind and in the conduct of the listening public.[217]

The exemplarity of romance distinguished it, in many romancers' eyes, from mendacious tales.[218] *San* and *science* are conjoined in romance for transmission to the public through the exemplary *maniere* of the protagonists. Examples thus insure *translation* of both *chevalerie* and *clergie*.

> Qui saiges est de sapience,
> Bien doit espandre s'escience,
> Que teus la puisse recoillir,
> Don boins essanples puise issir.
> (*Athis* 1–4)[219]

[Those who are wise with wisdom ought to disseminate their knowledge so that others may receive it and, from them in turn, good examples may proceed.]

Jean Renart sees himself as one "ki boune parole assenlle / Por traire as gens en essamplaire" (*Escoufle* 6–7) [who composes eloquent speech to serve as an example for others].

The choice of material for exemplification depends in part on the qualities the romancer wishes to exemplify. This is obvious in *Floris et Liriopé,* where a long description of beauty, both good and bad (*Floris* 1–100), precedes the narrative; the narrative itself is intended to exemplify good and bad beauty: "D'une aventure ke je sai / De teil biautei vos conterai" (*Floris* 101–2) [I'll tell you an adventure I know that has to do with such beauty]. Similarly, the author of *Cristal et Clarie* prefaces his romance with an incipient art of love that Cristal's ten-year quest for Clarie will subsequently exemplify.[220]

Collections of examples were mined by preachers, moralists, and chroniclers in order to develop their subjects. Similar sources are used by romancers, much as the poets of the Second Rhetoric used *poetries* as sources for examples in both short and long poems.[221] Thus, the *Prophecies Merlin* states: "que Fedelic a fet translater por ce que li chevalier et les autres gens laies les entendent miex et i puissent prendre aucun essample, car asses en y a qui bien i veut entendre, et ce dit nostre conte en ceste matiere" (§I) [which Frederick had translated so that the knights and other lay persons might understand them better and draw examples from them, for there are enough for anyone willing to make an effort to understand; here is what one story relates on this subject]. How this was done may be observed in the Huth *Merlin,* in which a knight is told by Merlin: "En ceste chose vous devés vous regarder et prendre essample" (Huth *Merlin* II, 135) [you ought to see yourself in this thing and take it as an example]. The "thing" is the fact that the Lord giveth and the Lord taketh away, and what the knight does with his soul will determine how the Lord will deal with him.

The example bespeaks an idea like prowess, noble love, or grace, which, as Jauss has pointed out, leaves the example undefined ("unbestimmt").[222] That is, the example has not been applied to a specific context that it could explain, qualify, or judge. In narrative the example not only derives from the idea that originally occupies the author's mind while looking for narrative *matiere,* but also transmits that idea as the *matiere*'s truth. This requires making a distinction between the exemplary as showing the typical or the mean, and the exemplary as representative of the ideal.[223] Representatives of the ideal are not typical or mean but heroic, idealized, and extreme. The ideal as idea cannot achieve totality, for such totality would be truly archetypal. It can therefore represent only a specific manifestation of the idea in the configuration of heterogeneous narrative, that is, in the extraordinary, unique, and extreme achievements of romance heroes and heroines.[224]

Originality comes from the more profound revelation of an idea in narrative by adaptation. Adaptation reevaluates exemplary figures in traditional *matiere.* But the reevaluation must also integrate data in a manner acceptable to the audience envisaged by the author. An author as early as Alberic

de Pisançon felt confident in assuming, before an aristocratic audience, that
the life of Alexander the Great permitted a qualification of the wisdom of
Solomon on *omnia vanitas:* "Solaz nos faz' antiquitas / Que tot non sie vanitas!" (*Alex* AdeP 7–8)[225] [may antiquity console us in the fact that not all
is vanity]. And indeed, Solomon's wisdom was not immune to attack, when
context or auctorial intention permitted doubts or qualifications. The Bible
itself declares that his wisdom was subject to decline.[226] Thus, the *Queste*
and the Prose *Estoire* make much of Solomon's helplessness in the face of
his wife's ingenuity.[227] Exemplary figures, even when given the most lavish
praise and endowed with the finest qualities, could slip into human error,
weakness, or sin. That too was exemplary, since the distance between ideal
description and uncertain conduct was instructive.

> Çou est la letre, mes la glose
> Puet on atorner faussement,
> Sor cui c'on veut; mais longement
> Ne se tient nule doreüre
> A envers d'une laveüre.
>
> (*Ille* P 10–14)

[This is the letter, but the gloss can be wrongly applied to anyone. But
gild will not hold long in the wash.]

Amplification centers on the identification of suitable, cogent examples
of chivalric ideals. The ideals become examplary qualities, and their opposites, defects, introduced as descriptions at suitable points *(loci)* in the *matiere*.

> De la Table Reonde estoit,
> An la cort molt grant los avoit;
> De tant com il i ot esté,
> N'i ot chevalier si loé,
> Et fu tant biax qu'an nule terre
> N'estovoit plus bel de lui querre.
> Molt estoit biax et preuz et genz
> Et n'avoit pas .xxv. anz;
> Onques nus hom de son aage
> Ne fu de si grant vaselage;
> Que diroie de ses bontez?
>
> (*Erec* 83–93)[228]

[He was of the Round Table and renowned at court. For all the time he
had been there, there was no knight so esteemed; and he was so handsome that none more handsome need be sought anywhere. He was very
handsome, worthy, and noble, yet was only twenty-five years old. Never

did a man of his age possess better knighthood. What could I even begin
to say about his moral and social qualities?]

Such abstractions eliminate villeins like the cowherd in *Yvain* who cannot
comprehend the language of romance;[229] only those to whom noble abstractions are meaningful will heed and understand such language.

Degrees of perfection in the realization of an ideal, as well as topical emphases permitting differentiation among personages and romances, allowed
for variation and gradation within a single context—for *specialitas* within
generalitas.[230] Systematic analysis reveals carefully thought out conceptions
of courtly values and their moral or social character.[231] And the union of
abstract exemplary material with the *estrange* as marvel could produce profoundly moving images more redolent of those of modern depth psychology
than of character analysis in eighteenth- and nineteenth-century novels.

The combination of the ideal and of diverse narrative leads, in rhetorical
terms, to the *chria* or *usus*—that is, to a combination of the proverb, moral,
or *sentence,* and an illustrative tale.[232]

> Ki bien vodreit reisun entendre
> Ici purreit ensample prendre:
> Tels purcace le mal d'autrui
> Dunt tuz li mals revert sur lui.
> (*Lais* Eq 307–10)

[Whoever would like to attend to a good narrative could draw an example
from this one, to wit: they who seek to bring misfortune on others bring
the whole misfortune down on themselves.]

A reciprocal relation is established between an agent, his or her actions, and
a proverbial statement invented to define the agent's characteristics and the
context for which he or she was invented.[233] Thus, the *Alexandre* makes the
death of Alexander into an admonition not to entrust serfs with noble respon-
sibilities,[234] which fits the aristocratic ethos of the romance.

> Qui vers de riche istoire veut entendre et oïr,
> Pour prendre bon example de prouece acueillir,
> De connoistre reison d'amer et de haïr,
> De ses amis garder et chierement tenir,
> Des anemis grever, c'on n'en puisse eslargir,
> Des ledures vengier et des biens fes merir,
> De haster quant leus est et a terme soffrir,
> Oëz dont le premier bonnement a loisir.
> (*Alex* APar I.1–8)[235]

[If you wish to hear and listen to a noble story in order to find good examples of acquiring prowess, understanding the basis of love and hate,
keeping friends and holding them dear, bringing ineluctable harm on enemies, avenging wrongs and rewarding good deeds, making haste when appropriate and waiting patiently for the right time—if so, then listen to the
first part attentively and receptively.]

Such an ideal audience would readily meet the requirements of effective discourse: "docilem, benivolum, adtentum auditorem habere volumus" (*Ad Her*
I.iv.7)[236] [we wish to have our hearer receptive, well-disposed, and attentive].

Topical amplifications may have implications for the entire romance out
of which they are drawn, including parts that the author of the amplification did not write.

> Li restors du paon tous les autres comprent
> Et donne a tous les veus biauté et parement
> C'est .i. drois mireoirs qui figureement
> Moustre le fait passé et donne ensengnement
> Que chascuns des bons face ou miex ou ensement
> Encore en iert de preus par cest remirement
> Car a toute riens faut Cause et conmencement
> Et mains grans biens avient a poi de movement.
>   (*Restor* 2061–68)

[The restoration of the peacock comprehends all other parts of the romance, adorning and beautifying everything. A true mirror, it represents
figuratively the past deed, giving lessons as to how each of the worthy
might do better or as well. Good men will come from reflection in such a
mirror, for everything requires a cause and a beginning, and many a great
good comes from small impulse.]

The effect is analogous to the imposition of new meaning onto a conventional fable, like Marie de France's morals in her *Fables*. Similarly, the reinterpretation of Lancelot's knighthood in the Vulgate *Queste* revises the
meaning of his career in the *Lancelot* Proper. Another illustration would be
Guillaume de Lorris' reading of the Narcissus fable in Ovid.

> Dames, cest essemple aprenez,
> Qui vers voz amis mesprenez;
> Car, se vos les laissiez morir,
> Deus le vos savra bien merir.
>   (*Rose* 1507–10/1505–8)

[Ladies, heed this example, you who wrong those who love you. For if
you let them die, God will make you pay for it.]

These words, addressed to women, become universal in the fable by the fact that Narcissus, a man, exemplifies them. And they in turn raise intriguing questions as to the sex addressed by the two active and passive complexes or agents in the dream vision, the lover and the rose.

Glossing may serve to clarify specific topical adaptations of the abstract ideals that are meant to elucidate obscurities in the sources. Such mental glossing was expected from the audience as part of its reflection on narrative significance. Marie de France's "gloser la letre" generalizes the principle. By *gloser,* the author makes the exemplary significance of a given *matiere* evident through more or less explicit topical amplifications. That is, the author may digress from the narrative for a didactic excursus; or he or she may render the narrative exemplary and display through the persons and actions what its meaning may be. Such explicit and implicit glosses enhance the public's appreciation of and its reflection on the *matiere.* Author and public are both reader and interpreter of a given *matiere* in the transmission of which they cooperate.

Here we touch on a fundamental feature of romance composition: "analogical composition." This technique seeks "diversity in its detail while fixing and reiterating in the audience's minds the theme or problem whose elaboration is the author's task."[237] Repeated topical descriptions emphasize a theme to the exclusion or subordination of others; they bestow on diverse marvelous adventures patterns or molds which reflect auctorial design. The adventure may be incomplete as far as its narrative beginning, middle, or end—its concrete narrative totality—is concerned; but is has the elements of a shape—a *samblance*—that give it meaning and significance in the context of the romance's *san.* These "relationships of kind," or *conjointures* of parts, emerge in the mind's eye as the telling progresses.[238]

Modes of Literal and Allegorical Signification: Histoire *and* Poème

Chronologically, there is a kind of drift from exemplary toward allegorical romance. The latter subordinates the play of diverse adventures to the reflection of abstract images. In the overall construct, analogy may produce designs of dazzling complexity and coherence in the diversity or strangeness of dreamlike or visionary representations. Romance uses both exemplary and allegorical modes. A romance is exemplary insofar as it relates events that transpire in (pseudo)historical times and places. Such exemplarity is founded on paradigmatic representation.

On the other hand, allegory or, more correctly, visionary images in romance signaled developments in paradigmatic representation that were to culminate in the late medieval *Dit.* The romances usually recognized as allegorical—notably the *Rose* and the *Queste*—are allegorical because of their reliance on visionary adventures. Yet medieval publics, to whom much that today seems exotic would have been familiar, could find exemplary romances far enough removed from the ordinary to be dreamlike.

> Cil ki *Partonopé* trova
> E ki les vers fist e rima,
> Mult se pena de bien dire,
> Si dist il bien de cele matire;
> Cume de fable et de menceonge
> La matire resemble sounge,
> Kar iceo ne put unkes estre.
> (*Edmund* 25–31)

[He who wrote *Partonopeu,* who put it into verse and line, strove to express himself well, and he did so with that *matiere.* As in fable or in lie, the *matiere* is like a dream, for such things could never be.]

These words have considerable weight as criticism when directed against romances like *Partonopeu de Blois,* although their weight is somewhat less when balanced against some of what passed as history in twelfth-century vernacular. In fact such histories influenced the composition of romance at a time when the historicity of Geoffrey of Monmouth and British fables about Arthur and his expected return was debated. Turning from pretence of historical veracity (even if the truth was largely topical) to dream visions whose truth was necessarily topical was a natural consequence of criticism of romance in the twelfth-century tradition[239] and of the marvelous in romance *matiere* itself. For the marvel whose mystery has not entirely dissipated may be true by allegory, an extraordinary occurrence assuming significance in a mode other than that of marvelous representation.

Authors and publics in the Middle Ages were aware of these differing modalities. Readers of the *Ovide moralisé* could thus perceive the change in the *Philomena* ascribed to Chrétien and in the twelfth-century *Pyrame et Tisbé* when they were incorporated into it and glossed. The former was *historia;* when allegorized, the tale became *poema.*

L'office du poete est de convertir les faiz et histoires passées en autres especes par oblicques et destournées figuracions par aucun beau et aourné langaige. Pour ceste raison . . . est dit, que Lucan ne fut point poete, pour ce qu'il est cogneü avoir mis par escript ses euvres plus par maniere d'ystoires que poetiquement. (*Ov mor* comm p. 20)

[The task of the poet is to turn past deeds and histories into other modes by digressive, indirect configurations that use some fine, ornate manner of expression. For this reason . . . it is said that Lucan was not a poet, as he is known to have written his works more in the historical than the poetic mode.]

The distinction antedates the emergence of romance.[240] The *matière poétique* seeks to *acorder la fable au voir* by *mutatio,* or the transformation into another mode largely parallel to or interlaced with, yet distinct from, that of the original *matiere* (fabulous or not) of the *estoire.*[241] This is what happens to the Arthurian legend in the *Queste del saint graal.* Similarly, in the *Ovide moralisé:*

> Qui ceste fable veult savoir,
> Bien en puet ramener a voir
> La sentence en mainte maniere.
> (I.3797–99)

[He who wants to know this fable can bring its meaning back to truth in a number of ways.]

The author of the allegory was also a glossator.

Glossing occurs not only in the *Ovide moralisé* and the *Queste,* but occasionally in romance too,[242] as part of the topical adaptation of source material. The accommodation of the characters, their milieu, and their actions to contemporary ideals and practices achieves the euhemeristic reduction of the Celtic supernatural or strangeness to the customs of French feudalism and courtesy—a practice the *Ovide moralisé* itself utilizes on its historical level.[243] But glossing adapts the historical level to different, more abstract contexts by astrological, moral, and allegorical readings. The transformations are systematic and distinct, yet discursive, when a mythological fable is transformed into a scientific, moral, or theological paradigm.

> Apollo l'[= Daphne] ama longuement,
> C'est Phebus, que l'Integument,[244]
> Selonc la paienne creence,
> Apele dieu de sapience,
> Qui tout enseigne et endouctrine:
> Solaus, qui art et enlumine,
> C'est sapience et charité,
> Qui doit estre en virginité.
> (*Ovide mor* I.3125–32)

[Apollo loved her a long time. He is Phebus, whom the Integument, according to the pagan faith, calls the god of wisdom, who provides teaching and instruction in all things. The sun which burns and gives light is wisdom and charity, which should be present in virginity.]

Similar transformations occur in the *Queste.* For example, the devil, disguised as a woman, attempts to seduce Perceval.

Ele t'apela por ce qu'ele doutoit que le solaux ne t'eschaufast trop. . . . Car
quant li solaux, par quoi nos entendons Jhesucrist, la veraie lumiere, eschaufe
le pecheor del feu del Saint Esperit, petit li puet puis forfere la froidure ne la
glace de l'anemi, por qu'il ait fichié son cuer el haut soleil. (*Queste* p.
114.15–21)[245]

[She called you because she feared that you would receive too much warmth
from the sun. . . . For when the sun, by which we understand Jesus Christ,
the true light, warms the sinner with the fire of the Holy Ghost, the cold and
ice of the devil avail little in doing him harm provided he has fixed his heart
on the high sun.]

The *Queste* derives from the *Lancelot* Proper, and, ultimately, from Chrétien's *Charrette,* as the *Ovide moralisé* does from the profane tales and significations of Ovid's *Metamorphoses.* Each new work reinterprets its
antecedents by means of historical, moral, and theological descriptions,
digressions, glosses, and other interpolations. Similar transformations occur in the allegorization of romance in Huon de Mery's *Tornoiement An-
techrist* and in the *Roman de la rose.* In the latter, only a brief falling asleep
and awakening remain from the historical level, a *chiquenaude* that propels
the dream into its topical and moral developments. The *Queste* also turns
"history" as *samblance* into *senefiance,* even to the point of suppressing narrative events in favor of their underlying signification (*Queste* p.
251.24–30).[246] It has become a "poem" in the medieval sense of the word.

Allegorization also relies on topical invention. The representation of the
grail in the *Queste* is an amplification by accumulation *(interpretatio)* of
descriptive attributes and properties.[247] The same applies to the expositions
of the knights' adventures. "Et li serpenz qui la porte, ce est l'Escriture mauvesement entendue et mauvesement espose, ce est ypocrisie et heresie et in-
iquitez et pechié mortel, ce est li anemis meismes" (*Queste* p. 103.7–9) [and
the serpent that carries her represents the Scriptures wrongly understood and
incorrectly interpreted, it is hypocrisy, heresy, iniquity, and mortal sin, it
is the devil himself]. Or in the prose *Estoire:*

Or repairet li contes a rainmexel qui estoit repris et enracineiz en terre. Si dit
qu'il crut et montepliait duurement, tant que il fuit grans arbres, en petit tempz.
Et quant il fuit grans et umbrables, si fuit toz blans comme noif, en la tronce
dedens et es brainches et es foilles, et en l'acorce. Et c'estoit significance de
virginiteit; car virginiteis est une virtus par coi li cors est tenus nes et li ame
blanche. Et ceu qu'il estoit blans en totes choses, si signifioit que celle qui l'avoit
planteit, estoit tote virge a celle hore qu'elle le plantoit. . . . Et sachies qu'entre
pucelage et virginiteit ne sont mies une chose meysmes, ançois i ait grans deser-
ance. (*Estoire* II, 457–58/I.126.8–15)

[Now the tale returns to the twig which had begun to grow again rooted in the ground. It says that it grew so well that it became a tall tree in a short while. And when it was tall and shady, it was all white like snow in the trunk, branches, leaves, and bark. And this signified virginity. For virginity is a virtue by which the body is kept clean and the soul white. And that it was totally white signified that she who had planted it was a pure virgin at the time of planting. . . . And know that chastity and virginity are not at all the same; rather there is a great distinction between them.]

This elaboration of narrative found in the *Queste* (pp. 213.14–214.6) by the *Estoire* author is a religious and moral evaluation in the allegorical mode. The allegorical gloss also appears in the secular contexts of arms and love.

> Esmerez sist cel jor ou destrier d'Orquanie,
> A son col un escu, que fu fès en Hongrie,
> A un leonet d'or, que forment reflambie;
> Ou chantel de l'escu, droiz est que gel vos die,
> Ot point un colombel, blans con flor espanie;
> Li leonciaus desoz de l'emfant senefie
> Que il doit estre frans de par chevalerie,
> Envers son anemi plainz de grant felonnie,
> Et li colombiaus blans douçour et cortoisie,
> Et que vers son ami mout forment s'umelie.
>
> (*Florence* 702–11)

[Esmerez was mounted that day on a destrier from Orkanie. From his neck hung a shield made in Hungary, which bore the brightly shining image of a gilden lionet. On the shield's upper quarter—it is right that I tell you this—was painted a dove white as a flower in bloom. The lionet beneath it signifies that the young man should be of noble knighthood, felonious toward his enemies; and the white dove represents gentility and courtesy, signifying thereby that he should humble himself greatly before his friends.]

Similarly, Bucifal's colors not only are marvelous, as we have observed, but also counterpoint the variegated regalia of Alexander the Great himself.

> Et sist sor un destrier de diverse semblance;
> La teste ot plus vermelle que n'est tains de garance,
> Le col et les costés ot blans par demonstrance,
> La crope ot pumelee par autre diference,
> Les quatre piés ot noirs, ce fu senefiance.
> Onques plus hardis rois de lui ne porta lance,
> Par sa proëce a il sor tout le mont poissance;

Onques teus rois ne fu, s'en Dieu eüst creance.
Trop sot d'astronomie et plus de ningremance,
Assés sot de fisique, apris l'ot en s'enfance.
(Alex APar III.5151–60)

[He was mounted on a destrier of diverse appearance. Its head was redder
than purple dye, its neck and ribs were clearly white, its crup was distinctly mottled, the four feet black, and this had a meaning. Never did a
more courageous king bear lance, and he dominated the whole world
through his prowess. Nor would ever a king have been his equal if he had
had faith in God. He was well versed in astronomy, and even more so in
necromancy, and knew a great deal about medicine, which he learned in
his youth.]

The marvelous horse is a virtual emblem of the extraordinary qualities and
accomplishments of its rider. The invention of attributes to fit a marvel is,
in brief compass, of the same kind as the allegorical amplifications cited from
Florence de Rome, the *Estoire del saint graal,* the *Queste,* and the *Ovide
moralisé.*

Multicolored, even artificially colored horses no doubt enhanced the emblematic conspicuousness of such descriptions in romance. For example, after Enide completes the quest with Erec, she rides a multicolored horse. It
is neither black, like the one she rode during the quest, nor sorrel.[248] A sharp
green line separates the symmetrical black and white sides of its head, a division analogous to that in her own life between a dark quest and the bright
joy exemplified in Erec's recuperation and the "surplus" (5208) they recover
by a return to happy sexual love. The contrast also marks the difference between Enide's fate and Dido's. Dido loved and was abandoned by Eneas
(*Eneas* 5294), but Enide followed her husband, who went on, like Eneas
(*Erec* 5296–98), to conquest and a crown. Chrétien's description of the
"bonté" of Enide's horse anticipates the outpouring of "bonté" during and
after the reconciliation between Erec and Enide.

Un palefroi de grant bonté,
Soëf anblant, gent et bien fet,
Li a l'an hors au perron tret;
Li palefroiz fu biax et buens.
(*Erec* 5268–71)

[A very fine palfrey, of gentle gait, noble, and well shaped, was brought
to her at the mounting block. The palfrey was beautiful and good.]

Enide too may partake of the joy of the court and finally be a queen as Erec
is a king. Just as Enide's beauty provides the narrative and topical *conjoin-*

ture in the first part of the romance,[249] her *bonté* informs the second part: "Belle Enide, bonne Enide."[250] Such "bounty" is eminently green, and indeed sexual in the reunion of husband and wife. But the bounty is not familial. Rather it is magnanimous, producing joy in the brilliant majesty of court and coronation at Brandigan and Nantes.

The coronation of Erec evokes the memory of Alexander the Great and Bucifal. Erec is said to surpass him and all emperors of Rome in largess (*Erec* 6611–23); and his robe, the decoration for which Macrobius inspired, as we have seen, portrays the four arts of the quadrivium, much as Alexander's prowess comprehends astronomy, magic, and medicine. Erec's robe was made by four fays (*Erec* 6682–83), and contains marvelous beasts of many colors.

> La pane qui i fu cosue
> Fu d'unes contrefetes bestes
> Qui ont totes blondes les testes
> Et les cors noirs come une more,
> Et les dos ont vermauz desore,
> Les vantres noirs et la coe inde.
> (*Erec* 6732–37)

[The cloth sewn into it represented beasts whose heads were blond, whose bodies were black as a Moorish woman's, whose backs were red on top, black on the underside, and whose tail was indigo.]

And withal he bears a green scepter—"toz d'une esmeraude anterine" (*Erec* 6812) [made entirely from one emerald]—also covered with the images of all manner of beasts. The audience would no doubt note the implied allegory of the emerald scepter that is analogous to and anticipated by the verdant line that divides the head of Enide's horse.

The distinction between allegorical and historical romance is analogous to the romancers' own distinction between *matiere* which is *coverte* or *oscure* and that which is *aperte* or *voire*. The distinction is common in allegorical romances, where imaginative, ambagious narrative is interlaced with discursive commentary or gradual elucidation by topical elements, like the god of love's discourse or the configuration of abstractions in the adventures of Guillaume de Lorris' *Rose*. By the conclusion,

> La verité, qui est coverte,
> Vos sera lores toute aperte
> Quant espondre m'orroiz le songe,
> Car il n'i a mot de mençonge.
> (*Rose* 2073–76/2071–74)

[The truth, now covered, will then be fully open to you, when you will have heard me set forth the dream—for there is not a false word in it.]

Guillaume's own "version coverte" is the dream; the "version aperte" is his own life, from which, in the words of the *Ovide moralisé* commentary, it is a digression. The two coalesce as Guillaume draws from his love the *matiere* of an art of love (21–44). The topical abstractions of a courtly lover inform the obscure dream as Alexander's virtues do Bucifal's colors, or as Enide's beauty and bounty inform the descriptions in *Erec:* "Quoique la densité significative de l'allégorie soit très variable, cette figure constitue, dans le texte, une glose intégrée à l'expression."[251] The drift from *estoire* to *poème* moves the mode of representation from metonymic identity *(idemptitas)* between attributes and the *matiere* they qualify to the metaphorical alterity *(similitudo* or *contrarietas)* of allegorical modes.[252] Just as, according to Gautier d'Arras, critical judgment can distinguish solid gold from gilding, it can also separate the given romance's representation of its *matiere* from fabulous nonsense. Any fable, rightly read, can show the good to follow or the evil to eschew, "Nes . . . fables as Sarasins" (*Partonopeu* 104)[253] [even Saracen fable], since all fables can be made to praise or blame through topical invention: "S'en porra l'en pranre toz tens / Et bons examples et bons sens" (*Partonopeu* 93–94) [and one can always draw from it both good examples and good signification]. But the profitable instruction is frequently "parfont et repus" (*Partonopeu* 102) [deep and hidden], as in the dream world to which Denis Piramus likened the *Partonopeu* itself. Instruction must therefore be found and drawn out of the *matiere,* as Marie de France, another inventor of dream worlds, says in the Prologue to the *Lais. Partonopeu de Blois* itself states:

> C'est del sage home la costume
> Qu'il porgart cascune parole,
> Et de la sage et de la fole
> Eslise le sens par voisdie,
> Sel traie hors de la folie.
>   (124–28)

[Wise men are wont to consider every word, and to elicit sense from both wise and foolish speech through their ingenuity, and to extract it from foolishness.]

Here we encounter anew the *Ovide moralisé*'s intention, "acorder la fable au voir." This is the task of "poets" and "historians" alike. It is by such accommodation that the author brings the parts of his or her opus into *conjointure.*

Roman: Ordre and Parties

Car bien i savra retorner quant il en sera temps et leus.
—Tristan *§386 n.1*

[For he will know how to return there at the right time and place.]

The word *roman* acquired a variety of denotations and connotations, from "the French language" to "romance genre," any one of which could be used singly or in conjunction with other meanings.

> Jehans qui en maint bien s'afaite
> Et pluisor bele rime a faite,
> Nos a un romanç commenchié.
> Assés briément l'a romanchié
> Des aventures de Bretaigne.
> Bien cuic que des mellors ataingne.
> Del roi Artu et de ses houmes
> Est cis roumans que nos lisoumes.
> (*Rigomer* 1–8) [1].

[Jehan, who devises many good things, and has made many a fine line of verse, has begun a French romance for all of us. He has rather briefly Romanced it about the adventures of Britain. I think that it reports the best ones. This French romance we are reading is about Arthur and his men.]

The double meanings of "language" and "a work in the Romance language" go back to the beginnings of vernacular *estoire*. [2] But here Jehan means something more specific—something that suggests his notion of romance was similar to Renaut de Beaujeu's: a *bele conjointure* or the orderly arrangement of narrative parts. Jehan's *Rigomer* centers on a marvel from which the romance derives and with which it begins (*Rigomer* 16–17) to spin out and intertwine adventures and lays (*Rigomer* 6429–34). The romance achieves its *bele conjointure* through the orderly disposition of narrative parts.

How did marvel and truth conjoin in romance? We have seen that each element has its own coherence.[3] The marvel or mythic level in Arthurian romance is analogous to Propp's narrative structure as confrontation, domination, and attribution.[4] But Propp's terminology is unsuitable for matter not derived directly from folklore, as is the case with romance. Rainer Warning has therefore proposed Greimas' terms "confrontation," "domination," and "possession" to adapt the phenomena to medieval romance.[5] In particular, domination resolves the confrontation of differing worldviews, and reflects national, dynastic, imperial, religious, or aristocratic presuppositions that contribute to a given romance's *san*. As in early vernacular histories, romances fostered contexts reflecting chivalric and courtly ideals. They read the contexts out of earlier *matieres* as their *surplus de san* (a technique Marie de France and her contemporaries learned from antiquity), as practiced in the *romans d'antiquité* and Ovidian *contes,* and further construed these *matieres* as an aristocratic version of arms, love, and rectitude. Thus, as Warning has demonstrated, all romance has a thematic level of coherence analogous to Fourquet's "niveau de cohérence courtoise." When mythic and courtly levels are brought together, they do not necessarily coalesce—they may not even be coherent separate parts—but they complete each other like an alloy or *concors discordia*. Their relation is a matter of order.

Order of Parts in Romance Narrative

Both historical and allegorical romances, unlike early *chansons de geste,*[6] rely on chronological and topographic coordinates to arrange data extracted from source material, which is itself adapted to the auctorial concept of the significance or the truth of the narrative. "Tout li a en ordre conté / De l'aventure la verté" (*Amadas* 6637–38)[7] [he told her in precise order the truth of the adventure]. There are two principal kinds of order for the Middle Ages: natural order and artificial order.[8] These terms from medieval Latin poetics correspond to the romancers' concern for what we may call *ci endroit* and *or endroit,* that is, the spatial and temporal coordinates of the narrative.

Natural Order of Narrative and Narrative Signification

Natural order resembles annalistic records in its insistence on a chronological sequence of events occurring within specific geographical limits like a region, town, or monastic foundation. The arts of poetry and prose describe natural order in narrative as normal temporal and spatial sequence, that is, the "natural" order in which events occur, and the topographic sequence of places occupied during that time.

> Linea stratae
> Est ibi dux, ubi res et verba sequuntur eumdem
> Cursum nec sermo declinat ab ordine rerum.
> *(Poetria nova* 88–90)

[Nature's smooth road points the way when "things" and "words" follow the same sequence, and the order of discourse does not depart from the order of occurrence.]

The *linea stratae*— or the *droite voie*[9]—of narrative fixes time and space at the beginning ("Certus praelimitet ordo / Unde praearripiat cursum stylus" [*Poetria nova* 56–57] [let a definite order chart in advance at what point the pen will take up its course]), moves through middle ("his utere velis. / Hunc portum teneas, hic fixa sit anchora mentis" [1061–62] [have recourse to those sails, occupy this harbour, cast the mind's anchor here]), to reach the end ("Jam mare transcurri, Gades in littore fixi" [2066] [Now I have crossed the sea; I have fixed my Cadiz on the shore]). It is a linear, horizontal structure that shapes the sequence of time and place, whether these are construed objectively, subconsciously, or topically.

The *Ducs* by Benoît de Sainte-Maure does not begin just with the departure of the Danes from Scandinavia. It extends back to their forefathers' departure from Troy (*Ducs* 645–62) and reaches down to the Norman domination in twelfth-century France and Britain.[10] Each successive reign forms a segment in the sequence, just as each reign frames and divides itself into a succession of adventures and marvels. The progression was to culminate in the reign of Henry II. For Benoît, chronology and geography conjoin to fix narrative parts, for example, through the death of one duke or king and the ascendency of another.

> En la kalende de fevrer,
> La u la lune est seze dite,
> Truis senz faille sa mort escrite;
> En France regnout Loeïs.
> Ci me repos e ci fenis,
> Mais n'achieve pas mis travaiz.
> Or vient l'estoire des granz faiz
> A translater e a escrivre,
> U mervilles avra a dire.
> *(Ducs* 14774–82)

[On the calends of February, when the moon is said to be in its sixteenth day, I find certain report of his death. Louis was reigning in France. Here I rest and stop, but my labor does not cease. Now it is time to transcribe and set down the history of the great deeds, in which there will be marvels to relate.]

Similarly, significant chronological divisions may mark a given life.

> Conté, retrait e dit vos ai
> Sum ce qu'en l'estoire en trovai,
> Confaitement n'en quel maniere
> Rout Richart Normendie arriere.
> Des or diron com il la tint
> Ne saveir que puis li avint.
> (*Ducs* 19541–46)

[I have told, related, and said, according to what I found in the history, how and in what way Richard won Normandy back. Now I shall tell how he held it and find out what happened to him subsequently.]

Again with attention to seriatim sequence, the *Troie* clearly marks its beginning, middle, and end: the origins of the war — the war — the aftermath of the war (see *Troie* 28767–74). Everything is "en ordre mot a mot" (*Troie* 283) [in order, word for word]. Temporal order determines chronological consistency. And it permits appropriate emphases, allowing, for example, the midpoint to acquire more than simply structural significance.[11]

Chronological and geographical order are more complex when viewed as topoi. They raise questions subsumed under *quomodo, ante rem, cum re, post rem,* as well as the more general *tempus* and *locus*.[12] They also preclude patchwork narrative structure,[13] like the parataxis in *chansons de geste* and in Beroul's *Tristan*. In the latter work, *pans,* or narrative patches, are sewn together with little regard for time-space coordinates, which are loose or nonexistent; the *negotia* are pieced together as disparate adventures.[14]

Invention establishes narrative *ordo* as natural, that is, as a chronologically and geographically determined sequence of events: "seriemque sub ordine certo / Interior praescribit homo" (*Poetria nova* 45–46) [he mentally outlines the successive steps in a definite order]. Thus in romance: "La soume de leur assambler / Vous voel tout en ordre conter" (*Amadas* 7449–50)[15] [I wish to resume their gathering in proper order]. This also holds true in episodes and other fragments.

> La bataille que après vint,
> Que mout redura puis e tint,

> Dirai en ordre mot a mot,
> E ço que chascuns i fist tot.
>   (*Troie* 281–84)[16]

[I shall report in order, word for word, the ensuing battle, which lasted a long time, and everything each one achieved in it.]

It has long been recognized that Benoît roughly ordered the sequence of events and participants in the battles he amplified to conform with the catalogues of battles and participants in his sources.[17]

Time's guardians among today's scholars, though, have detected occasional slips in some narratives.[18] Moreover, romance may deliberately confuse time, spreading fog on murky landscapes to reflect the mind of the protagonists.[19] But even in cases like these, coherence and understanding do derive from reference to normal chronology and "real" topography; the usual topical sequence of events is referred to by Matthew of Vendôme's "ordinaria successio" (*Ars vers* 4.13) as an array of topically coherent and discrete occurrences. Emphasis on time and place in a romance's framework of seasons, places, and settings — the season topic *(tempus)*— contributes to both narrative and topical clarity.[20]

Allegorical romances like Guillaume de Lorris' *Rose* also have an order corresponding to chronology in the waking world.

> Ou vintieme an de mon aage,
> Ou point qu'Amors prent le paage
> Des juenes genz, couchiez m'estoie
> Une nuit, si con je soloie.
>
> . . . .
>
> Avis m'iere qu'il estoit mais,
> Il a ja bien cinc anz ou mais,
> Qu'en mai estoie, ce sonjoie,
> Ou tens amoreus, plein de joie.
>   (*Rose* 21–24, 45–48)

[In my twentieth year, when Love levies its toll on young men, I had gone to bed one night as usual. . . . It seemed to me that it was May, five or more years ago, and I dreamed that it was Maytime, the season of love full with joy.]

Within the dream sequence, natural order does not, of course, follow the sun. Rather, it follows stages called *aventures (Rose* 2267/2255) in an elaborate and circumstantial *gradus amoris* marked by a succession of descriptive settings. However, all that transpires, as in biography itself, derives its order from the temporal, topographic, and psychological commonplaces of waking experience.

Time and place function as narrative coordinates. Horace signaled their importance in linking and division.

> Et properantis aquae per amoenos ambitus agros,
> Aut flumen Rhenum aut pluvius describitur arcus.
> Sed *nunc* non erat *his locus.*
>
> (*Ad Pisones* 17–19)[21]

[And a rainbow or the Rhine river or rushing waters winding through pleasant fields are described. But it was not the "place" for them now.]

Matthew of Vendôme emphasizes time and place in topical description, insisting that their placement be pertinent (*Ars vers* 1.110).[22] Opportunity therefore defines the *locus.* Since the *locus* in narrative, as a feature of *ordo,* includes chronological and topographic sequence, even in dream vision, the reader was to note them in order better to follow and understand the narrative.

> Sic nimirum in doctrina fieri oportet, ut videlicet prius historiam discas et rerum gestarum veritatem, a principio repetens usque ad finem *quid* gestum sit, *quando* gestum sit, *ubi* gestum sit, et *a quibus* gestum sit, diligenter memoriae commendes. Haec enim quattuor praecipue in historia requirenda sunt, persona, negotium, *tempus* et *locus.* (*Didascalicon* pp. 113.24–114.4; emphasis mine)

[So too, in fact, must it be in your instruction. First you learn history and diligently commit to memory the truth of the deeds that have been performed, reviewing from beginning to end *what* has been done, *when* it has been done, *where* it has been done, and *by whom* it has been done. For these are the four things which are especially to be sought for in history (i.e., narrative)—the *person,* the *business done,* the *time,* and the *place.* (pp. 135–136, emphasis mine)]

Although these words apply to the study of Scripture, they are applicable to any kind of *historia,* and thus of *estoire,* including chronicle and romance.[23]

French romance tends to emphasize a specific time—springtime, Pentacost, Ascension, at a prominent court or castle — to mark the beginning as a state of inaction before the call to adventure suddenly resounds or a marvel intrigues the court.

> E ja sabes vos veramens,
> Et aves o vist moltas ves,
> Q'ieu [Arthur] non manjaría peres,

> Qe cort tan esforsada tenga,
> Entro qe aventura venga
> O calque estraina novela
> De cavaler o de piusela.
>
> *(Jaufre* 146–52)

[And you already know for sure and have often seen that I (Arthur) will not eat for any reason, however grand my court, until an adventure comes, or some strange report about a knight or a maiden.]

The discovery of the marvel's source marks the end of the sequence of adventures; the passage from the court to the marvel and back restores and further enhances the original inaction. The account of that cycle is the narrative that locates and relocates the protagonists seeking the marvel through adventures. Thus, *loci* are markers in a chronological and topographic system.

Chrétien's romances exemplify this definition of *loci,* as they displace characters in time and space: straightforward movement away from and return to the court *(Erec, Charrette);* alternating movement between or among two or more centers, such as Arthur's court, the German imperial court, Constantinople *(Cligés);* encircling movement *(Yvain);* apparent meandering (Calogrenant in *Yvain, Perceval).* Similarly, the prose romancers fit the principal questers into a geographical network—Arthur's courts, Corbenic, the Joyeuse Garde, Sorelois, etc.—all of which are interlocked by the Vulgate's imposition of a typological framework onto what appears to be a careful, accurate temporal sequence: the right knight at the right place at the right time,[24] as Vinaver and Bogdanow have demonstrated in their studies of the Vulgate and the post-Vulgate cycles.[25] Furthermore, Köhler has shown the correlation between the questing knight and the achievement of adventure, and thus of narrative representation and character realization.[26] All this illustrates the *persona, negotium, locus,* and *tempus* fundamental to *historia,* according to Hugh of Saint Victor.

Artificial or Contrived Order of Narrative and Narrative Signification

Chronological and geographical sequence may also be arranged in artificial order, as Vergil did in the *Aeneid* and Chrétien de Troyes in *Yvain.* The account of Aeneas' arrival at Carthage precedes that of the destruction of Troy and most of the adventures pursuant to the flight from that city to Carthage. Similarly, Calogrenant's presence at Arthur's court precedes the chronologically earlier adventures he relates there about his defeat at the fountain. The intention that determines such an arrangement of parts may be either struc-

turally or rhetorically informed. If structural, it makes the arrangement artful; if rhetorical, more effective. Thus, order obtains on the narrative level
as well as on that of *san*.[27]

The distinction between natural and artificial order offers medieval terminology for the two levels of coherence identified by Fourquet. *Matiere* and
san in the given romance are an amalgam; the disposition of the one is accommodated to that of the other. They may indeed coalesce; or they may
counterpoint one another as distinctly, but also as artfully, as the different
melodies and poems in a motet. The language and methodology of medieval
and modern critics often seem widely divergent; yet the principle of artificial
order, surely today the most widely debunked notion in medieval poetic theory, shows itself to reflect the preoccupations of scholars like Jean Fourquet
and Rainer Warning, whose accommodation of actantial and thematic critical
theories is, in the last analysis, a more elegant identification of natural and
artificial order in the *Aeneid*, Chrétien de Troyes' distinction between *matiere*
and *san,* and Marie de France's elaboration of a *surplus de sen* from *matiere.*

As we have seen, Ernest Gallo identified natural and artificial order on
two levels in the commentary on the *Aeneid* attributed to Bernardus Silvestris. In the literal *historia,* Vergil employs artificial disposition of the chronological order by having Aeneas recount the Fall of Troy and his flight in books
II and III. But Bernardus' reading of the epic also brings out the natural order of man's rise from sin, represented by the sea storm and fright of book
I, to the vigorous assertion of will as virtue overcomes vice by book VI, where
the commentary ends.

Bernardus' reading is not idle or superficial, nor is the method used unique
to the imposed allegory of glosses. Other medieval works also show the doubling of orders, notably the Prose *Lancelot* and the complete *Roman de la
rose.* The former represents Lancelot's career in straight chronological sequence. But the appraisal of his career makes an abrupt change at the beginning of the *Queste del saint graal.* The love for Guenevere that made Lancelot
the best knight in the world emerges as a sin preventing him from having
realized his real worth. "Or gardes que tu peusses puis avoir fet, se tu eusses
toutes ces vertuz sauvees en toi que Nostre Sires i avoit mises. Tu n'eusses
mie failli a achever les aventures dou Saint Graal" (*Queste* p. 126.27–30)
[now consider what you could have accomplished subsequently had you
preserved all those virtues which Our Lord had bestowed on you. You would
not have failed to achieve the adventures of the Holy Grail]. The reevaluation of Lancelot begins when, early in the *Queste,* a maiden announces to
him that "Vos estiez hier matin li mieldres chevaliers dou monde. . . . Mes
qui ore le diroit, len le devroit tenir a mençongier; car meillor i a de vos"
(*Queste* pp. 12.31–13.2) [yesterday morning you were the best knight in the

world. . . . But anyone saying that now should be held a liar; for there is one better than you]. "Overnight" the narrative has slipped from the literal courtly *san* of the natural order to the allegorical moral *san* of the artificial order. The change has the powerful effect of reverberating back through the entire *Lancelot* Proper, just as the maiden begins to reevaluate Lancelot's life. In contrast to Bernardus Silvestris' reading of Vergil, we have in the Prose *Lancelot* natural literal order together with artificial order on the level of *san*.

In a not dissimiliar way, Jean de Meun rehearses the sequence of adventures in Guillaume de Lorris' *Rose* and thus, by the reduplication, produces a new reading of the Lover's progress, controverting the intention expressed in Guillaume's Prologue. Genius pronounces the condemnation of the Garden of Deduit.

> Pour Deu, seigneur, prenez ci garde:
> Qui bien la verité regarde,
> Les choses ici contenues,
> Ce sont trufles et fanfelues.
> Ci n'a chose qui seit estable,
> Quanqu'il i vit est corrompable.
> Il vit queroles qui faillirent,
> Et faudront tuit cil qui les firent.
> Ausinc feront toutes les choses
> Qu'il vit par tout laienz encloses.
> (*Rose* 20349–58/20319–28)

[For God's sake, my lords, heed what you see here. If you carefully consider the truth of the matter, the things contained therein are deceptive and worthless. Nothing is sure, everything he saw is subject to corruption. He saw carols that came to an end, as will all the dancers. So will it be with everything he saw enclosed therein.]

This effectively turns the Garden of Deduit inside out, placing its action in the very world of age, corruption, and death that Guillaume separates it from by the garden wall. Jean's adaptation is a gloss on Guillaume's text, like the maiden's on Lancelot's past in the *Queste,* rather than a distinct commentary.

What these romances achieve finds support in Matthew of Vendôme. Poets should follow topical principles that improve upon or correct source *materia;* they should not imitate those who "fabulas circinantes poeticas verbum verbo sigillatim exprimunt, tanquam super auctores metrice proposuerunt commentare" (*Ars vers* 4.1) [ransack poems word for word for images, just as if they were setting out to write a verse commentary on their authors]. Rather they must seek out what makes the narrative verisimilar, and follow that route assiduously, deleting from or adding to their *materia* in conformity with intention. "Si me couvient ainsinc paler, / Se par le dreit m'en veuil aler" (*Rose* 15193–94/15163–64) [and I must speak so if I wish to keep to the right path]. The *droite voie* in the Prose *Lancelot* and Jean de Meun's *Rose* is achieved by an artificial order on the level of *san*. Jean elicits that *surplus de san* from his courtly predecessor as deftly and effectively as the *Queste* author did from Chrétien's *Charrette* in the Prose *Lancelot*.

Integration of *Matiere* and *San:* Transition and Jointing in the Juxtaposition of Narrarive Parts

The prominence in medieval poetics of natural and artificial order raised problems of transition as well as of the jointing of parts. Natural and artificial order have to do principally with broad concerns like the arrangement of beginning, middle, and end, concerns that govern internal coherence and the lack of discrepancy—what C. O. Brink has named the "basic law of unity" enunciated by Horace in verses 151–52 of the *Ad Pisones:* "Sic veris falsa remiscet, / Primo ne medium, medio ne discrepet imum"[28] [thus does it blend true with false without discrepancy between beginning and middle or between middle and end]. These lines reflect a broad concern for the surface arrangement of parts, as well as for texture, that is, the character, quality, and purpose of the *series* and *iunctura* that loom large in both Horace and in the medieval arts of poetry and prose that derive from him.[29]

Multiple narrative strands may impede the author attempting to relate simultaneous events: "Tot ensemble dire ne puis, / Mais tot vos conterai en ordre" (*Rose* 698–99/696–97) [I can't relate everything at once, but I'll tell you everything in order]. Two principal kinds of jointing characterize such composition: parataxis and interlace (asyndetic and polysyndetic conjunctions).[30] The former appears in Marie de France's *Lais,* where distinct, independent tales are set down in succession.

> Ki divers cuntes veut traitier
> Diversement deit comencier
> E parler si rainablement
> K'il seit pleisibles a la gent.
> Ici comencerai *Milun*
> E musterai par brief sermun
> Pur quei e coment fu trovez
> Li lais ki issi est numez.
> > (*Lais* Milun 1–8)

[He or she who wishes to treat different stories ought to begin in different ways and speak so reasonably as to be pleasing. Here I shall begin *Milun* and show briefly why and how the lay that goes by that name was invented.]

On the other hand, Arthurian romance beginning with Chrétien will link such adventures in a quest. In the prose romances, it became common to insert narratives, some of which are called lays,[31] to explain the causes or the origins of the adventures knights encounter. A radial pattern emerges within the larger sequences, like the epicycles in the Prose *Sept sages de Rome*.[32] The beginning of the one adventure is described in a flashback, the knight's encounter with the adventure serves as a middle that joins the two disparate narratives, and the end is the achievement of the adventure. Parataxis becomes encasement or imbrication, that is, the encasing of lesser parts in greater ones. The time-place coordinates, in relation to particular knights and their qualities *(persona* and *maneries)* and the actual adventures *(negotia),* are basic constituents of such writing.[33] Thus, the simple principle of beginning, middle, and end proliferates into a potentially complex and interdependent encasement of parts *(enchevêtrement),* a patchwork that has acquired the order and design of a mosaic.[34]

The design itself acquires a high degree of complexity in the interlace patterns of the great prose cycles. Yet even there a sense of tripartite division into beginning, middle, and end obtains, fitting the typological pattern of Fall, Redemption, and Destruction in the Vulgate cycle. The post-Vulgate cycle makes a division into three parts of equal length. Even the post-Vulgate tripartition is not arbitrary, as Fanni Bogdanow has convincingly argued.[35] Structurally, the three parts are seen to organize thematic emphasis by deploying interlacing designs, encasement, and varieties of jointing: they are internally polysyndetic.

Returning to parataxis in terms of order, we may see how Gautier d'Arras carefully adapts it in the *Eracle* to spatial and temporal coordinates by artificial narrative order. To begin with, he alludes to the romance's composition in the conventional sense as delineation of beginning, middle, and end within the three separate tales that make up the plot.[36] However, Gautier understands beginning, middle, and end as the paratactically conjoined narrative blocks that constitute the three parts of the romance. Each block is recounted separately, without interruption or significant infratextual correlation.[37]

> Ichis [Eracle] mist sainte glise en pais
> Si li conquist si grant anour
> Com de le crois Nostre Signor.
> Ne voel pas ci entrelacier
> L'ahan qu'il ot au porcacier,
> Qu'ensi ne vait pas le matire;

> Ains dirai l'uevre tote entire
> De nostre empereor Laïs
> Et de sa feme Atanaïs,
> Et de l'honor vous dirai puis
> Qu'Eracles ot, et se jou puis,
> Aprés dirai de cele crois
> U Nostre sire fu destrois,
> Con fu perdue par foiblece
> Et reconquise par proueche.
>   (*Eracle* 2900–2914)

[He (Eracle) restored peace to the Holy Church. And he gained for it the honor of possessing the cross of Our Lord. I don't wish to insert here the travail he endured to win it, for that's not how the *matiere* goes. Rather I'll recount the whole work about our emperor Lais and his wife Athanais; afterward, I'll tell you of the honor achieved by Eracle, and then, if possible, about the cross on which Our Lord was hung, how it was lost through weakness and regained with prowess.]

Eracle possessed three "gifts" or talents: the intuitive ability to judge horses, women, and precious stones. The demonstration of those talents constitutes the beginning of the romance, the drama of Athanais the middle, and the defeat of the pagans the end; within each part there may be equally sharp subdivisions: the three proofs of Eracle's gifts in the first part and the different victories in the third.[38] The whole constitutes a paratactic juxtaposition corresponding, as Gautier says in the foregoing passage, to three *matieres:* first, choice of stones, horses, and women; second, marriage; and third, the recovery of the Cross.

Another variety of parataxis was the genealogical framework borrowed from vernacular histories.[39] Genealogy orders temporal progression in the *Horn,* including its alleged predecessor and potential continuation (1–5, 5225–39); the incipient sequence *Ipomedon-Protheselaus* (*Protheselaus* 31–62, 12693–97), presented as an addition to the *Thebes;* and the Huon de Bordeaux cycle.[40] Robert de Boron intended to use both paratactic jointing and genealogical sequence in his grail cycle. Although he planned each part in order, he states at the conclusion to the *Joseph* that he had to set aside four parts: the tales of Alain, Petrus, Moysés, and the "Riches Peschierres" (*Estoire* RoB 3461–80).

> Ces quatre choses rassembler
> Couvient chaucune, et ratourner
> Chascune partie par soi
> Si comme ele est.
>   (*Estoire* RoB 3481–84)

[It is proper to collect each of these narratives, and aptly round off each part by itself.]

But a fifth "chose" must be recounted first, although *ordre*—here natural order—locates it after the aforementioned parts: the grail story itself.

> Ausi cumme d'une partie
> Leisse, que je ne retrei mie,
> Ausi couvenra il conter
> La quinte, et les quatre oublïer,
> Tant que je puisse revenir
> Au retreire plus par loisir
> Et a ceste uuevre tout par moi,
> Et chascune mestre par soi.
> (*Estoire* RoB 3501–8)[41]

[Just as I leave off one part which I do not tell, so it is proper to tell the fifth part, leaving out the four others until I can return to relating this work more easily and completely, while setting each part separately.]

The fifth part may survive as the *Merlin* fragment and, in changed shape, the Didot *Perceval*.[42] The sequence in Robert's cycle suggests paratactic aggregates juxtaposed and distinguished by *persona, negotium, locus,* and *tempus.*

The post-Vulgate *Graal* abstracts the beginning, middle, and end sequence from the narrative in order to achieve a simple, recognizable mathematical division among the author's three books,[43] probably determined by page- and line-counting for verse and stichometry for prose. This "assenement" (Huth *Merlin* I, 280) [apportionment] provides for a comprehensive beginning, middle, and end: "Et la premiere partie fenist il au commenchement de ceste queste, et la seconde el commenchement dou graal, et la tierche fenist il . . . apriès la mort de Lanscelot, a chelui point meisme qu'il devise de la mort le rói March" (Huth *Merlin* I, 280) [and he completed the first part at the beginning of this quest, and the second at the beginning of the grail, and he finished the third . . . after Lancelot's death, precisely there where he relates Marc's death]. Each part is a narrative whole; each appears to have contained a coherent, discrete narrative block.

The mathematical apportionment admits different substructures within the three broad, mathematical segments of beginning, middle, and end, including both subordinate narrative strands and links to the entire Vulgate cycle.[44] The post-Vulgate was conceived as a branch of the Vulgate rather than a replacement. "Et cel anelet li avoit douné la Damoisiele del Lac, si coume la *grant hystore de Lanscelot* le devise, cele meisme ystoire qui doit estre departie de mon livre, ne mie pour chou qu'il . . . n'i apartiegne et que elle n'en soit traite, mais pour chou qu'il covient que les trois parties de mon livre soient ingaus"[45] [and the Maiden of the Lake had given him that ring, as the *High Tale of Lancelot* reports—that very tale which should be separated from my book, not because the latter . . . isn't part of it or drawn out of it, but because the three parts of my book have to be of equal length]. This seems to be true for the different versions of the Prose *Tristan* as well, which may incorporate sections of the Vulgate, be interpolated into it as *incidences,* or establish cross-references.[46]

Turning now to imbrication in terms of order, we can see that Froissart uses the term *intervalles* to designate adventures inserted into another adventure or sequence of events.[47] In one place, he excludes the *intervalles* between a departure and an arrival.

> Or esçou drois c'on me demande
> De monsigneur Melyador;
> Comment il chevauce des or
> Avoecques les .II. damoiselles,
> Qui sont jones, frices et belles,
> Le chemin par devers Norcgalles.
> Faire ne vous voel intervalles.
> Tant ont chevaucié et erré
> Qu'il sont en Norgales entré.
> (*Meliador* 18170–78)

[Now is it proper to ask me about my lord Meliador, how he goes riding from then on with two maidens who are young, sprightly, and beautiful, on the road to North Wales. I don't want to provide you with any "intervals." They rode and traveled until entering North Wales.]

His usage recalls the term *incidence* in the Guillaume cycle, which uses parataxis to accommodate new *matiere,* simultaneity, spatial separation, or a larger cast of characters, as well as the circumstances of manuscript production.[48] *Intervalles* as *incidences* may be interlaced, or quite literally sewn into the manuscript.[49] They may also be inserted by the scribe in the new copy.

Parataxis by *incidences* and *intervalles* facilitates additions to a given romance:
—as part of the original conception, as in Gautier d'Arras or Chrétien de Troyes, who often included two or more sequences or adventures;[50]
—as a continuator's additions to an extant romance, as in the successive branches of the Seven Sages of Rome cycle;
—as a compiler's reconstitution of narrative parts from one or more sources, as in prose compilations.

It also facilitates excision equally well—which may not imply rejection, but rather a decision to emphasize one part instead of another, as in Robert de Boron's preference for the "fifth part" of the *Estoire* to its other branches.

While parataxis may derive in part from oral tradition, both it and interlace were common devices in medieval historiography.[51] Interlace fits space-time coordinates to character and action.[52] It is an obvious solution to the problem of accounting for simultaneous but spatially or otherwise separate sequences.

> A ffin
> Me couvient l'une istoire traire,
> Ains que une autre preigne a retraire,
> Car je ne puis pas, ce me semble,
> Tres toutes deviser ensemble,
> Et tout en un temps maintes choses,
> Quoyque de renc soient descloses,
> En diverses marches aviennent,
> Si ne peut on, si comme elz viennent,
> Dire ensemble, tout en un mont,
> Ce qu'en un temps vient par le mond.
> (*Mutacion* 13694–704)

[I must conclude one history before beginning another. For I don't believe I can relate them all together, nor recount many different things at once. Although they occur simultaneously, they take place in different regions, so that it is impossible to relate at one and the same time all that happened in the world at any given moment.]

Thus, William of Malmesbury interlaces the different principalities and kingdoms of England and France into a coherent chronology,[53] much as Benoît de Sainte-Maure reconstructed the independent reigns of Norman dukes, British kings, and French kings.

> Ci n'os vuil or plus avant dire
> Que ne m'esloig de ma matire.
> La me convient a revertir,
> E qui des or voudra oïr,
> Saveir mun cum li dus Guilleaume
> Conquist la terre e le reiaume
> Sor Heiraut.
> (*Ducs* 38725–31)

[I don't want to say any more here lest I stray away from my *matiere*. I ought to return to it; and whoever will want to hear from now on will find out how Duke William won the land and kingdom by defeating Harold.]

The next degree of difficulty involves the interlacing of complete narrative strands. This loosens the stiffer chronological and geographic constraints of encasement on structure and plot, just as the *brisure* loosened the octosyllabic couplet.[54]

> Por ce, si cum sunt avenues,
> Avum cez choses ci teisues,
> Dites, mostrees clerement
> Que ne sevent gaires la gent
> Conment li reis Ewart fu nez,
> Cum il fu puis reis coronnez,
> Mais ci en puet le veir oïr.
> Or nos besoigne revertir
> A ce dum traite avuns l'estoire,
> Dum ele escrit ne fait memoire.
> (*Ducs* 30271–80)

[Therefore we have woven these events in here just as they happened, telling and showing them clearly; for hardly anyone knows how king Ewart was born and then crowned king. But here the truth can be heard. Now we must return to the source of our history which it writes and records.]

Rather than opting for parataxis like Gautier d'Arras, which would have imposed strict constraints on the placing of simultaneous narrative strands and totally locked complex *matiere* into compartments, the prose romances follow the example of chroniclers like Benoît. In doing so, they achieve the freer flow of separate narratives permitted by interlace. Even the mathematical limits of the post-Vulgate structure admit intertwining narrative streams into its borders. This is true also in the non-Arthurian prose cycle of the *Sept sages de Rome*.[55]

Interlace was used in verse romance to preserve natural order, as illustrated by Chrétien's use of *vers* in the first part of *Erec*. The amalgamation of two distinct adventures—the Hunt for the White Stag and the Sparrow Hawk contest—required interlacing the two. As we have seen, a common knit links them cohesively and coherently, but without the *jointure*'s being apparent, as it is in the later prose romances. The distinction between hidden and visible interlace is analogous, as we have seen (pp. 22–23), to that between *iunctura occulta* and *aperta* for metaphorical additions to narrative. Interlace is an elaborate technique in prose romance used within an overall plan to preserve the order of beginning, middle, and end. Thus, the Vulgate Lancelot-Grail accounts for the beginning and end of the adventures in Logres by interlacing three plans: the Arthurian plan, the grail plan, and God's plan. Prefiguration and typological fulfillment establish coherence and order among the three.[56] Beginning and end are separated by a long, "adventurous" middle ground, containing the intertwining quests of Lancelot and many other knights, and various parallel sequences typologically correlated with the main Arthurian *matiere* centering on Lancelot and culminating in the exploits of Galaad. There are in effect two contextual foci, love and grace, Camelot and Corbenic, analogous to those in Gautier de Châtillon's *Alexandreis* (see above, pp. 45–46). The disparity focuses on the name Lancelot/Galaad, and the failure of the Round Table to amalgamate the Arthurian and grail worlds necessitates a double conclusion: the one for the *chevaliers celestieux* at Sarras, the other for the Round Table on Salisbury Plain.

The adaptation of beginning, middle, and end to typological prefiguration and fulfillment required *jointures* with sacred history. The *Estoire* and the *Merlin,* added later to the cycle, elaborate this conception from the *Queste.* The *Merlin* recounts the beginning of the adventures in Logres, preparing for the post-Vulgate's more emphatic and structurally striking beginning with the Dolorous Stroke, an episode which functions both within its own framework and within the larger framework of which the *Mort Artu* and especially the *Queste* are the conclusions (*Estoire* II, 311–12/I.80–81). Like the quests that are interwoven into the Arthurian labyrinth, great genealogies also link beginnings and ends. "Salemons, la buenne eureuse virgene ne sera pas fins de ton lingnage [Mary, and thus Christ, are its middle], ains sera fins uns chevalier qui pasera de bontet et de cevalerie tous chiaus qui devant lui auront estet et qui a celui tans porteront armes." (*Estoire* II, 472/I.132.9–12)[57] [Solomon, the blessed virgin will not be the last of your line. Rather the last member will be a knight surpassing in nobility of life and chivalry all those who will have gone before him, and who will bear arms in his time.]. One sees how, through his family, Galaad enters into one typological pattern including Solomon and Christ, of which he is at the chronological end; and also into another almost hagiographical pattern that embraces all knights, and of which, Christ-like, he fulfills the promise and the potential. But as we are told only that part of Christ's life spent on the cross at the beginning of the *Estoire,* so we see only that part of the grail world which impinges on Arthur and the Round Table; similarly, the *Queste* and the *Estoire* reveal only that part of the aftermath of Eden that points to Christ and Galaad. The three great losses—Eden, Christ, the grail—provide another vast design. The simple poetic idea of beginning, middle, and end thus finally rests in God Himself, "li coumenchemens et la fins de toutes coses" (*Estoire* II, 264/I.66.28–29) [the beginning and the end of all things]. The technique underscores great truths in their archetypal simplicity and material multiplicity, functioning like the poetic archetype in Chartrain images of Creation, nature, and artistry. Indeed, the *Estoire* claims that the whole

Arthurian cycle derives from a little book given to the author by Christ during an ecstatic vision. A hierarchy patterned on biblical typology links complex narrative strands that interlace, inbricate, or otherwise join beginnings, middles, and ends on various levels in a vast, meaningful plan of salvation.

Other Arthurian romances trace labyrinthine narratives on the principle of greater and lesser wholes interlaced.[58] With the conception of the whole in mind the author of *Escanor* could exclaim:

> Et qui bel conmence et define,
> L'uevre en est plus bele et plus fine
> Et de plus grant noblece asez.
> $(1-3)^{59}$

[If one begins and ends well, the work is more beautiful, exquisite, and much more noble.]

A particularly difficult task, given the fact that the *Escanor*'s *materia remota* was allegedly incomplete and that additions could not easily fill the gaps (25896–909).

The organization and gradation of narrative strands and parts in the *Escanor* escaped its editor: "Au premier aspect," he wrote, "il est aisé de voir que le défaut capital de cette œuvre, qui malgré sa longueur n'est cependant pas ennuyeuse, est l'absence d'un but final vers lequel se dirige toute l'action et qui concentre l'intérêt sur un seul point, au lieu de le disperser sur des épisodes qui ne se relient pas suffisamment entre eux."[60] His conception of narrative threads held together by a common denouement neglects the fact that, here, the denouement is multistranded as a result of *glissements* like those Zink has identified in *Guillaume de Dole*.[61] Romances often begin at court with what amounts to a "denouement," with narrative threads unwinding into the adventurous forests like branches from a trunk.

The romancers frequently describe their work as a whole held together by appropriate links to a common source, but without implying that a common unilateral conclusion, or "nouement," occurs. The *Rigomer* expresses the principle figuratively, but clearly.

> Or vos en ai grantment conté
> Et ne pourquant ai oblïé
> Mout del millor et del plus bel,
> Mais par celui qui fist Abel,
> Or ai talent que me ravoie
> A ço que oblïé avoie;
> Car sans cestui oublïement
> Ne poons traire a finement
> De chou que avons commencié.

> Dont avon trop mal commencié;
> Car qui de l'abre velt parler,
> Ne li convient pas oblïer
> Qu'il ne parot de la racine.
> (10583–95)

[Now I have told you a great deal; and yet, I have neglected the best and most beautiful part. But in the name of Him who made Abel, I wish now to return to what I neglected. For without that part which I neglected to tell we cannot conclude what we have begun. Thus we have made a bad beginning. For in speaking of the tree one must not forget to talk of the root].

The structural image of the tree had already been used in the Vulgate cycle in the same sense.[62]

In composition founded on jointing and interlace, links assume great importance. They are frequently identified by the narrator, even in the briefest narratives: "De la dame vus voil mustrer / Que Guigemar pot tant amer" (*Lais* Gui 655–56) [I want to tell you something of the lady whom Guigemar loved so much]; "De li lairomes aïtant, / De Melïon dirons avant" (*Melion* 203–4) [we'll leave him now and speak henceforth about Meliun]; "Or me covient aillors entendre / Et dou bon rei Artu parler" (*Mantel* 46–47) [now I must turn to another subject and tell about good King Arthur]. This is also the case in so-called realist romance or *roman rose*.

> Or s'en vet, or la consaut Diex!
> Si fera il, gel sai de voir.
> Or referoit mout bon savoir
> Comment ses freres se contint.
> (*Dole* 4108–11)[63]

[Now she leaves—God help her! And He will, I know for sure. Now it would be well to know how her brother was faring.]

> Del castellain chi vous lairai
> Et de la dame vous dirai,
> Qui est de joie raemplie
> Plus c'onques ne fu en sa vie.
> (*Couci* 3711–14)

[Here I'll leave off telling about the castellan and take up the lady's story, the lady who had more joy than ever in her life.]

Finally, we find jointing in romanced epic: "Or lairai des barons que en mer sunt entré, / Si dirai de Florence, que tant ot grant biauté" (*Florence* 3345–46)

[Now I'll leave the barons who have gone to sea; I'll tell of Florence who was so very beautiful].

Another device to link narrative parts is the cross-reference: "Che fu li chevaliers qui a la roine parla a Quincparcorentin et a la dame de Roestoc ensamble le jor que Hector mut en la queste de mon seignor Gauvain. Si li encarcha tout ensi com li contes devisa la ou il parla a la roine" (*Lancelot* lxa. 34)[64] [he was the knight who spoke both to the queen and the lady of Roestoc at Quincparcorentin, the day Hector set out in quest of my lord Gauvain. And he entrusted him with everything, as the tale related where it spoke about the queen]. Such announcements, explicit foreshadowings, prefigurations, and predictions are not peculiar to Arthurian and grail romances. In the *Alexandre* they prepare the time, place, and circumstances of Alexander's death and the conclusion of the romance. Flashback serves the same purpose: "Il sist el cheval noir que li tramist la fee / Por cui amor passa un bras de mer salee" (*Alex* APar III. 1840–41) [he sat on the black horse sent him by the fay, for whose love he crossed a branch of salt water]. The announcement may be covert as well, but nonetheless effective, as Kurt Lewent showed for *Flamenca*. In all this cross-movement, the apposite and coherent linking of narrative parts is a matter of *iunctura*.[65]

The prominence of the adventure as a literary unit (especially the *aventure merveilleuse*) permitted both the linking of disparate material (adventures encountered in a quest, for example) and the superficially incomplete narrative (which relies on the *faille*).[66] A marvel's irrationality or inscrutability might justify incompleteness. So might the fact that the privileged moment of adventure stands out in the ordinary chronological sequence of events. Many of the major episodes in romance evince incompleteness or inscrutability: the quest for the Golden Fleece in the *Troie*, the love of Lancelot and Guenevere in the *Charrette*, the grail history in the Vulgate cycle.[67] The digressive character of such material suggests that its incorporation into narrative relies on formal and thematic criteria. Authors amplify *matiere* by using figural and tropical devices.

Ornament as a Principle of Arrangement and Jointing

Neither the principle of beginning, middle, and end nor that of interlace and juxtaposition is sufficient to comprehend all kinds of narrative order in romance.[68] We noted above the use of figural and tropical order in chronological and spatial sequences. Artificial order allowed for diverse arrangements of parts such as, for example, interlace. The parts may be independent of one another in chronology and geography, as the quests of Perceval and Gauvain in Chrétien's *Conte du graal* illustrate. Moreover, the elucidation of matter often required topical arrangement to make the narrative show forth the preconceived patterns or models that express its truth. At this level of composition the amalgamation of *matiere* and *san* in *conjointure* takes place. What terms referred to and defined *ordre* in the twelfth and thirteenth centuries?

The use of interlace has been attributed to emphasis in the arts of poetry and prose on digression and artificial order.[69] But they explicitly distinguish digression as amplification from natural and artificial order;[70] artificial order in narrative is not used for the plot of the Vulgate cycle, which obviously uses interlace freely. Interlace is not only digression, but also parallelism and bifurcation.

The application of topical and figurative language to the expression of truth identifies the poetic activity as artful deflection from direct discourse[71] in order to make *matiere* more elegant, to clothe its truth in a pleasing exterior, or to express the truth more appositely. This means that, from the sentence to the complete work, order in *matiere* is poetic to the extent that tropical and figural deflections occur.

Since artificial order originally described syntax, it became closely related to tropical and figural language.[72] When amplification and abbreviation extended tropes and figures to larger segments of discourse, and even the entire work (as in allegory or extended metaphor), the tropes and figures became a mine of formal suggestions for arrangement. Narrative instances of figural and tropical arrangement are:

—*frequentatio* as accumulation, which is an especially prominent kind of *interpretatio* because of its relation to Chartrain notions of emanation;[73]
—motif bifurcation or multiplication as *adiunctio;*
—motif, topical, analogical, and other material or thematic variations as *interpretatio,* or restatement;
—different kinds of repetitions, climactic effects, conversions and determinations of a morphological nature;[74]
—conjunctive and disjunctive patterns like parataxis, polysyndeton, chiasmus, division of material into episodic or subepisodic units, or, on the other hand, compression of disparate material into single, whole units;
—isocolon as arithmetic composition, as in the post-Vulgate tripartite division, or in even more subtle and complex arrangements;[75]
—contrasts analogous to antithesis, oxymoron, litotes, irony;[76]
—expression of a part for an inexpressible whole, as in synecdochic, metonymic, or allegorical amplifications like the *Roman de la rose* and the grail romances, as well as episodic segments of romances using amplified forms of comparison like *imago, enargia,* and *chria.*[77]

By contrast emphasis, fusion, allusion, and other devices for abbreviation could also color the work's manner and disposition.[78]

This is not to imply the imposition of neat formal patterns onto straightforward narrative. We may see how effective such artificiality would be by examining the catalogues of tropes and figures with which some have pretended, to their own disappointment, to get at the significance of rhetorical devices in romance. Of course, representative kinds of amplification and abbreviation do recur in romance.[79] But the catalogues of tropes and figures that demonstrate this are of dubious critical value. Even if they identify more or less accurately the devices used, they do not, of and by themselves, facilitate our appreciation of them in context. This is because the close relation between topical intention and a specific device used for amplification or abbreviation is lost when the latter is divorced from its narrative place and purpose. In effect, classification takes apart what the author has put together; it makes us read the ornamentation as merely typical of a figure or trope rather than as apt expression of content.

For example, if the Wheel of Fortune is introduced into narrative and described, it has been customary merely to identify it as a commonplace,[80] or locate it in broad thematic or historical categories of different kinds of fortune.[81] But this moves it away from the work it appears in, making us overlook the fact that a commonplace is construed as inherent in *matiere* and thus peculiar to and fittingly drawn from it. The great Wheel of Fortune in Arthur's dream in the *Mort Artu* is a readily comprehensible image of the *mesaventure* of the king's downfall from the throne as a fall from the Wheel itself (*Mort* §§176.57–177.2).[82] The description of the Wheel, conjoined to Gauvain's appeal to Arthur in a dream to desist from war (*Mort* §176.8–38), is an amplification as pertinent to the *matiere* as Hector's appearance to Aeneas in Vergil. They are parts in an array of commonplace images and devices in an appropriate narrative context.

The skilled writer does what C. O. Brink says Horace did with the *Ad Pisones:* "From the writers of the textbooks he takes what they have to teach about the technicalities of *delectus verborum* and *compositio* and he applies the 'rules' to his own purpose."[83] *Amo, amas, amat* as paradigm for the present tense of *amare* may be uninspiring when conjugated or practiced in the grammar class; but knowledge of the paradigm is essential to its apposite use in appropriate discourse. The same is true for rhetorical paradigms, including the devices for ornamentation. Practice makes them so much a part of instinct that the writer does not have to think step-by-step through them, as we do. The devices are tools or implements the skilled, talented artisan uses so often that they become almost natural.

> La tâche de l'écrivain . . . consiste à appliquer les règles d'un métier transmis de maître à apprenti, comme un art vénérable que l'on ne saurait exercer légitimement en dehors des rites enseignés. A tout fait d'expression préexiste un système. Celui-ci peut être la rhétorique, dont le caractère propre est d'être à la fois doctrinaire, explicite et fragmentaire.

But Paul Zumthor appends this important clarification: "en ce que les relations entre éléments n'y sont pas prédéterminées et que l'utilisateur dispose d'une grande liberté d'agencement."[84] The freedom of the master permits the invention of the masterpiece using the art that he or she has acquired by study and exercise. Tropes and figures suggest that the authors conceived, in principle, the manner of composition and form of the sentence, largely by the application of those devices learned in the abstract, studied in the authors, and used in student compositions for surface texture *(series)* and combination *(iunctura)*. [85] Geoffrey of Vinsauf makes the application explicit when he relates ornamentation to dilation.

> Ecce habemus exemplo praedicto [i.e., in the instruction on amplification] qualiter ex brevitate prolixitas generetur. Ibidem etiam videre possumus quod clausula rudis quibusdam ornatibus informetur et quod sententia facilis verborum difficultatibus aggravatur. . . . Si quis igitur habuerit prae manibus materiam brevem, non desperet eam extendere. Poterit enim ex modis praedictis [= devices for amplification] et postdicendis [= tropes and figures] quantum placuerit eam dilatare. (*Documentum* II. 2.70)[86]

> [Here we have in the aforementioned example instruction on generating length from brevity. We may also observe there that a plain sentence is informed by certain ornaments and that a simple sentence may be made weighty by difficult ornamentation. . . . If one has a brief matter, don't despair of lengthening it. One may dilate as much as one wishes by drawing on the aforementioned devices and those that follow.]

One amplifies, therefore, by using the tropes and figures of thought and diction. These words stress anew Horace's emphasis on ornate *series* and *iunctura,* both adapted to *sententia,* that is, the meaning the author elicits from a *materia* and expresses by the means chosen for amplification or abbreviation.

Arrangement of the *inventa* in romance could thus be understood as tropical and figural deflection from natural order in narrative. For example, Geoffrey of Vinsauf's instruction on circumlocution as amplification recalls the interlace structure of adventures and quests in the prose romances,[87] as in Dante's allusion to the *Arturi regis ambages pulcerrime* [most beautiful ambages of King Arthur], which links Geoffrey's words and prose romance structure. The constant medieval preoccupation with linking and texture, as juxtaposition of homogeneous and heterogeneous parts, was read into Horace's *tantum series iuncturaque pollet*.[88] The circuitous paths of Arthurian ambages interweave fine patches of various colors and parts. The polysyndetic character — specifically, the liberal use of conjunctions — recalls the use if *incidences* in the thirteenth-century epic *recueils*. The "procédé des *incidences* consiste à insérer au milieu d'une chanson [de geste], un autre poème racontant des faits supposés contemporains de ceux qu'elle apporte."[89] Deliberate open-ending *(failles)* could permit, implicitly, the never-ending tale.[90] The technique appears in cyclic romance in the terminology for narrative divisions and junctures.

> Ensi est li dus remés en prison el Val sans Retor o les .III. compaignons qui molt le confortoient a lor pooirs. Mes ore laisse li contes a parler d'eus tous et retorne a parler de Lancelot.
>
> Ensi comme vous avés oï fu Lancelos honorés a Escalon dont les tenebres estoient ostees par sa proece. (*Lancelot* xxiii *.13–14–xxiv* .1)

> [Thus did the duke remain imprisoned in the Valley of No Return with his three companions, who consoled him as well as they could. But now the tale stops speaking about all of them and returns to the story of Lancelot. Just as you have heard, Lancelot was honored at Escalon, where, by his prowess, he had dispersed the shadows.]

The prose *Sept sages de Rome* also uses the technique liberally.[91] Artful syntax illustrates structural principles like those used in the prose cycles. Polysyndeton as a figure of speech for the interconnection of words, phrases, and sentences may also describe the linking of narrative parts admired by Dante.

The opposite of polysyndeton is asyndeton — the deliberate omission of connectives, or parataxis.[92] But asyndeton may also suggest artificial groupings of parts of speech, including *adiunctio* and *disiunctio*. *Disiunctio* describes parallel but, respectively, synonymous or asynonymous statements: "The knights are rich, the ladies wealthy" or "The lords feast, the peasants starve." By *adiunctio* a number of phrases may be connected by one word. Transposed to narrative, *adiunctio* describes the interlaced pattern in the first part of Chrétien's *Erec*. Arthur achieves the hunt for the white stag and Erec achieves the sparrowhawk adventure. Chrétien links them by their conclusion, the object of each episode, that is, the most beautiful woman — Enide herself. Chrétien underscores the close parallel between narrative and syntactic structuring by a metaphorical *adiunctio* describing the consummation of the marriage between Erec and Enide at the conclusion to part I of

the romance. It is a syntactic conjunction of the principal images that serve
as *matiere* for the two adjoined *vers*.

> Cers chaciez qui de soif alainne
> Ne desirre tant la fontainne,
> N'espreviers ne vient a reclain
> Si volantiers quant il a fain,
> Que plus volantiers n'i venissent,
> Einçois que il s'antre tenissent
> (*Erec* 2027–32)

[A stag pursued by hunters and panting with thirst doesn't desire the fountain, nor does the famished sparrowhawk respond to the call more willingly than they came to their embrace.]

The separate but parallel metaphors come together, adjoined by the literal
conjugal union of Erec and Enide.[93] The description fits the structure of the
passage cited as well as the entire first part of Chrétien's poem: the formal
elaboration of the narrative is a figural amplification with topical stylization
analogous to the metaphorical restatement, in one sentence, of the consummation. One could hardly find a better romance example of the movement
from *thema* through amplificatory *informatio* to *omne materiae spatium* and
back again.

A similar procedure is used for the adventures in Guillaume de Lorris' part
of the *Roman de la rose*,[94] except that in this romance the metaphor extends
throughout the narrative. The juxtaposition of the Lover and Love in the
dream produces, first, Love's description of the Lover's adventures and con-
solations, then, second, the dream vision that rehearses the adventures in
an exemplary sequence pointing to the anticipated winning of the Rose by
Love. In *Erec* two images come together as two analogous narratives interlace; in the *Rose* a literal love story coalesces with a metaphorical story, each
centering on the image of Rose.

> C'est cele qui tant a de pris
> E tant est dine d'estre amee
> Qu'el doit estre Rose clamee.
> (*Rose* 42–44)

[She who is so esteemed and so worthy of being loved that she should be
called Rose.]

In fact, a trinity of roses — the "real life" lady, the dream lady, the flower —
restates in different modes the same object, the object of Guillaume's triune
quest as author, dreamer, and lover.

Figural arrangements may also produce contrastive or independent developments from a common beginning, which is called narrative *disiunctio*. In the
Lancelot Proper, for example, two shields are brought to Arthur's court, each
precipitating a distinct narrative sequence.[95] The first shield is Gauvain's,
and it begins Hector's quest for him (*Lancelot* lxa. 3–6); the second is the
split shield that marks the consummation of Lancelot and Guenevere's love
(adiunctio) (*Lancelot* lviiia. 13–16).[96] The second shield functions in a manner analogous to the spear stub Lancelot withdraws from a wounded knight
when he comes to Arthur's court[97] to be knighted and falls in love with Guenevere. It is also linked to Lancelot's later imprisonment by the Lady of Malehot, which precedes Galehot's effort to win Guenevere for Lancelot. Galehot's
sickness and death follow the closing of the split shield, as does the death
of the Lady of Malehot. Broken lances and shields run through this vast,
frequently discontinuous narrative, serving to bind it together in an immense
coniunctio. This kind of interlacing between narrative parts illustrates *hyper-
baton,* or the great separation of sequential material by interweaving parts
of other sequences.

Other parallel sequences reach across narrative space in formal patterns
underscoring meaningful aspects of the work's *san*.[98] Two examples: (1)
Lancelot breaks out of Morgain's prison when a rose he sees in the garden
reminds him of Guenevere, and he does so by pulling the bars apart; in the
Charrette episode he does the same to enter Guenevere's chamber. (2) Blood
as a means to heal is used for Agravain in the *Lancelot* Proper, as well as
for the leprous lady and the Maimed King in the *Queste*. Each episode adds
a weapon to the conclusion: Escalibor, the Espee as estranges renges, the
bleeding lance. Here the terms *complexio,* or parallel parts in separate sequences, and *distributio,* or scattered rehearsal of the same pattern, describe
the structure of these episodes. J. H. M. Taylor has identified these properties in late medieval romance as stratification, systemization, and patterning.[99]

In the deliberate, artificial disposition of their material, the prose romancers
adapt principles of composition which earlier writers like Chrétien, Gautier
d'Arras, and Robert de Boron used, extending tropical and figural sentence
structures to larger narrative parts. The principle still obtains, even if later
generations of romancers were no longer aware of its origins, but merely
followed the example of the twelfth-century romances they imitated and
adapted.

Horace proclaimed, and medieval schools taught, that "Dixeris egregie no-
tum si callida verbum / reddiderit iunctura novum" (*Ad Pisones* 47–48) [you
will express yourself best if an ingenious jointing renders a common word
new]. His injunction follows directly on the discussion of narrative *ordo*.

> Ordinis haec virtus erit et venus . . .
> ut iam nunc dicat iam nunc debentia dici,
> pleraque differat et praesens in tempus omittat;
> hoc amet, hoc spernat promissi carminis auctor.
> *in verbis etiam* . . . .
>
> (*Ad Pisones* 42–46; emphasis mine)

[This is the force and beauty of order . . . that it expresses what must be said in the right time and place, while setting aside other matters, omitting them for the present; this is what the author of the commissioned poem should cling to, that is what he or she should reject. In syntax as well . . . .]

The lines illustrated for the Middle Ages a principle of *ordo* founded on the close correlation between syntactic and narrative arrangement in *conjointure.*

Structuring of this kind may well support contrastive adaptation of the same *matiere,* as in Chrétien's and Hartmann's different versions of Erec's quest. Hartmann's *surplus de san* effected changes and deletions based on a figural principle different from Chrétien's. Both poets have much the same episodic sequence in the quest, except that Hartmann reduces the two encounters with robber knights *(conduplicatio)* to one episode while also suppressing the night camp in the woods. But there is another more fundamental difference between the two, which goes to the very heart of their readings of the quest, a difference made apparent in their choices for ornamental amplification. In a digression not found in Chrétien, Hartmann establishes at the outset that Erec is guilty of *verligen (recreantise)* (*Erec* H 2924–98, especially 2966–73). Each succeeding episode becomes an explicit illustration of Erec's *verligen,* either by his misconduct in the marriage bed or by his petty, testy treatment of Enît during the quest; the whole climaxes when Erec admits his wrong and asks Enît's forgiveness. "Nû vergap si imz an der stat, / Wan er sis vriuntlîchen bat" (*Erec* H 6802–3) [now she forgave him on the spot, since he asked her to do so lovingly.] Each adventure in the quest is therefore part of an exemplary *interpretatio,* or diversified restatement of the same idea. In contrast, Chrétien begins with an antithetical coupling: Erec is guilty of *recreantise* (*Erec* 2492–2504); but then, abruptly, Enide blames herself for uttering her *parole* (*Erec* 2585–2606). The latter development is not found in Hartmann. The uncertainty this antithesis produces regarding Erec's guilt makes the quest into something more than the reiterated confirmation of an original auctorial pronouncement. The narrative moves in stages. First, there is a gradual shift of Enide's *parole* from blame to love, as, second, Erec evolves from silence to pardon and from blame to love, in carefully graded stages.[100] The parallel *gradatio* climaxes in the pardon scene.

Hartmann's characters remain sharp and mostly unaltered throughout the quest; Erec's pique betrays his sense of guilt as much as does his request for pardon at the end, while Enît's fidelity and humility triumph. In principle, Erec's request for pardon exemplifies and confirms Hartmann's condemnation of *verligen* at the outset of the marital crisis. Erec's promise to improve leads to victory in the *Joie de la cort* episode. The reconciliation completes the *interpretatio* set forth in the discrete episodic parts of the quest in the German poem. But Chrétien is more subtle and "artificial." The antithesis that sets the problem at the beginning of the quest is gradually overcome by mutual understanding. The reconciliation occurs when the narrative *gradatio*, like the closing shield in the Prose *Lancelot*, brings husband and wife together again as before. In Hartmann, the *interpretatio* is formally repetitive, accumulative, synonymous. In Chrétien the thematic lines are more fluid, the development evinces more texture as parts gradually blend into other parts and, finally, into a whole which expresses the equality of spouses who have renewed their love. A different kind of amplification in each romance controls the elaboration of narrative parts in both discrete episodes and total plot drawn from a common *conte d'avanture.*

To take another example, in Chrétien's *Charrette,* as in *Erec,* Chrétien uses *gradatio* to elaborate his plot: Lancelot's gradual emergence in the quest is echoed in the belated revelation of his name after the progressive revelation of his qualities.[101] The *Lancelot* Proper uses this device to prefigure or prophesy darkly the grail mysteries prior to the *Queste,* as, for example, in the circumstances of Lancelot's becoming a knight, the interpretation of a dream of Arthur's by Helie de Toulouse, and the scattered adventures prefiguring Galaad and the visits to Corbenic in the *Agravain.*[102] In the Prose *Charrette* itself, the desire to fill in what seemed to be lacunae in Chrétien is obvious. But the author is ornamental in doing so. The doubling of tombs in the cemetery episode distinguishes that of Lancelot's grandfather, Galaad le fort (which Lancelot opens, as in Chrétien), from that of Symeon (which is reserved for Lancelot's son Galaad). The *conduplicatio* may be an imitation of the same device in Chrétien's romance: two combats with Meleagant, two visits to Guenevere, two searches for Gauvain. Moreover, Chrétien uses *occupatio* to pass over Gauvain's adventures with only brief accounts of their beginning and end. A number of manuscripts of the Vulgate describe Gauvain's quest in detail,[103] thus restructuring this brief account as *disiunctio:* the two quests are formally parallel and of common beginning, but they produce contrasting results.

Topical Order and Narrative Configuration

Ordo produces a *figura,* the mirror the author uses to reflect the viewer, in either an enhancing or a condemnatory manner. That vision is communicated by means of features that express auctorial conception in Geoffrey of Vinsauf's sense of the archetypal status of the work. That status is made "visible" *(sensilis)* by deployment of topical amplifications and abbreviations. They provide the figural or topical configuration of *materia* as topical order.

Topical order is the result of both choice and arrangement of descriptions of persons and things. "Narration at its most characteristic is a type of description."[104] Description, whether as a static totality or a sequential progression, determines "identity," which "in romance is at once a *given,* a *process,* and a *goal*":[105] the static representation of topical totality, progressive elaboration in narrative of topical arguments, and the exemplary illustration of that totality in discrete parts. These features of topical invention imply an order, as well as the stages or *gradus* that make up that order. The *gradus amoris* is the most familiar scheme, although others are found in romance; in fact, there are potentially as many as there are "givens," "processes," and "goals" to be depicted. Variety in the stages in different examples derives from context and, in particular, from the circumstances that express the context— whether, for example, love is represented as flirtation, friendship, or conjugal affection.[106] There are thus both static or constant and dynamic or variable elements in a given *gradus.*

We may illustrate and clarify these three elements of *gradus* by Alixandre's cup in *Cligés,* the "composition" of which is analogous to romance composition.[107] The cup Arthur gives Alixandre has three notable features: fine material, excellent workmanship, and precious stones. The precious stones are fit into the wrought gold, crowning it with ornamental beauty. Artificially added, they are amplifications materially different from the *matiere* in which they are placed. They are a *surplus.* Further, although the *matiere* itself is valuable, its "raw" value is enhanced by shaping so as to receive that which is most valuable, yet different—the precious stones. The *surplus de san* suggested by the ornamental stones requires a well-shaped object to arrange and display them.[108] Similarly, the attractive *matiere* of romance requires a shape suitable for topical ornamentation; it gives order and quality to the amplificatory additions. Like the goldsmith who shaped the gold and added the precious stones to the cup, Chrétien sought ornamental amplifications that would be pleasing and meaningful in the *conjointure* of his *matiere.*

Static Description in Narrative Economy

Topical invention magnifies an object while focusing on its prominent features. Similarly, description, by its emphasis on the paramount quality of a person or thing, is the most obvious technique for topical amplification, although all devices are common. As we have seen, topical amplification is what Matthew of Vendôme means by *descriptio*, and we should use the word in that sense for romance. Static topical developments from narrative *matiere*, like the stones in the *Cligés* cup, were construed by the romancers not as impositions but rather as enhancement of *ceo k'i ert:* "Funzione ornamentale, espressione dell'ingegno umano e trasmissione di un sapere, spesso, convergono in queste descrizioni"[109] [ornamental function, expression of human genius, and transmission of knowledge often converge in these descriptions]. As such, they contribute to the romance's *conjointure* both by their location and by their inherent significance apart from and greater than it; they stand out as discrete entities, even to the extent of being transferable,[110] as the following lines on a maiden's beauty illustrate.

> Et se je onques fis devise
> En biauté que Diex eüst mise
> En cors de feme ne en face,
> Or me replaist que une en face,
> Que ja n'en mentirai de mot.
> (*Perceval* 1805–9)

[And if I ever described the beauty which God bestowed on the person
and face of a woman, it pleases me now to do so again for I'll not include
a single mendacious word.]

Yet Blancheflor's unique but conventional excellence was lifted by the anonymous author of *Cristal et Clarie.*

> Mais se je onques fis devise
> En beauté, que Deus eüst mise
> En cors de feme ne en face,
> Or me replaist que une an face,
> Que ja de mot n'en mentirai.
> (*Cristal* 2403–7)[111]

[But if I ever described the beauty which God bestowed on the person and
face of a woman, it pleases me now to do so again for I'll not include a
single mendacious word.]

Like the precious stones in Alixandre's cup in *Cligés*, the *Cristal* borrowing
is a commonplace fitted into a new *matiere*, and into a narrative as different

from Blancheflor's as the latter's is from those of her descriptive sisters elsewhere in Chrétien's romances, of whom she is nonetheless a mirror image.

There is a distinction between description and *matiere* in the initial conception of the work. "Telx fu mesire Gauvain et si frere com je vos ai dit: si m'en tairai atant et revendrai a ma matere" (*Lancelot* lxix.7)[112] [such were my lord Gauvain and his brothers as I have told you. And I shall leave it at that and return to my *matiere*]. Topical amplifications like these are seen as departing from direct discourse to give the personage a descriptive type and topical classification. Afterward there is a return to the narrative *matiere,* fashioned to hold the amplifications as the gold in Alixandre's cup was shaped to receive precious stones.

The commonplace elucidates and makes coherent originally obscure *matiere.* The technique taught in composition classes allowed for original invention of *matiere,* its elucidation by deliberate amplification within implicit contexts.[113] Hilka found the use of description in Aimon de Varennes' *Florimont* more sparing than in the other *romans d'antiquité.*[114] But classification by frequency or length is alien to the professed concerns of romancers. A short description may well be effective amplification, as Chrétien states.[115] Even abbreviation emphasizes, and is therefore functional embellishment.[116]

The audience is important here. Medieval audiences clearly enjoyed descriptions that met and satisfied their predilections; thus, the Prose *Lancelot* introduces an extensive description of the young Lancelot for those who take pleasure in descriptions of beautiful children: "ne sa fachons ne fait pas a oublier en conte, mais a retraire oiant toute gent qui de grant biauté d'enfant voldront oïr parler" (*Lancelot* ixa.3) [his features should not be left out of a story, but depicted for those who like to hear told the beauty of young people]. Similarly, Thomas d'Angleterre says he had to invent topical amplifications that would meet his audience's expectations.[117] Otherwise, its response might be like that of a maiden listening to a poem in Froissart's *Meliador:* "Ceste parole n'est pas mienne, / Car onques n'amai par tel art" (20353–54)[118] [those are not my words, for my art of love was never such]. Chrétien's own critical response to the Tristan legend demonstrates the possibility of sweeping rejections.[119] On the other hand, his justification of the descriptions of Cligés and Fenice suggests that audiences did not always take to description. In such cases art came into conflict with public taste. "Or ne vous soit d'escouter grief / Se je de li un poi paroil" (*Jehan* 250–51) [may it not displease you if I say a little about her]. "Un poi" is over a hundred lines (252–374)! Nevertheless, amplification makes the *matiere* comprehensible, expresses, and even overstates,[120] its truth, as the author perceived it—it is the "raison por quoi" (*Lancelot* xxa.1) [reason why]. *Raison* in its narrative, cognitive, and discursive connotations unites romance *matiere* and *san* by amplifications.[121]

To take another witness, in *Fergus* the narrator comments on the possibility, efficacy, and appropriateness of descriptive passages before introducing the same Blancheflor description recycled in *Cristal et Clarie*.

> Et se onques nus faire pot
> Devise de nule pucele
> Qui tant fust avenans et biele,
> Or i vel mon sens apuier
> Un petitet sans anuier.
> Ne faç pas ensi com cil font
> Qui vont mentant par tot le mont;
> Si anuie, ço saciés bien,
> Ja de li ne mentirai rien,
> Ains en dirai la verité
> Ensi com il m'est aconté.
>   (*Fergus* 1522–32)

[And if anyone ever succeeded in describing a maiden who was so fair and beautiful, now do I wish briefly to apply my wits to that task, without boring you. I don't do as those who lie so much everywhere; at the risk of boring, rest assured that I shall utter no lies about her, but rather tell the truth just as it is told to me.]

The only truth in such description is, of course, topical truth. The veracity of topical amplifications derives from their credibility and suitability. Kurt Lewent's commentary on the art of description in *Flamenca* suggests a criterion for amplification consonant with medieval notions of topical efficacy: descriptions do not exist for their own sake, but have significance for the plot in which they are located.[122] They do not stand alone, but rather contribute, together with the *materia remota,* to the work's *materia propinqua,* like the stones in Alixandre's cup.

Topical description is obvious when the author dwells upon and systematically elaborates a point. Expressions like *afiert a, ajouter a, convient a, enter, ajoindre, revenir a, gloser* are common introductions to such developments.[123] In the *Escanor,* a digression on the Wheel of Fortune is terminated in order to press on to the description of a tournament.

> Mais de tel chose ne covient
> En ma matere pluz parler,
> Car d'aillors m'ai mult a meller
> D'autres choses que je dirai,
> Car du tornoi vouz conterai
> Qui devant Bauborc conmenca.
>   (*Escanor* 4892–97)[124]

[But it doesn't behoove me to dwell any longer on that subject in my *matiere*, for I have a lot of other things to take up; for I am going to relate the tournament that began before Bauborc.]

Elsewhere in *Escanor* a detailed description, over six hundred lines long, represents the bed, bedroom, and wife of Branz des Illes (*Escanor* 15578–16189). The narrator is convinced that the description is incomplete when he finally comes to locate bed and bedroom in the narrative:

> bien deviser les ouvraingnes
> Ne sarroie en .II. anz entiers.
> Et pour ce qu'il ne m'est mestiers
> De metre pluz m'entente ci,
> Vouz dirai ge le conte ainssi
> Conme Brianz fist atorner
> L'ostel pour le roi sejorner,
> Pour ce c'honnerer le voloit,
> Quar il dist que bien le valoit.
> (*Escanor* 16186–94)

[I could not describe all its special features in two full years. And since I must apply myself to what follows, I'll tell you how Brianz prepared the hostel to receive the king, since he wished to honor him as being most worthy of honor.]

The six hundred lines are incomplete, but sufficient.[125] The transition is easy and orderly. In *Escanor*, the reception of a king justifies a description worthy of such a host, hence the amplification.

Fortunately, Jean de Meun helps us understand the truncated description in *Escanor* and elsewhere when he cuts short another one of different kinds of mirrors and lenses because "Bon fait prolixité foïr" (*Rose* 18298 / 18268) [it is well to eschew prolixity]. His purpose is to write not a general treatise on vision or its defects, but on the defective vision of a lover. "Prolixity" is excess description. The examples provided in his text are sufficient for the average reader (18247–86 / 18217–56), and Nature, who is speaking here, can return to her subject.

Abbreviation, or avoidance of amplification, is justified by the fact that a given subject is not appropriate for topical development.

> Bien vos deïsse ou om la prent
> E ses vertuz dont ele a cent,
> Mais por l'interposicion
> Avient iço, que le laisson.
> (*Troie* 16677–80)

[I would tell you where she is taken, as well as detail her hundred virtues,
but it happens that we leave it out in order to avoid the digression outside
our subject.]

The description would "interpose" and thus be out of place. The author of
the *Atre périlleux* refuses to describe a castle, since there are more important
matters to deal with.

> Mais j'ai aillors m'entente mise
> Que a dire vous la devise
> Si com cele le devisa.
> (*Atre* 3995–97)

[But I have turned my attention away from relating to you her description
of it.]

Once more, audience intent is a factor alongside topical significance.

> Anuis seroit, se je voloie
> Tout deviser de cief en cief
> Seul de l'elme qu'il ot el cief
> Et del cercle et de la visiere.
> (*Atre* 3620–23)

[It would be tedious if I were to describe thoroughly only as much as the
helmet on his head or its circle and visor.]

His audience is already aware of how extraordinary the armor is. Hence,
the essential will suffice, as in this passage.

> Autre devise n'en voel faire
> Fors tant que sa biautés esclaire
> Trestous les lieus ou ele vient.
> (*Jehan* 4723–25)

[I don't want to describe any more, beyond asserting that her beauty illuminates every place she goes.]

After the expression of the abstract quality subsuming the person or action —
"Lour mes ne vous vol deviser / Fors tant qu'il orent biau disner" (*Jehan*
4759–60) [I don't wish to describe their meal any more than to say that it
was a fine dinner] — the romancers frequently fall back on the inexpressibility topic: "Nuls ne porroit compter ne dire la joie qui fu faite le jour: si m'en
tairai atant, sans plus parler" (*Laurin* ll. 6227–28) [no one could relate or

express the joy made that day. And I'll stop at that and say no more]. Certain amplifications would also have been disagreeable, despite obvious oratorical possibilities.

> Son frere prist a plaindre et a fort regreter,
> A gemir, a detordre, a braire, et a crïer,
> A maudire ses bras qui ont volu jouster.
> Moult se plaint longuement, mes plus n'en voel parler.
> *(Parfait* 2410–13)[126]

[He began to lament for his brother, to grieve, to moan, twist, wail, and cry out, to curse his arms that insisted on jousting. He laments for a very long time, but I don't wish to say any more about that.]

Adenet le Roi, who was not at all shy of lengthy description,[127] offers a definitive explanation for topical abbreviation as diminution.

> Bon fait legierement passer
> Ce que on ne puet amender
> Et chose qui n'est profitable
> Ne a deviser agreable.
> Se plus i ot, plus n'en dirai,
> Car d'autre chose a parler ai.
> *(Cleomadés* 16431–36)[128]

[It is well to pass over quickly what isn't amenable, profitable, or agreeable. What more there is I'll not say for I have other matters to talk about.]

Since topical amplification, like material additions, is meant to make evident *ceo k'i ert,* there must be a purpose behind lengthy descriptions.

> E nous dirai l'aresament,
> Los manjarz nil servizi gent
> Que sos ostes li fes la nueg,
> Que tornariaus a enueg.
> *(Jaufre* 6799–6802)

[And I'll not tell you how well they were received, nor the food and service his host offered him that night, because it would become tedious to you.]

Description serves to please as ornament. But when it is without substance or otherwise inappropriate, it becomes merely dilatory. Indeed, the relative ease with which such amplifications may be detached and classified under broad formal or thematic heads demonstrates their original distinctness from the source *matiere* as such and their static character. They dwell—in both senses of the word—on the *matiere*.[129]

Description is construed not only as addition but also as formal reference to context. Amplification is the author's principal contribution to his or her *matiere*. Through it the *surplus de san* not immediately apprehensible in the sources is drawn from the *matiere* as auctorial conception of source. But since the manner of statement is an essential part of the statement itself, the art of placing and developing the description comes to the fore. Here frequent allusions to auctorial *penser, avis, antancion, semblant* find their place. "Segnor, de la fontaine vos dirai mon pensé" (*Alex* APar III. 3624) [my lords, I'll tell you how I conceive of the fountain]. In describing a tent, Alexandre de Paris links the scene depicted on it to Alexander's desire to conquer the world.[130] Similarly, Benoît de Sainte-Maure could elaborate on Dares' catalogue of the Greek and Trojan heroes without the sense of writing lies or of falsifying his source.[131] For example, Dares describes Briseida as "formosam non alta statura candidam capillo flavo et molli superciliis iunctis oculis venustis corpore aequali blandam affabilem verecundam animo simplici piam" (*Dares* p. 17.7–10) [she was beautiful, not tall, fair, blond and soft-haired, with joined eyebrows, lovely eyes, fair shape, engaging, affable, modest, open, and devoted]. This becomes in the *Troie:*

> Briseïda fu avenant:
> Ne fu petite ne trop grant.
> Plus esteit bele et bloie et blanche
> Que flor de lis ne neif sor branche;
> Mais les sorcilles li joigneient,
> Que auques li mesaveneient.
> Beaus ieuz aveit de grant maniere
> E mout esteit bele parliere.
> Mout fu de bon afaitement
> E de sage contenement.
> Mout fu amee et mout amot,
> Mais sis corages li chanjot;
> E si ert el mout vergondose,
> Simple e aumosniere et pitose.
> (*Troie* 5275–88)

[Briseida was attractive, neither too short nor too tall. She was more beautiful, fair, and white-skinned than the lily or snow on the branch. But her eyebrows joined, which made her slightly less attractive. She had very fine, blue eyes, and her speech was most pleasant. She dressed well and conducted herself properly. She was greatly loved and returned that love in great measure; but she had an unsteady heart. And she is very modest, open, generous, and devoted.]

One notes how Benoît draws out of Dares' portrait impressions more appropriate to his own time, and adds, as *surplus de san,* Briseida's inconstancy. The addition permits his invention and narrative development of her betrayal of Troilus.[132]

Some of Benoît's descriptions are veritable set pieces, like those for Hector (*Troie* 5313–80) and Troilus (*Troie* 5393–5446); yet even for them Benoît adapts his source, as when he balances defects like Hector's stuttering and cross-eyes—"blaesum . . . strabum" (*Dares* p. 15.1–2)—by other, more commendable attributes.

> Se en lui rien mesaveneit,
> Par le bien faire le covreit:
> Ço savez bien, haute proëce
> Abaisse bien cri de laidece.
> (*Troie* 5323–26)[133]

[And if there were anything unattractive about him, he made up for it by his fine conduct. Rest assured that high prowess tends to eliminate a reputation for ugliness.]

Narrative texture derives from the qualities of the figures and actions represented within a context of prowess, love, or moral fortitude. Furthermore, texture is formally determined through the disposition and correlation of *personae* and their *negotia.* The elaboration of and emphasis on essential qualities fit into a topical order in narrative that conforms to a specific intention.[134] Narrative sequence derives therefore from simple abstractions artfully deployed, elaborated upon, and analyzed into constituent parts.[135]

> Mes s'au conter ne vos mescont,
> Il n'i a mot de vilainie,
> Ainz est contes de cortoisie
> Et de beaus moz et de plesanz.
> Nus, s'il n'est cortois et vaillanz,
> N'est dignes dou conte escouter
> Dont je vos vueil les moz conter.
> (*Meraugis* 26–32)

[But if I'm not mistaken, there were no villainous words in the story. Rather it contained courtesy, and fine, pleasing language. Only the courteous and valorous are worthy of listening to the story I want to tell you.]

The courteous tale in fine words—*beaus moz*—anticipates the conflict in *Meraugis* between inner worth as courtesy and external appearance as beauty; the entire romance combines in knights and ladies those two qualities and aspects of them or their antithetical defects in order to show that true beauty manifests courtesy.[136]

Now, texture is rhetorical coloration. As such it represents in a given work a spectrum of attributes that characterize general ideas in individual exemplars. In romance, these attributes are species of the general ideas most common to the genre's *san:* prowess, love, and rectitude.[137] When the narrative will show them forth, how it will knit them into a colorful and meaningful weave, are concerns proper to topical selection and distribution. We have observed that sensitivity to sharp contrasts was great enough to constrain Jean Renart to defend at some length the title and role of the ignoble kite in the *Escoufle* Epilogue: the noble end justifies and even ennobles the material means, much as Hector's valor offset his physical defects.

> Pour çou si di c'on ne doit mie
> Blasmer le rouman pour le non,
> C'on fait par bien povre seurnon
> A cort connoistre maint preudome,
> Çou'n est et la fins et la some.
> (*Escoufle* 9098–9102)

[So I maintain that the romance should not be blamed on account of its title. For many a worthy man is made known at court through a very poor surname, and that's the long and short of it.]

Something of the notion of Augustinian *sermo humilis* is apparent in these words: the meaning ennobles the subject matter.[138] The same transformation occurs with the grail. On the other hand, Gottfried von Straßburg reduced Thomas' account of Iseut's treatment of Tristan's wounds: medical details are a "rede, diu niht des hoves si" (*Tristan* Got 7954)[139] [speech not of the court]. And, more important in the *Escoufle,* the ring the bird snatches later identifies the lovers and their love—a topical feature as noble as the ring in the *Lai de l'ombre* that quickens, expresses, and ennobles another love.

The characteristics of the personages that determine material style and provide narrative texture can therefore be embodied in objects, families, nations, or cities—like Carthage, Troy, Priam's sons, the Golden Fleece, and the grail. The *Queste* employs multifarious epithets to refer to the grail.[140] They categorize the diverse adventures of the questing knights according to whatever intrinsic worth they may bring to the effort to achieve the grail.

Bien certes, Lancelot, por noient iriez en ceste queste, se vos ne vos baez a atenir de toz pechiez mortiex et a retrere vostre cuer des pensees terrianes et des deliz dou monde. Car bien sachiez que en ceste Queste ne vos puet vostre chevalerie riens valoir, se li Sainz Esperiz ne vos fet la voie en toutes les aventures que vos troverez. Car vos savez bien que ceste Queste est emprise por savoir au-cune chose des merveilles dou Saint Graal, que Nostre Sires a promis au verai chevalier qui de bonté et de chevalerie passera toz cels qui devant lui avront esté et qui aprés lui vendront. (*Queste* p. 116.2–11)

[Indeed Lancelot, it would avail you nothing to enter on this quest if you do not intend to abstain from all mortal sin and to withdraw your heart from earthly thoughts and worldly delights. For rest assured that your knighthood can avail you nothing on this quest, unless the Holy Spirit directs you through all the adversities you will encounter. For you must know that this quest has been undertaken to learn something of the marvels of the holy grail, which Our Lord promised to the true knight who will surpass all his predecessors and succes-sors in excellence and chivalry.]

The religious context permits the hermits and God's other prolocutors to qualify and condemn Gauvain and Hector as vehemently as the knights do villeins in *Guiron* (§§75, 120, 124). The grail is no more for their kind than is a sword for a villein. Just so, Dangier in the *Roman de la rose,* although personifying a potentially noble concept, remains a villainous villein, bear-ing a club, not a sword (*Rose* 3157/3141).

Dynamic Description in Narrative Economy

I am dwelling at some length on description in romance because the romances themselves do. Persons, things, and actions constitute the "presuppositions" of meaningful narrative for medieval writers. Description is therefore op-portune and systematic.[141] "De l'isle tout premierement vous doy je deviser la verité et l'estre de leans et de quoy ceulx servoient qui leans estoient" (*Folie Lanc* p. 95.1–2) [I ought first to provide a true description of the island and its contents, as well as of what its inhabitants did]. Like this one, most descrip-tions are additive. A tent in the *Rigomer* is followed from outside to inside, with different sections in each part (12789–92).[142] As topical inventions, such descriptions conform to a "principle of order" in the locus they occupy.

Actions follow the same procedure. The argument becomes "the act of 'plotting'. . . which must abide by, and thus illustrate, the principle of or-der."[143] Yvain's winning of Laudine shows how the sequence and complete-ness of topical order make an incredible event verisimilar.[144] No doubt, audience awareness that it is being made to believe and accept the incredible—the widow wedding publicly and willingly the very man who slew her beloved husband three days earlier—produces sophisticated comedy and disarms its moral faculties. But it is also true that the credibility rests on a complex but orderly topical arrangement of the marvelous features of Yvain's adventure. A topical order defines stages or *gradus* that organize the narrative parts within a whole; they inform and give a credible sequence to the plot.

Narrative *matiere* and description are combined in the *Rigomer* in a way that darkly foreshadows the order.

> Tres or devés entendre a moi,
> Qui veut de Rigomer oïr
> Et le cachier et le fuiir
> Et comment li tornois fina
> Et comment Gavains asouma
> Les mervelles et les encans.
> Teus ert dont liés, puis fu dolans,
> Qu'en poi d'eure grant cose avient.
> Jou di, que dire me convient:
> Tex estoit dont joians et liés,
> Puis fu dolans et coureciés.
> (*Rigomer* 13366–76)

[Henceforth you should heed me if you want to hear about Rigomer, about the pursuit and flight, how the tournament terminated and Gauvain put an end to the marvels and the enchantment. Some, happy then, afterward came to grief, for great things happen in a short space of time. I must say: some who were then joyous and happy later came to grief and vexation.]

The skill in such "plotting" consists in carefully placing and controlling the amplification of parts. It is a virtually geometrical process, and is occasionally so-called: "Entre Dieu et Nature le firent par compas" (*Gau d'Aupais* 162)[145] [God and nature drafted her shape], a comparison justified by the parallel activities of God, nature, and the artist. Such enhancement and topical plotting of persons and their actions were prominent in historical and hagiographical writing.

> Se de cez deus brément retrai,
> Si connois bien e vei e sai
> Que ce ne fait fors embelir,
> Enluminer et resplendir
> L'ovre e les faiz deu noble rei.
> (*Ducs* 42101–05)[146]

[If I speak briefly of these two, I recognize, see, and know that it serves only to embellish, illuminate, and adorn the task and deeds of the noble king.]

Exceptional persons are capable of exceptional deeds, and require therefore systematic topical delineation to bring out the traits that make their exceptionality comprehensible and their extraordinary deeds credible as unique excellence.[147]

The arts of poetry and prose propose some exemplary topical sequences, notably the *gradus amoris* and the description of persons and places. Romance organizes its narrative according to stages like the *gradus amoris:* combat — including duel, siege, imprisonment, and battle — questing, hospitality, penance, celebration, kinship and feudal relationships as well as their interactions, and others.[148] These motifs contain topoi; their elaboration by specific *argumenta* defines persons and events (heroes and marvels) of the *materia propinqua* in the context or contexts (the "evaluative perspectives") chosen for the work.[149]

Very little modern critical scholarship dealing with romance composition uses topical terminology correctly, although a number of studies provide the lineaments of such critical scholarship. For example, Bruckner's "context" for hospitality includes topoi appropriate to hospitality, just as her term motif fits topical argument. Similarly, her subunits are topical formulae for the disposition of arguments. Inclusion, rearrangement, or substitution within the formulae provides for both topical originality and natural and artificial order in topical sequence.[150] A topical conception of the stages in the rise from sin to virtue sequentially orders Bernardus Silvestris' commentary on the *Aeneid*.[151] By identifying the stages normally associated with repentance, and taking into account the historical and social evolution of the idea in the High Middle Ages, Payen succeeded in making significant analyses of romances based on their use of the topic as theme and motif, especially its adaptation to non-Christian *(romans d'antiquité)* and courtly contexts.[152] As discussed above, Chrétien's romances can be described as two-part arrangements fitting different commonplaces, usually those of falling in love, combat, or quest. The same is obviously true for other romances.[153]

The great prose romances illustrate various *gradus* in knighthood, love, and redemption that interlace between the death of Christ in the *Estoire* and the destruction of the Round Table in the *Mort Artu*. The *Queste* itself somewhat confuses the chronological and geographical coordinates that, in the *Lancelot* Proper, seem consistent and credible.[154] However, natural chronology and topography become irrelevant in the moral sphere, whose time is "eternal." Time takes on a different significance, as in Lancelot's twenty-four day coma (*Queste* p. 258.17–24). Geographical meeting places also display a consistent topical network. Much of the *Queste* plot includes dreams and visions, where time and place are visionary. In place of a *gradus amoris,* a different pattern obtains, with its own "natural chronology": the sequence of confession, trial and penance, and redemption orders the chronology and the topography, and thus the sequence of narrative parts. "Ainsi se manifeste le procédé de composition de l'auteur; il associe et combine ses épisodes non selon leur forme narrative, mais selon leur signification morale. Ce ne sont pas des fragments de 'chroniques' qu'il enchevêtre, mais des idées qu'il groupe." [155] Each questing knight has his own beginning, middle, and end within the plan of redemption. The quest junctures correlate the separate sequences in loose temporal succession. The entire romance fits into the typological plan of fulfillment and salvation which the Arthurian world is, finally, unable to achieve in the grail. [156]

The "atemporal" sequence of the *Queste* has therefore a rationale: it follows topical time, not chronological time, determined by the stages of penitence and illumination the knights achieve or fail to attain through the diverse adventures and marvels they encounter. Similarly, within the autobiographical time scheme of the *Rose*'s narrator, whose sleeping and waking represent only the beginning and end, an amplified midpoint—the dream—unrolls a complex *gradus amoris;* its parts are adventures which, like those in the *Queste,* have better and worse outcomes. This topical order, with its own time and space sequence, focuses on the rose as the goal of the lover's quest.

Propriety of Topical Description

Amplification is a means to complete incomplete or "corrupt" *matiere,* to perfect it by figurative and tropical devices. The sources that Chrétien describes as *corronpues* required topical amplification. A *matiere* may be incomplete because it lacks the amplificatory topics that explain its context. "Et por ce que je ne vos devisai onques la façon des freres, le vos deviserai je orendroit, tot ensi com li contes le vos devise" (*Lancelot* lxix.1) [since I have not yet described the features of his brothers, I shall do so now, just as the tale describes them to you]. The hyperbole we have noted in the description of marvels also appears in topical description. [157] When the description of objects or actions is most topical, it is almost always most abstract and general, as the person, thing, or event is located in its class or type.

> N'ot jusqu'au port de Macedoine
> Feme qui fust de sa beauté,
> Ainz fust autre jovenz viuté

> Qui fust demostrez lez sa face.
> Por ce me plest que je en face
> De li beles descriptïons.
>
> (*Meraugis* 44–49)

[There was no woman of her beauty from there to the port of Macedonia. Rather young women were of vile appearance beside her. So I'd like to make a beautiful description of her.]

The description is almost one hundred lines long. Similarly, in *Gui de Warewik,* the author asserts that he could not possibly describe Gui's daughter adequately, but that nevertheless it behooves him ("est raisun") to delineate her to some extent (52–55)

The propriety of topical inventions is one of the most difficult problems of composition: "Enprent un tel fet qe bien fet a descrire" (*TChev* 5246) [he undertakes something quite worthy of description]. Ingenuity, discrimination, and a sense of appropriate time and place will decide, for example, whether a hero is best described prior to an action or at some stage during the action—or whether his qualities should gradually emerge by appropriate topical additions at succeeding narrative *loci.* "Car la signification n'est pas dans l'image, mais dans l'enchaînement des images, elle n'est pas dans telle scène, mais dans l'aventure."[158] But opportunity, as an art, can only be called for, it cannot be taught.

Commentary may, however, evaluate the results. The evaluation will proceed with the most certainty if it does not neglect the topical moment's contribution to narrative significance and disposition. The solutions vary from work to work; they control adaptations by subsequent authors or scribes. The sovereign control of marvel, context, and narrative significance that marks the romances of Chrétien de Troyes stands over against the historical verification sought by Wace and Benoît de Sainte-Maure, and the elaboration of an incipient courtliness and romantic love in Roman *matiere* by precious Ovidian play in the *Thèbes* and *Eneas.* Later romancers imitated Chrétien's high sense of fictionality[159] in the name of received truths; others whimsically looked back to an Arthurian, Roman, or French past whose utopian splendor was no longer accessible except in the imagination.[160] In all these works, however, topical ordering of parts as plotting gives the texture—the romance text—as a *conjointure* more or less *bele,* but always an art.

8

Emergence of Romance

> *Mes quanque par bone raison*
> *Veaut Deux conjoindre e atremper,*
> *Forz et bons et sages senz per,*
> *Ja ne voudra ne n'a volu*
> *Que ce seit jamais dissolu;*
> *Ja n'i vaudra corrupcion.*
> (Rose 19092–97/19062–67)

> *[But whatever God wished for good reason to conjoin and blend, He, strong, wise, and without peer, will never wish, nor has He ever wished, that it ever become corrupt.]*

Auctorial Interventions and Emergent Romance

At the outset of this study it was argued that there are three complementary approaches to the art of medieval romance: analysis of representative texts,[1] historical survey of the constitution of the genre,[2] and inference from recorded statements. I have taken the last approach. Although it is evident that one cannot ignore the other two, taken by themselves they have certain defects which my approach can help overcome.

The study of selective or representative romances as well as the historical survey of texts can be only partially satisfactory in understanding the emergence and evolution of medieval French romance. This is because, first, chronology is notoriously uncertain. The chronology of major, seminal authors is controversial, as the scholarship on Chrétien's romances, the Tristan poems, *Perlesvaus,* and the different versions of the prose romances illustrates. Other works that have received less attention are still dated according to the sometimes dubious standards of earlier scholarship. Furthermore, we are very much in the dark about the real knowledge authors had of one another's work and their respective chronologies. Did Chrétien or Robert de Boron first write a grail romance? Did the later author know the work of the earlier one? Study of the evolution and originality of romance is impossible without a firm chronology and solid evidence of real intertextual reflection by authors.

Therefore, it seems useful to have a third frame of reference for historical criticism of medieval French romance: the evidence of auctorial interventions for the art of romance as it was generally received and delineated in some of its more striking ramifications. As tedious and atomistic as this must sometimes be, it nonetheless is valid critical scholarship. It is also the source of unexpected insights into the medieval art and into auctorial and audience expectations in the twelfth, thirteenth, and early fourteenth centuries.

Modern critical insights are equally useful in this kind of critical scholarship, especially when offered by those few critics who take the trouble to include medieval literature in their purview. Jauss' theory of the constitution of medieval genres, for example, helps to explain the emergence of *roman* as *conjointure* from *conte* and *estoire*. Generically, romance evinces the coherent disposition of the disparate material of marvelous adventures in coherent topical recreations. The art of romance results from "un exercice intellectuel . . . , une méthode de travail, une forme d'analyse du passé et de ses sources, une activité intellectuelle, la mise en roman, dont la forme romanesque est, non pas le but, mais la conséquence."[3] *Mise en roman* by the kind of invention we have identified in this study is furthermore discernible in a historical process the main lines of which Zink sets forth in his important article. Having dealt in my study with the formal foundations of the art of romance, we must now follow in Zink's footsteps and historically contextualize that art as it emerged in the works that represent it. The historical emergence of romance shows it generic characteristics.[4]

Since the word *roman* had a broad semantic range, it served as a lexical conduit for traditions as varied as those of medieval Latin poetics, medieval historiography, the marvelous sources of Celtic, antique, national, and other *matières,* and the specific demands of various segments of largely aristocratic audiences, especially the patrons. These traditions allowed for experimentation, adaptation, and correction in fashioning and transmitting narrative *matiere.* But once *conjointure* as "the poet's own coherent arrangement of disparate material"[5] became a generally accepted meaning for the word *roman,* it acquired generic integrity. The word *roman* replaced the more learned *conjointure.*

Critics have proposed more differentiated definitions, or, more precisely, descriptions of *conjointure* as *roman,* wherein "jointing"[6] is construed as ar-

ticulation: *conjointure* "établit un lien entre la suite des événements et la peinture des caractères, aboutit parfois à une architecture un peu secrète du
roman."[7] This description identifies the different elements that go into Chrétien's *conjointures:* marvelous adventures, representative characters, their
coordination and articulation in preconceived topical schemes. Jean Frappier has emphasized the way these elements come together: "une liaison in-
terne entre le déroulement des aventures et les sentiments des personnages,
une motivation de leurs actes, et aussi une structure plus serrée de l'intrigue
orientée graduellement vers une finalité riche de sens."[8] The interweave of
marvelous and conventional motivations and their encounter in the principal
characters—here Jauss' emphasis upon the hero who defines the romance
by material style comes to the fore—orient the plot toward a conclusion.
The conclusion need not be only in time and place, as we saw in the foregoing chapter. More important, the conclusion realizes the topical potential
and the significance of the main characters, closing the work when it is sufficient as an example of a social or religious ethic.

Articulation as *conjointure* can be described in both modern and medieval terminology, a fact that suggests their fundamental compatibility—their
reciprocal historical validity—in spite of the different critical presuppositions
and the diverse horizons of expectation that may separate a Chrétien de
Troyes from his modern interpreters. Medieval and modern terminologies
do not always coincide. For example, Guillaume de Lorris' *Roman de la rose*
is to medieval audiences an *estoire* or romance rather than a *Dit*, the *Lai
d'Aristote* or the *Vair palefroi* is a lay rather than a fabliau, and *Ille et Galeron* is a lay rather than a romance. The terminological differences may dis-
close the vagaries of generic distinction in the Middle Ages. But they also
reveal medieval awareness of genre in the transmission of received material.

In the final analysis, the real distinction indicated by auctorial interventions is less one between genres—or differently designated kinds of writing—
than one between ways of joining and jointing, between the juxtaposition
and articulation of different material styles. Narrative articulation makes
romance's *conjointure mout bele* and its *san mout bon*. The means of articulation may indeed evolve to such an extent that it becomes necessary to
distinguish one class of texts from another. This is what Chrétien did when
he distinguished romance *conjointure* and the storyteller's *contes*. The *Roman de Troie,* Chrétien's œuvre, the Lancelot-Grail cycle, and *Guillaume
de Dole,* are all different ways of articulating romance *conjointure.*[9] When
a romance *conjointure* is not *mout bele* as *conjointure*, we have one of two
things: a hodgepodge or a new genre. Just so, Guillaume de Lorris will prepare for the *Dit* by making romance into a topical art of love, thus opening
the way for the *traitié*—the treatise as a combination of distinct parts not
in a plot but in an argument or an anatomy.

Transition from Chronicle to Dream Vision

Romance derived its art from the art of poetry and prose clerics learned in the schools. That art established no specific *matiere* or genre. It was applicable to lyric, the *Dit,* the fabliau, as much as it was to romance. It showed how to exemplify, in various matters, modes, and forms, prevailing cultural views in religious, moral, social, or dynastic contexts. The common scholastic art makes romance's origins, as well as its disappearance, obscure. For the same clerics who made the expression *mise en roman* mean something more specific than "write in French" also invented vernacular history in the twelfth century and the *Dit* in the thirteenth and fourteenth.

After the fact, as it were, *roman* slowly emerges from the awareness of *estoire* as romance. At the other chronological end, writers begin to speak of the *Dit.* We have seen that the *Roman de la rose* itself, although very influential in the elaboration of the *Dit,* is still called by its authors a *roman,* and even an *estoire.*[10] Romance is therefore a transitional genre between 1150 *estoire* and 1300 *Dit.* The transition may be illustrated by the extreme kinds of *estoire* and *Dit,* that is, by annals and the treatise. The former relates events in chronological succession. This is indeed its only compositional principle, since choice of contents may otherwise be entirely haphazard or willful. In the *Dit conjointure* becomes what Jacqueline Cerquiglini calls *montage,* the different parts and modes of which come together in horizontal discontinuity.

Annals tend to record the extraordinary and the ordinary as they occur in temporal sequence. In evolving toward the chronicle the extraordinary tends more and more to predominate and the record to become a succession of marvelous adventures. The chronicle is no different in this respect from hagiography. A succession of royal biographies is a secular *légende dorée* or *vies de princes,* a collection of extraordinary yet exemplary lives. Hagiography, moreover, tends to orient the saint's life toward a goal, whether a miracle or martyrdom. Concentration on the extraordinary in a life and its topical stages is decisive for romance. In it, historical record-keeping becomes composition as choice and arrangement of material to fit a specific intention. This privileges the marvel or marvels and the personages who confront and know them. Topical investigation of the mystery in marvels — mystery in the medieval sense of mystery and signification — points to what Marie de France calls the search for and invention of "ceo k'i ert."

It is difficult to be sure how conscious early writers were of attempting something new or of merely conforming to received traditions of narrative composition. Geoffrey Gaimar explicitly postulated a new kind of history in the *Engleis,* one including aristocratic interest in love, courtesy, the hunt, and knightly combat. To develop these new social, and thus topical, emphases writers applied the art they learned in schools. Histories and romances preserved the memory of past adventures in which writers detected an ostensibly hidden, chivalric truth or rationale—the *raisun* of the adventures. That they had difficulties with certain truths suggests different audiences and contrasting truths, making for quantitative and qualitative differences in matter, style, and opinion. This is not the same as appreciation of formal artistry. Jehan Bodel admitted that the Matter of Britain, for all its "vanity," was *plesant,* just as Christine de Pizan admired Jean de Meun's artistry while decrying the causes it was made to serve.

Since so much of romance reminded audiences of dreams, the Macrobian principles of truth in dreams could be made to serve romance truths. Romance tended to appropriate the allegorical mode,[11] replacing presumed historicity with moral or social ideals exemplified in adventures whose truth was apprehended by the "heart." The techniques for such changes and adaptations are already in use in twelfth-century romance: the colors of horses, the euhemerization of mystery, the glossing of *matiere* as the invention of *ceo k'i ert.* Huon de Mery saw his *Tornoiement* in the tradition of both Raoul de Houdenc's allegorical poems and Chrétien's romances, which led him into the forest of Broceliande to discover the knights of the Round Table engaged in a psychomachia. Later prose romance radically revised earlier emphases on disturbing moralities by imposing religious contexts onto old plots. Others, such as the borderline case *Cristal et Clarie,* blend the frontiers between romance and *Dit.* The *Dit* tends to make *san* the organizing principle for content. As conceptualization of *san* progressed, the *matiere* became the concept and *san* prevailed over *récit.* If Marie de France saw her *Lais* as a *matiere* containing a *surplus de san* revealed by topical invention as *ceo k'i ert,* the *Dit* may be characterized as a *san* with a *surplus de matiere* revealing *ceo k'i ert* as parts in a montage or *forma tractandi.*[12]

The distinction is evident if one compares Guillaume de Lorris and Richard de Fornival. Guillaume's narrative centers on a mystery, the Rose; added topical developments make the work into an instructive treatise delivered by the god of Love, and illustrated in the adventures of the Lover. The topical order the god of Love sets forth informs the actual quest for the Rose.[13] Richard de Fornival disserts on the nature of love in general, and his love in particular as it exemplifies that more general conception; to do so he deploys bestiary images as a *surplus de matiere* culled from various sources according to the epistolary scheme of a *salut d'amour.* But the lady narrator in the *Response au bestiaire* uses the same images to counter his argument in favor of a different vision of love. The essential change is that, in Fornival's *Bestiaire,* the example is adapted to the organization of an argument illustrating a thesis or a position, as in a sermon; in romance, the ideas are elicited from the *matiere* to make it exemplary, a *matiere* that retains its historical coordinates of time and space.

Here we may again appreciate the importance of *bele conjointure* for romance as Chrétien de Troyes understood it: the coherent combination of disparate material—White Stag and Sparrow Hawk adventures followed by a multipartitioned quest in *Erec,* or the storm giant and the fountain fay adventures also followed by a quest in *Yvain.* The arrangement of this material is made meaningful by both chronological and spatial sequence, and by the *maniere* of the protagonists delineated by credible topical programs that pattern their marvelous adventures. The problem for the writer was to retain topical texture in and coherence among the parts. Poetics provided the traditional notions of *series* and *iunctura* in *compositio,* which facilitated adaptation and amalgamation of narrative *matieres.*

The adventures evoked by the marvel also represent the romancer's search for the archetypal. The failure to define love and the divine, sometimes even to name or identify referents for images like the Rose and the grail, fits the archetypal, "ideagenous" character of romance narratives. When Jean de Meun, adapting Andreas Capellanus, proposed a definition of love, the Rose, a *mystère* in Guillaume de Lorris, became a rationalization and even a topical place identified by Reason. Idea turned to concept, and myth as truth became a story illustrating a lesson.

Romance, whether emergent or evolving, is, like every literature, subject to the circumstances in which and for or against which it is produced.[14] These impinge upon the composition of specific works through the quest for *verité.* Herein lies the generic question of romance as it emerges in succeeding works as part of social, political, and moral history.

The experiment—or experience—seems to have been "creative" for most of the Middle Ages.[15] Romance explored both subjective and objective, psychological and historical complexities, seeking to harmonize opposites in the *concors discordia* of their *conjointures.*[16] Although often selective and reductive, romances evince common concern for prowess, love, and rectitude— the contexts that seemed, to the romancers and their favorably disposed publics and benefactors, to be fundamental subjects of the genre.[17] Scribal intervention is significant after ca. 1250. The adaptation of the poetic paradigm to romance, in place of the oral paradigm that produced the early *chansons de geste,* established a tradition which persisted into the sixteenth century in France.

Intertextuality and the Romance Horizons of Expectation

The art of romance is a technique for inventing and elaborating narrative. Although the art of invention antedated the romances, neither a specific theory nor a formal art of romance emerged until after they ceased to be written and a new epic literature emerged in the Renaissance.[18] Rather, the art of romance was adapted from traditional techniques to a new language and new sources. The tradition was learned and Latin, the adaptation to the art of romance was effected by imitation and revisions using the works and words of other romancers as models and the taste of aristocratic publics.[19] "Anthologizing" in *recueils* might also make explicit potential intertextual links.[20]

The unique excellence of the romance protagonists was an auctorial statement which bespoke the unique excellence of a particular combination of *matiere* and *san* in *bele conjointure*. The very uniqueness of representation in discrete romances maintained tradition while contributing dynamically to its elaboration. Romances not only emerged as integrated wholes, both in conception and in realization, they also continued to establish the integrity of the genre by implicit reflection on narrative and ethical potentialities in new and old *matieres*. Intertextuality in the "intertexte, " that is, "l'ensemble des textes que l'on peut rapprocher de celui que l'on a sous les yeux,"[21] plays a fundamental role in the emergence and the constitution of the romance genre. The *mouvance* of the *intertexte*,[22] or *ré-écriture—repetitio* as *renovatio*—implied a network of structural, linguistic, and social relationships that define romance as the work of their various intersections in texts.[23]

For us the texts are artifacts; in the Middle Ages they illustrated stages in a dynamic process of social and moral reflection elaborated in textual commentary and correction. The intertext acquired intertextuality when it was perceived that not only previous matter and models but also potential matter and models had a place in the invention of romance.[24] Topical invention termed the potential text the *status archetypus*. It preceded the new *status sensilis*. Translation, in medieval terms, was the perception of the *status archetypus* of a given *materia*. The available tradition was subject to correction within the image of the *translatio* of *chevalerie* and *clergie*.

The notion of "correction" basic to medieval poetics implies intertextuality. Reflection on the art of romance and romance *matieres,* and the history of that reflection as preserved in the recorded statements of romance, are the history of the constitution of a genre in texts. The recorded statements define the *Sitz im Leben,* or "social function and communicative achievement,"[25] of romance. As auctorial statements, they express intention and criticism by explicit demarcation of social or moral groups, and offer social and historical as well as formal reasons for correction.[26] It is possible to show how social norms determine stylistic features of romance, now that we recognize, with historians, that style for the Middle Ages was material, and thus that the representation of persons and things was made to fit social norms and expectations.[27]

As a transition between history and treatise,[28] and thus between two modes of stating truth, romance derives its validity from effective appeal to the imagination of audiences untrained in scholastic conceptualization and distinction, yet familiar with the tradition of *roman* as a work in the vernacular that dealt with problems in the medieval world raised by the ideals of God, nation or family, chivalry, and noble love. How indeed could the younger sons and daughters who are the *dramatis personae* of so many romances find consolation in a God, nation, or family that denied them a share in a world reserved only for elder brothers, the greater nobility, or the often ignoble wealthy?[29] The tournament, as *Erec,* some historians, and ecclesiastical strictures suggest, was no more viable a solution than bread and circuses had been in ancient Rome, nor were the grail and courtly love. But the romances show valor as worthy; they base it on intrinsic qualities, the essence of which could be discussed and aspired to, and the reality of which many wished for and needed in order to foster faith in the realization of dreams. The precarious social position of new knights and clerics, who shared in the imaginative union of *chevalerie* and *clergie,* could find at least psychological compensation and a raison d'être in romance.[30] And where reality conflicted with dream, there remained the dream, the ideal, the *status archetypus* which could find renewed expression in new romances.

An explicitly escapist intention in romance surfaces in Benoît's *chambre de beauté* and at the beginning of Chrétien's *Yvain.*[31] In the second half of the thirteenth century, after the Vulgate and post-Vulgate cycle had depicted the condemnation of secular knighthood which Chrétien had idealized for the newly emergent chivalric nobility of the twelfth century,[32] romance authors — and, presumably, their publics — began to opt for adventure romance without reference to rigorous morality, but also without social or political underpinnings.[33] Thus, *Claris et Laris* exalts the traditional values of romance *san* but does not use them to condemn contemporary vices.[34] Pageant and entertainment, the ritual of the aristocracy, entered narrative for their own sake, replacing both moral rigorism and introspection on chivalric *san.*[35] The flight from intellectual, moral, and social reality led from *Claris et Laris* to *Jehan de Saintré* as much as to *Don Quixote,* from castles in France and Britain to castles in Spain.

Myth of Romance

How does it happen, wonders anxiously the fourteenth-century author of the *Tresor amoureux,* that children of the same parents are so different from one another in real qualities and worth (*Tres am* 3091–3104)? "Parce que bons arbres se doit par reson porter bon fruit. Si auient aucunes fois quil

couuient quen cest arbre faille aucunes resons aussi conme plusseurs sevent"[36]
[for a good tree ought to bear good fruit. And yet it is well known that on
occasion that very tree fails to live up to expectation]. The children of Henry
II Plantagenet offered a striking illustration of this problem in the twelfth
and thirteenth centuries. So did the knights of the Round Table in the prose
cycles. But even the Arthurian myth—*vain* and *plesant* for some even while
they were attributing its ideals to Charlemagne and Rome—implied intrinsic worth that could influence action. That was the myth the rise and decline
of which we may follow in twelfth- and thirteenth-century romance. Before
the act of writing, then, lies the myth.

The myth was, like the archetypes for the arts of poetry and prose, ration-
alized by euhemerization, by the invention of its *surplus de san*. A comparison of the "Roman" adaptations with their major sources reveals to what
extent topical notions of love, expressed with Ovidian eloquence and adorned
with chivalric virtues, inform and shape narrative elaboration.[37] The authors
did not feel that they were corrupting the *matiere* by such additions and
modifications.

> Ne di mie qu'aucun bon dit
> N'i mete, se faire le sai,
> Mais la matire en ensivrai.
> (*Troie* 142–44)

[This is not to say that I won't introduce some amplificatory flourishes, if
I can, but I will follow the source for them.]

What the inventions might be depended on the author and his or her public,
including patrons, loved ones, and friends. It was this public that accounts
for the need felt for adaptations, restatements, and scribal interventions.
Some, like Jean Maillart, invited criticism. Chrétien protested against "tam-
pering" at the end of *Yvain*. *Yvain* remained relatively secure, at least in
France; the *Charrette* and *Perceval* did not enjoy the immunity he sought.

The *chansons de geste* themselves—the *matière de France*—adapted the
epic tradition to the new romance art that derived from rhetorical and other
learned traditions independent of formulaic epic. The new *chansons* acquired
a topicality that, to those like Jehan Bodel, rendered them true. His *Saisnes*
illustrates this, as do *Partonopeu de Blois*, Adenet le Roi's adaptations, and
the Huon de Bordeaux cycle; courtly love and chivalric virtues receive topical elaboration, as oral formulae and motifs give way to topical amplifications in octosyllabic couplets or monorhymed Alexandrine *laisses*. The
thirteenth-century grouping of *gestes* into "families" establishes topical subdivisions within the *matière de France* itself. Some of the earliest "French"

vernacular writing is part of the emergence of Anglo-Norman historical writing. Geiffrei Gaimar's *Engleis* incorporated both chronicle and lay into a composite, chronologically disposed work that, in its original conception, included the Golden Fleece, the siege of Troy, and an adaptation of Geoffrey of Monmouth's *Historia regum Britanniae*.[38] Geoffrey's *Historia*, widely regarded in the twelfth and thirteenth centuries as historical, also inspired adaptations — the *Bruts* — the most important of which is Wace's. Wace in turn furthered vernacular history in the *Rou*, depicting the origins and rise of the Norman dynasty. Benoît de Sainte-Maure began again the same task, but, like Wace's *Rou*, his *Chronique des ducs de Normandie* remained unfinished. Still, Benoît came near to realizing the universal history he designed for the *Troie*. His sequence of events corresponds to that in Wace's *Rou*, except that he takes the Norman beginnings back beyond Denmark to Troy. The universal history Gaimar had planned and, perhaps, completed, Benoît sought to emulate; but only two fragments of the plan were written, the *Troie* and the *Chronique*.

In addition to the chronicles, there began to appear works that are more in the nature of biography, as in saints' lives[39] like Guernes de Pont-Sainte-Maxence's *Thomas Becket*. Jordan Fantosme, the *Pseudo-Turpin*, *Guillaume le maréchal*, the histories of the Fourth Crusade by Villehardouin and Robert de Clari, as well as Joinville's *Vie de Saint-Louis* also fall into this grouping. Since the Middle Ages reckoned hagiography as part of history, works like Joinville's were comparable to saints' lives like Guernes', and by extension, to the whole corpus of medieval hagiography. Since vernacular hagiography accommodated vernacular epic techniques and topical invention, it facilitated the transition from *chansons de geste* to romance techniques, while influencing the art of romance narrative itself.

Genre and Romance

The evidence for grouping the *chansons de geste* and saints' lives apart from other writing because of their moral value, and Jehan Bodel's classification of French *matiere*, that is, the more literary *chanson de geste*, with romance, brings up the problem of genre for the Middle Ages. What is romance? Can it be recognized as a genre in any useful yet historically accurate sense? Could not all of medieval historiography, including hagiography, fall into its net, as many *chansons de geste* seem to have done by the thirteenth century? Are the different versions of *Barlaam et Josaphat* romance? What about the *Saisnes* and *Guillaume le maréchal*?

Since generic distinctions in the Middle Ages are usually hazy, they rarely satisfy modern, scientific criteria for definition. Yet recorded statments show that the emergence of works we call romance after 1150 did make authors aware of discrete *romans* that were broadly categorized, evaluated, and compared with one another. The evaluations assign the limits to this study and justify the designation romance for the works treated in it based on ethical or social criteria.

As the notion of material style might lead us to expect, generic distinctions were made on the basis of *matieres*—that is, on social, dynastic, or moral criteria. For example, the saint's life was distinguished from romance because it spoke of God.

> Ne voil pas en fables d'Ovide,
> Seinnurs, mestre mun estuide,
> Ne ja, sachez, ne parlerum
> Ne de Tristram ne de Galerun;
> Ne de Renard ne de Hersente
> Ne voil pas mettre m'entente,
> Mes voil de Deu et sa vertu,
> Ki est pussant et tutjurz fu,
> E de ses seinz, les Set Dormanz,
> Ki tant furent resplendisanz
> Devant la face Jesu Crist.
> (*Set dorm* 51–61)

[I don't want to apply myself to Ovidian fables, my lords, and rest assured that we shall never talk of Tristan or of Galeron; I will not apply myself to stories about Renart and Hersente. Rather I will speak of God and his virtue, He who is and always was powerful, and of His saints, the Seven Sleepers, who stood so radiant before the face of Jesus Christ.]

The justification for the alleged superiority of hagiography over romance is its veracity. But veracity stems less from the historicity of events and their documentation, as we may observe in the *Set dormans* itself, than from "Deu" and "sa vertu" revealed through the principal figures in the narrative. The *matiere* of the saint's life possessed intrinsic merit that raised it above and distinguished it from other *matieres*. The *chansons de geste* of the *cycle du Roi* take on a similar aureole, revealing God and His strength, and some "authorities" recognized the distinction. One had only to pattern the figure according to the idea to make even fictional inventions true. The saint's life had to conform to topical expectations of sainthood.[40]

Romance *matiere* was a threat to the integrity of the hagiographic example. So the anonymous *Vies des pères* branded romance matter harmful to the soul.

Leissiez Cliges et Perceval,
Qui les cuers tue et met a mal,
Et les romanz de vanité.[41]

[Set aside Cligés and Perceval, stories which slay and harm the heart, and romances on vain and empty subjects.]

Another contemporary work, the *Poème moral,* proclaimed epic itself to be vain.

Kar ce c'atient a l'ame, ce qu'atient a Jhesu,
Se bien seit li jugleres les dois movoir menu,
S'il moi dist que Rolant abatit Fernagu . . . ?[42]

[For what does it have to do with the soul or with Jesus if the jongleur plays skillfully and tells me that Roland struck down Fernagus?]

The condemnation of the *Partonopeu* because it resembles a "sounge" (*Edmund* 30)[43] recognizes the place of the marvel in *matiere* and composition, but denies the ethical validity of secular *san.*

The same moral underpinning is found in Jehan Bodel's validation of the *matière de France.* Despite its strictures this work made possible the topical embellishment of truth of any viable sort in any appropriate *matiere,* from Ovid through Celtic fables to dream visions. For Bodel does not question the *art* of Arthurian romance; rather, he attacks the presumed superiority of the British king that art seems to uphold. The distinction is of the same kind as that made by the hagiographers between their matter and all others that are not moral or religious. *Chansons de geste* evolved toward romance as the material tended to absorb topical subjects and marvels common in twelfth-century romance. The *Saisnes,* with its amplifications on love and chivalry, illustrates the transition, and justifies the juxtaposition of French matter and those of Rome and Britain in Bodel's Prologue. The absorption of the *chanson de geste* occurred after romance, as *roman,* had been recognized as a designation for tales of love and chivalry set forth in *bele conjointure.* But the romancers had insisted that their *matiere,* which was meaningless and often unacceptable in their sources, was susceptible of embellishment, elucidation, and euhemerization in a broadly courtly context. Such adaptation distinguished romance during the hundred fifty years it dominated European vernacular literature. The very attacks on romance that we have examined here are evidence that these works had acquired a certain integrity and that, taken together, they constituted in people's minds a group. This does not mean that they represented for them what we would today call a genre.

The problem for modern readers derives from the fact that the Middle Ages did not have a theoretical conception of genre;[44] further, no generally acknowledged terminological distinction was made between epic, romance, hagiography, and history in the time of the *romans d'antiquité*.[45] After Chrétien de Troyes, however, there was awareness of romance *(roman)* as a class of writing distinct from history, hagiography, and Fabliau. Although the characteristics of *roman* as romance were neither constant nor imposed, the word did identify and determine a class of writings recognized by romancers, their publics, and their detractors. These characteristics influenced what would be written as and designated *roman,* and fashioned public taste and expectations. A genre had been established from notions of composition in medieval Latin poetics, vernacular historiography and hagiography, and current social and moral ideals.[46] Beginning with Chrétien de Troyes, the elucidation of old matter and the discovery of chivalric truths in extraordinary marvels produced a kind of writing which united matter and truths in extraordinary narratives whose aristocratic heroes and heroines mirrored and exemplified prowess, love, or moral fortitude.

Since the evidence suggests that medieval audiences tended to identify with models of conduct that emerged or remained steadfast in a haphazard world,[47] romance offered a suitable medium for exemplary narrative that addressed the concerns and faiths of the nobility. The unique excellence of romance heroes and heroines did not preclude imaginary emulation by audiences, and provided confirmation of qualities that could find expression in individual efforts to achieve a model existence, in tournament and war, or in love and marriage.

Conjointure and Romance Fiction

Matiere and *san* come together in the *conjointure. Conjointure* often requires turning "natural" into "artificial" order. The fundamental pattern is deflection from normal order in the sentence. Such techniques include the tropes, and these in turn suggest two parallel, superimposed levels of order—*matiere* and *san.* Syntagmatic and paradigmatic correlation brings about the unification of *matiere* and *san* in the conjunction of narrative and topical parts at suitable places *(ci endroit* and *or endroit)* in a narrative and contextual whole.

The key to the totality of *conjointure* is the use of analogy as enhanced by interpretive amplification and abbreviation. These techniques are applied to the context and design of the work as much as are tropical and figural ornamentation in the sentence. Directly or obliquely, they restate the essential elements of the theme in analogical adventures derived from a *matiere* that may have been either expressive of a different *san* (as in the *Aeneid* for the *Eneas* author), or *depeciee* and *corronpue* (as in the storytellers' *contes* about Erec), that is, lacking the topical coherence that the new work seeks to achieve by amplifications and abbreviations.

We can appreciate the tremendous implications for romance of Chrétien's term *conjointure,* the nature of which might have escaped us but for the allusion to the *premier vers* in *Erec.* The *vers* signals a *jointure*—what the *Erec* Prologue announces as the most beautiful feature of the romance. The total *conjointure* of the romance's first part combines, "beautifully," two *vers* or *contes.* The combination invents the romance's *bele conjointure* as it reveals Enide's exemplary beauty. The conjunction, *ci endroit* and *or endroit,* has less to do with chronological beginnings and endings than with the collocation of topical parts of *ceo k'i ert.* When Chrétien achieved that kind of narrative, he had given to *estoire* a principle of composition dependent not on historical referents but on "archetypal" ones (which were probably evident to him in history anyway). He had invented the romance configuration.[48]

Romance *conjointure* is, then, a *figura.* By the careful ordering of source material and topical increments, the work becomes a model of conduct founded on social, moral, or religious ideals the author, patron, or audience deemed valid, and which the one or the other desired to see represented in marvelous adventures. The record of *matieres* and *sans* (*san* in the plural) is the history of the emergence and evolution of medieval romance as a genre.

Discrete groups of works also reflect romance as *figura.* We have observed it in authors like Bernardus Silvestris, who views human fate and redemption in the diverse modes of his various works, one of which—the *Cosmographia*—was called a complete art of poetry and prose by Gervase of Melkley, Geoffrey of Vinsauf, and other thirteenth-century masters. Chrétien's opus shows the same succession of inventions, wherein a model of love and knighthood receives constant renewal and original exposition. The great prose romances of the thirteenth century, adapting a series of diverse and even contradictory models of conduct, continue to use the principle of *figura,* with critical implications for audience evaluation of the secular ideals espoused in most verse romances. Verse romance itself, in the thirteenth century, counters the model of asceticism fostered in the prose, by new and diverse treatments of social and aristocratic ideals. In all these romances the principle of *figura* as *conjointure*—the union, in modern terms, of actantial and thematic schemes of composition—reflects the history of a genre in the process of constitution, reconstitution, and elaboration[49] according to the same art.

Unfortunately and ironically, the vicissitudes of manuscript transmission, the vagaries of scribal intervention, and the reevaluations of later authors and publics expose the *conjointure* to the very critique that inspired *conjointure* itself. *Contes,* as romance, are still subject to the charge that they are *depecies* and *corronpus,* that the work's *status archetypus* is imperfectly apprehended or faultily expressed in its *status sensilis.* Scribal intervention or amplificatory *desjoindre* may be loudly decried or humbly accepted. *Conjointure* and *desjointure* realize romance through a process of topical adaptation set forth and studied in medieval poetics, authorized for Marie de France by Priscian and the *romans d'antiquité,* and for Chrétien by Macrobius.[50]

In the final analysis, it is the topical *reprise* that permits the coalescence of *matiere* and *san* in the romance, whether the narrative illustrates *conjointure* or *desjointure.* As romance emerged from chronicle sequences, the type illustrated by the principal figures began to stylize the adventures they encountered in the different narrative parts. Romances tended to show a sequence of recurring types in the midst of variety—*san* in *aventures merveilleuses;* such stylization held together even the divergent strands of interlacing prose romance—from the all-informing typology of the Fall to the specific patterns of sin, redemption, and virtue, or falling in love and love service, or chivalric self-assertion, in the lives and adventures of knights and ladies. Norris Lacy identified this system in Chrétien, and Rainer Warning implied its validity for romance in general.

Patterns in a variety of romances use *reprises* to fashion exemplary mirrors that communicate signification. The freedom from delimited *conjointure* they allowed may or may not have been perceived by Chrétien himself when he wrote the *Perceval;* in any case, the constant construction and deconstruction, illustrated in the careers of Perceval and Gauvain, used the *faille*[51]—quests that turn away and move off to the side of their goal. Jean Renart introduced the principle of narrative *glissement,* shifting the plot from one central figure and *san* to another.[52] And yet there are patterns that reflect, with the accuracy or distortion of mirrors, the fundamental search for meaning in diversity, for a topically valid identity. The history of that quest—the medieval romancers' quest—is the history of the emergence of romance with the techniques of a traditional art.

Notes

Bibliography

Index

Notes

Preface

1. See notably Taylor 1987.
2. Robertson 1962 p. 6.

Introduction

1. Nitze 1953 p. 74; cf. Nitze in Loomis 1959 p. 270.
2. Cf. Micha in Loomis 1959 p. 358–59.
3. Zink 1981; cf. D. Kelly 1969c.
4. Trimpi 1971 p. 3; cf. Curtius 1938 pp. 433–48; Poirion 1972 p. 10.
5. Cf. Naumann 1970 p. 23, especially n. 6 (p. 35).
6. Jauss *GRLMA* IV.1, 125–28.
7. Jauss *GRLMA* I, 110.
8. See Tyssens 1966 pp. 688–89; Stempel 1972; Ringger 1973 pp. 34–35; Uitti 1975; Stevens 1978; Grigsby 1980; Lacy 1980 p. 34–66; Scholz 1980 pp. 1–12; Pemberton 1984; Halász 1985; Baumgartner 1987b pp. 176–77; Krueger 1987; Taylor 1987 pp. 285–86, 287–92. But cf. Gallais 1988 p. 641.
9. *Paris* pp. 608.17–609.10, 618.10–619.3. Cf. Stempel 1972; Ringger 1973 pp. 34–35; Stevens 1978; Zink 1981 p. 22; Jonin 1982; Pemberton 1984; Baumgartner 1987b pp. 176–77; Krueger 1987; Taylor 1987 pp. 285–86, 287–92.
10. Ménard 1969 pp. 463–521. Cf. Moos *FIM* pp. 751–59.
11. Gallais 1964b pp. 479–81; Zumthor *GRLMA* I, 90. Cf. Warning *GRLMA* IV.1, 25–30; Uitti in D. Kelly 1985c pp. 199–204; T. Hunt 1988 pp. 126–29.
12. Leupin 1982b pp. 25–35; D. Kelly 1988c; Hult 1989 pp. 79–84. Cf. Schmale 1985 p. 113.
13. *FIM* 1988.
14. Hult 1986b p. 93.
15. Cf. Badel 1975 p. 83.
16. Cf. *Florimont* 1034–36; *Rigomer* 7757–58. A patron could "authorize" a romance; cf. *Escoufle* 9058–61.
17. Badel 1975 p. 89.
18. Halpersohn 1911 especially pp. 28–42; Brinkmann 1964a; T. Hunt 1970, 1972; Badel 1975 pp. 84–85 and 92–93; Zink 1981 pp. 3–4; Stempel *GRLMA* XI.1, 710–12.
19. See Maddox 1978 pp. 14–24.
20. Schmolke-Hasselmann 1980a pp. 21–25. Cf. Isidore of Seville's example as well as Zumthor 1955, especially pp. 175–78; Chenu 1957a; D. Kelly 1978a pp. 87–95; Scholz 1980.

21. *Didascalicon* p. 58.15–21; *Ars vers* 3.52, and 4.11 with 4.21–23, and A. E. Galyon, trans., pp. 13 and 117 n. 21; D. Kelly 1970b p. 199 n. 65.

22. *Ars vers* 4.14–16 and 20–26.

23. See below, pp. 41–42.

24. Foulet and Uitti 1981 p. 247.

25. Similarly, on *ordo*, see Hugh of Saint Victor, *Didascalicon* p. 58.6–15.

26. Ruch 1963; Nitze 1914 pp. 486–88; D. Kelly 1970b pp. 179–87; Bardon 1986.

27. Haidu 1973a pp. 54–55; Payen 1981 p. 281; Zink 1984.

28. B. Cerquiglini 1978 pp. 93–96.

29. Dronke 1974 p. 13; cf. Hardison 1976; Minnis 1984 pp. 1, 7–8; Hult 1986b pp. 93–94; Moos 1988 pp. xliv–xlv.

30. See Zumthor *GRLMA* I, 75.

31. As do Zumthor *GRLMA* I, 57–91; Warning *GRLMA* IV.1, 25–59; Méla 1984; Moos *FIM* p. 767 n. 83. Cf. also Zumthor 1973; Haidu 1977; Huchet 1990. Speech-act theory is used to evaluate authorial interventions by Schlieben-Lange *GRLMA* XI.1, 755–96.

32. See Pemberton 1984. Specimen illustrations are found in Ringger 1973 pp. 15–63; Taylor 1987 pp. 287–92.

33. *De vulg* I.x.2.13; see Ihle 1983 pp. 24–25.

34. Robertson 1951b pp. 670–71; D. Kelly 1970b p. 181.

35. Jauss *GRLMA* I, 110. Cf. Guenée 1982 pp. 3–4.

36. Voelker 1886; *GRLMA* I; *FEW* X, 452–53, 455; Köhler 1977 pp. 8–9; D. Kelly 1983c p. 406, and 1984c pp. 33–37. Examples of *roman* as language: *Alex* APar I.31; *Beaudous* 287; *Becket* 6174; *Brut* 13792; *Cesar* pp. 35 fol. 4v°, 36 fol. 5r°; *Conseil* 857; *Dolopathos* fr p. 4; *Engleis* 6437; *Espine* 6; *Espurgatoire* 3, 2299; *Fables* Ep. 2, 12; *Guil Palerne* 9659; *Joufroi* 2332; *Lais* Pro 30; *Meliador* 11679; *Meraugis* 4334; *Merlin* S p. 19 var. 4; *Octavian* 6; *Ovide mor* I.16; *Perlesvaus* 8866, 10189; *Protheselaus* 12711; *Rigomer* 4; *Rou* III.5298, 5300; *Silence* 1662; *Tristan* p. 1 MS 756/ Pro 4: "en françois"; *Troie* 37, 39; *Tyolet* 34. As "genre": *Atre* 6673; *Becket* 151, 161, 6161; *Bel inc* 4, 6247; *Brut* 3823, 14866; *Cesar* p. 35 fol. 4r°; *Charrette* 2, 7101; *Chev épée* 803; Didot *Perc* E 2675, D 1981; *Dolopathos* fr pp. 3 (but cf. n. 1), 65–66; *Eledus* 4353; *Elucidation* 2; *Escoufle* 9074; *Fergus* 7011; *Flamenca* 4477; *Florence* 20 and, in MS 24384, 705; *Joufroi* 4397; *Lycorne* 8543, 8548; *Manekine* 22; *Perceval* Cont I U 17118 var.; *Rigomer* 3, 8, 17, 6431; *Rose* 37; *Rou* III.153, 5311; *Sept sages* V 245; *Venjance* Nev 1936. In general, see Godefroy VII, 230–31; *T-L* VIII, 1438–44.

37. *GRLMA* I, 112; cf. Faral 1913 pp. 392, 418–19.

38. *GRLMA* I, 119; cf. Haug 1973; Wolf 1977, especially pp. 276–77, 282–83; Kay 1985; Zink 1987; Taylor 1987 pp. 325–26.

39. *GRLMA* I, 125.

40. Halpersohn 1911; Gallais 1964b; Baader 1966 pp. 11–73, 319–48; Mölk 1969 p. ix; Badel 1975; Schmolke-Hasselmann 1980a pp. 21–25; Gallais 1988 pp. 639–1011. Cf. P. J. Jones 1933; Gsteiger 1959; Naumann 1970 pp. 23–34; Haug 1985.

41. W. Foerster in *Cliges* F pp. xxi–xxvii.

42. Cf. *Ars vers* 1.110.

43. On my reading and translation, see D. Kelly 1983a pp. 14–16. Most scholars think Chrétien is referring here to Macrobius' *Commentum in Somnium Scipionis;* see most recently T. Hunt 1981a.

44. T. Hunt 1981a pp. 211–13; cf. Peron 1989 pp. 300–303.

Chapter 1. *Conjointure*

1. See Nitze 1914 pp. 486–88; Köhler 1962 pp. 14–15 and n. 37 (p. 231); Hart 1981b pp. 59–60.

2. See Godefroy II, 239; IV, 648–51; IX, 157–58; X, 46–47; *T-L* II, 695–96; IV, 1721–38; *FEW* II, 1053–55.

3. *Charrette* 7098–7112; *Yvain* 6804–8. Cf. Burgess 1984 pp. 9–12.

4. Cf. Topsfield 1981 p. 2.

5. *Eneas* II, p. 210 var.; *Estoire* II, 159–60/I.28.24–31, 476/I.133.25–27; *Meliacin* 530–36; *TChev* 1022 and 1034, 2560. Cf. also the *Iter* p. xlii.41–43. For *coagmentare* in this sense in Late Latin, see J. E. Sandys, ed., in *Orator* pp. 87–88n.

6. *Rose* 1213–15/1211–13. See also Godefroy IV, 649; *T-L* IV, 1731.17–36 and 42–46; *FEW* V, 68. Cf. Knapp 1972. On *beau,* see Bruyne 1946 passim s.v. *beau, beauté,* etc.; Ducháček 1976; Matoré 1980.

7. *Genèse* B 128–37 (p. 64).

8. *Athis* MS C 3603–12; *Eneas* II, pp. 241–42 var.; *Flamenca* 4510–14; *Genèse* A 566–84 (pp. 41–42).

9. D. Kelly 1969c pp. 126–27; cf. Hart 1981b pp. 80–81 and n. 55 (p. 86); *Eneas* II, p. 210 var.

10. See above, p. 16.

11. Prose *Estoire* II, 430/I.115.26 [naturelement conjoindre]. Cf. Freeman 1979 pp. 128–34.

12. Godefroy IV, 651; see Laurie 1984.

13. Hart 1981a, 1981b. Cf. Uitti 1981.

14. Loomis 1949 pp. 68–103; D. Kelly 1970b pp. 195–98; Luttrell 1974 pp. 159–71.

15. Loomis 1949 pp. 290–93; Frappier 1968a pp. 155–56; Frappier 1969 pp. 85–106.

16. *Eneas* II, pp. 241–42 var.; *Troie* V, p. 152 (s.v. *desjoindre*).

17. *FEW* III, pp. 96–97; Godefroy II, p. 602; *T-L* II, p. 1625. Cf. Leupin 1982a.

18. D. Kelly 1984b, 1985a.

19. Cf. *Flamenca* 4857–62; *Guil maréchal* 14824–28. For an example involving syntax, see *Chron rim* 9702–5.

20. D. Kelly 1970b pp. 180–81. Cf. Gallais 1988 pp. 733–34.

21. *Tristan* Th D835–84; cf. D. Kelly 1969a p. 11. Similarly *Troie* 42–44.

22. Loomis 1949 pp. 38–58 is a useful introductory survey of these processes; see also Duggan *GRLMA* XI.1, 297.

23. Cf. Lausberg 1960 §292. On *texere* cf. *Dialogus* ll. 789–90. William of Malmesbury uses *texere* (§§I.1, 120), *sarcire* (§I.2), *intexere* (§§I.5, 112), *retexere* (§II.465), etc. For *interponere* see *ThLL* VII.i.2246.71–2247.52.

24. D. Kelly 1984b pp. 126–35.

25. See also *Lancelot* VIII.liva.17; cf. *Lancelot* K pp. 571.25–31 and 365.35–366.3, respectively.

26. Cf. Chrétien's description of the tree graft in *Cligés* 6317–21, 6325–29.

27. D. Kelly 1983c pp. 410–11.

28. On these terms see Lausberg 1960 §324 (1); cf. §854.

29. Cf. Brugger 1941 (1943) pp. 126–28.

30. Cf. *Cligés* 18–23.

31. *Didascalicon* p. 16.12. See D. Kelly 1984b p. 134.

32. Ruch 1963 pp. 254–55; see the fundamental discussion of the term in Vinaver 1970a pp. 105–28.

33. Cf. Nitze 1954 p. 181. Cf. in general *ThLL* VII.ii.649.80–651.83, 656.5–73, and s.v. *coniunctio* IV.327.57–328.39 and *coniungere* IV.335.43–336.25.

34. Cf. Brink 1963 II, 135–37.

35. Ruch 1963 p. 255.

36. See Rostagni 1930 p. 14.

37. *Comm* Hor IV, 458.33, 457.23.

38. Ruch 1963 pp. 254–55.

39. *Porphyry* 346.20–21; also in the *Pseudo-Acron* II, 316.10–19; *Comm* Hor I, 426.6, IV, 460.1–2. On "sentence" in antiquity and the Middle Ages, see Charpin 1988.

40. *Accessus* Prudentii pp. 19.5–7, 20.5–7, Homeri p. 25.6–7, etc. See D. Kelly 1970b pp. 184–85.

41. *Pseudo-Acron* II, 350.13–15; cf. *Comm* Hor IV, 459.32–460.4. See Nitze 1954; Quadlbauer 1962 §§30c, 37a, 37a3, 37c2–3; D. Kelly 1970b pp. 182–83.

42. *Metalogicon* p. 56.12–14. See Bolgar 1954 pp. 196, 417–18; Freeman 1976 pp. 158–59.

43. Robertson 1951b pp. 684–86; Nitze 1954.

44. Cf. Ollier 1974d pp. 221–22; Méla 1984 p. 16.

45. *Comm* Utrecht p. 64.155–59.

46. *Didascalicon* p. 125.15–17.

47. Anitchkof 1929 p. 192.

48. Cf. Lausberg 1960 §923.

49. *Comm* Hor IV, 472.29–73.3; emphasis mine.

50. Latham p. 150 s.v. *disjunctura*. On *iunctura acer* see Bardon 1986.

51. *L-S* pp. 590–91; *ThLL* V.i.1384.66–1385.2, 1387.3–42, 1388.84–1389.7.

52. D. Kelly 1970b pp. 185–86; D. Kelly 1984b. Cf. Marti 1941 pp. 248–49.

53. T. Hunt 1972 pp. 338–39 n. 14; but cf. D. Kelly 1978c p. 243 n. 39.

54. Cf. *Ad Pisones* 1–37; *Scholia* pp. 1.30–2.22; *Dialogus* ll. 1268–85, 1289–93, 1295–1315.

55. Cf. *De. planctu* VIII.213–23. See also D. Kelly 1970b pp. 181–82; J. Cerquiglini 1978.

56. Nitze 1953 pp. 76–79; Maddox 1978 pp. 29–30; Frappier *GRLMA* IV.1, 203.

57. On this commonplace, see below, pp. 41–42.

58. Cf. Ruch 1963 pp. 251–52.

59. Cf. *Alex* APar I.41. On such parataxis, see Vàrvaro 1963.

60. D. Kelly 1969a pp. 9–13.

61. See Köhler 1962 pp. 12–13.

62. Cf. above, pp. 24–25, from *Poetria nova* 843. Cf. Ruch 1963 pp. 255–56, 260–67; Hart 1981b pp. 66–67.

63. Cf. Köhler 1970 pp. 100–108; Payen 1964 pp. 574–75.

64. Cf. *Rigomer* 6429–34.

65. Lods 1974 p. 356; Ménard 1979 pp. 59–68.

66. Köhler 1962 pp. 14–15.

67. Nitze 1914 p. 455 n. 2; D. Kelly 1970b pp. 187–89. See *Alex* APar I.1, 30, 42, 57, 144, 3073; II.383, 1292, 3100; IV. 1698; *Cassidorus* §§35, 45; *Dole* 1334, 3179, 3196, 4126, 4142, 4586, 4595, 4652, 5229; *Eneas* 8432; *Engleis* 6486, 6504; *Flamenca* 7080; *Florence* 2097, 5041; *Guil maréchal* 3719, 18569, 18572; *Laurin* 7407, 7414, 7417, 14445–50, 14468; *Meliacin* 4911–12, 5078–79; *Parfait* 45, 987, 3905; *Partonopeu* Cont 1467; *Poire* 905; *Prise* 1229, 1250; *Restor* 2636; *Rou* II.3; *Silence* 2, 15; *Vengement* 48, 53–54, 1793; *Venjance* Nev 38, 43–44; *Venjance* (2) 35, 40, 43.

68. D. Kelly 1970b pp. 188–89, 1978b pp. 143–48.

69. Cf. *TChev* 26, 443, 1320, 6642–44, 6665, 6959, 6987 (part of a letter); *Violette* 6163–65, 6242–44. See Faral 1910 p. 319 (§242); D. Kelly 1970b pp. 187–98.

70. Vinaver 1970b; Baumgartner 1987b pp. 179–80. On the amalgam of the *Charrette* and *Yvain,* see Sargent-Baur 1987a and 1987b.

71. *Alex* APar III.15; *Beaudous* 284–90; *Cassidorus* §205; *Claris* 3; *Cleomadés* 93; *Cligés* 22; *Dolopathos* fr pp. 3–4, 65–66; *Escoufle* 36–37; *Florimont* 33–39, 9207–16; *Guil Palerne* 9659; *Guiron* Pro 338, pp. 176–77; Huth *Merlin* II, 57–58; *Lais* Pro 15–16, 30; *Lancelot* lxxxiv.72; *Silence* 1667; *Sone* Epistle p. 552.19; *Tyolet* 29–34.

72. *Alex* APar III.15; *Beaudous* 286–89; *Dolopathos* fr pp. 4, 65–66; *Guiron* Pro 338, p. 179; *Joufroi* 2330–32; *Lais* Pro 30; *Perlesvaus* ll. 8866, 10188–89; *Pierre* p. 1.7–8; *Rou* III.5297–5300; *Troie* 35–37, 139–44, 30303–4.

73. Cf. *Beaudous* 283–89.

74. Cf. Bogdanow 1966 pp. 121–22; Frappier *GRLMA* IV.1, 292, 316–17. See *Guiron* Pro 338 pp. 176–80.

75. *Fergus* 7004–11; *Guil Palerne* 9652; *Joufroi* 4397; *Perceval* Cont IV.6987; *Poire* 1609.

76. Ruch 1963 p. 253.

77. Van Coolput 1987a.

78. Ruch 1963 p. 253.

Chapter 2. Antecedent Paradigms of Invention: Literary Paradigm

1. See especially Faral 1924 pp. 99–103; Brinkmann 1928 pp. 29–81; Bruyne 1946 II, 14–49; Curtius 1954 pp. 481–85; Bagni 1968 pp. 19–32; Gallo 1971; Klopsch 1980; D. Kelly 1991 pp. 47–50.

2. Boesch 1936 p. 21; McKeon 1942 pp. 28–29; McKeon 1946; Bruyne 1946

I, 46, 224; Delhaye 1958 pp. 67–71; Wolter 1959 pp. 64–80; Bagni 1968 pp. 23–32;
T. Hunt 1970; Scaglione 1970 pp. 37–38; Zumthor *GRLMA* I, 57–91; Trimpi 1971
p. 3; Knapp 1973 pp. 443–50; Gössmann 1974 p. 85; D. Kelly 1991 pp. 47–57.

    3. Mariétan 1901, especially pp. 124–94; Bagni 1968 pp. 32–45; Ward 1972;
Dahan 1980 pp. 175–85; Klopsch 1980 pp. 94–100; H.-W. Goetz in Schmale 1985
pp. 167–79.

    4. Gregory 1955 pp. 247–78; Delhaye 1958 pp. 67–71; Ward 1972 pp. 249–50,
258; Dronke 1973 pp. 319–20.

    5. See in general Bruyne 1946 II, 146–72; Wetherbee 1969 pp. 91–99; Knapp
1980 pp. 587–89; Minnis 1984 pp. 139–45.

    6. See *Accessus* pp. 51.40–46; *Dialogus* ll. 549–64; *Didascalicon* p. 54.10–21
(Hugh ranks history with poetry; see Wolter 1959 pp. 61–62); *Comm Aen* pp.
2.15–3.3. Bruyne 1946 II, 206–76; McKeon 1946; Green 1967 p. 6; Bagni 1968 pp.
32–42, 155–57; Wetherbee 1972 pp. 144–51; Gompf 1973; Knapp 1973 pp. 445–47;
Gössmann 1974 p. 85–92; Wetherbee 1976 pp. 56–57; Gallo 1978 p. 76; Lubienski-
Bodenham 1979; Klopsch 1980 pp. 66–71, 94–100; Lynch 1988 pp. 108–12.

    7. Faral 1924 pp. 99–101; Klopsch 1980 p. 154 n. 205; Wetherbee 1972; D.
Kelly 1991 pp. 61–62. That Alain may have criticized Gautier and Joseph does not
alter the validity of this statement; see below, pp. 40–41, 60–61.

    8. Faral 1924 p. 101; Salmon 1963; Bagni 1968 pp. 24–28, and cf. pp. 91 and
112–13; Klopsch 1980 p. 121.

    9. Faral 1924 p. xi n. 1; Brinkmann 1928.

    10. Reichel 1909; Faral 1936; Trimpi 1974 pp. 61–62, 75–81; B. Harbert in
Anth; Faulhaber 1978 p. 106. On commentaries see Hélin 1951; *CTC;* Ward 1978;
R. J. Hexter 1986; on florilegia see Rouse 1979; and Martin 1979 on John of Salis-
bury's personal collection.

    11. McKeon 1946 p. 231. Cf. Caplan 1970 pp. 165–66; T. Hunt 1970 pp. 8–15.

    12. D. Kelly 1966a pp. 270–76; Dronke 1973.

    13. See R. W. Hunt 1948; Klopsch 1980 pp. 48–64; G. Przychocki in *Accessus
Ov;* Allen 1982; Minnis 1984. On the importance of the *accessus* in the twelfth century, see Quain 1945; Quain traces them back to the philosophers, but that does
not preclude the influence of the schools in the interim (p. 263).

    14. Bruyne 1946 I, 304–5; Silverstein 1948 p. 97–98, especially n. 34; Dronke
1974 pp. 32–47; Wetherbee 1976; D. Kelly 1978a pp. 26–56; Lynch 1988 (with
additional bibliography).

    15. R. W. Hunt 1948 pp. 98–100; Lausberg 1960 §§1–11; Bagni 1968 pp.
48–51; Zumthor *GRLMA* I, 59.

    16. Ward 1972; Allen 1973, 1982; M. C. Woods 1986.

    17. Boesch 1936 pp. 13–15; Marti 1941; Hélin 1951 pp. 410–12; Bagni 1968
pp. 127–30; Ward 1972 pp. 247–61.

    18. See Bolgar 1954 pp. 196–200.

    19. Cf. *Partonopeu* 77–134.

    20. See Salmon 1963 pp. 74–78; Vinaver 1964 pp. 490–95; Leff 1983 p. 34;
D. Kelly 1991 pp. 85–88.

    21. On this passage, see L. Gompf in *Ylias* p. 14.

22. *Ars poet* pp. 3–4. See Salmon 1963 pp. 75–76; Caplan 1970 pp. 261–62. On the identification of these works, see L. Gompf ed. of *Ylias* p. 14.

23. *Ars poet* p. 1.9–11. Cf. Liebeschütz 1926 pp. 134–35; D. Kelly 1991 pp. 61–64.

24. Because of its eloquence. See *Cosmographia* I.iii.474.

25. Liebeschütz 1926 p. 139.

26. Examples in *Accessus; Dialogus*. See in general R. W. Hunt 1948; Allen 1982 pp. 5–10; Minnis 1984 pp. 15–33.

27. On "plot-outline" and invention, see Trimpi 1971 pp. 33–34, 43–48.

28. Cf. Trimpi 1974 p. 25: "form *(vis)* and matter *(materia)* are combined in a 'quality' *(corpus)*." Cf. *Dialogus* p. 25.426–33.

29. On *compendium* as the work reduced to its essentials *(brevitas)*, or "quality" as *corpus*, see Quadlbauer 1977 p. 71 and n. 12.

30. *Comm* Utrecht p. 67.212; *Dialogus* ll. 222–23; cf. *Etymologiae* XIX.xix.4. The idea is implicit in *Ad Her* II.xxii. See also Bruyne 1946 II, 148 *(mater verborum)*; Dronke 1973 p. 325.

31. *Parisiana Poetria* 2.1–14. See also Bruyne 1946 II, 18–23.

32. *Accessus* pp. 43.106–7 and 39.1–43.106. Cf. p. 26.11–13, 30.5–6 *(De Ponto)*, 35.5–6 *(Tristium)*, 36.11; and *Comm* Utrecht p. 67.211–23.

33. Cf. D. Kelly 1983b pp. 114–17. For similar examples in the *vitae vergilianae*, see *Vitae*.

34. *Dialogus* ll. 426–29, 581–85 (cf. "quaedam"), 645–53, 759–62. Cf. *ThLL* VIII.448.61–63.

35. See also Quadlbauer 1977 pp. 91–92, especially n. 46. For the invention of words, see R. W. Hunt 1943 pp. 211–14.

36. Cf. *Accessus* p. 19.12–13; R. W. Hunt 1948 p. 94 n. 1; Wolter 1959 pp. 73–74; Zumthor *GRLMA* IV.1, 72; Stump 1978 pp. 79, 151–52.

37. See Stump 1978 pp. 17, 237–61. Cf. Ward 1972 pp. 248–49, 258, 271.

38. Marti 1941 pp. 250–51.

39. Demats 1970 p. 217; cf. Tuve 1966 pp. 18–22.

40. See Lausberg 1960 §292. Cf. Macrobius in Dronke 1974 p. 71.

41. On the terminology see Lausberg 1960 §§66–138; Trimpi 1974 pp. 65–67.

42. Cf. *Dialogus* ll. 700–703.

43. Trimpi 1974 pp. 80–81.

44. Bagni 1968 pp. 51–53; D. Kelly 1969c pp. 119–30; Dronke 1973 pp. 327–29; Dronke 1974 pp. 72–73; Hardison 1976 p. 7; Haidu 1977; D. Kelly 1978a pp. 29–45; D. Kelly 1991 pp. 64–68. On Geoffrey of Vinsauf's importance, see Gallo 1978 p. 69.

45. Dronke 1973 p. 337.

46. Matthew of Vendôme expresses this in several ways and for different stages in composition *(Ars vers* 3.49–52); see Bruyne 1946 II, 31–33; D. Kelly 1991 pp. 66–67.

47. Steinen 1966 p. 335. See also Bruyne 1946 II, 59, 62. Cf. *Cosmographia* I.ii; *De planctu* VIII.199–246; *Alda* 387–92, 407–8. See Nims 1974 pp. 216, 220–21; Trimpi 1974 p. 55 n. 65; Faulhaber 1978 pp. 98–99; Klopsch 1980 pp. 128–29.

48. See Brinkmann 1928 pp. 8–10; Boesch 1936 p. 24 n. 68; Bruyne 1946 I,

142–43, and II, 75–92; Curtius 1954 pp. 527–29; Lubac 1959 II.ii.41–60; Dronke 1973 pp. 327–28; J. B. Friedman 1974; Ward 1979 pp. 71–72. See as well the fine appreciation in Frappier 1968b pp. 142–44, 433–34. For examples, see *Dialogus* ll. 300–302, 320–21; *Didascalicon* pp. 113.18–21; 116.18–25, 118.8–19.8, 119.24–20.3; *Summa* pp. 26, 65; *Dictier* p. 267.

49. Cf. also *Documentum* II.3.1–3. On this notion, derived from Chartrain speculation on creation and invention, see Bruyne 1946 II, 38–39, 40–41; Gregory 1955 pp. 68–97; Nims 1974 pp. 225–26; Wetherbee 1976 pp. 46–49, 58. Cf. Haug 1978 pp. 68–69.

50. D. Kelly 1991 p. 37 n. 2.

51. *Cosmographia* I.ii.1. Cf. in general Liebeschütz 1926; Bruyne 1946 II, 263–79; Silverstein 1948 p. 104–14; Gregory 1955 pp. 100, 175.

52. See Green 1956 pp. 663–64; Green 1967 pp. 7–9. Cf. *Rose* 16005–64 / 15975–16034.

53. Cf. *Cosmographia* I.ii.1.10–17. Cf. Pickens 1984 p. 496; Baumgartner 1986 pp. 12–13 on *reconter*.

54. Curtius 1954 pp. 467–68; Gompf 1973 pp. 54–55; cf. D. Kelly 1988c; Langer 1990, especially ch.3.

55. See *De planctu* XVIII.68–91; *Alexandreis* X.6–167; *Architrenius* I.234–47. Cf. Wetherbee 1969 p. 115.

56. McKeon 1946 p. 224; Curtius 1954 pp. 210–20; Jordan 1967 pp. 33–34; Wetherbee 1972 pp. 66–73, 243–44.

57. Cf. *De planctu* VIII.124–246. See Cilento 1961 pp. 255–56, 276.

58. On *imitatio* as projection, see McKeon 1936; Ghellinck 1941; Botte 1942; Bruyne 1946 II, 280–301; Wolter 1959 pp. 72–73; D. Kelly 1978a pp. 30–31; Bruns 1980 p. 116.

59. On mental and physical *materia* (commonly distinguished as *materia / materies* or vice versa), see *ThLL* s.v. *Materia/materies*, VIII.448.61–81 et seq; *NGML* s.v *materia* cols. 250–53; Godefroy X, 132; *T-L* V, 1256–61; *FEW* VI, 481–84. Cf. Yates 1966; Caplan 1970 especially pp. 228–31, 239–40; Trimpi 1971 p. 26; Nims 1974 p. 221; Wetherbee 1976 pp. 46–47; D. Kelly 1978a pp. 30–33.

60. *Summa* pp. 66–67. Cf. *Parisiana Poetria* ch. 2; and Laugesen 1962 pp. 251–57.

61. Cf. Trimpi 1974 pp. 51–61, on "analysis" and "synthesis" in invention.

62. Bruyne 1946 II, 59; cf. also II, 22; Du Cange IV, 320 s.v. *materiatus* (1): "opus quodvis arte elaboratum," with an example from Hugh of Saint Victor. For other examples, see *Accessus* pp. 25.1–26.10; *Perceval* Cont III 33120–24.

63. Bruyne 1946 II, 38–39.

64. Ghellinck 1941. Cf. Keen 1973 pp. 309–10.

65. See the *Anticlaudianus* I.154–70; and Manitius 1931 pp. 923–24; Raynaud de Lage 1951 pp. 20–23; Cilento 1961 pp. 245, 270.

66. See *Ars vers* 4.1–48. cf. D. Kelly 1991 pp. 50–52.

67. Bolgar 1954 pp. 196–97; Trimpi 1974 pp. 61–65, and cf. pp. 54–57; D. Kelly 1983a pp. 11–13.

68. *Summa* pp. 66–67; cf. W. Kronbichler, ed., *Summa* pp. 14–15.

69. Cf. *Poetria nova:* "longum succingere thema" (702). See also Du Cange IV, 320: "materialia themata."

70. Cf. Brinkmann 1928 pp. 46–47; Bruyne 1946 II, 20–21. For an example, see J. Stohlmann in *Hist troy* pp. 20–76.

71. *Dialogus* ll. 222–26. See above, p. 31, on Horace's *abdita rerum.*

72. E.g., *Accessus* pp. 29.12–14, 31.9–17.

73. Quadlbauer 1962 §37a3; cf. §§37a in general and 44o1; Bagni 1968 p. 132; D. Kelly 1991 pp. 65–67.

74. See *Poetria nova* 720–30, 1681–85, 1761–63; *Documentum* II.2.45–70. Gallo 1978 pp. 73–76.

75. Cilento 1961 p. 256. Cf. Green 1956 p. 670; D. Kelly 1983b pp. 114–25.

76. See Charland 1936 pp. 109–226; Gilson 1932 pp. 93–154; Caplan 1970 pp. 57–60; Jaffe 1974 pp. 44–45; Zink 1976 pp. 221–61; Jennings 1978.

77. Bruyne 1946 II, 256.

78. *Glosae* §174.

79. Quadlbauer 1962 §§37a, 37a3, 37c2–3; Scaglione 1972 p. 97; D. Kelly 1970b; Vance 1972; Dronke 1973 pp. 327–37; Freeman 1979 pp. 11–12.

80. Lausberg 1960 §§950–53.

81. Cf. Hardison 1976 pp. 6–7.

82. Cf. Bagni 1968 p. 70 n. 10; D. Kelly 1991 p. 38.

83. Stock 1972 p. 14. Cf. Quain 1945 pp. 225–26; Silverstein 1948 p. 95; Green 1956 pp. 651–52; Wetherbee 1972 pp. 36–37; Dronke 1974.

84. Dronke 1974 pp. 119–43. Cf. Steinen 1966 pp. 373–83; Wetherbee 1972 pp. 162–86.

85. See Harich 1987, especially pp. 234–36. Cf. Brinkmann 1964b pp. 421–23. A similar model appears in *Athis;* see E. Baumgartner 1988b pp. 6–11.

86. Stock 1972 pp. 20–21.

87. Rohr 1962. Cf. Batany 1970; Trimpi 1974 pp. 51–55; Nims 1974 pp. 218–20. Cf. Benjamin 1972 pp. 28–29.

88. Harich 1987 pp. 158–61.

89. Harich 1987 pp. 220–22.

90. D. Kelly 1969c pp. 127–30; Klopsch 1980 p. 94.

91. Cf. Quadlbauer 1986; for similar amplifications in Bernardus Silvestris' *Mathematicus,* see Liebeschütz 1926 pp. 142–43.

92. Cf. *Comm* Utrecht p. 68.253–54 on *continuationes,* and above, pp. 22–24.

93. Jeauneau 1957.

94. H. Caplan, ed., *Ad Her* p. 32 n. *c.*

95. Riposati 1947 pp. 234–63; Trimpi 1971 pp. 25–27.

96. See in general Trimpi 1974 pp. 5–14, and cf. p. 34 (including n. 42).

97. Trimpi 1974 p. 15; cf. also pp. 106–10; and Melville *GRLMA* XI.1, 207–27.

98. Jordan 1967 p. 37.

99. Lausberg 1960 §§263–81.

100. *De inv* I.xix.27; *Ad Her* I.viii.12–13; Barwick 1928; Lausberg 1960 §§289–92; Stump 1978 p. 151 n. 69.

101. Riposati 1947 pp. 39–40.

102. Faral 1924 pp. 48–54, 86–98; Lausberg 1960 §290; Bornscheuer 1976 pp. 170–71.

103. Knapp 1973 p. 468–69. Cf. Bruyne 1946 II, 32–33; D. Kelly 1983b p. 104.

104. Cf. Marti 1941 pp. 251–52.

105. McKeon 1942 pp. 28–29; Caplan 1970 pp. 79–104; Kleinschmidt 1974 pp. 11–26.

106. Vinaver 1964 pp. 487–97; Leff 1983 pp. 33–34.

107. Bruyne 1946 II, 239; cf. *Poetria nova* 1842–52. Instruction by example loomed large in medieval critical evaluation; see Marti 1941 pp. 250–52; Bruyne 1946 II, 281–82; D. Kelly 1991 p. 41.

108. For background, see Faral 1924 pp. 61–85; Trimpi 1974 pp. 20–23.

109. *FEW* III, 255; Godefroy IX, 577 (not in *T-L*). Cf. Huguet III, 758–59: "exprimer, dire," "s'exprimer." On what follows, see D. Kelly 1986 pp. 108–10.

110. *ThLL* V.ii.1145–49; Blaise p. 320; Souter p. 132; Lausberg 1960 §§409 and 438. Cf. Bruyne 1946 II, 33–35.

111. *Praeexercitamina* §16 VI (p. 434). In *ThLL* V.ii.1146.34–35, from *rhet* 6, 16 p. 555, 2.

112. Cf. Trimpi 1974 p. 77; Stump 1978 pp. 15–26. On this terminology, see D. Kelly 1991 pp. 73–74.

113. Bagni 1968 p. 60. Cf. *Epistolae* §23 (p. 12).

114. Vinaver 1964 p. 488. Cf. Trimpi 1974 pp. 45–46.

115. Vinaver 1964 p. 488. Cf. Ohly 1958; Caplan 1970 pp. 121–22; Guiette 1978 pp. 29–56.

116. McKeon 1942 p. 28 n. 2; Yates 1966 especially pp. 1–104; Caplan 1970 pp. 83, 196–246; Evans 1971 especially pp. 266–69.

117. *Ars vers* 3.52. Yates 1966 pp. 30–31; D. Kelly 1978a p. 32. Cf. Vance 1973 pp. 5–13.

118. See Yates 1966 pp. 9–10.

119. Yates 1966 p. 11. Cf. Caplan 1970 pp. 207–8. On Aristotle's original intention with memory, see Bornscheuer 1976 pp. 52–60; Stump 1978 p. 16.

120. Vance 1972 p. 554; cf. especially pp. 546–48.

121. Faral 1924 pp. 77–79; Gallo 1974 pp. 53–58.

122. Manitius 1931 pp. 740–41, 742; Solmson 1941 pp. 48–50; McKeon 1942 pp. 28–29; Leff 1978; Quadlbauer 1986.

123. Müller 1981 pp. 2–6; D. Kelly 1983b p. 104 n. 12. Cf. Thoss 1972 p. 32–34.

124. Thoss 1972.

125. Curtius 1954 pp. 89–115.

126. Valesio 1980 pp. 37–38.

127. Trimpi 1974 p. 65; D. Kelly 1978a pp. 71–73; D. Kelly 1983b pp. 107–13.

128. Quadlbauer 1962, 1984. See also Faral 1924 pp. 86–89; Bruyne 1946 II, 41–43.

129. Laugesen 1962; D. Kelly 1991 p. 71.

130. Lausberg 1960 §§1078–79; Quadlbauer 1962 §§1–3.

131. Curtius 1954 pp. 80–82.

132. Auerbach 1958 pp. 25–53. Cf. Jauss *GRLMA* I, 131–34.

133. Caplan 1970 pp. 80–82, 119–20.

134. Quadlbauer 1962 §§46b–d; cf. §87j. See also Laugesen 1962 pp. 270–71; Kleinschmidt 1974 pp. 14–18; D. Kelly 1978c p. 237. Cf. Kurdziałek 1971 pp. 66–67; Corti 1978.

135. Trimpi 1974 pp. 64–75. Cf. Quadlbauer 1962 §44g.

136. Bruyne 1946 II, 239.

137. Quadlbauer 1962 §44g.

138. Trimpi 1974 p. 67; cf. Trimpi 1973 p. 28.

139. *Parisiana poetria* 2.87–123; cf. also 1.122–34. On the relation between memory and topoi, see Laugesen 1962 p. 251–52; Yates 1966 p. 31; Evans 1971.

140. Cf. Trimpi 1974 p. 65.

141. Duby 1978a and 1978b. See Haidu 1984.

142. Bruyne 1946 II, 31–35, 245–46; Quadlbauer 1962 §§37a, 56f; Trimpi 1974.

143. Laugesen 1962 pp. 270–71; cf. Quadlbauer 1962 §§32–35.

144. Caplan 1970 p. 83; see *Parisiana Poetria* 2.90–123.

145. The word appears in *Ars vers* 1.31; see Quadlbauer 1962 §37c.

146. Quadlbauer 1962 §§25e, 37c2, 44l–n. Cf. Matthew's definition of verse *Ars vers* 1.1.

147. Bruyne 1946 II, 273; cf. Trimpi 1971 p. 5. On *aequitas* and description, see Trimpi 1974 pp. 67–69; Quadlbauer 1962 §25o n. 41.

148. Vitz 1975; Marshall 1979; D. Kelly 1980.

149. On its origins in panegyric, see Bezzola 1944 II, 239; Kleinschmidt 1974.

150. On *electio,* see *Parisiana Poetria* ch. 2.

151. Cf. *Documentum* II.3.48–101. Determination is by modifiers; see Gallo 1978 pp. 71–72.

152. Faral 1924 pp. 63–67; D. Kelly 1978a pp. 43–44.

153. Gallo 1978 pp. 79–81; D. Kelly 1983b pp. 107–13. This is true when dealing with *negotia* as well; see Bagni 1968 pp. 71–72, 73.

154. Marti 1941 p. 253; Bagni 1968 pp. 37–38; Dronke 1973 pp. 317–18; Nims 1974 pp. 223–24.

155. Vinaver 1964 p. 493; cf. Quain 1945 pp. 225–26; Trimpi 1971 pp. 21–27; Trimpi 1974 pp. 5–40.

156. Klinck 1970 p. 8.

157. Faral 1924 pp. 65–67. See Klinck 1970 pp. 10–40 on the meanings of *interpretatio.*

158. On these lines, see Wetherbee 1969 pp. 114–18.

159. Vinaver 1964 p. 489. For historical background, see Trimpi 1974 pp. 52–61, 65–66.

160. Rohr 1962; Tuve 1966 pp. 21–22; D. Kelly 1978a pp. 82–84, 87–95.

161. *Ars vers* 3.52. Cf. Benjamin 1963 pp. 14–22.

162. Klopsch 1980 p. 159; D. Kelly 1983b p. 104. Cf. Knapp 1975 p. 60.

163. D. Kelly 1966a and 1991 pp. 38–39.

164. *Ars vers* §§1.65, 67, and 3.50. Cf. Trimpi 1974 pp. 61–75; Gallo 1978 pp. 80–83. On the emergence of these terms, see Quadlbauer 1962 §44r–v; Mölk 1968 pp. 177–99.

165. Gregory 1955 pp. 213–14; Cilento 1961 p. 264; Brinkmann 1964b p. 424; Stock 1972 pp. 126–27; Scaglione 1980.

166. Vinaver 1970a pp. 49–149.

167. See below, pp. 282–90; on ornament, Gallo 1971 pp. 150–66.

168. Picone 1982 pp. 2–6; Ihle 1983.

169. D. Kelly 1991 pp. 43–44, 50–52.

170. Trimpi 1974 pp. 73–81.

171. Dronke 1974 pp. 126–27.

172. *Poetria nova* 1796, 1825, 1831; cf. *Laborintus* 597–686; *De vulg* II.vi.7. See Faral 1924 pp. 101–3, and the examples pp. 61–98; Curtius 1954 pp. 158–64; Klopsch 1980 p. 158 n. 218.

173. See M. C. Woods 1986.

174. *Ars vers* 4.3–5. Cf. Harich 1987 pp. 8, 253.

175. Cf. L. J. Friedman 1965 pp. 170–71.

176. Cf. Stock 1972 pp. 36–61.

177. Brink 1963 II, 94–101.

178. See M. C. Woods 1986; D. Kelly 1984d pp. 174, 179–82.

179. Brinkmann 1971 pp. 322–24; Stock 1972 pp. 44–45; Demats 1973 pp. 19–20; Dronke 1974 p. 21.

180. Gompf 1973 pp. 55–59.

181. Lacy 1980 pp. 109–10; emphasis Lacy's.

182. Trimpi 1971 p. 55; cf. *Dialogus* ll. 645–53.

183. See Quadlbauer 1977 pp. 83–86.

184. Lausberg 1960 §§950–53. Cf. Faulhaber 1978 pp. 99–101.

185. See Quadlbauer 1977.

186. *Scholia* p. 5. See also *Comm* Serv II, 4.89–5.96; *Comm* Utrecht ll. 148–60; *Dialogus* ll. 191–200.

187. *Comm Aen* pp. 1.15–2.10; cf. Gallo 1978 pp. 74–76; Minnis 1984 pp. 150–53.

188. *Comm Aen* p. 3.9–11.

189. Stock 1972 p. 231.

190. Dronke 1973 p. 333–"imaginatively" in the medieval sense of artistic imagination (pp. 329–30).

191. See Liebeschütz 1926, especially pp. 110–11.

192. Cf. *Ars vers* 4.1.

193. Tuve 1966 p. 22.

194. See *Ducs* 207–63; *Troie* 23191–214. Cf. Tattersall 1981.

195. D. Kelly 1991 p. 95. Cf. Baumgartner 1987c pp. 45–46.

196. Benjamin 1963 p. 16.

Chapter 3. Antecedent Paradigms of Invention: Historiographic Paradigm

1. Faral 1913; Faral 1924 passim in Introduction; Brinkmann 1928; Vinaver 1964; Colby 1965.

2. Jauss 1977b pp. 329–30. Cf. Poirion 1978 pp. 219–24; Poirion 1986b.
3. Cf. Southworth 1973 p. 166.
4. Zumthor *GRLMA* IV.1, 70; Zink 1984.
5. Jauss *GRLMA* I, 125–29; Zink 1981 p. 4.
6. Köhler 1976 pp. 321–22; Frappier *GRLMA* I, 148. Cf. Raible 1972 especially pp. 135–38.
7. See Köhler 1970; Duby 1978b pp. 363–70.
8. But not "Latin romance"; cf. Knapp 1980 pp. 627–28.
9. Moos 1976.
10. Zumthor *FEW* IX, 122–23.
11. Gallais 1971a p. 71; Zumthor 1985 p. 12.
12. See, e.g., *T-L* VIII especially 1441.8–22; *FEW* X, 453 and 455.
13. J. Gildea, ed., in *Durmart* II, 29–30; cf. by contrast the observations of Lewis 1964 pp. 208–15; Ruhe 1985.
14. See Boesch 1936 pp. 75–80; Lofmark 1972a. For Spanish romance see Gumbrecht 1974; Deyermond 1975 pp. 238–39.
15. See Loomis 1949 pp. 22–24; Loomis 1959 pp. 57–60; Lacroix 1971 pp. 50–57; Busby 1987 pp. 57–63.
16. Cf. Loomis 1959 p. 59 and n. 1; Lacroix 1971 pp. 45–49. *Melusine* JdA p. 14.1–2 and *Ombre* 390–91 cite an oral report.
17. See Loomis 1949 p. 22. On the hostility toward jongleurs among historians, see Spörl 1935 pp. 57–58. But cf. as well Duggan *GRLMA* XI.1, 304–7.
18. See *Rou* II.1354–73, and III.6367–98. Modern techniques are analogous; cf. Vansina 1961.
19. See Uitti 1973 p. 235; Suard 1979; C. M. Jones 1990. The time at which the change occurred is disputed; see, for example, Calin and Duggan 1981.
20. Foulon 1958, especially pp. 370–73.
21. Cf. Faral 1910 p. 288 (§84a); Rychner 1955 pp. 48–67, 126–28; Lord 1960 pp. 25–26; Vansina 1961 pp. 80–83. On the problem of originality and "audience domination," cf. Frappier 1957 pp. 2–3; Ngal 1977.
22. See also *Gormont* 146, 418.
23. See Rychner 1955 p. 36; Delbouille 1959; Bäuml 1979.
24. Gallais 1964b p. 345. Cf. Simon 1958 pp. 62–63; E. Roach in *Melusine* Co p. 15 on vv. 85–92; Gallais 1988 pp. 780–82.
25. Lofmark 1972a p. 43; Lofmark 1972b.
26. Martin 1979; Petit 1985b pp. 789–807.
27. See Hélin 1951; Busby 1989.
28. Cormier 1973; L. G. Donovan 1975; Talarico 1981; Blask 1984; Petit 1985b.
29. Cf. *Olifant* 1–30.
30. See especially *Tornoiement* 410–13, 1844–51. Cf. Jauss *GRLMA* I, 135.
31. See D. Kelly 1978b pp. 139–40.
32. Cf. Köhler 1964a.
33. This is commonplace enough in the *Lais* to be taken as paradigmatic; see Pro 34–38, Eq 1–8; see also *Doon* 1–6, 281–86; *Espine* 1–14, 503–12; *Graelent* 727–32; *Guingamor* 668–78; *Lecheor* 19–36; *Nabaret* 46–48. For Marie see Rych-

ner ed. in *Lais* pp. xiv–xv; Ménard 1979 p. 56; for the anonymous lays, see Braet 1985 pp. 283–88. Cf. as well *Claris* 4659–74; Didot *Perc E* ll. 1475–79, 2672–73, and *D* ll. 1255–57, 1978–80; *Dole* 1–3; *Melusine* JdA p. 34.6–9.

34. *Ducs* 10506–10.

35. Huth *Merlin* II, 100. See Vansina 1961 p. 1.

36. See below, pp. 240–42.

37. *Cligés* 28–42; *Ducs* 42680, 43201–12. Cf. Loomis 1949 pp. 16–17 on Geoffrey of Monmouth; Uitti 1973 pp. 150–51 on Wace; and, in general, Köhler 1970 pp. 37–65.

38. D. Kelly 1970a p. 281. Cf. Vansina 1961 p. 5; Ollier 1974d p. 229. See *Engleis* 3232–34, 4084–86; *Espurgatoire* 3–6, 185–88; *Silence* 2657–58.

39. On this topic, see Lacroix 1971 pp. 16–28, 63–64. See also *Brut* 5171–84; *Dolopathos* fr p. 345 (on Godefroy de Bouillon); *Ducs* 27623–30, 38291–302; *Rou* Appendice 1–40 (II, 309–10). II.1524–25, III.1–166; *Voyage* 467–69.

40. Zink 1981 pp. 23–26.

41. Cf. also *Escoufle* 35–45. See also *Epervier* 1–10, 225–29; *Manekine* 37–38, 7339–42; *Perceval* Cont II 29350–57 (and note pp. 539–40); *Silence* 2657–58.

42. *Rou* III.95–106. Cf. Delehaye 1927 pp. 61–62; Gallais 1964b p. 346; Maddox 1977b pp. 165–66.

43. Cf. her *Lais* Pro 9–22, Eq 1–11; *Espine* 11–14; Huth *Merlin* I, 33, 85–86, 275.

44. *Ducs* 42675–80, 43201–12; *Rou* III.7841–44.

45. Cf. Schulz 1909 pp. 16–23; Spörl 1935 p. 57; Lacroix 1971 pp. 45–49. See also *Florimont* 10215–16; *Gille* 4233–34 (cf. 4848, 5519–20); *Guil maréchal* 3669–80, 3885–89, 4477–80, 8867; but cf. 3165–80.

46. *Sept sages* V 1–2. Cf. K. D. Uitti in D. Kelly 1985c pp. 230–31.

47. Cf. *Joseph d'A* ll. 393–402/311–18; *Merlin* M 75.96–101/S19.35–20.2.

48. *Lancelot* lxxia.48, iv*.22 (end of *Charrette* episode), xliii.6, l.60, *Meliador* 7234–40; *Merlin* S 321.36–43; *Mort* §2.9–12; *Queste* pp. 279.30–280.3; *Tristan* §§206 n.4, 330, 557, 604, 621 (pp. 426–27), and p. 243 n.3, 557; *Tyolet* 23–38.

49. Huth *Merlin* I, 175; II, 100, 113–14, 127.

50. Cf. Foulon 1958 pp. 341–434 for the *Saisnes;* Curtius 1960 pp. 245–46.

51. Jauss 1963; Delbouille 1969 p. 1172 n. 1.

52. Cf. Batany 1974 pp. 57–58.

53. Delbouille *GRLMA* I, 3–56.

54. Poirion 1972; Ollier 1974b; Harf-Lancner 1984 pp. 7–8.

55. On the problem of written vs. oral *chansons de geste,* see Calin and Duggan 1981. See also Bonjour 1957; Frappier 1957 pp. 10–13; Tyssens 1967 pp. 19–24; Duggan 1973 pp. 1–15.

56. Cf. Desmond 1979 pp. 4–5.

57. Faral 1910 pp. 87–118.

58. See Vansina 1961; Dorson 1972. Cf. as well the observations of Duggan 1973 pp. 213–16.

59. On oral education and the aristocracy, see Delehaye 1927 pp. 11 et passim; Bezzola 1944 II, 338–40; III, 74–80; Grundmann 1958; Zumthor 1985 p. 16.

60. Pope 1952 §22; Haidu 1982 pp. 39–42; Stock 1983.

61. Zumthor *GRLMA* I, 75–76; Beer 1976 pp. 1–11; Zink 1984; Zumthor 1984a pp. 170–74.

62. *Ducs* 25820–52; *Paris* pp. 392.16–393.1; *TChev* 4662–63; *Tristan* Pro p. 2/Pro 8–17. Cf. W.-D. Stempel in *GRLMA* XI.1, 719.

63. See Bender 1967; Köhler 1968; Duggan *GRLMA* XI.1, 285–31.

64. Jauss 1963 pp. 66–67; Jauss 1977a p. 315; Pickens 1977 pp. 113–21; R. T. Pickens in D. Kelly 1985c pp. 273–74.

65. See below, pp. 89–91.

66. Faral 1910 pp. 66–86; Vitz 1990 pp. 24–25.

67. Cf. *Alex* APar III.7449–62 on Narcissus. Cf. Faral 1910 pp. 44–60, 167–221; Pirot 1972 especially pp. 323–542; Duggan 1989b.

68. Vitz 1990 p. 23. Cf. *Florence* 5246–48.

69. See Faral 1910 p. 219–20.

70. Burrow 1973 p. 351. See Bonjour 1957; Gallais 1964a pp. 193–94; Zink 1981 p. 7 on "oralité fictive"; Scholz 1980 pp. 98–103; Vitz 1990.

71. Delbouille 1959; Tyssens 1966; Duggan 1973 pp. 26–33, 175, 214–15; Scholz 1980; Duggan 1989a and 1989b. But the gaps are wide apart between Duggan who extends the oral tradition down to Adenet le Roi and W. Calin who deems all oral versions to be lost; see Calin and Duggan 1981 pp. 233–36, 248–49, 252–53. Zumthor 1984b and 1987 on romance orality suggest a median between formulaic oral and literacy.

72. Ollier 1974a pp. 28–29; Bonjour 1957 pp. 253–55. Cf. *Dialogus* ll. 767–68.

73. Tyssens 1966 pp. 686–87, 693–95.

74. Van Emden 1975.

75. Loomis 1949 pp. 12–24; Ménard 1979 pp. 51–52; J. D. Janssens 1988 pp. 295–98.

76. See, for example, Lagorio 1970 pp. 29–37; Lagorio 1971; Ménard 1979 pp. 48–49; Lozachmeur 1980a; and Lozachmeur 1980b I, 224–25.

77. *Espine* 6–9; *Guil Palerne* 9658–59.

78. Cf. Schmolke-Hasselmann 1980a p. 24.

79. *Cleomadés* 15918–20, 18533–35; *Jaufre* 85–90; *Melusine* JdA pp. 308–10; *Parfait* 51–52.

80. *Brut* 13620–24; *Cleomadés* 15264–70; *Florimont* 1682–83; *Graelent* 727–30; *Gui* 8568; *Guil d'A* 3308–10; *Perceval* Cont I, ASP 1107–8; *Tydorel* 17–18, 232. Vansina 1961 terms "témoignages" such reports, but excludes them from oral tradition as such (pp. 22–23).

81. Diverres 1970, 1980; and Schmolke-Hasselmann 1980a pp. 228–32; Dembowski 1983 pp. 105–49; Diverres 1989. Cf. Zink 1980; Ainsworth 1988. Passages like the following transpose persons and events contemporary with Froissart into pseudohistory. "Une en y ot qui bien chanta, / Ce me dist cilz qui l'escouta. / Je volz lors sa cançon avoir / Et le desirai a savoir; / Cilz legierement le me dist" (*Meliador* 30642–46) [one of those there sang well according to one person who heard her. I asked for the song, desiring to know it. He recited it to me easily]. Froissart had in fact relocated Wenceslas de Brabant's verse in Arthurian times. Not dissimilar is

Machaut's transposition of the birth of Pierre de Lusignan into a mythograph in the *Prise d'Alexandrie*. Such transpositions fit the notion of *poète* in Middle French; see Zumthor 1955 pp. 180–83, and p. 70 above. Benoît de Sainte-Maure may have transposed Eleanor of Aquitaine (or some other queen) to invent Briseida; see Zumthor 1955 pp. 180–83; D. Kelly 1988c p. 36.

82. This occurs in medieval chronicles and hagiography; see Delehaye 1927 pp. 71–72. Cf. *Abladane* p. 478.100–108 (cf. pp. 498–500); *Brut* 1597–99, 5071–74, 5171–84; *Estoire* III, 125/I.208.5–7; III, 142/I.216.30–32; III, 275/I.282.33–36; *Guiron* §§254, 256; *Hist reg* p. 251/92.43–45 ("Saltus Goemagog"), 327/142.7–10, 329/144–45.25–26, 473/257.91–94; Huth *Merlin* I, 94; *Lais* DA 7–10; *Lanzelet* 7046–48, 7992–8005; *Manekine* 7659–62; *Meliador* 14759–62, 28983–29007; *Melusine* Co 1891–98, 6652–55; *Melusine* JdA pp. 67.8–10, 260.11–12, 307.9–12; *Merlin* M 47.58–60/S 53.12–14; *Perceval* Cont III 42638–41; *Robert* 5055–61; *Tristan* §291a (p. 216) (in *Erec* Pr p. 146.156–63). Cf. Bozóky 1985 pp. 80–81.

83. Loomis 1959 p. 52. On his influence, see Meneghetti 1979.

84. For example *Claris,* the Didot *Perc, Mort.* See Dean 1972 pp. 282–84; Meneghetti 1979 pp. xxiii–xxix on his influence on genealogies.

85. Bullock-Davies 1966.

86. Loomis 1949 pp. 22–24.

87. Bezzola 1944 II, 318–20; Marx 1952 pp. 4–5, 56–58; Kellermann 1956; Gallais 1967; Gallais 1988 pp. 795–805. See *Durmart* 15084–126, 15131.

88. See Frappier *GRLMA* IV.1, 208.

89. See Fourrier 1960 pp. 473–74; D. Kelly 1970a pp. 280–81.

90. Cf. *Florimont* 2417–20, 10815–42, and in general Risop 1895 pp. 439–41; Fourrier 1960 pp. 477–78; D. Kelly 1976 p. 18. See also *Melusine* JdA p. 302.1–2.

91. Cf. *Wistasse* 2205.

92. *Restor* 1497–542.

93. See below, pp. 89–90.

94. Following Vansina 1961 p. 50.

95. Cf. Vansina 1961 pp. 53–54 on "traditions figées" ("témoignages" or "textes figés"), not subject to the freedom usually associated with formulaic invention; cf. Rychner 1955 pp. 33–34. Is this because of the disappearance of the scôp or bard in the Romance-language world? Cf. Faral 1910 pp. 2–24.

96. Such *mouvance* is an extremely important variable in the medieval text; it carries on the oral adaptability of "text" to reception. See Vansina 1961 pp. 71–77.

97. Zumthor 1984b, 1987.

98. Zumthor 1972 pp. 70–75; Zumthor 1985 p. 15. See Rychner 1955 p. 33; Duggan 1973 p. 211 on "improvisational systems" and memory; Marichal 1961; Gallais 1964b pp. 479–82; Bruns 1980.

99. Zumthor 1972 p. 71.

100. The "quasi-abstraction" is analogous to Geoffrey of Vinsauf's *status archetypus.*

101. Zumthor 1972 p. 507. See also Raible 1972, especially pp. 132–38; Bruyne 1946 II, 294.

102. Trimpi 1974 p. 40. Cf. Riquer 1971; Haug 1973; Kibler 1979; Schmolke-Hasselmann 1980a pp. 32–34; Baumgartner 1990.

103. W. Roach *(Perceval)*, J. Rychner *(Lanval)*, P. Dembowski *(Ste-Marie)*, R. Mortier *(Roland)*, R. T. Pickens (Jaufre Rudel). Cf. Foulet and Speer 1979 pp. 50–51; Dembowski 1981 pp. 23–24.

104. See Roques 1952 and his ed. of *Erec* pp. xxxvii-li. The approach is not invalidated by the editorial defects. But there is no consensus: Foulet and Speer 1979 p. 58; Reid 1976; T. Hunt 1979; Hult 1986a; Uitti 1988.

105. Vinaver 1939.

106. See E. Löseth in *Tristan* pp. iii-xxvi; L.-F. Flutre in *Perceforest;* R. Lathuillère ed. *Guiron* pp. 35 et passim. On the *Perceval* Continuations, see also Wrede 1952; Roach 1956; Gallais 1988.

107. See M.-R. Jung 1968; Badel 1980 pp. 144–45; Hult 1981; Hult 1986b pp. 34–55.

108. Ed. F. A. G. Cowper in *Ille* pp. xxiv-xxv; cf. Le Gentil 1950; F. P. Sweetser ed. in *Blancandin* pp. 11–28.

109. *Estoire* II, 4–5/I.3.19–22. Cf. Frappier 1970 pp. 17–26; Riquer 1971 pp. 34–36; Scholz 1980 pp. 137–38; Baumgartner 1987c p. 44.

110. E. Kennedy 1970 p. 531. Cf. Vinaver in *Balain* p. xvii; Micha 1963 pp. 493–99; Gallais 1964a; Frappier on the replacement of Perceval by Galaad in the Prose *Lancelot* in 1968b pp. 132–33, 452–55; E. Kennedy 1986. See also Klebs 1899 pp. 323–511; Guenée 1977 pp. 5–7; Hult 1986b pp. 59–74.

111. Gallais 1964a p. 223. Cf. Roach 1956; Gallais 1964b pp. 481–82; Riquer 1971 pp. 35–36. On the complexity of the "editor's" role, see Taylor 1987 pp. 281–86.

112. Gallais 1964a pp. 182–83. See now Gallais 1988.

113. On the major branches and variant versions of the *Perceval* Continuations, see Wrede 1952; Roach 1956 and *Perceval* Cont I-IV; Gallais 1988. Cf. as well in this context R. O'Gorman ed. in *Joseph d'A* Mid Fr pp. 261–63; Wallen 1972 and 1982; Triaud 1985. A. Hilka's edition of *Perceval* shows changes wrought on Chrétien's torso by subsequent scribes; see especially pp. 457–80; and the analyses of *Guiron* (R. Lathuillère) and the Prose *Tristan* (E. Löseth).

114. See also *Meraugis* 5933–38. Cf. Scholz 1980 pp. 135–37; C. M. L. Lévy in *Floriant* Pr p. 29.

115. See Bogdanow 1966 pp. 60–63.

116. Knapp 1975 p. 7–8.

117. See the useful discussions of the relation between *inventio artium* and *translatio artium* in Worstbrock 1965 pp. 2, 20; Freeman 1979 pp. 24–56; Burns 1985a.

118. Bezzola 1944 II, 430; cf. Haug 1973 pp. 129–31.

119. Cf. Wolter 1959 pp. 67–69; Zumthor 1972 pp. 346–51; D. Kelly 1974 pp. 147–48.

120. Spörl 1935 pp. 13–17; Köhler 1970 pp. 45–46; Pickering 1967. Cf. Köhler 1964b.

121. In general, see Wolter 1959; Lammers 1965; Lacroix 1971; Ray 1974; Beer 1976; Guenée 1977; Tyson 1979; Guenée 1982; *GRLMA* XI.1, especially G. Melville pp. 157–228 and H. Hofmann pp. 367–687.

122. On *narratio fabulosa*, see above pp. 63–66. Cf. Raynaud de Lage 1976 pp. 127–28, including bibliography; Fleishman 1983.

123. Köhler 1962 pp. 213–23; Woledge and Clive 1964 pp. 32–43.

124. Ghellinck 1946 II, 92.
125. Guenée 1973 p. 1004. Cf. as well Keuck 1934; Spörl 1935 p. 18; Schmale 1985 pp. 105–23 and 179–94 (by H.-W. Goetz); Hofmann GRLMA XI.1, 375–77.
126. Cf. Pickering 1967 I, 46–88; Marichal 1968 pp. 463–65.
127. Keuck 1934 pp. 57–63, 69–76; Chenu 1957b pp. 64–66; Guenée 1973 pp. 1006–8, 1010–11. Cf. Köhler 1970 pp. 5–11.
128. Bezzola 1944; Chenu 1957b pp. 87–88; Brandt 1966; Kleinschmidt 1974; Bloch GRLMA XI.1, 135–56; Bosl 1977 pp. 35–36; Duby 1978b pp. 369–70. Cf. also K. Hauck in Lammers 1965 pp. 165–99; Poirion 1978. On John of Salisbury see Spörl 1935 pp. 80–81, 108; Hofmann GRLMA XI.1, 430–64.
129. Zumthor 1972 pp. 346–51; Lacy 1977 pp. 150–58.
130. Bezzola 1942 p. 14; Bezzola 1944 II, 430; Wolter 1959 p. 56; Köhler 1970 pp. 45–46; Stempel GRLMA XI.1, 707–18. On later vernaculer historiography, see Marchello-Nizia 1982; and relevant sections of GRLMA XI.1
131. Wolter 1959 pp. 75–76.
132. Ray 1974 p. 55. Cf. Kleinschmidt 1974; Melville GRLMA XI.1, 157–228.
133. Bogdanow 1966 p. 5; cf. Beer 1976 pp. 47–68.
134. Cf. Payen 1970; L.G. Donovan 1975 p. 200; Payen 1980; Petit 1985b pp. 251–326.
135. Schulz 1909 pp. 120–34; Wolter 1959; Kleinschmidt 1974; Ward 1977; Schmale 1985 pp. 68–84, 167–79 (by H. W. Goetz).
136. Marti 1941 pp. 246–47; Moos 1976.
137. Lacroix 1971 p. 35; Baumgartner 1987c. Cf. Etymologiae I.xlii.1.
138. Zink 1981 pp. 10–23. See the references to remembrer in the Ducs 41874, 44515.
139. On the Brut see I. Arnold ed. I, lxxix-lxxxvi. Cf. Hist reg pp. 219/71, 383–84/189–90 (on Merlin's prophecies), 496/274–75, 536/303. That the technique remained characteristic of (pseudo)historical writing is evident in Perceforest 70:481–522.
140. See Short 1977; Struss in GRLMA XI.1, 961–62, 969–70.
141. Cf. Beer 1976 p. 70. Brut 104, 1067–70, 1528–36, 1617–18, 3401–6, 5071–88, 6325–28, 11117–18, 12961–62, 13275–93; Ducs 21525–30, 26900–922, 37289–302, 38720–32, 38879–84, 42659–62.
142. Cf. Hist reg pp. 252/92.14–17, 282/113.19–22, 290/118.2–6, 327/143.18–20, 330/145.37–40, 372/180.43–45.
143. See Kretzschmar 1980 pp. 23–26.
144. Struss in GRLMA XI.1, 990–91; but cf. pp. 992–93.
145. Brut 5171–84.
146. Frappier 1957.
147. Frappier 1957 p. 19.
148. Zumthor GRLMA IV.1, 62. See Ducs 9603–16.
149. Cf. De gestis §§8, 134; TChev 1329–34.
150. See below, pp. 154–59.
151. Faral 1913 pp. 307–88; Wehrli 1961 pp. 430–31.
152. D. Kelly 1978c pp. 237–39; cf. Zumthor GRLMA IV.1, 62; Beer 1976 pp. 40–44; Gier GRLMA XI.1, 842–43.

153. Kleinschmidt 1974 pp. 14–18. Cf. Tyson 1979 pp. 197–98.

154. Wolter 1959 pp. 74–78; Kleinschmidt 1974; Melville *GRLMA* XI.1, 202–3.

155. Schulz 1909 pp. 67–83; Wolter 1959 pp. 59–64; Lacroix 1971 pp. 167–91; Kleinschmidt 1974 pp. 22–90.

156. Zumthor *GRLMA* IV.1, 62–65; Dembowski 1976 p. 120. Cf. Becker 1943 p. 503.

157. D. Kelly 1978c pp. 233–35; D. Kelly 1984c pp. 34–37.

158. Foulet and Uitti 1981 pp. 245–49.

159. D. Kelly 1983a pp. 10–16.

160. Wehrli 1961 pp. 433–34; cf. Struss *GRLMA* XI.1, 964–68 on *Becket*.

161. See Zink 1981 pp. 21–22; Moos 1988 pp. 52–60.

162. For the special case of the narrative lay, see Riquer 1955 pp. 1–19; Frappier 1961; Pickens 1978b. On the complexity of the problem in the wider sense of romance adopted here, see Deyermond 1975 pp. 232–34; Taylor 1987 pp. 278–86.

Chapter 4. *Conte: Matiere* and *San*

1. Vàrvaro 1967; Vinaver 1970a pp. 15–38; Ruhe 1979a pp. 132–37. Cf. Hofer 1954 pp. 99–108; Poirion 1972.

2. Stach 1952; Duby 1973 pp. 103–10.

3. Halpersohn 1911 pp. 33–42, and n. 72 (p. 68).

4. E. Faral ed. in *Conquête* I, 9 n. 4; cf. Tyssens 1966 pp. 689–93; O'Gorman 1970 p. 454.

5. Cf. Baumgartner 1987c pp. 40–42; Warren 1988 pp. 230–46.

6. Cf. also *Alex* APar I.2045; *Alix orp* p. 17.1; *Bliocadran* 642–47; *TChev* 768, 1121. Cf. Gallais 1988 pp. 778–95, 813–17.

7. Todorov 1969; Zumthor 1972 pp. 65–70; Pemberton 1984 p. 482. Cf. Van Coolput 1986 pp. 189–217. But see as well Baumgartner 1987b pp. 175–77, and 1990 pp. 43–61.

8. Cf. Scholz 1980 pp. 60, 63–64, 125–35.

9. Burgess 1984 pp. 10–11, especially n. 2. For other works, see Gallais 1964a p. 204; Ollier 1974a pp. 27–28; Schmolke-Hasselmann 1980a p. 21–25.

10. See, for example, K. Warnke, in *Espurgatoire* pp. xlvii-xlviii.

11. Cf. Quadlbauer 1962; Gallais 1964b pp. 338–47; Allen 1973 pp. 34–35; Jauss *GRLMA* I, 108; Klopsch 1980 pp. 112–20; Knapp 1980; Hofmann *GRLMA* XI.1, 371–73.

12. Frappier 1961 p. 33 n. 4 (quoting E. Hoepffner).

13. Frappier 1961 p. 26.

14. See Riquer 1955; Frappier 1961 pp. 24–28; Baader 1966 pp. 11–36; Baum 1969; Ménard 1979 pp. 52–59, 97–99.

15. See Baader 1966 pp. 11–12; Ringger 1973 pp. 25–48.

16. Cf. Gier 1977b p. 72.

17. Cf. pp. 11, 70–71, above.

18. Huth *Merlin* I, 98; cf. *Merlin* M 23.19–66, 31.11–13, 36.2–4, 69.2–4/S II, 27.30–28.15; 35.24–26, 41.5–7, 70.19–21, 108.36–37.

19. Leupin 1982b pp. 37–43. Cf. also Pickens 1984 pp. 498–500; Baumgartner

1987b pp. 172–75; Pickens 1988 pp. 33–39; and *Estoire* III, 102–3/I.195.32–36; *Guiron* §§192, 268; *Melusine* Co 6503–34; *Perceforest* 91:207–8. Further evidence for this is the naming of Dares as author in succeeding versions of the *De excidio;* see L. Gompf in *Ylias* pp. 6–10.

    20. Cf. Gallais 1964b p. 337.

    21. Bruyne 1946 II, 281.

    22. See *Alex* APar II, ix–xi; for *TChev* see II, 1–18. Cf. Frappier *GRLMA* IV.1, 150–52, 156, 166.

    23. See Pickens 1978a pp. 203–4; Pickens 1978b pp. 378–84. On the practice of *assemblage,* see Delbouille 1927, 1960; Tyssens 1967; Palermo 1960. Cf. *Engleis* 2327–32; 6434–38; *Estoire* RoB 3481–3514; Huth *Merlin* I, 33; *Mort* §1.9–10; *Rigomer* 6429–34; *Silence* 1660–69; *Tristan* pp. 403–4.

    24. *Lais* Chev 5–6, Pro 39–40, Yo 3–4.

    25. *Lais* Pro 9–22, El 2–4, 21–28, Guig 1–2.

    26. Cf. Schmolke-Hasselmann 1980a pp. 116–77; D. Kelly 1984c. See Loomis 1949 pp. 15–16 on William of Malmesbury.

    27. *Anjou* 38–39; *Escoufle* 3738. See Stimming 1888 pp. 333–34, 342.

    28. Zink 1979 pp. 17–26.

    29. Maddox 1978 pp. 26–32; Poirion 1982 p. 6.

    30. *Alex* APar III, 3407–14, 3515–44; *Blanc chev* 139–45; *Claris* 24804–30; *Guil maréchal* 13853–63; Huth *Merlin* I, 31–33; *Melior* 1–12; *Merlin* M 19.36–50, 24.10–15/S 23.15–25, 28.38–29.3; *Mule* 41–49, 440–49, 490–95; *Troie* 129–31; *Venjance* Nev 1488–92.

    31. Fourquet 1956; cf. Baumgartner 1982 pp. 559–60. *Mule* 1–16.

    32. Even in Arthurian matter; see the *Meriadoc,* so close to Bodel's language even in Latin: "Legencium igitur consulens utilitati illam compendioso perstringere stilo statui, sciens quod maioris sit precii breuis cum sensu oracio quam multiflua racione uacans locucio" (p.1).

    33. Cf. *Lais* Yo 5–6: "En pensé ai e en talent / Que d'Iwenec vus die avant"; *Cesar* p. 35 fol. 4r°.

    34. *Cesar* p. 35 fol. 4r°; *Durmart* 13–16; *Escanor* 4–7; *Florimont* 27–30; *Lais* Yo 5–6; *TChev* 1324–25; *Tornoiement* 16–21. Cf. *Parfait* 18–20; *Partonopeu* Cont 3059–64. Marie's "command" may have included *Yvain;* see Sargent-Baur 1987a.

    35. Frappier 1972 pp. 363–67, 370; Ruhe 1985.

    36. D. Kelly 1970a pp. 279–82. For a similar separation between a written source in England and the oral report of that source's content, see *Guil d'A* 11–17 and 3308–10; yet the author "Chrétien" says that he read the *estoire* (46).

    37. Cf. *Joufroi* 2324–32.

    38. *Tornoiement* 19–21. Cf. Godefroy VI, 300–301; *T-L* VII, 1533–38.

    39. Cf. *Florimont* 9207–16.

    40. See Ponti 1988 pp. 184–87. Cf. the historians, and *Brut* 5071–88; *Estoire* III, 269, 270–71/I.280 var. 4, 280.30–32.

    41. *Escoufle* 958–63; *Estoire* II, 128–29/I.21.9–15; *Perceval* Cont I MQ 16801–08, T 12671–78; *Tristan* Got 12648–56, 16909–22.

42. *Troie* 913–20. Cf. J. Stohlmann in *Hist troy* pp. 139–214; Baumgartner 1987c.

43. On the Greek fragments, see Eisenhut 1983 pp. 12–18. *Perceforest* also claims a Greek antecedent; see Taylor 1987 p. 281.

44. Cf. *Troie* 103.

45. Colby 1965 pp. 20–21; see her catalogues, pp. 14–19.

46. Huth *Merlin* I, 31–33; *Joseph d'A* ll. 372–78/293–98; *Merlin* M 73.62–84/S 19.15–27.

47. E. Vinaver in *Balain* p. xvii; E. Kennedy 1970. Cf. Pauphilet 1968 pp. 157–90. For a specimen study of this kind of composition, see Pickens 1984.

48. Ferrier 1954 pp. 7–21.

49. See above, pp. 44–45, 62–66.

50. Cf. Chenu 1957b pp. 66–67.

51. Brinkmann 1964b pp. 419–35; Matarasso 1979; Picone 1982 pp. 2–6 on *ambages.*

52. There was no distinction in Chrétien's time based on etymology; see Frappier 1972 pp. 349–50; Gier 1977b.

53. Frappier 1972 pp. 366–67.

54. Köhler 1962 pp. 14–15; Uitti 1973 pp. 134–37; Frappier 1972; Ollier 1974a pp. 30–32; Haug 1978 pp. 65–69.

55. Rychner 1969 II, 1134; but see Gier 1977b pp. 66–72.

56. Frappier 1972 pp. 368–69; cf. pp. 338, 355 n. 1, 363; and Frappier *GRLMA* IV.1, 350.

57. Frappier 1972 p. 368; cf. Pauphilet 1968 pp. 169–71.

58. Frappier 1972 p. 368.

59. Frappier pp. 368–69.

60. In Jodogne 1964a p. 84. The subject is complex; cf. Haug 1978 pp. 86–87; Vitz 1978 pp. 405–7.

61. In Jodogne 1964a p. 85; cf. Jauss *GRLMA,* I, 113; Gosman 1984 p. 83.

62. *Erec* 5841–43; see Bezzola 1947 pp. 195–98. For examples in *Perceforest* and the *Sept sages* cycle, see Niedzielski 1978a pp. 124–27; Palermo 1983; Taylor 1987; Halász 1986. For *chansons de geste,* see Engel 1910.

63. Rychner 1972 p. 270; see Haug 1978 pp. 22–25. Cf. Sargent-Baur 1987a.

64. On the origins of the dichotomy *matiere-san,* see Bruyne 1946 I, 282–84. Cf. also *Melusine* JdA pp. 311.31–312.3.

65. See especially Jauss *GRLMA* I, 107–38. On auctorial *gré,* see Hult 1989 pp. 91 and n. 31 (p. 269).

66. Ferrier 1954 pp. 54–78. See the examples of *Flamenca* and the *Cent nouv,* especially xxvi and xcix.

67. D. Kelly 1984c pp. 44–45.

68. M. Delbouille ed. in *Aristote* pp. 16–21.

69. Cf. *Brun* 11–12, 244; *Meraugis* 24–29 (cf. 310–15). See Stanesco 1989.

70. See also *Guiron* p. 181.

71. R. Lathuillère ed. in *Guiron* pp. 16–17; cf. Bogdanow 1966 pp. 194–95.

72. See also *Alex* APar I.2, 42–55, 57–61; *Dole* 5645–48; *Epervier* 9–10; *Joufroi* 89–90; *Mort* §115.103–10; *Perceforest* I.2175/74:45 and 46; *TChev* 2297. See, as *oppositio* to Ydoine, the portrait of the deceitful woman (*Amadas* 3568–3656).
73. *Alex* APar II.1355–56; *Fouke* p. 3.1–8.
74. D. Kelly 1984c pp. 37–41. Cf. Burgess 1970 p. 28; Gier 1977b pp. 65–66, 68; Burgess 1987 pp. 35–49.
75. Foulet and Uitti 1981 p. 246.
76. Foulet and Uitti 1981 p. 247.
77. Foulet and Uitti 1981 p. 247 n. 9; see Poirion 1982 p. 64.
78. Zumthor 1972 p. 123. Cf. *Partonopeu* 101–6.
79. See above, pp. 39–40. Cf. Marie's *Fables* Pro 1–26.
80. Vernet 1955 p. 670 vv. 23–24; cf. Wetherbee 1972 pp. 28–29.
81. Köhler 1962 pp. 11–12; Zink 1981 pp. 19–23.
82. See M. J. Donovan 1961; T. Hunt 1974; Ménard 1979 p. 18; Hult 1986b pp. 95–97.
83. D. Kelly 1984c pp. 34–36. Cf. Köhler 1970 pp. 47–48.
84. See below, pp. 222–26.
85. Cf. D. Kelly 1969b pp. 260–61 on the omitted *matiere*.
86. Bechtoldt 1935; Koenig 1973; Uitti 1973 pp. 217–18; Gier 1977b pp. 67–71.
87. *Alex B* 3497–98; *Bel inc* 1–10; *Dolopathos* fr pp. 5–7; *Ducs* 42062–71; *Guiron* pp. 175–80; *Hunbaut* 32–33; *Joseph d'A* ll. 31–32/23–25; *Levrier* 1–54; *Prise* 1228–29; *Rose* 16165–76/16135–46, 16211–21/16181–91; *Tristan* p. 402; *Violette* 1–43.
88. On these senses, see Nitze 1915; Köhler 1962 pp. 15–17; Maddox 1977b pp. 164–66. See also *Blanc chev* 1484–88; *Guil Palerne* 1–22; *Partonopeu* 91–134, 7250–52, and Cont 117–18; *Perceforest* 88:505–7; *Restor* 1666–72; *Richars* 1–6.
89. Cf. *Cassidorus* §§488–89; *Ducs* 14793–804.
90. Gier 1977b p. 70. On the diversity of terms used to describe mental operations, see Chenu 1957a.
91. *Alex* APar I.2028–30 and *B* 3367–69; *Levrier* 1–64 (several examples).
92. Cf. *Hunbaut* 32–45; *Meliador* 20094–131.
93. See *Lais* Pro 28–32, and Baader 1966 pp. 136–37; Freeman 1979 pp. 21–44.
94. Glunz 1937 pp. 65–66; Curtius 1954 p. 50; Wolter 1959 p. 54–55; Lubac 1959 I.1, 295 n. 7. Cf. *Fables* Pro 23–26; and Badel 1975 pp. 92–93.
95. *Alex* APar IV.1556; *Vengement* 33–34.
96. Cf. Dronke 1973 p. 338.
97. *De vulg* II.iv.8. See Colish 1968 pp. 269–72; Vinaver 1925 p. 29.
98. Cf. *Narcisus* 111–14.
99. *Bel inc* 1931–36; *Ducs* 467–70; *Estoire* III, 64/I.180.12–15. Cf. A. Henri in *Cleomadés* Vol. V.2, pp. 643–44.
100. *Queste* pp. 44.28–29 etc. Cf. *Lancelot* iv.14.
101. Nitze 1915 pp. 19–22, 27.
102. Curtius 1954 pp. 388–89; Köhler 1962 pp. 15–17; Köhler 1970 pp. 49–51; Uitti 1973 pp. 142–43; Badel 1975 pp. 83–84, 89–92; Ménard 1979 pp. 17–18.
103. *Alex* APar IV.1609–14; *Athis* 1–11; *Beaudous* pp. viii-ix (vv. 1–88); *Dur-*

mart 1–12; *Erec* 1–12; *Fables* Pro 1–6, 21–26; *Guil Palerne* 1–22; *Ignaure* 1–4, 11–14; *Levrier* 1–38; *Ovide mor* I.1–14; *Partonopeu* 91–134; *Protheselaus* 3–6; *Restor* 1–8; *Troie* 1–6; *Venjance Nev* 2–6.

104. *Dolopathos* fr pp. 6–7; *Escoufle* 35–46; *Lais* Pro 11–22; *Melusine* Co 44–46.

105. *Beaudous* 283–92; *Troie* 33–39.

106. *Escoufle* 43–45.

107. Huth *Merlin* I, 86; *Merlin* M 43.37–44.28/S 48.3–27 (Merlin's prophecies).

108. *Erec* 6679–80; see D. Kelly 1983a pp. 14–15.

109. *Dolopathos* fr pp. 5–7; *Eledus* 1189, 2440, 2567, 2684–2705.

110. *Alex* APar I.280–81; *Manekine* 30–33.

111. Köhler 1970 pp. 41–43. Cf. Schalk 1959 pp. 139–44.

112. See also *Athis* 223–26.

113. *Alex* APar I.1659–69; *Estoire* III, 33–34/I.172.7–22; *Sept sages* V 272.

114. *Restor* 1666–72.

115. *Partonopeu* 4605–8.

116. *Estoire* I.45.1–4; *Laurin* ll. 13333–74; *Ovide mor* II.3217–23. Cf. *Ducs* 25820–6468.

117. *Aristote* 3–5; *Beaudous* 293–96; *Bel inc* 1933–36; *Gui* 15–18.

118. *Alex* APar III.5159–60; *Bel inc* 1933; *Meliacin* 626–34.

119. *Alex* APar II.2536–38; *Ovide mor* I.8–36.

120. Cf. *Alex* APar III.5159–60; *Athis* 319–22; *Bel inc* 1933–34; *Brut* 5205–6; Huth *Merlin* II, 198; *Queste* p. 155.9–11; *Troie* 13357–60.

121. *Alex* APar III.529–32.

122. *Alex* APar I.340–42; *Lais* Pro 1–2.

123. *Fables* Pro 22; *Levrier* 1; *Prise* 1228–29.

124. See Baumgartner 1982; D. Kelly 1983c.

125. Wetherbee 1972 p. 24–25. Cf. Spörl 1935 pp. 80–87.

126. Köhler 1962 p. 16; Mickel 1975; Pickens 1978b pp. 372–73.

127. *Anjou* 8063; *Blanc chev* 1595; *Charrette* 23, 28–29; *Dolopathos* fr pp. 3–4; *Ducs* 2123–26; *Emp* 43–44; *Escoufle* 29–30; *Fables* Pro 1–4, 22, 35; *Florimont* 17; *Guil d'A* 1–3; *Guiron* pp. 176–77, 178, 181–82; *Joufroi* 4396–4402; *Lais* Pro 13–16; *Meraugis* 1–5, 338–39; *Perceval* Cont III 42642; *Restor* 294; *Rigomer* 6432; *Rose* 6324–26/6294–96; *Silence* 1880, 3140; *Tristan* pp. 1–2, 402–5.

128. *Yvain* 150–72. Cf. *Poetria nova* 46–47; Brault 1972; Cline 1972.

129. *Estoire* RoB 3161–62; *Florimont* 5–6; *Guil maréchal* 22; *Jaufre* 14–20; *Manekine* 25–27; *Rigomer* 6438–40.

130. *Ducs* 2133–34; *Epervier* 9–10; *Floriant* 6240–48; *Florimont* 47–52, 113–19, 9263–72; *Manekine* 4–6; *Partonopeu* Cont 117–20.

131. Lindberg 1976. My thanks to my colleague for his help. Cf. Schleusener-Eichholz 1985.

132. See Haidu 1973b.

133. Cf. Schmolke-Hasselmann 1980a pp. 160–69.

134. Ollier 1974a pp. 32–36; Pickens 1978a pp. 201–11; Pickens 1978b pp. 372–77; Schmolke-Hasselmann 1980a pp. 152–60; Grimbert 1988.

135. Haug 1978 pp. 5–16; Gier 1979b pp. 13–14, 17–18; Liborio 1979 pp. 30–31;

Poirion 1980; Schmolke-Hasselmann 1980b. The most thoroughgoing intertextual statement is found in Jean de Meun; see Wetherbee 1971. Cf. Loomis 1949 pp. 39–40.

136. On later reception see Schmolke-Hasselmann 1980a, especially part I: "Die Auseinandersetzung mit Chrestien," pp. 26–177; Badel 1975 pp. 85–86, 93; Bozóky 1985 p. 82; Wolf 1989. And *Couci* 1–47; *Durmart* 1–12; *Manekine* 1–29; *Richars* 5–32.

137. See Köhler 1962 pp. 9–10; Köhler 1970 pp. 12–18. In *Alex* APar IV.1610–14; *Beaudous* p. vii (107–20); *Meraugis* 30–32; *Partonopeu* Cont 3046–70; *Thèbes* 13–18.

138. See Badel 1975 p. 86 n. 12; *Gille* 816–22; *TChev* 13–17. See also *Dialogus* ll. 835–37: "materiam libri sui componendi . . . , quem experimento propriae naturae . . . in se recognovit."

139. Are these the *loci* of topical invention wherein the audience and the romance figure discover common attributes?

140. Contrast the lady in *Meliador* who, upon hearing a ballade, announces: "onques n'amai par tel art" (20354); see D. Kelly 1978a p. 249. Cf. Brault 1975 p. 51.

141. Frappier 1963. But see T. Hunt 1981b; whether Hunt is right or not the conclusion holds: the lovers are exemplary, either *in bono* or *in malo*.

142. Vinaver 1971 pp. 31–32; Lacy 1980 pp. 52–57; Zink 1981 pp. 21–23; Grimbert 1988 pp. 2–8.

143. In Vinaver 1925 p. 96; cf. Vinaver 1970a p. 166. A number of studies have been devoted to Dinadan; see Van Coolput 1986 p. 156 n. 129.

144. Vinaver 1970a pp. 175–77; cf. Baumgartner 1975 especially pp. 182–87, 252–59; Payen 1979.

145. *Donnei* 141–78; *Fables* Pro 23–26; *Ovide mor* I.31–33; *Partonopeu* 91–134.

146. *Claris* 1–114. Cf. Badel 1975 p. 87; D. Kelly 1983c pp. 415–17. Cf. *Durmart* 4332–40; *Guil maréchal* 5143–48.

147. Ruhe 1979a pp. 155–59, 1979b.

148. *Guil Palerne* 18–20; *Guiron* p. 175; *Merlin* M 23.36–37/S 28.10; *Troie* 24399; cf. *Queste* p. 37.28–29. See as well the numerous examples in *T-L* V, 1378–79, 1382–83. Cf. also Ollier 1974a p. 29; Gier 1977b pp. 69–70.

149. Cf. *FEW* VI, 698–99; D. Kelly 1970a p. 281 and n. 12; Maddox 1978 pp. 20–22; Gier 1979a p. 94. On the "mémoire des textes," see Burns 1985b.

150. *Joseph d'A* ll. 31–32/23–25; var.: "de me donner sens et memoyre pour conduyre ceste matere a fin" (*Joseph d'A* p. 5 var. 31). See *Florence* 4283–84; *Merlin* M 23.35–39/S 27.40–28.3; *Paris* p. 507.6–7; *Rigomer* 15919–22; *Queste* p. 37.28–29. Cf. *Humbaut* 222–23; *Rose* 134–38, 401/399.

151. *Merlin* M 16.19–24/S 18.29–34; Huth *Merlin* I, 3–4 (cf. II, 196).

152. Cf. Wetherbee 1976 pp. 45–46.

153. *Rose* 2073–76/2071–74. See Van den Boogaard 1985.

154. *Cosmographia* I.ii.14; cf. D. Kelly 1978a pp. 31–32. Note also *Poetria nova* 120–21: "ars . . . ludit quasi quaedam praestigiatrix."

155. Cf. *Charrette* 28–29; *Perceval* 62.

156. *Beaudous* 305–28; *Fables* Pro 1–40.

157. *Ducs* 264–67, 22267–70.

158. Peron 1989 p. 312. Cf. *Beaudous* p. viii (vv. 147–48); WatrC xxix.1–9 (on which D. Kelly 1978a pp. 109–10); *Yvain* 150–68. Cf. pp. 000–00 above (with slightly different translation).

159. *Ducs* 2127–34, 28723–26, 42043–53. Cf. Marti 1941 p. 250; Curtius 1954 pp. 467–68; Gompf 1973 pp. 58–59.

160. *Aristote* 44–58, 516–27; *Berinus* §1 (p. 3); *Claris* 4667–74; *Ducs* 2134, 39690–96; *Gui* 18. See Ollier 1974a pp. 34–36.

161. Cf. *FEW* IV, 685–86, 688; *Guiron* p. 175. See Hanning 1974.

162. See D. Kelly 1984b pp. 120–21. Cf. *Estoire* I, 131; Huth *Merlin* II, 198; *Partonopeu* 309–14.

163. *Sens* is a synonym for *engin* in v. 4. Cf. also *Amadas* 7124–29; *Anjou* 8061–8104; *Dolopathos* fr pp. 6–7; *Emp* 43–45; *Galeran* 2278–79; *Melusine* Co 125–41; *Meraugis* 310–13; *Partonopeu* 124–34, Cont 3056–58; *Prise* 1227–29.

164. See *Ovide mor* I.59–64; *Venjance* (3) §44. Contrast *Troie* 23214–15.

165. DuCange VI, 419–20, especially s.v. *subtiliare* (2); Godefroy VII, 563–66, 585; X, 706, 721; *T-L* IX, 984–91; *FEW* XII, 365–67.

166. *Perceforest* 74:56.

167. On *rudis,* cf. Stock 1972 p. 81; and Godefroy VII, 259; X 598; *T-L* VIII, 1529–31; *FEW* X, 540–42.

168. *Dolopathos* fr p. 7.

169. See *Guiron* p. 175; *Partonopeu* 4653–58. Cf. Curtius 1954 pp. 477–78; Jodogne 1964b p. 88; Badel 1975 pp. 89–90.

170. Köhler 1962 p. 9. Cf. H. R. Jauss's use of *Erwartungshorizont* in *GRLMA* I, 119.

171. *Ducs* 2127–29, 2157–64, 14793–804. See *Dole* 5643–52; *Lais* Pro 43–56. Cf. *Troie* 13457–94, and Simon 1958 pp. 60–70, 106–8; Kupper *GRLMA* XI.1, 820–23.

172. See below, p. 224. *Atre* 1–6; *Bel inc* 1–5; *Couci* 8245–49; *Escanor* 4–14, 18–21, 48–57; *Florimont* 8–9, 9211–16, 13637–40; *Joufroi* 83–88; *Partonopeu* 10609–44; *Rose* 40–44; *Violette* 48–64, 6637–39. For antecedents, see Bezzola 1944 II, 369–77, 461–67; Zumthor 1975 pp. 172–73.

173. Frappier 1972 p. 341; but see Haug 1978 p. 24, 69. On the patron, see Grundmann 1936; Bumke 1979; for French examples see also Lejeune 1954, 1958, 1977 pp. 204–8; Legge 1959, 1963 passim; Tyson 1979.

174. Köhler 1970 ch. 2. See *Alex* APar I.37–61; *Couronnement* 4–5; *Durmart* 15093–126; *Perceval* Cont II 26086–100; *Rou* II.1354–73; *Saisnes* 25–26.

175. For contemporary commentary, see Faral 1910; Fletcher 1966 pp. 137–42, 178–92. Cf. *Galeran* 4810–13; *Rou* II.1354–73, III.6373–98.

176. Freeman 1979 pp. 179–80 n. 18.

177. *Atre* 3396, 4728–29; *Brun* 1190, 2724, 3648–49; *Brut* 3401–6, 13275–93; *Cesar* p. 35 fol. 4r°; *Claris* 21750; *Dolopathos* fr p. 108; *Escoufle* 454, 1306–13, 2652; *Florence* MS 24384, v. 4136; *Floriant* 6452, 6586; *Floris* 1594; *Horn* 1644; *Laurin* ll. 7911–16, 9386–87, 10549; *Mantel* 1–5; *Marques* pp. 56 (53a4), 74 (62a2), 83 (66d1), 90 (70b1); *Rigomer* 3024–26, 6548–50, 7325–27, 7907–9, 11243–46, 11609–12; *Ovide mor* I.1496, II.4088, 5077, IV.4312; *Partonopeu* Cont 2412; *Per-*

ceval Cont I *T* 1674 (= *E* 4988), *L* 9354–55, *A* 9308; *Perceval* Cont II 32292; *Protheselaus* 7328–39; *Rose* 5634/5604, 6419/6389, 11488/11458, 15395/15365; *Silence* 3138; *Troie* 3144, 13400, 20034, 27439.

178. Cf. *Lais* Chait 33–34, Milun 22; *Lycorne* 8552–58; *Meliador* 3412–14, 18118–23, 22963–67; *Perceval* Cont II 28006–7.

179. Cf. Frappier *GRLMA* IV.1, 306; *Perceval* Cont II 26086–101.

180. See Mölk 1969 §4, vv. 7–16; §8, vv. 25–29; §9, vv. 10–16; §15, vv. 8–15; §20, vv. 13–27; §21, vv. 13–15; §22, vv. 8–11; §24, vv. 37–41.

181. On Adenet's sources, see A. Henry ed. in *Berte* pp. 16–49. Cf. *Gau d'Aupais* 3–6.

182. Greif 1886 passim; Faral 1913 pp. 3–157. But cf. L. G. Donovan 1975 pp. 217–27 for the *Thèbes;* and Nolan 1980 and Cormier 1988, 1989 for the *Aeneid* glosses and the *Eneas; TChev* Vol. II, pp. 62–63, and vv. 6657–64.

183. See the analogous examples in *T-L* II, 1412.51–1413.19; *FEW* VIII, 334 (s.v. *depecer* col. a).

184. As in *Brut* 1223–30.

185. Cf. *Guil maréchal* 3593–98.

186. See D. Kelly 1970a p. 280; Burgess 1984 pp. 11–12. Cf. alongside those to follow *Anseïs de Carthage* 12 and *Bueve de Hanstone* 11, both cited in Jodogne 1964b pp. 96–97; *Perceval* H p. 459, vv. 93–95.

187. Cf. *Tristan* MS 12599 (p. 191); §283a (p. 207).

188. Cf. Huth *Merlin* II, 57–58. On this division, see Bogdanow 1966 pp. 60–87; Ryding 1971 pp. 31–32.

189. Cf. Frappier 1972 p. 354.

190. These lines are missing in the Short (*L* 7934–35, *ASP* 7926–27) and Long (*E* 18000–18001) redactions. See also, for example, *Chev deus espees* 3531–45, 6290–93, 10460–61; Didot *Perc D* 116–18, 1783–85, *E* 132–34, 2392–95, and *Durmart* 15–16, 1571–73, 6073–76, 9097–9100; *Eracle* 6121–23; *Helcanus* §5 (p. 9); *Rose* 6184–89/6154–59; *Sone* 14793–96.

191. Cited from Bruyne 1946 II, 91.

192. Brugger 1941 (1943) pp. 126–28.

193. D. Kelly 1969a; cf. above, pp. 101–3, and on *divers,* pp. 26–31.

194. D. Kelly 1970b pp. 191–94.

195. Guenée 1977 pp. 9–13.

196. See above, p. 73.

197. Cf. also *Silence* 3138, 6678. See also *Guil d'A* 13–17; *Lycorne* 8550–58.

198. Often only as quotes or comparisons; but see also *Melusine* Co 93–117; *Poire* 2978–80; *Venjance* (3) §1. The prose romances do this extensively; see E. Kennedy 1970. The example of the *Rose* is well documented.

199. See also *Berinus* §§4, 148. See also n. 182 above.

200. L. G. Donovan 1975 pp. 189–257 and passim; Petit 1985b pp. 21–137.

201. Angeli 1971 pp. 101–41; Poirion 1978; Shirt 1982; Huchet 1984. Cf. *Restor* 66–68, 291–96, 2681–91.

202. D. Kelly 1969a pp. 14–15.

203. L. Constans ed. in *Troie* I, 234–63; Hansen 1971 pp. 6–10.

204. *Troie* 5093–98, 24904–7. Cf. Greif 1886 pp. 12–57.

205. Also *Troie* 648–49 in the plot resumé.

206. Most such references are topical, as in *Manekine* 2875–79. However, see *Abenteuer* pp. 105 (49b), 106 (49c); *Amadas* 1407–8; *Berinus* §576; *Cleomadés* 15914–32, 18505–18; *Couci* 5438–39; *Cristal* 6427–30; Didot *Perc* E 132–34, 250–52, 2392–95, 2639–42, and D 116–18, 218–21, 1251–57, 1783–85; *Durmart* 6073–76, 9097–9100; *Estoire* p. 158.19–22; *Estoire* RoB 3155–58; *Florimont* 3887–93; *Folie Lanc* 5.579–93, 7.416–18; *Guiron* pp. 176–77, 181–82, §§4, 288; *Helcanus* §§5 (p. 9), 282 (p. 331); Huth *Merlin* II, 172–73; *Joseph d'A* ll. 393–96/311–12; *Manekine* 8481–82; *Meliador* 30574–79; *Melusine* JdA pp. 10.14–16, 14.2–5, 16.29–31; *Merlin* M 17.4–5/S 20.13–14, 457.14–15; *Perceval* Cont I E 264–65, E 881–83, E 3989–90, E 5481–83, E 9154–63, T 5574–83, L 7083–90, A 7051–58, M 17157–64, T 13061–68, L 7541–44, A 7503–6, AL 7991–95, T 13817–21, M 18055–59, T 13754–57; *Perceval* Cont II E 20001–2; *Perceval* Cont III 39681–83; *Perlesvaus* ll. 3625–26, 4392–94, 8868–69; *Richars* 1687–88; *Rigomer* 6429–34, 12910–16, 14280, 16347–52.

207. *Alex* AdeP 27–32; *Alex déca* 61–66; *Alex* APar 166–94; *Alex* B 77–80 (cf. A 62–68), 7264–65 (cf. A 3707–8), L 135–40; *Florimont* 3883–93 (cf. pp. cvi-cix). The paternity is retained in *TChev* 46–509. Cf. Frappier 1964b pp. 16–17.

208. Loomis 1949 pp. 45–50. For an exception, see Cadot 1976 pp. 440–47.

209. Greif 1886 p. 33. Compare, for example, the child in Ulysse's dream (*Troie* 29827–58) with the candle-tree child (*Perceval* Cont II 31421–505; Didot *Perc* pp. 203–4; *Durmart* 1507–48), and the giant of Saint Michael's Mount borrowed from Geoffrey of Monmouth (*Brut* 11404–15).

210. I.e., Dares at this juncture. Cf. Greif 1886 p. 16.

211. On Antenor, see M.-R. Jung 1984 and 1985.

212. Greif 1886 p. 55 (§68.5) for references.

213. See above, p. 89.

214. See Tattersall 1981; Baumgartner 1988a pp. 9–10 and 1988b pp. 3–4. Cf. *Florence* 1–13; and, in general, Seifert 1977 pp. 234–36.

215. Spörl 1935 pp. 18–20. See McCormick 1975; Krüger 1976; Tillmann-Bartylla *GRLMA* XI.1, 324. Cf. Wolter 1959 p. 79.

216. Frappier *GRLMA* IV.1, 506–7.

217. *Troie* IV, 435, in MS *G;* J. R. Reinhard ed. in *Amadas* pp. iii-iv; Huot 1987 pp. 19–35. Cf. as well the insertion of Merlin's prophecies into Wace's *Brut* (p. 389 var.), *Fouke* pp. 59.39–61.7, and *Guiron* §212 n. 2.

218. A. Foulet ed. in *Alex* AdeP pp. 1–2, APar pp. ix-xviii; *TChev* 1333–42. Cf. Meyer 1886. See also *Florimont* 103–10.

219. Delbouille 1927, 1960; Riquer 1968.

220. Riquer 1968 pp. 123, 184, 227.

221. Van Emden 1975 p. 114.

222. Delbouille 1927, 1960.

223. Delbouille 1927; Tyssens 1967. Cf. Palermo 1960.

224. F. Meunier ed. *Godin* pp. xi-xvi.

225. Klebs 1899; Delbouille 1969 pp. 1176–86; Köhler *GRLMA* I, 400–401; Frappier *GRLMA* IV.1, 167–70.

226. On hagiographic cycles, see Delehaye 1927 pp. 37–38; on late epic, C. M. Jones 1990.

227. Sparnaay 1933 I, 72–73; D. Kelly 1970b pp. 195–97; Pirot 1972 pp. 469–75. Cf. Sturm-Maddox 1971; *Eracle* 2903–14.

228. G. Hutchings in *Charrette* H, e.g., pp. xxx-xxxiii; Kennedy 1970 pp. 524–25.

229. See *Perceval* H pp. 455–80.

230. A. Henry ed. in *Cleomadés* II, 661–74.

231. Cf. Schmolke-Hasselmann 1980a p. 27 n. 45, pp. 41–42.

232. Monfrin 1963 pp. 161–62.

233. On this sense of *perfectio*, see Calcidius' commentary on *Timaeus*, ch. 222, and Liebeschütz 1926 p. 136 n. 107.

234. On the passage from *unir* to *parfaire*, see *Becket* 148–60; *Estoire* II, 539/I.160.24; *Folie Lanc* p. 60.587–90 (cf. *Tristan* §287a n. 1); *Melusine* JdA p. 307.2–14. See *T-L* VII, 249.9–14; cf. *FEW* VIII, 239 ("compléter qch en y ajoutant ce qui manque" s.v. *perficere*) and XIV, 47 ("réunir les données d'un récit . . . joindre deux ou plusieurs choses de même nature" or "différentes pour n'en faire qu'une" s.v. *unire*.).

235. See above, p. 124.

236. Cf. *Parfait* 1–53; *Restor* 133–53.

237. *Accomplir: Ovide mor* I, 20–22; *dire mot a mot: Perceval* Cont II 25281–83; *Tristan* §282a (p. 190); *fournir: Becket* 144, 163; *Cleomadés* 18460 (= *parfournir*); *Sone* 14795. Cf. *Mort* §1; *Tristan* §570.

238. Pickens 1978b p. 375.

239. Godefroy V, 763–64; *T-L* VII, 252–53; and *Engleis* 2251; *Rose* 10584–88/10554–58.

240. Cf. *Becket* 151–55; *Brun* 1852–59; *Mort* §204.8–13; *Perceval* Cont III 42657–65 (see also p. 344 and 386 n. 42638–68); *Perceval* Cont IV 6984–7020; *Troie* 132–37.

241. Adams 1974; Shirt 1975; but cf. J. Janssens 1987.

242. Cf. T. B. W. Reid ed. *Yvain* R 5061f. note (p. 211); D. Kelly 1984b pp. 123–24.

243. The geographical discrepancy is between not conflicting but complementary passages; Chrétien's *Charrette* is not a geography!

244. Bloomfield 1970 p. 38.

245. Examples: *Parfait* 2932–40; *TChev* 6639–43, 6674–77. See Blumenfeld-Kosinski 1988 pp. 88–90; and above, pp. 89–91.

246. Cf. *Chev deus espees* 12346–52; *Troie* 132–37.

247. Busby 1980b; Schmolke-Hasselmann 1980a p. 31 (cf. pp. 86–91).

248. Didot *Perc* E 1471–72; D 1251–52.

249. *Guiron* pp. 176–80, 182–83; Huth *Merlin* II, 57–58, 172–73; *Rose* 6324–26/6294–96; *Tristan* §287a n. 1 (p. 211). On the *Brait*, see Bogdanow 1966; Baumgartner 1975 p. 97 n. 40.

250. *Tristan* §§41, 388a, 502, etc.; see Bogdanow 1966. See as well *Waldef* 23–24.
251. See Bogdanow 1966 pp. 64–87, 272–73; D. Kelly 1966b pp. 22–24; Sargent-Baur 1987a and 1987b. Cf. *Guiron* §§256, 262; *Perceforest* IV.xxxi.434–39 (cf. note 705/435, p. 1178)/90:353–54; 91:195 ("les croniques"); *Tristan* §§190 n. 6, 204 n. 3, 231a n. 4, 252, 282a, 293a (pp. 218–19), 318 n. 1, 387, 392, 396, 475, 502, 534 n. 5, 545.
252. *Perceval* Cont I Vol. 3.2, p. 215.
253. *Perceval* Cont I Vol. 2, p. 601.
254. Cf. *ThLL* V.i 1351.53–55 s.v. *discretio;* Godefroy IX, 328; *T-L* II, 1546–47.
255. On *simplece* in descriptions, see also pp. 226–28.
256. Cf. *Eledus* 11–18; *Perceval* Cont I E 262–66, 881–88; *Troie* 4855–60. See Gallais 1964a pp. 214–20.
257. On such elaboration, see Rohr 1962 pp. 320–25.
258. *Amadas* 1406–8; *Cleomadés* 15926–32; *Manekine* 8481–82; *Merlin* M 46.62–71/S 51.32–38; *Perceforest* 89:356; *Tristan* §§282a, 480 n. 1; *Waldef* 5023–28, 6013–14. See Ménard 1969 pp. 493–94; Taylor 1987 p. 285; and under abbreviation below, pp. 295–97.
259. *Amadas* 7427–32, 7449–50; *Anjou* 47–48; *Athis* 13778–80; *Cleomadés* 17408–21; *Oiselet* 8; *Sept sages* V 249–52; *TChev* 4245–54, 4271–73; *Tornoiement* 3127 ("a la parsome"); *Troie* 5327.
260. *Lanzelet* 6912–13 (on Arthur's predicted return).
261. *Estoire* II, 18–19/I.7.4–7; *Rigomer* 12910–16.
262. *Chev épée* 12–17; *Couci* 5438–42; *Fergus* 4072–80; *Helcanus* §43 (p. 69); *Ovide mor* I.1615–21; *Perceval* Cont I E 2072–77.
263. *Estoire* II, 9/I.5.1–2. See Leupin 1982b pp. 23–35; D. Kelly 1988c pp. 29–31.
264. Cf. as well *Estoire* RoB 3161–64.
265. On what follows, see D. Kelly 1984d.
266. See above, p. 62.
267. Leupin 1982a; D. Kelly 1985a pp. 212–15; Hult 1986b.
268. Zink 1979 pp. 45–68; cf. Baumgartner 1981 pp. 92–95 and 1986 pp. 16–18, especially n. 20 (p. 21); D. Kelly 1984d pp. 180–82; Burns 1985a pp. 1–2.
269. Vinaver 1966 pp. 13–23; Matarasso 1979.
270. See Woledge and Clive 1964 pp. 37–38; Struss *GRLMA* IV.1, 370–71, 373–75. Cf. *Joseph d'A* Mid Fr p. 285; and, on the *Elucidation*'s "branches," A. W. Thompson ed. *Elucidation* pp. 75–76.
271. *Brut* 104, 1067–70, 1528–36, 1617–18, 6327–28, 8015, 11118, 12961–62; *Cleomadés* 17408–13; Didot *Perc* E 2392–94, 2640–41, D 1783–84; *Dolopathos* fr pp. 66, 430 (from *Dolopathos* lat p. 107.17–25); *Escanor* 25898–909; *Escoufle* 9048–51; *Epervier* 27; *Florence* MS 24384 vv. 1247, 3569; *Floriant* 8276–78; *Gliglois* 2630; *Guingamor* 8; *Lycorne* 8556–61; *Melusine* Co 6233–38; *Perceval* Cont I E 8950 (but cf. *T* 5370 and the *MQ* vars.), *L* 8244–46 (*M* 18308–10, *T* 14058–60); *Perceval* Cont II 29190–91; *Rigomer* 12140; *Sept sages* V 835–36; *Tristan* §§103, 104 and n. 3, 171 n. 2, 182, 307 n. 8 (p. 239); *Troie* 725–26, 10310–12, 14127–28, 14578, 20148–49, 22547, 27275–76, 27682.
272. *Chev deus espees* 9315–17; *Claris* 8682–83, 19897–98; *Cleomadés* 1507–9,

2713–14, 8211–16, 8384–91, 8974–75, 13914, 15914–17, 17119–20, 18505–35; *Dolopathos* lat p. 107.17–20; *Fergus* 17–18; *Florimont* 854, 9130; *Guil d'A* 33–34; *Helcanus* §§189 (pp. 238–39), 195 (p. 245), 196 (p. 245), 208 (p. 256), 282 (p. 331); *Lanzelet* 9275–76, 9292–95; *Meliador* 7123, 7228–29; *Oiselet* 4; *Partonopeu* Cont 3915–16; *Perceval* Cont III 39582–84; *Queste* p. 105.1–2; *Rigomer* 16347–52; *TChev* 6404–18; *Tristan* §172; *Troie* 4225–26, 5087–88, 29575–94.

273. *Becket* 4392, 5878; *Cleomadés* 17798–99, 18358–59, 18460–61, 18505–35; *Estoire* II, 503–4, 514, 516/I.145.1–22, 150.24–26, 151.13–15; *Gille* 5525; *Ovide mor* IV.2009–10; *Parfait* 374–75; *Troie* 24405. Cf. *Perlesvaus* ll. 4392–94.

274. Frappier 1968b pp. 142–46, 433–34, 450; *GRLMA* IV.1, 584–89.

275. Frappier *GRLMA* IV.1, 316; E. Kennedy 1986; Baumgartner 1981 pp. 13–16. Cf. E. Kennedy in *Lancelot* K vol. II, pp. 89–90; *Lancelot* Vol. VII, pp. 462–76.

276. Frappier 1968b p. 145.

277. Vinaver 1966 p. 15; E. Kennedy 1973 pp. 181–84. Cf. Zumthor 1978; Leupin 1979; Burns 1988. See *Tristan* §§20 n. 1, 23 n. 1.

278. D. Kelly 1969b; Chase 1983; Van Coolput 1986 pp. 18–38; Schmid 1986; Caulkins 1987 (with bibliography). See *Estoire* II, 402–3, 471–73, III, 114–17, 269–71, 302–3/I.106.25–107.14, 132.1–14, 202.30–204.11, 280.14–281.5, 293.20–294.3; *Guiron* §288; *Queste* p. 251.22–30, 265.15–266.9. God is the beginning and end of all things, including the narrative. The *Estoire* purports to have first been written by Jesus Christ (II, 9/I.5.7); see also *Estoire* II, 264/I.66.28–29, and cf. II, 312–13/I.81.14–29.

279. Pickford 1960; L.-F. Flutre in *Perceforest* 70:475–76, 521–22; Taylor 1987.

280. The tendency was already present in historical writing. On *entrelacement* as *intrication,* see C. E. Pickford in *Alix orp* pp. xxii–xxiv. Cf. also *Lanzelet* 9426–31; and Tattersall 1981; Baumgartner 1987c pp. 46–47 and 1988b.

281. D. Kelly 1976 pp. 16–17; Pemberton 1984 pp. 486–87. Cf. the *Berinus* Prologue §1 (p. 3); *Guiron* §288; *Lancelot* xxa.12; *Melusine* Co 1777–92; *Sone* 21314–19; *Tristan* §185a.

282. See *Claris* 5659–65; *Cleomadés* 6592–98, 11798, 15100–102, 17767–72; *Guiron* §229; *Manekine* 6689–96; *Meliador* 30103–4; *Ovide mor* IV.3154–55.

283. Huth *Merlin* I, 85; II, 254; *TChev* 6162–69; *Troie* 30301–2. Cf. *Horn* 5238–39.

284. D. Kelly 1969b pp. 261–65. See *Hunbaut* 1264–65; *Meliador* 30574–79.

285. The *droite voie* can be both straight (i.e., the shortest distance) and correct (i.e., most credible). For the latter sense, see *Chev deus espees* 12349–52; *Perceval* Cont I *A* 7775–82 (*L* 7803–6) *L* 7991–93 (*A* 7991–93, *T* 13817–19, *M* 18055–57), *T* 13754–57); Huth *Merlin* II, 137 ("une autre voie"); *Lancelot* xxiva.33; *Manekine* 58–61; *Poire* 339–46; *Tristan* §293a. Cf. *Tristan* Th Douce 879–83.

286. Ihle 1983. See below, pp. 269–82.

287. Didot *Perc* E 1471–79, D 1251–57; *Escanor* 4892–97; *Estoire* II, 123, 533/I.20.8–9, 158.19–22; *Guiron* p. 182, §132; *Lancelot* lxxxix.1; *Mance* 1715–16; *Meliador* 5241–44, 28861–62; *Merlin* M 17.4–5/S 20.12–14, 335.17–20; *Ovide mor* IV.224–28; *Perceval* Cont II 20001–4, 28778–79; *Perceval* Cont III 37119–23;

Tristan §§37, 106 n. 2, 258, 278, 332 (cf. §160 justifying an inclusion because "apartient a nostre ystoire" or "matiere").

288. *Lancelot* S I, 19 n. 3 (by a scribe); *Ovide mor* II.4580–94.

289. *Parfait* 13; *Restor* 9–11, 66–68, 277–301, 2685–87; *Tristan* Th Sneyd[1] 729–30.

290. Cf. *Lancelot* via.7, xxa.12.

291. *Lancelot* liiia.7.

292. See A. Micha ed. *Lancelot* Vol. ix, p. 200.

293. Vinaver 1966 p. 12; Baumgartner 1986 p. 12. Cf. *Lancelot* xlviii.24. On the incomplete Dyalogus story in the Prose *Sept sages,* see D. Kelly 1985a pp. 212–213. Cf. also *Tristan* §§296a nn. 1 and 2, 335 n. 1, 393 n. 3, 508 n. 2.

294. Cf. *Eracle* 6121–31; *Estoire* RoB 3155–64, 3461–514.

295. *Couci* 5438–39; *Cristal* 6427–30; Didot *Perc* E 248–52, D 217–20; *Durmart* 1569–74, 6073–76, 9097–100; *Estoire* II, 439, 533/I.119.7–14, 158.19–22; *Estoire* RoB 3155–64; *Florimont* 3883–93; *Folie Lanc* p. 60.588–90; *Guiron* §§4, 288; *Helcanus* §5 (p. 9); Huth *Merlin* II, 172–73; *Lancelot* civ.9; *Manekine* 2875–79; *Meliador* 30574–79; *Merlin* p. 20.13–14; *Perceval* Cont II 20001–4; *Perlesvaus* ll. 3625–26, 4392–94; *Queste* p. 251.28–30; *Sone* 14793–96, 21316–18; *Tristan* §§306 (pp. 236–37 and n. 6), 421 n. 3 (cf. §441 n. 1), 466 n. 4, 493 n. 7; *Troie* 45–74 (on "Omer"), 2061–67, 5577–82, 20148–49, 27273–76.

296. Often this has to do with names or time spans. *Alex* APar II.4, 1723; *Anjou* 85; *Berinus* §280; *Cassidorus* §404; *Claris* 19897–98; *Cleomadés* 1507–9, 2713–14, 8211–16, 8384–87, 8974–75, 13914, 15914–17, 17119, 17408–43; *Dolopathos* fr p. 66; *Durmart* 839–40; *Escoufle* 9048–51; *Fergus* 17–18; *Florence* MS 24384 v. 1247; *Florimont* 854, 9130–31; *Gliglois* 2630; *Guingamor* 8; *Lais* Chait 34, Mil 22; *Laurin* l. 10549; *Meliador* 3413–14, 7213, 18122–23, 22963–67; *Rigomer* 12140; *Sept sages* V 836; *Troie* 725–26, 4225–26, 29575–94.

297. See *Erec* 19–22; *Folie Lanc* p. 60.592. See Gallais 1988 ch. XI.

298. Loomis 1949 p. 40. Cf. Baumgartner 1985 pp. 10–14; *Perceval* Cont I L 8299–8310 and M 18363–74.

299. *Alex* A 254–55, 368–71, 4540; *Alex* APar II.972–73, IV.1233–35; *Dole* 5332–50, 5507–12; *Florence* MS 24384 v. 1025; *Gille* 11–20, 2413–16, 5211–15; *Prise* 577; *Vengement* 33, 151–52, 242–46, 546–47; *Venjance* (2) 133; *Waldef* 18–24, 45–54. See Poirion 1980.

300. Loomis 1949 p. 41. Similarly Faral 1913 p. 74 on *Eneas.*

301. Nims 1974 p. 219.

302. See *Troie* 1635–42, 2028–44, 2061–67.

303. Lacy 1980 p. 80.

304. Lacy 1980 p. 116.

Chapter 5. *Estoire: Aventure merveilleuse*

1. See Schmale 1985 pp. 110–11.

2. Gallais 1964b pp. 339–42; Gumbrecht *GRLMA* XI.1, 903–5; Meneghetti 1989. Cf. the juxtaposition *devoir-merveille* in *Perc* Cont I (Gallais 1988 pp. 870–75).

3. Fourquet 1956. See also Marx 1952 pp. 87–88; Frappier 1961 pp. 29–32; Köhler 1970 p. 12; Warning *GRLMA* IV.1, 25–59; Hanning 1972 pp. 9–10; Poirion 1973; Boklund 1977a; Haug 1978; Poirion 1978; Maddox 1980 pp. 92–93; Poirion 1982 p. 65; Harf-Lancner 1984 pp. 7–10; Dubost 1988 especially pp. 66–68.

4. Cf. Thoss 1972 p. 30; E. Kennedy 1973 pp. 173–75; Frappier *GRLMA* IV.1, 210–11; Dufournet and Castellani 1988. For the fay as illustration see Westoby 1985.

5. Haidu 1973b p. 717. Zumthor *GRLMA* I, 87, and IV.1, 69.

6. See Zumthor *GRLMA* I, 66–67; Dembowski 1978 p. 145. Cf. Struss *GRLMA* XI.1, 951–1023, on contingency in events and their integration into received historical models.

7. Cf. Priscian *Praeexercitamina* §1–4 I (pp. 430–31).

8. Cf. *Ad Her* I.xvii.27, II.xix. On inventing one's own examples, see IV.i-vii and pp. xvi-xvii. The *Ad Her* considers his invention of original examples to be unique, since, he asserts, most rhetoricians borrow from others.

9. Bloch 1977.

10. Zink 1981 p. 12; cf. p. 21. See also Sturm-Maddox 1971 pp. 247–48; Haidu 1972b; Haug 1973; Cadot 1976; Poirion 1986a.

11. E. Vinaver in *Balain* pp. xxii-xxiii.

12. Poirion 1973; Wolf 1977 pp. 264–66; Payen 1978; Stanesco 1985.

13. Cf. Baumgartner 1985 pp. 18–20; Dinshaw 1988 pp. 91–93. Contrast *Joufroi* 4333–44; *Paris* p. 470.18–21; *Troie* 1643–49.

14. Contrast with Hue de Rotelande's "crude formulation," discussed in Krueger 1987 p. 123. Cf. Méla 1984 pp. 15–16.

15. Köhler 1970 pp. 77–78, 100–104; cf. Boiron and Payen 1970 pp. 22–26.

16. Guiette 1978 pp. 29–56; D. Kelly 1983a; D. Kelly 1988a.

17. Haidu 1972a, especially pp. 36–37.

18. Matoré 1980 pp. 229–31; Poirion 1986b.

19. Stimming 1888 pp. 333–34, 342 *(estranh)*; Jauss 1953; Frappier 1961 pp. 33–34; R. Lathuillère ed. *Guiron* pp. 136–44; Sienaert 1978 pp. 192–93; Poirion 1982 p. 82; Marache 1988; Peron 1989. See *Cleomadés* 12–18.

20. Ménard 1969 pp. 376–416; Köhler 1970 p. 46; Carasso-Bulow 1976 pp. 11–12; Sienaert 1978 pp. 17–24; Poirion 1982 pp. 4–6. Cf. Fourrier 1960 p. 489; and see in general Ducháček 1960 pp. 104–10.

21. Zumthor 1972 p. 138; cf. also Carasso-Bulow 1976 pp. 15–34; Poirion 1982 pp. 3–4.

22. See the reflections of Dubost 1988, who asserts that "Chrétien de Troyes, comme les autres auteurs du Moyen Age, ne connaissait que la *merveille,* terme à vaste capacité romantique . . . " (p. 49).

23. Frappier *GRLMA* IV.1, 210–11; cf. Marache 1988 on "les effets de sens du mot" (p. 130).

24. See Lefèvre *GRLMA* IV.1, 271; and Struss *GRLMA* IV.1, 363–64, 367.

25. Ménard 1979 pp. 182–86; Ihle 1983 pp. 23–26.

26. Carasso-Bulow 1976 pp. 22–23; Frappier *GRLMA* IV.1, 315–16; Leupin 1982a. Other examples: the flower maidens (*Alex* APar III.2898–2900) and other marvels Alexander encounters in India (III.996); the varieties of places that make

the brave turn cowardly and vice versa (_Alex_ APar I.2517–38; _Meraugis_ 3694–3744) or that reveal false love (_Lancelot_ lxxxiii.6); the Fountain of Marvels (_Folie Lanc_ pp. 49.96–108, 117.746–50).

27. See J. Rychner ed. _Lais_ pp. xvii-xix; Boiron and Payen 1970 pp. 23–24; D. Kelly 1971 pp. 332–34; Poirion 1982 pp. 52–55. Cf. _Lancelot_ via.1–2.

28. _Alex_ APar II.1961–73. See also _Dole_ 5320–21. Cf. _Folie Lanc_ p. 63.101–3 (Lancelot throws a giant out a window); Huth _Merlin_ II, 15; _TChev_ 2786 (Alexander swims across a swift current); _Waldef_ 1041–42, 11424–28 (a man's beauty), 5691–96 (a madman), 11639–42 (a large army), 21327–32 (a great blow).

29. Huth _Merlin_ I, 243. Cf. _Alex_ APar III.6736–37; _Erec_ 3108–9; _Lancelot_ xxixa.7; _Waldef_ 16842–48, 17219–22, 21249–54.

30. Rousset 1956 pp. 29–30; D. Kelly 1974 pp. 148–49; Taylor 1987 pp. 285–86; Dubost 1988 pp. 68–69. See _Atre_ 2882–87 (bad night in forest); _Ducs_ 19525–40; Huth _Merlin_ I, 203–13; _Meliacin_ 4227–30 (recognition); _Parfait_ 2657–58 (blows); _Partonopeu_ 735–36 (a good wind); _Perceforest_ 89:361–63 (including note 1 to p. 361 and note 1 to p. 362), 363–64; _Pierre_ pp. 69.9–11, 72.23–26; _TChev_ 5790–5864; _Tristan_ §102.7–9.

31. Pauphilet 1950 pp. 105–6; Rousset 1956 p. 32; Baader 1966 pp. 106–7; Sargent-Baur 1972; Ménard 1979 pp. 88–91; Poirion 1982 pp. 4–6.

32. _Rou_ III.5323–26.

33. Kellermann 1936 pp. 113, 115–16.

34. See Lyons 1965 passim; cf. as well, on the "tournament" as subgenre, _GRLMA_ IV.1, 446–48 (R. Lejenue) and 477–78 (J.-C. Payen).

35. Köhler 1970 pp. 66–72. Alexander has an analogous encounter in _TChev_ 7019–40.

36. _Guil maréchal_ 1531–50, 2395–2421. Cf. Huth _Merlin_ II, 231; _Mort_ §3 (Arthur has tournaments).

37. Cf. _Alix orp_ p. 6.10–16; _Meliador_ 12605–16.

38. See _Mort_ §§100–101; see also Huth _Merlin_ I, 227. Cf. Van Coolput 1987a pp. 99–106.

39. _Erec_ 533–46. Cf. _Escoufle_ 1858–63.

40. Incest in _Anjou; Manekine._ Homosexuality (accusation of) in _Eneas_ 8567–621; _Lais_ Lan 277–86; _Perc Cont_ IV 1554–1601. Women knights: the Amazons in the various Alexander romances, including _TChev_ 4690–93 (Candea governed by women), 6138–91; and _Claris_ 27742–75; _Eneas_ 6907–34, 6984–993; _Perceforest_ 89:364–65; _Silence,_ especially 2257–2400.

41. Huth _Merlin_ I, 21–31, 93, 153–54, 160, 164–65, 279–80; II, 76–77, 80, 96–98, 100, 155, 158; _Merlin_ M 16.1–41/S 18.21–19.1; the _Profecies_ illustrate his vision. See Zumthor 1943; Thorpe 1973; Frappier _GRLMA_ IV.1, 191–94.

42. _Alex_ APar III.3232–46.

43. Cf. Hansen 1971 pp. 28–31. On Benoît's use of Ovid, see Greif 1886 pp. 16–19.

44. D. Kelly 1984d pp. 172–73.

45. Lacroix 1971 pp. 75–79. See Schulz 1909 pp. 138–39; Rousset 1956. For antiquity, see Kroll 1924 pp. 54–57.

46. Lacroix 1971 p. 75. Cf. Lofmark 1972a pp. 57–61; Keen 1973 pp. 290, 293, 307; E. Kennedy 1973 p. 175.

47. *Ducs* 39873–84; *Rou* III.337–40. Cf. also *Guil maréchal* 485–92.

48. Delehaye 1927 pp. 47–50, 210; Rousset 1956 pp. 32–34; Wehrli 1961 pp. 430–31; Altman 1975 pp. 5–7; Poirion 1982 pp. 7–18.

49. Kleinschmidt 1974; Gier 1979b pp. 12–13. Cf. Trimpi 1974 pp. 97–98.

50. *Rou* III.5323–26. See Brinkmann 1964b p. 401; Tubach 1980.

51. Baader 1966 p. 114–15; D. Kelly 1974 pp. 153–55. For similar phenomena in *chansons de geste,* see Gsteiger 1959 p. 217.

52. Legge 1963 pp. 29–31.

53. Fourrier 1960 pp. 392–98.

54. Poirion 1978 p. 227. See *Claris* 24804–30, 25016–29; *Folie Lanc* p. 93.509–11; *Guil maréchal* 1531–50, 1883–94, 2395–2421, 5983–89; Huth *Merlin* I, 151; *Meliacin* 2275–81; *Merlin* S 235.39–236.4; *Yvain* 2166–71, and the hero's "reconquest" of Laudine's castle and love at the end of the romance.

55. On *certain,* see p. 141, above.

56. Didot *Perc* E 1909–44/D 1558–90; *Lancelot* lxxia.48; *Mort* §3; *Queste* p. 278.5–7. See D. Kelly 1984b pp. 128–30; Pickens 1984 pp. 507–8.

57. Cited from William of Newburg in Lacroix 1971 p. 75 n. 166. Cf. Rousset 1956 pp. 26–29; Guiette 1978 pp. 29–45. Cf. *Prise* 1563–74.

58. Keen 1973 p. 297; Tubach 1980 p. 7.

59. D. Kelly 1978a pp. 37–39. Cf. Jauss 1983 p. 454.

60. Cited from C. G. Jung 1971 p. 416/p. 388; see in general Jung's *Synchronizität als ein Prinzip akausaler Zusammenhänge* and *Über Synchronizität.* My purpose here is to identify common features in a certain kind of experience, not to impose, or reject, a modern, psychoanalytic reading of medieval texts.

61. Benjamin 1972 p. 26.

62. Cf. Bell 1976 pp. 474–75. For analogous developments in romance, see *Melusine* JdA pp. 19–21; *Perceforest* IV.xxi-xxiii and n. 475/82 (pp. 1163–64)/90: 341–44.

63. *Alex* APar III.3407–14; *Folie Lanc* p. 141.2–7; Huth *Merlin* I, 148. See Carasso-Bulow 1976 p. 24.

64. Cf. *Alex* APar I.402–8, III.3524–29, IV.13–14; *Estoire* II, 175, 448, 503, III, 160/I.32.31–33, 122.14–21, 145.1–4, 226.11–23; *Folie Lanc* pp. 49.96–108, 93.509–16; *Guil maréchal* 6107–12, 13853–63; *Joseph d'A* ll. 489–91/391–93; *Merlin* M 19.36–42/S 23.15–20; *Mule* 41–49, 440–48, 490–92; *St-Louis* §§128–29, 297–98. On the limitations of such historical inquiry, see Guenée 1973 pp. 1008–11.

65. Hugh of Saint Victor, cited from Bruyne 1946 II, 237 n. 2.

66. D. Kelly 1978a pp. 26–56. Cf. *Meliacin* 214–19.

67. Frappier 1964b pp. 24, 33; Poirion 1982 p. 95.

68. Köhler 1970 pp. 85–88; Ménard 1979 pp. 86–87. The distinction may, of course, be hazy, given the alterity of modern and medieval perceptions of what is natural and unnatural. An extraordinary rainfall, a natural disaster to us, is extraordinary to Alexander's men, whereas monsters in the desert seem as natural as elephants (*Alex* APar III.3139–44, 3254–61).

69. Levenson 1979.
70. Cf. Jodogne 1964a pp. 79–80; Köhler 1970 pp. 67–69; D. Kelly 1976; Ribard 1980a.
71. Cf. *Partonopeu* Cont 1696–1704.
72. D. Kelly 1984c p. 41.
73. *Alex* APar III.7359, 7787–88, 7817; *Guiron* §152; *Parfait* 3509–13; *Paris* p. 454.13 ("desaventure"); *Restor* 603–5; *Waldef* 20504–24. See Patch 1927; Köhler 1973.
74. Brinkmann 1964b pp. 422–23; Köhler 1970 pp. 66–91, 195–205; Köhler 1973 pp. 28–30; L. G. Donovan 1975 pp. 47, 77; Köhler 1976 pp. 332–33; D. Kelly 1976 pp. 12–16. *Alex* APar III.3720–29; *Guil maréchal* 11014–21, 11745–50, 12105–10, 13321–28, 15834–48, 17501–4; *Merlin* M §§1–16/S pp. 1–20; *Paris* p. 575.14–20. Cf. Merlin's prophecies and typology in the *Lancelot,* especially iv.
75. Especially lays: *Desiré* 1–4, 762–64; *Doon* 281–86; *Epervier* 225–27; *Espine* 503–4; *Graelent* 727–30; *Guingamor* 1–5, 675–78; *Ignaure* 14–18; *Lais* Gui 22–26, Eq 3–9, Fr 515–18, Bsc 315–18, Lan 1–4, DA 1–6, 253–54, Yo 555–58, Laus 1–2, 157–59, El 25–28; *Tydorel* 1–3. See also *Guiron* §104; and above, pp. 121–25.
76. See pp. 75–78. Also *Berinus* §1 (pp. 1–2); *Cleomadés* 87–90; Didot *Perc* E 1476–77, 2672–73, D 1255–56, 1978–80, Appendix AD 504–7; *Dole* 5643–52; *Dolopathos* fr pp. 6–7; *Epervier* 1–8; *Erec* 23–26; *Escoufle* 26–30; *Espine* 11–14; *Lais* Pro 34–38; *Lancelot* xliii.6, l.60c (= 61a), cvi.25; *Manekine* 7339–42; *Meliador* 30510–12; *Troie* 102–4.
77. See above, p. 50; and D. Kelly 1986; Peron 1989 pp. 296–303.
78. For romance examples, see the dream adventures in *Bel inc* 4551–84, 4634–53. Cf. Faral 1913 pp. 381–82.
79. *Vies* 35, in Mölk 1969 §75.
80. Köhler 1962 p. 233 nn. 51–52 (cf. pp. 17–19); D. Kelly 1985b p. 76.
81. Cf. above on Caradoc's joy, pp. 137–38.
82. Jauss 1953; Frappier *GRLMA* IV.1, 352; D. Kelly 1986.
83. Kellermann 1936 p. 69–70; Lyons 1965 pp. 12–13; Gallais 1988 pp. 645–46.
84. Carasso-Bulow 1976 pp. 70–72; Schmolke-Hasselmann 1980a p. 50; Poirion 1982 p. 19. Cf. *Amadas* 4725–49; *Guiron* §113.
85. Cf. Warning *GRLMA* IV.1, 49–54 on this "ironische Erzählweise."
86. *Alex* APar III.994–97, 2296–97, 2898–2900, 3139–44, 3254–61, 3334–37, 3407–19, 3561–62, 3585–94, 3706–29, 6946–52, 7153–56, 7250; *TChev* 6428–31, 6600–6607. Cf. *St-Louis* §190. See Sullivan 1985a and 1985b; Baumgartner 1988a.
87. Lausberg 1960 §§579, 909–10. Cf. Frappier *GRLMA* IV.1, 352; Peron 1989 pp. 300–301.
88. Gallo 1971 p. 206.
89. Ménard 1969 pp. 391–92; Curtis 1979. Cf. Jauss 1953 p. 62.
90. Pickering 1970; Mahler 1974.
91. D. Kelly 1966b pp. 156–62.
92. Carasso-Bulow 1976, especially pp. 15–19; Poirion 1982.
93. Knapton 1975 pp. 15–16. Cf. *Lais* Mil 1–2; and Dubost 1988 pp. 49–50, 54.

94. See Frappier 1964b p. 24.

95. Lausberg 1960 §290; Moos 1988 pp. 26–30; Peron 1989 p. 295 n. 6.

96. Cf. *De inv* p. 56 n. *c.* On "confecta ex rerum varietate" as "from a variety of *materials*" (my emphasis), see *De inv* p. 56 n. *b.*

97. Köhler 1970 p. 46. Cf. Raynaud de Lage 1976 p. 158; Zink 1979 pp. 40–41, 44; Poirion 1982.

98. F. Meunier ed. *Godin* pp. xi–xvi; Palermo 1983; Taylor 1987 pp. 274–80.

99. D. Kelly 1978b.

100. *Alex* APar I.2517–74; Huth *Merlin* II, 155; *Meraugis* 3694–744. Cf. Brugger 1941 (1949) pp. 332–35.

101. Jauss 1953.

102. Freeman 1979 pp. 112–18; Freeman in D. Kelly 1985c pp. 98–115, 120–23, 129–31.

103. D. Kelly 1984c pp. 44–45.

104. Hauvette 1933.

105. See *Cligés* 2724–52. For Fénice, see *Cligés* 2675–2705.

106. See as well *Perceforest* 89:375–76.

107. Especially in thirteenth-century romance, although there are beginnings in Chrétien (Keu, Esclados, Mabonagrain). See Schmolke-Hasselmann 1980a pp. 64–72.

108. Zumthor *GRLMA* I, 66.

109. Frappier 1961 pp. 27, 30, 34; D. Kelly 1974 pp. 148–49.

110. Rousset 1956 p. 29. Cf. Carasso-Bulow 1976 pp. 19–21.

111. Köhler 1970 pp. 66–128; Köhler 1976 pp. 339–41. See below, pp. 240–46.

112. *Guil maréchal* 1893–94; *Yvain* 358–66. Cf. Köhler 1970 pp. 78–83; Boklund 1977b pp. 239–42.

113. Frappier 1961 p. 34; see Ménard 1979 p. 180.

114. *Paris* p. 405.9–13; *Pierre* pp. 36.21–37.1; cf. *Waldef* 18145–50.

115. D. Kelly 1970a p. 278. I incorrectly denied this for Melior; see *Partonopeu* 1125 and vars. *Fée* may indeed be a positive designation for a beautiful man or woman, as in *Waldef* 3286–87, 3385–86. See Harf-Lancner 1984 p. 8.

116. See D. Kelly 1984d.

117. Köhler *GRLMA* IV.1, 93–94.

118. Brinkmann 1928 pp. 109–18; D. Kelly 1985c pp. 38–47; D. Kelly 1986. The examples are numerous: *Flamenca* 1579–82; *Floriant* 2887–921; *Florimont* 4485–88, 6003–28; *Floris* 183–284, 349–52; *Gau d'Aupais* 162–66; *Guiron* §§117, 130; *Jehan* 247–364, 565–82; *Meraugis* 43–141; *Perceval* 1805–29 (adapted in *Fergus* 1519–32, *Cristal* 2403–8); *Sone* 12923–50; *Tornoiement* 1405–25. Another procedure is to emphasize the peculiar in stock description, as in the *Troie* portrait catalogue (5093–582 and *Troie* Pr §§70–73) or in the romances on Melusine and her sons.

119. See Micha, *GRLMA* IV.1, 377–79.

120. Lejeune *GRLMA* IV.1, 438. Cf. pp. 438–40; and Zink 1979 pp. 17–44; *Paris* pp. 391.4–392.5.

121. See Reinhard 1927 pp. 18–44; Brugger 1941, 1951; Köhler 1966 p. 89; Poirion 1982 p. 85. On this, cf. the project based on S. Thompson's motif index, in Lichtblau 1985.

122. Colby 1965; D. Kelly 1988b.
123. Cf. Bruckner 1980b.
124. D. Kelly 1983a pp. 17–18.
125. *Mort* §3.16–25; *Queste* p. 154.20–22.
126. Matarasso 1979 pp. 131–35.
127. *Lancelot* cvi.9–10 (Long pp. 182–83; Short pp. 267–68).
128. See also *Alex* APar I.402–8.
129. Similarly, unique occurrences announce Arthur's death in the *Lancelot* lx.12, lxvi.37–38.
130. *Lancelot* K pp. 149.16–151.15, 158.22–161.14; *Lancelot* xxiia.2–5, 24–29.
131. *Joseph d'A* ll. 682–87/549–50. See Köhler 1970 pp. 66–88.
132. This is what I call "unique excellence"; see below pp. 232–34, and D. Kelly 1978a pp. 184–85. Cf. Allen 1984.
133. Cf. Huth *Merlin* I, 248, 254; II, 180; *Paris* pp. 395.14–17 and 456.21.
134. Köhler 1970 pp. 77–78.
135. Cf. *Pirame* and Chrétien's *Philomela* in the *Ovide mor,* and Cadot 1976.
136. Faral 1913 pp. 73–109; Sienaert 1978 p. 88–89.
137. Cf. Guiette 1978 pp. 73–83.
138. *Alex* APar III.3393–3421; *Folie Lanc* p. 112.481–94; *Guiron* §23; Huth *Merlin* I, 218. See Poirion 1982 pp. 71–75, 80–81 and Godefroy III, 92; IX 450; *T-L* III, 182–87.
139. On *faé,* see *Atre* p. 294, s.v. *faé.* Cf. *Parfait* 3466–67 and Godefroy III, 695–96; *T-L* III, 1553–54. See Harf-Lancner 1984 pp. 63–77.
140. *Queste* p. 15.27–30.
141. *Queste* pp. 277.20–279.7.
142. D. Kelly 1985a.
143. Poirion 1986b.
144. Cf. Sienaert 1978 p. 205; Zumthor *GRLMA* IV.1, 72–73.
145. Cf. also *Ars vers* 1.64–71, 1.110, 4.13.
146. Poirion 1978 pp. 221–24.
147. Cf. Poirion 1982 p. 4. Again, there are numerous examples: *Alex* APar III.2933–36, 3706–8; *Blanc chev* 139–42; *Parfait* 2657–58.
148. Tuve 1966 p. 22. Cf. Uitti 1973 pp. 25–27 on "mythic participation"; Suard 1978.
149. Ménard 1969 pp. 389–416.
150. Bruyne 1946 II, 77; cf. II, 76–77, 248. See also Ducháček 1976 p. 108; Guiette 1978 pp. 48–49; Poirion 1978 p. 219; Poirion 1986b p. 31.
151. See *ThLL* I, 735–40; *M W* I, 212–13 (also s.v. *admiror*); *Guiron* §110; Huth *Merlin* II, 9–10; *Parfait* 949–52.
152. See J. Bédier in *Tristan* Béd I, 258 and n. 3.
153. Cf. Gier 1982 p. 543.
154. *Lais* Pro 28–33.
155. Thorpe 1973.
156. *Guiron* §54; *Mort* §3; *Perceforest* I.6359–835, 12380–3021/74:69–73, 80–85.

157. Faral 1913 pp. 328–35; Sullivan 1985a; Van Coolput 1987b.
158. Cf. *Ombre* 226–67.
159. *Alex* APar II.2831–33; *Lais* Laüs 147, Mil 127–31.
160. Köhler 1970 pp. 68–72; D. Kelly 1971 p. 335. Cf. *Jaufre* 1267–71; *Tyolet* 13–24.
161. D. Kelly 1978d p. 305; Matarasso 1979 pp. 134–35.
162. *Folie Lanc* pp. 89–90.336–46; *Lancelot* lxxia.48.
163. *Parfait* 1822–23. See above, pp. 151–52.
164. Locatelli 1951; Köhler 1970 pp. 66–67.
165. Poirion 1978.
166. On this verb in the sense of "to be in suspense," see *T-L* V, 1547.20–22 and 1549.9–43.
167. Kellermann 1936 pp. 60–84; D. Kelly 1966b pp. 150–64; Warning *GRLMA* IV.1, pp. 30–44; Lacy 1978 p. 155; Ménard 1979 pp. 196–99; M. T. Bruckner in D. Kelly 1985c pp. 157–62. But cf. Schmolke-Hasselmann 1980a p. 44.
168. See also *Thèbes* 27–32, 161–64, 833–38, 1881–920, 2055–80, 2364–80, 2889–2910, 5053–80. The will of the gods is well known in the *Eneas;* cf. also the fears of Lavine's mother 3285–3524, Latins 6545–72, and Turnus 5810–19, 9604–12, 9643–68. The destruction of Laurente permits the rebirth of Troy as Rome. See Cormier 1973; Haug 1973 pp. 137–38; Poirion 1978.
169. See also *Troie* 27548–60. On *destinee/destine*, see D. Kelly 1976 pp. 12–13; and Godefroy II, 659; IX, 652; *T-L* II, 1767–69.
170. Frequent in the Lancelot-Grail cycle; the *Mort* §176 will suffice as example. See Frappier 1964a pp. 538–39, 542–43, 552.
171. D. Kelly 1969b; Vinaver 1970a pp. 129–49; Schmolke-Hasselmann 1980a pp. 41–47.
172. Kellermann 1936 pp. 69–72.
173. Nitze 1953 p. 79–80 and below, pp. 189–91.
174. Fourquet 1956; Köhler 1970 pp. 100–106. Cf. Warning *GRLMA* IV.1 pp. 30–59; Lichtblau 1985.
175. Cf. above, p. 45. See Rohr 1962; Stock 1972; Haug 1973 p. 136; D. Kelly 1978a pp. 30–32, 42–45.
176. D. Kelly 1974 p. 158. See also *Parfait* 14–17; *Perlesvaus* ll. 10, 3873–74; *Troie* 2825–62.
177. Cf. the effect of the grail on Galaad's flesh, *Queste* pp. 277.33–278.2.
178. Cf. Vinaver 1970a p. 128; D. Kelly 1984b.
179. Ihle 1983 pp. 33–40.
180. See notably the surveys in Loomis 1949 pp. 371–72, 387–88; Roques 1955, 1956; Gossen 1959; Loomis 1963; Bogdanow 1966 pp. 1–22. On the Round Table, which underwent similar transformations, see Eberlein-Westhues 1979; Schmolke-Hasselmann 1982; Baumgartner 1987a pp. 19–20.
181. Worstbrock 1965.
182. Bloomfield 1970 p. 106.
183. Bloomfield 1970 p. 110. Cf. Köhler 1970 pp. 77–78.
184. Frappier 1968b pp. 264–88; Köhler 1973 pp. 29–30. Cf. D. Kelly 1976.

185. Cf. E. Vinaver in *Balain* pp. xxv-xxvii; Bogdanow 1966; Van Coolput 1986 pp. 74–75. Cf. Maurer 1964.

186. Zink 1979.

187. Köhler 1962 pp. 213–23; Köhler 1970 pp. 181–235; Zumthor 1975 pp. 238–39.

188. D. Kelly 1974, 1984d.

189. Fourquet 1956 p. 301.

190. Köhler 1970 pp. 67, 69.

191. Cf. Gallais 1971b; Ruberg 1963. See, for example, *Alex* APar III and *TChev* in India; *Dole* 4679–85; *Escoufle* 3736–41; *Mance* 1430–33; *Rigomer* 10973–80.

192. Köhler 1970 pp. 236–61; Frappier 1961 pp. 31–37. Cf. *Richars* 33–45, 71–74.

193. Frappier 1961 p. 32; cf. Pickens 1977 p. 105–8. Cf. Ribard 1970.

194. Köhler 1970 pp. 68–69, 87–88; Warning *GRLMA* IV.1, 30–44; Lacy 1972; Haidu 1974.

195. *Alex* APar I.402–8, III.992–97; *Claris* 24804–30; *Dole* 4694–99; *Espine* 282–84; *Estoire* II, 514/I.150.20–26; *Fet* pp. 397–401 (cf. *Iter*); *Folie Lanc* pp. 49.97–108, 141.3–7; Huth *Merlin* I, 132; II, 44, 216; *Joseph d'A* ll. 489–92/391–93; *Merlin* M 19.36–42/S 23.15–20, 374.35–375.1; *Mule* 41–49, 440–48, 490–92; *Prise* 1080–84; *Queste* pp. 16.16–31, 28.18–29; *Venjance Nev* 1488–92. Cf. *Huon* 4619–26, 4718–25.

196. Köhler 1970 pp. 102–4; Le Rider 1978; Maddox 1978 p. 29.

197. Schmolke-Hasselmann 1980a p. 44.

198. Quoted from D. Kelly 1978b p. 139. Cf. *Melior* 1–12 (quoted above, p. 190), and, on King Caradoc of Vannes, in Szkilnik 1988.

199. Ménard 1969 pp. 311–14; Köhler 1970 pp. 5–36; Schmolke-Hasselmann 1980a pp. 51–57.

200. *Bel inc* 201–5; *Charrette* 222–23; *Perceval* 889–93.

201. *Amadas* 171–90; *Ipomedon* 116–42.

202. In general, see Ménard 1969 pp. 459–61; Köhler 1970 pp. 112–15, 133–35; Schmolke-Hasselmann 1980a pp. 61–63. On Dinadan, see Köhler 1970 pp. 82–83; Vinaver 1970 pp. 163–77; Baumgartner 1975 pp. 182–87, 252–59; Payen 1979; Chênerie 1986 p. 495 (with additional bibliography n. 228).

203. Ménard 1969 pp. 459–61; Vinaver 1970 pp. 167–69.

204. Ménard 1969 pp. 315–32; D. Kelly 1983c.

205. *Mance* 1050–58; *Durmart* 578–654. See Ménard 1969 pp. 387–89; Ribard 1969 pp. 179–80; D. Kelly 1976.

206. Köhler 1962 pp. 213–23; Bogdanow 1966 pp. 197–221; D. Kelly 1976.

207. *Amadas* 2542–44; *Florimont* 3895–4052; *Folie Lanc; Lancelot* cv.38; *Partonopeu* 5354–56; *Yvain* 2806–9.

208. Cf. as well *Jaufre* 9995–10000; for analogous marvels, see *Perceforest* I.5982–6031/74:68–69; 88:489.

209. Köhler 1970 p. 83.

210. Payen 1968 pp. 328–29; Burgess 1970 pp. 46–55; Köhler 1970 pp. 67–69; E. Kennedy 1973 p. 173; Ollier 1975 p. 183; Ménard 1979 p. 86; Köhler *GRLMA*

IV.1, 89. See *Atre* 2756–60; *Espine* 375–81; *Estoire* II, 434/I.116.38–117.11; *Folie Lanc* p. 93.509–16; *Guil maréchal* 1883–94; *Guiron* §213; Huth *Merlin* II, 10, 101, 231, 244; *Mantel* 758–59; *Merlin* S 320.11–322.4, 374.24–27; *Tyolet* 9–24.

211. Köhler 1970 p. 100; D. Kelly 1978a pp. 184–85. Cf. Benjamin 1963 p. 16 on the extreme.

212. Warning *GRLMA* IV.1, 30–33.

213. Köhler 1970 pp. 67–72, 105–6; Lacy 1980 p. 6. See *Estoire* II, 448/I.122.14–18; Huth *Merlin* I, 151; *Partonopeu* Cont 2852–54; *Pierre* p. 2.8–10.

214. Cf. also *Guiron* §§2 (Arthur), 31 (Bademagu).

215. Zumthor 1968 p. 87.

216. Payen 1973; Zink 1979.

217. Lacy 1980 pp. 62–64.

218. Pickens 1977 pp. 125–27, 133–36, and cf. pp. 137–42.

219. On Gauvain in this respect, see Busby 1980b pp. 388–93.

220. Ruberg 1963; D. Kelly 1971 pp. 335–36.

221. Ruberg 1963 pp. 124–27; Sturm-Maddox 1971 pp. 241–44; Haidu 1974 pp. 139–46; Ollier 1974d pp. 228–32; L. G. Donovan 1975 pp. 191–200; Pickens 1977 pp. 108–21; D. Kelly 1984a; Meneghetti 1984 especially pp. 210–17.

222. *Melusine* JdA pp. 46–47.

223. Cf. Pickens 1977 pp. 116–18. On the various names for the "Buens Chevaliers" in *Perlesvaus*, see Schmid 1986 pp. 146–59.

224. See above, pp. 56–57.

225. Kellermann 1936 pp. 61–64.

226. Sargent-Baur 1973. Cf. Accarie 1979 pp. 27–30.

227. *Perceval* 3572–3611, 4646–83, 6392–6433. Cf. Huchet 1988.

228. Matarasso 1979; Baumgartner 1981 pp. 97–107; Ihle 1983 pp. 72–91.

229. In *Fergus* 1177–88 the hero in effect replaces his father by the knight who dubs him; yet he wonders whether a person of his birth can seek love (2686–2700).

230. Guiette 1978 pp. 48–49; Ménard 1979 pp. 168–69.

231. Frappier 1964 pp. 36–37; Ménard 1979 pp. 186–89. The grail in the *Queste* is the most obvious example; see also *Melusine* JdA pp. 2–5, 310–11.

232. See above, pp. 148–49.

233. Zumthor 1972 pp. 359–60, 363.

234. Zumthor 1972 p. 360.

235. See H. R. Jauss' principle of alterity (1977a).

236. Bosl 1977 pp. 30–32.

237. Cf. *Rose* 470/468.

238. Poirion 1986a pp. 57–58.

239. Bogdanow 1966 p. 150.

240. Bogdanow 1966 pp. 246.161–65. Cf. Huth *Merlin* I, 264–65.

241. Cf. *Iter, Voyage.*

242. Ruhe 1979a, 1979b. Cf. Ihle 1983 chs. II and IV.

243. D. Kelly 1974 p. 158. Cf. *Mule* 444–48.

244. Cf. Riquer 1956; Frappier 1961 pp. 31–36.

245. R. Lathuillère ed. in *Guiron* pp. 154–55. Cf. the analogous use of "epicycles" in the Seven Sages cycle, on which see Palermo 1959 pp. 243–45 and 1960.
246. D. Kelly 1984d p. 172.
247. See Pickens 1977 pp. 101–5.

Chapter 6. *Estoire: Verité* and *Senefiance*

1. E. Vinaver in *Balain* pp. xxi-xxii.
2. Goldin 1975. Cf. M. R. Jung 1976.
3. Poirion 1982 p. 122; cf. Warning 1983 pp. 71–75.
4. Frappier *GRLMA* IV.1, 346.
5. Baker 1924; Simon 1958 (1959) pp. 104–5; Schmale 1985 pp. 112–15.
6. Gier 1977a pp. 18–19, 29–33. Cf. Baker 1924 especially pp. 146–52; P. J. Jones 1933 pp. 24–25; Hürsch 1934; Uitti 1967 pp. 271–74; Waltz 1970 pp. 24–30; Vitz 1978 pp. 403–5, 407 n. 13; Gumbrecht 1979 pp. 54–56; Gumbrecht *GRLMA* XI.1, 899–901.
7. Gumbrecht 1979 pp. 61–63. Cf. *Becket* 6176–80; *Marguerite* 729–39.
8. And therefore improved rather than incited to imitation. See Waltz 1965 pp. 176–203; Baehr 1968; Jauss 1968 pp. 159–63; Gier 1977a pp. 10–34; Mölk 1978 pp. 354–55; Tubach 1980.
9. K. Hauck in Lammers 1965; Schmale 1985 pp. 116–17.
10. *Rou* II.1361–72. Cf. A. J. Holden in *Rou*, vol. III, pp. 123–24; Schmale 1985 pp. 121–22.
11. *Alex* APar IV.1652–74; *Durmart* 5–12; *Oiselet* 172–95/158–83; *Rose* 156–68, 470/468, 1930–40/1928–38; *Thèbes* 13–18. Cf. Köhler 1962 pp. 9–10; Köhler 1970 pp. 11–14, 48–49; Köhler 1976 pp. 326–28.
12. Poirion 1972 pp. 13–14.
13. Cf. Viscardi 1967 pp. 13–14.
14. Lazar 1964; Topsfield 1975; Warning 1983.
15. Frappier 1959b; D. Kelly 1978a pp. 185–86; Meneghetti 1975, 1979. See *Brut* 10493–520; *Ducs* 27593–96; *Engleis* 6481–6520.
16. Glunz 1937 pp. 60–65; Köhler 1970; Ménard 1976; Köhler *GRLMA* IV.1, 89–90.
17. *Brut* 10735–72. Cf. *TChev* P106–9 (p. 122); D. Kelly 1978a pp. 19–20; Press 1985; Ainsworth 1988 pp. 195–96. On histories, see Wolter 1959 pp. 75–76.
18. Jauss 1963 pp. 66–67; Jodogne 1964a pp. 79, 81–82; Cormier 1974 pp. 151–56; Petit 1985a.
19. Grundmann 1952; Köhler 1976 p. 327, 329–31; Burgess 1981a; Poirion 1982 p. 6.
20. *De vulg* II.ii.7, II.iv.8; cf. I.x.2. See Colish 1968 pp. 269–72; Frappier 1968a pp. 61–62.
21. Badel 1975 pp. 89–93. See above on *san/sans*, pp. 106–14.
22. *Brut* 7–8; *Cristal* 1897–99; *Melusine* JdA p. 159.18; *Sone* 16283–86. Cf. *FEW* XIV, 288: "conformité de l'idée avec son objet . . . ; conformité d'un récit avec

un fait . . . (sens ca. 1200)"; and Marchello-Nizia 1982; H.-W. Goetz in Schmale 1985 pp. 172–73.

23. *Melusine* JdA pp. 34–35. Cf. Jonin 1982 pp. 177–81.

24. Jauss 1953; M. R. Jung 1976; D. Kelly 1986.

25. Cf. Haug 1978 p. 71; Bruckner 1980b; Baumgartner 1984a; Gosman 1984.

26. On *certain* and *senefiance*, see *Queste* p. 67.13–17. See above, pp. 141, 155, and, in general, on *certain* and its derivatives, Godefroy II, 23–24; IX, 21; *T-L* II, 131–34; and on *senefiance*, Godefroy VII, 355–56; *T-L* IX, 435–41; as a sign, it is related to the medieval senses of *merveille*.

27. Vinaver 1970c pp. 116–17.

28. See I. Arnold in *Brut* p. 809.

29. Köhler 1966 pp. 94–96; Uitti 1972 pp. 77–78, 93; Köhler 1976 p. 327; Haug 1978 pp. 65–70.

30. Cf. Worstbrock 1965; Stempel *GRLMA* XI.1, 718.

31. See above, pp. 110–14. Cf. also Knapp 1980 pp. 584–87.

32. Vinaver 1970c p. 117. Cf. Bezzola 1944 II, 366; Lewis 1966; Frappier 1968a pp. 12–13; Kleinschmidt 1976; Haidu 1977 pp. 883–86; Duby 1978b; Zink 1979 pp. 26–32.

33. Zumthor *GRLMA* I, 90. Cf. Ainsworth 1988 pp. 187–88.

34. Köhler 1970 p. 51; cf. p. 83. See also Ohly 1965.

35. *Anjou* 33; *Dolopathos* fr pp. 4–7; *Escoufle* 10–34; *Espine* 1–14; *Florimont* 43–46, 861–65; *Guil d'A* 11–15; *Lais* Eli 27–28; *Lycorne* 8548–61; *Melusine* JdA p. 254.19–22; *TChev* 6646–64.

36. See also *Manekine* 45–48; *P Aug* 105–7; *TChev* 6647–50; *Turpin* Pro 10–14. Cf. Badel 1975 p. 91.

37. Cf. *P Aug* vv. 99–107. See Köhler 1962 pp. 213–23; Woledge and Clive 1964 p. 34; Poirion *GRLMA* IV.1, 75–76; Speer and Foulet 1980 pp. 361–63; Chassé 1985.

38. Woledge and Clive 1964 pp. 38–39. Cf. Uitti 1985.

39. Schmolke-Hasselmann 1980a pp. 4–5, 21.

40. Frappier 1968b p. 132; Poirion *GRLMA* IV.1, 76–81; E. Kennedy 1986 pp. 270–72.

41. See Bogdanow 1966.

42. See Curtis 1969 pp. 10–23; Baumgartner 1975 pp. 48–52, 90–91; Van Coolput 1986 pp. 116–51.

43. Poirion 1978 p. 215.

44. D. Kelly 1977 pp. 131, 141 n. 1.

45. Cf. similar words in the *Gesta Ambaziensium Dominorum*, cited by Bezzola 1944 II, 336 n. 1. Cf. Knapp 1980 pp. 585–86.

46. See Greif 1886; Lumiansky 1958; R. Jones 1972 pp. 43–59; Uitti 1973 pp. 142–44; Sullivan 1985b. Cf. Raynaud de Lage 1976 pp. 127–59.

47. See above, pp. 52–54; and, in general, Trimpi 1973 pp. 25–29.

48. Cf. Taylor 1987 p. 281.

49. *Alex* APar IV.1486–89; *Charrette* 7111–12; *Lycorne* 8548–61; *Yvain* 6804–8. Cf. Köhler 1962 p. 12.

50. The *Epistola ad Aristotelem;* see *TChev* P46–47 and the note to these lines (Vol. II, p. 99).

51. See B. Foster with I. Short in *TChev* Vol. II, pp. 58–61.

52. Poirion 1972 pp. 14–15; Köhler 1976 p. 325; D. Kelly 1978c pp. 237–39; E. R. Woods 1978 pp. 75–78; Köhler *GRLMA* IV.1, 85–86; Frappier *GRLMA* IV.1, 209–10; Schmolke-Hasselmann 1980a pp. 207, 246–48. Cf. Köhler 1970 p. 22, 54–61.

53. Is Charlemagne's Saxon war a counterpart to Arthur's victory over the Saxons in Arthurian romance or legend? Cf. Bezzola 1944 II, 334–35; Kleinschmidt 1974 pp. 60–61, 169–70; M. R. Jung 1976 pp. 431–33; Keller 1985. Legitimization by genealogy is common in oral traditions too, from which Jean Bodel borrowed part of his *matiere;* see Vansina 1961 pp. 83–92.

54. For other *chansons de geste,* see Gsteiger 1959 pp. 218–20; Tyssens 1966 p. 689.

55. Warren 1988.

56. Cf. in this context Köhler 1962 pp. 9–15; Ollier 1974b pp. 210–11; Schmolke-Hasselmann 1980a pp. 232–48.

57. *Vies des pères* in U. Mölk 1968 §75; D. Kelly 1985b.

58. Cf. *Escanor* 15–21. For similar instances of romance topics in *chansons de geste,* see E. R. Woods 1977; Grunmann-Gaudet 1979.

59. *Dole* 24–29; see Zink 1979 pp. 26–32. Cf. *Brun* 243–44.

60. Köhler 1962 pp. 17–18.

61. Cf. Ollier 1974c pp. 352–61.

62. Bloch 1977 pp. 2–3. Cf. Kleinschmidt 1976; Stock 1983.

63. Cf. Duby 1978a, 1978b.

64. Examples of diverse authorities are found in Stock 1983.

65. See also *Richars* 20–21 and note (p. 193). Cf. also v. 91 note, and Struss *GRLMA* IV.1, 375.

66. Schmolke-Hasselmann 1980a pp. 246–48. Cf. Frappier 1964a pp. 25–30.

67. The noun and verb, or the concepts they represent, are very frequent, deriving their significance from *intentio, intendere,* in the *accessus* (see above pp. 37–38). *Alex déca* 1–3; *Anjou* 12–20; *Beaudous* 299–304; *Becket* 115–20; *Berinus* §1; *Brun* 11–12; *Cleomadés* 4; *Desiré* 1–2; *Fables* Ep 20–22; *Floriant* 9–17; *Florimont* 15–18; *Galeran* 896–97; *Guil de Palerne* 4665–68; *Guiron* p. 177 §132 n. 1; *Lais* Pro 23–30; *Levrier* 61–64, 77–78; *Lycorne* 8562–65; *Manekine* 6044–46; *Perceval* 61–67; *Perceval* Cont I EU 3222–25; *Restor* 293–96; *Richars* 5–6, 46; *Silence* 2354–58; *Venjance* (3) §2. The examples do not distinguish between specific and general intention, between those dealing with *matiere* or *san,* or synonymous words and expressions like *panser, pourpos, voil faire, pour ceo, dirai a quel fin, cure, pour moustrer ensengnement,* etc.

68. D. Kelly 1966b; Borsari 1983, especially ch. I; Bruckner 1986.

69. Jauss *GRLMA* I, 121–25; Köhler *GRLMA* IV.1, 82–103; Bumke 1979; Haidu 1982; and, in general, studies in *Rezeptionskritik.*

70. Cf. Kleinschmidt 1974 and 1976; Schmidt 1977; Scholz 1980 pp. 9–14; Krueger 1987 pp. 123–25; Huot 1990.

71. Gallais 1964b pp. 333–38; Lough 1978 pp. 7–30; and, especially, Bumke 1979; Kupper *GRLMA* XI.1, 820–24. On the influence of patrons on the two versions of *Meliador,* see Diverres 1987.

72. *Comm Aen* p. 31.20–21; cf. *De inv* i.25.36. Cf. Lausberg 1960 §§373, 1146 on application.

73. *Alex* AdeP 9–26; *Alex déca* 1–3; *Alex* APar I.11, 30–31. On the prose romances, see above, pp. 75–78.

74. Cf. Pauphilet 1950 p. 153.

75. Cf. Pagani 1976.

76. Gunn 1952 p. 166.

77. Cf. as well the *Charrette* 7098–7112.

78. Brandt 1966; Duby 1978b; Struss *GRLMA* XI.1, 964–70.

79. Gumbrecht *GRLMA* XI.1, 869–950; Struss *GRLMA* XI.1, 951–1023. For romance, cf. Warning *GRLMA* IV.1, 33–39; Lacy 1980 pp. 67–72, 115–16; Allen 1982; T. Hunt 1986 p. 13.

80. Fleischman 1983 pp. 291–92.

81. Dragonetti 1987. See now *FIM.*

82. Warning *GRLMA* IV.1, 35–36; D. Kelly 1966b pp. 162–65, 172–86; Lacy 1980 pp. 67–112.

83. Foerster and Breuer 1914 pp. 43*-45*.

84. D. Kelly 1969c p. 137; Köhler *GRLMA* IV.1. 87–88; T. Hunt 1986 p. 26.

85. Poe 1984. Cf. Godefroy VI, 567; X, 476; *T-L* VIII, 210–17, 221–23; *FEW* X, 105–18, especially §2a.

86. *Alex* APar I.275–76; *Espurgatoire* 189; *Fables* LXX.71–74; *Floire* 2856, 3103; *TChev* 375.

87. On the following, cf. Paul 1967.

88. *Couci* 1–50; *Escoufle* 6–30; *Jaufre* 21; *Partonopeu* 91–135.

89. *Alex* APar IV.1652–74; *Dole* 8–15. Cf. Köhler *GRLMA* IV.1, 86–88.

90. See Zumthor 1973 p. 15; Ollier 1975 pp. 183–84.

91. Köhler 1962 pp. 11–14. Cf. *Becket* 16–25; *Dolopathos* fr pp. 5–7; *Durmart* 1–12; *Escanor* 19885–93; *Partonopeu* 7364–72; *Rose* 6300–6303/6270–73. *Raison* is allied to *droit* in *Guiron* p. 179. As antonym to *raison* in this sense: "acoison sans droiture" (*Estoire* II, 464/I.129.12–15).

92. See above on Thomas's *Tristan,* pp. 120–21. Cf. *Amadas* 1–20.

93. *Bel inc* 1–7; *Couci* 1–10, 51–54; *Florimont* 9213–14; *Joufroi* 1–88 (but cf. 4345–93); *Partonopeu* 10609–14; *Poire* 16–20, 2981–84; *Rose* 40–44; *Waldef* 75–92, 7142–47. Cf. Grigsby 1968; Ruhe 1979a p. 140(-41) n. 14; Anderson *GRLMA* IV.1, 283, 288, 290; Krueger 1987 pp. 126–29.

94. *Dolopathos* fr pp. 4–5; *Sept sages* V 1–6.

95. Zink 1981 pp. 24–25.

96. D. Kelly 1978a pp. 109–10. *Anjou* 1–22; *Escoufle* 10–25; *Fables* Pro 21–26, XXXVII.59–64; *Meraugis* 10–16; *Sept sages* V 9–13.

97. *Tresor* II.vi, II.viii.2. See Ollier 1974b pp. 225–29; Gosman 1984.

98. Hanning 1972; Köhler 1976; Bloch 1977; Larmat 1979. Cf. Huon de Mery on Chrétien's *bel françois* (*Tornoiement* 3529).

99. Ollier 1976 pp. 353–57; Lacy 1980 pp. 38–66; T. Hunt 1986. Cf. Owen 1970.

100. Köhler 1970 pp. 112–13; Haupt 1971; Schmolke-Hasselmann 1980a pp. 66–67.

101. See above, p. 121.

102. Ollier 1976 pp. 348–50; Busby 1980b; Schmolke-Hasselmann 1980 pp. 86–115; Busby 1988.

103. Ollier 1976 pp. 351–52; Burns 1988.

104. See Steadman 1968 pp. 28–30; Baumgartner 1981 pp. 81–82.

105. Cf. Paul 1967; Vitz 1975; D. Kelly 1983b pp. 107–13.

106. DuCange VI, 260; *FEW* XI, 634–37, especially in earlier examples. Cf. L-S p. 1702: "simple, plain, uncompounded, unmixed . . . ; simple in a moral sense, without dissimulation, open, frank, straightforward, direct, guileless, artless, honest, sincere, ingenuous, etc." Thus, it seems incorrect to translate *simplece* as only "simple-mindedness" (as does Robertson 1951a p. 49 n. 72). For an obvious negative example, see *Paris* p. 444.22–23.

107. *Melusine* JdA p. 156.37–38. Cf. *Yder* 3667–73; Colby 1965 pp. 43, 48–49.

108. D. Kelly 1978a pp. 37–38; T. Hunt 1981b.

109. Cf. Blaise p. 382 s.v. I *grossus;* Allen 1982 pp. 16–18. The only French example in this sense noted is the *Rose* passage; see *T-L* IV, 704.6–12; *FEW* IV, 278.

110. Lausberg 1960 §258.

111. Grundmann 1958 (but cf. his 1936); Maddox 1978 pp. 22–24. Various levels of comprehension and senses of intertextuality are suggested by Jean de Meun's references in the *Rose*.

112. Kerényi 1971 p. 65.

113. As in *Cassidorus;* cf. Bossuat 1946 pp. 63–69; Speer 1978. See also Vinaver 1925 p. 29.

114. Rohr 1978 pp. 45–60.

115. Zumthor *GRLMA* I, 66; Ihle 1983 p. 127.

116. Rohr 1962; Frappier 1964b p. 49; Haidu 1973a pp. 64–65.

117. Tuve 1966 p. 22.

118. Cf. J. Cerquiglini 1978 pp. 88–90; D. Kelly 1983a p. 10.

119. Gallais 1971b; Köhler 1976 pp. 332–33, 335–37; Hanning 1977. This is not the same as psychocritical approaches, where the methods of modern psychoanalysis are applied to medieval images and narratives much as they would be to dreams, folktales, and other narrative and imaginary "sources"; cf. Wolfzettel 1985 (with bibliography, to which add Aubailly 1986; Chandès 1986; Huchet 1990).

120. Vitz 1975 pp. 428, 438; Ménard 1976 pp. 299–300; D. Kelly 1978a pp. 184–85; D. Kelly 1980; Moos 1988 pp. x, xxvi.

121. D. Kelly 1978a pp. 69–84; D. Kelly 1978d pp. 290–91.

122. See especially Brugger 1941 pp. 25–27; Battaglia 1968 pp. 41–43; Jauss 1968; Kleinschmidt 1974; Ollier 1975 pp. 185–86; Vitz 1975 pp. 439–43; Bosl 1977; Lacy 1980 pp. 7, 27–33; Gosman 1981; Jauss 1983; Wolfzettel 1990a.

123. Especially *Rose* 15260/15230. Ollier 1976 pp. 337–41, 344–47; Ménard 1979 pp. 206–9; D. Kelly 1983b pp. 111–13. Vitz 1973 pp. 49–75 has noted that they may be discretely or harmoniously fragmented.

124. Jauss 1968; Schmolke-Hasselmann 1977; Taylor 1987 pp. 318–20.

125. Cf. D. Kelly 1987 pp. 203–4.

126. Köhler 1970; cf. on Perceval, Payen 1968 pp. 392–402. Gumbrecht points out the absence of the concept of "development" ("Entwicklung") in medieval historiogaphy (*GRLMA* XI.1, 877–78). Hence, "individual" features could not "develop" or "evolve," they could only "change" as mutability.

127. Köhler 1970 p. 99.

128. Köhler 1970 pp. 91, 99–101.

129. D. Kelly 1983b pp. 109–11.

130. Ruberg 1963; Hahn 1988.

131. Speer 1981, 1983.

132. On women, see Hansen 1971.

133. Boklund 1977b pp. 239–40; Lacy 1980 p. 4; see above, pp. 170–74.

134. Hanning 1972 pp. 11–12; Warning *GRLMA* IV.1, 39–41; Hanning 1977 p. 240; Lacy 1980 p. 6.

135. *Ars vers* 1.60; see above, pp. 52–53 and 56–57; and cf. Vitz 1975 p. 443; Steinen 1966 pp. 368–73, 375; D. Kelly 1980, 1984a.

136. *Perceforest* 70:517; cf. M. R. Jung 1976 pp. 445–49.

137. Ruberg 1963 pp. 127–34; Schon 1966; Ollier 1974d pp. 230–32. Cf. Bosl 1977 pp. 24–25.

138. On this see now Schmolke-Hasselmann 1980a pp. 130–39, 208–22, and 1981a; Freeman 1983; Owen 1984.

139. D. Kelly 1985a p. 213.

140. *Guil maréchal* 2563–76. Cf. Brugger 1941 pp. 22–39.

141. Bogdanow 1966 pp. 5–13, 200–206.

142. Cf. Brugger 1941 (1943) pp. 123–73; Busby 1980a, 1980b; Schmolke-Hasselmann 1980a; Baumgartner 1987a.

143. Lofmark 1972a pp. 52–55.

144. D. Kelly 1971 pp. 354–55. Cf. Wolfzettel 1988a.

145. Lewent 1933 pp. 21–25, 35; Brugger 1941 pp. 22–44; Köhler 1959, especially pp. 42–70; Vitz 1975 pp. 427–31; Ménard 1979 pp. 195–96; Busby 1980a; Lacy 1980 pp. 6–10; Schmolke-Hasselmann 1980a p. 82.

146. D. Kelly 1976 pp. 13–16.

147. D. Kelly 1977 especially pp. 131–33.

148. Cf. Haidu 1973a pp. 56, 67–68; Van Coolput 1978.

149. Vàrvaro 1963; D. Kelly 1977. Cf. Speer 1981 pp. 312–13.

150. See also *Cligés* 152–64. See Ménard 1976 pp. 292–93; D. Kelly 1978b p. 139; Niedzielski 1978b. Cf. Lacy 1980 pp. 2–3; Chênerie 1986 pp. 104–13. On knights who become hermits, see A. J. Kennedy 1981.

151. Badel 1969 pp. 85–86, 171. Cf. Payen 1968 p. 280; Ménard 1979 pp. 121–22; Talarico 1981.

152. Vitz 1975 pp. 431–34. Cf. Steadman 1968; D. Kelly 1987.

153. D. Kelly 1968; cf. Corti 1978, 1983.

154. Bogdanow 1973; Speer 1974; McMunn 1978; Speer 1978; D. Kelly 1984a, 1986.

155. Bogdanow 1966 pp. 197–221. For verse romance see Schmolke-Hasselmann 1980a pp. 82–85.

156. Bogdanow 1966 pp. 197–221; Van Coolput 1986.

157. See E. Vinaver in *Balain* pp. xvii-xx.

158. D. Kelly 1974 p. 157.

159. Speer 1974 p. 481.

160. Speer 1974 p. 481; cf. pp. 480–81.

161. See Pickens 1977 pp. 21–56; Wolfzettel 1988a.

162. Adler 1975.

163. D. Kelly 1966b; cf. *Charrette* 365–77.

164. A similar dwarf appears in the *Bel inconnu;* see Haidu 1972b p. 43.

165. Schmolke-Hasselmann 1977; Kind 1979 pp. 122–203; Busby 1985; D. Kelly 1989. On *Flamenca,* see Lewent 1933 pp. 20–21.

166. Cf. Woledge 1969 pp. 1273–74.

167. Ménard 1969 pp. 459–60; Vinaver 1970a p. 167; D. Kelly 1983c p. 410.

168. Ménard 1969 pp. 460–61; Baumgartner 1975 pp. 182–87; Payen 1979.

169. Schmolke-Hasselmann 1980a pp. 208–22; Schmolke-Hasselman 1981a; Owen 1984. On incongruous combinations in *Marques de Rome* and the Seven Sage cycle in general, see Speer 1981 pp. 309–11.

170. On the Beau Couard, see Brugger 1941, 1951; Ménard 1969 pp. 387–89.

171. See Harf-Lancner 1984; *Melusine* Co 1353–1472; *Melusine* JdA pp. 78–81.

172. On paradox as *mirabilia,* see Pickens 1977 p. 102.

173. Like Vermineux in *Perceforest* 88:499–500. Cf. Bruckner 1977 p. 61.

174. Burgess 1981a p. 266–67.

175. Lewent 1933 pp. 11, 63–64, 80–83. Durmart's change from *failli* to *chevalier* is just as rapid; see *Durmart* 590–622. On the relation between character and language, see Solterer 1985. Cf. D. Kelly 1986 pp. 112–13.

176. Cf. Pickens 1977 pp. 57–100.

177. Cf. Lavaud and Nelli 1960 p. 310 n. 3; D. Kelly 1986 p. 114. On Gauvain, see Busby 1980b pp. 346–47, and 1988.

178. Zumthor *GRLMA* I, 66.

179. See especially Marx 1952 pp. 77–78; Köhler 1962 pp. 205–12; Jodogne 1964a; Ménard 1967 pp. 390–91; Köhler 1970 pp. 66–88, 91–96; Schmolke-Hasselmann 1980a pp. 73–75; Poirion 1982 p. 75.

180. Cf. Frappier 1964b; Cormier 1974; Raynaud de Lage 1976 pp. 55–86, 127–59; Raynaud de Lage *GRLMA* IV.1, pp. 171, 176, 178–80; Petit 1985a, 1985b.

181. Cf. Wolter 1959 pp. 75–78.

182. *Claris* 14–88; *Perceforest* I.10715–42/74:76–77; I.10804–8/74:77 n. 1; I.11034–42/74:78, 92, 94; 89:367–68; *Yvain* 12–32. On ideals in *translatio,* see Worstbrock 1965.

183. Pickens 1978a p. 206.

184. See L.-F. Flutre in *Perceforest* 74: 59–60, especially pp. 59 n.3 and 60 n. 1.

185. Marx 1952 p. 5; E. Kennedy 1970.

186. Reinhard 1933; Marx 1952 pp. 79–82. Cf. Loomis 1949 pp. 48–49.

187. Eberwein-Westhues 1979; Schmolke-Hasselmann 1982; Baumgartner 1987a.

188. Cf. Ollier 1976 pp. 332–33.

189. Cf. *Hist reg* pp. 370–71/179.18–21. *Estoire* III, 42 (MS 2455). In *Perceval* the maxims of the mother, Governal, and the hermit play a similar role; see Le Rider 1978 pp. 19–30.

190. Cf. Haidu 1972b.

191. Loomis 1949 pp. 213–14. For similar examples, see Baumgartner 1987a pp. 28, 30; *Alex* APar I.571–72; *Athis* P61–74 (II p. 427); *Berinus* §§384 (p. 382), 435 (pp. 23–24), 511 (pp. 106–7); *Dolopathos* fr pp. 42, 428; *Melusine* JdA p. 303.2–24; *Sept sages* V 185–88; *Troie* 10374–82.

192. A. W. Thompson in *Elucidation* pp. 37–50; and in Loomis 1959 pp. 208–9. See also the *Perceforest*'s far more extensive and coherent narrative drawn from the motif of rape in Darnant.

193. *Gille* 3611–16; *Melusine* Co 5911–16; *Rou* III.2189–94.

194. Cf. *Melusine* JdA p. 86.6–8.

195. Cf. Gössmann 1974 p. 39; Duby 1978b pp. 327–51. See now Maddox 1991.

196. D. Kelly 1978a pp. 88–91.

197. Cf. *Ducs* 27453–62 (the wake).

198. Besides the examples in Godefroy II, 326–27; IX 231; and *T-L* II.943–44, and *Lancelot* IX, p. 180 (s.v. "coutumes") and, in general, pp. 176–93, note the following specific examples: Ceremonies requiring the bearing of arms: *Lancelot* xiva.2, lviia.6; *Lycorne* 6693–95; *Meliador* 23408–13; *Mort* §12.8–13. Dubbing: *Abenteuer* p. 91; *Lancelot* xxiia.28; *Partonopeu* 7433–40; *Perceval* 1626–28; *Yder* 467–72. Protocol at feasts: *Abenteuer* p. 43; *Brut* 10445–58; *Cleomadés* 17339–44; *Lancelot* xxa.5; *Rigomer* 27–30. Tournaments: *Guiron* pp. 211, 216. Quintains: *Alex* APar I.571–72; *Lancelot* vi.3, xxa.3. Burials: *Dolopathos* fr p. 428; Huth *Merlin* II.10, 71; *Lancelot* xxxvii*.32, l.59; *Troie* 10374–82. Procedure in battle and duel: *Guiron* p. 189; *Lancelot* xliii.23 n. a; *Meliador* 26890–98; *Perceval* 2721–29 (cf. Halász 1980). Upbringing and education: *Dolopathos* fr p. 42; *Sept sages* V 186–92. Wearing the crown: *Meliacin* 43–58. Marriage: *Cleomadés* 16982–97; *Helcanus* §295; *Horn* 4137–45. Procedure for criminal prosecution and punishment, often adapted to the crime (murder, adultery, etc.): *Lais* Mil 60–64 (cf. Bloch 1977). Lodging of guests, length of stay, and hospitality: *Berinus* §511; *Mort* §25.50–55 (cf. Bruckner 1980a). Duration of a quest: *Artus* p. 165.26–38; *Queste* p. 23.16–25 (cf. D. Kelly 1971 pp. 334–43). Changes in the names of towns and countries, peoples, religious orders, etc.: *Melusine* JdA p. 146.17–21, 268.14–15.

199. Ménard 1976 pp. 302–5.

200. See *Perceval* 413–81 and *Bliocadran*; and T. E. Kelly 1974 pp. 47–48, 52–61; Schmid 1986.

201. Cf. Larmat 1979 pp. 51–52; Maddox 1986.

202. *Ducs* 9834–38, 14815–20, 15797–808; *Engleis* 6049–70; *Guil maréchal* 11073–84, 15025–30; *Mutacion* 23610–29; *Prise d'Al* 43–68; *St-Louis* §§18, 555–57, 689. Cf. Spörl 1935 pp. 56, 80; Bezzola 1944 II, 439–44; Simon 1958 (1959) pp. 103–9; Wolter 1959 pp. 59–64; Allen 1982 pp. 248–87; Rüsen *GRLMA* XI.1, 44–45.

203. See Ginsberg 1983.

204. Cf. *Ducs* 34899–905.

205. On this, cf. Waltz 1970 pp. 25–26, 28–29; Schmale 1985 p. 117.

206. *Alexis* 616–20. Cf. Vitz 1975 pp. 433–34.

207. P. J. Jones 1933 pp. 24–25; Waltz 1970 p. 28–30; Gier 1977a p. 19; Vitz 1978; and above, p. 206.

208. Jodogne 1964b pp. 92–94; Ollier 1976 pp. 337–38, 353–55.

209. Walther 1927 p. 150 n. 1. Cf. Köhler 1962 pp. 10–12; Köhler 1970 pp. 49–51.

210. Nitze 1915; Jodogne 1964b pp. 91–92; T. Hunt 1972 pp. 320–21; Zink 1981 pp. 9–10.

211. Cf. *Escoufle* 5880–81.

212. Zumthor 1972 p. 117. Cf. Hanning 1972 p. 13; Warning *GRLMA* IV.1, 39–40; Vitz 1975 pp. 438–41; Zink 1981 pp. 19–23.

213. Cf. Walther 1927 on sermons; Stierle 1972. Joinville uses them in conversation with Louis IX; see *St-Louis* §§555–57, 689. In general, see Gumbrecht *GRLMA* XI.1, 869–950. The best, most thorough study of the *exemplum,* its varieties, and uses is now Moos 1988.

214. D. Kelly 1976 pp. 9–10. This is true throughout the Seven Sages cycle: *Cassidorus* §§98, 101, 122, 127, 245, 373–74, 445, 486, 488; *Dolopathos* fr p. 167. They are also used in the *semblances* of the *Queste;* see Baumgartner 1981 pp. 79–82.

215. On *science* as source of verses that form exemplary persons in the audience, see *Alex* APar I.1–8, 42–61, and IV.1661–68; *Amadas* 1419–26; *Anjou* 26–34; *Aristote* 57, 453–54; *Athis* 1–4, D6067–74 (I, 210); *Beaudous* 293–328; *Berinus* §1 (p. 3); *Blanc chev* 11–19, 1569–74, 1595–99; *Dolopathos* fr pp. 4–7; *Donnei* 141–60; *Durmart* 15957–79; *Epervier* 7–10; *Escoufle* 6–9; *Gui* 12915–19; *Guiron* p. 182; *Ignaure* 1–4; *Lais* Eq 307–10; *Levrier* 63–64, 1613–16; *Mance* 20–24; *Oiselet* 135–37/121–23; *Partonopeu* 91–134; *Perceforest* I.2086–89/71:376; *Venjance* Nev 1–6. On prose in general see Woledge and Clive 1964 pp. 28–32. Cf. Payen 1969 pp. 1092–96 on exemplarity in love; Gosman 1981 pp. 168–69.

216. Variant on heart and eyes or ears; see Brault 1972; Cline 1972.

217. Cf. Frappier 1959a; Maddox 1977a.

218. *Anjou* 35–46; *Brut* 9751–52, 9788–98; *Cleomadés* 6590–98; *Erec* 1–22; *Escanor* 10–17, 25898–909; *Rigomer* 3340–43; *Sept sages* V 1–6. Cf. Köhler 1962 pp. 11–12; Ollier 1976 p. 357. Some fables are construed as the correct version (*Rigomer* 6441–44).

219. Other examples: *Alex* APar IV.1610–34; *Beaudous* pp. viii-ix (vv. 141–88); *Erec* 4–12; *Lais* Pro 1–8. See Nitze 1915.

220. D. Kelly 1978a pp. 99–100; D. Kelly 1984c pp. 42–44. Cf. Busby 1989.

221. Patterson 1935 I, 10–15; D. Kelly 1991 p. 161 and *n.* 354.

222. Jauss *GRLMA* I, 111 (general remarks in context of genre).

223. Gumbrecht *GRLMA* XI.1, 884–85. Cf. Tuve 1966 p. 21–22; Benjamin 1963 p. 16.

224. Cf. *Ducs* 38287–302; *Queste* p. 220.20–30; L.-F. Flutre in *Perceforest* 74:70–71.

225. See Frappier *GRLMA* IV.1, 153; Zink 1981 p. 10 n. 16; D. Kelly 1984c p. 47.

226. 1 Kings xi. Cf. the analogous decline of Cassidorus (Speer 1974).

227. *Queste* p. 220.20–30. D. Kelly 1984b pp. 120–21. Cf. *Sept sages* V 249–52.
228. *Amadas* 1419–26.
229. See Vance 1987 pp. 55–65. Cf. Köhler *GRLMA* IV.1, 87–88; Boklund 1977b
pp. 248–49; Schmolke-Hasselmann 1980a pp. 234–36.
230. D. Kelly 1983b pp. 111–13; and above, pp. 55–56, 231–32; Vance 1987
pp. 85–88.
231. Köhler 1959; Rohr 1962.
232. *Blanc chev* 17–19, 1569–74, 1595–99; Huth *Merlin* II, 135; *Jehan* 39–48;
Rose 1507–10/1505–8. Cf. Ollier 1976 pp. 329–57.
233. On use of proverbs, see Ollier 1976; Schulze-Busacker 1985.
234. *Alex* APar IV.1661–68.
235. Frappier *GRLMA* IV.1, 161–62.
236. Lausberg 1960 §§266–79.
237. Lacy 1980 p. 110. See Vinaver 1971 pp. 99–122.
238. Lacy 1980 p. 110. Cf. Pickens 1977 pp. 17–56; D. Kelly 1984d pp. 174–80;
Wolf 1989.
239. Köhler 1962 pp. 12–13, 17–19, 215–23; Southworth 1973 pp. 27–28; D.
Kelly 1985b.
240. Sanford 1931; K. Langosch in *Registrum* 162 note (p. 211); Marti 1941 pp.
246–49; Bruyne 1946 II, 307–8; Gompf 1973 pp. 55–61; Moos 1976; Knapp 1980
pp. 593, 607–24. One finds the full range in Froissart; see Ainsworth 1988.
241. Demats 1973; Picone 1982. The distinction goes back at least to Hrabanus
Maurus, as the *Ov mor* comm points out (p. 20); see Bruyne 1946 I, 341–43; Zumthor 1955 pp. 178–83. It is implicit in Isidore, *Etymologiae* VII.vii.10.
242. *Charrette* 4550–53; *Escoufle* 5880–81; *Lais* Pro 9–16.
243. Demats 1973 pp. 101–3.
244. On this term, see Jeauneau 1957; Wetherbee 1972 pp. 36–48.
245. On the terminology, see Matarasso 1979 pp. 108–10.
246. Cf. Dante's refusal to discuss Beatrice's death as foreign to his subject, in
Vita nuova XXVIII. On *semblance,* see Baumgartner 1981 p. 76 n. 16.
247. Ihle 1983 pp. 33–40.
248. See Bezzola 1947 pp. 194–98. Cf. Soredamors' "doreüre sore" (*Cligés* 970),
which emblematizes her beauty and her love (777–83, 954–79).
249. D. Kelly 1970b p. 196–97.
250. Sargent-Baur 1973.
251. Zumthor *GRLMA* I, 70. Cf. Ribard 1980b.
252. Cf. Gervase of Melkley's *Ars poet* p. 6.6–7.
253. Cf. *Dolopathos* fr pp. 4–6; *Donnei* 141–78; *Escoufle* 6–30.

Chapter 7. *Roman: Ordre* and *Parties*

1. *Dolopathos* fr pp. 65–66.
2. *Rou* III.5298–5300.
3. Fourquet 1956.

4. Warning *GRLMA* IV.1, 31; Haidu 1974b pp. 134–38. From "Celtisant" scholarship, see Schoepperle 1913 pp. 185–86; Marx 1952 pp. 90–92; Vendryes 1950; Haug 1970.

5. See Warning *GRLMA* IV.1, 31–33.

6. Zumthor *GRLMA* I, 87; cf. n. 14 below.

7. Godefroy X, 239; *T-L* VI, especially 1202.29–1203.45.

8. They are not outdated: see Bloomfield 1980 p. 214; Schmolke-Hasselmann 1981b.

9. On this expression, see Burns 1988; cf. *Lancelot* lxxxvii.5.

10. Baumgartner 1986 pp. 8–12. Cf. Wace *Rou* III.18, 91, and Appendice 157–76 (Vol. II, pp. 313–14).

11. On midpoint in romance (especially Chrétien's), see Freeman 1979, especially pp. 57–127; Sullivan 1985a; and, in D. Kelly 1985c, pp. 109–15 (M. A. Freeman), 142–48 (M. T. Bruckner), and 219–27 (K. D. Uitti).

12. *Didascalicon* p. 114.1–4; Minnis 1984 p. 17. Cf. Ruberg 1963 pp. 139–44; Baumgartner 1986.

13. *Alex* APar I.32–41.

14. Rychner 1955 pp. 68–125; Vàrvaro 1963. On the oral and written narrator figure, see Bik 1972; Pemberton 1984 pp. 491–96.

15. Cf. *Amadas* 6601–2, 6611–12; *TChev* 311.

16. Cf. *Troie* 611–12.

17. Greif 1886 p. 55 (§68.2: "Bei den Kampfschilderungen ging er schablonen-mäßig zu Werke"); Warren 1988 pp. 55–119.

18. Schenk 1980. To his notes add T. B. W. Reid in *Yvain* R pp. 210–11, nn. 4908f. and 5061f; Adams 1974; Shirt 1975. See also Lot 1954 pp. 29–64; Pauphilet 1968 pp. 163–67.

19. Ménard 1967; Micha 1973; Schenk 1980; D. Kelly 1988b.

20. Dronke 1959 pp. 166–69. Cf. L. J. Friedman 1965 pp. 176–77; Pickens 1977 pp. 17–56; Schmolke-Hasselmann 1981b. The place in romance of the season topic (= *tempus*) has been recognized and commented upon, especially for courtly lyric; see Hoepffner 1934.

21. Emphasis mine, to underscore *nunc* and *locus* as topoi. See Brink 1963 II, 99; *Porphyry* p. 345.13–14; *Pseudo-Acron* p. 311.9–12, 312.2–4.

22. Thoss 1972 pp. 37, 50.

23. R. W. Hunt 1948 p. 94.

24. Matarasso 1979; Baumgartner 1987b pp. 187–90. In *Escoufle,* Richar de Montivilliers appears in the Holy Land and the Holy Roman Empire to save both from their enemies. These are the fortuitous but meaningful encounters of adventure. Description fits the narrative to context.

25. Bogdanow 1966, especially pp. 13–22; Vinaver 1970a pp. 129–61; Vinaver 1971 pp. 68–98.

26. Köhler 1970 pp. 89–90; see also Ruberg 1963 pp. 127–39.

27. Cf. Bagni 1968 p. 77 and n. 17; Moos 1976; Quadlbauer 1977; Gallo 1978 pp. 73–76; D. Kelly 1991 pp. 70–71. Cf. Brinkmann 1964b pp. 410–11.

28. Cf. *Silence* 1663–69.

29. D. Kelly 1970b pp. 179–87; cf. Bloomfield 1980.

30. Vinaver 1964. Cf. in Altman 1975 the distinction between diametrical and gradational oppositions in hagiography.

31. R. Lathuillère in *Guiron* pp. 19–20; Ferrier 1954 pp. 7–21. See *Rigomer* 2730–34, 6433–34; *Tristan* §§63 and n. 1/616.28–29, 80, 178 n. 1 (p. 130).

32. See Palermo 1959 pp. 243–45; and his 1960. Cf. Micha 1984; Baumgartner 1987b pp. 182–84; Micha 1987 pp. 129–42.

33. Lot 1918 pp. 29–64; Ruberg 1963 pp. 139–44, whose analysis is applicable to the French original. But cf. Micha 1980 pp. 141–57. This temporally and topographically coherent use of parataxis contrasts with the use of the device in *chansons de geste* and Beroul; see above, p. 266.

34. The sense is apparent in Latin; see Niermeyer s.v. *compositio* (1–2). Cf. Vinaver 1970b; Lacy 1980 pp. 113–17.

35. Bogdanow 1966 p. 221.

36. *Eracle* 2746, 5110–18; cf. *Ille* 5828–29: "Por qant por li le commençai / Et por le conte le finai," a reference to his beginning and ending patrons. Cf. Becker 1935 pp. 286–90.

37. Cf. *Eracle* 2746. Cf. Rauhut 1955 p. 343; Renzi 1964 especially pp. 147–49. But see now Zumthor 1984a; Wolfzettel 1990a on the blocks as *gradus*.

38. Failure to recognize these formal distinctions leads to confusion among segments; see Becker 1935 pp. 288–89.

39. Becker 1934 pp. 46–71; Becker 1943; Schmid 1986.

40. The *Brut* is itself a genealogy; see also M. K. Pope and T. B. W. Reid in *Horn* Vol. II, pp. 3–4; L.-F. Flutre in *Perceforest* 74:46–49, 89:381–82; Crane 1986 chs. 1–2.

41. Cf. also *Estoire* RoB 3509–14; *Enf Gauvain* 156–67, 170–74, 186–92, 355–60. On the confusing branching indicated in the *Elucidation* 14–24, 339–82; and the *Estoire* II, 13–14/I.5.36–6.4; *Merlin* M 91.59–69, see Leupin 1982b pp. 27–29; Gallais 1988 pp. 732–33.

42. W. Roach in Didot *Perc* pp. 113–25; *Merlin* M 91.59–69.

43. Cf. Bogdanow 1966 pp. 220–21; and above, pp. 127–28.

44. Bogdanow 1966 pp. 16–22. The idea was perhaps already present in the Vulgate; see Vinaver 1966 pp. 10–13; Vinaver 1970a pp. 138–49. Cf. Taylor 1987: "division into books supposes organisatory principles far more complex than the narrator explicitly allows" (p. 282).

45. Bogdanow 1966 p. 62 n. 1.

46. Ruhe 1979a pp. 137–59; Van Coolput 1986 pp. 6–11; Baumgartner 1987b pp. 182–84. Cf. Taylor 1987 pp. 273–78.

47. Cf. Dembowski 1980 pp. 128–29.

48. Delbouille 1927, 1960; Tyssens 1967.

49. Cf. Palermo 1960.

50. D. Kelly 1970b pp. 195–98; Bruckner 1980b.

51. Cf. Schulz 1909 pp. 98–108; Lacroix 1971 pp. 84–105, 125–28.

52. Vinaver 1970a pp. 138–49; see also Speer 1974.

53. Cf. Schulz 1909 pp. 98–100; Lacroix 1971 pp. 87–88.

54. Frappier 1964c, 1965; cf. Ollier 1978.

55. D. Kelly 1978b.

56. Tuve 1966 pp. 426–36. Cf. Taylor 1987 pp. 308–18; Szkilnik 1991.

57. Elaborated in *Tristan en prose* and elsewhere; see Van Coolput 1986 pp. 18–38; Caulkins 1987.

58. D. Kelly 1969b, 1984b. For *Perceforest,* see Lods 1951 on "sources"and "composition" (pp. 37–94, 182–96).

59. Cf. *Amadas* 21–23; *Dolopathos* fr p. 7.

60. H. Michelant ed. in *Escanor* p. xxi.

61. On *glissement* in *Escanor,* see Adams 1987 p. 155.

62. *Lancelot* lxxia.48.

63. Cf. *Escoufle* 5047–51, 5208–15, 6158–61, 8516–23. This is related to *glissement;* see Zink 1979.

64. *JA DEVISÉ, OŸ,* etc.: *Abenteuer* pp. 15(U25o), 55–56(33d); *Abladane* p. 479.124–26; *Berinus* §§154 (p. 134), 446 (p. 36); *Cassidorus* §§222, 235, 499; Didot *Perc D* 139.1–2; *Ducs* 47, 121, 136, 42464–76; *Estoire* III, 72–73/I.182.23–31; *Florence* 5776–79; *Folie Lanc* pp. 47.1–3, 121.3–5, 136.1–5; Huth *Merlin* I, 207; *Lancelot* ixa.1, lxxii.7 (see also S II, 28–29); *Laurin* ll. 1907–12; *Merlin* S 166.23–26; *Mort* §4.1–5; *Queste* pp. 263.27–30, 264.3–7, 266.16–18. *DEVISERA,* etc.: *Abenteuer* p. 134; *Abladane* pp. 427.61–64, 478.79–81; *Berinus* §487 (p. 79); *Cassidorus* §§203, 468; Didot *Perc D* 140.27–28; *Durmart* 3320–22; *Estoire* II, 168, 301, III, 112/117–18 and var. 10, 30 var. 5, 77.26–27; *Estoire* RoB 3461–514; Huth *Merlin* I, 148, 199, 253, 258; II, 57; *Lancelot* ia.1, xxiia.2, lx*.12, lxxviii.57, lxxxiv.72, lxxxvii.5, lxxxix.11; *Laurin* ll. 6067–70; *Meliador* 28827–31; *Merlin* S 94.27–31, 215.3–9, 245.18–246.15; *Rigomer* 7919–21; *Mort* §39.21–24; *Partonopeu* 10622–46; *Troie* 27548–60. On discontinuity *(desjointure),* see D. Kelly 1984b and 1985a and above, pp. 17–19, 23–24; it is often related to interlace at the moment of return: *Lancelot* liv.7.

65. Lewent 1933 pp. 81–83; Gosman 1988. On Froissart's description of *ordenance* as *conjointure* in *Meliador,* see Dembowski 1980 pp. 126–29.

66. See above, p. 17.

67. Vinaver 1970a pp. 129–49; Ihle 1983; D. Kelly 1984d pp. 172–73.

68. Warning *GRLMA* IV.1, 30. Cf. Vance 1987 pp. 87–88 on the relation, in Eco's terms, between the "heap" and the "labyrinth."

69. Leyerle 1967 pp. 5–6; Vinaver 1970a pp. 134–36; D. Kelly 1984d pp. 180–81.

70. Cf. Quadlbauer 1977 pp. 90–92.

71. Moos 1976 pp. 107–9. Cf. Conrad of Hirsau's criticism of those who do not practice such deflection, *Dialogus* p. 49.1264–85.

72. See above on *ornatus,* pp. 58–61; cf. Vinaver 1970b p. 153.

73. See above, p. 45; and Stock 1972 pp. 155–57; cf. Faral 1924 p. 67.

74. Angeli 1971 pp. 114–18 (on *Eneas*); L. G. Donovan 1975 pp. 121–23,

246–55; Lacy 1978 pp. 155–57; Ruhe 1979a pp. 142–55; Warning *GRLMA* IV.1, 33–39; Scholz 1980 pp. 139–67; Bozóky 1985; Burns 1985a, 1985b; Ruhe 1985 pp. 294–97; Baumgartner 1987b pp. 180–82.

75. See Hart 1981a, 1981b; Sullivan 1985a; Freeman, pp. 109–16, Bruckner, pp. 142–48, and K. D. Uitti, pp. 223–27, in D. Kelly 1985c.

76. Haidu 1968; Ribard 1970; Pickens 1977 pp. 101–36; Ménard 1979 pp. 211–12.

77. D. Kelly 1978a p. 34; Ihle 1983 pp. 23–26; Monson 1987.

78. Ménard 1979 pp. 190–212; Ihle 1983 pp. 26–30.

79. See A. Hilka in *Florimont* pp. cxiv-cxxxviii; Bertolucci 1959, 1960; Arbusow 1963 especially pp. 21–29.

80. E.g., by A. Hilka in *Perceval* H p. 715 n. 4646–47.

81. As in Patch 1927; Pickering 1967.

82. Frappier 1968b pp. 256–88.

83. Brink 1963 I, 190.

84. Zumthor *GRLMA* I, 90.

85. Brink 1963 II, 290.

86. D. Kelly 1991 p. 78. Cf. *Parisiana Poetria* 1.19–22, 6.395–99; *Ars poet* pp. 49.18–19, 67.15–22; Worstbrock 1985.

87. Ihle 1983 pp. 66–67.

88. Brink 1963 II, 135–37, 290, on order, texture, and combination. Cf. *Documentum* II.3.154–62, and above, pp. 21–26.

89. Delbouille 1927 p. 621.

90. Vinaver 1966 pp. 11–13; Leupin 1982; D. Kelly 1985a pp. 212–13.

91. Speer 1983; D. Kelly 1984b pp. 143–48; Niedzielski 1978a.

92. Vàrvaro 1963 p. 205; cf. Vinaver 1970a pp. 81–82.

93. *Conjointure* is also sexual union, here an image of structure, trope, and rhetorical figure.

94. D. Kelly 1978a pp. 86–87 on the lover's dream of "adventures" and the plot of the dream vision; a dream serves the same purpose in Jean de Meun's continuation (18304–498/18274–468).

95. Cf. Poirion 1981 pp. 114, 116; Rockwell 1988 on *departir*.

96. See Poirion 1982 p. 94.

97. See Chênerie 1984; Suard 1984.

98. Cf. Lacy 1972.

99. Taylor 1987 pp. 302–8. On this subject, see Vinaver's observations in 1964 pp. 494–503, 1966 pp. 11–24. On broken swords, see Baumgartner 1984b pp. 11–12, especially n. 11 (p. 14).

100. This is *insinuatio,* that is, the introduction and justification of what first appears reprehensible.

101. D. Kelly 1966b.

102. Frappier 1968b pp. 75–131.

103. *Lancelot* S IV, 182.34–195.30; G. Hutchings in *Charrette* H pp. 122–31.

104. Bloomfield 1980 p. 211.

105. Hanning 1972 p. 11 (his emphasis). For illustrations, see Deist 1986.

106. Cf. Kellermann 1970; R. Jones 1972 on different loves in the *romans d'anti-quité;* Accarie 1979; Hahn 1988.

107. Freeman 1979 pp. 149–53. Cf. an analogous image in *Ars vers* 2.11.

108. Cf. Bruyne 1946 II, 33–34. See his appreciation of architectural beauty p. 91. On such *entrelardement* and *maniere,* see Taylor 1987 pp. 283–85.

109. Peron 1989 p. 297. Cf. Zumthor *GRLMA* IV.1, 70–72; Thoss 1972 pp. 75–77; L. G. Donovan 1975 pp. 121–23, 138–47; Maddox 1977a; D. Kelly 1987.

110. L. Foulet 1925; Lyons 1965 pp. 77–78, 151; D. Kelly 1984c pp. 43–44; Sullivan 1985a. See also Schröder 1986. For historiography, cf. Bezzola 1944 II.2, 334, 364–66; Wolter 1959 p. 74.

111. On the art of the *Cristal* plagiaries see Busby 1989. Cf. *Cligés* 2677–84.

112. *Meraugis* 1185–91; *Parfait* 282–85. Cf. Lacy 1978 pp. 151–52.

113. Lyons 1965 pp. 11–16; Thoss 1972 pp. 108–9; Burgess 1985.

114. In *Florimont* p. cxiv.

115. Colby 1965 pp. 96–97.

116. Gallo 1971 pp. 188–95; Ihle 1983 p. 127. Cf. Pauphilet 1968 pp. 179–86.

117. Cf. Bertolucci Pizzorusso 1959 pp. 54–57.

118. See D. Kelly 1978a p. 249.

119. Cf. Weber 1976; T. Hunt 1981b.

120. See above on exaggeration, pp. 50, 160–63.

121. See above, pp. 222–26.

122. Lewent 1933 p. 28; cf. D. Kelly 1986.

123. *Eracle* 6121–48; *Estoire* II, 428–29/I.114.35–115.3 (on the turning island); *Estoire* RoB 3155–64; *Lais Chai* 235–36; *Lancelot* lxxia.48; *Restor* 2681–91.

124. On the tournament as a subgenre of romance, see Payen *GRLMA* IV.1, 477–78.

125. See above on sufficiency, pp. 137–45. In *Meliacin* 1346–1807, Girard d'A-miens links another long description of beds with that of a servant giant, two beautiful young people, and three stages in a *gradus amoris.*

126. *Dolopathos* fr pp. 63–64; *Melusine* JdA pp. 28.32–29.15. Cf. *Ars vers* 1.64–71; *Poetria nova* 622–23.

127. Cf. Micha *GRLMA* IV.1, 463–64.

128. On avoiding description of the reprehensible, see *Ars vers* 1.59. See also *Guil maréchal* 4431–56.

129. Pickering 1967 I, 18 n. 3, 33. Cf. Brault 1972.

130. *Alex* APar I.2052–70; *TChev* 5379. See Baumgartner 1988b pp. 5–6.

131. Cf. F. Meister in *Dares* pp. xxii–xxiii.

132. Greif 1886 pp. 35–77; D. Kelly 1988c pp. 31–36.

133. Cf. Paul 1967 pp. 412–13, 426–28; Vitz 1975; and *De amore* pp. 60–62.

134. D. Kelly 1983b p. 109; D. Kelly 1991 pp. 70–71.

135. D. Kelly 1978a pp. 34–35 (example of *Epistolae*).

136. Adler 1947; Blumenfeld-Kosinski 1988; D. Kelly 1989.

137. Rohr 1962; Zumthor *GRLMA* IV.1, 71; Vitz 1975; D. Kelly 1983b; Busby 1985.

138. Auerbach 1958 pp. 24–63; Quadlbauer 1962 §6b.

139. Cf. J. Bédier in *Tristan* Béd I, 97 n. 2.
140. Ihle 1983 pp. 33–40.
141. See Trimpi 1971 p. 49 n. 68; Maddox 1977a especially pp. 68–73; D'Alessandro 1986.
142. See Faral 1913 pp. 338–39.
143. Trimpi 1971 p. 55.
144. D. Kelly 1983a pp. 16–20.
145. See also *Rose* 16766–67/16736–37. Cf. Hart 1981a pp. 268–71.
146. *Ducs* 44064–70. Cf. Schulz 1909 pp. 120–34; Becker 1934 pp. 51–55; Kleinschmidt 1974.
147. Kleinschmidt 1974.
148. Dronke 1959 pp. 166–69; Köhler 1960; Ruberg 1963; L. J. Friedman 1965; Ohly 1965; D. Kelly 1971 pp. 331–43; Hanning 1972; Vance 1972; Hanning 1977 pp. 223–33; Shirt 1977; Ménard 1979 pp. 121–30; Bruckner 1980a; Halász 1980; Schulze-Busacker 1981; Shirt 1981; Zumthor *GRLMA* IV.1, 70–71; Maddox 1986; Taylor 1987 pp. 306–8.
149. Pickens 1977 p. 62. Cf. Brinkmann 1964b p. 402; Burgess 1981b.
150. Bruckner 1980a pp. 178–83; Bruckner 1980b pp. 105–6.
151. Poirion 1978 pp. 225–27.
152. Payen 1968.
153. Cf. Lacy 1978 pp. 154–57; Gier 1979b pp. 16–19.
154. Pauphilet 1968 pp. 163–67.
155. Pauphilet 1968 p. 167. Cf. Baumgartner 1981; Frappier 1964b p. 45; Matarasso 1979.
156. Lagorio 1970 p. 38; Ruberg 1963 pp. 152–56; Matarasso 1979; Baumgartner 1981; Van Coolput 1986.
157. See above, pp. 161–63.
158. Poirion 1983 p. 196; cf. his 1978 p. 229; and Ollier 1976 p. 335.
159. Uitti 1972 pp. 80–81; Haug 1978.
160. Cf. *Claris* 1–114, and D. Kelly 1983c pp. 414–17.

Chapter 8. Emergence of Romance

1. As in Vinaver 1970a and 1971; Adler 1975; Schmolke-Hasselmann 1980a; Haug 1985.
2. As in *GRLMA* IV and most introductory manuals.
3. Zink 1981 p. 11. Cf. Zink 1987a pp. 5–6; Taylor 1987 pp. 293–332.
4. See Haug 1973 pp. 130–31.
5. Luttrell 1974 p. 68.
6. Topsfield 1981 p. 23; see above, pp. 15–17.
7. Frappier 1968a p. 59.
8. Frappier *GRLMA* IV.1, 206.
9. Vinaver 1970a; Poirion in *GRLMA* IV.1, 79–80; Zink 1981.
10. See J. Cerquiglini 1980 p. 164.

11. Tuve 1966 especially ch. 5; Zink 1981 pp. 23–27.

12. J. Cerquiglini 1980 pp. 158–59; Allen 1982.

13. O'Leary 1980.

14. Besides E. Köhler's numerous studies, see Bumke 1979; Haidu 1984.

15. See Taylor 1987 pp. 267–332; and the lists of adaptations, compilations, insertions, and other varieties of romance proliferation from the thirteenth century on in Woledge 1954.

16. Cf. Zumthor *GRLMA* I, 66; Méla 1984 pp. 18–20.

17. Cf. Köhler 1977.

18. Frappier 1968a pp. 13–16; Ryding 1971 pp. 9–18.

19. Jauss *GRLMA* I, 107–38; Köhler 1977; Bumke 1979; Bruckner 1987; Taylor 1987 pp. 308–29; D. Kelly 1988c; Wolfzettel 1990b; and the bibliography in Bumke 1982.

20. Bruckner 1987 p. 231. Cf. Huot 1987; Short 1988.

21. Riffaterre 1981 p. 4.

22. Zumthor 1981.

23. Poirion 1981; Bruckner 1987.

24. Cf. Riffaterre 1981 p. 6; cf. D. Kelly 1984a pp. 94–95.

25. Jauss 1979 p. 209. Cf. Crane 1986.

26. Köhler 1977.

27. See Jauss *GRLMA* I, 112–13.

28. Cf. Köhler *GRLMA* IV.1, 82–103; J. Cerquiglini 1980; Zink 1981 pp. 4–5.

29. Cf. Köhler 1964b.

30. Köhler 1970; Ward 1979.

31. See the reflections of Haidu 1977; and, on Jean Renart, Zink 1979 pp. 42–44; Sullivan 1985a.

32. Duby 1978b pp. 352–70; Flori 1979; Sargent-Baur 1984. But see as well Ménard 1976 and Chênerie 1986 pp. 18–31.

33. Cf. Zink 1979 pp. 17–44; Ruhe 1979a, 1979b.

34. D. Kelly 1983c.

35. Dembowski 1983 pp. 105–49; Ainsworth 1988.

36. B. N. fr. 22550 41r–v. See Bosl 1977 p. 32. Cf. Ainsworth 1988 pp. 197–98.

37. See Faral 1913; Hansen 1971; L. G. Donovan 1975; Petit 1985a, 1985b.

38. Legge 1963 pp. 29–31; Bell 1976.

39. See Jodogne 1964a pp. 56–59.

40. Nichols 1969; cf. Gier 1977a.

41. In Mölk 1969 §75 vv. 33–35; cf. as well §76; D. Kelly 1985b; Taylor 1987 pp. 267–68. Contrast *Melusine* Co 17–46.

42. In Mölk 1969 §64 vv. 3145–47; see also vv. 2309–12 and §75 vv. 23–35; and Faral 1910 pp. 46–47, 171, 173, 176 n. 4; P. J. Jones 1933 pp. 26–28, 43–47; Bruyne 1946 II, 139.

43. Cf. *Ille* P931–36 (p. 32); see Renzi 1964 pp. 59–61.

44. Cf. Jauss *GRLMA* I, 108.

45. Marichal 1968 pp. 452–54.

46. Zumthor *GRLMA* IV.1, 60–73; cf. Poirion 1981 pp. 110–11, 117–18.
47. Cf. Haidu 1974a pp. 2–4.
48. Frappier *GRLMA* IV.1, 206.
49. Warning *GRLMA* IV.1, 25–59.
50. D. Kelly 1983a pp. 25–26; Uitti 1983.
51. See Leupin 1982a.
52. Zink 1979 pp. 66–68; cf. also Zink 1981 p. 25.

Bibliography

Abbreviations

Blaise: Albert Blaise and Henri Chirat. *Dictionnaire latin-français des auteurs chrétiens*. Strasbourg: Latin chrétien, 1954.

Bloch: Oscar Bloch and Walther von Wartburg. *Dictionnaire étymologique de la langue française*. 5th ed. rev. Paris: Presses Universitaires de France, 1968.

CTC: *Catalogus translationum et commentariorum — Mediaeval and Renaissance Latin Translations and Commentaries: Annotated Lists and Guides*. Ed. Paul Oskar Kristeller, F. Edward Cranz, and Virginia Brown. Union Académique Internationale. Washington, DC: Catholic University of America Press, 1960–.

DuCange: C. D. DuCange. *Glossarium mediae et infimae latinitatis*. New, enlarged ed. 10 vols. Paris: Libairie des Sciences et des Arts, 1937–38.

FEW: Walther von Wartburg. *Französisches etymologisches Wörterbuch*. Leipzig and Berlin: Teubner; Basel: Zbinden, 1928–.

FIM: *Fälschungen im Mittelalter*. Internationaler Kongreß der Monumenta Germaniae Historica München, 16.–19. September 1986. Monumenta Germaniae Historica: Schriften, 33.1–5. Hannover: Hahnsche Buchhandlung, 1988. Vol. V.

Godefroy: Frédéric Godefroy. *Dictionnaire de l'ancienne langue française et de tous ses dialectes du IXe au XVe siècle*. 10 vols. Paris: Vieweg, Bouillon, 1881–1902.

GRLMA: *Grundriß der romanischen Literaturen des Mittelalters*. Heidelberg: Winter, 1968–.

Huguet: Edmond Huguet. *Dictionnaire de la langue française du seizième siècle*. 7 vols. Paris: Champion, Didier, 1925–67.

Latham: R. E. Latham. *Revised Medieval Latin Word-List from British and Irish Sources*. London: British Academy, Oxford University Press, 1965.

L-S: Charlton T. Lewis and Charles Short. *A Latin Dictionary*. Oxford: Clarendon Press, 1879, 1969,

MW: *Mittellateinisches Wörterbuch bis zum ausgehenden 13. Jahrhundert*. Munich: Beck, 1967–.

NGML: *Novum glossarium mediae latinitatis ab anno DCCC usque ad annum MCC*. Copenhagen: Munksgaard, 1957–.

Niermeyer: *Mediae latinitatis lexicon minus*. Ed. J. F. Niermeyer, C. van de Kieft, and G. S. M. M. Lake-Schoonebeek. Leiden: Brill, 1984.

Souter: Alexander Souter. *A Glossary of Later Latin to 600 A.D.* Oxford: Clarendon Press, 1949.

ThLL: Thesaurus linguae latinae. Leipzig: Teubner, 1900–.

T-L: Tobler-Lommatzsch Altfranzösisches Wörterbuch. Berlin: Wiedmann; Wiesbaden: Steinen, 1925–.

Primary Literature

In some references to primary works, more than one edition has been cited. This is because either the available editions are unreliable and therefore the evidence of both is desirable; or there are two good editions, either of which may be used by the scholar; or the variant readings are interesting. In all cases, the first-listed edition is quoted and/or cited first, unless the reference is not found in it. When a reference is identical in both editions (as in the beginning of the *Rose*), only one reference is given. When the passage is found in only one edition, the reference is clear enough for the reader to identify the edition being used. Translations that are not my own are identified with the appropriate edition. Translations used are cited with the work translated; all other translations are my own.

Abenteuer: Die Abenteuer Gawains, Ywains und Le Morholts mit den drei Jungfrauen aus der Trilogie (Demanda) des Pseudo-Robert de Borron: die Fortsetzung des Huth-Merlin nach der allein bekannten Hs. Nr. 112 der Pariser National Bibliothek. Ed. H. Oskar Sommer. Beihefte zur Zeitschrift für romanische Philologie, 47. Halle: M. Niemeyer, 1913.

Abladane: "*Le Roman d'Abladane.*" Ed. L.-F. Flutre. *Romania* 92 (1971): 458–506.

Accessus: Accessus ad auctores, Bernard d'Utrecht, Conrad d'Hirsau Dialogus super auctores. Ed. R. B. C. Huygens. Leiden: Brill, 1970. Pp. 19–54.

Accessus Ov: Accessus Ovidiani. Ed. Gustavus Przychocki. Symbolae ad veterum auctorum historiam atque ad medii aevi studia philologica, 1. Cracow: Nakładem Akademii Uniejętności, 1911.

Ad Her: Ad C. Herennium de ratione dicendi (Rhetorica ad Herennium). Ed. and trans. Harry Caplan. Loeb Classical Library. Cambridge: Harvard University Press; London: Heinemann, 1968.

Ad Pisones: Ars poetica. In *Q. Horati Flacci opera,* ed. Edward C. Wickham and H. W. Garrod. 2d ed. Oxford: Clarendon Press, 1901.

Aeneid: Aeneidos. In *P. Vergili Maronis opera,* ed. R. A. B. Mynors. Oxford: Clarendon Press, 1969.

Alda: Guillaume de Blois, *Alda.* Ed. Marcel Wintzweiller. In Gustave Cohen, *La "comédie latine" en France au XIIᵉ siècle.* Collection latine du moyen âge. 2 vols. Paris: Belles Lettres, 1931. Vol. I, pp. 107–51.

Alex A/Alex B: The Medieval French "Roman d'Alexandre," Vol. I: *Text of the Arsenal and Venice Versions.* Ed. Milan S. La Du. Elliott Monographs, 36. New York: Kraus, 1965.

Alex AdeP: Albéric de Pisançon, *Alexandre.* Ed. Alfred Foulet. In *The Medieval French "Roman d'Alexandre."* Elliott Monographs, 38. New York: Kraus, 1965. Vol. III, pp. 37–60.

Alex APar: The Medieval French "Roman d'Alexandre," Vol. II: Version of Alexandre de Paris. Text. Ed. E. C. Armstrong et al. Elliott Monographs, 37. New York: Kraus, 1965.

Alex déca: Alexandre décasyllabique, ed. Alfred Foulet. In The Medieval French "Roman d'Alexandre." Elliott Monographs, 38. New York: Kraus, 1965. Vol. III, pp. 61–100.

Alexandreis: Galteri de Castellione Alexandreis. Ed. Marvin L. Colker. Thesaurus mundi, 17. Padua: Antenore, 1978.

Alexis: La vie de Saint Alexis. Ed. Christopher Storey. Textes littéraires français, 148. Geneva: Droz, 1968.

Alix orp: Alixandre l'orphelin. Ed. Cedric E. Pickford. French Classics. Manchester: Manchester University Press, 1951.

Amadas: Amadas et Ydoine. Ed. John R. Reinhard. Classiques français du moyen âge, 51. Paris: Champion, 1974.

Anjou: Jehan Maillart, Le roman du Comte d'Anjou. Ed. Mario Roques. Classiques français du moyen âge, 67. Paris: Champion, 1931.

Anth: A Thirteenth-Century Anthology of Rhetorical Poems: Glasgow MS Hunterian V.8.14. Ed. Bruce Harbert. Toronto: Pontifical Institute of Medieval Studies, 1975.

Anticlaudianus: Alain de Lille, Anticlaudianus. Ed. R. Bossuat. Textes philosophiques du moyen âge, 1. Paris: Vrin, 1955.

———: Alan of Lille, Anticlaudianus or the Good and Perfect Man. Trans. James J. Sheridan. Toronto: Pontifical Institute of Mediaeval Studies, 1973.

Architrenius: Johannes de Hauvilla, Architrenius. Ed. Paul Gerhard Schmidt. Munich: Fink, 1974.

Aristote: Henri d'Andeli, Le lai d'Aristote. Ed. Maurice Delbouille. Bibliothèque de la Faculté de Philosophie et Lettres de l'Université de Liège, 123. Paris: Belles Lettres, 1951.

Ars poet: Gervase of Melkley, Ars poetica. Ed. Hans-Jürgen Gräbener. Forschungen zur romanischen Philologie, 17. Münster: Aschendorff, 1965.

Ars vers: Matthew of Vendôme, Ars versificatoria. In Mathei Vindocinensis opera, ed. Franco Munari. Storia e letteratura, 171. Rome: Storia e letteratura, 1988. Vol. III.

———: Matthew of Vendôme, The Art of Versification. Trans. Aubrey E. Galyon. Ames: Iowa State University Press, 1980.

Artus: Le livre d'Artus, ed. H. Oskar Sommer. In The Vulgate Version of the Arthurian Romances. Washington, DC: Carnegie Institution, 1913. Vol. VII.

Athis: Li romanz d'Athis et Prophilias. Ed. Alfons Hilka. Gesellschaft für romanische Literatur, 29 and 40. Dresden: Gesellschaft für romanische Literatur; Halle: M. Niemeyer, 1912–16.

Atre: L'âtre périlleux. Ed. Brian Woledge. Classiques français du moyen âge, 76. Paris: Champion, 1936.

Balain: Le roman de Balain. Ed. M. Dominica Legge. Manchester: Manchester University Press, 1942.

Beaudous: Beaudous. In Robert de Blois, *Sämtliche Werke,* ed. Jacob Ulrich. 3 vols. Berlin: Mayer & Müller, 1889–95. Vol. I.

Becket: Guernes de Pont-Sainte-Maxence, *La vie de Saint Thomas Becket.* Ed. Emmanuel Walberg. Classiques français du moyen âge, 77. Paris: Champion, 1964.

Bel inc: Renaut de Beaujeu, *Le bel inconnu.* Ed. G. Perrie Williams. Classiques français du moyen âge, 38. Paris: Champion, 1929.

Berinus: Berinus. Ed. Robert Bossuat. Société des Anciens Textes Français. 2 vols. Paris: SATF, 1931–33.

Berte: Berte aus grans piés. In Adenet le Roi, *Œuvres,* ed. Albert Henry. Université Libre de Bruxelles: Travaux de la Faculté de Philosophie et Lettres, 23. Brussels: Presses Universitaires de Bruxelles; Paris: Presses Universitaires de France, 1963. Vol. IV.

Blanc chev: Jean de Condé, *Li lays dou Blanc Chevalier.* In Baudouin de Condé and Jean de Condé, *Dits et contes,* ed. Auguste Scheler. 3 vols. Brussels: Devaux, 1866–67. Vol. II, pp. 1–48.

Blancandin: Blancandin et l'Orgueilleuse d'amour. Ed. Franklin P. Sweetser. Textes littéraires français, 112. Geneva: Droz; Paris: Minard, 1964.

Bliocadran: Bliocadran: A Prologue to the "Perceval" of Chrétien de Troyes. Edition and Critical Study. Ed. Lenora D. Wolfgang. Beihefte zur Zeitschrift für romanische Philologie, 150. Tübingen: M. Niemeyer, 1976.

Brun: Brun de la Montaigne. Ed. Paul Meyer. Société des Anciens Textes Français. Paris: Firmin Didot, 1875.

Brut: Wace, *Le roman de Brut.* Ed. Ivor Arnold. Société des Anciens Textes Français. 2 vols. Paris: SATF, 1938–40.

Cassidorus: Le roman de Cassidorus. Ed. Joseph Palermo. Société des Anciens Textes Français. Paris: Picard, 1963–64.

Cent nouv: Les cent nouvelles nouvelles. Ed. Franklin P. Sweetser. Textes littéraires français, 127. Geneva: Droz; Paris: Minard, 1966.

Cesar: Li roumanz de Julius Cesar: ein Beitrag zur Cäsargeschichte im Mittelalter. Ed. Paul Hess. Winterthur: P. G. Keller, 1956.

Charrette: Chrétien de Troyes, *Le chevalier de la charrete.* Ed. Mario Roques. Classiques français du moyen âge, 86. Paris: Champion, 1970.

Charrette H: Le roman en prose de Lancelot du Lac: Le conte de la charrette. Ed. Gweneth Hutchings. Paris: Droz, 1938.

Chev deus espees: Li chevaliers as deus espees. Ed. Wendelin Foerster. Halle: Niemeyer, 1877.

Chev epee: Le chevalier à l'épée. In *Two Old French Romances,* Part I: *"Le chevalier à l'épée" and "La mule sans frein,"* ed. R. C. Johnston and D. D. R. Owen. Edinburgh and London: Scottish Academic Press, 1972.

Chron rim: Philippe Mouskes, *Chronique rimée.* Collection des chroniques belges inédites. Brussels: Hayez, 1836–38.

Claris: Li Romans de Claris et Laris. Ed. Johann Alton. Bibliothek des litterarischen Vereins in Stuttgart, 169. Tübingen: H. Laupp, 1884.

Cleomadés: Cleomadés. In Adenet le Roi, *Œuvres,* ed. Albert Henry. Université Libre de Bruxelles: Travaux de la Faculté de Philosophie et Lettres, 46. 5 vols. Brussels: Editions de l'Université de Bruxelles, 1971. Vol. V.1–2.

Cligés: Chrétien de Troyes, *Cligés.* Ed. Alexandre Micha. Classiques français du moyen âge, 84. Paris: Champion, 1957.

Cligès F: Chrétien de Troyes, *Cligès.* Ed. Wendelin Foerster. Halle: Niemeyer, 1884.

Comm Aen: Commentum quod dicitur Bernardi Silvestris super sex libros Eneidos Virgilii — The Commentary on the First Six Books of the "Aeneid" of Vergil Commonly Attributed to Bernardus Silvestris. Ed. Julian Ward Jones and Elizabeth Frances Jones. Lincoln and London: University of Nebraska Press, 1977.

Comm Hor: Scholia in Horatium. Ed. H. J. Botschuyver. Amsterdam: Van Bottenburg, 1935–42. Vols. I, III-IV.

Comm Serv: Servianorum in Vergilii carmina commentariorum, Vol. II: *Quod in Aeneidos libros I et II explanationes continet.* Ed. Edward Kennard Rand et al. Lancaster: American Philological Society, 1946.

Comm Utrecht: Accessus ad auctores, Bernard d'Utrecht, Conrad d'Hirsau Dialogus super auctores. Ed. R. B. C. Huygens. Leiden: Brill, 1970. Pp. 55–69.

Conquête: Geoffroy de Villehardouin, *La conquête de Constantinople.* Ed. Edmond Faral. Classiques de l'histoire de France au moyen âge, 18–19. 2 vols. Paris: Belles Lettres, 1961.

Conseil: Le lai du conseil. Ed. Albert Barth. In *Romanische Forschungen* 31 (1912): 799–872.

Cor: The Anglo-Norman Text of "Le lai du cor." Ed. C. T. Erickson. Anglo-Norman Text Society, 24. Oxford: Blackwell, 1973.

Cosmographia: Bernardus Silvestris, *Cosmographia.* Ed. Peter Dronke. Textus minores, 53. Leiden: Brill, 1978.

Couci: Jakemes, *Le roman du Castelain de Couci et de la Dame de Fayel.* Ed. John E. Matzke and Maurice Delbouille. Société des Anciens Textes Français. Paris: SATF, 1936.

Couronnement: Le couronnement de Louis. Ed. E. Langlois. 2d ed. Classiques français du moyen âge, 22. Paris: Champion, 1969.

Cristal: Cristal und Clarie. Ed. Hermann Breuer. Gesellschaft für romanische Literatur, 36. Dresden: Niemeyer, 1915.

Dares: Daretis Phrygii de excidio Troiae historia. Ed. F. Meister. Leipzig: Teubner, 1873.

De amore: Andreas Capellanus, *De amore libri tres.* Ed. E. Trojel. Copenhagen: Gadiana, 1892.

De cons: Boethius, *The Consolation of Philosophy.* Ed. and trans. "I. T." Rev. by H. F. Stewart. Loeb Classical Library. Cambridge: Harvard University Press; London: Heinemann, 1968.

De gestis: William of Malmesbury, *De gestis regum Anglorum libri quinque.* Ed. William Stubbs. Rolls Series, 90. 2 vols. London, 1877; rpt. Wiesbaden: Kraus, 1964.

De inv: Cicero, *De inventione—De optimo genere oratorum—Topica.* Ed. H. M. Hubbell. Loeb Classical Library. Cambridge: Harvard University Press; London: Heinemann, 1960.

De planctu: Alain de Lille, *De planctu Naturae.* Ed. Nikolaus M. Häring. *Studi medievali* 19 (1978): 797–879.

———: Alan of Lille, *The Complaint of Nature.* Trans. Douglas M. Moffat. Yale Studies in English, 36. New York: H. Holt, 1908.

De vulg: De vulgari eloquentia. Ed. Pier Vincenzo Mengaldo. In Dante, *Opere minori.* 2 vols. Milan and Naples: Ricciardi, 1979. Vol. II, pp. 1–237.

Desiré: Le lai de Desiré. In *Les lais anonymes des XIIe et XIIIe siècles,* ed. Prudence Mary O'Hara Tobin. Publications romanes et françaises, 143. Geneva: Droz, 1976. Pp. 157–205.

Dialogus: Conrad of Hirsau, *Dialogus super auctores.* In *Accessus ad auctores, Bernard d'Utrecht, Conrad d'Hirsau Dialogus super auctores,* ed. R. B. C. Huygens. Leiden: Brill, 1970. Pp. 71–131.

Dictier: "L'art de dictier. " In Eustache Deschamps, *Œuvres complètes,* ed. Gaston Raynaud. Société des Anciens Textes Français. Paris: Firmin Didot, 1891. Vol. VII, pp. 266–92.

Didascalicon: Hugh of Saint Victor, *Didascalicon: de studio legendi.* Ed. Charles Henry Buttimer. Catholic University of America Studies in Medieval and Renaissance Latin, 10. Washington, DC: Catholic University of America Press, 1939.

———: Hugh of Saint Victor, *The "Didascalicon": A Medieval Guide to the Arts.* Trans. Jerome Taylor. Records of Civilization: Sources and Studies. New York and London: Columbia University Press, 1961.

Didot *Perc: The Didot "Perceval" according to the Manuscripts of Modena and Paris.* Ed. William Roach. Philadelphia: University of Pennsylvania Press, 1941.

Documentum: Geoffrey of Vinsauf, *Documentum de modo et arte dictandi et versificandi* (short version). In Edmond Faral, *Les arts poétiques du XIIe et du XIIIe siècle: recherches et documents sur la technique littéraire du moyen âge.* Bibliothèque de l'Ecole des Hautes Etudes, 238. Paris: Champion, 1924. Pp. 263–320.

Dole: Jean Renart, *Le roman de la rose ou de Guillaume de Dole.* Ed. Félix Lecoy. Classiques français du moyen âge, 91. Paris: Champion, 1979.

Dolopathos fr: *Li romans de Dolopathos.* Ed. Charles Brunet and Anatole de Montaiglon. Paris: P. Jannet, 1856.

Dolopathos lat: Johannes de Alta Silva, *Dolopathos sive De rege et septem sapientibus.* Ed. Alfons Hilka. Sammlung mittellateinischer Texte, 5. Heidelberg: C. Winter, 1913.

Donnei: "Le Donnei des amants. " Ed. Gaston Paris. *Romania* 25 (1896): 497–541.

Doon: Le lai de Doon. In *Les lais anonymes des XIIe et XIIIe siècles,* ed. Prudence Mary O'Hara Tobin. Publications romanes et françaises, 143. Geneva: Droz, 1976. Pp. 319–33.

Ducs: Benoît de Sainte-Maure, *Chronique des ducs de Normandie.* Ed. Carin Fahlin; glossary with Östen Södergård. Bibliotheca Elcmaniana Universitatis

Regiae Upsaliensis, 56, 60, 64. 3 vols. Uppsala: Almqvist & Wiksells, 1951–67.

Durmart: Durmart le galois. Ed. Joseph Gildea. 2 vols. Villanova, PA: Villanova Press, 1965–66.

Edmund: Denis Piramus, *La vie seint Edmund le rei.* Ed. Hilding Kjellman. Göteborgs kungl. Vetenskaps- och Vitterhetssamhälles Handlingar, 5te följden, sef. A. Göteborg: Elanders, 1935. Vol. 4.3.

Eledus: Le roman d'Eledus et Serene. Ed. John Revell Reinhard. University of Texas Studies. Austin: University of Texas Press, 1923.

Elucidation: The Elucidation: A Prologue to the Conte del graal. Ed. Albert Wilder Thompson. New York: Institute of French Studies, 1931.

Emp: Edition critique des versions en vers et en prose de la légende de l'Empereur Constant, avec une étude linguistique et littéraire. Ed. James Coveney. Publications de la Faculté des Lettres de l'Université de Strasbourg, 126. Paris: Belles Lettres, 1955.

Eneas: Eneas. Ed. J.-J. Salverda de Grave. Classiques français du moyen âge, 44, 62. 2 vols. Paris: Champion: 1925–29.

Enf Gauvain: "Les Enfances Gauvain: fragments d'un poème perdu." Ed. Paul Meyer. *Romania* 39 (1910): 1–32.

Engleis: Geffrei Gaimar, *L'estoire des Engleis.* Ed. Alexander Bell. Anglo-Norman Text Society, 14–16. Oxford: Blackwell, 1960.

Epervier: Le lai de l'épervier. Ed. Gaston Paris. *Romania* 7 (1878): 1–21.

Epistolae: Epistolae duorum amantium: Briefe Abaelards und Heloises? Ed. Ewald Könsgen. Mittellateinische Studien und Texte, 8. Leiden and Cologne: Brill, 1974.

Eracle: Gautier d'Arras, *Eracle.* Ed. Guy Raynaud de Lage. Classiques français du moyen âge, 102. Paris: Champion, 1976.

Erec: Chrétien de Troyes, *Erec et Enide.* Ed. Mario Roques. Classiques français du moyen âge, 80. Paris: Champion, 1966.

Erec H: Hartmann von Aue, *Erec.* Ed. Albert Leitzmann. 4th ed. by Ludwig Wolff. Altdeutsche Textbibliothek, 39. Tübingen: Niemeyer, 1967.

Erec Pr: *Erec: roman arthurien en prose publié d'après le ms. fr. 112 de la Bibliothèque Nationale.* Ed. Cedric E. Pickford. Textes littéraires français, 87. 2d ed. rev. and corrected. Geneva: Droz; Paris: Minard, 1968.

Escanor: Gérard d'Amiens, *Der Roman von Escanor.* Ed. Henri Michelant. Bibliothek des litterarischen Vereins in Stuttgart, 178. Tübingen: Laupp, 1886.

Escoufle: Jean Renart, *L'Escoufle.* Ed. Franklin Sweetser. Textes littéraires français, 211. Paris and Geneva: Droz, 1974.

Espine: Le lai de l'espine. In *Les lais anonymes des XIIe et XIIIe siècles,* ed. Prudence Mary O'Hara Tobin. Publications romanes et françaises, 143. Geneva: Droz, 1976. Pp. 255–88.

Espurgatoire: Marie de France, *Das Buch vom Espurgatoire S. Patrice.* Ed. Karl Warnke. Bibliotheca normannica, 9. Halle: Niemeyer, 1938.

Estoire: Le Saint-Graal ou le Joseph d'Arimathie, première branche des romans de la Table Ronde. Ed. Eugène Hucher. 3 vols. Le Mans, 1874; Geneva: Slatkine, 1967.

— — —: *Lestoire del saint graal*. In *The Vulgate Version of the Arthurian Romances*, ed. H. Oskar Sommer. Washington: Carnegie Institution, 1909. Vol. I.

Estoire RoB: Robert de Boron, *Le roman de l'Estoire dou graal*. Ed. William A. Nitze. Classiques français du moyen âge, 57. Paris: Champion, 1927.

Etymologiae: Isidore of Seville, *Etymologiarum sive originum libri XX*. Ed. W. M. Lindsay. 2 vols. Oxford: Clarendon Press, 1911.

Fables: Marie de France, *Die Fabeln*. Ed. Karl Warnke. Bibliotheca Normannica, 6. Halle: Niemeyer, 1898.

Fergus: Guillaume le clerc, *The Romance of Fergus*. Ed. Wilson Frescoln. Philadelphia: William H. Allen, 1982.

Fet: Li fet des Romains: compilé ensemble de Salluste et de Suétoine et de Lucan. Ed. L.-F. Flutre and K. Sneyders de Vogel. 2 vols. Paris: Droz; Groningen: J. B. Wolters, n.d.–1938.

Flamenca: Le roman de Flamenca. Ed. Ulrich Gschwind. Romanica Helvetica, 86AB. 2 vols. Bern: Francke, 1976.

Floire: Floire et Blancheflor. Ed. Margaret M. Pelan. Publications de la Faculté des Lettres de l'Université de Strasbourg: textes d'études, 7. 2d ed. Paris: Belles Lettres, 1956.

— — —: *Le conte de Floire et Blancheflor*. Ed. Jean-Luc Leclanche. Classiques français du moyen âge, 105. Paris: Champion, 1980

Florence: Florence de Rome. Ed. A. Wallensköld. Société des anciens textes français. Paris: Firmin-Didot, 1907. Vol. I.

Florence 24384: *Florence de Rome*. Ed. A. Wallensköld. Société des anciens textes français. Paris: Firmin-Didot, 1909. Vol. II.

Floriant: Floriant et Florete. Ed. Harry F. Williams. University of Michigan Publications: Language and Literature, 23. Ann Arbor: University of Michigan Press; London: Geoffrey Cumberlege, Oxford University Press, 1947.

Floriant Pr: *Le roman de Floriant et Florete ou Le chevalier qui la nef maine*. Ed. Claude M. L. Lévy. Ottawa: Editions de l'Université d'Ottawa, 1983.

Florimont: Aimon de Varennes, *Florimont*. Ed. Alfons Hilka. Gesellschaft für romanische Literatur, 48. Göttingen: Niemeyer, 1932.

Floris: Robert de Blois, *Floris et Liriopé*. Ed. Wolfram von Zingerle. Altfranzösische Bibliothek, 12. Leipzig: Reisland, 1891.

Folie Lanc: La folie Lancelot: A Hitherto Unidentified Portion of the Suite du Merlin Contained in MSS. B. N. fr. 112 and 12599. Ed. Fanni Bogdanow. Beihefte zur Zeitschrift für romanische Philologie, 109. Tübingen: Niemeyer, 1965.

Folie Ox: La Folie Tristan d'Oxford. Ed. Ernest Hoepffner. 2d ed. Publications de l'Université de Strasbourg: textes d'études, 8. Rodez: P. Carrère, 1943.

Fouke: Fouke le fitz Waryn. Ed. E. J. Hathaway, P. T. Ricketts, C. A. Robson, and A. D. Wilshere. Anglo-Norman Texts, 26–28. Oxford: Blackwell, 1975.

Galeran: Galeran de Bretagne. Ed. Lucien Foulet. Classiques français du moyen âge, 37. Paris: Champion, 1925.

Gau d'Aupais: Gautier d'Aupais. Ed. Edmond Faral. Classiques français du moyen âge, 20. Paris: Champion, 1919.

Genèse: Schöpfung und Sündenfall in der altfranzösischen Genesisdichtung des Evrat. Ed. Reinhold R. Grimm. Europäische Hochschulschriften. Reihe XIII: Französische Sprache und Literatur, 39. Bern: H. Lang; Frankfurt and Munich: P. Lang, 1976.

Gille: Gautier de Tournay, *L'histoire de Gille de Chyn.* Ed. Edwin B. Place. Northwestern University Studies in the Humanities, 7. Evanston and Chicago: Northwestern University, 1941.

Gliglois: Gliglois. Ed. Charles H. Livingston. Harvard Studies in Romance Languages, 8. Cambridge: Harvard University Press, 1932.

Glosae: Guillaume de Conches, *Glosae super Platonem.* Ed. Edouard Jeauneau. Textes philosophiques du moyen âge, 13. Paris: Vrin, 1965.

Godin: La chanson de Godin. Ed. Françoise Meunier. Université de Louvain: recueil de travaux d'histoire et de philologie, ser. 4, fasc. 14. Louvain: Bibliothèque de l'Université–Publications universitaires de Louvain, 1958.

Gormont: Gormont et Isembart. Ed. Alphonse Bayot. Classiques français du moyen âge, 14. Paris: Champion, 1931.

Graelent: Le lai de Graelent. In *Les lais anonymes des XIIᵉ et XIIIᵉ siècles,* ed. Prudence Mary O'Hara Tobin. Publications romanes et françaises, 143. Geneva: Droz, 1976. Pp. 83–125.

Gui: Gui de Warewik. Ed. Alfred Ewert. Classiques français du moyen âge, 74–75. 2 vols. Paris: Champion, 1932–33.

Guil d'A: Chrétien de Troyes, *Guillaume d'Angleterre.* Ed. Maurice Wilmotte. Classiques français du moyen âge, 55. Paris: Champion, 1927.

Guil maréchal: L'histoire de Guillaume le maréchal, comte de Striguil et de Pembroke. Ed. Paul Meyer. 3 vols. Paris: Renouard, 1891–1901.

Guil Palerne: Guillaume de Palerne. Ed. H. Michelant. Société des anciens textes français. Paris: Firmin-Didot, 1876.

Guingamor: Le lai de Guingamor. In *Les lais anonymes des XIIᵉ et XIIIᵉ siècles,* ed. Prudence Mary O'Hara Tobin. Publications romanes et françaises, 143. Geneva: Droz, 1976. Pp. 127–55.

Guiron: Guiron le courtois: étude de la tradition manuscrite et analyse critique. Ed. Roger Lathuillère. Publications romanes et françaises, 186. Geneva: Droz, 1966.

Helcanus: Le roman de Helcanus. Ed. Henri Niedzielski. Textes littéraires français, 121. Geneva: Droz, 1966.

Hist reg: Geoffrey of Monmouth, *Historia regum Britanniae.* Ed. Acton Griscom. Together with a literal translation of the Welsh Manuscript N° LXI of Jesus College, Oxford, by Robert Ellis Jones. London, New York, Toronto: Longmans, Green, 1929.

— — —: Geoffrey of Monmouth, *Historia regum Britanniae.* In Edmond Faral, *La légende arthurienne.* 3 vols. Paris: Champion, 1929. Vol. III, pp. 63–303.

Hist troy: Anonymi Historia troyana Daretis Frigii: Untersuchungen und kritische Ausgabe. Ed. Jürgen Stohlmann. Beihefte zum "Mittellateinischen Jahrbuch," 1. Wuppertal, Ratingen, Düsseldorf: A. Henn, 1968.

Horn: Thomas, *The Romance of Horn.* Ed. Mildred K. Pope. Rev. and completed by T. B. W. Reid. Anglo-Norman Texts, 9–10, 12–13. 2 vols. Oxford: Blackwell, 1955–64.

Hunbaut: The Romance of Hunbaut. Ed. Margaret Winters. Davis Medieval Texts and Studies, 4. Leiden: Brill, 1984.

Huon: Huon de Bordeaux. Ed. Pierre Ruelle. Université Libre de Bruxelles: Travaux de la Faculté de Philosophie et Lettres, 20. Brussels: Presses Universitaires de Bruxelles; Paris: Presses Universitaires de France, 1961.

Huth *Merlin: Merlin, roman en prose du XIIIᵉ siècle, publié avec la mise en prose du poème de Merlin de Robert de Boron d'après le manuscrit appartenant à M. Alfred H. Huth.* Ed. Gaston Paris and Jacob Ulrich. Société des anciens textes français. 2 vols. Paris: Firmin-Didot, 1886.

Ignaure: Le lai d'Ignaure ou Lai du prisonnier. Ed. Rita Lejeune. Académie Royale de Langue et de Littérature Françaises de Belgique: textes anciens, 3. Brussels: Palais des Académies; Liège: H. Vaillant-Carmanne, 1938.

Ille: Gautier d'Arras, *Ille et Galeron.* Ed. Frederick A. G. Cowper. Société des anciens textes français. Paris: Picard, 1956.

Ipomedon: Hue de Rotelande, *Ipomedon.* Ed. A. J. Holden. Bibliothèque française et romane, 17. Paris: Klincksieck, 1979.

Iter: Iter Alexandri Magni ad paradisum. Ed. Alfons Hilka. In *"La prise de Defur" and "Le voyage d'Alexandre au paradis terrestre."* Elliott Monographs, 35. New York: Kraus, 1965. Pp. xli–xlviii.

Jaufre: Jaufre. Ed. Clovis Brunel. Société des anciens textes français. 2 vols. Paris: SATF, 1943.

Jehan: Philippe de Remi, *Jehan et Blonde.* Ed. Sylvie Lécuyer. Classiques français du moyen âge, 107. Paris: Champion, 1984.

Joseph d'A: "The Modena Text of the Prose *Joseph d'Arimathie.*" Ed. William Roach. *Romance Philology* 9 (1956): 313–42.

— — —: *Der Prosaroman von Joseph von Arimathia.* Ed. Georg Weidner. Oppeln: Franck, 1881.

Joseph d'A Mid Fr: "The Middle French Redaction of Robert de Boron's *Joseph d'Arimathie.*" Ed. Richard O'Gorman. *Proceedings of the American Philosophical Society* 122 (1978): 261–85.

Joufroi: Joufroi de Poitiers. Ed. Percival B. Fay and John L. Grigsby. Textes littéraires français, 183. Geneva: Droz, 1972.

Laborintus: Eberhard the German, *Laborintus.* In Edmond Faral, *Les arts poétiques du XIIᵉ et du XIIIᵉ siècle: recherches et documents sur la technique littéraire du moyen âge.* Bibliothèque de l'Ecole des Hautes Etudes, 238. Paris: Champion, 1924. Pp. 336–77.

Lais: Marie de France, *Les lais.* Ed. Jean Rychner. Classiques français du moyen âge, 93. Paris: Champion, 1968.

Lancelot: Lancelot. Ed. Alexandre Micha. Textes littéraires français 247, 249, 262, 278, 283, 286, 288, 307, 315. 9 vols. Paris and Geneva: Droz, 1978–83.

Lancelot K: *Lancelot do Lac: The Non-Cyclic Old French Prose Romance.* Ed. Elspeth Kennedy. 2 vols. Oxford: Clarendon Press, 1980.

Lancelot S: *Le livre de Lancelot del Lac.* In *The Vulgate Version of the Arthurian*

Romances, ed. H. Oskar Sommer. 8 vols. Washington, DC: Carnegie Institution, 1910–12. Vols. III–V.

Lanzelet: Ulrich von Zatzikhoven, *Lanzelet.* Ed. K. A. Hahn. Deutsche Neudrucke, Reihe: Texte des Mittelalters. Frankfurt, 1845; rpt. Frankfurt and Berlin: de Gruyter, 1965.

Laurin: Le roman de Laurin fils de Marques le sénéchal: Text of MS. B. N. f. fr. 22548. Ed. Lewis Thorpe. University of Nottingham Research Publication, 2. Cambridge: W. Heffer, [1958].

Lecheor: Le lai du lecheor. In *Les lais anonymes des XII* et *XIII* siècles, ed. Prudence Mary O'Hara Tobin. Publications romanes et françaises, 143. Geneva: Droz, 1976. Pp. 347–58.

Levrier: Jean de Condé, *Li dis dou levrier.* In Baudouin de Condé and Jean de Condé, *Dits et contes,* ed. Auguste Scheler. 3 vols. Brussels: Devaux, 1866–67. Vol. II, pp. 303–53.

Lycorne: Le romans de la Dame a la lycorne et du Biau chevalier au lyon. Ed. Friedrich Gennrich. Gesellschaft für romanische Literatur, 18. Dresden: Niemeyer, 1908.

Mance: Jean de Condé, *Li dis dou Chevalier a le mance.* In Baudouin de Condé and Jean de Condé, *Dits et contes,* ed. Auguste Scheler. 3 vols. Brussels: Devaux, 1866–67. Vol. II, pp. 167–242.

Manekine: La Manekine. In Philippe de Remi, sire de Beaumanoir, *Œuvres poétiques,* ed. Hermann Suchier. Société des anciens textes français. Paris: Firmin Didot, 1884. Vol. I.

Mantel: "Le conte du *Mantel.*" Ed. F.-A. Wulff. *Romania* 14 (1885): 343–80.

Marcabru: Marcabru, *Poésies complètes.* Ed. J.-M.-L. Dejeanne. Bibliothèque Méridionale, ser. I. Toulouse: E. Privat, 1909. Vol. 12.

Marguerite: Wace, *La vie de sainte Marguerite.* Ed. Elizabeth A. Francis. Classiques français du moyen âge, 71. Paris: Champion, 1932.

Marques: Le roman de Marques de Rome. Ed. Johann Alton. Bibliothek des litterarischen Vereins in Stuttgart, 187. Tübingen: H. Laupp, 1889.

Meliacin: Girard d'Amiens, *Le roman du cheval de fust, ou de Meliacin.* Ed. Paul Aebischer. Textes littéraires français, 212. Geneva: Droz, 1974.

Meliador: Jean Froissart, *Meliador.* Ed. Auguste Longnon. Société des anciens textes français. 3 vols. Paris: Firmin Didot, 1895–99.

Melion: Le lai de Melion. In *Les lais anonymes des XII* et *XIII* siècles, ed. Prudence Mary O'Hara Tobin. Publications romanes et françaises, 143. Geneva: Droz, 1976. Pp. 289–318.

Melior: Melior et Ydoine. Ed. Paul Meyer. *Romania* 37 (1908): 236–44.

Melusine Co: Coudrette, *Le roman de Mélusine ou Histoire de Lusignan.* Ed. Eleanor Roach. Bibliothèque française et romane, B 18. Paris: Klincksieck, 1982.

Melusine JdA: Jean d'Arras, *Mélusine.* Ed. Louis Stouff. Publications de l'Université de Dijon, 5. Dijon: Bernigaud et Privat, 1932.

Meraugis: Raoul de Houdenc, *Meraugis de Portlesguez.* Ed. Mathias Friedwagner. Halle: Niemeyer, 1897.

Meriadoc: "Historia Meriadoci" and "De ortu Waluuanii." Ed. J. Douglas Bruce.

Hesperia: Ergänzungsreihe, 2. Göttingen: Vandenhoeck & Ruprecht; Baltimore: Johns Hopkins University Press, 1913.

Merlin M: Robert de Boron, *Merlin*. Ed. Alexandre Micha. Textes littéraires français, 281. Paris and Geneva: Droz, 1980.

— — — S: *Lestoire de Merlin*. Ed. H. Oskar Sommer. In *The Vulgate Version of Arthurian Romances*. Washington, DC: Carnegie Institution, 1908. Vol. II.

Metalogicon: Ioannis Saresberiensis episcopi Carnotensis Metalogicon libri IV. Ed. Clemens C. I. Webb. Oxford: Clarendon Press, 1929.

Mort: La Mort le roi Artu. Ed. Jean Frappier. 3d ed. Textes littéraires français, 58. Geneva: Droz; Paris: Minard, 1964.

Mule: La mule sans frein. In *Two Old French Gauvain Romances,* Part I: *"Le chevalier à l'épée" and "La mule sans frein,"* ed. R. C. Johnston and D. D. R. Owen. Edinburgh and London: Scottish Academic Press, 1972.

Mutacion: Christine de Pizan, *Le livre de la mutacion de Fortune*. Ed. Suzanne Solente. Société des anciens textes français. 4 vols. Paris: Picard, 1959–66.

Nabaret: Le lai de Nabaret. In *Les lais anonymes des XIIe et XIIIe siècles,* ed. Prudence Mary O'Hara Tobin. Publications romanes et françaises, 143. Geneva: Droz, 1976. Pp. 359–64.

Narcisus: "Der altfranzösische Narcisuslai." Ed Alfons Hilka. *Zeitschrift für romanische Philologie* 49 (1929): 633–75.

Octavian: Octavian: altfranzösischer Roman nach der Oxforder Handschrift Bodl. Hatton 100. Ed. Karl Vollmöller. Altfranzösische Bibliothek, 3. Heilbronn: Henninger, 1883.

Oiselet: "Le lai de l'oiselet." Ed. Gaston Paris. In *Légendes du moyen âge*. 2d ed. Paris: Hachette, 1904. Pp. 271–91.

— — —: *"Le lai de l'oiselet."* Ed. Raymond Weeks. In *Medieval Studies in Memory of Gertrude Schoepperle Loomis*. Paris: Champion; New York: Columbia University Press, 1927. Pp. 341–53.

Olifant: Baudouin de Condé, *Li contes de l'olifant*. In Baudouin de Condé and Jean de Condé, *Dits et contes,* ed. Auguste Scheler. 3 vols. Brussels: Devaux, 1866–67. Vol. I, pp. 233–43.

Ombre: Jean Renart, *Le lai de l'ombre*. Ed. Félix Lecoy. Classiques français du moyen âge, 104. Paris: Champion, 1983.

Orator: M. Tulli Ciceronis ad M. Brutum Orator. Ed. John Edwin Sandys. Cambridge: University Press, 1885.

Osith: "An Anglo-French Life of St. Osith." Ed. A. T. Baker. *Modern Language Review* 6 (1911): 476–502; 7 (1912): 74–93, 157–92.

Ov mor comm: Le commentaire de Copenhague de l'"Ovide moralisé," avec l'édition critique du Septième Livre. Ed. Jeannette T. M. van 't Sant. Amsterdam: H. J. Paris, 1929.

Ovide mor: L'Ovide moralisé. Ed. C. de Boer. Verhandelingen der koninklijke Akademie van Wetenschappen te Amsterdam. Afdeeling Letterkunde, n.s. 15, 21, 30.3, 37, 43. Amsterdam: Müller, 1915–38.

P Aug: "Mélanges de poésie française, III. Prologue en vers français d'une histoire perdue de Philippe-Auguste." Ed. Paul Meyer. *Romania* 6 (1877): 494–98.

Parfait: Jean de la Mote, *Le parfait du paon.* Ed. Richard J. Carey. University of North Carolina Studies in the Romance Languages and Literatures, 118. Chapel Hill: University of North Carolina Press, 1972.

Paris: "Der altfranzösische Roman Paris et Vienne." Ed. Robert Kaltenbacher. *Romanische Forschungen* 15 (1904): 321–688a[a].

Parisiana Poetria: John of Garland, *The "Parisiana Poetria."* Ed. Traugott Lawler. Yale Studies in English, 182. New Haven and London: Yale University Press, 1974.

Partonopeu: Partonopeu de Blois. Ed. Joseph Gildea and Leon Smith. 2 vols. Villanova: Villanova University Press, 1967–70.

Perceforest: "Etudes sur le roman de *Perceforêt.*" Ed. L.-F. Flutre. *Romania* 70 (1948–49): 474–522; 71 (1950): 374–92, 482–508; 74 (1953): 44–102; 88 (1967): 475–508; 89 (1968): 355–86; 90 (1969): 341–70; 91 (1970): 189–226.

———: *Le roman de Perceforest. Première partie.* Ed. Jane H. M. Taylor. Textes littéraires français, 279. Geneva: Droz, 1979.

———: *Perceforest: Quatrième partie.* Ed. Gilles Roussineau. Textes littéraires français, 343. 2 vols. Paris and Geneva: Droz, 1987.

Perceval: Chrétien de Troyes, *Le roman de Perceval ou Le Conte du graal.* Ed. William Roach. 2d ed. Textes littéraires français, 71. Geneva: Droz; Paris: Minard, 1959.

Perceval Cont I: The Continuations of the Old French "Perceval" of Chrétien de Troyes: The First Continuation, Vol. I: *Redaction of Mss TVD.* Ed. William Roach. Vol. II: *Redaction of Mss EMQU.* Ed. William Roach and Robert H. Ivy, Jr. Vol. III, Part 1: *Redaction of Mss ALPRS.* Ed. William Roach. Part 2: *Glossary of the First Continuation,* by Lucien Foulet. Philadelphia: American Philosophical Society, 1949–55.

Perceval Cont II: The Continuations of the Old French "Perceval" of Chrétien de Troyes, Vol. IV: *The Second Continuation.* Ed. William Roach. Philadelphia: American Philosophical Society, 1971.

Perceval Cont III: The Continuations of the Old French "Perceval" of Chrétien de Troyes, Vol. V: *The Third Continuation by Manessier.* Ed. William Roach. Philadelphia: American Philosophical Society, 1983.

Perceval Cont IV: Gerbert de Montreuil, *La continuation de Perceval.* Ed. Mary Williams and Marguerite Oswald. Classiques français du moyen âge, 28, 50, 101. 3 vols. Paris: Champion, 1922–75.

Perceval H: Chrétien de Troyes, *Der Percevalroman.* Ed. Alfons Hilka. Halle: Niemeyer, 1932.

Perlesvaus: Le haut livre du graal: Perlesvaus. Ed. William A. Nitze, T. Atkinson Jenkins, et al. 2 vols. Chicago, 1932–37; New York: Phaeton, 1972.

Philomena: Chrétien de Troyes, *Philomena.* Ed. C. de Boer. Paris: P. Geuthner, 1909.

Pierre: La belle Maguelone. Ed. Adolphe Biedermann. Paris: Champion; Halle: Niemeyer, 1913.

Piramus: Piramus et Tisbé. Ed. C. de Boer. Classiques français du moyen âge, 26. Paris: Champion, 1921.

Poetria nova: Geoffrey of Vinsauf, *Poetria nova.* In Edmond Faral, *Les arts poétiques du XIIe et du XIIIe siècle: recherches et documents sur la technique litté-raire du moyen âge.* Bibliothèque des Hautes Etudes, 238. Paris: Cham-pion, 1924. Pp. 194–262.

— — —: Geoffrey of Vinsauf, *Poetria nova.* Trans. Margaret F. Nims. Toronto: Pon-tifical Institute of Medieval Studies, 1967.

Poire: Thibaut, *Li romanz de la poire.* Ed. Friedrich Stehlich. Halle: Niemeyer, 1881.

Porphyry: Pomponii Porphyrionis commentarii in Q. Horatium Flaccum. Ed. Wil-helm Meyer. Leipzig: Teubner, 1874.

Praeexercitamina: Priscian, *Praeexercitamina.* In *Grammatici latini,* ed. Heinrich Keil. Leipzig: Teubner, 1859. Vol. III, pp. 430–40.

Prise: "La prise de Defur" and "Le voyage d'Alexandre au paradis terrestre." Ed. Law-ton P. G. Peckham and Milan S. La Du. Elliott Monographs, 35. New York: Kraus, 1965. Pp. 1–72.

Prise d'Al: Guillaume de Machaut, *La prise d'Alexandrie ou Chronique du roi Pierre Ier de Lusignan.* Ed. M. L. de Mas Latrie. Publications de la Société de l'Orient Latin: série historique, 1. Geneva: Fick, 1877.

Prison: Baudouin de Condé, *Li prisons d'amours.* In Baudouin de Condé and Jean de Condé, *Dits et contes,* ed. Auguste Scheler. 3 vols. Brussels: Devaux, 1866–67. Vol. I, pp. 267–377.

Prophecies: Les prophécies de Merlin: Edited from MS. 593 in the Bibliothèque Muni-cipale of Rennes. Ed. Lucy Allen Paton. Modern Language Association of America Monograph Series 1.1–2. 2 vols. New York, 1926–27; rpt. New York: Kraus, 1966.

Protheselaus: Hue de Rotelande, *Protheselaus.* Ed. Franz Kluckow. Gesellschaft für romanische Literatur, 45. Göttingen: Gesellschaft für romanische Literatur; Halle: Niemeyer, 1924.

Pseudo-Acron: Pseudoacronis scholia in Horatium vetustiora. Ed. Otto Keller. 2 vols. Leipzig: Teubner, 1902–4.

Queste: La queste del saint graal. Ed. Albert Pauphilet. Classiques français du moyen âge, 33. Paris: Champion, 1980.

Registrum: Das "Registrum multorum auctorum" des Hugo von Trimberg: Unter-suchungen und kommentierte Textausgabe. Ed. Karl Langosch. Germanische Studien, 235. Berlin: E. Ebering, 1942.

Restor: Jean Le Court, dit Brisebare, *Le restor du paon.* Ed. Richard J. Carey. Textes littéraires français, 119. Geneva: Droz, 1966.

Richars: Richars li biaus. Ed. Anthony J. Holden. Classiques français du moyen âge, 106. Paris: Champion, 1983.

Rigomer: Jehan, *Les mervelles de Rigomer.* Ed. Wendelin Foerster and Hermann Breuer. Gesellschaft für romanische Literatur, 19, 39. 2 vols. Dresden: M. Niemeyer, 1908–15.

Robert: Robert le diable. Ed. E. Löseth. Société des anciens textes français. Paris: Firmin Didot, 1903.

Roland: Les textes de la Chanson de Roland. Ed. Raoul Mortier. 10 vols. Paris: La Geste Francor, 1940–44.

Rose: Guillaume de Lorris and Jean de Meung, *Le roman de la rose.* Ed. Ernest Langlois. Société des anciens textes français. 5 vols. Paris: Firmin Didot, 1914–24.

— — —: Guillaume de Lorris and Jean de Meun, *Le roman de la rose*. Ed. Félix Lecoy. Classiques français du moyen âge, 92, 95, 98. 3 vols. Paris: Champion, 1965–70.

Rou: Wace, *Le roman de Rou*. Ed. A. J. Holden. Société des anciens textes français. 3 vols. Paris: Picard, 1970–73.

Saisnes: Jean Bodel, *Saxenlied*. Ed. F. Menzel and E. Stengel. Ausgaben und Abhandlungen aus dem Gebiete der romanischen Philologie, 99–100. 2 vols. Marburg: Elwert, 1906–9.

Saturnalia: Ambrosii Theodosii Macrobii Saturnalia. Ed. J. Willis. Leipzig: Teubner, 1963.

Scholia: Scholia Vindobonensia ad Horatii artem poeticam. Ed. J. Zechmeister. Vienna: [s.p.], 1877.

Sept sages Pr: *Deux rédactions du roman des Sept sages de Rome*. Ed. Gaston Paris. Société des anciens textes français. Paris: Firmin Didot, 1876.

Sept sages V: *Le Roman des sept sages de Rome: A Critical Edition of the Two Verse Redactions*. Ed. Mary B. Speer. Edward C. Armstrong Monographs on Medieval Literature, 4. Lexington: French Forum, 1989.

Set dorm: Chardri, *La vie des set dormanz*. Ed. Brian S. Merrilees. Anglo-Norman Text Society, 35. London: Anglo-Norman Text Society, Westfield College, 1977.

Silence: Heldris de Cornuälle, *Le roman de Silence*. Ed. Lewis Thorpe. Cambridge: Heffer, 1972.

Somnium: Macrobius, *Commentarii in Somnium Scipionis*. Ed. J. Willis. Leipzig: Teubner, 1963.

Sone: Sone de Nausay. Ed. Moritz Goldschmidt. Bibliothek des litterarischen Vereins in Stuttgart, 216. Tübingen: Litterarischer Verein, 1899.

St-Louis: Jean, sire de Joinville, *Histoire de Saint Louis, Credo et Lettre à Louis X*. Ed. and trans. Natalis de Wailly. Paris: Firmin Didot, 1874.

Summa: Konrad von Mure, *Die "Summa de arte prosandi."* Ed. Walter Kronbichler. Geist und Werk der Zeiten, 17. Zürich: Fretz und Wasmuth, 1968.

TChev: Thomas of Kent, *The Anglo-Norman "Alexander" ("Le roman de toute chevalerie")*. Ed. Brian Foster with Ian Short. Anglo-Norman Text Society, 29–31, 32–33. 2 vols. London: Anglo-Norman Text Society, 1976–77.

Thèbes: Le roman de Thèbes. Ed. Guy Raynaud de Lage. Classiques français du moyen âge, 94, 96. 2 vols. Paris: Champion, 1966–71.

Timaeus: Timaeus a Calcidio translatus commentarioque instructus. Ed. J. H. Waszink. In *Plato latinus*. Corpus platonicum medii aevi. London: Warburg Institute; Leiden: Brill, 1962. Vol. IV.

Tornoiement: Huon de Mery, *Li tornoiemenz Antecrit*. Ed. Georg Wimmer. Ausgaben und Abhandlungen aus dem Gebiete der romanischen Philologie, 76. Marburg: Elwert, 1888.

Tres am: Le trésor amoureux. In Jean Froissart, *Œuvres*, ed. M. Aug. Scheler. Brussels: Devaux, 1872. Vol. III, pp. 52–281.

Tresor: Brunetto Latini, *Li livres dou tresor*. Ed. Francis J. Carmody. University of

California Publications in Modern Philology, 22. Berkeley and Los Angeles: University of California Press, 1948.

Tristan: Quotes are from *Le roman en prose de Tristan, le roman de Palamède et la compilation de Rusticien de Pise: analyse d'après les manuscrits de Paris.* Ed. E. Löseth. Bibliothèque de l'Ecole des Hautes Etudes, 82. Paris: Bouillon, 1980.

——: Second quotes, when available, are from *Le Roman de Tristan en prose.* Ed. Renée L. Curtis. Arthurian Studies, 12–14. 3 vols. Cambridge: D. S. Brewer, 1985. Or from *Le Roman de Tristan en prose.* Ed. Philippe Ménard. Textes littéraires français, 353. Geneva: Droz, 1987.

Tristan Béd: Thomas, *Le roman de Tristan.* Ed. Joseph Bédier. Société des anciens textes français. 2 vols. Paris: Firmin Didot, 1902–5.

Tristan Ber: Beroul, *The Romance of Tristran.* Ed. A. Ewert. 2 vols. Oxford: Blackwell, 1939–70.

Tristan Got: Gottfried von Straßburg, *Tristan.* Ed. Gottfried Weber, with Gertrud Utzmann and Werner Hoffmann. Darmstadt: Wissenschaftliche Buchgesellschaft, 1967.

Tristan Th: Thomas d'Angleterre, *Les fragments du roman de Tristan.* Ed. Bartina H. Wind. Textes littéraires français, 92. Geneva: Droz; Paris: Minard, 1960.

Troie: Benoît de Sainte-Maure, *Le roman de Troie.* Ed. Léopold Constans. Société des anciens textes français. 6 vols. Paris: Firmin Didot, 1904–12.

Troie Pr: *Le roman de Troie en prose.* Ed. L. Constans and E. Faral. Classiques français du moyen âge, 29. Paris: Champion, 1922.

Turpin: The Old French Johannes Translation of the "Pseudo-Turpin Chronicle." Ed. Ronald N. Walpole. Berkeley, Los Angeles, London: University of California Press, 1976.

Tydorel: Le lai de Tydorel. In *Les lais anonymes des XIIe et XIIIe siècles,* ed. Prudence Mary O'Hara Tobin. Publications romanes et françaises, 143. Geneva: Droz, 1976. Pp. 207–26.

Tyolet: Le lai de Tyolet. In *Les lais anonymes des XIIe et XIIIe siècles,* ed. Prudence Mary O'Hara Tobin. Publications romanes et françaises, 143. Geneva: Droz, 1976. Pp. 227–53.

Vengement: Gui de Cambrai, *Le vengement Alixandre.* Ed. Bateman Edwards. Elliott Monographs, 23. New York: Kraus, 1965.

Venjance (1), (2), (3), (4), (5): *Five Versions of the Venjance Alixandre.* Ed. Edward Billings Ham. Elliott Monographs, 34. New York: Kraus, 1965.
   1. The Venice *Venjance,* pp. 1–12.
   2. The Parma *Venjance,* pp. 13–46.
   3. Jean Wauquelin, *Venjance,* pp. 47–75.
   4. *Venjance* in *Renart le contrefait,* pp. 76–78.
   5. Besançon *Venjance,* pp. 79–82.

Venjance Nev: Jehan le Nevelon, *La venjance Alixandre.* Ed. Edward Billings Ham. Elliott Monographs, 27. New York: Kraus, 1965.

Violette: Gerbert de Montreuil, *Le roman de la violette ou de Gerart de Nevers.* Ed.

Douglas Labaree Buffum. Société des anciens textes français. Paris: Champion, 1928.

Vita nuova: Dante, *Vita nuova.* Ed. Domenico De Robertis. In *Opere minori.* 2 vols. Milan and Naples: Ricciardi, 1984. Vol. I.1, pp. 1–247.

Vitae: Vitae vergilianae. Ed. J. Brummer. Leipzig: Teubner, 1912.

Voyage: Voyage d'Alexandre. Ed. Lawton P. G. Peckham and Milan S. La Du. Elliott Monographs, 35. New York: Kraus, 1965. Pp. 73–90.

Waldef: Le roman de Waldef (Cod. Bodmer 168). Ed. A. J. Holden, Bibliotheca Bodmeriana: textes, 5. Cologny-Geneva: Fondation Martin Bodmer, 1984.

WatrC: Watriquet de Couvin, *Dits.* Ed. Auguste Scheler. Brussels: Devaux, 1868.

Wistasse: Li romans de Wistasse le moine, édité d'après le manuscrit, fonds français 1553, de la Bibliothèque Nationale, Paris. Ed. Denis Joseph Conlon. University of North Carolina Studies in the Romance Languages and Literatures, 126. Chapel Hill: University of North Carolina Press, 1972.

Yder: The Romance of Yder. Ed. and trans. Alison Adams. Arthurian Studies, 8. Cambridge: D. S. Brewer; Totowa, NJ: Biblio, 1983.

Ylias: Joseph Iscanus, *Werke und Briefe.* Ed. Ludwig Gompf. Mittellateinische Studien und Texte, 4. Leiden and Cologne: Brill, 1970. Pp. 77–211.

Yvain: Chrétien de Troyes, *Le chevalier au lion (Yvain).* Ed. Mario Roques. Classiques français du moyen âge, 89. Paris: Champion, 1982.

Yvain R: Chrétien de Troyes, *Yvain (Le chevalier au lion).* Ed. Wendelin Foerster and T. B. W. Reid. Manchester: Manchester University Press, 1942.

Secondary Literature

Accarie, Maurice 1979: "Faux mariage et vrai mariage dans les romans de Chrétien de Troyes." *Annales de la Faculté des Lettres et Sciences Humaines de Nice* 38: 25–35.

Adams, Alison 1974: "Godefroi de Leigni's Continuation of *Lancelot.*" *Forum for Modern Language Studies* 10: 295–99.

Adams, Alison 1987: "The Shape of Arthurian Verse Romance (to 1300)." In *The Legacy of Chrétien de Troyes,* ed. N. J. Lacy, D. Kelly, and K. Busby. Faux titre, 31. Amsterdam: Rodopi. Vol. I, pp. 141–65.

Adler, Alfred 1947: "The Themes of 'The Handsome Coward' and of 'The Handsome Unknown' in *Meraugis de Portlesguez.*" *Modern Philology* 44: 218–24.

Adler, Alfred 1975: *Epische Spekulanten: Versuch einer synchronen Geschichte des altfranzösischen Epos.* Theorie und Geschichte der Literatur und der schönen Künste: Texte und Abhandlungen, 33. Munich: W. Fink.

Ainsworth, Peter F. 1988: "The Art of Hesitation: Chrétien, Froissart and the Inheritance of Chivalry." In *The Legacy of Chrétien de Troyes,* ed. N. J. Lacy, D. Kelly, and K. Busby. Faux titre, 37. Amsterdam: Rodopi. Vol. II, pp. 187–206.

Allen, Judson B. 1973: "Commentary as Criticism: Formal Cause, Discursive Form, and the Late Medieval Accessus." *Acta Conventus Neo-Latini Lovaniensis,* ed. J. IJsewijn and E. Keßler. Humanistische Bibliothek: Abhandlungen, 20. Leuven: University Press, Munich: Fink. Pp. 29–48.

Allen, Judson B. 1982: *The Ethical Poetic of the Later Middle Ages: A Decorum of Convenient Distinction.* Toronto, Buffalo, London: University of Toronto Press.

Allen, Judson B. 1984: "Grammar, Poetic Form, and the Lyric Ego: A Medieval *A priori.*" In *Vernacular Poetics in the Middle Ages,* ed. L. Ebin. Studies in Medieval Culture, 16. Kalamazoo: Medieval Institute. Pp. 199–226.

Altman, Charles F. 1975: "Two Types of Opposition and the Structure of Latin Saints' Lives." *Medievalia et Humanistica* n.s. 6: 1–12.

Angeli, Giovanna 1971: *L'"Eneas" e i primi romanzi volgari.* Documenti di filologia, 15. Milan and Naples: Ricciardi.

Anitchkof, Eugène 1929: "Le Saint Graal et les rites eucharistiques." *Romania* 55: 174–94.

Arbusow, Leonid 1963: *Colores rhetorici: eine Auswahl rhetorischer Figuren und Gemeinplätze als Hilfsmittel für akademische Übungen an mittelalterlichen Texten.* 2d ed. by Helmut Peter. Göttingen: Vandenhoeck & Ruprecht.

Aubailly, Jean-Claude 1986: *La fée et le chevalier: essai de mythanalyse de quelques lais féeriques des XIIe et XIIIe siècles.* Essais, 10. Paris: Champion.

Auerbach, Erich 1958: *Literatursprache und Publikum in der lateinischen Spätantike und im Mittelalter.* Bern: Francke.

Baader, Horst 1966: *Die Lais: zur Geschichte einer Gattung der altfranzösischen Kurzerzählungen.* Analecta Romanica, 16. Frankfurt: Klostermann.

Badel, Pierre-Yves 1969: *Introduction à la vie littéraire du moyen âge.* Bordas Etudes, 30. Paris, Brussels, Montréal: Bordas.

Badel, Pierre-Yves 1975: "Rhétorique et polémique dans les prologues de romans au moyen âge." *Littérature* 20: 81–94.

Badel, Pierre-Yves 1980: *Le Roman de la rose au XIVe siècle: étude de la réception de l'œuvre.* Publications romanes et françaises, 153. Geneva: Droz.

Baehr, Rudolf 1968: "Das Alexiuslied als Vortragsdichtung." In *Serta Romanica: Festschrift Gerhard Rohlfs.* Tübingen: Niemeyer. Pp. 175–99.

Bagni, Paolo 1968: *La costituzione della poesia nelle artes del XII-XIII secolo.* Università degli Studi di Bologna. Facoltà di lettere e filosofia: Studi e ricerche, n.s. 20. Bologna: Zanichelli.

Baker, A. T. 1924: "Saints' Lives Written in Anglo-French: Their Historical, Social and Literary Importance." In *Essays by Divers Hands, being the Transactions of the Royal Society of Literature of the United Kingdom* n.s. 4: 119–56.

Bardon, H. 1986: "*Iunctura callidus acri (Perse 5, 14),*" *Rivista di cultura classica e medioevale* 28: 3–6.

Barwick, K. 1928: "Die Gliederung der narratio in der rhetorischen Theorie und ihre Bedeutung für die Geschichte des antiken Romans." *Hermes* 63: 261–87.

Batany, Jean 1970: "Paradigmes lexicaux et structures littéraires au moyen âge." *Revue d'histoire littéraire de la France* 70: 819–35.

Batany, Jean 1974: " 'Home and Rome,' A Device in Epic and Romance: *Le Couronne-ment de Louis* and *Ille et Galeron.*" *Yale French Studies* 51: 42–60.

Battaglia, Salvatore 1968: *Mitografia del personaggio.* Milan: Rizzoli.

Baum, Richard 1969: "Les troubadours et les lais." *Zeitschrift für romanische Philologie* 85: 1–44.

Baumgartner, Emmanuèle 1975: *Le "Tristan en prose": essai d'interprétation d'un roman médiéval.* Publications romanes et françaises, 133. Geneva: Droz.

Baumgartner, Emmanuèle 1979: "Du *Tristan* de Béroul au *Roman en prose de Tristan:* étude comparée de l'idéologie et de l'écriture romanesques à partir de l'épisode de la forêt de Morois." In *Der altfranzösische Prosaroman: Funktion, Funktionswandel und Ideologie am Beispiel des "Roman de Tristan en prose,"* ed. E. Ruhe and R. Schwaderer. Kolloquium Würzburg 1977. Beiträge zur romanischen Philologie des Mittelalters, 12. Munich: Fink. Pp. 11–45.

Baumgartner, Emmanuèle 1981: *L'arbre et le pain: essai sur "La Queste del saint graal."* Paris: SEDES.

Baumgartner, Emmanuèle 1982: "Jeux de rimes et roman arthurien." *Romania* 103: 550–60.

Baumgartner, Emmanuèle 1984a: "Arthur et les chevaliers *envoisiez.*" *Romania* 105: 312–25.

Baumgartner, Emmanuèle 1984b: "Joseph d'Arimathie dans le *Lancelot en prose.*" In *Lancelot.* Actes du Colloque des 14 et 15 janvier 1984. Göppinger Arbeiten zur Germanistik, 415. Göppingen: Kümmerle. Pp. 7–15.

Baumgartner, Emmanuèle 1985: "Géants et chevaliers." In *The Spirit of the Court,* ed. G. S. Burgess and R. A. Taylor. Selected Proceedings of the Fourth Congress of the International Courtly Literature Society (Toronto 1983). Cambridge: D. S. Brewer. Pp. 9–22.

Baumgartner, Emmanuèle 1986: "Temps linéaire, temps circulaire et écriture romanesque (XIIᵉ–XIIIᵉ siècles)." In *Le temps et la durée dans la littérature au moyen âge et à la Renaissance.* Actes du Colloque organisé par le Centre de Recherche sur la Littérature du Moyen Age et de la Renaissance de l'Université de Reims (novembre 1984). Paris: Nizet. Pp. 7–21.

Baumgartner, Emmanuèle 1987a: "Rois et chevaliers: du 'Lancelot en prose' au 'Tristan en prose.' " In *Tristan et Iseut: mythe européen et mondial,* ed. D. Buschinger. Actes du Colloque des 10, 11 et 12 janvier 1986. Göppinger Arbeiten zur Germanistik, 474. Göppingen: Kümmerle. Pp. 19–31.

Baumgartner, Emmanuèle 1987b: "Les techniques dans le roman en prose." In *The Legacy of Chrétien de Troyes,* ed. N. J. Lacy, D. Kelly, and K. Busby. Faux titre, 31. Amsterdam: Rodopi. Vol I, pp. 167–90.

Baumgartner, Emmanuèle 1987c: "Vocabulaire de la technique littéraire dans le *Roman de Troie* de Benoît de Sainte-Maure." *Cahiers de lexicologie* 51: 39–48.

Baumgartner, Emmanuèle 1988a: "L'orient d'Alexandre." *Bien dire et bien aprandre* 6: 7–15.

Baumgartner, Emmanuèle 1988b: "Peinture et évidence: la description de la tente dans les romans antiques du XIIᵉ siècle." In *Sammlung-Deutung-Wertung:*

Ergebnisse, Probleme, Tendenzen und Perspektiven philologischer Arbeit.
   Mélanges Wolfgang Spiewok. Amiens: Université de Picardie, Centre d'E-
   tudes Médiévales; Stuttgart: Sprint. Pp. 3–11.
Baumgartner, Emmanuèle 1990: *La harpe et l'épée: tradition et renouvellement dans*
   le «Tristan» en prose. Paris: SEDES.
Bäuml, Franz H. 1979: "Der Übergang mündlicher zur artes-bestimmten Literatur
   des Mittelalters: Gedanken und Bedenken." In *Oral Poetry: das Prob-*
   lem der Mündlichkeit mittelalterlicher epischer Dichtung. Wege der
   Forschung, 555. Darmstadt: Wissenschaftliche Buchgesellschaft. Pp.
   238–50.
Bechtoldt, Heinrich 1935: "Der französische Wortschatz im Sinnbezirk des Verstandes
   (Die geistliche und lehrhafte Literatur von ihren Anfängen bis zum Ende
   des 12. Jahrhunderts)." *Romanische Forschungen* 49: 21–180.
Becker, Philipp August 1934: *Der gepaarte Achtsilber in der französischen Dichtung.*
   Abhandlungen der philologisch-historischen Klasse der sächsischen Akademie
   der Wissenschaften, 43.1. Leipzig: Hirzel.
Becker, Philipp August 1935: "Von den Erzählern neben und nach Chrestien de
   Troyes. I-III." *Zeitschrift für romanische Philologie* 55: 257–92, 385–445,
   513–60.
Becker, Philipp August 1943: "Die Normannenchroniken: Wace und seine Bearbeiter."
   Zeitschrift für romanische Philologie 63: 481–519.
Beer, Jeanette M. A. 1976: *A Medieval Caesar.* Etudes de philologie et d'histoire,
   30. Geneva: Droz.
Bell, Alexander 1976: "Gaimar as Pioneer." *Romania* 97: 462–80.
Bender, Karl-Heinz 1967: *König und Vasall: Untersuchungen zur Chanson de geste*
   des XII. Jahrhunderts. Studia romanica, 13. Heidelberg: C. Winter.
Benjamin, Walter 1963: *Ursprung des deutschen Trauerspiels.* Frankfurt: Suhrkamp.
Benjamin, Walter 1972: "Lehre vom Ähnlichen." In *Zur Aktualität Walter Benja-*
   mins, ed. Siegfried Unseld. Suhrkamp Taschenbuch, 150. Frankfurt: Suhrkamp. Pp. 23–30.
Benton, John F. 1981: "Collaborative Approaches to Fantasy and Reality in the Literature of Champagne." In *Court and Poet,* ed. G. S. Burgess. Selected Proceedings of the Third Congress of the International Courtly Literature Society
   (Liverpool 1980). ARCA: Classical and Medieval Texts, Papers and Monographs, 5. Liverpool: F. Cairns. Pp. 43–57.
Bertolucci, Valeria 1960: "Commento retorico all'*Erec* e al *Cligés.*" *Studi mediolatini*
   e volgari 8: 9–51.
Bertolucci Pizzorusso, Valeria 1959: "La retorica nel Tristano di Thomas." *Studi medi-*
   olatini e volgari 6-7: 25–61.
Bezzola, Reto R. 1942: "Der französisch-englische Kulturkreis und die Erneuerung
   der europäischen Literatur im 12. Jahrhundert." *Zeitschrift für romanische*
   Philologie 62: 1–18.
Bezzola, Reto R. 1944: *Les origines et la formation de la littérature courtoise en Oc-*
   cident (500–1200). 3 vols. Paris: Champion, 1944–63.
Bezzola, Reto R. 1947: *Le sens de l'aventure et de l'amour (Chrétien de Troyes).* Paris:
   Jeune Parque.

Bik, Elisabeth J. 1972: "Les interventions d'auteur dans le *Tristan* de Béroul." *Neophilologus* 56: 31–42.

Blask, Dirk Jürgen 1984: *Geschehen und Geschick im altfranzösichen Eneas-Roman.* Romanica et Comparatistica 2. Tübingen: Stauffenburg.

Bloch, R. Howard 1977: *Medieval French Literature and Law.* Berkeley, Los Angeles, London: University of California Press.

Bloch, R. Howard 1990: "New Philology and Old French." *Speculum* 65: 38–58.

Bloomfield, Morton W. 1970: *Essays and Explorations: Studies in Ideas, Language, and Literature.* Cambridge: Harvard Univ. Pr.

Bloomfield, Morton W. 1980: "Episodic Juxtaposition or the Syntax of Episodes in Narration." In *Studies in English Linguistics for Randolph Quirk.* London and New York: Longman. Pp. 210–20.

Blumenfeld-Kosinski, Renate 1988: "Arthurian Heroes and Convention: *Meraugis de Portlesguez* and *Durmart le Galois.*" In *The Legacy of Chrétien de Troyes,* ed. N. J. Lacy, D. Kelly, and K. Busby. Faux titre, 37. Amsterdam: Rodopi. Vol. II, pp. 79–92.

Boesch, Bruno 1936: *Die Kunstanschauung in der mittelhochdeutschen Dichtung von der Blütezeit bis zum Meistergesang.* Bern and Leipzig: Haupt.

Bogdanow, Fanni 1966: *The Romance of the Grail: A Study of the Structure and Genesis of a Thirteenth-Century Arthurian Prose Romance.* Manchester: Manchester University Press; New York: Barnes and Noble.

Bogdanow, Fanni 1973: "The Transformation of the Role of Perceval in Some Thirteenth Century Prose Romances." *Studies in Medieval Literature and Languages in Memory of Frederick Whitehead.* Manchester: Manchester University Press. New York: Barnes & Noble. Pp. 47–65.

Boiron, Françoise, and Jean-Charles Payen 1970: "Structure et sens du 'Bel Inconnu' de Renaut de Beaujeu." *Moyen âge* 76: 15–26.

Boklund, Karin M. 1977a: "On the Spatial and Cultural Characteristics of Courtly Romance." *Semiotica* 20: 1–37.

Boklund, Karin M. 1977b: "Socio-sémiotique du roman courtois." *Semiotica* 21: 227–56.

Bolgar, R. R. 1954: *The Classical Heritage and Its Beneficiaries.* Cambridge: Cambridge University Press.

Bonjour, Adrien 1957: "Poésie héroïque du moyen âge et critique littéraire." *Romania* 78: 243–55.

Bornscheuer, Lothar 1976: *Topik: zur Struktur der gesellschaftlichen Einbildungskraft.* Frankfurt: Suhrkamp.

Borsari, Anna Valeria 1983: *Lancillotto liberato: una ricerca intorno al "fin amant" e all'eroe liberatore.* Università di Bologna: Pubblicazioni della Facoltà di Magistero n.s. 12. Florence: Nuova Italia.

Bosl, Karl 1977: "Leitbilder und Wertvorstellungen des Adels von der Merowingerzeit bis zur Höhe der feudalen Gesellschaft." In *The Epic in Medieval Society: Aesthetics and Moral Values,* ed. H. Scholler. Tübingen: Niemeyer. Pp. 18–36.

Bossuat, Robert 1946: "Un débat d'amour dans le roman de *Cassidorus.*" *Etudes romanes dédiées à Mario Roques.* Paris: Droz. Pp. 63–75.

Botte, D. B. 1942: "Imitatio." *Archivum latinitatis medii aevi* 16: 149–54.

Bozóky, Edina 1985: "De la parole au monument: marquer la mémoire dans la littérature arthurienne." In *Jeux de mémoire: aspects de la mnémotechnie médiévale,* ed. B. Roy and P. Zumthor. Etudes médiévales. Montreal: Presses de l'Université de Montréal; Paris: Vrin. Pp. 73–82.

Braet, H. 1985: "Les lais 'bretons,' enfants de la mémoire." *Bulletin bibliographique de la Société Internationale Arthurienne* 37: 283–91.

Brandt, William J. 1966: *The Shape of Medieval History: Studies in Modes of Perception.* New Haven and London: Yale University Press.

Brault, Gerard J. 1972: "Chrétien de Troyes' *Lancelot:* The Eye and the Heart." *Bulletin bibliographique de la Société Internationale Arthurienne* 24: 142–53.

Brault, Gerard J. 1975: "Isolt and Guenevere: Two Twelfth-Century Views of Woman." In *The Role of Woman in the Middle Ages,* ed. R. T. Morewedge. Papers of the Sixth Annual Conference of the Center for Medieval and Renaissance Studies, State University of New York at Binghamton, 6–7 May 1972. Albany: State University of New York Press. Pp. 41–64.

Brink, C. O. 1963: *Horace on Poetry.* 3 vols. Cambridge: Cambridge University Press, 1963–82.

Brinkmann, Hennig 1928: *Zu Wesen und Form mittelalterlicher Dichtung.* Halle: Niemeyer; rpt. Darmstadt: Wissenschaftliche Buchgesellschaft, 1979.

Brinkmann, Hennig 1964a: "Der Prolog im Mittelalter als literarische Erscheinung." *Wirkendes Wort* 14: 1–21. Rpt. in his *Studien zur Geschichte der deutschen Sprache und Literatur.* 2 vols. Düsseldorf: Schwann, 1966. Vol. II, pp. 79–105.

Brinkmann, Hennig 1964b: "Wege der epischen Dichtung im Mittelalter." *Archiv für das Studium der neueren Sprachen und Literaturen* 200: 401–35.

Brinkmann, Hennig 1971: "Verhüllung ('integumentum') als literarische Darstellungsform im Mittelalter." In *Der Begriff der repraesentatio im Mittelalter: Stellvertretung, Symbol, Zeichen, Bild,* ed. A. Zimmermann. Miscellanea Mediaevalia, 8. Berlin and New York: de Gruyter. Pp. 314–39.

Brinkmann, Hennig 1980: *Mittelalterliche Hermeneutik.* Darmstadt: Wissenschaftliche Buchgesellschaft.

Bruckner, Matilda Tomaryn 1977: "*Florimont:* Extravagant Host, Extravagant Guest." *Studies in Medieval Culture* 11: 57–63.

Bruckner, Matilda Tomaryn 1980a: *Narrative Invention in Twelfth-Century French Romance: The Convention of Hospitality (1160–1200).* French Forum Monographs, 17. Lexington: French Forum.

Bruckner, Matilda Tomaryn 1980b: "Repetition and Variation in Twelfth-Century French Romance." In *The Expansion and Transformations of Courtly Literature,* ed. N. B. Smith and J. T. Snow. Athens: University of Georgia Press. Pp. 95–114.

Bruckner, Matilda Tomaryn 1986: "An Interpreter's Dilemma: Why Are There So Many Interpretations of Chrétien's *Chevalier de la charrette?*" *Romance Philology* 40: 159–80.

Bruckner, Matilda Tomaryn 1987: "Intertextuality." In *The Legacy of Chrétien de*

Troyes, ed. N. J. Lacy, D. Kelly, and K. Busby. Faux titre, 31. Amsterdam: Rodopi. Vol. I, pp. 223–65.

Brugger, Ernst 1941: " 'Der schöne Feigling' in der arthurischen Literatur." *Zeitschrift für romanische Philologie* 61: 1–44; 63 (1943): 123–73, 275–328; 65 (1949): 121–92, 289–433.

Brugger, Ernst 1951: "Nachtrag zu 'Der schöne Feigling in der arthurischen Literatur.' " *Zeitschrift für romanische Philologie* 67: 289–98.

Bruns, Gerald L. 1980: "The Originality of Texts in a Manuscript Culture." *Comparative Literature* 32: 113–29.

Bruyne, Edgar de 1946: *Etudes d'esthétique médiévale.* Rijksuniversiteit te Gent: Werken uitgegeven door de Faculteit van de Wijsbegeerte en Letteren, 97–99. 3 vols. Bruges: de Tempel.

Bullock-Davies, Constance 1966: *Professional Interpreters and the Matter of Britain.* Cardiff: University of Wales Press.

Bumke, Joachim 1979: *Mäzene im Mittelalter: die Gönner und Auftraggeber der höfischen Literatur in Deutschland 1150–1300.* Munich: C. H. Beck.

Bumke, Joachim, ed. 1982: *Literarisches Mäzenatentum: ausgewählte Forschungen zur Rolle des Gönners und Auftraggebers in der mittelalterlichen Literatur.* Wege der Forschung, 598. Darmstadt: Wissenschaftliche Buchgesellschaft.

Burgess, Glyn S. 1970: *Contribution à l'étude du vocabulaire pré-courtois.* Publications romanes et françaises, 110. Geneva: Droz.

Burgess, Glyn S. 1981a: "Symbolism in Marie de France's *Laüstic* and *Le Fresne.*" *Bulletin bibliographique de la Société Internationale Arthurienne* 33: 258–68.

Burgess, Glyn S. 1981b: "The Theme of Beauty in Chrétien's *Philomena* and *Erec et Enide.*" In *An Arthurian Tapestry: Essays in Memory of Lewis Thorpe,* ed. K. Varty. Glasgow: French Department of the University of Glasgow. Pp. 114–28.

Burgess, Glyn S. 1984: *Chrétien de Troyes: Erec et Enide.* Critical Guides to French Texts, 32. London: Grant & Cutler.

Burgess, Glyn S. 1985: "Social Status in the *Lais* of Marie de France." In *The Spirit of the Court,* ed. G. S. Burgess and R. A. Taylor. Selected Proceedings of the Fourth Congress of the International Courtly Literature Society (Toronto 1983). Cambridge: D. S. Brewer. Pp. 69–78.

Burgess, Glyn S. 1987: *The "Lais" of Marie de France: Text and Context.* Athens: University of Georgia Press.

Burns, E. Jane 1985a: *Arthurian Fictions: Rereading the Vulgate Cycle.* Columbus: Ohio State University Press, for Miami University.

Burns, E. Jane 1985b: "La répétition et la mémoire du texte." In *Jeux de mémoire: aspects de la mnémotechnie médiévale,* ed. B. Roy and P. Zumthor. Etudes médiévales. Montreal: Presses de l'Université de Montréal; Paris: Vrin. Pp. 65–71.

Burns, E. Jane 1988: *"La voie de la voix:* the Aesthetics of Indirection in the Vulgate Cycle." In *The Legacy of Chrétien de Troyes,* ed. N. J. Lacy, D. Kelly, and K. Busby. Faux titre, 37. Amsterdam: Rodopi. Vol. II, pp. 151–67.

Burrow, J. A. 1973: "Bards, Minstrels, and Men of Letters." In *The Mediaeval World,* ed. D. Daiches and A. Thorlby. Literature and Western Civilization, 2. London: Aldus. Pp. 347–70.

Busby, Keith 1980a: "Caractérisation par contraste dans le roman de *Hunbaut.*" *Studia Neophilologica* 52: 415–24.

Busby, Keith 1980b: *Gauvain in Old French Literature*. Degré Second, 2. Amsterdam: Rodopi.

Busby, Keith 1985: *"Le roman des eles* as Guide to the *sens* of *Meraugis de Portlesguez."* In *The Spirit of the Court,* ed. G. S. Burgess and R. A. Taylor. Selected Proceedings of the Fourth Congress of the International Courtly Literature Society (Toronto 1983). Cambridge: D. S. Brewer. Pp. 79–89.

Busby, Keith 1987: "The Character and the Setting." In *The Legacy of Chrétien de Troyes,* ed. N. J. Lacy, D. Kelly, and K. Busby. Faux titre, 31. Amsterdam: Rodopi. Vol. I, pp. 57–89.

Busby, Keith 1988: "Diverging Traditions of Gauvain in Some of the Later Old French Verse Romances." In *The Legacy of Chrétien de Troyes,* ed. N. J. Lacy, D. Kelly, and K. Busby. Faux titre, 37. Amsterdam: Rodopi. Vol. II, pp. 93–109.

Busby, Keith 1989: *"Cristal et Clarie:* A Novel Romance?" In *Convention and Innovation in Literature,* ed. T. D'haen, R. Grübel, and H. Lethen. Utrecht Publications in General and Comparative Literature, 24. Amsterdam and Philadelphia: J. Benjamins. Pp. 77–103.

Cadot, A. M. 1976: "Du récit mythique au roman: étude sur *Piramus et Tisbé."* *Romania* 97: 433–61.

Calin, William, and Joseph J. Duggan 1981: "Un débat sur l'épopée vivante." *Olifant* 8: 227–316.

Caplan, Harry 1970: *Of Eloquence: Studies in Ancient and Medieval Rhetoric*. Ithaca and London: Cornell University Press.

Carasso-Bulow, Lucienne 1976: *The Merveilleux in Chrétien de Troyes' Romances*. Histoire des idées et critique littéraire, 153. Geneva: Droz.

Caulkins, Janet Hillier 1987: "Chelinde et la naissance du *Tristan en prose."* *Moyen âge* 93: 41–50.

Cerquiglini, Bernard 1978: "La parole étrange." *Langue française* 40: 83–98.

Cerquiglini, Jacqueline 1978: "Espace du texte, espace du sens: bilan des recherches sémiotiques en moyen français." In *Sémantique lexicale et sémantique grammaticale en moyen français,* ed. Marc Wilmet. Colloque organisé par le Centre d'Etudes Linguistiques et Littéraires de la Vrije Universiteit Brussel, 28–29 septembre 1978. Brussels: V. U. B. Centrum voor Taal- en Literatuurwetenschap. Pp. 81–95.

Cerquiglini, Jacqueline 1980: "Le clerc et l'écriture: le *voir dit* de Guillaume de Machaut et la définition du *dit."* In *Literatur in der Gesellschaft des Spätmittelalters.* Begleitreihe zum *GRLMA,* 1. Heidelberg: Winter. Pp. 151–68.

Chandès, Gérard 1986: *Le serpent, la femme et l'épée. Recherches sur l'imagination symbolique d'un romancier médiéval: Chrétien de Troyes.* Faux titre, 27. Amsterdam: Rodopi.

Charland, Th.-M. 1936: *Artes praedicandi: contribution à l'histoire de la rhétorique au moyen âge.* Publications de l'Institut d'Etudes Médiévales d'Ottawa, 7. Paris: Vrin; Ottawa: Institut d'Etudes médiévales.

Charpin, François 1988: "La notion de phrase: l'héritage des anciens." In *L'héritage des grammairiens latins de l'Antiquité aux Lumières,* ed. I. Rosier. Actes du Colloque de Chantilly, 2–4 septembre 1987. Paris: Société pour l'Information Grammaticale. Pp. 57–68.

Chase, Carol J. 1983: "Sur la théorie de l'entrelacement: ordre et désordre dans le *Lancelot en prose.*" *Modern Philology* 80: 227–41.

Chassé, Dominique 1985: "La mise en mémoire des informations narratives: le système du vers et le système de la prose." In *Jeux de mémoire: aspects de la mnémotechnie médiévale,* ed. B. Roy and P. Zumthor. Etudes médiévales. Montreal: Presses de l'Université de Montréal; Paris: Vrin. Pp. 57–64.

Chênerie, Marie-Luce 1984: "L'aventure du chevalier enferré, ses suites et le thème des géants dans le *Lancelot.*" In *Approches du Lancelot en prose,* ed. J. Dufournet. Collection Unichamp, 6. Paris: Champion. Pp. 59–100.

Chênerie, Marie-Luce 1986: *Le chevalier errant dans les romans arthuriens en vers des XIIᵉ et XIIIᵉ siècles.* Publications romanes et françaises, 172. Geneva: Droz.

Chenu, M.-D. 1957a: "*Spiritus:* le vocabulaire de l'âme au XIIᵉ siècle." *Revue des sciences philosophiques et théologiques* 41: 209–32.

Chenu, M.-D. 1957b: *La théologie au douzième siècle.* Etudes de philosophie médiévale, 45. Paris: Vrin.

Cilento, Vincenzo 1961: *Medio evo monastico e scolastico.* Milan and Naples: Ricciardi.

Cline, Ruth H. 1972: "Heart and Eyes." *Romance Philology* 25: 263–97.

Colby, Alice M. 1965: *The Portrait in Twelfth-Century French Literature: An Example of the Stylistic Originality of Chrétien de Troyes.* Histoire des idées et critique littéraire, 61. Geneva: Droz.

Colish, Marcia L. 1968: *The Mirror of Language: A Study in the Medieval Theory of Knowledge.* Yale Historical Publications: Miscellany, 88. New Haven and London: Yale University Press.

Cormier, Raymond J. 1973: *One Heart One Mind: The Rebirth of Virgil's Hero in Medieval French Romance.* Romance Monographs, 3. University: Romance Monographs.

Cormier, Raymond J. 1974: "The Problem of Anachronism: Recent Scholarship on the French Medieval Romances of Antiquity." *Philological Quarterly* 53: 145–57.

Cormier, Raymond J. 1988: "Qui détient le rameau d'or devant Charon? (*Enéide,* VI.405–407)." *Rheinisches Museum für Philologie* n.s. 131: 151–56.

Cormier, Raymond J. 1989: "An Example of Twelfth Century *Adaptatio:* The *Roman d'Eneas* Author's Use of Glossed *Aeneid* Manuscripts." *Revue d'histoire des textes* 19: 277–89.

Corti, Maria 1978: "Structures idéologiques et structures sémiotiques au XIIIᵉ siècle." *Travaux de linguistique et de littérature* 16.1: 93–105.

Corti, Maria 1983: "Structures idéologiques et structures sémiotiques dans les *ser-*

mones ad status du XIIIᵉ siècle." In *Archéologie du signe,* ed. L. Brin-d'Amour and E. Vance. Recueil d'Etudes Médiévales, 3. Toronto: Pontifical Institute of Mediaeval Studies. Pp. 145–63.

Crane, Susan 1986: *Insular Romance: Politics, Faith, and Culture in Anglo-Norman and Middle English Literature.* Berkeley, Los Angeles, London: University of California Press.

Curtis, Renée L. 1969: *Tristan Studies.* Munich: Fink.

Curtis, Renée L. 1979: "L'humour et l'ironie dans le *Tristan en prose* (tomes I et II)." In *Der altfranzösische Prosaroman: Funktion, Funktionswandel und Ideologie am Beispiel des "Roman de Tristan en prose,"* ed. E. Ruhe and R. Schwaderer. Kolloquium Würzburg 1977. Beiträge zur romanischen Philologie des Mittelalters, 12. Munich: Fink. Pp. 77–103.

Curtius, Ernst Robert 1938: "Zur Literarästhetik des Mittelalters I-III." *Zeitschrift für romanische Philologie* 58: 1–50, 129–232, 433–79.

Curtius, Ernst Robert 1954: *Europäische Literatur und lateinisches Mittelalter.* 2d ed. Bern: Francke.

Curtius, Ernst Robert 1960: *Gesammelte Aufsätze zur romanischen Philologie.* Bern and Munich: Francke.

Dahan, Gilbert 1980: "Notes et textes sur la poétique au moyen âge." *Archives d'histoire doctrinale et littéraire du moyen âge* 55: 171–239.

D'Alessandro, Domenico 1986: "La descrizione in Chrétien de Troyes: i segni di demar-cazione." *AION: Annali Istituto Universitario Orientale – Napoli,* Sezione romanza, 18: 553–66.

Dean, Ruth 1972: "The Fair Field of Anglo-Norman: Recent Cultivation." *Medievalia et humanistica* n.s. 3: 279–97.

Deist, Rosemarie 1986: *Die Nebenfiguren in den Tristanromanen Gottfrieds von Straß-burg, Thomas' de Bretagne und im "Cligès" Chrétiens von Troyes.* Göppinger Arbeiten zur Germanistik, 435. Göppingen: Kümmerle.

Delbouille, Maurice 1927: "Le système des 'incidences': observations sur les manuscrits du cycle épique de Guillaume d'Orange." *Revue belge de philologie et d'histoire* 6: 617–41.

Delbouille, Maurice 1959: "La chanson de geste et le livre." In *La technique litté-raire des chansons de geste.* Actes du Colloque de Liège (septembre 1957). Bibliothèque de la Faculté de Philosophie et Lettres de l'Université de Liège, 150. Paris: Belles Lettres. Pp. 295–407.

Delbouille, Maurice 1960: "Dans un atelier de copistes: en regardant de plus près les manuscrits B¹ et B² du cycle épique de Garin de Monglane." *Cahiers de civilisation médiévale* 3: 14–22.

Delbouille, Maurice 1969: "Apollonius de Tyr et les débuts du roman français." In *Mélanges Rita Lejeune.* 2 vols. Gembloux: Duculot. Vol. II, pp. 1171–1204.

Delehaye, Hippolyte 1927: *Les légendes hagiographiques.* 3d ed. rev. Subsidia hagiographica, 18. Brussels: Société des Bollandistes.

Delhaye, Ph. 1958: " 'Grammatica' et 'ethica' au XIIᵉ siècle." *Recherches de théologie ancienne et médiévale* 25: 59–110.

Demats, Paule 1970: "D'*amoenitas* à *deduit:* André le Chapelain et Guillaume de

Lorris." In *Mélanges Jean Frappier.* 2 vols. Publications romanes et françaises, 112. Geneva: Droz. Vol. I, pp. 217–33.

Demats, Paule 1973: *Fabula: trois études de mythographie antique et médiévale.* Publications romanes et françaises, 122. Geneva: Droz.

Dembowski, Peter F. 1976: "Literary Problems of Hagiography in Old French." *Medievalia et humanistica* n.s. 7: 117–30.

Dembowski, Peter F. 1978: "La position de Froissart-poète dans l'histoire littéraire: bilan provisoire." *Travaux de linguistique et de littérature* 16.1: 131–47.

Dembowski, Peter F. 1980: "Considérations sur *Meliador.*" In *Etudes Jules Horrent.* Liège: [s.p.]. Pp. 123–31.

Dembowski, Peter F. 1981: "Intertextualité et critique des textes." *Littérature* 41: 17–29.

Dembowski, Peter F., 1983: *Jean Froissart and His "Meliador": Context, Craft, and Sense.* Edward C. Armstrong Monographs on Medieval Literature, 2. Lexington: French Forum.

Desmond, Morgan Joseph 1979: "The Concept of Narrative among Twelfth-Century Vernacular Hagiographers: A Comparison of the *Vie de Sainte Marguerite,* the *Vie de Saint Gilles,* and the *Vie de Sainte Osith* with Their Latin Sources." Diss. University of Wisconsin—Madison.

Deyermond, A. D. 1975: "The Lost Genre of Medieval Spanish Literature." *Hispanic Review* 43: 231–59.

Dinshaw, Carolyn 1988: "Readers in/of *Troilus and Criseyde.*" *Yale Review of Criticism* 1.2: 81–105.

Diverres, A. H. 1970: "The Irish Adventures in Froissart's *Meliador.*" In *Mélanges Jean Frappier.* 2 vols. Publications romanes et françaises, 112. Geneva: Droz. Vol. I, pp. 235–51.

Diverres, A. H. 1980: "Les aventures galloises dans *Meliador* de Froissart." In *Mélanges Charles Foulon.* 2 vols. Rennes: Institut de Français, Université de Haute-Bretagne; Liège: Marche Romane. Vol. II, pp. 73–79.

Diverres, A. H. 1987: "The Two Versions of Froissart's *Meliador.*" In *Studies Brian Woledge.* Publications romanes et françaises, 180. Geneva: Droz. Pp. 37–48.

Diverres, A. H. 1989: "Froissart's Travels in England and Wales." *Fifteenth-Century Studies* 15: 107–22.

Donovan, L. G. 1975: *Recherches sur "Le roman de Thèbes."* Paris: SEDES.

Donovan, Mortimer J. 1961: "Priscian and the Obscurity of the Ancients." *Speculum* 36: 75–80.

Dorson, Richard M., ed. 1972: *African Folklore.* Garden City: Doubleday-Anchor.

Dragonetti, Roger 1987: *Le mirage des sources: l'art du faux dans le roman médiéval.* Paris: Seuil.

Dronke, Peter 1959: "The Text of Carmina burana 116." *Classica et mediaevalia* 20: 159–69.

Dronke, Peter 1973: "Mediaeval Rhetoric." In *The Mediaeval World,* ed. D. Daiches and A. Thorlby. Literature and Western Civilization, 2. London: Aldus. Pp. 315–45.

Dronke, Peter 1974: *Fabula: Explorations into the Uses of Myth in Medieval Platonism.* Mittellateinische Studien und Texte, 9. Leiden and Cologne: Brill.

Dubost, Francis 1988: "Merveilleux et fantastique dans *Le Chevalier au lion*." In *Le Chevalier au lion de Chrétien de Troyes: approches d'un chef-d'œuvre*, ed. Jean Dufournet. Collection Unichamp, 20. Paris: Champion. Pp. 47–76.

Duby, Georges 1973: *Hommes et structures du moyen âge*. Ecole Pratique des Hautes Etudes—Sorbonne. VIe section: Sciences Economiques et Sociales. Le savoir historique, 1. Paris and The Hague: Mouton.

Duby, Georges 1978a: *Medieval Marriage: Two Models from Twelfth-Century France*. Trans. E. Forster. Johns Hopkins Symposia in Comparative History, 11. Baltimore and London: Johns Hopkins University Press.

Duby, Georges 1978b: *Les trois ordres ou l'imaginaire du féodalisme*. Bibliothèque des histoires. Paris: Gallimard.

Ducháček, Otto 1960: *Le champ conceptuel de la beauté en français moderne*. Opera Universitatis Brunensis: Facultas philosophica, 71. Prague: Státní Pedagogické Nakladatelství.

Ducháček, Otto 1976: "Esquisse du champ sémantique de la beauté dans le français du XIIe siècle." *Kwartalnik Neofilologiczny* 23: 105–18.

Dufournet, Jean, and Marie-Madeleine Castellani 1988: "Temps liturgique et temps folklorique dans la *Manekine* de Philippe de Beaumanoir." In *Le nombre du temps: en hommage à Paul Zumthor*. Paris: Champion. Pp. 63–72.

Duggan, Joseph J. 1973: *The Song of Roland: Formulaic Style and Poetic Craft*. Publications of the Center for Medieval and Renaissance Studies UCLA, 6. Berkeley, Los Angeles, London: University of California Press.

Duggan, Joseph J. 1989a: "Oral Performance of Romance in Medieval France." In *Continuations: Essays on Medieval French Literature and Language in Honor of John L. Grigsby*. Birmingham: Summa. Pp. 51–61.

Duggan, Joseph J. 1989b: "Performance and Transmission, Aural and Ocular Reception in the Twelfth- and Thirteenth-Century Vernacular Literature of France." *Romance Philology* 43: 49–58.

Eberlein-Westhues, Hildegard 1979: "König Arthurs 'Table Ronde': Studien zur Geschichte eines literarischen Herrschaftszeichens." In *Der altfranzösische Prosaroman: Funktion, Funktionswandel und Ideologie am Beispiel des "Roman de Tristan en prose,"* ed. E. Ruhe and R. Schwaderer. Kolloquium Würzburg 1977. Beiträge zur romanischen Philologie des Mittelalters, 12. Munich: Fink. Pp. 184–269.

Eisenhut, Werner 1983: "Spätantike Troja-Erzählungen—mit einem Ausblick auf die mittelalterliche Troja-Literatur." *Mittellateinisches Jahrbuch* 18: 1–28.

Engel, Gustav 1910: *Die Einflüsse der Arthurromane auf die Chansons de geste*. Diss. Halle. Halle: Hohmann.

Evans, Gillian R. 1971: "Two Aspects of *Memoria* in Eleventh and Twelfth Century Writings." *Classica et mediaevalia* 32: 263–78.

Faral, Edmond 1910: *Les jongleurs en France au moyen âge*. Bibliothèque de l'Ecole des Hautes Etudes, 187. Paris: Champion.

Faral, Edmond 1913: *Recherches sur les sources latines des contes et romans courtois du moyen âge*. Paris; rpt. Geneva and Paris: Slatkine, 1983.

Faral, Edmond 1924: *Les arts poétiques du XIIe et du XIIIe siècle: recherches et documents sur la technique littéraire du moyen âge*. Bibliothèque de l'Ecole des Hautes Etudes, 238. Paris: Champion.

Faral, Edmond 1936: "Le manuscrit 511 du 'Hunterian Museum' de Glasgow: notes sur le mouvement poétique et l'histoire des études littéraires en France et en Angleterre entre les années 1150 et 1225." *Studi medievali* n.s. 9: 18–121.

Faulhaber, Charles B. 1978: "The Letter-Writer's Rhetoric: The *Summa dictaminis* of Guido Faba." In *Medieval Eloquence: Studies in the Theory and Practice of Medieval Rhetoric*, ed. James J. Murphy. Berkeley, Los Angeles, London: University of California Press. Pp. 85–111.

Ferrier, Janet M. 1954: *Forerunners of the French Novel: An Essay on the Development of the "Nouvelle" in the Late Middle Ages*. Manchester: Manchester University Press.

Fleischman, Suzanne 1983: "On the Representation of History and Fiction in the Middle Ages." *History and Theory* 22: 278–310.

Fletcher, Robert Huntington 1966: *The Arthurian Material in the Chronicles, Especially Those of Great Britain and France*. 2d ed. Burt Franklin Bibliography and Reference Works, 88. New York: Burt Franklin.

Flori, Jean 1979: "Pour une histoire de la chevalerie: l'adoubement dans les romans de Chrétien de Troyes." *Romania* 100: 21–53.

Foerster, Wendelin, and Hermann Breuer 1914: *Kristian von Troyes: Wörterbuch zu seinen sämtlichen Werken*. Romanische Bibliothek, 21. Halle: Niemeyer.

Foulet, Alfred, and Mary Blakely Speer 1979: *On Editing Old French Texts*. Edward C. Armstrong Monographs on Medieval Literature, 1. Lawrence: Regents Press of Kansas.

Foulet, Alfred, and Karl D. Uitti 1981: "The Prologue to the *Lais* of Marie de France: A Reconsideration." *Romance Philology* 35: 242–49.

Foulet, Lucien 1925: "*Galeran* et les dix compagnons de Bretagne." *Romania* 51: 116–21.

Foulon, Charles 1958: *L'œuvre de Jehan Bodel*. Travaux de la Faculté des Lettres et Sciences Humaines de Rennes, ser. 1:2. Paris: Presses Universitaires de France.

Fourquet, Jean 1956: "Le rapport entre l'œuvre et la source chez Chrétien de Troyes et le problème des sources bretonnes." *Romance Philology* 9: 298–312.

Fourrier, Anthime 1960: *Le courant réaliste dans le roman courtois en France au moyen âge; I: Les débuts (XIIe siècle)*. Paris: Nizet.

Frappier, Jean 1957: "Réflexions sur les rapports des chansons de geste et de l'histoire." *Zeitschrift für romanische Philologie* 73: 1–19.

Frappier, Jean 1959a: "Variations sur le thème du miroir, de Bernard de Ventadour à Maurice Scève." *Cahiers de l'Association Internationale des Etudes Françaises* 11: 134–58.

Frappier, Jean 1959b: "Vues sur les conceptions courtoises dans les littératures d'oc et d'oïl au XIIe siècle." *Cahiers de civilisation médiévale* 2: 135–56.

Frappier, Jean 1961: "Remarques sur la structure du lai: essai de définition et de classement." In *La littérature narrative d'imagination, des genres littéraires aux techniques d'expression.* Colloque de Strasbourg, 23–25 avril 1959. Paris: Presses Universitaires de France. Pp. 23–39.

Frappier, Jean 1963: "Structure et sens du Tristan: version commune, version courtoise." *Cahiers de civilisation médiévale* 6: 255–80, 441–54.

Frappier, Jean 1964a: "Le personnage de Galehaut dans le *Lancelot en prose.*" *Romance Philology* 17: 535–54.

Frappier, Jean 1964b: "Remarques sur la peinture de la vie et des héros antiques dans la littérature française du XIIᵉ et du XIIIᵉ siècle." In *L'humanisme médiéval dans les littératures romanes du XIIᵉ au XIVᵉ siècle,* ed. Anthime Fourrier. Colloque organisé par le Centre de Philologie et de Littératures romanes de l'Université de Strasbourg du 29 janvier au 2 février 1962. Actes et Colloques, 3. Paris: Klincksieck. Pp. 13–54.

Frappier, Jean 1964c: "Sur la versification de Chrétien de Troyes: l'enjambement dans *Erec et Enide.*" *Romance Studies* 32: 41–49.

Frappier, Jean 1965: "La brisure du couplet dans *Erec et Enide.*" *Romania* 86: 1–21.

Frappier, Jean 1968a: *Chrétien de Troyes: l'homme et l'œuvre.* New ed. Connaissance des lettres, 50. Paris: Hatier.

Frappier, Jean 1968b: *Etude sur La Mort le roi Artu, roman du XIIIᵉ siècle: dernière partie du Lancelot en prose.* Publications romanes et françaises, 70. 2d ed. Geneva: Droz.

Frappier, Jean 1969: *Etude sur Yvain ou le Chevalier au lion de Chrétien de Troyes.* Paris: SEDES.

Frappier, Jean 1970: "Pour le commentaire d'*Erec et Enide:* notes de lecture." *Marche romane* 20.4: 15–30.

Frappier, Jean 1972: "Le prologue du *Chevalier de la charrette* et son interprétation." *Romania* 93: 337–77.

Freeman, Michelle A. 1976: "Problems in Romance Composition: Ovid, Chrétien de Troyes, and the *Romance of the Rose.*" *Romance Philology* 30: 158–68.

Freeman, Michelle A. 1979: *The Poetics of "Translatio studii" and "Conjointure": Chrétien de Troyes's "Cligés."* French Forum Monographs, 12. Lexington: French Forum.

Freeman, Michelle A. 1983: "*Fergus:* Parody and the Arthurian Tradition." *French Forum* 8: 197–215.

Friedman, John Block 1974: "The Architect's Compass in Creation Miniatures of the Later Middle Ages." *Traditio* 30: 419–29 + 12 figures.

Friedman, Lionel J. 1965: "Gradus amoris." *Romance Philology* 19: 167–77.

Gallais, Pierre 1964a: "Formules de conteur et interventions d'auteur dans les manuscrits de la *Continuation-Gauvain.*" *Romania* 85: 181–229.

Gallais, Pierre 1964b: "Recherches sur la mentalité des romanciers français du moyen âge." *Cahiers de civilisation médiévale* 7: 479–93; 13 (1970): 333–47.

Gallais, Pierre 1967: "Bléhéri, la cour de Poitiers et la diffusion des récits arthuriens sur le continent." In *Moyen âge et littérature comparée.* Société Française de Littérature Comparée: Actes du Septième Congrès National, Poitiers 27–29 mai 1965. Paris: Didier. Pp. 47–79.

Gallais, Pierre 1971a: "De la naissance du roman: à propos d'un article récent." *Cahiers de civilisation médiévale* 14: 69–75.

Gallais, Pierre 1971b: "Littérature et médiatisation, réflexions sur la genèse du genre romanesque." *Etudes littéraires* 4: 39–73.

Gallais, Pierre 1988: *L'imaginaire d'un romancier français de la fin du XIIe siècle (description de la "Continuation-Gauvain")*. Faux titre, 33, 34, 36, 39. 4 vols. Amsterdam and Atlanta, GA: Rodopi, 1988–89.

Gallo, Ernest 1971: *The "Poetria nova" and Its Sources In Early Rhetorical Doctrine*. De proprietatibus litterarum: series maior, 10. The Hague and Paris: Mouton.

Gallo, Ernest 1974: "Matthew of Vendôme: Introductory Treatise on the Art of Poetry." *Proceedings of the American Philosophical Society* 118: 51–92.

Gallo, Ernest 1978: "The Grammarian's Rhetoric: The *Poetria nova* of Geoffrey of Vinsauf." In *Medieval Eloquence: Studies in the Theory and Practice of Medieval Rhetoric*, ed. James J. Murphy. Berkeley, Los Angeles, London: University of California Press. Pp. 68–84.

Ghellinck, Jean de 1941: "Imitari, imitatio." *Archivum latinitatis medii aevi* 15: 151–59.

Ghellinck, Jean de 1946: *L'essor de la littérature latine au XIIe siècle*. Museum Lessianum: section historique, 4–5. 2 vols. Brussels: Edition universelle; Paris: Desclée de Brouwer.

Gier, Albert 1977a: *Der Sünder als Beispiel: zu Gestalt und Funktion hagiographischer Gebrauchstexte anhand der Theophiluslegende*. Bonner romanistische Arbeiten, 1. Frankfurt, Bern, Las Vegas: Peter Lang.

Gier, Albert 1977b: "Das Verwandtschaftsverhältnis von afr. *sens* und *sen.*" *Romanistisches Jahrbuch* 28: 54–72.

Gier, Albert 1979a: "Zu einer neuen Interpretation von Chrétiens *Erec et Enide.*" *Zeitschrift für romanische Philologie* 95: 92–103.

Gier, Albert 1979b: "Zum altfranzösischen Artusroman: literarisches Spiel und Aufhebung der Zeitgesetze." *Lendemains 16: Zeitschrift für Frankreichforschung + Französischstudium* 4 (November): 11–24.

Gier, Albert 1982: "Noch einmal: *Chievrefoil*, V. 51–78." *Zeitschrift für romanische Philologie* 98: 540–46.

Gilson, Etienne 1932: *Les idées et les lettres*. Paris: Vrin.

Ginsberg, Warren 1983: *The Cast of Character: The Representation of Personality in Ancient and Medieval Literature*. Toronto, Buffalo, London: University of Toronto Press.

Glunz, Hans H. 1937: *Die Literarästhetik des europäischen Mittelalters: Wolfram-Rosenroman-Chaucer-Dante*. Bochum-Langendreer: Pöppinghaus.

Goldin, Frederick 1975: "The Array of Perspectives in the Early Courtly Love Lyric." In *In Pursuit of Perfection: Courtly Love in Medieval Literature*. Port Washington and London: Kennikat. Pp. 51–100.

Gompf, Ludwig 1973: "Figmenta poetarum." In *Literatur und Sprache im europäischen Mittelalter: Festschrift für Karl Langosch*. Darmstadt: Wissenschaftliche Buchgesellschaft. Pp. 53–62.

Gosman, Martin 1981: "L'élément féminin dans le *Roman d'Alexandre:* Olympias et Candace." In *Court and Poet,* ed. G. S. Burgess. Selected Proceedings of the Third Congress of the International Courtly Literature Society (Liverpool 1980). ARCA: Classical and Medieval Texts, Papers and Monographs, 5. Liverpool: F. Cairns. Pp. 167–76.

Gosman, Martin 1984: "Alexandre le Grand et le statut de la noblesse ou le plaidoyer pour la permanence: prolégomènes à l'histoire d'une légende." In *Non nova, sed nove: mélanges Willem Noomen.* Groningen: Bouma. Pp. 81–93.

Gosman, Martin 1988: "La genèse du *Roman d'Alexandre:* quelques aspects." *Bien dire et bien aprandre* 6:25–44.

Gossen, Carl Theodor 1959: "Zur etymologischen Deutung des Grals." *Vox romanica* 18: 177–219.

Gössmann, Elisabeth 1974: *Antiqui und Moderni im Mittelalter: eine geschichtliche Standortbestimmung.* Veröffentlichungen des Grabmann-Institutes n.s. 23. Munich, Paderborn, Vienna: F. Schöningh.

Green, Richard Hamilton 1956: "Alan of Lille's *De planctu Naturae." Speculum* 31: 649–74.

Green, Richard Hamilton 1967: "Alan of Lille's *Anticlaudianus:* ascensus mentis in Deum." *Annuale mediaevale* 8: 3–16.

Gregory, Tullio 1955: *Anima mundi: la filosofia di Guglielmo di Conches e la scuola di Chartres.* Pubblicazioni dell'Istituto di Filosofia dell'Università di Roma, 3. Florence: Sansoni.

Greif, Wilhelm 1886: *Die mittelalterlichen Bearbeitungen der Trojanersage: ein neuer Beitrag zur Dares- und Dictysfrage.* Ausgaben und Abhandlungen aus dem Gebiete der romanischen Philologie, 61. Marburg: Elwert.

Grigsby, John L. 1968: "The Narrator in *Partonopeu de Blois, Le Bel Inconnu,* and *Joufroi de Poitiers." Romance Philology* 21: 536–43.

Grigsby, John L. 1980: "The Ontology of the Narrator in Medieval French Romance." In *The Nature of Medieval Narrative,* ed. M. Grunmann-Gaudet and R. F. Jones. French Forum Monographs, 22. Lexington: French Forum. Pp. 159–71.

Grimbert, Joan Tasker 1988: *"Yvain" dans le miroir: une poétique de la réflexion dans le "Chevalier au lion" de Chrétien de Troyes.* Purdue University Monographs in Romance Languages, 25. Amsterdam and Philadelphia: J. Benjamins.

Grundmann, Herbert 1936: "Die Frauen und die Literatur im Mittelalter: ein Beitrag zur Frage nach der Entstehung des Schrifttums in der Volkssprache." *Archiv für Kulturgeschichte* 26: 129–61.

Grundmann, Herbert 1952: "Sacerdotium-regnum-studium: zur Wertung der Wissenschaft im 13. Jahrhundert." *Archiv für Kulturgeschichte* 34: 5–21.

Grundmann, Herbert 1958: *"Litteratus-illitteratus:* der Wandel einer Bildungsnorm vom Altertum zum Mittelalter." *Archiv für Kulturgeschichte* 40: 1–65.

Grunmann-Gaudet, Minnette 1979: "From Epic to Romance: The Paralysis of the Hero in the *Prise d'Orange." Olifant* 7: 22–38.

Gsteiger, Manfred 1959: "Notes sur les préambules des chansons de geste." *Cahiers de civilisation médiévale* 2: 213–20.

Guenée, Bernard 1973: "Histoires, annales, chroniques: essai sur les genres historiques au moyen âge." *Annales: économies, sociétés, civilisations* 28: 997–1016.

Guenée, Bernard 1977: *Le métier d'historien au moyen âge: études sur l'historiographie médiévale.* Publications de la Sorbonne: Etudes, 13. Paris: La Sorbonne.

Guenée, Bernard 1982: "Histoire et chronique: nouvelles réflexions sur les genres historiques au moyen âge." In *La chronique et l'histoire au moyen âge,* ed. D. Poirion. Colloque des 24 et 25 mai 1982. Cultures et civilisations médiévales, 2. Paris: Presses de l'Université de Paris—Sorbonne. Pp. 3–12.

Guiette, Robert 1978: *Forme et senefiance: études médiévales recueillies.* Publications romanes et françaises, 148. Geneva: Droz.

Gumbrecht, Hans Ulrich 1974: "Literary Translation and Its Social Conditioning in the Middle Ages: Four Spanish Romance Texts of the 13th Century." *Yale French Studies* 51: 205–22.

Gumbrecht, Hans Ulrich 1979: "Faszinationstyp Hagiographie: ein historisches Experiment zur Gattungstheorie." In *Deutsche Literatur im Mittelalter—Kontakte und Perspektiven: Hugo Kuhn zum Gedenken.* Stuttgart: J. B. Metzler. Pp. 37–84.

Gunn, Alan M. F. 1952: *The Mirror of Love: A Reinterpretation of "The Romance of the Rose."* Lubbock: Texas Tech Press.

Hahn, Stacey Layne 1988: "Patterned Diversity: Hierarchy and Love in the Prose *Lancelot."* Diss. University of Wisconsin—Madison.

Haidu, Peter 1968: *Aesthetic Distance in Chrétien de Troyes: Irony and Comedy in "Cligés" and "Perceval."* Histoire des idées et critique littéraire, 87. Geneva: Droz.

Haidu, Peter 1972a: *Lion-queue-coupée: l'écart symbolique chez Chrétien de Troyes.* Histoire des idées et critique littéraire, 123. Geneva: Droz.

Haidu, Peter 1972b: "Realism, Convention, Fictionality and the Theory of Genres in *Le Bel Inconnu." Esprit créateur* 12: 37–60.

Haidu, Peter 1973a: "Humor and the Aesthetics of Medieval Romance." *Romanic Review* 64: 54–68.

Haidu, Peter 1973b: "Texts, Pretextuality and Myth in the *Folie Tristan d'Oxford." Modern Language Notes* 88: 712–17.

Haidu, Peter 1974: "Narrativity and Language in Some XIIth Century Romances." *Yale French Studies* 51: 133–46.

Haidu, Peter 1977: "Repetition: Modern Reflections on Medieval Aesthetics." *Modern Language Notes* 92: 875–87.

Haidu, Peter 1982: "Le sens historique du phénomène stylistique: la sémiose dissociative chez Chrétien de Troyes." *Europe* 60 (no 642, October): 36–47.

Haidu, Peter 1984: "Romance: Idealistic Genre or Historical Text?" In *The Craft of Fiction: Essays in Medieval Poetics,* ed. L. A. Arrathoon. Rochester: Solaris. Pp. 1–46.

Halász, Katalin 1980: *Structures narratives chez Chrétien de Troyes*. Studia Romanica Universitatis Debreceniensis de Ludovico Kossuth nominatae: series litteraria, 7. Debrecen: Kossuth Lajos Tudományegyetem.

Halász, Katalin 1985: "Le narrateur et sa fonction interprétative: le *Conte du graal et Perlesvaus.*" In *Analyses de romans*. Studia Romanica Universitatis Debreceniensis de Ludovico Kossuth nominatae: series litteraria, 11. Debrecen: Kossuth Lajos Tudományegyetem. Pp. 3–25.

Halász, Katalin 1986: "The Intermingling of Romance Models in a 13th-Century Prose Romance: *Le roman de Laurin.*" *Forum for Modern Language Studies* 22: 273–83.

Halpersohn, Rubin 1911: *Über die Einleitungen im altfranzösischen Kunstepos*. Diss. Heidelberg. Berlin: Schiftan.

Hanning, Robert W. 1972: "The Social Significance of Twelfth-Century Chivalric Romance." *Medievalia et Humanistica* n.s. 3: 3–29.

Hanning, Robert W. 1974: "*Engin* in Twelfth-Century Romance: An Examination of the *Roman d'Enéas* and Hue de Rotelande's *Ipomedon.*" *Yale French Studies* 51: 82–101.

Hanning, Robert W. 1977: *The Individual in Twelfth-Century Romance*. New Haven and London: Yale University Press.

Hansen, Inez 1971: *Zwischen Epos und höfischem Roman: die Frauengestalten im Trojaroman des Benoît de Sainte-Maure*. Beiträge zur romanischen Philologie des Mittelalters, 8. Munich: Fink.

Hardison, O. B., Jr., 1976: "Toward a History of Medieval Literary Criticism." *Medievalia et Humanistica* n.s. 7: 1–12.

Harf-Lancner, Laurence 1984: *Les fées au moyen âge. Morgane et Mélusine: la naissance des fées*. Nouvelle Bibliothèque du moyen âge, 8. Paris: Champion.

Harich, Henriette 1987: *Alexander epicus: Studien zur Alexandreis Walters von Châtillon*. Dissertationen der Karl-Franzens-Universität Graz, 72. Graz: dbv-Verlag.

Hart, Thomas Elwood 1981a: "Chrestien, Macrobius, and Chartrean Science: The Allegorical Robe as Symbol of Textual Design in the Old French *Erec.*" *Mediaeval Studies* 43: 250–96.

Hart, Thomas Elwood 1981b: "The *Quadrivium* and Chrétien's Theory of Composition: Some Conjunctures and Conjectures." *Symposium* 35: 57–86.

Hauck, Karl 1965: "Haus- und sippengebundene Literatur mittelalterlicher Adelsgeschlechter von Adelssatiren des 11. und 12. Jahrhunderts her erläutert." In *Geschichtsdenken und Geschichtsbild im Mittelalter: ausgewählte Aufsätze und Arbeiten aus den Jahren 1933 bis 1959*. Wege der Forschung, 21. Darmstadt: Wissenschaftliche Buchgesellschaft. Pp. 165–99.

Haug, Walter 1970: "Vom Imram zur Aventiure-Fahrt: zur Frage nach der Vorgeschichte der hochhöfischen Epenstruktur." *Wolfram-Studien* 1: 264–98.

Haug, Walter 1973: "Struktur und Geschichte: ein literaturtheoretisches Experiment an mittelalterlichen Texten." *Germanisch-romanische Monatsschrift* n.s. 23: 129–52.

Haug, Walter 1978: "*Das Land, von welchem niemand wiederkehrt*": Mythos, Fik-

tion und Wahrheit in Chrétiens "Chevalier de la charrete," im "Lanzelet" Ulrichs von Zatzikhoven und im "Lancelot"-Prosaroman. Untersuchungen zur deutschen Literaturgeschichte, 21. Tübingen: Niemeyer.

Haug, Walter 1985: *Literaturtheorie im deutschen Mittelalter: von den Anfängen bis zum Ende des 13. Jahrhunderts. Eine Einführung.* Darmstadt: Wissenschaftliche Buchgesellschaft.

Haupt, Jürgen 1971: *Der Truchseß Keie im Artusroman: Untersuchungen zur Gesellschaftsstruktur im höfischen Roman.* Philologische Studien und Quellen, 57. Berlin: E. Schmidt.

Hauvette, Henri 1933: *La "Morte vivante": étude de littérature comparée.* Paris: Boivin.

Hélin, Maurice 1951: "Recherche des sources et tradition littéraire chez les écrivains latins du moyen âge." In *Mélanges Joseph de Ghellinck.* 2 vols. Museum Lessianum: section historique, 14. Gembloux: Duculot. Vol. II, pp. 407–20.

Hexter, Ralph J. 1986: *Ovid and Medieval Schooling: Studies in Medieval School Commentaries on Ovid's "Ars amatoria," "Epistulae ex Ponto," and "Epistulae Heroidum."* Münchener Beiträge zur Mediävistik und Renaissance-Forschung, 38. Munich: Arbeo.

Hoepffner, E. 1934: " 'Matière et sens' dans le roman d'*Erec et Enide.*" *Archivum romanicum* 18: 433–50.

Hofer, Stefan 1954: *Chrétien de Troyes: Leben und Werke des altfranzösischen Epikers.* Graz and Cologne: H. Böhlaus.

Huchet, Jean-Charles 1984: *Le roman médiéval.* Paris: Presses Universitaires de France.

Huchet, Jean-Charles 1988: "Le nom et l'image: de Chrétien de Troyes à Robert de Boron." In *The Legacy of Chrétien de Troyes,* ed. N. J. Lacy, D. Kelly, and K. Busby. Faux titre, 37. Amsterdam: Rodopi. Vol. II, pp. 1–16.

Huchet, Jean-Charles 1990: *Littérature médiévale et psychanalyse: pour une clinique littéraire.* Paris: Presses Universitaires de France.

Hult, David F. 1981: "Gui de Mori, lecteur médiéval." *Incidences* 5.1: 53–70.

Hult, David F. 1986a: "Lancelot's Two Steps: A Problem in Textual Criticism." *Speculum* 61: 836–58.

Hult, David F. 1986b: *Self-Fulfilling Prophecies: Readership and Authority in the First "Roman de la rose."* Cambridge: Cambridge University Press.

Hult, David F. 1989: "Author/Narrator/Speaker: The Voice of Authority in Chrétien's *Charrete.*" In *Discourses of Authority in Medieval and Renaissance Literature,* ed. K. Brownlee and W. Stephens. Hanover, NH, and London: University Press of New England, for Dartmouth College. Pp. 76–96, 267–69.

Hunt, R. W. 1943: "Studies on Priscian in the Eleventh and Twelfth Centuries." *Mediaeval and Renaissance Studies* 1: 194–231.

Hunt, R. W. 1948: "The Introductions to the 'Artes' in the Twelfth Century." In *Studia mediaevalia in honorem admodum reverendi patris Raymundi Josephi Martin.* Bruges: De Tempel. Pp. 85–112.

Hunt, Tony 1970: "The Rhetorical Background to the Arthurian Prologue: Tradition and the Old French Vernacular Prologues." *Forum for Modern Language Studies* 6: 1–23.

Hunt, Tony 1972: "Tradition and Originality in the Prologues of Chrestien de Troyes." *Forum for Modern Language Studies* 8: 320–44.

Hunt, Tony 1974: "Glossing Marie de France." *Romanische Forschungen* 86: 396–418.

Hunt, Tony 1979: "Chrestien de Troyes: The Textual Problem." *French Studies* 33: 257–71.

Hunt, Tony 1981a: "Chrestien and Macrobius." *Classica et mediaevalia* 33: 211–27.

Hunt, Tony 1981b: "The Significance of Thomas's *Tristan.*" *Reading Medieval Studies* 7: 41–61.

Hunt, Tony 1986: *Chrétien de Troyes: Yvain (Le Chevalier au lion)*. Critical Guides to French Texts, 55. London: Grant & Cutler.

Hunt, Tony 1988: "*Texte* and *Prétexte: Jaufre* and *Yvain.*" In *The Legacy of Chrétien de Troyes*, ed. N. J. Lacy, D. Kelly, and K. Busby. Faux titre, 37. Amsterdam: Rodopi. Vol. II, pp. 125–41.

Huot, Sylvia 1987: *From Song to Book: The Poetics of Writing in Old French Lyric and Lyrical Narrative Poetry*. Ithaca and London: Cornell University Press.

Huot, Sylvia 1990: "Medieval Readers of the *Roman de la rose:* The Evidence of Marginal Notations." *Romance Philology* 43: 400–420.

Hürsch, Melitta 1934: "Alexiuslied und christliche Askese." *Zeitschrift für französische Sprache und Literatur* 58: 414–18.

Ihle, Sandra Ness 1983: *Malory's Grail Quest: Invention and Adaptation in Medieval Prose Romance*. Madison: University of Wisconsin Press.

Jaffe, Samuel Peter 1974: *Nicolaus Dybinus' "Declaracio oracionis de beata Dorothea": Studies and Documents in the History of Late Medieval Rhetoric*. Beiträge zur Literatur des XV. bis XVIII. Jahrhunderts, 5. Wiesbaden: F. Steiner.

Janssens, J. D. 1988: "The Influence of Chrétien de Troyes on Middle Dutch Arthurian Romances: A New Approach." In *The Legacy of Chrétien de Troyes*, ed. N. J. Lacy, D. Kelly, and K. Busby. Faux titre, 37. Amsterdam: Rodopi. Vol. II, pp. 285–306.

Janssens, Jan 1987: "The 'Simultaneous' Composition of *Yvain* and *Lancelot:* Fiction or Reality?" *Forum for Modern Language Studies* 23: 366–76.

Jauss, Hans-Robert 1953: "Die Defigurierung des Wunderbaren und der Sinn der Aventüre im *Jaufre.*" *Romanistisches Jahrbuch* 6: 60–75.

Jauss, Hans-Robert 1963: "Chanson de geste et roman courtois (analyse comparative du *Fierabras* et du *Bel Inconnu*)." In *Chanson de geste und höfischer Roman*. Heidelberger Kolloquium, 30. Januar 1961. Studia romanica, 4. Heidelberg: Winter. P. 61–77.

Jauss, Hans-Robert 1968: "Die klassische und die christliche Rechtfertigung des Häßlichen in mittelalterlicher Literatur." In *Die nicht mehr schönen Künste: Grenzphänomene des Ästhetischen*, ed. H.-R. Jauss. Poetik und Hermeneutik, 3. Munich: Fink. Pp. 143–68.

Jauss, Hans-Robert 1977a: *Alterität und Modernität der mittelalterlichen Literatur: Gesammelte Aufsätze 1956–1976*. Munich: W. Fink.

Jauss, Hans-Robert 1977b: "Littérature médiévale et expérience esthétique: actualité des *Questions de littérature* de Robert Guiette." *Poétique* 31: 322–36.

Jauss, Hans-Robert 1979: "The Alterity and Modernity of Medieval Literature." *New Literary History* 10: 181–229.

Jauss, Hans-Robert 1983: "Das Vollkommene als Faszinosum des Imaginären." In *Funktionen des Fiktiven,* ed. D. Heinrich and W. Iser. Hermeneutik und Poetik, 10. Munich: W. Fink. Pp. 443–61.

Jeauneau, Edouard 1957: "L'usage de la notion d'*integumentum* à travers les gloses de Guillaume de Conches." *Archives d'histoire doctrinale et littéraire du moyen âge* 32: 35–100.

Jennings, Margaret 1978: "The *Ars componendi sermones* of Ranulph Higden." In *Medieval Eloquence: Studies in the Theory and Practice of Medieval Rhetoric,* ed. James J. Murphy. Berkeley, Los Angeles, London: University of California Press. Pp. 112–26.

Jodogne, Omer 1964a: "Le caractère des œuvres 'antiques' dans la littérature française du XIIe et du XIIIe siècle." In *L'Humanisme médiéval dans les littératures romanes du XIIe au XIVe siècle,* ed. A. Fourrier. Colloque organisé par le Centre de Philologie et de Littératures romanes de l'Université de Strasbourg du 29 janvier au 2 février 1962. Actes et colloques, 3. Paris: Klincksieck. Pp. 55–85.

Jodogne, Omer 1964b: "La personnalité de l'écrivain d'oïl du XIIe au XIVe siècle." In *L'Humanisme médiéval dans les littératures romanes du XIIe au XIVe siècle,* ed. A. Fourrier. Colloque organisé par le Centre de Philologie et de Littératures romanes de l'Université de Strasbourg du 29 janvier au 2 février 1962. Actes et colloques, 3. Paris: Klincksieck. Pp. 87–106.

Jones, Catherine M. 1990: " 'La Tresse': Interlace in the *chanson de geste.*" *French Forum* 15: 261–75.

Jones, Paul John 1933: *Prologue and Epilogue in Old French Lives of Saints before 1400.* Diss. University of Pennsylvania. Philadelphia: University of Pennsylvania.

Jones, Rosemarie 1972: *The Theme of Love in the "Romans d'antiquité."* Modern Humanities Research Association Dissertation Series, 5. London: Modern Humanities Research Asso.

Jonin, Pierre 1982: "Le *je* de Marie de France dans les *Lais.*" *Romania* 103: 170–96.

Jordan, Robert M. 1967: *Chaucer and the Shape of Creation: The Aesthetic Possibilities of Inorganic Structure.* Cambridge: Harvard University Press.

Jung, Carl-Gustav 1944: *Psychologie und Alchemie.* Psychologische Abhandlungen, 5. Zürich: Rascher.

Jung, Carl-Gustav 1971: *Erinnerungen, Träume, Gedanken,* Ed. A. Jaffé. Olten, Freiburg-i.-Br.: Walter. Trans. Richard and Clara Winston, *Memories, Dreams, Reflections.* New York: Pantheon. 1963.

Jung, Marc-René 1968: "Gui de Mori et Guillaume de Lorris." *Vox romanica* 27: 106–37.

Jung, Marc-René 1976: "Lecture de *Jaufre.*" In *Mélanges Carl Theodor Gossen.* Bern: Francke; Liège: Marche Romane. Pp. 427–51.

Jung, Marc-René 1984: "L'exil d'Anténor." In *Mittelalterstudien Erich Köhler zum Gedenken.* Heidelberg: C. Winter. Pp. 103–19,

Jung, Marc-René 1985: "*De Lamedonte filio Hectoris.*" In *Variorvm mvnera florvm: Latinität als prägende Kraft mittelalterlicher Kultur. Festschrift Hans F. Haefele.* Sigmaringen: J. Thorbecke. Pp. 219–29.

Kay, Sarah 1985: "The Tristan Story as Chivalric Romance, Feudal Epic and Fabliau." In *The Spirit of the Court,* ed. G. S. Burgess and R. A. Taylor. Selected Proceedings of the Fourth Congress of the International Courtly Literature Society (Toronto 1983). Cambridge: D. S. Brewer. Pp. 185–95.

Keen, Maurice 1973: "Mediaeval Ideas of History." In *The Mediaeval World,* ed. D. Daiches and A. Thorlby. Literature and Western Civilization, 2. London: Aldus. Pp. 285–314.

Keller, Hans-Erich 1985: "Literary Patronage in the Time of Philip Augustus." In *The Spirit of the Court,* ed. G. S. Burgess and R. A. Taylor. Selected Proceedings of the Fourth Congress of the International Courtly Literature Society (Toronto 1983). Cambridge: D. S. Brewer. Pp. 196–207.

Kellermann, Wilhelm 1936: *Aufbaustil und Weltbild Chrestiens von Troyes im Percevalroman.* Beihefte zur Zeitschrift für romanische Philologie, 88. Halle: Niemeyer; rpt. Darmstadt: Wissenschaftliche Buchgesellschaft, 1967.

Kellermann, Wilhelm 1956: "Le problème de Breri." In *Les romans du graal dans la littérature des XIIᵉ et XIIIᵉ siècles.* Colloques internationaux du Centre National de la Recherche Scientifique, 3. Paris: Editions du CNRS. Pp. 137–48.

Kellermann, Wilhelm 1970: "Les types psychologiques de l'amour dans les romans de Chrétien de Troyes." *Marche romane* 20.4: 31–39.

Kelly, Douglas 1966a: "The Scope of the Treatment of Composition in the Twelfth- and Thirteenth-Century Arts of Poetry." *Speculum* 41: 261–78.

Kelly, Douglas 1966b: *Sens and Conjointure in the "Chevalier de la charrette."* Studies in French Literature, 2. The Hague and Paris: Mouton.

Kelly, Douglas 1968: "Courtly Love in Perspective: The Hierarchy of Love in Andreas Capellanus." *Traditio* 24: 119–47.

Kelly, Douglas 1969a: "*En uni dire (Tristan* Douce 839) and the Composition of Thomas's *Tristan.*" *Modern Philology* 66: 9–17.

Kelly, Douglas 1969b: "Multiple Quests in French Verse Romance: *Mervelles de Rigomer* and *Claris et Laris.*" *Esprit créateur* 9: 257–66.

Kelly, Douglas 1969c: "Theory of Composition in Medieval Narrative Poetry and Geoffrey of Vinsauf's *Poetria nova.*" *Mediaeval Studies* 31: 117–48.

Kelly, Douglas 1970a: "The Composition of Aimon de Varennes' *Florimont.*" *Romance Philology* 23: 277–92.

Kelly, Douglas 1970b: "The Source and Meaning of *conjointure* in Chrétien's *Erec* 14." *Viator* 1: 179–200.

Kelly, Douglas 1971: "La forme et le sens de la quête dans l'*Erec et Enide* de Chrétien de Troyes." *Romania* 92: 326–58.

Kelly, Douglas 1974: "*Matiere* and *genera dicendi* in Medieval Romance." *Yale French Studies* 51: 147–59.

Kelly, Douglas 1976: "Fortune and Narrative Proliferation in the *Berinus.*" *Speculum* 51: 6–22.

Kelly, Douglas 1977: " 'Senpres est ci et senpres la': Motif Repetition and Narrative Bifurcation in Beroul's *Tristan.*" In *Voices of Conscience: Essays James D. Powell and Rosemary Hodgins.* Philadelphia: Temple University Press. Pp. 131–42.

Kelly, Douglas 1978a: *Medieval Imagination: Rhetoric and the Poetry of Courtly Love.* Madison: University of Wisconsin Press.

Kelly, Douglas 1978b: "Motif and Structure as Amplification of Topoi in the *Sept sages de Rome* Prose Cycle." In *Studies on the Seven Sages of Rome and Other Essays in Medieval Literature Dedicated to the Memory of Jean Misrahi.* Honolulu: Educational Research Associates. Pp. 133–54.

Kelly, Douglas 1978c: "Topical Invention in Medieval French Literature." In *Medieval Eloquence: Studies in the Theory and Practice of Medieval Rhetoric,* ed. J. J. Murphy. Berkeley, Los Angeles, London: University of California Press. Pp. 231–51.

Kelly, Douglas 1978d: "*Translatio studii:* Translation, Adaptation, and Allegory in Medieval French Literature." *Philological Quarterly* 57: 287–310.

Kelly, Douglas 1980: "Psychologie/pathologie et parole dans Chrétien de Troyes." *Œuvres et critiques* 5.2: 31–37.

Kelly, Douglas 1983a: "The Logic of the Imagination in Chrétien de Troyes." In *The Sower and His Seed: Essays on Chrétien de Troyes,* ed. R. T. Pickens. French Forum Monographs, 44. Lexington: French Forum. Pp. 9–30.

Kelly, Douglas 1983b: "La spécialité dans l'invention des topiques." In *Archéologie du signe,* ed. L. Brind'Amour and E. Vance. Recueil d'études médiévales, 3. Toronto: Pontifical Institute of Mediaeval Studies. Pp. 101–25.

Kelly, Douglas 1983c: "*Tout li sens du monde* dans *Claris et Laris.*" *Romance Philology* 36: 406–17.

Kelly, Douglas 1984a: "Les fées et les arts dans la représentation du Chevalier de la charrette." In *Lancelot,* ed. D. Buschinger. Actes du Colloque des 14 et 15 janvier 1984. Göppinger Arbeiten zur Germanistik, 415. Göppingen: Kümmerle. Pp. 85–97.

Kelly, Douglas 1984b: "L'invention dans les romans en prose." In *The Craft of Fiction: Essays in Medieval Poetics,* ed. L. A. Arrathoon. Rochester: Solaris. Pp. 119–42.

Kelly, Douglas 1984c: "Obscurity and Memory: Sources for Invention in Medieval French Literature." In *Vernacular Poetics in the Middle Ages,* ed. L. Ebin. Studies in Medieval Culture, 16. Kalamazoo: Medieval Institute, Western Michigan University. Pp. 33–56.

Kelly, Douglas 1984d: "The Rhetoric of Adventure in Medieval Romance." In *Chrétien de Troyes and the Troubadours: Essays Leslie Topsfield.* Cambridge: St. Catharine's College. Pp. 172–85.

Kelly, Douglas 1985a: "*Disjointure* and the Elaboration of Prose Romance: The Example of the Seven Sages of Rome Prose Cycle." In *The Spirit of the Court,* ed. G. S. Burgess and R. A. Taylor. Selected Proceedings of the Fourth Congress of the International Courtly Literature Society (Toronto 1983). Cambridge: D. S. Brewer. Pp. 208–16.

Kelly, Douglas 1985b: "Romance and the Vanity of Chrétien de Troyes." In *Romance: Generic Transformation from Chrétien de Troyes to Cervantes,* ed. K. Brownlee and M. S. Brownlee. Hanover, and London: University Press of New England. Pp. 74–90.

Kelly, Douglas, ed. 1985c: *The Romances of Chrétien de Troyes: A Symposium.* Edward C. Armstrong Monographs on Medieval Literature, 3. Lexington: French Forum.

Kelly, Douglas 1986: "Exaggeration, Abrupt Conversion, and the Uses of Description in *Jaufre* and *Flamenca.*" In *Studia occitanica in memoriam Paul Remy.* 2 vols. Kalamazoo: Medieval Institute, Western Michigan University. Vol. II, pp. 107–19.

Kelly, Douglas 1987: "The Art of Description." In *The Legacy of Chrétien de Troyes,* ed. N. J. Lacy, D. Kelly, and K. Busby. Faux titre, 31. Amsterdam: Rodopi. Vol. I, pp. 191–221.

Kelly, Douglas 1988a: "Le jeu de la vérité." In *Le Chevalier au lion de Chrétien de Troyes: approches d'un chef-d'œuvre,* ed. J. Dufournet. Collection Unichamp, 20. Paris: Champion. Pp. 105–17.

Kelly, Douglas 1988b: "Le lieu du temps, le temps du lieu." In *Le nombre du temps: en hommage à Paul Zumthor.* Nouvelle Bibliothèque du moyen âge, 12. Paris: Champion. Pp. 123–26.

Kelly, Douglas 1988c: "Le patron et l'auteur dans l'invention romanesque." In *Théories et pratiques de l'écriture au moyen âge,* ed. E. Baumgartner and C. Marchello-Nizia. Actes du Colloque Palais du Luxembourg-Sénat, 5 et 6 mars 1987. Littérales, 4. Paris: Paris X-Nanterre; Fontenay/St. Cloud: ECS. Pp. 25–39.

Kelly, Douglas 1989: "Description and Narrative in Romance: The Contextual Coordinates of *Meraugis de Portlesguez* and the *Bel Inconnu.*" In *Continuations: Essays John L. Grigsby.* Birmingham, AL: Summa. Pp. 83–93.

Kelly, Douglas 1991: *The Arts of Poetry and Prose.* Typologie des sources du moyen âge occidental 59 (A-V.A.2*). Turnhout: Brepols.

Kelly, Thomas E. 1974: *Le Haut Livre du graal: Perlesvaus. A Structural Study.* Histoire des idées et critique littéraire, 145. Geneva: Droz.

Kennedy, Angus J. 1981: "The Portrayal of the Hermit-Saint in French Arthurian Romance: The Remoulding of a Stock-Character." In *An Arthurian Tapestry: Essays Lewis Thorpe.* Glasgow: French Department of the University. Pp. 69–82.

Kennedy, Elspeth 1970: "The Scribe as Editor." In *Mélanges Jean Frappier.* Publications romanes et françaises, 112. 2 vols. Geneva: Droz. Vol. I, pp. 523–31.

Kennedy, Elspeth 1973: "The Role of the Supernatural in the First Part of the Old French Prose *Lancelot.*" In *Studies Frederick Whitehead.* Manchester: Manchester University Press. Pp. 173–84.

Kennedy, Elspeth 1986: *Lancelot and the Grail: A Study of the Prose "Lancelot."* Oxford: Clarendon Press.

Kerényi, Karl 1971: *Der antike Roman: Einführung und Textauswahl*. Libelli, 315. Darmstadt: Wissenschaftliche Buchgesellschaft.

Keuck, Karl 1934: *Historia: Geschichte des Wortes und seiner Bedeutungen in der Antike und in den romanischen Sprachen*. Diss. Münster. Emsdetten: Lechte.

Kibler, William W. 1979: "The *Roland* after Oxford: The French Tradition." *Olifant* 6: 275–92.

Kind, Maureen Ellen 1979: "The Quest and Structure in Medieval Romance: *Durmart le Galois, Meraugis de Portlesguez,* and the *Atre périlleux.*" Diss. University of Wisconsin—Madison.

Klebs, Elimar 1899: *Die Erzählung von Apollonius aus Tyrus: eine geschichtliche Untersuchung über ihre lateinische Urform und ihre späteren Bearbeitungen*. Berlin: Reimer.

Kleinschmidt, Erich 1974: *Herrscherdarstellung: zur Disposition mittelalterlichen Aussageverhaltens, untersucht an Texten über Rudolf I. von Habsburg*. Bibliotheca Germanica, 17. Bern and Munich: Francke.

Kleinschmidt, Erich 1976: "Minnesang als höfisches Zeremonialhandeln." *Archiv für Kulturgeschichte* 58: 35–76.

Klinck, Roswitha 1970: *Die lateinische Etymologie des Mittelalters*. Medium Aevum: philologische Studien, 17. Munich: Fink.

Klopsch, Paul 1980: *Einführung in die Dichtungslehren des lateinischen Mittelalters*. Darmstadt: Wissenschaftliche Buchgesellschaft.

Knapp, Fritz Peter 1972: "Die häßliche Gralbotin und die victorinische Ästhetik." *Sprachkunst* 3: 1–10.

Knapp, Fritz Peter 1973: "Vergleich und Exempel in der lateinischen Rhetorik und Poetik von der Mitte des 12. bis zur Mitte des 13. Jahrhunderts." *Studi medievali* n.s. 3, 14: 443–511.

Knapp, Fritz Peter 1975: *Similitudo: Stil- und Erzählfunktion von Vergleich und Exempel in der lateinischen, französischen und deutschen Großepik des Hochmittelalters*. Philologica Germanica, 2. Vienna and Stuttgart: Braumüller.

Knapp, Fritz Peter 1980: "Historische Wahrheit und poetische Lüge: die Gattungen weltlicher Epik und ihre theoretische Rechtfertigung im Hochmittelalter." *Deutsche Vierteljahrsschrift für Literaturwissenschaft und Geistesgeschichte* 54: 581–635.

Knapton, Antoinette 1975: *Mythe et psychologie chez Marie de France dans "Guigemar."* North Carolina Studies in the Romance Languages and Literatures, 142. Chapel Hill: University of North Carolina, Department of Romance Languages.

Koenig, Daniel 1973: *"Sen" / "sens" et "savoir" et leurs synonymes dans quelques romans courtois du 12ᵉ et du début du 13ᵉ siècle*. Publications universitaires européennes, série XIII: Langue et littérature françaises, 22. Bern: H. Lang; Frankfurt: P. Lang.

Köhler, Erich 1959: "Zur Entstehung des altprovenzalischen Streitgedichts." *Zeitschrift für romanische Philologie* 75: 37–88.

Köhler, Erich 1960: "Le Rôle de la 'coutume' dans les romans de Chrétien de Troyes." *Romania* 81: 386–97.

Köhler, Erich 1962: *Trobadorlyrik und höfischer Roman: Aufsätze zur französischen und provenzalischen Literatur des Mittelalters.* Neue Beiträge zur Literaturwissenschaft, 15. Berlin: Rütten & Loening.

Köhler, Erich 1964a: "Narcisse, la fontaine d'Amour et Guillaume de Lorris." In *L'Humanisme médiéval dans les littératures romanes du XIIe au XIVe siècle,* ed. A. Fourrier. Colloque organisé par le Centre de Philologie et de Littératures romanes de l'Université de Strasbourg du 29 janvier au 2 février 1962. Actes et colloques, 3. Paris: Klincksieck. Pp. 147–66.

Köhler, Erich 1964b: "Observations historiques et sociologiques sur la poésie des troubadours." *Cahiers de civilisation médiévale* 7: 27–51.

Köhler, Erich 1966: *Esprit und arkadische Freiheit: Aufsätze aus der Welt der Romania.* Frankfurt and Bonn: Athenäum.

Köhler, Erich 1968: *"Conseil des barons" und "jugement des barons": epische Fatalität und Feudalrecht im altfranzösischen Rolandslied.* Sitzungsberichte der Heidelberger Akademie der Wissenschaften: philosophisch-historische Klasse, 4. Heidelberg: C. Winter.

Köhler, Erich 1970: *Ideal und Wirklichkeit in der höfischen Epik: Studien zur Form der frühen Artus- und Graldichtung.* Beihefte zur Zeitschrift für romanische Philologie, 97. 2d ed. Tübingen: Niemeyer.

Köhler, Erich 1973: *Der literarische Zufall, das Mögliche und die Notwendigkeit.* Munich: W. Fink.

Köhler, Erich 1976: "Il sistema sociologico del romanzo francese medievale." *Medioevo romanzo* 3: 321–44.

Köhler, Erich 1977: "Gattungssystem und Gesellschaftssystem." *Romanistische Zeitschrift für Literaturgeschichte—Cahiers d'histoire des littératures romanes* 1: 7–22.

Kretzschmar, William A., Jr. 1980: "Three Stories in Search of an Author: The Narrative Versions of Havelok." *Allegorica* 5.2: 20–97.

Kroll, Wilhelm 1924: "Der Stoff der Dichtung." In his *Studien zum Verständnis der römischen Literatur.* Stuttgart: Metzler. Pp. 44–63.

Krueger, Roberta L. 1987: "The Author's Voice: Narrators, Audiences, and the Problem of Interpretation." In *The Legacy of Chrétien de Troyes,* ed. N. J. Lacy, D. Kelly, and K. Busby. Faux titre, 31. Amsterdam: Rodopi. Vol.I, pp. 115–40.

Krüger, Karl Heinrich 1976: *Die Universalchroniken.* Typologie des sources du moyen âge occidental, 16 (A-I.2*). Turnhout: Brepols.

Kurdziałek, Marian 1971: "Der Mensch als Abbild des Kosmos." In *Der Begriff der repraesentatio im Mittelalter: Stellvertretung, Symbol, Zeichen, Bild,* ed. A. Zimmermann. Miscellanea Mediaevalia, 8. Berlin and New York: de Gruyter. Pp. 35–75.

Lacroix, Benoît 1971: *L'historien au moyen âge.* Conférence Albert-le-Grand 1966. Montréal: Institut d'Etudes Médiévales; Paris: Vrin.

Lacy, Norris J. 1972: "Thematic Structure in the *Charrette.*" *Esprit créateur* 12: 13–18.

Lacy, Norris J. 1977: "The Form of the *Brut*'s Arthurian Sequence." In *Jean Misrahi Memorial Volume: Studies in Medieval Literature.* Columbia: French Literature Publ. Co. Pp. 150–58.

Lacy, Norris J. 1978: "The Composition of *L'Escoufle.*" *Res publica litterarum* 1: 151–58.

Lacy, Norris J. 1980: *The Craft of Chrétien de Troyes: An Essay on Narrative Art.* Davis Medieval Texts and Studies, 3. Leiden: Brill.

Lagorio, Valerie M. 1970: "Pan-Brittonic Hagiography and the Arthurian Grail Cycle." *Traditio* 26: 29–61.

Lagorio, Valerie M. 1971: "St. Joseph of Arimathea and Glastonbury: A 'New Pan-Brittonic Saint.' " *Trivium* 6: 59–69.

Lammers, Walther 1965: *Geschichtsdenken und Geschichtsbild im Mittelalter: ausgewählte Aufsätze und Arbeiten aus den Jahren 1933 bis 1959.* Wege der Forschung, 21. Darmstadt: Wissenschaftliche Buchgesellschaft.

Langer, Ullrich 1990: *Divine and Poetic Freedom in the Renaissance: Nominalist Theology and Literature in France and Italy.* Princeton: Princeton University Press.

Larmat, Jean 1979: "*Le Roman de Tristan en prose,* manuel de courtoisie." In *Der altfranzösische Prosaroman: Funktion, Funktionswandel und Ideologie am Beispiel des "Roman de Tristan en prose,"* ed. E. Ruhe and R. Schwaderer. Kolloquium Würzburg 1977. Beiträge zur romanischen Philologie des Mittelalters, 12. Munich: Fink. Pp. 46–76.

Laugesen, Anker Teilgård 1962: "La roue de Virgile: une page de la théorie littéraire au moyen âge." *Classica et mediaevalia* 23: 248–73.

Laurie, H. C. R. 1984: "Chrétien's 'bele conjointure.' " In *Actes du 14ᵉ Congrès International Arthurien.* 2 vols. Rennes: Presses Universitaires de Rennes 2. Vol. I, pp. 379–96.

Lausberg, Heinrich 1960: *Handbuch der literarischen Rhetorik: eine Grundlegung der Literaturwissenschaft.* 2 vols. Munich: Hueber.

Lavaud, René, and René Nelli, trans. 1960: *Les troubadours: Jaufre, Flamenca, Barlaam et Josaphat.* Bibliothèque Européenne. Bruges: Desclée de Brouwer.

Lazar, Moshé 1964: *Amour courtois et "fin'amours" dans la littérature du XIIᵉ siècle.* Bibliothèque française et romane, 8. Paris: Klincksieck.

Leff, Michael C. 1978: "The Logician's Rhetoric: Boethius' *De differentiis topicis, Book IV.*" In *Medieval Eloquence: Studies in the Theory and Practice of Medieval Rhetoric,* ed. J. J. Murphy. Berkeley, Los Angeles, London: University of California Press. Pp. 3–24.

Leff, Michael C. 1983: "The Topics of Argumentative Invention in Latin Rhetorical Theory from Cicero to Boethius." *Rhetorica* 1: 23–44.

Le Gentil, Pierre 1950: "A propos d'Amadas et Ydoine (version continentale et version insulaire)." *Romania* 71: 359–73.

Legge, M. Dominica 1959: "The Influence of Patronage on Form in Medieval French Literature." In *Stil- und Formprobleme in der Literatur.* Vorträge des VII. Kongresses der Internationalen Vereinigung für moderne Sprachen und Literaturen in Heidelberg. Heidelberg: C. Winter. Pp. 136–41.

Legge, M. Dominica 1963: *Anglo-Norman Literature and Its Background.* Oxford: Clarendon Press.

Lejeune, Rita 1954: "Rôle littéraire d'Aliénor d'Aquitaine et de sa famille." *Cultura neolatina* 14: 5–57.

Lejeune, Rita 1958: "Rôle littéraire de la famille d'Aliénor d'Aquitaine." *Cahiers de civilisation médiévale* 20: 201–17.

Le Rider, Paule 1978: *Le chevalier dans le Conte du graal de Chrétien de Troyes.* Bibliothèque du moyen âge. Paris: SEDES.

Leupin, Alexandre 1979: "Les enfants de la Mimésis: différence et répétition dans la 'Première Continuation du Perceval.' " *Vox romanica* 38: 110–26.

Leupin, Alexandre 1982a: "La faille et l'écriture dans les continuations du *Perceval.*" *Moyen âge* 88: 237–69.

Leupin, Alexandre 1982b: *Le graal et la littérature: étude sur la Vulgate arthurienne en prose.* Lausanne: L'Age d'homme.

Levenson, J. L. 1979: "The Narrative Format of Benoît's *Roman de Troie.*" *Romania* 100: 54–70.

Lewent, Kurt 1933: "Zum Inhalt und Aufbau der 'Flamenca.' " *Zeitschrift für romanische Philologie* 53: 1–86.

Lewis, C. S. 1964: *The Discarded Image: An Introduction to Medieval and Renaissance Literature.* Cambridge: Cambridge University Press.

Lewis, C. S. 1966: "Imagination and Thought in the Middle Ages." In his *Studies in Medieval and Renaissance Literature.* Cambridge: Cambridge University Press. Pp. 41–63.

Leyerle, John 1967: "The Interlace Structure of *Beowulf.*" *University of Toronto Quarterly* 37: 1–17.

Liborio, Mariantonia 1979: " 'Qui petit semme petit quelt' ": l'itinerario poetico di Chrétien de Troyes." *Quaderno di lingua e letteratura francese* 1: 29–90.

Lichtblau, Karin 1985: "Index des motifs narratifs dans la littérature profane allemande des origines à 1400." *Bulletin bibliographique de la Société Internationale Arthurienne* 37: 312–20.

Liebeschütz, Hans 1926: "Kosmologische Motive in der Bildungswelt der Frühscholastik." *Vorträge der Bibliothek Warburg 1923–1924.* Leipzig and Berlin: Teubner. Pp. 83–148.

Lindberg, David C. 1976: *Theories of Vision from Al-Kindi to Kepler.* University of Chicago History of Science and Medicine. Chicago and London: University of Chicago Press.

Locatelli, Rossana 1951: "L'avventura nei romanzi di Chrétien de Troyes e nei suoi imitatori." *ACME: Annali della Facoltà de Filosofia e Lettere dell'Università di Milano* 4: 3–22.

Lods, Jeanne 1951: *Le roman de Perceforest: origines-composition-caractères-valeur et influence.* Publications romanes et françaises, 32. Geneva: Droz; Lille: Giard.

Lods, Jeanne 1974: review of Richard Baum, *Recherches sur les œuvres attribuées à Marie de France,* Annales Universitatis Saraviensis, Reihe: Philosophische Fakultät, 9 (Heidelberg: C. Winter, 1968), in *Cahiers de civilisation médiévale* 14: 355–58.

Lofmark, Carl 1972a: "Der höfische Dichter als Übersetzer." In *Probleme mittelhochdeutscher Erzählformen,* ed. P. F. Ganz and W. Schröder. Marburger Kolloquium 1969. Berlin: E. Schmidt. Pp. 40–62.

Lofmark, Carl 1972b: "Wolfram's Source References in 'Parzival.'" *Modern Language Review* 67: 820–44.

Loomis, Roger Sherman 1949: *Arthurian Tradition and Chrétien de Troyes*. New York and London: Columbia University Press.

Loomis, Roger Sherman, ed. 1959: *Arthurian Literature in the Middle Ages: A Collaborative History*. Oxford: Clarendon Press.

Loomis, Roger Sherman 1963: *The Grail from Celtic Myth to Christian Symbol*. Cardiff: University of Wales Press; New York: Columbia University Press.

Lord, Albert B. 1960: *The Singer of Tales*. Harvard Studies in Comparative Literature, 24. Cambridge: Harvard University Press.

Lot, Ferdinand 1954: *Etude sur le Lancelot en prose*. Bibliothèque de l'Ecole des Hautes Etudes, 226. Paris: Champion.

Lough, John 1978: *Writer and Public in France from the Middle Ages to the Present Day*. Oxford: Clarendon Press.

Lozachmeur, Jean-Claude 1980a: "A propos de l'origine du nom de *Mabonagrain*." *Etudes celtiques* 17: 257–62.

Lozachmeur, Jean-Claude 1980b: "Le problème de la transmission des thèmes arthuriens à la lumière de quelques correspondances onomastiques (I)." In *Mélanges Charles Foulon*. 2 vols. Rennes: Institut de Français, Université de Haute-Bretagne; Liège: Marche Romane. Vol. I, pp. 217–25.

Lubac, Henri de 1959: *Exégèse médiévale: les quatre sens de l'Ecriture*. Théologie: études publiées sous la direction de la Faculté de Théologie S. J. de Lyon—Fourvière, 41–42, 59. Paris: Aubier, 1959–64.

Lubienski-Bodenham, H. 1979: "The Origins of the Fifteenth Century View of Poetry as 'Seconde Rhétorique.'" *Modern Language Review* 74: 26–38.

Lumiansky, R. M. 1958: "Structural Unity in Benoit's *Roman de Troie*." *Romania* 79: 410–24.

Luttrell, Claude 1974: *The Creation of the First Arthurian Romance: A Quest*. Evanston: Northwestern University Press.

Lynch, Kathryn L. 1988: *The High Medieval Dream Vision: Poetry, Philosophy, and Literary Form*. Stanford: Stanford University Press.

Lyons, Faith 1965: *Les éléments descriptifs dans le roman d'aventure au XIIIe siècle (en particulier "Amadas et Ydoine," "Gliglois," "Galeran," "L'Escoufle," "Guillaume de Dole," "Jehan et Blonde," "Le Castelain de Couci")*. Publications romanes et françaises, 84. Geneva: Droz.

McCormick, Michael 1975: *Les annales du haut moyen âge*. Typologie des sources du moyen âge occidental, 14. (A-I.3). Turnhout: Brepols.

McKeon, Richard 1936: "Literary Criticism and the Concept of Imitation in Antiquity." *Modern Philology* 34: 1–35.

McKeon, Richard 1942: "Rhetoric in the Middle Ages." *Speculum* 17: 1–32.

McKeon, Richard 1946: "Poetry and Philosophy in the Twelfth Century: The Renaissance of Rhetoric." *Modern Philology* 43: 217–34.

McMunn, Meradith Tilbury 1978: "Psychological Realism and the Representation of Medieval Children in the *Roman de Kanor*." In *Studies on the Seven Sages of Rome and Other Essays in Medieval Literature Dedicated to the Mem-*

ory of Jean Misrahi. Honolulu: Educational Research Associates. Pp. 181–200.

Maddox, Donald 1977a: "Nature and Narrative in Chrétien's *Erec et Enide.*" *Mediaevalia* 3: 59–82.

Maddox, Donald 1977b: "The Prologue to Chrétien's *Erec* and the Problem of Meaning." In *Jean Misrahi Memorial Volume: Studies in Medieval Literature.* Columbia SC: French Literature Publ. Co. Pp. 159–74.

Maddox, Donald 1978: *Structure and Sacring: The Systematic Kingdom in Chrétien's "Erec et Enide."* French Forum Monographs, 8. Lexington: French Forum.

Maddox, Donald 1980: "Trois sur deux: théories de bipartition et de tripartition des œuvres de Chrétien." *Œuvres et critiques* 5.2: 91–102.

Maddox, Donald 1986: "Lancelot et le sens de la coutume." *Cahiers de civilisation médiévale* 29: 339–53.

Maddox, Donald 1991: *The Arthurian Romances of Chrétien de Troyes: Once and Future Fictions.* Cambridge Studies in Medieval Literature, 12. Cambridge: Cambridge University Press.

Mahler, Annemarie E. 1974: "The Representation of Visual Reality in *Perceval* and *Parzival.*" *PMLA* 89: 537–50.

Manitius, Max 1931: *Geschichte der lateinischen Literatur des Mittelalters,* Vol. III: *Vom Ausbruch des Kirchenstreites bis zum Ende des zwölften Jahrhunderts.* Handbuch der Altertumswissenschaft, 9.2.3. Munich: C. H. Beck.

Marache, Bernard 1988: "Le mot et la notion d'aventure dans la 'conjointure' et le 'sen' du *Chevalier au lion.*" In *Le Chevalier au lion de Chrétien de Troyes: approches d'un chef-d'œuvre,* ed. Jean Dufournet. Collection Unichamp, 20. Paris: Champion. Pp. 119–38.

Marchello-Nizia, Christiane 1982: "L'historien et son prologue: forme littéraire et stratégies discursives." In *La chronique et l'histoire au moyen âge.,* ed. D. Poirion. Colloque des 24 et 25 mai 1982. Cultures et civilisations médiévales, 2. Paris: Presses de l'Université de Paris — Sorbonne. Pp. 13–25.

Marichal, Robert 1961: "Critique des textes." In *L'histoire et ses méthodes,* ed. C. Samaran. Encyclopédie de la Pléiade, 11. Paris: Gallimard. Pp. 1247–1366.

Marichal, Robert 1968: "Naissance du roman." In *Entretiens sur la renaissance du 12ᵉ siècle,* ed. M. de Gandillac and E. Jeauneau. Paris and The Hague: Mouton. Pp. 449–92.

Mariétan, Joseph 1901: *Problème de la classification des sciences d'Aristote à St-Thomas.* St-Maurice: Imp. St-Augustin; Paris: Félix Alcan.

Marshall, Linda E. 1979: "The Identity of the 'New Man' in the 'Anticlaudianus' of Alan of Lille." *Viator* 10: 77–94.

Marti, Berthe Marie 1941: "Literary Criticism in the Mediaeval Commentaries on Lucan." *Transactions and Proceedings of the American Philological Association* 72: 245–54.

Martin, Janet 1979: "Uses of Tradition: Gellius, Petronius, and John of Salisbury." *Viator* 10: 57–76.

Marx, Jean 1952: *La légende arthurienne et le graal.* Bibliothèque de l'Ecole des Hautes

Etudes: section des sciences religieuses, 64. Paris: Presses universitaires de France.

Matarasso, Pauline 1979: *The Redemption of Chivalry: A Study of the "Queste del saint graal."* Histoire des idées et critique littéraire, 180. Geneva: Droz.

Matoré, Georges 1980: "Remarques sur beau et beauté en ancien français." In *Etudes André Laüly.* Nancy: Université de Nancy II. Pp. 225–32.

Maurer, Friedrich 1964: *Leid: Studien zur Bedeutungs- und Problemgeschichte besonders in den großen Epen der staufischen Zeit.* Bibliotheca Germanica, 1. 3d ed. Bern and Munich: Francke.

Méla, Charles 1984: *La reine et le Graal: la "conjointure" dans les romans du Graal de Chrétien de Troyes au "Livre de Lancelot."* Paris: Seuil.

Ménard, Philippe 1967: "Le temps et la durée dans les romans de Chrétien de Troyes." *Moyen âge* 73: 375–401.

Ménard, Philippe 1969: *Le rire et le sourire dans le roman courtois en France au moyen âge (1150–1250).* Publications romanes et françaises, 105. Geneva: Droz.

Ménard, Philippe 1976: "Le chevalier errant dans la littérature arthurienne: recherches sur les raisons du départ et de l'errance." In *Voyage, quête, pèlerinage dans la littérature et la civilisation médiévales.* Senefiance, 2. Aix-en-Provence: CUER-MA; Paris: Champion. Pp. 289–311.

Ménard, Philippe 1979: *Les Lais de Marie de France: contes d'amour et d'aventure du moyen âge.* Littératures modernes, 19. Paris: Presses universitaires de France.

Meneghetti, Maria Luisa 1975: "L' 'Estoire des Engleis' di Geffrei Gaimar fra cronaca genealogica e romanzo cortese." *Medioevo romanzo* 2: 232–46.

Meneghetti, Maria Luisa 1979: *I fatti di Bretagna: cronache genealogiche anglonormanne dal XII al XIV secolo.* Vulgares eloquentes, 9. Padua: Antenore.

Meneghetti, Maria Luisa 1984: "Duplicazione e specularità nel romanzo arturiano (dal 'Bel Inconnu' al 'Lancelot-Graal')." In *Mittelalterstudien Erich Köhler zum Gedenken.* Studia romanica, 55. Heidelberg: C. Winter. Pp. 206–17.

Meneghetti, Maria Luisa 1989: "Meraviglioso e straniamento." In *Il meraviglioso e il verosimile tra antichità e medioevo,* ed. D. Lanza and O. Longo. Biblioteca dell' "Archivum romanicum," Ser. I. Storia-letteratura-paleografia, 221. Florence: L. S. Olschki. Pp. 227–35.

Meyer, Paul 1886: *Alexandre le Grand dans la littérature française du moyen âge.* Bibliothèque française du moyen âge, 4–5. 2 vols. Paris: Vieweg.

Micha, Alexandre 1963: "Les manuscrits du *Lancelot en prose:* troisième article." *Romania* 84: 478–99.

Micha, Alexandre 1973: "Temps et conscience chez Chrétien de Troyes." In *Mélanges Pierre Le Gentil.* Paris: SEDES/CDU. Pp. 553–60.

Micha, Alexandre 1980: *Etude sur le "Merlin" de Robert de Boron: roman du XIIIe siècle.* Publications romanes et françaises, 151. Geneva: Droz.

Micha, Alexandre 1984: "Sur un procédé de composition de *Lancelot:* les récits rétrospectifs." In *Approches du Lancelot en prose,* ed. J. Dufournet. Collection Unichamp, 6. Paris: Champion. Pp. 7–23.

Micha, Alexandre 1987: *Essais sur le cycle du Lancelot-Graal*. Publications romanes et françaises, 179. Geneva: Droz.

Mickel, Emanuel J., Jr. 1975: "The Unity and Significance of Marie's 'Prologue.' " *Romania* 96: 83–91.

Minnis, A. J. 1984: *Medieval Theory of Authorship: Scholastic Literary Attitudes in the Later Middle Ages*. London: Scolar Press.

Mölk, Ulrich 1968: *Trobar clus trobar leu: Studien zur Dichtungstheorie der Trobadors*. Munich: Fink.

Mölk, Ulrich, ed. 1969: *Französische Literarästhetik des 12. und 13. Jahrhunderts*. Sammlung romanischer Übungstexte, 54. Tübingen: Niemeyer.

Mölk, Ulrich 1978: "La *Chanson de saint Alexis* et le culte du saint en France aux XIᵉ et XIIᵉ siècles." *Cahiers de civilisation médiévale* 21: 339–55.

Monfrin, Jacques 1963: "Humanisme et traductions au moyen âge." *Journal des savants*. Pp. 161–90.

Monson, Don A. 1987: "La 'surenchère' chez Chrétien de Troyes." *Poétique* 70: 231–46.

Moos, Peter von 1976: "*Poeta* und *historicus* im Mittelalter: zum Mimesis-Problem am Beispiel einiger Urteile über Lucan." *Beiträge zur Geschichte der deutschen Sprache und Literatur* (Tübingen) 98: 93–130.

Moos, Peter von 1988: *Geschichte als Topik: das rhetorische Exemplum von der Antike zur Neuzeit und die "historiae" im "Policraticus" Johanns von Salisbury*. Ordo: Studien zur Literatur und Gesellschaft des Mittelalters und der frühen Neuzeit, 2. Hildesheim, Zürich, New York: G. Olms.

Müller, Wolfgang G. 1981: *Topik des Stilbegriffs: zur Geschichte des Stilverständnisses von der Antike bis zur Gegenwart*. Impulse der Forschung, 34. Darmstadt: Wissenschaftliche Buchgesellschaft.

Naumann, Bernd 1970: "Vorstudien zu einer Darstellung des Prologs in der deutschen Dichtung des 12. und 13. Jahrhunderts." In *Formen mittelalterlicher Literatur: Siegfried Beyschlag zu seinem 65. Geburtstag*. Göppinger Arbeiten zur Germanistik, 25. Göppingen: Kümmerle. Pp. 23–37.

Ngal, M. aM 1977: "Literary Creation in Oral Civilizations." *New Literary History* 8: 335–44.

Nichols, Stephen G., Jr. 1969: "The Interaction of Life and Literature in the *peregrinationes ad loca sancta* and the *chansons de geste*." *Speculum* 44: 51–77.

Niedzielski, Henri 1978a: "La formation d'un cycle littéraire au moyen âge: exemple des *Sept sages de Rome*." In *Studies on the Seven Sages of Rome and Other Essays in Medieval Literature Dedicated to the Memory of Jean Misrahi*. Honolulu: Educational Research Associates. Pp. 119–32.

Niedzielski, Henri 1978b: "Helcanus: A Child Prodigy?" In *Studies on the Seven Sages of Rome and Other Essays in Medieval Literature Dedicated to the Memory of Jean Misrahi*. Honolulu: Educational Research Associates. Pp. 173–80.

Nims, Margaret F. 1974: "*Translatio:* 'Difficult Statement' in Medieval Poetic Theory." *University of Toronto Quarterly* 43: 215–30.

Nitze, William A. 1914: "The Romance of Erec, Son of Lac." *Modern Philology* 11: 445–89.

Nitze, William A. 1915: "*Sans* et *matière* dans les œuvres de Chrétien de Troyes." *Romania* 44: 14–36.

Nitze, William A. 1953: "Arthurian Problems." *Bulletin bibliographique de la Société Internationale Arthurienne* 5: 69–84.

Nitze, William A. 1954: "Conjointure in *Erec*, vs. 14." *Modern Language Notes* 69: 180–81.

Nolan, Barbara 1980: "The Judgment of Paris in the *Roman d'Eneas:* A New Look at Sources and Significance." *Classical Bulletin* 56: 52–56.

O'Gorman, Richard F. 1970: "The Prose Version of Robert de Boron's *Joseph d'Arimathie.*" *Romance Philology* 23: 449–61.

Ohly, Friedrich 1958: "Vom geistigen Sinn des Wortes im Mittelalter." *Zeitschrift für deutsches Altertum und deutsche Literatur* 89: 1–23.

Ohly, Friedrich 1965: "Die Suche in Dichtungen des Mittelalters." *Zeitschrift für deutsches Altertum und deutsche Literatur* 94: 171–84.

O'Leary, Susan Jane 1980: "A Semiotics of Allegory (An Allegory of Semiotics): A Study of Guillaume de Lorris' *Roman de la rose.*" Diss. University of Wisconsin-Madison.

Ollier, Marie-Louise 1974a: "The Author in the Text: The Prologues of Chrétien de Troyes." *Yale French Studies* 51: 26–41.

Ollier, Marie-Louise 1974b: "Demande sociale et constitution d'un 'genre': la situation dans la France du XII\^{e\} siècle." *Mosaic* 8: 207–16.

Ollier, Marie-Louise 1974c: "Les discours en 'abyme' ou la narration équivoque." *Medioevo romanzo* 1: 351–64.

Ollier, Marie-Louise 1974d: "Nom, désir, aventure: les structures latentes d'un roman courtois." *Far-Western Forum* 1: 221–32.

Ollier, Marie-Louise 1975: "Le roman courtois: manifestation du dire créateur." In *La lecture sociocritique du texte romanesque,* ed. G. Falconer and H. Mitterand. Toronto: Hakkert. Pp. 175–88.

Ollier, Marie-Louise 1976: "Proverbe et sentence: le discours d'autorité chez Chrétien de Troyes." *Revue des sciences humaines* 41: 329–57.

Ollier, Marie-Louise 1978: "Le présent du récit: temporalité et roman en vers." *Langue française* 40: 99–112.

Owen, D. D. R. 1970: "Profanity and Its Purpose in Chrétien's *Cligés* and *Lancelot.*" *Forum for Modern Language Studies* 6: 37–48.

Owen, D. D. R. 1984: "The Craft of Guillaume le Clerc's *Fergus.*" In *The Craft of Fiction: Essays in Medieval Poetics,* ed. L. A. Arrathoon. Rochester: Solaris. Pp. 47–81.

Pagani, Walter 1976: "Ancora sul prologo dell'*Erec et Enide.*" *Studi mediolatini e volgari* 24: 141–52.

Palermo, Joseph 1959: "A la recherche du 'seigneur devant nommé' du roman de *Kanor.*" *Romance Philology* 12: 243–51.

Palermo, Joseph 1960: "Les limites du roman de *Cassidorus*: l'apport des manuscrits de Bruxelles." *Romance Philology* 14: 22–27.

Palermo, Joseph 1983: "The Arthurian Element in the Cycle of the *Sept sages de Rome.*" *Society of the Seven Sages Newsletter* 10: 9–16.

Parkes, M. B. 1973: "The Literacy of the Laity." In *The Mediaeval World,* ed. D.

Daiches and A. Thorlby. Literature and Western Civilization, 2. London: Aldus. Pp. 555–77.

Patch, Howard R. 1927: *The Goddess Fortuna in Mediaeval Literature.* Cambridge: Harvard University Press; rpt. New York: Octagon, 1967.

Patterson, Warner Forrest 1935: *Three Centuries of French Poetic Theory: A Critical History of the Chief Arts of Poetry in France (1328–1630).* 2 vols. University of Michigan Publications: Language and Literature, 14–15. Ann Arbor: University of Michigan Press.

Paul, Jacques 1967: "L'éloge des personnes et l'idéal humain au XIIIe siècle d'après la chronique de fra Salimbene." *Moyen âge* 73: 403–30.

Pauphilet, Albert 1950: *Le legs du moyen âge: études de littérature médiévale.* Melun: d'Argences.

Pauphilet, Albert 1968: *Etudes sur la Queste del Saint Graal attribuée à Gautier Map.* Paris: Champion.

Payen, Jean-Charles 1964: "L'art du récit dans le *Merlin* de Robert de Boron, le *Didot Perceval* et le *Perlesvaus.*" *Romance Philology* 17: 570–85.

Payen, Jean-Charles 1968: *Le motif du repentir dans la littérature française médiévale (des origines à 1230).* Publications romanes et françaises, 98. Geneva: Droz.

Payen, Jean-Charles 1969: "Les valeurs humaines chez Chrétien de Troyes." In *Mélanges Rita Lejeune.* 2 vols. Gembloux: Duculot. Vol. II, pp. 1087–1101.

Payen, Jean-Charles 1970: "Structure et sens du 'Roman de Thèbes.'" *Moyen âge* 76: 493–513.

Payen, Jean-Charles 1973: "Structure et sens de *Guillaume de Dole.*" In *Etudes Félix Lecoy.* Paris: Champion. Pp. 483–98.

Payen, Jean-Charles 1978: "L'enracinement folklorique du roman arthurien." *Travaux de linguistique et de littérature* 16.1: 427–37.

Payen, Jean-Charles 1979: "Le *Tristan en prose,* manuel de l'amitié: le cas Dinadan." In *Der altfranzösische Prosaroman: Funktion, Funktionswandel und Ideologie am Beispiel des "Roman de Tristan en prose,"* ed. E. Ruhe and R. Schwaderer. Kolloquium Würzburg 1977. Beiträge zur romanischen Philologie des Mittelalters, 12. Munich: Fink. Pp. 104–30.

Payen, Jean-Charles 1980: "La mise en roman de la matière antique: le cas du *Roman de Thèbes.*" In *Etudes Jules Horrent.* Liège: [n.p.]. Pp. 325–32.

Payen, Jean-Charles 1981: "Rhétorique ou poétique de l'imaginaire? sur la fonction de l'allégorie à la fin du moyen âge (à propos d'un livre récent)." *Studi francesi* 74: 280–85.

Pemberton, Lyn 1984: "Authorial Interventions in the *Tristan en prose.*" *Neophilologus* 68: 481–97.

Peron, Gianfelice 1989: "Meraviglioso e verosimile nel romanzo francese medievale: da Benoît de Sainte-Maure a Jean Renart." In *Il meraviglioso e il verosimile tra antichità e medioevo,* ed. D. Lanza and O. Longo. Biblioteca dell'"Archivum romanicum," Ser. I. Storia-letteratura-paleografia, 221. Florence: L. S. Olschki. Pp. 293–323.

Petit, Aimé 1985a: *L'anachronisme dans les romans antiques du XIIe siècle.* Lille: Atelier National de Reproduction de Thèses, Université de Lille III.

Petit, Aimé 1985b: *Naissances du roman: les techniques littéraires dans les romans antiques du XIIe siècle.* Lille: Atelier National Reproduction des Thèses, Université de Lille III; Paris and Geneva: Champion-Slatkine.

Pickens, Rupert T. 1977: *The Welsh Knight: Paradoxicality in Chrétien's "Conte del graal."* French Forum Monographs, 6. Lexington: French Forum.

Pickens, Rupert T. 1978a: "History and Meaning in the *Lais* of Marie de France." In *Studies on the Seven Sages of Rome and Other Essays in Medieval Literature Dedicated to the Memory of Jean Misrahi.* Honolulu: Educational Research Associates. Pp. 201–11.

Pickens, Rupert T. 1978b: "La poétique de Marie de France d'après les prologues des *Lais.*" *Lettres romanes* 32: 367–84.

Pickens, Rupert T. 1984: " 'Mais de çou ne parole pas Crestiens de Troies . . .': A Re-Examination of the Didot-*Perceval.*" *Romania* 105: 492–510.

Pickens, Rupert T. 1988: "Histoire et commentaire chez Chrétien de Troyes et Robert de Boron: Robert de Boron et le livre de Philippe de Flandre." In *The Legacy of Chrétien de Troyes,* ed. N. J. Lacy, D. Kelly, and K. Busby. Faux titre, 37. Amsterdam: Rodopi. Vol. II, pp. 17–39.

Pickering, F. P. 1967: *Augustinus oder Boethius? Geschichtsschreibung und epische Dichtung im Mittelalter — und in der Neuzeit.* 2 vols. Philologische Studien und Quellen, 39 and 80. Berlin: Schmidt, 1967–76.

Pickering, F. P. 1970: *Literature and Art in the Middle Ages.* Glasgow: University Press; Coral Gables: University of Miami Press.

Pickford, Cedric Edward 1960: *L'évolution du roman arthurien en prose vers la fin du moyen âge d'après le manuscrit 112 du fonds français de la Bibliothèque Nationale.* Paris: Nizet.

Picone, Michelangelo 1982: "Dante e la tradizione arturiana." *Romanische Forschungen* 94: 1–18.

Pirot, François 1972: *Recherches sur les connaissances littéraires des troubadours occitans et catalans des XIIe et XIIIe siècles: les "sirventes-ensenhamens" de Guerau de Cabrera, Guiraut de Calanson et Bertrand de Paris.* Memorias de la Real Academia de Buenas Letras de Barcelona, 14. Barcelona: Real Academia de Buenas Letras.

Poe, Elizabeth Wilson 1984: *From Poetry to Prose in Old Provençal: The Emergence of the "Vidas," the "Razos," and the "Razos de trobar."* Birmingham: Summa.

Poirion, Daniel 1972: "Chanson de geste ou épopée? remarques sur la définition d'un genre." *Travaux de linguistique et de littérature* 10.2: 7–20.

Poirion, Daniel 1973: "L'ombre mythique de Perceval dans le *Conte du graal.*" *Cahiers de civilisation médiévale* 16: 191–98.

Poirion, Daniel 1978: "De l' 'Enéide' à l' 'Eneas': mythologie et moralisation." *Cahiers de civilisation médiévale* 19: 213–29.

Poirion, Daniel 1980: "Fonction de l'imaginaire dans l'*Escoufle.*" In *Mélanges Charles Foulon.* 2 vols. Rennes: Institut de Français, Université de Haute-Bretagne; Liège: Marche Romane. Vol. I, pp. 287–93.

Poirion, Daniel 1981: "Ecriture et ré-écriture au moyen âge." *Littérature* 41: 109–18.

Poirion, Daniel 1982: *Le merveilleux dans la littérature française du moyen âge.* Que sais-je? 1938. Paris: Presses universitaires de France.

Poirion, Daniel 1986a: *Résurgences: mythe et littérature à l'âge du symbole (XII*e *siècle)*. Paris: Presses universitaires de France.

Poirion, Daniel 1986b: "Théorie et pratique du style au moyen âge: le sublime et la merveille." *Revue d'histoire littéraire de la France* 86: 15–32.

Ponti, Annalisa 1988: "I 'Tristani' di Thomas e Béroul: prospettivismo monologico e prospettivismo dialogico." *Medioevo romanzo* 13: 183–202.

Pope, M. K. 1952: *From Latin to Modern French with Especial Consideration of Anglo-Norman: Phonology and Morphology*. Rev. ed. Publications of the University of Manchester, 229: French Ser., 6. Manchester: Manchester University Press.

Press, A. R. 1981: "The Precocious Courtesy of Geoffrey Gaimar." In *Court and Poet*, ed. G. S. Burgess. Selected Proceedings of the Third Congress of the International Courtly Literature Society (Liverpool 1980). ARCA: Classical and Medieval Texts, Papers and Monographs, 5. Liverpool: F. Cairns. Pp. 267–76.

Quadlbauer, Franz 1962: *Die antike Theorie der genera dicendi im lateinischen Mittelalter*. Österreichische Akademie der Wissenschaften: Philosophisch-historische Klasse, Sitzungsberichte, 241.2. Graz, Vienna, Cologne: Böhlaus.

Quadlbauer, Franz 1977: "Lukan im Schema des *ordo naturalis/artificialis:* ein Beitrag zur Geschichte der Lukanbewertung im lateinischen Mittelalter." *Grazer Beiträge* 6: 67–105.

Quadlbauer, Franz 1984: "Optimus Orator / Perfecte Eloquens: zu Ciceros formalem Rednerideal und seiner Nachwirkung." *Rhetorica* 2: 103–19.

Quadlbauer, Franz 1986: "Ovidkritik bei Matthaeus von Vendôme und ihre poetologisch-rhetorischen Hintergründe." In *Kontinuität und Wandel: lateinische Poesie von Naevius bis Baudelaire. Franco Munari zum 65. Geburtstag*. Hildesheim: Weidmann. Pp. 424–45.

Quain, Edwin A. 1945: "The Medieval Accessus ad auctores." *Traditio* 3: 215–64.

Raible, Wolfgang 1972: "Vom Autor als Kopist zum Leser als Autor: Literaturtheorie in der literarischen Praxis." *Poetica* 5: 133–51.

Rauhut, Franz 1955: "Das Psychologische in den Romanen Gautiers von Arras." *Wissenschaftliche Zeitschrift der Friedrich-Schiller-Universität Jena/Thüringen: Gesellschafts- und sprachwissenschaftliche Reihe* 5: 343–52.

Ray, Roger D. 1974: "Medieval Historiography through the Twelfth Century: Problems and Progress of Research." *Viator* 5: 33–59.

Raynaud de Lage, Guy 1951: *Alain de Lille: poète du XII*e *siècle*. Université de Montréal: Publications de l'Institut d'Etudes Médiévales, 12. Montréal: Institut d'Etudes Médiévales; Paris: Vrin.

Raynaud de Lage, Guy 1976: *Les premiers romans français et autres études littéraires et linguistiques*. Publications romanes et françaises, 138. Geneva: Droz.

Reichel, Georgius 1909: *Quaestiones progymnasmaticae*. Diss. Leipzig. Leipzig: Typis Roberti Noske Bornensis.

Reid, T. B. W. 1976: "Chrétien de Troyes and the Scribe Guiot." *Medium Aevum* 45: 1–19.

Reinhard, John Revell 1927: *The Old French Romance of Amadas et Ydoine: An Historical Survey*. Durham: Duke University Press.

Reinhard, John Revell 1933: *The Survival of Geis in Mediaeval Romance*. Halle: M. Niemeyer.

Renzi, Lorenzo 1964: *Tradizione cortese e realismo in Gautier d'Arras*. Università di Padova: Pubblicazioni della Facoltà di Lettere e Filosofia, 42. Padua: CEDAM.

Ribard, Jacques 1969: *Un ménestrel du XIVᵉ siècle: Jean de Condé*. Publications romanes et françaises, 104. Geneva: Droz.

Ribard, Jacques 1970: "Le lai du *Laostic*: structure et signification." *Moyen âge* 76: 263–74.

Ribard, Jacques 1980a: "A propos de l'épilogue de 'Renart le nouvel': quelques réflexions sur l'allégorie de Fortune." In *Alain de Lille, Gautier de Châtillon, Jakemart Giélée et leur temps*. Actes du Colloque de Lille octobre 1978. Lille: Presses universitaires de Lille. Pp. 307–20.

Ribard, Jacques 1980b: "Ecriture symbolique et visée allégorique dans *Le Conte du graal.*" *Œuvres et critiques* 5.2: 103–9.

Riffaterre, Michael 1981: "L'intertexte inconnu." *Littérature* 41: 4–7.

Ringger, Kurt 1973: *Die "Lais": zur Struktur der dichterischen Einbildungskraft der Marie de France*. Beihefte zur Zeitschrift für romanische Philologie, 137. Tübingen: M. Niemeyer.

Riposati, Benedetto 1947: *Studi sui "Topica" di Cicerone*. Edizioni dell'Università Cattolica del S. Cuore: Pubblicazioni, 22. Milan: Vita e Pensiero.

Riquer, Martín de 1955: "La 'aventure,' el 'lai' y el 'conte' en María de Francia." *Filología romanza* 2: 1–19.

Riquer, Martín de 1968: *Les chansons de geste françaises*. Trans. Irénée Cluzel. 2d ed. Paris: Nizet.

Riquer, Martín de 1971: "La influencia de la transmisión manuscrita en la estructura de las obras literarias medievales." In *Historia y estructura de la obra literaria*. Coloquios celebrados del 28 al 31 de marzo de 1967. Anejos de Revista de Literatura, 31. Madrid: Consejo Superior de Investigaciónes Científicas. Pp. 31–37.

Risop, Alfred 1895: "Ungelöste Fragen zum Florimont." In *Abhandlungen Herrn Prof. Dr. Adolf Tobler*. Halle: M. Niemeyer. Pp. 430–63.

Roach, William 1956: "Les continuations du Conte del graal." In *Les romans du graal dans la littérature des XIIᵉ et XIIIᵉ siècles*. Strasbourg, 29 mars–3 avril 1954: Colloques Internationaux du Centre National de la Recherche Scientifique, 3. Paris: CNRS. Pp. 107–18.

Robertson, D. W., Jr. 1951a: "The Doctrine of Charity in Mediaeval Literary Gardens: A Topical Approach through Symbolism and Allegory." *Speculum* 26: 24–49.

Robertson, D. W., Jr. 1951b: "Some Medieval Literary Terminology, with Special Reference to Chrétien de Troyes." *Studies in Philology* 48: 669–92.

Robertson, D. W., Jr. 1962: *A Preface to Chaucer: Studies in Medieval Perspectives*. Princeton: Princeton University Press.

Rockwell, Paul V. 1988: "Departures: Sens and Departir in the Prose *Lancelot*. Metaphors of Mediation in Twelfth- and Thirteenth-Century Romance." Diss. University of Wisconsin—Madison.

Rohr, Rupprecht 1962: "Zur Skala der ritterlichen Tugenden in der altprovenzalischen und altfranzösischen höfischen Dichtung." *Zeitschrift für romanische Philologie* 78: 292–325.

Rohr, Rupprecht 1978: *Matière, sens, conjointure: methodologische Einführung in die französische und provenzalische Literatur des Mittelalters.* Darmstadt: Wissenschaftliche Buchgesellschaft.

Roques, Mario 1952: "Le manuscrit fr. 794 de la Bibliothèque Nationale et le scribe Guiot." *Romania* 73: 177–99.

Roques, Mario 1955: " 'Graal' dans les parlers d'oïl." *Romance Philology* 9: 196–201.

Roques, Mario 1956: "Le nom du graal." In *Les romans du graal dans la littérature des XIIe et XIIIe siècles.* Strasbourg 29 mars–3 avril 1954: Colloques Internationaux du Centre National de la Recherche Scientifique, 3. Paris: Editions CNRS. Pp. 1–14.

Rostagni, Augusto 1930: *Arte poetica di Orazio: introduzione e commento.* Turin: Chiantore.

Rouse, R. H. 1979: "*Florilegia* and Latin Classical Authors in Twelfth- and Thirteenth-Century Orléans." *Viator* 10: 131–60.

Rousset, Paul 1956: "Le sens du merveilleux à l'époque féodale." *Moyen âge* 62: 25–37.

Ruberg, Uwe 1963: "Die Suche im Prosa-Lancelot." *Zeitschrift für deutsches Altertum und deutsche Literatur* 92: 122–57.

Ruch, M. 1963: "Horace et les fondements de la 'iunctura' dans l'ordre de la création poétique (*A. P.,* 46–72)." *Revue des études latines* 41: 246–69.

Ruhe, Ernstpeter 1979a: "Repetition und Integration: Strukturprobleme des *Roman de Tristan en prose.*" In *Der altfranzösische Prosaroman: Funktion, Funktionswandel und Ideologie am Beispiel des "Roman de Tristan en prose,"* ed. E. Ruhe and R. Schwaderer. Kolloquium Würzburg 1977. Beiträge zur romanischen Philologie des Mittelalters, 12. Munich: Fink. Pp. 131–72.

Ruhe, Ernstpeter 1979b: "Thesen zum Ende der Gattungsgeschichte des höfischen Romans." In *Der altfranzösische Prosaroman: Funktion, Funktionswandel und Ideologie am Beispiel des "Roman de Tristan en prose,"* ed. E. Ruhe and R. Schwaderer. Kolloquium Würzburg 1977. Beiträge zur romanischen Philologie des Mittelalters, 12. Munich: Fink. Pp. 173–83.

Ruhe, Ernstpeter 1985: "*Inventio* devenue *troevemens:* la recherche de la matière au moyen âge." In *The Spirit of the Court,* ed. G. S. Burgess and R. A. Taylor. Selected Proceedings of the Fourth Congress of the International Courtly Literature Society (Toronto 1983). Cambridge: D. S. Brewer. Pp. 289–97.

Rychner, Jean 1955: *La chanson de geste: essai sur l'art épique des jongleurs.* Publications romanes et françaises, 53. Geneva: Droz; Lille: Giard.

Rychner, Jean 1969: "Le prologue du *Chevalier de la charrette* et l'interprétation du roman." In *Mélanges Rita Lejeune.* 2 vols. Gembloux: Duculot. Vol. II, pp. 1121–35.

Rychner, Jean 1972: "Encore le prologue du *Chevalier de la charrette.*" *Vox romanica* 31: 263–71.

Ryding, William W. 1971: *Structure in Medieval Narrative*. De proprietatibus litterarum: series maior, 12. The Hague and Paris: Mouton.

Salmon, Paul 1963: "Über den Beitrag des grammatischen Unterrichts zur Poetik des Mittelalters." *Archiv für das Studium der neueren Sprachen und Literaturen* 199: 65–84.

Sanford, Eva Matthews 1931: "Lucan and His Roman Critics." *Classical Philology* 26: 233–57.

Sargent-Baur, Barbara Nelson 1972: "Petite histoire de Maboagrain (à propos d'un article récent)." *Romania* 93: 87–96.

Sargent-Baur, Barbara Nelson 1973: "Belle Enide, bonne Enide." In *Mélanges Pierre Le Gentil*. Paris: SEDES and CDN. Pp. 767–71.

Sargent-Baur, Barbara Nelson 1984: "Promotion to Knighthood in the Romances of Chrétien de Troyes." *Romance Philology* 37: 393–408.

Sargent-Baur, Barbara Nelson 1987a: "The Missing Prologue of Chrétien's *Chevalier au lion*." *French Studies* 41: 385–94.

Sargent-Baur, Barbara Nelson 1987b: "With Catlike Tread: The Beginning of Chrétien's *Chevalier au lion*." In *Studies Brian Woledge*. Publications romanes et françaises, 180. Geneva: Droz. Pp. 163–73.

Scaglione, Aldo 1970: *Ars grammatica: A Bibliographic Survey, Two Essays on the Grammar of the Latin and Italian Subjunctive, and a Note on the Ablative Absolute*. Janua linguarum: series minor, 77. The Hague and Paris: Mouton.

Scaglione, Aldo 1972: *The Classical Theory of Composition from Its Origins to the Present: A Historical Survey*. University of North Carolina Studies in Comparative Literature, 53. Chapel Hill: University of North Carolina Press.

Scaglione, Aldo 1980: "Rhetorical Factors as Clues to Form and Meaning." *Comparative Literature* 32: 337–54.

Schalk, Fritz 1959: "Zur Entwicklung der artes in Frankreich und Italien." In *Artes liberales: von der antiken Bildung zur Wissenschaft des Mittelalters*, ed. J. Koch. Studien und Texte zur Geistesgeschichte des Mittelalters, 5. Leiden and Cologne: Brill. Pp. 137–48.

Schenk, David P. 1980: "Vues sur le temps et l'espace chez Chrétien de Troyes." *Œuvres et critiques* 5.2: 111–17.

Schleusener-Eichholz, Gudrun 1985: *Das Auge im Mittelalter*. Münstersche Mittelalter-Schriften, 35. 2 vols. Munich: W. Fink.

Schmale, Franz-Josef 1985: *Funktion und Formen mittelalterlicher Geschichtsschreibung: eine Einführung*. Mit einem Beitrag von Hans-Werner Goetz. Darmstadt: Wissenschaftliche Buchgesellschaft.

Schmid, Elisabeth 1986: *Familiengeschichten und Heilsmythologie: die Verwandtschaftsstrukturen in den französischen und deutschen Gralromanen des 12. und 13. Jahrhunderts*. Beihefte zur Zeitschrift für romanische Philologie, 211. Tübingen: M. Niemeyer.

Schmidt, Paul Gerhard 1977: "Weltliche Dichtung des lateinischen Mittelalters und ihr Publikum." *Gymnasium* 84: 167–83.

Schmolke-Hasselmann, Beate 1977: " 'Camuse chose': das Häßliche als ästhetisches und menschliches Problem in der altfranzösischen Literatur." In *Die Mächte des Guten und Bösen: Vorstellungen im XII. und XIII. Jahrhundert über ihr Wirken in der Heilsgeschichte*, ed. A. Zimmermann and G. Vuillemin-Diem. Miscellanea mediaevalia, 11. Berlin, New York: de Gruyter. Pp. 442–52.

Schmolke-Hasselmann, Beate 1980a: *Der arthurische Versroman von Chrestien bis Froissart: zur Geschichte einer Gattung.* Beihefte zur Zeitschrift für romanische Philologie, 177. Tübingen: M. Niemeyer.

Schmolke-Hasselmann, Beate 1980b: "L'intégration de quelques récits brefs arthuriens (*Cor, Mantel, Espee*) dans les romans arthuriens du XIIIᵉ siècle." In *Le récit bref au moyen âge*, ed. D. Buschinger. Actes du Colloque des 27, 28 et 29 avril 1979, Université de Picardie: Centre d'Etudes Médiévales. Paris: Champion. Pp. 107–28.

Schmolke-Hasselmann, Beate 1981a: "Le roman de *Fergus:* technique narrative et intention politique." In *An Arthurian Tapestry: Essays in Memory of Lewis Thorpe*. Glasgow: French Department of the University. Pp. 342–53.

Schmolke-Hasselmann, Beate 1981b: "Untersuchungen zur Typik des arthurischen Romananfangs." *Germanisch-romanische Monatsschrift* n.s.31: 1–13.

Schmolke-Hasselmann, Beate 1982: "The Round Table: Ideal, Fiction, Reality." *Arthurian Literature* 2: 41–75.

Schoepperle, Gertrude 1913: *Tristan and Isolt: A Study of the Sources of the Romance.* New York University: Ottendorfer Memorial Series of Germanic Monographs, 3. Frankfurt: J. Baer; London: D. Nutt.

Scholz, Manfred Günter 1980: *Hören und Lesen: Studien zur primären Rezeption der Literatur im 12. und 13. Jahrhundert.* Wiesbaden: F. Steiner.

Schon, Peter M. 1966: "Das literarische Porträt im französischen Mittelalter." *Archiv für das Studium der neueren Sprachen und Literaturen* 202: 241–63.

Schröder, Werner 1986: "Der synkretistische Roman des Wirnt von Gravenberg: unerledigte Fragen an den *Wigalois.*" *Euphorion* 80: 235–77.

Schulz, Marie 1909: *Die Lehre von der historischen Methode bei den Geschichtschreibern des Mittelalters (VI.–XIII. Jahrhundert).* Abhandlungen zur mittleren und neueren Geschichte, 13. Berlin and Leipzig: Rothschild.

Schulze-Busacker, Elisabeth 1981: "Etude typologique de la complainte des morts dans le roman arthurien en vers du 12ᵉ au 14ᵉ siècle." In *An Arthurian Tapestry: Essays in Memory of Lewis Thorpe*. Glasgow: French Department of the University. Pp. 54–68.

Schulze-Busacker, Elisabeth 1985: *Proverbes et expressions proverbiales dans la littérature narrative du moyen âge français: recueil et analyse.* Nouvelle Bibliothèque du moyen âge, 9. Paris: Champion.

Seifert, Arno 1977: "Historia im Mittelalter." *Archiv für Begriffsgeschichte* 21: 226–84.

Shirt, David J. 1975: "Godefroi de Lagny et la composition de la *Charrete.*" *Romania* 96: 27–52.

Shirt, David J. 1977: "*Cligès:* Realism in Romance." *Forum for Modern Language Studies* 13: 368–80.

Shirt, David J. 1981: " 'Le Chevalier de la charrete': A World Upside Down?" *Modern Language Review* 76: 811–22.

Shirt, David J. 1982: "The Dido Episode in *Enéas:* The Reshaping of Tragedy and Its Stylistic Consequences." *Medium Aevum* 51: 3–17.

Short, Ian 1977: "An Early Draft of Guernes' 'Vie de Saint Thomas Becket.' " *Medium Aevum* 46: 20–34.

Short, Ian 1988: "L'avènement du texte vernaculaire: la mise en recueil." In *Théories et pratiques de l'écriture au moyen âge,* ed. E. Baumgartner and C. Marchello-Nizia. Actes du Colloque Palais du Luxembourg-Sénat, 5 et 6 mars 1987. Littérales, 4. Paris: Paris-X Nanterre, Centre de Recherches du Département de Français; Fontenay/St-Cloud: Centre Espace-Temps-Histoire. Pp. 11–24.

Sienaert, Edgard 1978: *Les Lais de Marie de France: du conte merveilleux à la nouvelle psychologique.* Essais sur le moyen âge. Paris: Champion.

Silverstein, Theodore 1948: "The Fabulous Cosmogony of Bernardus Silvestris." *Modern Philology* 46: 92–116.

Simon, Gertrud 1958: "Untersuchungen zur Topik der Widmungsbriefe mittelalterlicher Geschichtsschreiber bis zum Ende des 12. Jahrhunderts." *Archiv für Diplomatik, Schriftgeschichte, Siegel- und Wappenkunde* 4: 52–119; 5–6 (1959–60): 73–153.

Solmsen, Friedrich 1941: "The Aristotelian Tradition in Ancient Rhetoric." *American Journal of Philology* 62: 35–50, 169–90.

Solterer, Helen 1985: "*Sermo* and *joglar:* Language Games in *Flamenca.*" In *The Spirit of the Court,* ed. G. S. Burgess and R. A. Taylor. Selected Proceedings of the Fourth Congress of the International Courtly Literature Society (Toronto 1983). Cambridge: D. S. Brewer. Pp. 330–38.

Southworth, Marie-José 1973: *Etude comparée de quatre romans médiévaux: Jaufre, Fergus, Durmart, Blancandin.* Paris: Nizet.

Sparnaay, Hendrik 1933: *Hartmann von Aue: Studien zu einer Biographie.* 2 vols. Halle: M. Niemeyer, 1933–38; rpt. Darmstadt: Wissenschaftliche Buchgesellschaft, 1975.

Speer, Mary B. 1974: "Cassidorus: The Fallen Hero." *Romance Philology* 27: 479–87.

Speer, Mary B. 1978: "The *Dame-Pucelle* Debate in the *Roman de Cassidorus.*" In *Studies on the Seven Sages of Rome and Other Essays in Medieval Literature Dedicated to the Memory of Jean Misrahi.* Honolulu: Educational Research Associates. Pp. 155–72.

Speer, Mary B. 1981: "Beyond the Frame: Verisimilitude, *Clergie,* and Class in the *Roman de Marques de Rome.*" *Romance Philology* 35: 305–34.

Speer, Mary B. 1983: "Recycling the Seven Sages of Rome." *Zeitschrift für romanische Philologie* 99: 288–303.

Speer, Mary B., and Alfred Foulet 1980: "Is *Marques de Rome* a Derhymed Romance?" *Romania* 101: 336–65.

Spörl, Johannes 1935: *Grundformen hochmittelalterlicher Geschichtsanschauung: Studien zum Weltbild der Geschichtsschreiber des 12. Jahrhunderts.* Munich: Hueber.

Stach, Walter 1952: "Wort und Bedeutung im mittelalterlichen Latein." *Deutsches Archiv für Erforschung des Mittelalters* 9: 332–52.

Stanesco, Michel 1985: "Le secret de l'*estrange* chevalier: notes sur la motivation contradictoire dans le roman médiéval." In *The Spirit of the Court,* ed. G. S. Burgess and R. A. Taylor. Selected Proceedings of the Fourth Congress of the International Courtly Literature Society (Toronto 1983). Cambridge: D. S. Brewer. Pp. 339–49.

Stanesco, Michel 1989: " 'D'armes et d'amour': la fortune d'une *devise* médiévale." *Travaux de littérature* 2: 37–54.

Steadman, John M. 1968: " 'Courtly Love' as a Problem of Style." In *Chaucer und seine Zeit: Symposion für Walter F. Schirmer.* Buchreihe der Anglia: Zeitschrift für englische Literatur, 14. Tübingen: M. Niemeyer. Pp. 1–33.

Steinen, Wolfram von den 1966: "Les sujets d'inspiration chez les poètes latins du XIIe siècle." *Cahiers de civilisation médiévale* 9: 165–75, 363–83.

Stempel, Wolf-Dieter 1972: "Perspektivische Rede in der französischen Literatur des Mittelalters." In *Interpretation und Vergleich: Festschrift für Walter Pabst.* Berlin: F. Schmidt. Pp. 310–30.

Stevens, Martin 1978: "The Performing Self in Twelfth-Century Culture." *Viator* 9: 193–212 + 12 figures.

Stierle, Karlheinz 1972: "L'histoire comme exemple, l'exemple comme histoire: contribution à la pragmatique et à la poétique des textes narratifs." *Poétique* 10: 176–98.

Stimming, Albert 1888: "Über den Verfasser des Romans de Jaufre." *Zeitschrift für romanische Philologie* 12: 323–47.

Stock, Brian 1972: *Myth and Science in the Twelfth Century: A Study of Bernard Silvester.* Princeton: Princeton University Press.

Stock, Brian 1983: *The Implications of Literacy: Written Language and Models of Interpretation in the Eleventh and Twelfth Centuries.* Princeton: Princeton University Press.

Strauss, Leo 1967: *Jerusalem and Athens: Some Preliminary Reflections.* City College Papers, 6. New York: City College.

Stump, Eleonore 1978: *Boethius's "De topicis differentiis," Translated, with Notes and Essays on the Text.* Ithaca, and London: Cornell University Press.

Sturm-Maddox, Sara 1971: "The Love-Interest in *Le Bel Inconnu:* Innovation in the *roman courtois." Forum for Modern Language Studies* 7: 241–48.

Suard, François 1978: "L'utilisation des éléments folkloriques dans le lai du 'Frêne.' " *Cahiers de civilisation médiévale* 21: 43–52.

Suard, François 1979: *Guillaume d'Orange: étude du roman en prose.* Bibliothèque du XVe siècle, 44. Paris: Champion.

Suard, François 1984: "Lancelot et le chevalier enferré (XXIIa sq.)." In *Approches du Lancelot en prose,* ed. J. Dufournet. Collection Unichamp, 6. Paris: Champion. Pp. 177–96.

Sullivan, Penny 1985a: "Medieval Automata: The 'Chambre de beautés' in Benoît's *Roman de Troie." Romance Studies* 6: 1–20.

Sullivan, Penny 1985b: "Translation and Adaptation in the *Roman de Troie.*" In *The Spirit of the Court,* ed. G. S. Burgess and R. A. Taylor. Selected Proceedings of the Fourth Congress of the International Courtly Literature Society (Toronto 1983). Cambridge: D. S. Brewer. Pp. 350–59.

Szkilnik, Michelle 1988: "Les deux pères de Caradoc." *Bulletin bibliographique de la Société Internationale Arthurienne* 40: 268–86.

Szkilnik, Michelle 1991: *L'archipel du graal: Etude de l'"Estoire del Saint Graal."* Publications romanes et françaises, 196. Geneva: Droz.

Talarico, Kathryn Marie 1981: "*Fundare domum:* Medieval Descriptive Modes and the *Roman d'Eneas.*" *Yale French Studies* 61: 202–24.

Tattersall, Jill 1981: "Sphere or Disc? Allusions to the Shape of the Earth in Some Twelfth-Century and Thirteenth-Century Vernacular French Works." *Modern Language Review* 76: 31–46.

Taylor, Jane H. M. 1987: "The Fourteenth Century: Context, Text and Intertext." In *The Legacy of Chrétien de Troyes,* ed. N. J. Lacy, D. Kelly, and K. Busby. 2 vols. Faux titre, 31. Amsterdam: Rodopi. Vol. I, pp. 267–332.

Thorpe, Lewis 1973: "Merlin's Sardonic Laughter." In *Studies in Medieval Literature and Languages in Memory of Frederick Whitehead.* Manchester: Manchester University Press; New York: Barnes and Noble. Pp. 323–39.

Thoss, Dagmar 1972: *Studien zum locus amoenus im Mittelalter.* Wiener romanistische Arbeiten, 10. Vienna and Stuttgart: Braumüller.

Todorov, Tzvetan 1969: "La quête du récit." *Critique* 262: 195–214.

Topsfield, L. T. 1975: *Troubadours and Love.* Cambridge: Cambridge University Press.

Topsfield, L. T. 1981: *Chrétien de Troyes: A Study of the Arthurian Romances.* Cambridge: Cambridge University Press.

Triaud, Annie 1985: "Une version tardive de l'*Eneas.*" In *The Spirit of the Court,* ed. G. S. Burgess and R. A. Taylor. Selected Proceedings of the Fourth Congress of the International Courtly Literature Society (Toronto 1983). Cambridge: D. S. Brewer. Pp. 360–72.

Trimpi, Wesley 1971: "The Ancient Hypothesis of Fiction: An Essay on the Origins of Literary Theory." *Traditio* 27: 1–78.

Trimpi, Wesley 1973: "The Meaning of Horace's *ut pictura poesis.*" *Journal of the Warburg and Courtauld Institute* 36: 1–34.

Trimpi, Wesley 1974: "The Quality of Fiction: The Rhetorical Transmission of Literary Theory." *Traditio* 30: 1–118.

Tubach, Frederic C. 1980: "The Formation of the Miraculous as Narrative and Cultural Pattern: Remarks on the Religious Imagination of Gregory's *Dialogues.*" *Deutsche Vierteljahrsschrift für Literaturwissenschaft und Geistesgeschichte* 54: 1–13.

Tuve, Rosemond 1966: *Allegorical Imagery: Some Mediaeval Books and Their Posterity.* Princeton: Princeton University Press.

Tyson, Diane B. 1979: "Patronage of French Vernacular History Writers in the Twelfth and Thirteenth Centuries." *Romania* 100: 180–222.

Tyssens, Madeleine 1966: "Le jongleur et l'écrit." In *Mélanges René Crozet.* 2 vols. Poitiers: Société d'Etudes médiévales. Vol. I, pp. 685–95.

Tyssens, Madeleine 1967: *La geste de Guillaume d'Orange dans les manuscrits cycliques.* Bibliothèque de la Faculté de Philosophie et Lettres de l'Université de Liège, 178. Paris: Belles Lettres.

Uitti, Karl D. 1967: "The Old French *Vie de Saint Alexis:* Paradigm, Legend, Meaning." *Romance Philology* 20: 263–95.

Uitti, Karl D. 1972: "Remarks on Old French Narrative: Courtly Love and Poetic Form." *Romance Philology* 26: 77–93; 28 (1974–75): 190–99.

Uitti, Karl D. 1973: *Story, Myth, and Celebration in Old French Narrative Poetry 1050–1200.* Princeton: Princeton University Press.

Uitti, Karl D. 1975: "The Clerkly Narrator Figure in Old French Hagiography and Romance." *Medioevo romanzo* 2: 394–408.

Uitti, Karl D. 1981: "A propos de philologie." *Littérature* 41: 30–46.

Uitti, Karl D. 1983: "Vernacularization and Old French Mythopoesis with Emphasis on Chrétien's *Erec et Enide.*" In *The Sower and His Seed: Essays on Chrétien de Troyes,* ed. R. T. Pickens. French Forum Monographs, 44. Lexington: French Forum. Pp. 81–115.

Uitti, Karl D., 1985: "A Note on Historiographical Vernacularization in Thirteenth-Century France and Spain." In *Homenaje a Álvaro Galmés de Fuentes.* 2 vols. Oviedo: Universidad de Oviedo; Madrid: Gredos. Vol. I, pp. 573–92.

Uitti, Karl D. with Alfred Foulet 1988: "On Editing Chrétien de Troyes: Lancelot's Two Steps and Their Context." *Speculum* 63: 271–92.

Valesio, Paolo 1980: *Novantiqua: Rhetorics as a Contemporary Theory.* Bloomington: Indiana University Press.

Vance, Eugene 1972: "Le combat érotique chez Chrétien de Troyes: de la figure à la forme." *Poétique* 12: 544–71.

Vance, Eugene 1973: "Augustine's *Confessions* and the Grammar of Selfhood." *Genre* 6: 1–28.

Vance, Eugene 1987: *From Topic to Tale: Logic and Narrativity in the Middle Ages.* Theory and History of Literature, 47. Minneapolis: University of Minnesota Press.

Van Coolput, Colette-Anne 1978: "Le roi Marc dans le Tristan de Béroul." *Moyen âge* 84: 35–51.

Van Coolput, Colette-Anne 1986: *Aventures querant et le sens du monde: aspects de la réception productive des premiers romans du Graal cycliques dans le "Tristan en prose."* Mediaevalia Lovaniensia, 1.14. Leuven: Leuven University Press.

Van Coolput, Colette-Anne 1987a: "La réaction de quelques romanciers postérieurs." In *The Legacy of Chrétien de Troyes,* ed. N. J. Lacy, D. Kelly, and K. Busby. Faux titre, 31. Amsterdam: Rodopi. Vol. I, pp. 91–114.

Van Coolput, Colette-Anne 1987b: "Sur quelques sculptures anthropomorphes dans les romans arthuriens en prose." *Romania* 108: 254–67.

Van den Boogaard, Nico 1985: "Le *Roman de la rose* de Guillaume de Lorris et l'art de la mémoire." In *Jeux de mémoire: aspects de la mnémotechnie médiévale,* ed. B. Roy and P. Zumthor. Etudes médiévales. Montreal: Presses de l'Université de Montréal; Paris: Vrin. Pp. 85–90.

Van Emden, W. G. 1975: "Contribution à l'étude de l'évolution sémantique du mot 'geste' en ancien français." *Romania* 96: 105–22.

Vansina, Jan 1961: *De la tradition orale: essai de méthode historique*. Musée Royal de l'Afrique Centrale: Annales (série in 8°), Sciences Humaines, 36. Tervuren: Musée Royal de l'Afrique Centrale.

Vàrvaro, Alberto 1963: *Il "Roman de Tristan" di Béroul*. Università di Pisa: studi di filologia moderna, n.s. 3. Turin: Bottega d'Erasmo.

Vàrvaro, Alberto 1967: "La teoria dell'archetipo tristaniano." *Romania* 88: 13–58.

Vendryes, J. 1950: "Les éléments celtiques de la légende du graal." *Etudes celtiques* 5: 1–50.

Vernet, André 1955: "Une épitaphe inédite de Thierry de Chartres." In *Recueil de travaux Clovis Brunel*. Mémoires et documents publiés par la Société de l'Ecole des Chartes, 12. 2 vols. Paris: Société de l'Ecole des Chartes. Vol. II, pp. 660–70.

Vinaver, Eugène 1925: *Etudes sur le "Tristan" en prose: les sources, les manuscrits, bibliographie critique*. Paris: Champion.

Vinaver, Eugène 1939: "Principles of Textual Emendation." In *Studies Mildred K. Pope*. Manchester: Manchester University Press. Pp. 351–69.

Vinaver, Eugène 1964: "From Epic to Romance." *Bulletin of the John Rylands Library* 46: 476–503.

Vinaver, Eugène 1966: *Form and Meaning in Medieval Romance*. Presidential Address of the Modern Humanities Research Association. London: Modern Humanities Research Association; Leeds: W. S. Maney.

Vinaver, Eugène 1968: "La forêt de Morois." *Cahiers de civilisation médiévale* 11: 1–13.

Vinaver, Eugène 1970a: *A la recherche d'une poétique médiévale*. Paris: Nizet.

Vinaver, Eugène 1970b: "From Motive to Ornament." In *Medieval Literature and Folklore Studies: Essays Francis Lee Utley*. New Brunswick: Rutgers University Press. Pp. 147–53 and 359.

Vinaver, Eugène 1970c: "A Speech by the President of the International Arthurian Society at a Dinner Offered by the University of Wales on the Occasion of the Ninth International Arthurian Congress in Cardiff 13 August 1969." *Bulletin bibliographique de la Société Internationale Arthurienne* 22: 115–18.

Vinaver, Eugène 1971: *The Rise of Romance*. Oxford: Clarendon Press.

Viscardi, Antonio 1967: *Le letterature d'oc et d'oïl*. New ed. Milan: Sansoni.

Vitz, Evelyn Birge 1973: "The *I* of the *Roman de la rose*." *Genre* 6: 49–75.

Vitz, Evelyn Birge 1975: "Type et individu dans l' 'autobiographie' médiévale: étude d'*Historia calamitatum*." *Poétique* 24: 426–45.

Vitz, Evelyn Birge 1978: "*La vie de Saint Alexis:* Narrative Analysis and the Quest for the Sacred Subject." *PMLA* 93: 396–408.

Vitz, Evelyn Birge 1990: "Chrétien de Troyes: clerc ou ménestrel? problèmes des traditions orale et littéraire dans les cours de France au XIIᵉ siècle." *Poétique* 81: 21–42.

Voelker, P. 1886: "Die Bedeutungsentwicklung des Wortes Roman." *Zeitschrift für romanische Philologie* 10: 485–525.

Wallen, Martha Louise 1972: "The Art of Adaptation in the Fifteenth-Century *Erec et Enide* and *Cligès.*" Diss. University of Wisconsin—Madison.

Wallen, Martha Louise 1982: "Significant Variations in the Burgundian Prose Version of *Erec et Enide.*" *Medium Aevum* 51: 187–96.

Walther, J. Th. 1927: *L'exemplum dans la littérature religieuse et didactique au moyen âge.* Paris and Toulouse; rpt. Geneva: Slatkine, 1973.

Waltz, Matthias 1965: *Rolandslied—Wilhelmslied—Alexiuslied: zur Struktur und geschichtlichen Bedeutung.* Studia romanica, 9. Heidelberg: C. Winter.

Waltz, Matthias 1970: "Zum Problem der Gattungsgeschichte im Mittelalter: am Beispiel des Mirakels." *Zeitschrift für romanische Philologie* 86: 22–39.

Ward, John O. 1969: "Educational Crisis and the Genesis of Universities in Medieval Europe." *Teaching History* 3.4 (December): 5–18.

Ward, John O. 1972: "The Date of the Commentary on Cicero's 'De inventione' by Thierry of Chartres (ca. 1095–1160?) and the Cornifician Attack on the Liberal Arts." *Viator* 3: 219–73.

Ward, John O. 1977: "Classical Rhetoric and the Writing of History in Medieval and Renaissance Culture." In *European History and Its Historians,* ed. F. McGregor and N. Wright. Adelaide: Adelaide University Union Press. Pp. 1–10.

Ward, John O. 1978: "The Commentator's Rhetoric—From Antiquity to the Renaissance: Glosses and Commentaries on Cicero's *Rhetorica.*" In *Medieval Eloquence: Studies in the Theory and Practice of Medieval Rhetoric,* ed. J. J. Murphy. Berkeley, Los Angeles, London: University of California Press. Pp. 25–67.

Ward, John O. 1979: "Gothic Architecture, Universities and the Decline of the Humanities in Twelfth Century Europe." In *Principalities, Powers and Estates: Studies in Medieval and Early Modern Government and Society,* ed. L. O. Frappell. Adelaide: Adelaide University Union Press. Pp. 65–75.

Warning, Rainer 1983: "Moi lyrique et société chez les troubadours." In *Archéologie du signe,* ed. L Brind'Amour and E. Vance. Recueil d'Etudes Médiévales, 3. Toronto: Pontifical Institute of Medieval Studies. Pp. 63–100.

Warren, Glenda Leah 1988: "Translation as Re-Creation in the *Roman de Troie.*" Diss. University of Wisconsin—Madison.

Weber, Hubert 1976: *Chrestien und die Tristandichtung.* Europäische Hochschulschriften. Ser. 13: Französische Sprache und Literatur, 32. Bern: H. Lang; Frankfurt: P. Lang.

Wehrli, Max 1961: "Roman und Legende im deutschen Hochmittelalter." In *Worte und Werte: Bruno Markwardt zum 60. Geburtstag.* Berlin: de Gruyter. Pp. 428–43.

Westoby, Kathryn S. 1985: "A New Look at the Role of the Fée in Medieval French Arthurian Romance." In *The Spirit of the Court,* ed. G. S. Burgess and R. A. Taylor. Selected Proceedings of the Fourth Congress of the International

Courtly Literature Society (Toronto 1983). Cambridge: D. S. Brewer. Pp. 373–85.

Wetherbee, Winthrop 1969: "The Function of Poetry in the 'De planctu Naturae' of Alain de Lille." *Traditio* 25: 87–125.

Wetherbee, Winthrop 1971: "The Literal and the Allegorical: Jean de Meun and the 'de Planctu Naturae.' " *Mediaeval Studies* 33: 264–91.

Wetherbee, Winthrop 1972: *Platonism and Poetry in the Twelfth Century: The Literary Influence of the School of Chartres.* Princeton: Princeton University Press.

Wetherbee, Winthrop 1976: "The Theme of Imagination in Medieval Poetry and the Allegorical Figure 'Genius.' " *Medievalia et Humanistica* n.s. 7: 45–64.

Woledge, Brian 1954: *Bibliographie des romans et nouvelles en prose française antérieurs à 1500.* Publications romanes et françaises, 42. Geneva: Droz; Lille: Girard. *Supplément 1954–1973.* Publications romanes et françaises, 130. Geneva: Droz, 1975.

Woledge, Brian 1969: "Bons vavasseurs et mauvais sénéchaux." In *Mélanges Rita Lejeune.* 2 vols. Gembloux: Duculot. Vol. II, pp. 1263–77.

Woledge, Brian, and H. P. Clive 1964: *Répertoire des plus anciens textes en prose française depuis 842 jusqu'aux premières années du XIIIe siècle.* Publications romanes et françaises, 79. Geneva: Droz.

Wolf, Alois 1977: "Die 'adaptation courtoise': kritische Anmerkungen zu einem neuen Dogma." *Germanisch-romanische Monatsschrift* n.s. 27: 257–83.

Wolf, Alois 1989: " 'Non veni solvere sed adimplere . . .': zu den möglichen typologischen Hintergründen eines mittelalterlichen Gestaltungsprinzips." In *Paradeigmata: literarische Typologie des Alten Testaments,* Part I: *Von den Anfängen bis zum 19. Jahrhundert,* ed. F. Link. Berlin: Duncker & Humblot. Pp. 83–102.

Wolfzettel, Friedrich 1985: "Mediävistik und Psychanalyse: eine Bestandsaufnahme." In *Mittelalterbilder aus neuer Perspektive: Diskussionsanstöße zu amour courtois, Subjektivität in der Dichtung und Strategien des Erzählens,* ed. E. Ruhe and R. Behrens. Kolloquium Würzburg 1984. Beiträge zur romanischen Philologie des Mittelalters, 14. Munich: W. Fink. Pp. 210–39.

Wolfzettel, Friedrich 1988a: "Le *Roman d'Erec* en prose du XIIIe siècle: un anti-*Erec et Enide?*" In *The Legacy of Chrétien de Troyes,* ed. N. J. Lacy, D. Kelly, and K. Busby. Faux titre, 37. Amsterdam: Rodopi. Vol. II, pp. 215–28.

Wolfzettel, Friedrich 1988b: "Wahrheit der Geschichte und Wahrheit der Frau: *honor de feme* und weibliche *aventure* im altfranzösischen Roman." *Zeitschrift für romanische Philologie* 104: 197–217.

Wolfzettel, Friedrich 1990a: "La recherche de l'universel. Pour une nouvelle lecture des romans de Gautier d'Arras." *Cahiers de civilisation médiévale* 33: 113–31.

Wolfzettel, Friedrich 1990b: "Zum Stand und Problem der Intertextualitätsforschung im Mittelalter (aus romanistischer Sicht)." In *Artusroman und Intertextualität,* ed. F. Wolfzettel. Gießen: W. Schmitz. Pp. 1–17.

Wolter, Hans 1959: "Geschichtliche Bildung im Rahmen der artes liberales." In *Artes liberales: von der antiken Bildung zur Wissenschaft des Mittelalters,* ed. J. Koch. Studien und Texte zur Geistesgeschichte des Mittelalters, 5. Leiden and Cologne: Brill. Pp. 50–83.

Woods, Ellen Rose 1977: "The Ascendance of Love in *Aye d'Avignon.*" *Olifant* 5: 43–53.

Woods, Ellen Rose 1978: *Aye d'Avignon: A Study of Genre and Society.* Histoire des idées et critique littéraire, 172. Geneva: Droz.

Woods, Marjorie Curry 1986: "Poetic Digression and the Interpretation of Medieval Literary Texts." *Acta Conventus Neo-Latini Sanctandreani.* Proceedings of the Fifth International Congress of Neo-Latin Studies, St. Andrews 24 August to 1 September 1982. Medieval and Renaissance Texts and Studies, 38. Binghamton: Center for Medieval and Early Renaissance Studies, University Center at Binghamton, NY. Pp. 617–26.

Worstbrock, Franz Josef 1965: "*Translatio artium:* über die Herkunft und Entwicklung einer kulturhistorischen Theorie." *Archiv für Kulturgeschichte* 47: 1–22.

Worstbrock, Franz Josef 1985: "Dilatatio materiae: zur Poetik des 'Erec' Hartmanns von Aue." *Frühmittelalterliche Studien* 19: 1–30.

Wrede, Hilmar 1952: "Die Fortsetzer des Gralromans Chrestiens von Troyes." Diss. Göttingen.

Yates, Frances A. 1966: *The Art of Memory.* London: Routledge and Kegan Paul; Chicago: University of Chicago Press.

Zink, Michel 1976: *La prédication en langue romane avant 1300.* Nouvelle Bibliothèque du moyen âge, 4. Paris: Champion.

Zink, Michel 1979: *Roman rose et rose rouge: Le Roman de la rose ou de Guillaume de Dole de Jean Renart.* Paris: Nizet.

Zink, Michel 1980: "Froissart et la nuit du chasseur." *Poétique* 41: 60–77.

Zink, Michel 1981: "Une mutation de la conscience littéraire: le langage romanesque à travers des exemples français du XIIᵉ siècle." *Cahiers de civilisation médiévale* 24: 3–27.

Zink, Michel 1984: "Héritage rhétorique et nouveauté littéraire dans le 'roman antique' en France au moyen âge: remarques sur l'expression de l'amour dans le roman d'*Eneas.*" *Romania* 105: 248–69.

Zink, Michel 1987: "Chrétien et ses contemporains." In *The Legacy of Chrétien de Troyes,* ed. N. J. Lacy, D. Kelly, and K. Busby. Faux titre, 31. Amsterdam: Rodopi. Vol. I, pp. 5–32.

Zumthor, Paul 1943: *Merlin le prophète: un thème de la littérature polémique de l'historiographie et des romans.* Lausanne: Payot, 1943; rpt. Geneva: Slatkine, 1973.

Zumthor, Paul 1955: "Note sur les champs sémantiques dans le vocabulaire des idées." *Neophilologus* 39: 175–83, 241–49.

Zumthor, Paul 1968: "De la chanson au récit: 'La Chastelaine de Vergi.'" *Vox romanica* 27: 77–95.

Zumthor, Paul 1972: *Essai de poétique médiévale.* Paris: Seuil.

Zumthor, Paul 1973: "Le texte médiéval et l'histoire: propositions méthodologiques." *Romanic Review* 64: 5–15.

Zumthor, Paul 1975: *Langue, texte, énigme.* Paris: Seuil.

Zumthor, Paul 1978: "Le texte-fragment." *Langue française* 40: 75–82.

Zumthor, Paul 1981: "Intertextualité et mouvance." *Littérature* 41: 8–16.

Zumthor, Paul 1984a: "L'écriture et la voix: le roman d'Eracle." In *The Craft of Fiction: Essays in Medieval Poetics,* ed. L. A. Arrathoon. Rochester: Solaris. Pp. 161–209.

Zumthor, Paul 1984b: *La poésie et la voix dans la civilisation médiévale.* Collège de France: essais et conférences. Paris: Presses universitaires de France.

Zumthor, Paul 1985: "Les traditions poétiques." In *Jeux de mémoire: aspects de la mnémotechnie médiévale,* ed. B. Roy and P. Zumthor. Etudes médiévales. Montreal: Presses de l'Université de Montréal; Paris: Vrin. Pp. 11–21.

Zumthor, Paul 1987: *La lettre et la voix: de la "littérature" médiévale.* Paris: Seuil.

Index

Titles are indexed under author unless anonymous, in which case they are indexed under title.

447

TEXT AND DISPLAY LINES ARE SET IN SABON

Library of Congress Cataloging-in-Publication Data
Kelly, Douglas.
The art of medieval French romance / Douglas Kelly.
490 pp.   cm.
Includes passages in Old and Middle French with translations into English.
Includes bibliographical references and index.
ISBN 0-299-13190-4
1. French literature—To 1500—History and criticism.
2. Romances—History and criticism.   3. Narration (Rhetoric)
4. Rhetoric, Medieval.   I. Title.
PQ201.K45   1992
840.9′001—dc20   91-32465